Lecture Notes in Computer Science 12933

More information about this subseries at http://www.springer.com/series/7409

Carmelo Ardito · Rosa Lanzilotti ·
Alessio Malizia · Helen Petrie ·
Antonio Piccinno · Giuseppe Desolda ·
Kori Inkpen (Eds.)

Human-Computer Interaction – INTERACT 2021

18th IFIP TC 13 International Conference
Bari, Italy, August 30 – September 3, 2021
Proceedings, Part II

 Springer

Editors
Carmelo Ardito (iD)
Department of Electrical and Information
Engineering
Polytechnic University of Bari
Bari, Italy

Alessio Malizia (iD)
Computer Science Department
University of Pisa
Pisa, Italy

University of Hertfordshire
Hatfield, United Kingdom

Antonio Piccinno (iD)
Computer Science Department
University of Bari Aldo Moro
Bari, Italy

Kori Inkpen (iD)
Microsoft Research
Redmond, WA, USA

Rosa Lanzilotti (iD)
Computer Science Department
University of Bari Aldo Moro
Bari, Italy

Helen Petrie (iD)
Department of Computer Science
University of York
York, UK

Giuseppe Desolda (iD)
Computer Science Department
University of Bari Aldo Moro
Bari, Italy

ISSN 0302-9743   ISSN 1611-3349   (electronic)
Lecture Notes in Computer Science
ISBN 978-3-030-85615-1   ISBN 978-3-030-85616-8   (eBook)
https://doi.org/10.1007/978-3-030-85616-8

LNCS Sublibrary: SL3 – Information Systems and Applications, incl. Internet/Web, and HCI

This Springer imprint is published by the registered company Springer Nature Switzerland AG
The registered company address is: Gewerbestrasse 11, 6330 Cham, Switzerland

Welcome

It is our great pleasure to welcome you to the 18th IFIP TC13 International Conference on Human-Computer Interaction, INTERACT 2021, one of the most important conferences in the area of Human-Computer Interaction at a world-wide level. INTERACT 2021 was held in Bari (Italy) from August 30 – September 3, 2021, in cooperation with ACM and under the patronage of the University of Bari Aldo Moro. This is the second time that INTERACT was held in Italy, after the edition in Rome in September 2005. The Villa Romanazzi Carducci Hotel, which hosted INTERACT 2021, provided the right context for welcoming the participants, thanks to its liberty-period villa immersed in a beautiful park. Due to the COVID-19 pandemic, INTERACT 2021 was held in hybrid mode to allow attendees who could not travel to participate in the conference.

INTERACT is held every two years and is well appreciated by the international community, attracting experts with a broad range of backgrounds, coming from all over the world and sharing a common interest in HCI, to make technology effective and useful for all people in their daily life. The theme of INTERACT 2021, "Sense, Feel, Design," highlighted the new interaction design challenges. Technology is today more and more widespread, pervasive and blended in the world we live in. On one side, devices that sense humans' activities have the potential to provide an enriched interaction. On the other side, the user experience can be further enhanced by exploiting multisensorial technologies. The traditional human senses of vision and hearing and senses of touch, smell, taste, and emotions can be taken into account when designing for future interactions. The hot topic of this edition was Human-Centered Artificial Intelligence, which implies considering who AI systems are built for and evaluating how well these systems support people's goals and activities. There was also considerable attention paid to the usable security theme. Not surprisingly, the COVID-19 pandemic and social distancing have also turned the attention of HCI researchers towards the difficulties in performing user-centered design activities and the modified social aspects of interaction.

With this, we welcome you all to INTERACT 2021. Several people worked hard to make this conference as pleasurable as possible, and we hope you will truly enjoy it.

Paolo Buono
Catherine Plaisant

Preface

The 18th IFIP TC13 International Conference on Human-Computer Interaction, INTERACT 2021 (Bari, August 30 – September 3, 2021) attracted a relevant collection of submissions on different topics.

Excellent research is the heart of a good conference. Like its predecessors, INTERACT 2021 aimed to foster high-quality research. As a multidisciplinary field, HCI requires interaction and discussion among diverse people with different interests and backgrounds. The beginners and the experienced theoreticians and practitioners, and people from various disciplines and different countries gathered, both in-person and virtually, to learn from each other and contribute to each other's growth.

We were especially honoured to welcome our invited speakers: Marianna Obrist (University College London), Ben Shneiderman (University of Maryland), Luca Viganò (King's College London), Geraldine Fitzpatrick (TU Wien) and Philippe Palanque (University Toulouse 3 "Paul Sabatier").

Marianna Obrist's talk focused on the multisensory world people live in and discussed the role touch, taste and smell can play in the future of computing. Ben Shneiderman envisioned a new synthesis of emerging disciplines in which AI-based intelligent algorithms are combined with human-centered design thinking. Luca Viganò used a cybersecurity show and tell approach to illustrate how to use films and other artworks to explain cybersecurity notions. Geraldine Fitzpatrick focused on skills required to use technologies as enablers for good technical design work. Philippe Palanque discussed the cases of system faults due to human errors and presented multiple examples of faults affecting socio-technical systems.

A total of 680 submissions, distributed in 2 peer-reviewed tracks, 4 curated tracks, and 3 juried tracks, were received. Of these, the following contributions were accepted:

- 105 Full Papers (peer-reviewed)
- 72 Short Papers (peer-reviewed)
- 36 Posters (juried)
- 5 Interactive Demos (curated)
- 9 Industrial Experiences (curated)
- 3 Panels (curated)
- 1 Course (curated)
- 11 Workshops (juried)
- 13 Doctoral Consortium (juried)

The acceptance rate for contributions received in the peer-reviewed tracks was 29% for full papers and 30% for short papers. In the spirit of inclusiveness of INTERACT, and IFIP in general, a substantial number of promising but borderline full papers, which had not received a direct acceptance decision, were screened for shepherding.

Interestingly, many of these papers eventually turned out to be excellent quality papers and were included in the final set of full papers. In addition to full papers and short papers, the present proceedings feature's contributions accepted in the shape of posters, interactive demonstrations, industrial experiences, panels, courses, and descriptions of accepted workshops.

Subcommittees managed the reviewing process of the full papers. Each subcommittee had a chair and a set of associated chairs who were in charge of coordinating the reviewing process with the help of expert reviewers. Two new sub-committees were introduced in this edition: "Human-AI Interaction" and "HCI in the Pandemic". Hereafter we list the sub-committees of INTERACT 2021:

- Accessibility and assistive technologies
- Design for business and safety-critical interactive systems
- Design of interactive entertainment systems
- HCI education and curriculum
- HCI in the pandemic
- Human-AI interaction
- Information visualization
- Interactive systems technologies and engineering
- Methodologies for HCI
- Social and ubiquitous interaction
- Understanding users and human behaviour

The final decision on acceptance or rejection of full papers was taken in a Programme Committee meeting held virtually, due to the COVID-19 pandemic, in March 2021. The technical program chairs, the full papers chairs, the subcommittee chairs, and the associate chairs participated in this meeting. The meeting discussed a consistent set of criteria to deal with inevitable differences among many reviewers. The corresponding track chairs and reviewers made the final decisions on other tracks, often after electronic meetings and discussions.

We would like to express our strong gratitude to all the people whose passionate and strenuous work ensured the quality of the INTERACT 2021 program: the 12 sub-committees chairs, 88 associated chairs, 34 track chairs, and 543 reviewers; the Keynote & Invited Talks Chair Maria Francesca Costabile; the Posters Chairs Maristella Matera, Kent Norman, Anna Spagnolli; the Interactive Demos Chairs Barbara Rita Barricelli and Nuno Jardim Nunes; the Workshops Chairs Marta Kristín Larusdottir and Davide Spano; the Courses Chairs Nikolaos Avouris and Carmen Santoro; the Panels Chairs Effie Lai-Chong Law and Massimo Zancanaro; the Doctoral Consortium Chairs Daniela Fogli, David Lamas and John Stasko; the Industrial Experiences Chair Danilo Caivano; the Online Experience Chairs Fabrizio Balducci and Miguel Ceriani; the Advisors Fernando Loizides and Marco Winckler; the Student Volunteers Chairs Vita Santa Barletta and Grazia Ragone; the Publicity Chairs Ganesh D. Bhutkar and Veronica Rossano; the Local Organisation Chair Simona Sarti.

We would like to thank all the authors, who chose INTERACT 2021 as the venue to publish their research and enthusiastically shared their results with the INTERACT community. Last, but not least, we are also grateful to the sponsors for their financial support.

Carmelo Ardito
Rosa Lanzilotti
Alessio Malizia
Helen Petrie
Antonio Piccinno
Giuseppe Desolda
Kori Inkpen

IFIP TC13 – http://ifip-tc13.org/

Established in 1989, the Technical Committee on Human–Computer Interaction (IFIP TC 13) of the International Federation for Information Processing (IFIP) is an international committee of 34 member national societies and 10 Working Groups, representing specialists of the various disciplines contributing to the field of human–computer interaction. This includes (among others) human factors, ergonomics, cognitive science, and multiple areas of computer science and design.

IFIP TC 13 aims to develop the science, technology and societal aspects of human–computer interaction (HCI) by

- encouraging empirical, applied and theoretical research
- promoting the use of knowledge and methods from both human sciences and computer sciences in design, development, evaluation and exploitation of computing systems
- promoting the production of new knowledge in the area of interactive computing systems engineering
- promoting better understanding of the relation between formal design methods and system usability, user experience, accessibility and acceptability
- developing guidelines, models and methods by which designers may provide better human-oriented computing systems
- and, cooperating with other groups, inside and outside IFIP, to promote user-orientation and humanization in system design.

Thus, TC 13 seeks to improve interactions between people and computing systems, to encourage the growth of HCI research and its practice in industry and to disseminate these benefits worldwide.

The main orientation is to place the users at the center of the development process. Areas of study include:

- the problems people face when interacting with computing devices;
- the impact of technology deployment on people in individual and organizational contexts;
- the determinants of utility, usability, acceptability, accessibility, privacy, and user experience ...;
- the appropriate allocation of tasks between computing systems and users especially in the case of automation;
- engineering user interfaces, interactions and interactive computing systems;
- modelling the user, their tasks and the interactive system to aid better system design; and harmonizing the computing system to user characteristics and needs.

While the scope is thus set wide, with a tendency toward general principles rather than particular systems, it is recognized that progress will only be achieved through both general studies to advance theoretical understandings and specific studies on practical issues (e.g., interface design standards, software system resilience, documentation, training material, appropriateness of alternative interaction technologies, guidelines, integrating computing systems to match user needs and organizational practices, etc.).

In 2015, TC13 approved the creation of a Steering Committee (SC) for the INTERACT conference series. The SC is now in place, chaired by Anirudha Joshi and is responsible for:

- promoting and maintaining the INTERACT conference as the premiere venue for researchers and practitioners interested in the topics of the conference (this requires a refinement of the topics above);
- ensuring the highest quality for the contents of the event;
- setting up the bidding process to handle the future INTERACT conferences (decision is made at TC 13 level);
- providing advice to the current and future chairs and organizers of the INTERACT conference;
- providing data, tools, and documents about previous conferences to the future conference organizers;
- selecting the reviewing system to be used throughout the conference (as this affects the entire set of reviewers, authors and committee members);
- resolving general issues involved with the INTERACT conference;
- capitalizing on history (good and bad practices).

In 1999, TC 13 initiated a special IFIP Award, the Brian Shackel Award, for the most outstanding contribution in the form of a refereed paper submitted to and delivered at each INTERACT. The award draws attention to the need for a comprehensive human-centered approach in the design and use of information technology in which the human and social implications have been taken into account. In 2007, IFIP TC 13 launched an Accessibility Award to recognize an outstanding contribution in HCI with international impact dedicated to the field of accessibility for disabled users. In 2013, IFIP TC 13 launched the Interaction Design for International Development (IDID) Award that recognizes the most outstanding contribution to the application of interactive systems for social and economic development of people in developing countries. Since the process to decide the award takes place after papers are sent to the publisher for publication, the awards are not identified in the proceedings. Since 2019 a special agreement has been made with the *International Journal of Behaviour & Information Technology* (published by Taylor & Francis) with Panos Markopoulos as editor in chief. In this agreement, authors of BIT whose papers are within the field of HCI are offered the opportunity to present their work at the INTERACT conference. Reciprocally, a selection of papers submitted and accepted for presentation at INTERACT are offered the opportunity to extend their contribution to be published in BIT.

IFIP TC 13 also recognizes pioneers in the area of HCI. An IFIP TC 13 pioneer is one who, through active participation in IFIP Technical Committees or related IFIP groups, has made outstanding contributions to the educational, theoretical, technical, commercial, or professional aspects of analysis, design, construction, evaluation, and use of interactive systems. IFIP TC 13 pioneers are appointed annually and awards are handed over at the INTERACT conference.

IFIP TC 13 stimulates working events and activities through its Working Groups (WGs). Working Groups consist of HCI experts from multiple countries, who seek to expand knowledge and find solutions to HCI issues and concerns within a specific domain. The list of Working Groups and their domains is given below.

WG13.1 (Education in HCI and HCI Curricula) aims to improve HCI education at all levels of higher education, coordinate and unite efforts to develop HCI curricula and promote HCI teaching.

WG13.2 (Methodology for User-Centred System Design) aims to foster research, dissemination of information and good practice in the methodical application of HCI to software engineering.

WG13.3 (HCI, Disability and Aging) aims to make HCI designers aware of the needs of people with disabilities and encourage development of information systems and tools permitting adaptation of interfaces to specific users.

WG13.4 (also WG2.7) (User Interface Engineering) investigates the nature, concepts and construction of user interfaces for software systems, using a framework for reasoning about interactive systems and an engineering model for developing UIs.

WG 13.5 (Resilience, Reliability, Safety and Human Error in System Development) seeks a framework for studying human factors relating to systems failure, develops leading edge techniques in hazard analysis and safety engineering of computer-based systems, and guides international accreditation activities for safety-critical systems.

WG13.6 (Human-Work Interaction Design) aims at establishing relationships between extensive empirical work-domain studies and HCI design. It will promote the use of knowledge, concepts, methods and techniques that enable user studies to procure a better apprehension of the complex interplay between individual, social and organizational contexts and thereby a better understanding of how and why people work in the ways that they do.

WG13.7 (Human–Computer Interaction and Visualization) aims to establish a study and research program that will combine both scientific work and practical applications in the fields of human–computer interaction and visualization. It will integrate several additional aspects of further research areas, such as scientific visualization, data mining, information design, computer graphics, cognition sciences, perception theory, or psychology, into this approach.

WG13.8 (Interaction Design and International Development) is currently working to reformulate their aims and scope.

WG13.9 (Interaction Design and Children) aims to support practitioners, regulators and researchers to develop the study of interaction design and children across international contexts.

WG13.10 (Human-Centred Technology for Sustainability) aims to promote research, design, development, evaluation, and deployment of human-centered technology to encourage sustainable use of resources in various domains.

New Working Groups are formed as areas of significance in HCI arise. Further information is available at the IFIP TC13 website: http://ifip-tc13.org/.

IFIP TC13 Members

Officers

Chairperson

Philippe Palanque, France

Vice-chair for Awards

Paula Kotze, South Africa

Vice-chair for Communications

Helen Petrie, UK

Vice-chair for Growth and Reach out INTERACT Steering Committee Chair

Jan Gulliksen, Sweden

Vice-chair for Working Groups

Simone D. J. Barbosa, Brazil

Vice-chair for Development and Equity

Julio Abascal, Spain

Treasurer

Virpi Roto, Finland

Secretary

Marco Winckler, France

INTERACT Steering Committee Chair

Anirudha Joshi, India

Country Representatives

Australia
Henry B. L. Duh
Australian Computer Society

Austria
Geraldine Fitzpatrick
Austrian Computer Society

Belgium
Bruno Dumas
IMEC – Interuniversity
Micro-Electronics Center

Brazil
Lara S. G. Piccolo
Brazilian Computer Society (SBC)

Bulgaria
Stoyan Georgiev Dentchev
Bulgarian Academy of Sciences

Croatia
Andrina Granic
Croatian Information Technology
Association (CITA)

Cyprus
Panayiotis Zaphiris
Cyprus Computer Society

Czech Republic
Zdeněk Míkovec
Czech Society for Cybernetics
and Informatics

Finland
Virpi Roto
Finnish Information Processing
Association

France
Philippe Palanque and Marco Winckler
Société informatique de France (SIF)

Germany
Tom Gross
Gesellschaft fur Informatik e.V.

Ireland
Liam J. Bannon
Irish Computer Society

Italy
Fabio Paternò
Italian Computer Society

Japan
Yoshifumi Kitamura
Information Processing Society of Japan

Netherlands
Regina Bernhaupt
Nederlands Genootschap
voor Informatica

New Zealand
Mark Apperley
New Zealand Computer Society

Norway
Frode Eika Sandnes
Norwegian Computer Society

Poland
Marcin Sikorski
Poland Academy of Sciences

Portugal
Pedro Campos
Associacăo Portuguesa para o
Desenvolvimento da Sociedade da
Informação (APDSI)

Serbia
Aleksandar Jevremovic
Informatics Association of Serbia

Singapore
Shengdong Zhao
Singapore Computer Society

Slovakia
Wanda Benešová
The Slovak Society for Computer
Science

Slovenia
Matjaž Debevc
The Slovenian Computer Society
INFORMATIKA

Sri Lanka
Thilina Halloluwa
The Computer Society of Sri Lanka

South Africa
Janet L. Wesson & Paula Kotze
The Computer Society of South Africa

Sweden
Jan Gulliksen
Swedish Interdisciplinary Society for
Human-Computer Interaction
Swedish Computer Society

Switzerland
Denis Lalanne
Swiss Federation for Information
Processing

Tunisia
Mona Laroussi
Ecole Supérieure des Communications de
Tunis (SUP'COM)

United Kingdom
José Abdelnour Nocera
British Computer Society (BCS)

United Arab Emirates
Ahmed Seffah
UAE Computer Society

ACM

Gerrit van der Veer
Association for Computing
Machinery

CLEI

Jaime Sánchez
Centro Latinoamericano de Estudios en
Informatica

Expert Members

Julio Abascal, Spain
Carmelo Ardito, Italy
Nikolaos Avouris, Greece
Kaveh Bazargan, Iran
Ivan Burmistrov, Russia
Torkil Torkil Clemmensen, Denmark
Peter Forbrig, Germany
Dorian Gorgan, Romania

Anirudha Joshi, India
David Lamas, Estonia
Marta Kristin Larusdottir, Iceland
Zhengjie Liu, China
Fernando Loizides, UK/Cyprus
Ochieng Daniel "Dan" Orwa, Kenya
Eunice Sari, Australia/Indonesia

Working Group Chairpersons

**WG 13.1 (Education in HCI
and HCI Curricula)**

Konrad Baumann, Austria

**WG 13.2 (Methodologies
for User-Centered System Design)**

Regina Bernhaupt, Netherlands

WG 13.3 (HCI, Disability and Aging)

Helen Petrie, UK

**WG 13.4/2.7 (User Interface
Engineering)**

José Creissac Campos, Portugal

**WG 13.5 (Human Error, Resilience,
Reliability, Safety and System
Development)**

Chris Johnson, UK

**WG13.6 (Human-Work
Interaction Design)**

Barbara Rita Barricelli, Italy

WG13.7 (HCI and Visualization)

Peter Dannenmann, Germany

**WG 13.8 (Interaction Design
and International Development)**

José Adbelnour Nocera, UK

**WG 13.9 (Interaction Design
and Children)**

Janet Read, UK

**WG 13.10 (Human-Centred
Technology for Sustainability)**

Masood Masoodian, Finland

Conference Organizing Committee

General Conference Co-chairs

Paolo Buono, Italy
Catherine Plaisant, USA and France

Advisors

Fernando Loizides, UK
Marco Winckler, France

Technical Program Co-chairs

Carmelo Ardito, Italy
Rosa Lanzilotti, Italy
Alessio Malizia, UK and Italy

Keynote and Invited Talks Chair

Maria Francesca Costabile, Italy

Full Papers Co-chairs

Helen Petrie, UK
Antonio Piccinno, Italy

Short Papers Co-chairs

Giuseppe Desolda, Italy
Kori Inkpen, USA

Posters Co-chairs

Maristella Matera, Italy
Kent Norman, USA
Anna Spagnolli, Italy

Interactive Demos Co-chairs

Barbara Rita Barricelli, Italy
Nuno Jardim Nunes, Portugal

Panels Co-chairs

Effie Lai-Chong Law, UK
Massimo Zancanaro, Italy

Courses Co-chairs

Carmen Santoro, Italy
Nikolaos Avouris, Greece

Industrial Experiences Chair

Danilo Caivano, Italy

Workshops Co-chairs

Marta Kristín Larusdottir, Iceland
Davide Spano, Italy

Doctoral Consortium Co-chairs

Daniela Fogli, Italy
David Lamas, Estonia
John Stasko, USA

Online Experience Co-chairs

Fabrizio Balducci, Italy
Miguel Ceriani, Italy

Student Volunteers Co-chairs

Vita Santa Barletta, Italy
Grazia Ragone, UK

Publicity Co-chairs

Ganesh D. Bhutkar, India
Veronica Rossano, Italy

Local Organisation Chair

Simona Sarti, Consulta Umbria, Italy

Programme Committee

Sub-committee Chairs

Nikolaos Avouris, Greece
Regina Bernhaupt, Netherlands
Carla Dal Sasso Freitas, Brazil
Jan Gulliksen, Sweden
Paula Kotzé, South Africa
Effie Lai-Chong Law, UK

Philippe Palanque, France
Fabio Paternò, Italy
Thomas Pederson, Sweden
Albrecht Schmidt, Germany
Frank Steinicke, Germany
Gerhard Weber, Germany

Associated Chairs

José Abdelnour Nocera, UK
Raian Ali, Qatar
Florian Alt, Germany
Katrina Attwood, UK
Simone Barbosa, Brazil
Cristian Bogdan, Sweden
Paolo Bottoni, Italy
Judy Bowen, New Zealand
Daniel Buschek, Germany
Pedro Campos, Portugal
José Creissac Campos, Portugal
Luca Chittaro, Italy
Sandy Claes, Belgium
Christopher Clarke, UK
Torkil Clemmensen, Denmark
Vanessa Cobus, Germany
Ashley Colley, Finland
Aurora Constantin, UK
Lynne Coventry, UK
Yngve Dahl, Norway
Maria De Marsico, Italy
Luigi De Russis, Italy
Paloma Diaz, Spain
Monica Divitini, Norway
Mateusz Dolata, Switzerland
Bruno Dumas, Belgium
Sophie Dupuy-Chessa, France
Dan Fitton, UK
Peter Forbrig, Germany
Sandnes Frode Eika, Norway
Vivian Genaro Motti, USA
Rosella Gennari, Italy

Jens Gerken, Germany
Mareike Glöss, Sweden
Dorian Gorgan, Romania
Tom Gross, Germany
Uwe Gruenefeld, Germany
Julie Haney, USA
Ebba Þóra Hvannberg, Iceland
Netta Iivari, Finland
Nanna Inie, Denmark
Anna Sigríður Islind, Iceland
Anirudha Joshi, India
Bridget Kane, Sweden
Anne Marie Kanstrup, Denmark
Mohamed Khamis, UK
Kibum Kim, Korea
Marion Koelle, Germany
Kati Kuusinen, Denmark
Matthias Laschke, Germany
Fernando Loizides, UK
Andrés Lucero, Finland
Jo Lumsden, UK
Charlotte Magnusson, Sweden
Andrea Marrella, Italy
Célia Martinie, France
Timothy Merritt, Denmark
Zdeněk Míkovec, Czech Republic
Luciana Nedel, Brazil
Laurence Nigay, France
Valentina Nisi, Portugal
Raquel O. Prates, Brazil
Rakesh Patibanda, Australia
Simon Perrault, Singapore

Lara Piccolo, UK
Aparecido Fabiano Pinatti de Carvalho, Germany
Janet Read, UK
Karen Renaud, UK
Antonio Rizzo, Italy
Sayan Sarcar, Japan
Valentin Schwind, Germany
Gavin Sim, UK
Fotios Spyridonis, UK
Jan Stage, Denmark
Simone Stumpf, UK
Luis Teixeira, Portugal

Jakob Tholander, Sweden
Daniela Trevisan, Brazil
Stefano Valtolina, Italy
Jan Van den Bergh, Belgium
Nervo Verdezoto, UK
Chi Vi, UK
Giuliana Vitiello, Italy
Sarah Völkel, Germany
Marco Winckler, France
Dhaval Vyas, Australia
Janet Wesson, South Africa
Paweł W. Woźniak, Netherlands

Reviewers

Bruno A. Chagas, Brazil
Yasmeen Abdrabou, Germany
Maher Abujelala, USA
Jiban Adhikary, USA
Kashif Ahmad, Qatar
Muneeb Ahmad, UK
Naveed Ahmed, United Arab Emirates
Aino Ahtinen, Finland
Wolfgang Aigner, Austria
Deepak Akkil, Finland
Aftab Alam, Republic of Korea
Soraia Meneses Alarcão, Portugal
Pedro Albuquerque Santos, Portugal
Günter Alce, Sweden
Iñigo Aldalur, Spain
Alaa Alkhafaji, Iraq
Aishat Aloba, USA
Yosuef Alotaibi, UK
Taghreed Alshehri, UK
Ragaad Al-Tarawneh, USA
Alejandro Alvarez-Marin, Chile
Lucas Anastasiou, UK
Ulf Andersson, Sweden
Joseph Aneke, Italy
Mark Apperley, New Zealand
Renan Aranha, Brazil
Pierre-Emmanuel Arduin, France
Stephanie Arevalo Arboleda, Germany
Jan Argasiński, Poland

Patricia Arias-Cabarcos, Germany
Alexander Arntz, Germany
Jonas Auda, Germany
Andreas Auinger, Austria
Iuliia Avgustis, Finland
Cédric Bach, France
Miroslav Bachinski, Germany
Victor Bacu, Romania
Jan Balata, Czech Republic
Teresa Baldassarre, Italy
Fabrizio Balducci, Italy
Vijayanand Banahatti, India
Karolina Baras, Portugal
Simone Barbosa, Brazil
Vita Santa Barletta, Italy
Silvio Barra, Italy
Barbara Rita Barricelli, Italy
Ralph Barthel, UK
Thomas Baudel, France
Christine Bauer, Netherlands
Fatma Ben Mesmia, Canada
Marit Bentvelzen, Netherlands
François Bérard, France
Melanie Berger, Netherlands
Gerd Berget, Norway
Sergi Bermúdez i Badia, Portugal
Dario Bertero, UK
Guilherme Bertolaccini, Brazil
Lonni Besançon, Australia

Laura-Bianca Bilius, Romania
Kerstin Blumenstein, Austria
Andreas Bollin, Austria
Judith Borghouts, UK
Nis Bornoe, Denmark
Gabriela Bosetti, UK
Hollie Bostock, Portugal
Paolo Bottoni, Italy
Magdalena Boucher, Austria
Amina Bouraoui, Tunisia
Elodie Bouzekri, France
Judy Bowen, New Zealand
Efe Bozkir, Germany
Danielle Bragg, USA
Diogo Branco, Portugal
Dawn Branley-Bell, UK
Stephen Brewster, UK
Giada Brianza, UK
Barry Brown, Sweden
Nick Bryan-Kinns, UK
Andreas Bucher, Switzerland
Elizabeth Buie, UK
Alexandru Bundea, Germany
Paolo Buono, Italy
Michael Burch, Switzerland
Matthew Butler, Australia
Fabio Buttussi, Italy
Andreas Butz, Germany
Maria Claudia Buzzi, Italy
Marina Buzzi, Italy
Zoya Bylinskii, USA
Diogo Cabral, Portugal
Åsa Cajander, Sweden
Francisco Maria Calisto, Portugal
Hector Caltenco, Sweden
José Creissac Campos, Portugal
Heloisa Candello, Brazil
Alberto Cannavò, Italy
Bruno Cardoso, Belgium
Jorge Cardoso, Portugal
Géry Casiez, France
Fabio Cassano, Italy
Brendan Cassidy, UK
Alejandro Catala, Spain

Miguel Ceriani, UK
Daniel Cermak-Sassenrath, Denmark
Vanessa Cesário, Portugal
Fred Charles, UK
Debaleena Chattopadhyay, USA
Alex Chen, Singapore
Thomas Chen, USA
Yuan Chen, Canada
Chola Chhetri, USA
Katherine Chiluiza, Ecuador
Nick Chozos, UK
Michael Chromik, Germany
Christopher Clarke, UK
Bárbara Cleto, Portugal
Antonio Coelho, Portugal
Ashley Colley, Finland
Nelly Condori-Fernandez, Spain
Marios Constantinides, UK
Cléber Corrêa, Brazil
Vinicius Costa de Souza, Brazil
Joëlle Coutaz, France
Céline Coutrix, France
Chris Creed, UK
Carlos Cunha, Portugal
Kamila Rios da Hora Rodrigues, Brazil
Damon Daylamani-Zad, UK
Sergio de Cesare, UK
Marco de Gemmis, Italy
Teis De Greve, Belgium
Victor Adriel de Jesus Oliveira, Austria
Helmut Degen, USA
Donald Degraen, Germany
William Delamare, France
Giuseppe Desolda, Italy
Henrik Detjen, Germany
Marianna Di Gregorio, Italy
Ines Di Loreto, France
Daniel Diethei, Germany
Tilman Dingler, Australia
Anke Dittmar, Germany
Monica Divitini, Norway
Janki Dodiya, Germany
Julia Dominiak, Poland
Ralf Dörner, Germany

Julie Doyle, Ireland
Philip Doyle, Ireland
Fiona Draxler, Germany
Emanuel Felipe Duarte, Brazil
Rui Duarte, Portugal
Bruno Dumas, Belgium
Mark Dunlop, UK
Sophie Dupuy-Chessa, France
Jason Dykes, UK
Chloe Eghtebas, Germany
Kevin El Haddad, Belgium
Don Samitha Elvitigala, New Zealand
Augusto Esteves, Portugal
Siri Fagernes, Norway
Katherine Fennedy, Singapore
Marta Ferreira, Portugal
Francesco Ferrise, Italy
Lauren Stacey Ferro, Italy
Christos Fidas, Greece
Daniel Finnegan, UK
Daniela Fogli, Italy
Manuel J. Fonseca, Portugal
Peter Forbrig, Germany
Rita Francese, Italy
André Freire, Brazil
Karin Fröhlich, Finland
Susanne Furman, USA
Henrique Galvan Debarba, Denmark
Sandra Gama, Portugal
Dilrukshi Gamage, Japan
Jérémie Garcia, France
Jose Garcia Estrada, Norway
David Geerts, Belgium
Denise Y. Geiskkovitch, Canada
Stefan Geisler, Germany
Mirko Gelsomini, Italy
Çağlar Genç, Finland
Rosella Gennari, Italy
Nina Gerber, Germany
Moojan Ghafurian, Canada
Maliheh Ghajargar, Sweden
Sabiha Ghellal, Germany
Debjyoti Ghosh, Germany
Michail Giannakos, Norway

Terje Gjøsæter, Norway
Marc Gonzalez Capdevila, Brazil
Julien Gori, Finland
Laurent Grisoni, France
Tor-Morten Gronli, Norway
Sebastian Günther, Germany
Li Guo, UK
Srishti Gupta, USA
Francisco Gutiérrez, Belgium
José Eder Guzman Mendoza, Mexico
Jonna Häkkilä, Finland
Lilit Hakobyan, UK
Thilina Halloluwa, Sri Lanka
Perttu Hämäläinen, Finland
Lane Harrison, USA
Michael Harrison, UK
Hanna Hasselqvist, Sweden
Tomi Heimonen, USA
Florian Heinrich, Germany
Florian Heller, Belgium
Karey Helms, Sweden
Nathalie Henry Riche, USA
Diana Hernandez-Bocanegra, Germany
Danula Hettiachchi, Australia
Wilko Heuten, Germany
Annika Hinze, New Zealand
Linda Hirsch, Germany
Sarah Hodge, UK
Sven Hoffmann, Germany
Catherine Holloway, UK
Leona Holloway, Australia
Lars Erik Holmquist, UK
Anca-Simona Horvath, Denmark
Simo Hosio, Finland
Sebastian Hubenschmid, Germany
Helena Vallo Hult, Sweden
Shah Rukh Humayoun, USA
Ebba Þóra Hvannberg, Iceland
Alon Ilsar, Australia
Md Athar Imtiaz, New Zealand
Oana Inel, Netherlands
Francisco Iniesto, UK
Andri Ioannou, Cyprus
Chyng-Yang Jang, USA

Gokul Jayakrishnan, India
Stine Johansen, Denmark
Tero Jokela, Finland
Rui José, Portugal
Anirudha Joshi, India
Manjiri Joshi, India
Jana Jost, Germany
Patrick Jost, Norway
Annika Kaltenhauser, Germany
Jin Kang, Canada
Younah Kang, Republic of Korea
Jari Kangas, Finland
Petko Karadechev, Denmark
Armağan Karahanoğlu, Netherlands
Sukran Karaosmanoglu, Germany
Alexander Kempton, Norway
Rajiv Khadka, USA
Jayden Khakurel, Finland
Pramod Khambete, India
Neeta Khanuja, Portugal
Young-Ho Kim, USA
Reuben Kirkham, Australia
Ilan Kirsh, Israel
Maria Kjærup, Denmark
Kevin Koban, Austria
Frederik Kobbelgaard, Denmark
Martin Kocur, Germany
Marius Koller, Germany
Christophe Kolski, France
Takanori Komatsu, Japan
Jemma König, New Zealand
Monika Kornacka, Poland
Thomas Kosch, Germany
Panayiotis Koutsabasis, Greece
Lucie Kruse, Germany
Przemysław Kucharski, Poland
Johannes Kunkel, Germany
Bineeth Kuriakose, Norway
Anelia Kurteva, Austria
Marc Kurz, Austria
Florian Lang, Germany
Rosa Lanzilotti, Italy
Lars Bo Larsen, Denmark
Marta Larusdottir, Iceland

Effie Law, UK
Luis Leiva, Luxembourg
Barbara Leporini, Italy
Pascal Lessel, Germany
Hongyu Li, USA
Yuan Liang, USA
Yu-Tzu Lin, Denmark
Markus Löchtefeld, Denmark
Angela Locoro, Italy
Benedikt Loepp, Germany
Domenico Lofù, Italy
Fernando Loizides, UK
Arminda Lopes, Portugal
Feiyu Lu, USA
Jo Lumsden, UK
Anders Lundström, Sweden
Kris Luyten, Belgium
Granit Luzhnica, Austria
Marc Macé, France
Anderson Maciel, Brazil
Cristiano Maciel, Brazil
Miroslav Macík, Czech Republic
Scott MacKenzie, Canada
Hanuma Teja Maddali, USA
Rui Madeira, Portugal
Alexander Maedche, Germany
Charlotte Magnusson, Sweden
Jyotirmaya Mahapatra, India
Vanessa Maike, USA
Maitreyee Maitreyee, Sweden
Ville Mäkelä, Germany
Sylvain Malacria, France
Sugandh Malhotra, India
Ivo Malý, Czech Republic
Marco Manca, Italy
Muhanad Manshad, USA
Isabel Manssour, Brazil
Panos Markopoulos, Netherlands
Karola Marky, Germany
Andrea Marrella, Italy
Andreas Martin, Switzerland
Célia Martinie, France
Nuno Martins, Portugal
Maristella Matera, Italy

Radiah Rivu, Germany
Mehdi Rizvi, Italy
Judy Robertson, UK
Michael Rohs, Germany
Marco Romano, Italy
Anton Rosén, Sweden
Veronica Rossano, Italy
Virpi Roto, Finland
Debjani Roy, India
Matthew Rueben, USA
Vit Rusnak, Czech Republic
Philippa Ryan, UK
Thomas Ryberg, Denmark
Rufat Rzayev, Germany
Parisa Saadati, UK
Adrian Sabou, Romania
Ofir Sadka, Israel
Juan Pablo Saenz, Italy
Marco Saltarella, Italy
Sanjit Samaddar, UK
Ivan Sanchez Milara, Finland
Frode Eika Sandnes, Norway
Leonardo Sandoval, UK
Carmen Santoro, Italy
Pratiti Sarkar, India
Guilherme Schardong, Brazil
Christina Schmidbauer, Austria
Eike Schneiders, Denmark
Maximilian Schrapel, Germany
Sabrina Scuri, Portugal
Korok Sengupta, Germany
Marta Serafini, Italy
Marcos Serrano, France
Kshitij Sharma, Norway
Sumita Sharma, Finland
Akihisa Shitara, Japan
Mark Shovman, Israel
Ludwig Sidenmark, UK
Carlos Silva, Portugal
Tiago Silva da Silva, Brazil
Milene Silveira, Brazil
James Simpson, Australia
Ashwin Singh, India
Laurianne Sitbon, Australia

Mikael B. Skov, Denmark
Pavel Slavik, Czech Republic
Aidan Slingsby, UK
K. Tara Smith, UK
Ellis Solaiman, UK
Andreas Sonderegger, Switzerland
Erik Sonnleitner, Austria
Keyur Sorathia, India
Emanuel Sousa, Portugal
Sonia Sousa, Estonia
Anna Spagnolli, Italy
Davide Spallazzo, Italy
Lucio Davide Spano, Italy
Katta Spiel, Austria
Priyanka Srivastava, India
Katarzyna Stawarz, UK
Teodor Stefanut, Romania
Mari-Klara Stein, Denmark
Jonathan Strahl, Finland
Tim Stratmann, Germany
Christian Sturm, Germany
Michael Svangren, Denmark
Aurélien Tabard, France
Benjamin Tag, Australia
Federico Tajariol, France
Aishwari Talhan, Republic of Korea
Maurizio Teli, Denmark
Subrata Tikadar, India
Helena Tobiasson, Sweden
Guy Toko, South Africa
Brianna Tomlinson, USA
Olof Torgersson, Sweden
Genoveffa Tortora, Italy
Zachary O. Toups, USA
Scott Trent, Japan
Philippe Truillet, France
Tommaso Turchi, UK
Fanny Vainionpää, Finland
Stefano Valtolina, Italy
Niels van Berkel, Denmark
Jan Van den Bergh, Belgium
Joey van der Bie, Netherlands
Bram van Deurzen, Belgium
Domenique van Gennip, Australia

Paul van Schauk, UK
Koen van Turnhout, Netherlands
Jean Vanderdonckt, Belgium
Eduardo Veas, Austria
Katia Vega, USA
Kellie Vella, Australia
Leena Ventä-Olkkonen, Finland
Nadine Vigouroux, France
Gabriela Villalobos-Zúñiga, Switzerland
Aku Visuri, Finland
Giuliana Vitiello, Italy
Pierpaolo Vittorini, Italy
Julius von Willich, Germany
Steven Vos, Netherlands
Nadine Wagener, Germany
Lun Wang, Italy
Ruijie Wang, Italy
Gerhard Weber, Germany
Thomas Weber, Germany
Rina Wehbe, Canada
Florian Weidner, Germany
Alexandra Weilenmann, Sweden
Sebastian Weiß, Germany

Yannick Weiss, Germany
Robin Welsch, Germany
Janet Wesson, South Africa
Benjamin Weyers, Germany
Stephanie Wilson, UK
Marco Winckler, France
Philipp Wintersberger, Austria
Katrin Wolf, Germany
Kim Wölfel, Germany
Julia Woodward, USA
Matthias Wunsch, Austria
Haijun Xia, USA
Asim Evren Yantac, Turkey
Enes Yigitbas, Germany
Yongjae Yoo, Canada
Johannes Zagermann, Germany
Massimo Zancanaro, Italy
André Zenner, Germany
Jingjie Zheng, Canada
Suwen Zhu, USA
Ying Zhu, USA
Jürgen Ziegler, Germany

Partners and Sponsors

Partners

International Federation for Information Processing

In-cooperation with ACM   In-cooperation with SIGCHI

Sponsors

EULOGIC

Experis™
ManpowerGroup

exprivia

openwork
Just solutions

Contents – Part II

Designing for Smart Devices and IoT

Designing for the Elderly and Accessibility

Education and HCI

COVID-19 and HCI

Addressing the Challenges of COVID-19 Social Distancing Through Passive Wi-Fi and Ubiquitous Analytics: A Real World Deployment

Miguel Ribeiro[1,2]([✉]), Nuno Nunes[1,2], Marta Ferreira[1], João Nogueira[1], Johannes Schöning[2,3,4], and Valentina Nisi[1,2]

[1] Instituto Superior Técnico, University of Lisbon, Lisbon, Portugal
[2] ITI/LARSyS, Funchal, Portugal
`jose.miguel.ribeiro@tecnico.ulisboa.pt`
[3] University of Bremen, Bremen, Germany
[4] University of St. Gallen, Gallen, Switzerland

Abstract. During the COVID-19 pandemic, social distancing measures were employed to contain its spread. This paper describes the deployment and testing of a passive Wi-Fi scanning system to help people keep track of crowded spaces, hence comply with social distancing measures. The system is based on passive Wi-Fi sensing to detect human presence in 93 locations around a medium-sized European Touristic Island. This data is then used in website plugins and a mobile application to inform citizens and tourists about the locations' crowdedness with real-time and historical data. To understand how people react to this type of information, we deployed online questionnaires in situ to collect user insights regarding the usefulness, safety, and privacy concerns. Results show that users considered the occupancy data reported by the system as positively related to their perception. Furthermore, the public display of this data made them feel safer while travelling and planning their commute.

Keywords: Passive Wi-Fi · Survey · Mobile application · COVID-19

1 Introduction

Driven by the impact of the COVID-19 pandemic, governments worldwide were forced to impose lockdowns, promote work from home, and enforce other measures for citizens to keep social distancing slow-down the spread of the virus and flatten the curve to avoid overwhelming the healthcare systems. In this scenario, we saw the appearance of several technological applications emerging, ranging from symptom tracking [23,27] and pandemic planning [44] to digital contact tracing [30,31,41,43] and also reaching the field of information visualization platforms [11,46]. Especially in high-density urban areas, maintaining social distancing is intricate. After the first wave of the pandemic from February to

© IFIP International Federation for Information Processing 2021
Published by Springer Nature Switzerland AG 2021
C. Ardito et al. (Eds.): INTERACT 2021, LNCS 12933, pp. 3–24, 2021.
https://doi.org/10.1007/978-3-030-85616-8_1

May 2020, many countries in the northern hemisphere saw a decrease in infection rates leading to a return of many economic activities. Driven by the need to foster economic growth, many countries incentivized unconfinement measures, from mandatory use of masks and sanitation to enforcing capacity limitations in public spaces.

This paper describes a technology-based measure implemented in a touristic European Island after the first wave of the pandemic. The system evolved from an existing community based passive Wi-Fi infrastructure deployed as part of a tourism flow sensing research project [29]. The infrastructure uses a network of Wi-Fi routers to passively detect the presence of wireless-enabled devices in their range [36]. Through machine learning, the infrastructure estimates the presence and flow of people both historically and in real-time. Unlike existing systems (e.g., Google popular times), the system is open to the local community enabling the deployment of additional services, including ubiquitous analytics [39] adapted to the local context. Here, we describe how we adapted the original infrastructure to help citizens and visitors, including local businesses and health and tourism authorities, leveraging open information about people's presence and flow. The infrastructure was deployed on 93 specific points of interest (POIs), emphasizing touristic places and popular public locations like shopping centers.

Sensing human presence has been approached in several manners, from manual people counting, surveys to wearable trackers [7]. In the context of the pandemic, monitoring mobility at scale and in real-time was an important requirement. Several methods were attempted, from video processing [15,38], crowdsourcing smartphone applications [33], cell tower and call record, and non-intrusive wireless monitoring (NIWM) [5,21,37,42]. While most techniques require user knowledge or intervention in the data acquisition process, NIWM does not. Either via cell signals, Bluetooth, or Wi-Fi devices, the number of people in specific locations can be sensed automatically and anonymously using NIWM. However, this data is hard to validate, as users often do not know they are being monitored or are not actively involved in the data collection process. To overcome this challenge, the system described here collects human presence data anonymously and presents the results back to citizens transparent and accessible. In this paper, we present our design approach and discuss how users understand and react to this real-time information. We contribute to a deeper understanding of such a system's impact in helping people maintain social distancing and the broader implications in terms of accuracy of the methods employed and the safety and privacy concerns that such information could entail.

1.1 Contributions and Research Questions

The work described in this paper was the response to the regional call to action to help the community return to a "new normal". The passive Wi-Fi infrastructure already in place in the island [29] was capable of estimating the presence and flow of people in public spaces. The existing system provided an opportunity to adapt the information for citizens and tourists, to help them make informed decisions when planning and moving through public locations. The system was then adapted from a generic passerby counter to a system to reinforce the social distancing measures of COVID-19 situation in the following ways: i) increase the existing network of passive Wi-Fi sensors to 93 POIs covering not only touristic POIs but also essential public places such as shopping centers and squares; ii) developing a mobile application that could show this information to citizens and locals, together with COVID-19 safety measures and tourist information about POIs and attractions; and finally, iii) deploying an in situ survey to present the occupancy data and probe passerby about the accuracy of the displayed data, as well as the sense of safety, privacy, and satisfaction of the location. Through this research, the authors intend to answer the following research questions:

RQ1: Can we validate passive Wi-Fi data as a representation of occupancy of a POI for COVID-19 occupancy monitoring?
RQ2: Can occupancy data automatically collected via passive Wi-Fi increase the sense of safety and crowd awareness in public locations?
RQ3: Can we use this information to help citizens make informed decisions about when to visit public locations based on their occupation?

2   Related Work

This research is primarily motivated by two areas of prior work, combining non intrusive people sensing and data presentation to citizens to collect feedback. The area of people sensing has had in the past the attention of researchers mainly due to the unnecessary intervention of the people being sensed. The technologies and techniques vary and aim to target the masses with automated mechanisms that require little to no human intervention. Examples of this are found in video surveillance analysis, where the video feed of existing surveillance cameras can be processed to enable head counts by using convolutional neural networks to overcome the challenges of low resolution images and poor lighting [15]. Recently a study [38] was done using thermal imagery to tag people for COVID-19 with signs like high body temperature by automatically detecting the faces and the temperature of the people passing in front of a thermal camera.

Other efforts were done using big data of cell phone records [4,40] to detect mobility traces, interaction patterns and taking advantage of functionalities such as handover and cell (re)selection, which are used to maintain seamless coverage for mobile end-user equipment between cells. The study by Alsaeedy and Chong [2] uses those parameters to identify the regions at risk of infections with high human mobility by using the existing cellular network. Also, Ahmed in [1] proposed a similar framework to control the spread of COVID-19 using the cellular system by using the mobile identifiers of infected people and calculating the distances of other phones nearby in those cell towers to deliver that information to the clinical centers for close contacts of suspects.

Wi-Fi has been used in the pre-pandemic to detect gatherings and passerby, with studies being done in football games [5], universities campuses [3] and hospitals [37]. The motivations of many of these studies are diverse, some look at energy waste on scanning methods [3], realistic facility management and planning [37], while others looked at crowding factors, flock detection and waiting times, speed and frequent paths [21] and even social information like popularity of events (in the case of [4] singers in concerts). In the pandemic context, Wi-Fi has also been used to detect the contagion risk in public transport [10] by using multiple sensors that monitor the air quality, temperature humidity and use Wi-Fi probes to detect the people present thus creating an index for contagion risk. Another solution that employs Wi-Fi probe requests is presented in [42] with the goal to estimate indoor crowd densities based on dynamic fingerprints based on signal strength and proposing a crowd density estimation solution based on the positioning algorithm. The authors made experiments in a laboratory class and in three public social activities in a footbridge, railway and subway demonstrating how this can be used to estimate crowd density. Wi-fi was also proposed in a framework to monitor vital respiratory signs of patients by measuring the Wi-Fi frames reflected by the human body standing between a dedicated emitter and receiver and applying bandpass filtering to extract respiratory components of the patients [25].

2.1   Feedback via Voluntary Walk-Up Systems

While user surveys and online forms are viable ways for citizens to contribute with their opinions, the idea of gathering this type of information in situ without the need for a human interviewer opens opportunities for new studies. HCI brings new possibilities of presenting and gathering information from the users by providing interactive and attractive interfaces to grasp the passerby's attention often done via public displays. A recurrent problem with this method is that the users are often presented with automatically sensed information, that may not always represent the reality, and the user may feel the need to give an opinion or to even challenge the presented data. A classic example of this is the presentation of real-feel weather conditions or environmental parameters.

The area of surveying is essential to gather the citizens perspectives about different subjects of our society and products. Several approaches have been done to assess user satisfaction or inquiry through interactive technologies [6,19,20, 28]. One of the studies done in this area presents Roam.IO [18], which proposes a hybrid data approach combining data from IoT sensing with qualitative data contributed by citizens. The authors developed a public installation consisting of a tangible robot-like interface placed in passageways, to entice and encourage the public to walk-up and answer questions. The users are questioned to suggest what the data might represent and enrich it with subjective observations with success in user engagement with this apparatus.

2.2   Citizen Science

Several attempts have tried to tackle the problem of gathering data through citizens in ubiquitous ways [17,45]. This led to a range of interactive technologies, focused on human-centred data collection. An example is VoiceYourView [45] which uses speech recognition and natural language processing to provide feedback of how citizens perceive and feel about the public spaces around them.

Physical tangible mechanisms have also been used for public opinion gathering such as polling systems to urban voting and visualizations [24]. Another tangible approach was EmoBall [12] and Mood Squeezer [14] which allows for playfulness in office buildings where a lightweight technology was designed to ask people to reflect on their mood by squeezing a colored ball from a box set. VoxBox [16] presented a tangible system for gathering opinions in situ at an event through playful and engaging interaction via a large panel of interaction turning the questionnaire itself into a toy that made people want to fidget with it. CommunitySourcing [17] was also used to investigate the potential of community sourcing by designing, implementing and evaluating a vending machine that allowed users to earn credits by performing tasks using a touchscreen attached to the machine and physical rewards were dispensed through traditional vending mechanics. Similarly, SmallTalk [13] explored how tangible devices used as a toy with spinners, dials and buttons can be used to gather feedback from children in the context of a theater performance via a tangible survey system to capture what children thought of the performance they had seen. Recently Diethei [8] explored socio-psychological processes and motivations to share personal data during a pandemic.

3 Data and Deployment

This system's main components rely on the presence and flow sensing infrastructure, providing user information via dashboards, web plugins, a mobile app, and finally collecting in situ feedback. The sensing infrastructure is based on a network of passive Wi-Fi routers described below. This infrastructure then powers the two other components by enabling data to be processed and presented to the end-users. The presence and flow data is presented to different stakeholders in different formats, from a global dashboard mostly targeting authorities to web plugins (that can be included in websites) targeting local businesses, thus informing them of people's presence at different times. Then, the data is consumed by an official Tourism Board app that presents the list of safe locations to visit and at what times. Finally, the surveys are generated as interactive webpages that can be deployed on tablets in situ or accessed by mobile phones via a QR code. The survey is used to collect feedback from the users of those locations about the accuracy of the data, safety of the location and overall satisfaction.

3.1 Passive Wi-Fi Data Gathering

The presence data presented in the visualizations is gathered from a passive Wi-Fi platform [29, 36]. This infrastructure was originally designed to support a community-based Wi-Fi tracking system to understand mobility at scale. The original system provided several interactive dashboards [32, 34, 35] to help communities easily run systematic analysis of tourists' mobility patterns in the destinations, contributing in new ways in visualizing spatio-temporal mobility data.

This system is composed of Wi-Fi routers spread across all parishes of the region, as shown in Fig. 1. The data is collected in real-time by Wi-Fi routers

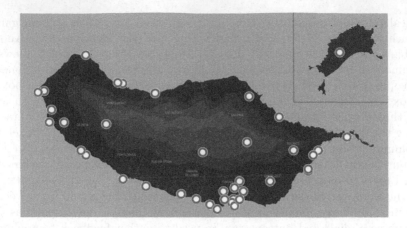

Fig. 1. Map of Madeira Islands (Portugal) showing the locations of the passive Wi-Fi routers deployed.

spread across multiple locations covering all regions' parishes. The data collected and sent to a central server includes a location identifier, a timestamp and an anonymous identifier (based on the MAC address) of each Wi-Fi enabled device present in a radius of approximately 80 m from the router (depending on the location and obstacles). The processed results are made available via an API that allows developing standalone implementations, thus providing real-time information about the number of devices detected in the last hours, location meta-data, and historical hourly data that serves as a comparison to the current counts.

The locations were chosen based upon common points of interest selected in coordination with the local tourism bureau and include governmental buildings close to the street, tourism offices, plazas, restaurants, cafes, and viewpoints where the routers were installed in the nearest facility. The routers placed in each location needed an electrical connection and internet access, thus posing challenges in terms of coverage and location. They had to be placed indoors close to outlets and on a suitable site provided by the existing building.

A challenge in adapting the infrastructure for COVID-19 security capacity was asking each site to provide the maximum safety number for each space. To overcome both challenges, the research team worked closely with local authorities to find and test a reasonable match between the router's range and the spaces' capacity. This process was tested initially in a private beach club, which provided very good conditions to evaluate the sensing infrastructure's accuracy. The club was only accessible via a controlled entrance and provided daily counts of admissions per hour and the maximum number of people inside the facilities on any given hourly period. This data was used as ground truth for several weeks to evaluate the accuracy of the machine learning methods used to estimate both the number of entrances and the total number of people inside the facility from the number of devices detected by the router. The ground truth facility had an overall capacity of 500 people and it was monitored with a single router located in the main entrance building. While this shows the simplicity and ease of deployment of the sensing infrastructure, not all the POIs could rely on the same level of accuracy since, in many places, there was no access control or no structured capacity defined. In these cases, the research team judged from inspection of maps and local screening based on signal strength measures. Finally, in some POIs, it was impossible to make the assessment, and hence the research team resorted to 60% of the maximum pre-pandemic capacity.

3.2   Dashboard and Web Plugins

Motivated by the rapid spread of COVID-19, and inspired by the social sensing paradigm, the contributions of this section lie in the implementation of an interactive platform based on the Wi-Fi tracking infrastructure, to visualize information related to this enriched dataset of spatio-temporal data. In particular, we here present the visualizations related to the COVID-19 disease diffusion and its effect on human mobility in the islands and describe the interactive data visualization application.

We designed and implemented a web-based interactive data visualization built using Web technologies, focusing on the visualizations related to the COVID-19 period, showing the data in percentages of the total for each location, in a way to preserve the counts of some routers that are located in private infrastructures. These data representations have been designed to present the human presence considering the period when the pandemic of COVID-19 was experienced in Portugal. In particular, as it is possible to see in Fig. 2, the presented data show the percentage of users in a specific area, in comparison with the last week before the day the state of emergency was declared in Portugal and the first case in Madeira Islands.

The dashboard presents an interactive visualization of human presence data during the COVID-19 outbreak, and to compare this data with the patterns of previous weeks. The visualized data is collected exploiting social sensing, and in particular, a community-based passive Wi-Fi tracking infrastructure, deployed in the Madeira Archipelago.

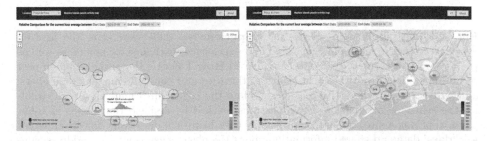

Fig. 2. (Left): Presents the information grouped by municipality; (Right) Zoomed view presents the ungrouped information focused on a specific area.

In addition to this, a web widget was also created being able to be embedded in websites, (which was also used for the in situ survey shown in Fig. 3) so that each institution that has a router in its facilities can also inform its visitors about the current status and historical trend for each hour. This widget is currently used in the Private Beach Club website informing their website visitors of their affluence in real-time.

3.3 Mobile Application

The final touchpoint consisted of a mobile application designed for the Health and Tourism authorities responsible for implementing the Islands' safe tourism system. This system relied on the airport (and port) PCR COVID-19 testing. The visitors could either upload the results of a COVID-19 PCR test to the app and then pass the health check at the airports' arrivals. Alternatively, they could perform a free PCR test on arrival and receive the test results via email. During the 14-day monitoring period, the visitors were also asked to fill out a voluntary epidemiological survey.

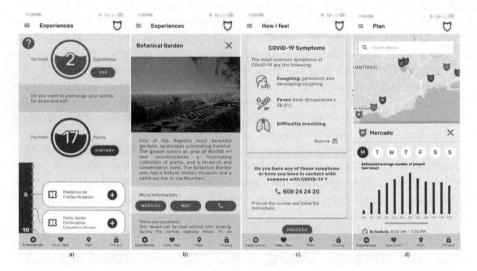

Fig. 3. Mobile application screens: a) **Experiences** - This view gives the user an overview of the current points collected and experiences exchange for points, as well as the history in a vertical chronological view; b) **How I Feel** - Shows the common user recommendations from the local health authorities and can call emergency numbers; c) **Plan** - This is where the user can explore the region in a map view and visualize the real-time occupancy of the locations marked by a shield that varies in color. Upon touching a site, the user is presented with historical occupancy for the different weekdays' data and shared information about the place, such as website, address, contacts, and schedule; d) **Privacy** - In this tab allows the user to view in a transparent manner how the information that is being presented is collected, and the ability to set notification permissions and geolocation (used to locate the user in the map).

Thus, the app was part of a more extensive safety system, which included testing all visitors, asking them to fill out an epidemiological survey and a daily follow up of COVID-19 related symptoms. To nudge visitors to perform the PCR test before arrival and as a way to incentivize daily epidemiological monitoring, the app also implemented a gamification mechanism that awarded users points each time they performed a COVID-19 safe activity.

Although the app's gamification component is beyond this paper's scope, it enabled a user to accumulate points by completing tasks and challenges of visiting safe locations. The points could then be exchanged for free experiences proposed by the local tourism office. The application interface starts by presenting the user with opening instructions for the first use, which helps the user navigate through the four main screens of the application and understand the points system, the challenges, and mechanics. Then the information is depicted in Fig. 3 and categorized into four tabs.

Both the real-time map data and the historical occupation charts are powered by the passive Wi-Fi infrastructure that collects data anonymously in these locations.

3.4 In Situ Survey

The in situ surveys were deployed in a total of four locations (described in more detail in Table 2). These surveys were used to present and collect information in selected POIs and survey the passerby's about the sense of safety and satisfaction of the location, and inquiry about privacy and safety concerns. This method also provided a way to crowdsource the accuracy of the information depicted, asking passersby to confirm the estimate and fine-tune the machine learning algorithms and the overall range and occupancy estimates.

The user interface was developed using web technologies suitable for responsive screen sizes and were deployed in a tablet to be answered via smartphone. The interface was designed as follows:

- To show the user the current location and current count (the system counts the number of devices in the Wi-Fi range and estimates the number of people based on a custom made algorithm) via a widget with an animated waveform gauge. The animation is supposed to draw attention to the screen (see Fig. 4, top left);
- Based on the real-time Wi-Fi counts, the interface shows an average hourly count history with the current hour highlighted (Fig. 4 Top);
- The interface shows the interactive survey. The survey gathers information about the users feeling about the occupancy levels of the location (as reported by the system interface), their safety perception, and the relevance of the real-time widget regarding their perceptions;
- The interface cycles through question panels when no interaction is recorded for 15 s. The cycling of the panels is designed to draw attention to the interactive screen;
- The system sends data to the database, when the user: answers all questions or does not interact for 15 s after having answered a question.

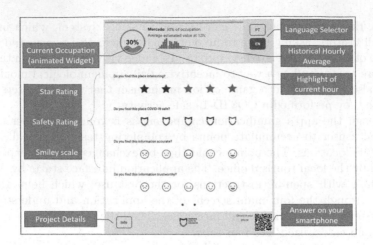

Fig. 4. In situ interactive survey Interface components diagram.

The survey had the option of two languages (English and Portuguese), has a QR-Code for the user to scan and answer the survey on their mobile phone thus avoiding physical touch with the tablet and has an "Info" button to show the project details and information about how the data is gathered and related privacy issues.

The survey questions are organised according to three kinds of answers, each one depicted by a specific icon: a star rating to rate the place interest, a shield to rate safety and a smiley for accuracy and trustworthiness score on a 5 point Likert scale We kept the number of questions low and succinct to maximize user engagement and a swift interaction with minimum effort. The questions are presented in Table 1, grouped into two tabs of questions that cycled between them.

Table 1. In situ survey questions

#	Question	Rating scale	Pannel	Connotation
Q1	Do you find this place interesting?	Star	1	Positive
Q2	Do you find this place COVID-19 safe?	Shield	1	Positive
Q3	Do you find this information accurate?	Smiley	1	Positive
Q4	Do you find this information trustworthy?	Smiley	1	Positive
Q5	Do you find this information useful?	Smiley	2	Positive
Q6	Do you find this information intrusive?	Smiley	2	Negative
Q7	Do you find this information improves safety?	Smiley	2	Positive
Q8	Do you find this information violates privacy?	Smiley	2	Negative

3.5   Deployment

The in situ survey was deployed in four POIs and took place during the months of September to December of 2020. The locations were the research institute cafe (where it was piloted for a week), a private beach club, the gift shop of one of the most popular tourist attractions (viewpoint) and a Hotel lobby. In all of these places a tablet was used on a stand to show the relevant information and prompt the users with the questions.

The locations, described in Table 2 were chosen for their characteristics of being locations that drew the attention of locals and tourists, and for their facilities that allowed an appreciate placement of the tablets indoors and in secure yet accessible spots in the premises.

Table 2. Location details

Type	Location	Limit	Nr Answers	Nr days
Research Institute	Restaurant/Bar	n/a	77	6
Touristic attraction (Viewpoint)	Gift Shop	n/a	28	128
Beach club	Entrance	500	90	131
Hotel	Reception	n/a	35	105
Total			230	–

4   Results

In this section, we will present the results from the in situ survey, relative to how the users classified the information provided and perceived their safety at the locations. Besides, we present the results of modeling the Wi-Fi counts with ground truth data in one site to estimate the real number of people present.

4.1   Passive Wi-Fi Ground Truth Validation

One of the four sites where the in situ survey was deployed, the private beach club, was used to provide ground truth to validate the data collected from the rest of the nodes of the passive Wi-Fi system and remodel the data to estimate the real number of people in the premises. To support the unconfinement of people after the first wave of COVID-19, the regional authorities asked all public sites to limit occupancy. For this specific site, the number of people inside the premises was limited to 500. Since the access was controlled electronically, this site provided unique conditions to evaluate the accuracy of the Wi-Fi sensor. The ground truth data corresponds to 356 data points covering 44 days between June and August. The whole premise was covered by a single Wi-Fi sensor placed in the main building after the entrance.

While the Wi-Fi counts help to show the peak times of occupation and the overall curve along the days of the week, those numbers are not exact counts.

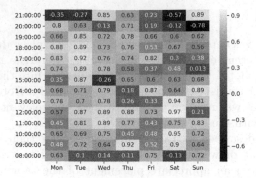

Fig. 5. Weekday and hourly correlations between the Wi-Fi counts and ground truth.

This is mainly due to people out of the Wi-Fi range having their wireless turned off, among other factors. To estimate the real number of people in the premises from the real-time Wi-Fi counts, we compared and created data models with the official hourly number of entrances and exits controlled via the electronic access control system. The time slot used for the comparisons was 60 min. For each hour and weekday, we computed the correlation between these variables. We tried to estimate the real number of people through data modeling. The data gathered in the private beach club shows strong Persons' correlations with the ground truth data. The correlation for the dataset is 0.64, and Fig. 5 shows the breakdown in weekdays and hours. In this analysis, each correlation is done using 6 data points. The low values in some isolated hours correspond to the beginning and end of the day, where abnormal movements may have occurred during the procedures of opening and closing of the facilities that did not provide correlations as good as the remaining hours.

We also attempted to model the number of actual people entering and exiting the premises against the router counts with several regression methods. The features were extracted by grouping the data hourly for each weekday. Each row represented one hour of data on a specific weekday from the location. The number of hours of ground truth varied, as also did the closing times. The total

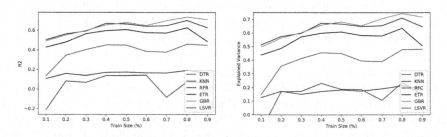

Fig. 6. Evolution of R2 (left) and explained variance (right) with incremental steps of train/test percentages for seven methods.

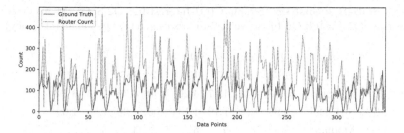

Fig. 7. Beach club ground truth counts vs router counts.

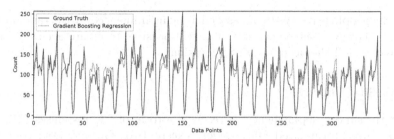

Fig. 8. Modeled router counts of the beach club to fit the ground truth data.

number of days was 44, ranging from 2020-06-15 to 2020-07-29. This resulted in 590 data points with the following features: *hour, weekday, count*. The Scikit-learn python library was used to test the following common methods used in regression:

– Decision Tree Regressor (DTR)
– K-Neighbors Regressor (KNR) – k = 100
– Random Forest Regressor (RFR) – Estimators = 100
– Extra Trees Regressor (ETR) – Estimators = 100
– Gradient Boosting Regressor (BGR) – Learning Rate = 0.1, Estimators = 100
– Linear Support Vector Regressor (LSVR) = Tolerance = 1e−4
– Epsilon Support Vector Regressor (SVR) – Degree = 3, Epsilon = 0.1

The parameter sweep was done for the train/test ratio, ranging from 10% to 90%, with step increments of 10%. These classifiers were run 1000 times for each of the steps and the average accuracy for each classifier was taken for the results shown in Fig. 6. The method that shows higher results when using the same dataset for trains and test (train size = 1) is the Gradient Boost Regression. Using this method, we plotted in Fig. 7 the original data points of router counts and ground truth, and in Fig. 8 the regression made using the Random Forest Regressor, with values of R2 and explained variance of 0.92.

These results show that the routers data can be reliably used to predict the real number of passersby in certain locations by modeling for each location, or location typology. The accuracy depends on how the router is installed, its range,

Table 3. Statistical analysis of replies (Q1-Interesting; Q2-Safe; Q3-Accurate; Q4-Trustworthy; Q5-Useful; Q6-Intrusive; Q7-Improves safety; Q8-Violates Privacy)

Parameter	Q1	Q2	Q3	Q4	Q5	Q6	Q7	Q8
N	185	182	174	163	172	155	155	149
Average	4.58	4.41	4.17	4.26	4.40	3.46	4.43	3.29
Std. Dev	0.95	1.09	1.19	1.13	1.08	1.60	1.01	1.69
Median	5	5	5	5	5	4	5	4

how many people leave Wi-Fi on, as well as being influenced by the random MAC addresses, however, as we can see, it is still possible to create accurate models that predict well the occupancy of a location.

4.2 In Situ Survey

During the survey deployment, we received a total of 230 responses. All of the questions were formulated affirmatively except two (Q6 and Q8), concerning privacy and intrusiveness. The user's answers can be interpreted as the higher the scales' rating, the better.

The statistics for the 230 replies to the eight questions are shown in Table 3. It shows that Q6(privacy) and Q8(intrusiveness) have more spread out standard deviations, while the remaining questions scored high averages, showing that the public information derived from the passive Wi-Fi data was correlated with the location's perceived occupancy. In general the users reported interest in the site, and felt COVID-19 safe. Since the survey could be abandoned without answering all of the questions, the total number of users that replied to all questions was 130. The answers regarding interest in the place (Q1), perceived safety in the place, accuracy of info, trustworthiness, usefulness, and improved safety of the place through the info provided (Q2, Q3, Q4, Q5, Q7), are all

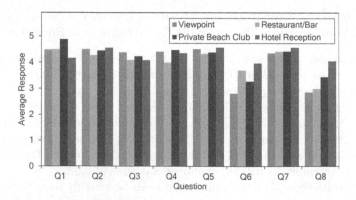

Fig. 9. Average question results across the different locations.

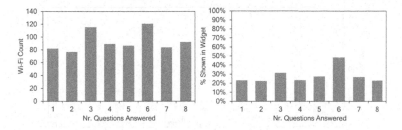

Fig. 10. Number of questions answered by Wi-Fi count(left) and percentage shown in the widget(right).

quite positive (between 4 and 5 Likert scale rating). The questions regarding intrusiveness of the information (Q6) and violation of privacy (Q8) recorded lower scores, compared to the previous answers, but still quite high, (between 3 and 4), according to the Likert scale. Since the questions were formulated in a negative form, high scores in these two questions indicate users perceptions of the information being intrusive and privacy violation.

Figure 9 shows the score distribution of the questions across the four locations is consistent across all sites, except for questions Q6 and Q8 regarding privacy and intrusiveness. For these questions, the Hotel and Bar show users being more concerned about privacy (Q8) and intrusiveness (Q6). To note that in all questions, the maximum standard deviation (SD) was 1.69 and only 2 questions had SDs above 1.19 in a 5 point Likert scale, which implies that most answers in these 2 questions ranged between ∼2.4 points of the scale, thus not being able to extract conclusions as strong and consistent as the remaining questions.

In Fig. 10 we present the number of questions answered compared to the number of Wi-Fi devices detected in the past 60 min to the reply and the occupation percentage shown in the widget. The results reveal no direct increase or decrease resulting from the percentage shown and the number of questions answered. Six, was the most prevalent number of questions answered when the location showed more occupancy.

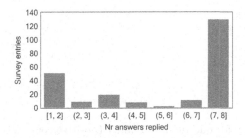

Fig. 11. Distribution of number of questions answered by each user.

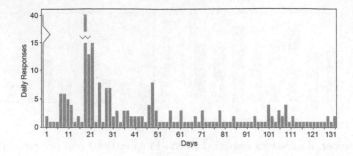

Fig. 12. Number of daily responses throughout the deployment (Broken Y axis).

Figure 11 shows the distribution of the number of questions answered by each user, revealing that the vast majority of users replied to all eight questions or just one single question before abandoning the survey. The deployment spanned from September to December of 2020. The number of daily responses varied considerably, as shown in Fig. 12, with a higher frequency happening in the initial days and then rapidly fading out through the deployment. To note that across the four locations, at least one response was recorded every day. We also plotted the replies for questions 1–5 and 7 against the percentage shown in the widget in Fig. 13. These were the questions with positive connotation aimed to understand the user's satisfaction with the location and the perception of accuracy of the data being presented.

Lastly, the language in which the questionnaires were answered may differentiate the users that answered from local and foreigners. The results presented in Fig. 14 (left) shows that the majority of survey entries were done in Portuguese, and that division is maintained across the users of the other locations, with the exception of the hotel reception, in which the majority of entries were done in English as seen in Fig. 14 (right).

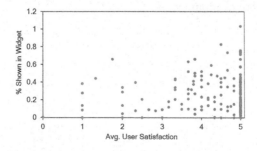

Fig. 13. Average reply for questions 1–5 and 7 (positive connotation) against the percentage shown in the widget.

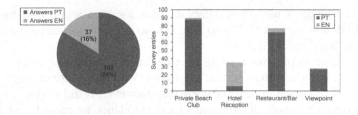

Fig. 14. Number of survey entries per language (left) and number of questions answered per survey language (right).

5 Discussion

As a low-cost technological solution to help unconfinement measures during the pandemic, the infrastructure described here provided some useful results and discussion points. Monitoring and modeling people's behavior is always a sensitive issue. The passive Wi-Fi approach is both anonymous and practical for providing real-time information about the people's presence, occupancy and flow. Previous research showed this method was effective in detecting people's presence and flow while preserving privacy [29,36]. Although Wi-Fi devices expose IDs that could potentially be used to track the owners, our dataset clearly shows that this is impractical with the high number (96%) of randomized IDs exposed in recent iOS and Android implementations. Although, to increase privacy, the system does not store device IDs, our past data shows the randomization percentage has risen significantly in the last years (56% since 2016). This is an important privacy by design feature, making passive Wi-Fi more trustworthy than other alternatives, e.g., using cameras [47] or access control systems or even active Wi-Fi logging [26]. Although systems like Google popular times provide similar information, these datasets are not publicly available and therefore, are not a practical solution for communities such as those described here. As drawbacks, the passive Wi-Fi system requires an infrastructure to operate (power, internet connection, backend for ML algorithms and provide real-time and historical data). While our results show a strong correlation between the passive Wi-Fi data and the ground truth, the system is naturally prone to inaccuracies. The location (including obstacles), the limited range, and dependency on having Wi-Fi enabled can naturally influence the system's accuracy. One could argue that such potential inaccuracies are a built-in feature as they end up increasing privacy protection (e.g., acting as a non-intentional mechanism to implement differential privacy [9]). Despite the limitations, our results clearly show that passive Wi-Fi is a viable alternative for capacity monitoring in the wild, answering RQ1.

Besides, the in situ surveys were a mechanism to understand people's reaction of this information. First, the survey results confirmed that users perceived the occupancy data displayed to be quite accurate, confirming from a user perspective our RQ1 (Q3–Q5). The results show that users were overall pleased with the information provided. From the answers regarding Q7 (safety improval) the average result of 4.43 shows that the users perceived that the system presented improved the citizens feeling of safety in that location while also finding the place COVID-safe (Q2), which also comes from a combination of the measures taken by the local authorities.

Secondly, our deployment confirms that in situ surveying is prone to the novelty effect, exciting users in the beginning, while not supporting long term engagement of the same number of users [22]. However, it did continue to engage some users over the whole deployment (4 months) since we recorded at least one answer per location over the period of 127 days. Finally, concerning privacy and intrusiveness (Q6 and Q8), the users express some negative concerns about the system as the Likert's scores are quite high (3 to 4) and the question phrased negatively. Further probing of the users would be necessary to understand their concerns in more details.

Future work should address differences between in situ and mobile app use of this same information. The mobile application has been released, being promoted mainly via touristic channels and was installed by over 9000 users in Google and Apple stores (Jan 2021 to Apr 2021). From the usage data, and the time spend in each screen, the users explored on average 13 locations of the interactive map and opened the hourly occupation charts, thus showing that the application was used to inform users of the real-time occupation in several locations. In addition, given the positive feedback of the data accuracy (Q3) and trustworthiness (Q4) from the in situ survey (the same rates shown in the app), the data shown in the mobile application enabled the users to make informed decisions about their commute plans around the region as per RQ3.

6   Conclusion

With this work, describe and evaluate the deployment of three components that aim to inform citizens about the real-time occupation of public spaces by using a passive Wi-Fi system. The challenge of estimating the real number of people from the Wi-Fi counts was modeled for a use case with accurate ground truth, that provides a solid base for modeling data accurately. The data modeling from the use case used for modeling here set the ground to update the rest of the Wi-Fi locations to be used in that way, opening the possibility of creating models for locations with similar characteristics once the basic info is provided, such as the capacity of the places, and the accuracy of how much of the passerby does the system capture, while adjusting the routers so to cover all ground necessary to estimate the number of people in that location.

The positive feedback of the survey system encourages future work to turn the web dashboard presented into a larger public display to be placed in the cities and inform citizens in real time about the presence of people in locations nearby with the updated models for each location. While the mobile application will also be updated to include quick user surveys that prompt users with questions about the experience of using the application and the general feel of the visited locations as well as feedback about the presented data.

References

1. Ahmed, A.M.: Designing a framework to control the spread of COVID-19 by utilizing cellular system. Kurdistan J. Appl. Res. **5**, 146–153 (2020). https://doi.org/10.24017/covid.16
2. Alsaeedy, A.A.R., Chong, E.K.P.: Detecting regions at risk for spreading COVID-19 using existing cellular wireless network functionalities. IEEE Open J. Eng. Med. Biol. **1**, 187–189 (2020). https://doi.org/10.1109/OJEMB.2020.3002447. Conference Name: IEEE Open Journal of Engineering in Medicine and Biology
3. Baniukevic, A., Jensen, C., Lu, H.: Hybrid indoor positioning with Wi-Fi and bluetooth: architecture and performance. In: 2013 IEEE 14th International Conference on Mobile Data Management (MDM), vol. 1, pp. 207–216 (2013). https://doi.org/10.1109/MDM.2013.30
4. Böhmer, M., Hecht, B., Schöning, J., Krüger, A., Bauer, G.: Falling asleep with angry birds, Facebook and kindle: a large scale study on mobile application usage. Presented at the (2011)
5. Bonné, B., Barzan, A., Quax, P., Lamotte, W.: WiFiPi: involuntary tracking of visitors at mass events. Presented at the (2013). https://doi.org/10.1109/WoWMoM.2013.6583443
6. Brignull, H., Rogers, Y.: Enticing people to interact with large public displays in public spaces. Interact **3**, 17–24 (2003)
7. Buettner, M., Prasad, R., Philipose, M., Wetherall, D.: Recognizing daily activities with RFID-based sensors. Presented at the (2009). https://doi.org/10.1145/1620545.1620553
8. Diethei, D., Niess, J., Stellmacher, C., Stefanidi, E., Schöning, J.: Sharing heartbeats: motivations of citizen scientists in times of crises. Association for Computing Machinery, New York (2021). https://doi.org/10.1145/3411764.3445665
9. Dwork, C.: Differential privacy: a survey of results. In: Agrawal, M., Du, D., Duan, Z., Li, A. (eds.) TAMC 2008. LNCS, vol. 4978, pp. 1–19. Springer, Heidelberg (2008). https://doi.org/10.1007/978-3-540-79228-4_1
10. Fatih, Şİ, Gökhan, A.N., Panić, S., Stefanović, Č, Yağanoğlu, M., Prilinčević, B.: Covid-19 risk assessment in public transport using ambient sensor data and wireless communications. Bull. Nat. Sci. Res. **10**(2), 43–50 (2020). https://doi.org/10.5937/bnsr10-29239
11. Florez, H., Singh, S.: Online dashboard and data analysis approach for assessing COVID-19 case and death data. F1000Research, vol. 9, no. 570, p. 10. 2020.12688/f1000research.24164.1
12. Fuentes, C., Rodríguez, I., Herskovic, V.: EmoBall: a study on a tangible interface to self-report emotional information considering digital competences. In: Bravo, J., Hervás, R., Villarreal, V. (eds.) AmIHEALTH 2015. LNCS, vol. 9456, pp. 189–200. Springer, Cham (2015). https://doi.org/10.1007/978-3-319-26508-7_19
13. Gallacher, S., Golsteijn, C., Rogers, Y., Capra, L., Eustace, S.: SmallTalk: using tangible interactions to gather feedback from children. Presented at the (2016). https://doi.org/10.1145/2839462.2839481
14. Gallacher, S., et al.: Mood squeezer: lightening up the workplace through playful and lightweight interactions. Presented at the (2015). https://doi.org/10.1145/2675133.2675170

15. Gao, C., Li, P., Zhang, Y., Liu, J., Wang, L.: People counting based on head detection combining Adaboost and CNN in crowded surveillance environment. Neurocomputing **208**, 108–116 (2016). https://doi.org/10.1016/j.neucom.2016.01.097

16. Golsteijn, C., et al.: VoxBox: a tangible machine that gathers opinions from the public at events. Presented at the (2015). https://doi.org/10.1145/2677199.2680588

17. Heimerl, K., Gawalt, B., Chen, K., Parikh, T., Hartmann, B.: CommunitySourcing: engaging local crowds to perform expert work via physical kiosks. Presented at the (2012). https://doi.org/10.1145/2207676.2208619

18. Houben, S., et al.: Roam-IO: engaging with people tracking data through an interactive physical data installation. In: Proceedings of the 2019 on Designing Interactive Systems Conference (DIS 2019), pp. 1157–1169. Association for Computing Machinery (2019). https://doi.org/10.1145/3322276.3322303

19. Houben, S., Weichel, C.: Overcoming interaction blindness through curiosity objects. In: CHI '13 Extended Abstracts on Human Factors in Computing Systems (CHI EA 2013), pp. 1539–1544. Association for Computing Machinery (2013). https://doi.org/10.1145/2468356.2468631

20. Ju, W., Sirkin, D.: Animate objects: how physical motion encourages public interaction. In: Ploug, T., Hasle, P., Oinas-Kukkonen, H. (eds.) PERSUASIVE 2010. LNCS, vol. 6137, pp. 40–51. Springer, Heidelberg (2010). https://doi.org/10.1007/978-3-642-13226-1_6

21. Kjærgaard, M.B., Wirz, M., Roggen, D., Tröster, G.: Mobile sensing of pedestrian flocks in indoor environments using WiFi signals. Presented at the (2012). https://doi.org/10.1109/PerCom.2012.6199854

22. Koch, M., von Luck, K., Schwarzer, J., Draheim, S.: The novelty effect in large display deployments-experiences and lessons-learned for evaluating prototypes. In: Proceedings of 16th European Conference on Computer-Supported Cooperative Work-Exploratory Papers. European Society for Socially Embedded Technologies (EUSSET) (2018). https://doi.org/10.18420/ecscw2018_3

23. Koehlmoos, T.P., Janvrin, M.L., Korona-Bailey, J., Madsen, C., Sturdivant, R.: COVID-19 self-reported symptom tracking programs in the united states: framework synthesis. J. Med. Internet Res. **22**(10), e23297 (2020). https://doi.org/10.2196/23297

24. Koeman, L., Kalnikaité, V., Rogers, Y.: "Everyone is talking about it!": a distributed approach to urban voting technology and visualisations. Presented at the (2015). https://doi.org/10.1145/2702123.2702263

25. Li, F., Valero, M., Shahriar, H., Khan, R.A., Ahamed, S.I.: Wi-COVID: a COVID-19 symptom detection and patient monitoring framework using WiFi. Smart Health **19**, 100147 (2021). https://doi.org/10.1016/j.smhl.2020.100147

26. Meneses, F., Moreira, A.: Large scale movement analysis from WiFi based location data. Presented at the (2012). https://doi.org/10.1109/IPIN.2012.6418885

27. Menni, C., et al.: Real-time tracking of self-reported symptoms to predict potential COVID-19. Nat. Med. **26**(7), 1037–1040 (2020). https://doi.org/10.1038/s41591-020-0916-2

28. Müller, J., Alt, F., Michelis, D., Schmidt, A.: Requirements and design space for interactive public displays. Presented at the (2010). https://doi.org/10.1145/1873951.1874203

29. Nunes, N., Ribeiro, M., Prandi, C., Nisi, V.: Beanstalk: a community based passive Wi-Fi tracking system for analysing tourism dynamics. Presented at the (2017). https://doi.org/10.1145/3102113.3102142

30. Oswald, M., Grace, J.: The COVID-19 contact tracing app in England and 'experimental proportionality'. SSRN Electron. J. (2020). https://doi.org/10.2139/ssrn.3632870

31. Park, Y.J., et al.: COVID-19 national emergency response center, epidemiology and case management team: contact tracing during coronavirus disease outbreak, South Korea, 2020. Emerg. Infect. Dis. **26**(10), 2465–2468 (2020). https://doi.org/10.3201/eid2610.201315

32. Prandi, C., Nisi, V., Ribeiro, M., Nunes, N.: Sensing and making sense of tourism flows and urban data to foster sustainability awareness: a real-world experience. J. Big Data **8**(1), 1–25 (2021). https://doi.org/10.1186/s40537-021-00442-w

33. Ram, N., Gray, D.: Mass surveillance in the age of COVID-19. J. Law Biosci. **7**, lsaa023 (2020). https://doi.org/10.1093/jlb/lsaa023

34. Redin, D., Vilela, D., Nunes, N., Ribeiro, M., Prandi, C.: ViTFlow: a platform to visualize tourists flows in a rich interactive map-based interface, pp. 1–2. IEEE (2017). https://doi.org/10.23919/SustainIT.2017.8379814

35. Ribeiro, M., Nisi, V., Prandi, C., Nunes, N.: A data visualization interactive exploration of human mobility data during the COVID-19 outbreak: a case study, pp. 1–6. IEEE (2020). https://doi.org/10.1109/ISCC50000.2020.9219552

36. Ribeiro, M., Nunes, N., Nisi, V., Schöning, J.: Passive Wi-Fi monitoring in the wild: a long-term study across multiple location typologies. Pers. Ubiquit. Comput., 1–15 (2020). https://doi.org/10.1007/s00779-020-01441-z

37. Ruiz-Ruiz, A.J., Blunck, H., Prentow, T.S., Stisen, A., Kjærgaard, M.B.: Analysis methods for extracting knowledge from large-scale WiFi monitoring to inform building facility planning. Presented at the (2014). https://doi.org/10.1109/PerCom.2014.6813953

38. Said, M., Samuel, M., Shannan, N., Bashir, F.M., Dodo, Y.: Novel vision-based thermal people counting tool for tracking infected people with viruses like COVID-19. J. Adv. Res. Dyn. Control Syst. **12**, 1115–1119 (2020). https://doi.org/10.5373/JARDCS/V12SP7/20202210

39. Shaw, P., Mikusz, M., Nurmi, P., Davies, N.: Tacita: a privacy preserving public display personalisation service. Presented at the (2018). https://doi.org/10.1145/3267305.3267627

40. Sohn, T., et al.: Mobility detection using everyday GSM traces. In: Dourish, P., Friday, A. (eds.) UbiComp 2006. LNCS, vol. 4206, pp. 212–224. Springer, Heidelberg (2006). https://doi.org/10.1007/11853565_13

41. Stevens, H., Haines, M.B.: TraceTogether: pandemic response, democracy, and technology. East Asian Sci. Technol. Soc. **14**(3), 523–532 (2020). https://doi.org/10.1215/18752160-8698301

42. Tang, X., Xiao, B., Li, K.: Indoor crowd density estimation through mobile smartphone Wi-Fi probes. IEEE Trans. Syst. Man Cybern. Syst. **50**(7), 2638–2649 (2020). https://doi.org/10.1109/TSMC.2018.2824903. Conference Name: IEEE Transactions on Systems, Man, and Cybernetics: Systems

43. Vedaei, S.S., et al.: COVID-SAFE: an IoT-based system for automated health monitoring and surveillance in post-pandemic life. IEEE Access **8**, 188538–188551 (2020).https://doi.org/10.1109/ACCESS.2020.3030194. Conference Name: IEEE Access

44. Whitelaw, S., Mamas, M.A., Topol, E., Spall, H.G.C.V.: Applications of digital technology in COVID-19 pandemic planning and response. Lancet Digital Health **2**(8), e435–e440 (2020). https://doi.org/10.1016/S2589-7500(20)30142-4

45. Whittle, J., et al.: VoiceYourView: collecting real-time feedback on the design of public spaces. Presented at the (2010). https://doi.org/10.1145/1864349.1864358

46. Wissel, B.D., et al.: An interactive online dashboard for tracking COVID-19 in U.S. counties, cities, and states in real time. J. Am. Med. Inform. Assoc. **27**(7), 1121–1125 (2020). https://doi.org/10.1093/jamia/ocaa071
47. Zhao, X., Delleandrea, E., Chen, L.: A people counting system based on face detection and tracking in a video, pp. 67–72. IEEE (2009). https://doi.org/10.1109/AVSS.2009.45

Hanging Out Online: Social Life During the Pandemic

Ashwin Singh[1]([⊠]) and Grace Eden[2]

[1] Living Lab, IIIT Delhi, New Delhi, India
ashwin17222@iiitd.ac.in
[2] Department of Human-Centered Design, IIIT Delhi, New Delhi, India
grace@iiitd.ac.in

Abstract. In March 2020, the government of India ordered a nationwide lockdown to prevent the spread of Covid-19. This led to the shutdown of educational institutes throughout the country, restricting all activities to online mediums. The shift has affected how students engage with each other, where rather than in-person interaction, they meet through a variety of online tools. In this paper, we discuss how the normal everyday routine of 'hanging out' with friends has been transformed during a prolonged lockdown of over ten months and counting. We investigate the opportunities and challenges students encounter when socializing online through various online modes including video calls, communal movie watching and social media. We discuss how social interaction; in particular, hanging out with friends has been transformed through these technologies and its implications for facilitating spontaneous interaction, negotiating intimacy, mutual understanding, and accessibility to different social groups. Finally, we conclude with a discussion of how these factors impact the transition from in-person to online modes of casual social interaction.

Keywords: Qualitative fieldwork · Covid-19 · Negotiating intimacy online

1 Introduction

During the Covid-19 pandemic, countries imposed nationwide lockdowns as a preventive measure against the spread of the disease [1]. In India, the closing of educational institutes affected over 34 million university and college-going students [2]. In addition, 71% of youth located in metropolis cities were spending the lockdown with their families [3]. With all academic activities restricted to online mediums and restrictions on "hanging out" in physical settings, the social lives of university students have been significantly affected. Now, it is only possible to hang out with friends online.

In this study, we present preliminary findings on how students maintain their social connections, what we refer to as "hanging out"; specifically how they make use of various technologies to interact with friends online while adapting to the

C. Ardito et al. (Eds.): INTERACT 2021, LNCS 12933, pp. 25–33, 2021.
https://doi.org/10.1007/978-3-030-85616-8_2

lockdown. Our aim is to understand which technologies facilitate communication amongst the students, with a focus on the role technologies play in mediating everyday social interaction [4]. In addition, we investigate the different ways in which students use computer-mediated communication (CMC) technologies to share their experiences with friends and how they manage those relationships.

We conduct a preliminary qualitative study to investigate the effects of the lockdown on the social life of university students; particularly the transformations brought about by CMC technologies and how they unfolded due to differences between in-person and computer-mediated interactions. We discuss these differences and their implications for opportunities for spontaneous social interaction. Next, we talk about the shifts in context and social accessibility of social interaction during the lockdown, followed by how students negotiate intimacy and configure their identity in CMC technologies. Finally, we conclude with a discussion of how students have adapted to the lockdown; discussing some challenges they encountered in the process.

2   Related Work

Our work builds upon three broad areas of computer-mediated communication, namely presence, presentation of self and common ground. Presence plays an important role in how students use different CMC technologies to socialize with their peers whereas self-presentation is key to how they construct their identity online. Lastly, we examine examples of how common ground is developed in the CMC technologies that students use and how these transform everyday social interactions.

2.1   Being Together Online

While presence is concerned with the sense of being transported to a space different from a physical environment, mediated presence refers to social interaction that takes place through the medium itself [5] and can be defined as the degree to which people overlook the mediated nature of an interaction [6]. For this paper, we discuss two aspects of mediated presence, namely co-presence and social presence. Co-presence refers to the sense of being together with other people [7] and is reflexive in nature [8]. Specifically, it relates to how people perceive others through the medium, as well as how they are perceived by others [8]. In computer-mediated interaction, the level of co-presence available plays an important role in determining the extent to which technologies provide people with a sense of being together. Social presence, on the other hand, is the moment-to-moment awareness of other people and participation with them [7]. Social presence influences the extent to which interpersonal relationships are facilitated by the medium [9]. Levels of social presence are said to increase when multiple modalities (such as audio and video), low latency (immediate feedback during an interaction), and personalisation are available [10]. In our research, we are interested to explore how support for social presence is used as a criteria when students select technologies for interacting with friends online.

2.2   Configuring Identity

Goffman's work on the presentation of self describes how people's roles differ depending upon the social context and the norms within it [11]. For example, people may underplay or overplay aspects of themselves such as vulnerability or formality to ensure compatibility with the idealised version of themselves that they wish to display to others. Self-presentation becomes particularly relevant in the use of social media where people's profiles are visible to their different social circles including friends, acquaintances, co-workers and family members [12]. Each of these groups rarely mingle together in the real world [13]. Thus, when these diverse groups are flattened into a shared online space, it results in a phenomenon referred to as context collapse [12]. This situation results in a limiting effect on how people present themselves to others. Instead, people adopt a plethora of measures to navigate these tensions, such as using multiple accounts or creating alternate accounts under pseudonyms or nicknames [14]. Recently, people have started using private Instagram accounts (known as Finstas) to create intimate spaces that are only accessible to a trusted group of friends. This creates an opportunity for people to create safe spaces where they can share alternate identities with smaller groups [15]. Having control over one's presentation of self plays a crucial role in regulating one's identity, allowing more room for disclosure and affording more agency [16].

2.3   Shared Experiences

Common ground also plays an important role in the development of shared experiences. It refers to the shared knowledge, beliefs and suppositions shared in common between a group of people [17]. Here, we discuss two dimensions of common ground - namely cultural common ground and personal common ground paying particular attention to the different roles they play in sustaining social interaction online. When people have an affiliation to a community that shares the same history and practices, for instance, students who belong to the same educational institution; they share a cultural common ground because their joint (or shared) knowledge is a result of their affiliation to the same institution [17]. On the other hand, personal common ground is constituted by joint personal events or experiences, which can act as shared bases for holding conversations [17]. Friends can share a personal common ground because they share personal experiences in the past, such as attending the same class, travelling, or hanging out together. These often are a result of events and experiences that occur during a typical day. However, individuals can have varying levels of personal common ground with different groups of people; for instance, people share a more extensive common ground with partners through the sharing of more private information as compared to their friends [17]. Challenges to the development of personal common ground is highlighted during the Covid-19 pandemic due to the shift from in-person to online interactions and the differing affordances of both in supporting shared experiences. Cultural and personal common ground form important contexts in which everyday social interactions are situated and are important for developing a trove of shared experiences that foster interpersonal relationships [17]. In what follows, we discuss how its absence during the lockdown has brought challenges to students' casual social interactions online.

3   Methodology

To understand how hanging out with friends has transformed students' casual social interactions during the lockdown, we conducted a preliminary qualitative study with five university students. Participants were recruited using convenience sampling [18] owing to the ease of accessibility during the lockdown period. Upon approval from our Institutional Review Board, we conducted semistructured interviews for between 45 min to 1 h with five participants (M = 3, F = 2) (Table 1). The aim of the interviews was to understand different student perspectives on how they foster their social relationships online - specifically their normal routine of just hanging out with each other.

Table 1. Description of participants.

Id	Age	Gender	Alias
P1	21	woman	Neetika
P2	21	man	Ketan
P3	21	man	Rahul
P4	20	woman	Preeti
P5	20	man	Madhur

During the interviews we asked participants to describe how they would hangout with their friends and acquaintances before the lockdown and how they hang out with them now, during the lockdown. We asked them to describe their use of different technologies - when they were used, who they were used with, and why they were used. Finally, we asked them to describe the challenges they encountered while socializing online and how they managed their relationships during the lockdown.

Interviews were conducted remotely and audio recorded using an online meeting tool. These were transcribed and anonymized with participant IDs. To analyze the data, we adopted an inductive coding approach to thematically code [19] the transcripts. In the first iteration, the first author identified high-level codes and for the second iteration, both authors performed line-by-line coding of the first round of high level categories. These refined codes were compared and discussed amongst the researchers to identify patterns and to reach consensus during remote data analysis sessions where the researchers discussed emerging themes, patterns and their significance to each other.

4   Findings

In this section, we present findings from the study in four subsections: First, we discuss how lack of **presence** has transformed spontaneous interaction over the lockdown period and how it affects the routine practice of hanging out with friends. Second, we examine contexts which give rise to social interaction and how technologies mediate them in a way that might compromise the continued development of **common ground**. Third, we discuss how students negotiate intimacy and their **presentation of self** to engage in joint personal experiences and manage their social relationships online. Finally, we summarize students' challenges when transitioning to the lockdown, including how online social interaction helped them during the transition period in the face of various technical and personal challenges.

4.1   Spontaneity of Social Interaction

In this section, we discuss how differences emerging from the affordances of in-person and mediated interactions affected online social interaction for students; particularly how the absence of a shared physical space has implications for spontaneity and situatedness of social interaction.

Participants associated their socializing experiences prior to the lockdown with "spontaneity" because they could simply "bump into each other" in shared physical settings. *"We were all living in a common space with similar schedules so there were naturally interactions between us while going to classes"* (Ketan). However, after the lockdown, the absence of shared physical spaces affected this spontaneity, making social interaction more planned. In this shift, co-presence is diminished; resulting in students no longer feeling that they're together with their friends. Rather, now they needed to make an effort to initiate conversations and chit chat with their friends. *"Now, you talk to people you explicitly want to talk to because that call button on your phone needs to be pressed. Spontaneity is good but it gets you in situations you don't want to be"* (Rahul). Here we see that the deliberate action required to communicate with others online has resulted in selective interactions with specific people, allowing for a greater sense of control in mediated settings as compared to in-person interactions.

All participants reported that their pre-lockdown socializing experiences were predominantly situated in their college surroundings. *"In college you would just sit and eat together and talk about nothing. Now that's very rare, right?"* (Neetika). During the lockdown, situatedness has shifted into virtual settings that mediate interaction between users. However, this shift has resulted in a decline in social interaction. *"My friend mentioned the same concern that there has been a sort of disconnect between us due to a reduction in communication during the lockdown"* (Ketan). The lack of shared physical space has reduced the frequency of casual everyday exchanges between people with the "disconnect" felt by most participants illustrating the inadequacies of computer-mediated communication when the goal of these interactions is aimed at fostering relationships rather than the less nuanced goal of exchanging information.

4.2 Shifts in Context and Social Accessibility

Before the lockdown the context which acts as the basis for people to socially interact with each other emerged from personal experiences that occurred in everyday situations, many of which were shared with other students from college. *"So we used to talk about our workload, TV shows, plans or even gossip about what's going around in college"* (Preeti). However, the dissolution of the ongoing establishment of in-person context and joint personal experiences has led to interactions which arise from a *"requirement"* to talk to college acquaintances to complete coursework online. *"I don't really get time to interact with people I'm not close to, unless it's something particular like coursework"* (Rahul). Interactions motivated by academic work from college indicate a shift in context and show how cultural common ground sustains some level of social interaction between people who were not close to each other. However, due to the lack of personal experiences together, there is less opportunity for spontaneous conversations to develop.

Another consequence of the shift to online mediums is seen in the different social groups people interact with both pre-lockdown and now. *"I think, before the lockdown, I used to socialize with my school friends less. It's definitely a lot more now since you reach everyone that way [online]"* (Neetika). Amidst the absence of in-person interaction access to people from different social groups (e.g. school and college friends) in the online mode has now flattened. Due to the affordances of computer-mediated communication technologies access across each of them is now the same whereas pre-lockdown these groups were associated with specific locations and circumstances. One result of this has been that students began reaching out to their old friends from school rather than trying to making new friends with college acquaintances online; something that would have developed more easily in-person.

4.3 Negotiating Intimacy

Technologies can facilitate interactions between people who share different types of personal common ground and students make decisions about which ones to use in order to negotiate different levels of intimacy with friends and partners. We examine instances of this negotiation across three different technologies, namely communal watching, video conferencing, and social media. Finally, we discuss how students overcome some of these tensions through how they configure and reveal their different online identities with different people.

Communal Watching: Students engaged in communal watching with their close friends and partners over popular technologies such as Netflix Party and streaming over Discord. While watching TV shows and movies together was framed as an intimate activity, the degree of intimacy is negotiated. *"Yeah, I use it [Netflix Party] quite often with my really close friends who watch the same shows that I do and we like to talk over chat"* (Neetika). *"Sometimes me and my girlfriend video call while watching a movie but keeping each other on mute so we're there* *together but not actually speaking to each other"* (Rahul). Neetika and her close friends use the chat feature on Netflix Party to engage in small talk throughout the film. Whereas Rahul and his girlfriend share a video call over Google Duo as the film plays only occasionally unmuting themselves to talk about the plot. These differences in the use of a communication side medium are intertwined with participants' mutually desired level of intimacy and associated social presence (e.g. small talk between friends or silent presence between partners).

Video Conferencing: In addition to its use in communal TV and movie watching, video conferencing is also used by students to talk to their close friends and partners; both being groups with whom they share an extensive personal common ground. Video conferencing affords a high degree of social presence due to the richness of both video and audio modalities alongside their synchronous nature which affords immediate feedback. These applications were described as intimate mediums where they felt comfortable interacting with not more than "three to four" people or they interacted one-on-one with their partner. While birthdays are a common occasion where large groups of people participate in video calls, some students said that it is often awkward for them due to a large number of people on the call that they do not know - this limits their self-presentation in a medium which affords a high degree of social presence.

Finstas: Another instance of context collapse occurred on Instagram, where students attempted to circumvent it by creating private secondary accounts known as Finstas (Fake Instagram accounts) to share their daily experiences with close friends. Madhur described his motivations for creating a Finsta referring to his account as a "repository of memories" whereas Neetika said that she wanted to socialise with her close friends beyond just texting or sharing memes. Finstas helped students indulge in self-disclosure with people they shared a deep personal common ground with. *"Sharing experiences personally helps me process them as well as make my peace with them and I think it's very wonderful that I am able to do so"* (Ketan). Being a member of the LGBTQIA+ community, Ketan used his Finsta as a rite of passage, creating artistic concepts using animation, visuals, and poetry to share his experiences with trusted friends who accept his identity in contrast to his family and the larger group of followers on his public Instagram account. Finstas make it possible to share personal experiences by giving students control over who has access to content so that they can express the most personal and intimate aspects of themselves.

4.4   Adjusting to Lockdown

At the start of the lockdown, there was a period of uncertainty where it was unclear how soon the restrictions on in-person interaction would be lifted. Meeting online continued month-to-month and with it the realization that "social distancing" would be with us for the near future. As a result, students began to adapt to the "new normal". *"So I got into the habit of calling people every two, three weeks and actively texting my close friends to keep in touch with them. So that's definitely something that developed over time and became stable by June [2020]"* (Neetika). Students would engage in conversations with their friends more often for emotional support. A common routine involved "checking-up" regularly to ensure that friends were doing alright. They discussed a fear of growing apart and expressed a desire to preserve their relationships. *"I do wish to keep in touch more frequently with my friends because our bonds are something that need to be kept alive despite the physical distances between us now"* (Ketan). However, online social interaction was described as draining and difficult to sustain over long periods of time. It has also been challenging for friends to interact with each other due to varying schedules and different time zones. These challenges also included consequences for personal privacy when students spent all their time at home. *"There is some noise in the background. People keep coming in and going out so it's difficult to maintain my personal space"* (Preeti). At home individual agency can be compromised, creating obstacles to freely interacting with friends which would otherwise be uninterrupted when meeting in-person. Further, students gender and sexual identity was threatened due to heteronormative beliefs held at home forcing them to conceal aspects of themselves to ensure their safety.

5   Discussion

In this work we investigated how social interaction has been transformed during the Covid-19 lockdown for university students. We found that current technologies lack support for spontaneous interaction because they cannot simulate a sense of being together in the same way as a physical space. This absence of shared physical space makes it difficult to feel emotionally connected leading to a change in students' interaction between their different social groups that are now equally accessible online. In fact, we found that students negotiate intimacy online by selecting which technologies to use with different people based upon their relationships with them (e.g. video, chat). These kinds of negotiations also allowed students to manage their personal identity when posting content on private Finsta accounts. Additionally, regular interactions between friends are used to check-in on each others' well-being. However, students still face challenges exercising agency and managing personal space because they spend more time at home where they can be easily distracted and where the boundaries between personal, social, and academic spaces have become increasingly indistinguishable. Added to this, queer students felt their identity was restricted when confined at home. Further, different schedules between geographically distributed friends made it difficult for them to meet. While the ongoing lockdown in India continues to transform how friends engage with each other our findings present opportunities to reconsider how technologies could be designed to accommodate 'hanging out'. To this end, our future work will involve a series of co-design workshops with a larger group of students to sketch out ideas for how to better support spontaneity, intimacy, and shared experiences when hanging out with friends in casual social interactions online.

Acknowledgments. Thanks and appreciation to our participants for contributing their valuable time. We also thank the Center for Design and New Media (A TCS Foundation Initiative supported by Tata Consultancy Services) at IIIT-Delhi for supporting this research.

References

1. Withnall, A.: India coronavirus: Modi announces 21-day nationwide lockdown, limiting movement of 1.4bn people. Independent (2020)
2. Education: from disruption to recovery. UNESCO, 2020. https://en.unesco.org/covid19/educationresponse
3. Kaul, A., Chapman, T.: Life in lockdown: a survey of India's urban youth. Observer Research Foundation, 2020. https://www.orfonline.org/wp-content/uploads/2020/07/ORF-Monograph-Life-In-Lockdown1.pdf
4. December, J., Randall, N.: World Wide Web 1997 Unleashed, 2nd edn. Sams, Indianapolis (1996)
5. Lee, K.M.: Presence, explicated. Commun. Theor. **14**(1), 27–50 (2004)
6. Lombard, M.: Direct responses to people on the screen: television and personal space. Commun. Res. **22**(3), 288–324 (1995)
7. Skarbez, R., Brooks, F.P., Jr., Whitton, M.C.: A survey of presence and related concepts. ACM Comput. Surv. **50**(6), 1–39 (2017)
8. Goffman, E.: Behavior in public places: notes on the social organization of gatherings, vol. 01 (1963)
9. Parker, E., Short, J., Williams, E., Christie, B.: The social psychology of telecommunication. In: Contemporary Sociology, vol. 7, no. 32 (1978)
10. Daft, R., Lengel, R.: Organizational information requirements, media richness and structural design. Manage. Sci. **32**, 554–571 (1986)
11. Goffman, E.: The Presentation of Self in Everyday Life, vol. 01. Harmondsworth, London (1956)
12. Marwick, A., Boyd, D.: I tweet honestly, I tweet passionately: Twitter users, context collapse, and the imagined audience. New Media Soc. **13**(1), 114–133 (2011)
13. Bowers, K.: Situationism in psychology: an analysis and a critique. Psychol. Rev. **80**, 307–336 (1973)
14. Marwick, A., Boyd, D.: Networked privacy: how teenagers negotiate context in social media. New Media Soc. **16**, 1051–1067 (2014)
15. Xiao, S., Metaxa, D., Park, J., Karahalios, K., Salehi, N.: Random, messy, funny, raw: finstas as intimate reconfigurations of social media, pp. 1–13 (2020)
16. Boyd, D., Marwick, A.: Boyd, D., Marwick, A.E.: Social privacy in networked publics: Teens' attitudes, practices, and strategies (September 22, 2011). A Decade in Internet Time: Symposium on the Dynamics of the Internet and Society, September 2011.
17. Clark, H.H.: Using Language. 'Using' Linguistic Books. Cambridge University Press, Cambridge (1996)
18. Bernard, H.: Research Methods in Anthropology: Qualitative and Quantitative Approaches, pp. 148–149 (2011)
19. Miles, M. B., Huberman, A. M.: Qualitative data analysis: An expanded sourcebook (2nd ed.). Thousand Oaks, CA: Sage (1994)

Investigating Italian Citizens' Attitudes Towards Immuni, the Italian Contact Tracing App

Cristina Bosco$^{(\boxtimes)}$ (ID) and Martina Cvajner (ID)

University of Trento, 38068 Rovereto, TN, Italy
`cris.bosco@icloud.com`, `martina.cvajner@unitn.it`

Abstract. This research investigates Italian citizens' attitudes towards the contact tracing app Immuni, promoted by the Italian government to track the spread of Covid19 and prevent possible future out-breaks. More specifically, this paper tries to uncover the factors that have motivated individuals to uptake the app or fail to do so. We have used a variety of qualitative methods: firstly, a virtual ethnography has been conducted, analyzing thematically 3013 tweets with the hashtag #Immuni. To further investigate the motivation behind either the adoption or the refusal of Immuni, twenty semi-structured interviews have been carried out with potential and actual users. A doctor and a health official have been also interviewed as secondary users. The results show that multiple factors shape users' attitudes towards Immuni and influence their willingness to adopt it. The most relevant have to do with the perceived benefits, perceived barriers, perceived efficacy of the app and the cues to action. The usability of the overall app is also discussed with a focus on some of the key issues identified by the users.

Keywords: User research · Contact tracing apps · Qualitative research methods

1 Introduction

In June 2020, the Italian government announced the launch of Immuni, a contact tracing app (hereafter, CTA) designed to help preventing Covid19's diffusion by tracking citizens' social exchanges and notifying them of potentially infected contacts [6]. By August 2020, only 5 million users had downloaded Immuni, 13% of the target population (all of people living in Italy above 14 years old) [1]. A marketing campaign - "Scarica Immuni Week" (Let's download Immuni) – was consequently launched (October 5–12, 2020). The campaign notwithstanding, in early February 2021, only 10 million Italians had downloaded the app. The effectiveness of CTAs is contingent upon their popularity. Previous studies

© IFIP International Federation for Information Processing 2021
Published by Springer Nature Switzerland AG 2021
C. Ardito et al. (Eds.): INTERACT 2021, LNCS 12933, pp. 34–42, 2021.
https://doi.org/10.1007/978-3-030-85616-8_3

have found that the spread of the virus could be controlled digitally if 56% of the overall population (80% of smartphone users) adopted the app [8]. Ferretti and colleagues [7] have argued that if 60% of the population adopted a CTA, a significant portion of asymptomatic contagions could be prevented. Why then has Immuni failed to gain adequate acceptance? This paper - through the combined use of a virtual ethnography conducted on Twitter, and semi-structured interviews with primary and secondary users - explores user motivations driving the acceptance' or the rejection - of Immuni.

2 Related Work

Being able to accurately and rapidly trace contacts is proven to be a key strategy in slowing down the spread of a virus. By identifying those in contact with an infected individual early enough, it becomes possible to quarantine them before they continue to spread the virus without overloading the national health system [5]. Digital contact tracing used together with manual tracing can fasten the process of tracing contacts and contribute to contain the spread of the virus. In addition, digital contact tracing presents some striking advantages compared to the alternative. In fact, while manual tracing requires specialized personnel and resources, on top of being extremely time consuming [9], digital contact, if well-implemented, can be cheaper and faster. Furthermore, it allows widening the range of people informed, indeed the contagion does not only occur among people who know each other but it might take place among strangers. Thus, with the employment of digital contact tracing, it becomes possible to reach and inform all those potential contacts that were nearly impossible to achieve by relying merely on memory.

Yet, the success or the failure of this system highly depends on how many people decide to uptake it. Since most European countries have opted for introducing the contact tracing system on a voluntary basis, it becomes extremely important to explore and understand what motivates people to either download or not download a contact tracing app.

There is, however, very little research carried out on users' attitudes towards CTAs. To our knowledge, the only study which tackles this issue qualitatively has been conducted in UK by Williams et al. [10]. The researchers run multiple focus groups to explore British citizens' attitudes towards the contact tracing app designed and developed by the National Health System (NHS). Several relevant themes emerged in their research, mainly participants expressed a lack of knowledge and appropriate information regarding contact tracing apps. In addition, they worried about their privacy and the use of their sensitive data and they showed concerns over the app's uptake arguing that the percentage of uptakes of the app was a crucial factor in its success, thus if not enough people downloaded the app, then it would have not been fully effective.

However, this study was conducted before an official app was released. The fact that the app did not exist but was only a proposal by the time the investigation was undertaken, makes it more difficult for the participants to have a clear idea of the actual app and its actual functioning. This research aimed to expand on this previous study by attempting to overcome this limitation. In fact, this study investigated users' attitudes towards Immuni, which was released and available for download prior the beginning of the data collection. Therefore, the participants had a clear idea of the contact tracing app as well as had the choice to either download it or not. This made possible to expand the research from behavioral intentions to actual behavior.

Furthermore, this research not only seeks to investigate users' motivation for up-taking contact tracing app, but also aims to expand on previous studies by adding the analysis of secondary users of the contact tracing app. Indeed, in this scenario, the users are not only those citizens who make use of Immuni, but also the contact-tracing operators who deal with the Immuni's health-related procedure and make the overall system function. They can be defined as secondary users, as they interact with primary users and interact with the system and they rely on primary users to obtain information to make the system function, following the definition provided by Alsos [2], and their contribution and insights on the procedure behind Immuni might be a key factor in the evaluation of the app itself and determining its success.

3   Immuni

Immuni is based on two different mechanisms: the generation of a random key of exposure and Bluetooth low energy (BLE). Once Immuni is installed on a device (Device1), it generates an exposure key that is temporary, random and changed daily. By using BLE, the phone transmits a signal that is generated by the random exposure key and which contains a rolling proximity identifier (ID of Device1). When another device with Immuni (Device2) receives this signal, both devices save the rolling proximity identifier locally, in their memory. If the user of Device 1 tests positive for Covid19, s/he can upload, with the external help of an operator, a random exposure key into Immuni's server, which derives the rolling proximity identifiers broadcasted recently by Device 1. At this point, Device 2, which periodically compares all the random keys shared in the server with locally saved rolling proximity identifiers, will find a match with Device 1 and it will – if the length of the contact and the distance between the devices is above certain thresholds - inform the user of potential exposure to the virus. Once risky exposure has been detected, Immuni advises the user to consult a general practitioner. It is the GP that may prescribe a precautionary quarantine or a nasal swab. If the test for Covid-19 is positive, the operators of the National Health Service can, with the user consent, insert the user's random temporary exposure key on Immuni's server, thus informing the other users potentially exposed.

4   Methods

4.1   Data Collection

The data were collected using three different methodologies:

– a virtual ethnography on tweets gathered from the launch of the app on 15th of June until the 12th of October, the end of the *"Scarica Immuni Week"*,
– twenty interviews with primary users run from 21st of October until the 27th of October
– two interviews with secondary users undertaken on the 5th of November

The virtual ethnography data were gathered from June 15 (the launch of the app) to October 12 (the conclusion of the Scarica Immuni Week). The relevant tweets were scraped from Twitter using the website www.vicinitas.io

All the tweets, posted within two days, having the #immuni specific hashtag were collected. The data set (N = 30,532) was subsequently cleaned, deleting all tweets not in Italian, duplicates, replies or retweets (around 25,500 of the tweets gathered). All surviving tweets were read to check their pertinence. The final data set consisted of 3,013 tweets. The authors followed Braun and Clarke's guidelines [4].

A thematic analysis of the tweets revealed several themes: (a) perceived benefits, (b) perceived barriers, (c) perceived efficacy, (d) cues to action, and (e) overall usability. These themes were used as a model for the 22 semi-structured interviews with primary users, collected between October 21–27, 2020. Along with socio-demographics, participants were asked questions about the perceived benefit (What, do you think, has encouraged people to download Immuni?), the perceived barriers (What do you think has encouraged people not to download Immuni?), the perceived efficacy (Would you say that Immuni has an active role in the fight against Covid19?), cues to action (How did you hear about Immuni?), and overall usability (Have you ever encountered problem using Immuni?). Participants were recruited by using two methods. Ten were recruited by posting the following notice on Instagram and Facebook: (Do you want to participate in a very cool initiative?), while ten were recruited by randomly searching for last names on the website www.paginebianche.it, the Italian national phone-book posted online. Simultaneously, the authors decided to interview two secondary users. On November 5, a physician and an employee of an ASL (the local unit of the national health service), both involved with Immuni, were interviewed concerning two main issues: a) How do you think Immuni fits within the contact tracing procedure? b) What do you think of Immuni and its efficacy?

The interviewed sample consisted of 11 men and 11 women. Almost half of the sample (N = 9) was in the 20–30 age cohort, while the remainder was evenly distributed. Among those 11 were Immuni users and 9 stated they did not download the app at the time of the interview. User evaluation of Immuni was defined as all factors (perceived benefits, perceived barriers and perceived efficacy) that have an impact on the overall evaluation of the Immuni as an effective CTA. Cues to action were defined as all the cues able to trigger the download of Immuni. Usability was employed as a general term covering all the usability aspects of the tool.

All material gathered in this study was in Italian, yet it was translated to be presented in English in this paper. This generates a series of implications concerning the validity of the report and the research itself as it is almost impossible to achieve a perfectly matching translation as many words and idiomatic expressions in Italian might not be fully translatable in English. In this regard, translation has been done by the researcher, who is fully proficient in both English and Italian, with the goal of achieving semantic and conceptual equivalence [3].

4.2   Data Analysis

Both datasets, consisting of tweets and interviews, were studied through inductive thematic analysis: a strict semantic logic, which exclusively paid attention to the meaning of words, was employed. All data were read to gain familiarity with the corpus and obtain a general understanding of it (phase 1). Subsequently, a systematic study of the textual corpus made identification of repeating patterns and the generation of codes possible. Themes and sub-themes emerged (phase 2). One of the researchers analyzed the data, while the second checked the results independently.

To guarantee the anonymity of the tweets' authors, all the collected data were anonymized. Interviewees were asked beforehand to give their informed consent and willingness to be recorded. They were informed that all data collected during the interview phase would be subsequently anonymized.

5   Results

5.1   Users' Overall Evaluation of the App

The user's evaluation is contingent upon three sub-themes: the perceived benefits arising from using the app, the perceived barriers encountered by the users when presented with Immuni, and the perceived efficacy of Immuni as a protective health measure. Concerning the benefits, the first sub-theme, the study documents how the benefits of Immuni are identified by the users mainly with tracing contacts effectively and contribution to prevent the spread of the virus. However, users show a variety of concerns regarding the use of Immuni, and these concerns acted as potential barriers that could prevent them from using it. The most significant one was the users' suspect that Immuni could impose automatically a quarantine to all of those notified by the system, even when healthy. *.. and above all, the fear of being in quarantine, without a real need to do so.* (Giovanni)[1]. The alleged quarantine imposed by Immuni was different from the one prescribed by their GP: it was not perceived as mandatory or as reliable as the one prescribed by a doctor, thus it could be easily avoided or dismissed by the users. *And the fact that an app is the one which informs you that you have*

---

[1] interview(24/10/2020).

to be in quarantine, and it is not your doctor, or a person whom you trust, or anybody else, it what convinces people not to download it (Lops)[2].

Some users perceived this (alleged) imposition and the fact that Immuni could trace contacts with other users as a violation of their individual freedom and a violation of their privacy. This belief might have encouraged some not to trust the app and therefore, it might have led not to download it. *#Immuni intrudes your privacy, it records your data and limits you freedom. Do not download it, for your own good and for those around you* (Fla)[3].

On the contrary, some participants showed no privacy fears or concerns claiming that they considered Immuni as a safe app and that they believed the data collected by Immuni to be safely protected. *I mean, even if I have it on my phone, Immuni is an app that does not collect any information about me and I know that the data collected on Immuni are used only for epidemiological purpose.* (Sara)[4].

Another important aspect concerning the barriers encountered was the digital divide among users. This was mainly related to age and economic status. From the data analysis, it was highlighted how elderly, who are not used to digital devices, might encounter some difficulties in both downloading Immuni and using it correctly. In addition to that, Immuni, as it was described in the introduction, requires a newer software to function correctly. Thus, all of those citizens with older phones, who cannot afford a new phone to have Immuni, are not be able to download and use the app. Therefore, both elderly and people coming from a lower socio-economic status might be systematically excluded from this health-related public service. Often, the two factors (user's older age and phone's incompatibility) are combined together for the elderly, who have difficulties in using digital devices and smartphones, but also own older phones which might not be compatible with Immuni. *Here you have some very old phones. For instance, my mum and dad, who are around 80s, don't have smartphones, what will they do then? You can sit down and teach them how to use it but it is too complicated. Thus, Immuni has zero efficacy with such an old population and these very old phones* (Salvatrice)[5].

Concerning the last sub-theme: the evaluation of the efficacy of Immuni, it has emerged that Immuni was perceived as ineffective because of its low rate of adoption. According to many, such a failure had occurred because its adoption was completely voluntary, encouraging many citizens not to download it. *Immuni was not imposed, thus it was not downloaded.* (Moody)[6]. It seems that many citizens would have preferred a more coercive method, wherein the government imposed Immuni to access some services and some public places *They (the government) should have forced us to download it. We all should have been forced, also those who cannot do it by themselves, like me for example. They*

---

[2] interview(26/10/2020).

[3] tweet(10/10/2020).

[4] interview(23/10/2020).

[5] interview(22/10/2020).

[6] interview(21/10/2020).

would have had to set up a public spot or office in which you can go and they help you out downloading it (Salvatrice)[7].

Finally, concerning the evaluation of Immuni as an effective tracing system, the integration with the national health system (SSN) was discussed. According to the data analyzed, users believed that Immuni was not properly integrated into the actual operations of the national health system. *Also because I know that there are some issues concerning the relation of Immuni with the ASL: I believe some operators don't know how to insert the codes* (Moody)[8]. Such a suspicion appears unfounded, at least under the technological point of view. The data collected with the secondary users have made clear that doctors in charge of contact tracing had been carefully instructed on the use of Immuni and were all capable of making the overall Immuni's system function correctly. *Immuni is so easy, it takes only 3 min, it is not long at all. It is a very small part of the all procedure of contact tracing, not so significant concerning the time required* (Contact tracing doctor)[9].

5.2 Cues to Action

The second main theme observed in the data gathered is the cues to action. Usually, they are either internal (physiological cues) or external (related to information transmitted by external factors such as friends, media, or institutions). This study has focused only on external cues.

Almost all people interviewed expressed their disappointment towards the Immuni's marketing campaign arguing that the app was not promoted enough and with enough insistence, and the marketing campaign, conducted by the government, did not neither reassure citizens' regarding their privacy fear nor explain adequately the functioning of the app *Minister @robersperanza, as you can see from this hundreds of comments, most of the population did not understand how Immuni works. Why there is no informative advertisements on TVs, newspapers?#COVID19italia @MinisteroSalute* (Mec)[10]. This might have contributed to both spread confusion regarding the app and also dismissing it as a not relevant tool *I think that if the government actually cared about this project, they would have done more to promote it* (Lops)[11].

5.3 Immuni's Usability

This theme concerns with all the characteristics of the app that can influence its perceived usability and can impact on the perception of the app itself. Among usability design choices, the sub-theme of notifications has emerged. At the beginning, users complained about push notifications being too frequent and too

---

[7] interview(22/10/2020).
[8] interview (21/10/2020).
[9] interview(5/11/2020).
[10] tweet(10/10/2020).
[11] interview(26/10/2020).

disruptive. In an app designed only to inform about possible contagions, notifications should only be informative and should represent an infrequent, thus relevant, phenomenon.

Subsequently, users started to express worries concerning lack of feedback. Notifications had become not only sporadic but also not very evident. One user claimed that he had been informed of a risky exposition only after he had entered the app. *I saw the notification only as I entered the app, I didn't receive any notification, I didn't get a notification like when you receive a message. Nothing like that* (Senator)[12]. This could be extremely problematic: although the app itself asks the user to check one's status every day, the user has nothing to do within the app, so s/he is not encouraged or even reminded of opening the app regularly *And the app says "open Immuni once a day to check its status", but if you open the app, there is nothing to do there, so why would I open it everyday?* (Demetra)[13]. Many have perceived Immuni as defined by a lack of feedback as it does not provide any external stimuli or outputs on whether the system is working appropriately.

6 Discussion

As countries are facing several difficulties in running a successful vaccination campaign and the number of infected citizens remains dangerously high, digital contact tracing could be now even more than in the past a fundamental tool in containing the virus. Investigating all the factors that influence users' perception and attitudes towards the Italian CTA has proved to be an extremely complex and challenging task. As a matter of fact, several multi-layered factors are involved in influencing users' views and opinions concerning Immuni.

We found that the overall evaluation of the app is affected by three main clusters: the perceived benefits, the perceived barriers and the overall efficacy of the tool. These three factors are highly intertwined and related with one and other. These findings are in line with previous research, which have found the importance of privacy concerns and doubts over the mass uptake of then app as two relevant factors impacting CTA' citizen's evaluation [10].

An external aspect that might have influenced users' perception of Immuni is the official marketing campaign as well as all the information circulating, both online and offline, regarding the app. Some have claimed that such a lousy campaign may have actually led to more reluctance and skepticism towards the app, as the communication failed in clarifying the purpose of the app and the way it worked. It also did not dispel the privacy fears of the citizens.

Concerning the overall usability, most people presented no issues in using the app, they found it simple to understand and easy to use. The main problems raised by primary users and by the virtual ethnography concerned with the design of exposure notification. Users are asked to check routinely the status of the app, but as there is no reminder or notification sent to the user, why would

---

[12] interview(25/10/2020).
[13] interview(21/10/2020).

s/he check the app every day? This proves to be a major usability barrier, as it might prevent some users from discovering quickly of their risky exposition.

In conclusion, our research can shed a light on citizens' attitudes towards CTAs and open up new avenues of research in the area of attitudes towards CTAs.

References

1. Agi.it, R.: Download, positivi, notifiche: i primi 3 mesi di immuni, September 2020. https://www.agi.it/cronaca/news/2020-09-14/immuni-download-positivi-notifiche-9663280/
2. Alsos, O.A., Svanæs, D.: Designing for the secondary user experience. In: Campos, P., Graham, N., Jorge, J., Nunes, N., Palanque, P., Winckler, M. (eds.) INTERACT 2011. LNCS, vol. 6949, pp. 84–91. Springer, Heidelberg (2011). https://doi.org/10.1007/978-3-642-23768-3_7
3. Behling, O., Law, K.S.: Translating questionnaires and other research instruments: problems and solutions. Sage **133** (2000)
4. Braun, V., Clarke, V.: Using thematic analysis in psychology. Qual. Res. Psychol. **3**(2), 77–101 (2006)
5. Dar, A.B., Lone, A.H., Zahoor, S., Khan, A.A., Naaz, R.: Applicability of mobile contact tracing in fighting pandemic (COVID-19): issues, challenges and solutions. Comput. Sci. Rev. **38**, 100307 (2020)
6. Falletti, E.: Privacy protection, big data gathering and public health issues: COVID-19 tracking app use in Italy. In: Big Data Gathering and Public Health Issues: COVID-19 Tracking App Use in Italy, 2 January 2021
7. Ferretti, L., et al.: Quantifying SARS-CoV-2 transmission suggests epidemic control with digital contact tracing. Science **368**(6491) (2020)
8. Hinch, R., et al.: Effective configurations of a digital contact tracing app: a report to nhsx. en, April 2020. https://github.com/BDI-pathogens/covid-19_instant_tracing/blob/master/Report
9. Verrall, A.: Rapid audit of contact tracing for COVID-19 in New Zealand, April 2020. https://apo.org.au/sites/default/files/resource-files/2020-04/apo-nid303350.pdf/
10. Williams, S.N., Armitage, C.J., Tampe, T., Dienes, K.: Public attitudes towards COVID-19 contact tracing apps: a UK-based focus group study. Health Expectations **24**(2), 377–385 (2020)

Social Companion Robots to Reduce Isolation: A Perception Change Due to COVID-19

Moojan Ghafurian[1]([✉]), Colin Ellard[2], and Kerstin Dautenhahn[1,3]

[1] Department of Electrical and Computer Engineering, University of Waterloo, Waterloo, ON, Canada
{moojan,kerstin.dautenhahn}@uwaterloo.ca
[2] Department of Psychology, University of Waterloo, Waterloo, ON, Canada
cellard@uwaterloo.ca
[3] Department of Systems Design Engineering, University of Waterloo, Waterloo, ON, Canada

Abstract. Social isolation is one of the negative consequences of a pandemic like COVID-19. Social isolation and loneliness are not only experienced by older adults, but also by younger people who live alone and cannot communicate with others or get involved in social situations as they used to. In such situations, social companion robots might have the potential to reduce social isolation and increase well-being. However, society's perception of social robots has not always been positive. In this paper, we conducted two online experiments with 102 and 132 participants during the self isolation periods of COVID-19 (May-June 2020 and January 2021), to study how COVID-19 has affected people's perception of the benefits of a social robot. Our results showed that a change caused by COVID-19, as well as having an older relative who lived alone or at a care center during the pandemic significantly and positively affected people's perception of social robots, as companions, and that the feeling of loneliness can drive the purchase of a social robot. The second study replicated the results of the first study. We also discuss the effects of Big 5 personality traits on the likelihood to purchase a social robot, as well as on participants' general attitude towards COVID-19 and adapting to the pandemic.

1 Introduction

Social isolation is a common issue among older adults, especially those with disabilities, and can affect health and quality of life. Lack of social support can lead to loneliness, which is a significant public health issue [15] and is associated with multiple negative health outcomes, such as depression [2,5], anxiety [42], and an increase in cardiovascular risk [46]. While social isolation is more common among older adults, pandemics such as COVID-19 can lead to an increase in social isolation not only in older adults [3], but among adults of all ages [14,48]. Social

C. Ardito et al. (Eds.): INTERACT 2021, LNCS 12933, pp. 43–63, 2021.
https://doi.org/10.1007/978-3-030-85616-8_4

isolation is an important consequence of COVID-19, along with many other negative consequences [14] such as an increase in family violence [47]. As concluded by Van Bavel et al. [49], action is required to mitigate these devastating effects.

Since the outbreak of COVID-19, many researchers have emphasized different benefits of using robots and artificially intelligent systems on mitigating the associated risks. These applications included using robots for medical education [17], managing the spread of COVID-19 in public areas by reducing human contact, disinfecting areas, providing security [53,54], and helping children to stay connected with each other [43]. We believe that another important application area is to use social robots as companions during a pandemic such as COVID-19. Social robots have the potential to act as companions and reduce social isolation, and have already been used successfully in providing care and support in many domains, such as by improving older adults' mood [50,51], reducing depression [1], and even reducing the need to use medication [45].

However, perception of social robots has not always been positive, and previously, prior to COVID-19, it has been reported that there is an increasing trend in people's negative attitudes towards robots [16]. It might also be difficult to perceive their benefits accurately, especially by those who do not have any experience of, or direct knowledge of anyone who has experienced loneliness and social isolation. One of the common concerns raised by many researchers and participants alike is that social robots may replace human companions. While this is a valid concern, social robots can be highly beneficial in situations where such human interaction is in fact prohibited, for example during a pandemic such as COVID-19, or for older adults who might be socially isolated, e.g., due to medical conditions. In these situations the presence of social robots could be positive and effective in reducing their loneliness and improving society's mental wellbeing.

While companion robots can be beneficial to reduce loneliness, they can only succeed if society has a positive attitude towards them. Specifically, people need to perceive the benefits of social robots and be willing to adopt them. It has been previously shown that lower social support can increase older adults' acceptance of social robots that are less intuitive to use [4]. But, a lower level of psychological well-being, such as emotional loneliness, life satisfaction, and depressive mood can reduce acceptance, depending on the robot and how intuitive it is to use [4]. We argue that the changes caused by COVID-19 has resulted in a higher level of attention to the consequences of social isolation, which could highlight the benefits of having a companion robot (for self or loved ones), and could change society's perception of them.

Therefore, we investigated how experience of social isolation due to COVID-19 has affected the perception of benefits of companion robots, and whether loneliness can affect the tendency to purchase a social robot (as an indicator of participants' intention to use it). We further asked what tasks people would prefer for a companion robot to carry out, and what aspects of a companion robot they perceived to be important.

Research Questions and Hypotheses:
This paper investigated seven research questions:

RQ1: Has a change due to COVID-19 affected people's perception of social companion robots?

RQ2: Has having an older relative who lives alone or at a care center during the pandemic affected people's perception of social companion robots?

RQ3: Can loneliness increase the likelihood of purchasing a companion robot?

RQ4: Do people have strong preferences for tasks of companion robots?

RQ5: Are social elements (e.g., showing emotions) perceived to be important for a companion robot, and how does the importance of such components compare with the technical accuracy of the robots?

RQ6: How do different personality types affect attitudes towards COVID-19, as well as attitudes towards social robots during the pandemic?

RQ7: Are the findings related to the perception of social robots due to COVID-19 and the effect of loneliness on purchase of a social robot robust and independent of the time that the study was conducted?

Our hypotheses were as follows.

H1: COVID-19 has caused people to reflect more about the consequences of social isolation, and has positively affected attitudes towards social companion robots, because the pandemic pointed out situations where social robots can fill gaps in the provision of social interaction, as opposed to robots being perceived negatively as replacements of human contact.

H2: For the same reason as in H1, having an older relative who either lives alone or at a care center has positively affected the attitude towards social robots.

H3: A change in perception of social robots can positively influence people's tendency to purchase one.

H4: Loneliness can be an important factor in adopting a social robot and can increase the tendency to purchase a social companion robot.

H5: Social elements such as robots' ability to show emotions, adapting its behaviour based on its users, etc., will be perceived to be as important as technical accuracy by people, since many studies have shown their advantages in experimental settings.

H6: The observed effects can be replicated at a later time, as we believe that these effects (e.g., change of perception of social robots due to COVID-19) are long-term, as a result of COVID-19, and independent of the time of the study.

2 Background

In previous studies, social robots were successfully used in many contexts, such as for increasing older adults' social engagement [34,41] and providing companionship [26,32]. They also helped with activities of daily living, such as helping older adults with dementia with the process of eating food [13], as well as supporting nurses in a hospital [37]. Furthermore, social robots have been able to help children with autism in many domains such as therapy and education [11,39], for example by increasing their social engagement [40], or even involving children in peer-learning scenarios, e.g., to improve children's writing skills [10].

However, despite their success in multiple domains and a variety of studies, many of the existing social robots have not been used much beyond the context of these studies. A part of this can be due to the existing challenges, such as having robots that can act fully autonomously, or concerns related to a robot's monetary cost [28,35] (as it is challenging to build affordable consumer robots [44]).

To be successfully adopted by their intended users, multiple factors are critical, which can be related to the robot (e.g., its appearance and design, its capabilities, etc.) and its users (e.g., users' acceptance, trust, attitude towards robots, and likelihood of adopting a robot). User acceptance is in fact essential for the success of social robots [44].

According to a recent study conducted in Europe [16], people have become more cautious in using robots, and their attitude towards autonomous robots has become more negative during the period 2012 to 2017. This study also showed that people are more comfortable with robots at workplaces, as opposed to the robots used in healthcare and those that are designed to help older adults. According to this study, participants' age, gender, and education level, and employment status could all affect one's attitude towards robots: men were found to have a more positive attitude towards robots and education was positively correlated with a positive attitude [16]. The growing anxiety in using robots was associated with the concern that the robots may replace humans and lead to losing one's job [8,27,29]. A negative attitude towards social robots can not only affect their acceptance [38] and adoption (as people with a highly negative attitude tend to avoid human–robot communication [30]), but also can affect people's interactions with the robot, and as shown by Nomura et al., users' self-expression towards the robots [30].

In general, society's perception and acceptance of social robots are affected by multiple factors. For example, de Graaf et al. recommended creating a clear purpose for robots, increasing robots' social capabilities, and considering the use context (e.g., living situation, time and location of use) to be important for developing social robots that are accepted by society [19]. In the context of healthcare, many factors such as a robot's design, personality, adaptability, humanness, size, and gender can affect how people react to it and affect users' acceptance [7]. Furthermore, it has been shown that the attitude towards social robots can significantly affect their acceptance [31].

There are multiple other factors that have been shown to affect acceptance of social robots, including but not limited to, feelings of social presence [21], perceived enjoyment [21], familiarity with robots [6], robots being functionally relevant [12], emotional displays (e.g., positive versus negative) [6], robots' ease of use [12], level of interaction between potential users and robots [33], the category label assigned to the robot (i.e., the way the robot is introduced, e.g., a "home appliance") [23], and even age [38].

Furthermore, previous studies showed different results regarding the impact of loneliness on the acceptance of robots: loneliness has been shown to be correlated with a more positive attitude towards robots (by increasing the perceived social presence) [24] and a more negative attitude (by decreasing anthropomorphic tendencies) [25] towards social robots. However, in many cases, social robots have been promising in reducing loneliness and social isolation, especially in older adults [36].

3   Experiment

To address our research questions, two online studies were conducted in May 2020 and January 2021 in Canada, both during the self isolation period of COVID-19. While both were conducted during the times that people have been self isolating, the time difference enables us to ensure that the findings are robust and independent of participants' level of experience with COVID-19.

3.1   Methodology

A questionnaire was designed and administered online on Amazon Mechanical Turk. The questionnaire measured different aspects of people's experience of COVID-19 and perception of robots, and was implemented in 5 sections as below:

Section 1 - Loneliness: Feeling of loneliness as measured through the 8-item UCLA Loneliness Scale Questionnaire (ULS-8) [20]

Section 2 - Big 5 Personality: Big 5 personality, i.e., personality measured through five different traits of Extroversion, Openness to experience, Conscientiousness, Extraversion, Agreeableness, and Emotionality (or Neuroticism) was measured using the TIPI Questionnaire [18]

Section 3 - Extroversion: The specific extroversion dimension of Big 5 was assessed via 24 items related to Extroversion from the 120-item Big 5 questionnaire (IPIP-120 Personality Test) [22], to ensure consistency and accuracy in the results of the Big 5 personality test. Note that the results of this questionnaire were used only for ensuring the consistency between TIPI and IPIP-120 results, as we preferred to avoid using all items from IPIP-120 (to avoid participant fatigue).

Section 4 - Perception of Social Robots: A questionnaire was designed, asking participants:

(a) whether they were likely to purchase a social robot if it is "affordable" for them (rated on a continuous scale from "not at all" to "very likely").

(b) if their perception of social robots as companions has changed due to COVID-19 (rated on a continuous scale from "Not Changed at All" to "Completely Changed"), with a follow up question asking them to explain why it has/has not changed (answer provided as a text entry).

(c) what task/tasks they preferred for a companion robot during COVID-19. The choices were: music/video, chitchat and joking, dancing, exercises, reminders (health related, e.g., medicine and appointments, or daily life/socially related), cooking, games, relaxation or meditation or breathing exercises, storytelling or reading together, and Other (we asked them to specify).

(d) what appearance they preferred a social robot to have. The choices were: Human-like, Animal-like, and Other (we asked them to specify).

(e) what were the elements in a social robot that were important to them. The choices were: Not making mistakes, Ability to show emotions, Not requiring much maintenance, Having a specific behaviour that they might like, Recognizing them, and Other (please specify).

All questions that were not rated on a continuous scale (i.e., preference about the robot's appearance, important elements for a social robot, and preferred tasks) were provided as multiple-choice questions, where participants could select as many responses as they wished, with the response of "Other" having a text entry to be completed.

Section 5 - Demographics: A questionnaire was designed to gather participants' demographics information, as well as other information that could affect their attitude and behaviour during COVID-19, which included: (a) age, (b) gender, (c) if participants had pets/type of pets, (d) number of people in their household, (e) number of children in their household, (f) if they have a relative who is over 80 and lives alone (if yes, how can a social robot help them?), (g) if they have a relative who is over 80 and lives in a care home (if yes, how can a social robot help them?), (h) how can a social robot help them stay connected with an older relative, (i) how they feel about social isolation and COVID-19 (responses ranged from their life is completely and negatively affected to their life is completely and positively affected), and how they feel about the way their life has changed, (k) aside from work communications, how many people did they connect with and if this number was changed due to COVID-19, (l) whether they have ever moved to a new country and lived there for a significant period for a purpose other than a holiday (as an indication of their ability to adapt to significant changes in their lives), (m) how stressed/anxious they were due to COVID-19, (n) how much they followed social isolation rules, and (o) if they thought there were differences between social robots and conversational virtual agents, to explain which one they prefer, and to explain why.[1]

On each page of the questionnaire, attention and sanity checks were added. For example, we presented the same question with the opposite direction of the scale for the answers, or questions with clear answers, such as "How much do you think that drinking water is liquid" or "Do you agree that Tuesdays are considered weekends in North America?".

Finally, we intended for participants to complete the study on a positive note. Thus, with the purpose of trying to change participants' mood after thinking about the questions mentioned above, we asked them about their favourite animal, favourite cartoon character, and favourite movie. These questions were included at the very end and served solely as an attempt to end the study on a positive note.

---

[1] Note that only a subset of these results, which were appropriate for the scope of this paper are discussed due to page limits.

3.2   Procedure

Upon reading the information letter and signing the consent form, participants were directed to the questionnaire. They completed the 5 sections of the questionnaire mentioned above. Afterwards they received the completion code and instructions on how to submit the HIT[2].

3.3   Participants

The first study was conducted May-June 2020. 110 participants were recruited on Amazon Mechanical Turk. Participation was limited to Canada[3] and those who had an approval rate over 97% (to minimize the risk of getting low quality responses) and had completed at least 100 HITs[4] (to ensure familiarity with the interface). Data of five participants were removed as they failed the attention checks. The data of three participants' were removed due to repeated participation. This finally resulted in 102 participants (41 Female, 61 Male; age: [18,66], mean: 34.6 yrs). The number of people in participants' household ranged from 1 to 8, with one not indicating a number and reporting "more than 5". The number of children in participants' household ranged from 0 to 6, with one not indicating a number and reporting "more than 5". The majority (68 participants) reported to have no children in their household.

The second study was conducted in January 2021. By checking the MTurk IDs prior to participation, we ensured that those who participated in the first study will not participate again. Recruitment criteria on Amazon Mechanical Turk was the same as before: 97% approval rate based on at least 100 HITs. But as country was also limited as before, we were not able to recruit more than 70 participants for the second study (who did not participate in the first one); therefore, the criteria was changed to an approval rate of 95% based on at least 50 HITs. A total of 138 participants were recruited (60 female, 77 male, and 1 unknown). Five participants failed the attention checks and their data were removed from the study. One participant's data was removed due to missing data. This left 132 participants (59 Female, 72 Male, and 1 unknown; age: [25,72], mean: 33.6 yrs). The reported number of people in participants' household ranged from 1 to 26. The number of children in participants' household ranged from 0 to 5.

Full Ethics clearance was received from the University of Waterloo's Research Ethics Committees prior to running the studies. Participants were notified about the nature of the questions under foreseeable risks in the consent form and were informed that the questions might make them think about different aspects of social isolation during COVID-19 and the feeling of loneliness. They were also

---

[2] Human Intelligence Task.

[3] Participation was limited to Canada, where rules on social distancing were precisely defined and followed by the majority of people.

[4] A Human Intelligence Task (HIT) is a task on Mechanical Turk (MTurk), which is completed by the volunteers on MTurk.

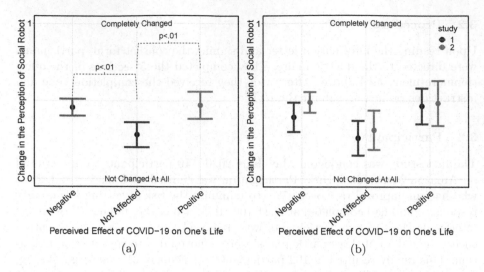

Fig. 1. Change in the perception of social robots as a result of the reported change in people's lives due to COVID-19 for (a) both studies combined, and (b) each study. 95% confidence intervals are visualized. Both a positive and a negative change significantly increased the change in perception of companion robots (see Table 1). Note that in study 2 the number of people who reported a positive change decreased, therefore, the smaller sample in the positive group could have led to a larger confidence interval. In study 1 we had 44, 29, and 29 participants in "Negative", "Not affected", and "Positive" groups, respectively. Whereas these numbers were 91, 23, and 18 in study 2.)

given the option to skip questions (without it affecting the remuneration) or to stop at any point.

4   Results

First, we will discuss how participants' perception of social robots changed as a result of COVID-19, and how participants' loneliness level and this change in perception affected the tendency of purchasing a social robot. Afterwards, we will discuss the tasks that the participants preferred for a social companion robot and the elements/capabilities that they considered to be important for the robots, along with their preferred appearance for a social robot. Finally, we will present results on how participants' personality affected adapting to COVID-19 in general. We did not observe any effect of having a pet, or the number of people and children living in participants' households on any of the measures, therefore these results are not discussed in this section.

4.1   COVID-19 and Perception Change

Experiencing a change in one's lifestyle as a result of the pandemic (whether positive or negative) led to a change in the perception of benefits of companion robots. This change was significantly higher than the change reported by those who indicated that their lives were not affected by COVID-19 (see Fig. 1).

Table 1. Linear Regression model predicting perception changed based on participants' lifestyle change due to COVID-19, and whether they had a relative over 80 who lives alone or at a care center. Age, gender, and Big 5 personality were controlled for but removed as they did not improve the model (neither had a significant effect on perception change).

Covariate	Estimate	SE	t	Pr $(> |t|)$
Intercept	219.086	105.725	2.072	<.05
Study	62.358	41.603	1.499	0.135
loneliness	−2.894	4.048	−0.715	0.475
feelIsolationNegative	158.686	50.591	3.137	<.01
feelIsolationPositive	178.476	61.531	2.901	<.01
OlderRelativeAloneTRUE	97.642	42.503	2.297	<.05

To study the significance of this difference, a linear model was fit to predict perception change, based on the change in participants' lifestyle, whether they had an older relative (over 80) who lived alone or at a care home, and study (i.e., time of the study). Table 1 shows the results. Both a positive ($t = 3.016, p < .01$) and a negative change ($t = 3.228, p < .01$) significantly affected the perception change (confirming H1). Further, having a relative who either lives alone or at a care center significantly and positively affected the perception change ($t = 2.322, p < .05$; confirming H2; also see Fig. 2). We did not see an effect of study (i.e., time of study) on perception change (supporting H6).

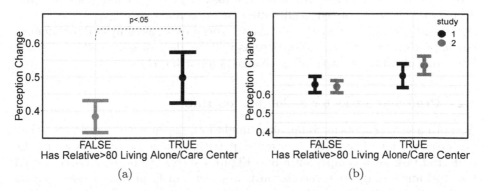

Fig. 2. Reported perception change based on whether the participants had an older relative who either lived alone or at a care center (a) for the combined data, and (b) for each study.

Table 2. Linear Regression model predicting the likelihood to purchase a social robot based on the loneliness level, study (time of the study), Big 5 personality traits, age, gender, and participants' perception change regarding social robots due to COVID-19. Loneliness and the change in perception were not correlated.

Covariate	Estimate	SE	t	Pr $(> |t|)$
Intercept	−135.271	350.043	−0.386	.700
Study	6.034	36.810	0.164	.870
Loneliness	15.570	4.368	3.564	<.001
Extraversion	11.906	15.266	0.780	.436
Agreeableness	24.378	16.952	1.438	.152
Conscientiousness	23.178	17.046	1.360	.175
Emotionality	0.447	17.600	0.025	.980
Openness	−54.713	17.878	−3.060	<.01
PerceptionChanged	0.395	0.057	6.883	<.0001
Gender:Male	90.861	39.554	2.297	<.05
Gender:DidNotShare	23.860	277.009	0.086	.931
Age	−1.661	1.629	−1.020	.309

This change in perception of the benefits of social robots due to COVID-19 also significantly affected the reported likelihood of purchasing a social robot ($t = 6.883, p < .0001$; confirming H3; see Table 2). Furthermore, loneliness, along with this perception change, significantly and positively affected the likelihood of purchasing a companion robot ($t = 3.564, p < .001$). Results are shown in Table 2 and Fig. 3. This confirmed H4. This likelihood was also affected by one of the Big 5 personality traits: openness ($t = −3.060, p < .01$), but unlike what was expected, as openness increased, the likelihood to purchase a social robot decreased. We also noticed gender differences as male participants reported a significantly higher likelihood to purchase a social robot as compared with female participants ($t = 2.297, p < .05$). Here as well, we did not see an effect of study (i.e., time of study) on perception change (supporting H6).

4.2   Preferred Tasks for a Companion Robot

Accepting social robots as companions might also depend on the tasks that they are designed for. Therefore we studied participants' responses related to the preferred task for a companion robot. Figure 4 shows the results. While we did not find any strong preference towards a specific task, playing games, getting involved in a chitchat, playing music, helping in exercises, and helping with reminders were considered as the most preferred tasks for a companion robot, while "dancing" was the least preferred.

We performed binomial tests to study whether the differences were significant. Dancing was selected significantly less than all other options ($p < .0001$),

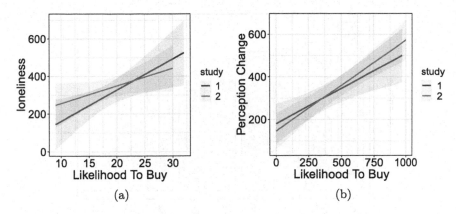

Fig. 3. Reported likelihood to purchase a social robot based on (a) the measured level of loneliness and (b) change in perception of social robots due to COVID-19 (see Table 2 for more details).

and getting involved in games was selected significantly more than helping with reminders ($p < .05$), relaxation ($p < .01$), cooking ($p < .01$), story telling ($p < .0001$), and dancing ($p < .0001$).

In addition, 18 participants selected other, either alone or along with other choices, four of whom indicated that they were not interested in using a companion robot and many others did not provide any explanation. The suggestions for "other" included cleaning the house, helping with household choirs, scheduling appointments, providing information about the weather and news, and giving random factoids.

4.3 Important Elements for a Companion Robot

We further studied different social and technical capabilities of robots and asked which one/ones the participants believed to be the most important in a companion social robot. We found "not requiring any maintenance" and "recognizing you' to be two of the important elements for social robots, and, interestingly, social capabilities such as "recognizing you", "ability to show emotions", and "having a specific behaviour that one prefers" to be considered even more important than technical soundness, i.e., "not making mistakes". Thus, it indicates that participants prefer a social companion robot that is technically robust but they do not necessarily ask for an advanced level of rational intelligent behaviour. The results are shown in Fig. 5.

We further conducted binomial tests to check whether the differences were significant. Among these elements, "not requiring much maintenance" and "recognizing you" were selected significantly more than all others (significance levels ranged from $p < .05$ to $p < .0001$; the difference between these two elements were not significant). Also, "Not making mistakes" was selected significantly less than all other elements (significance levels changed from $p < .05$ to $p < .0001$). This

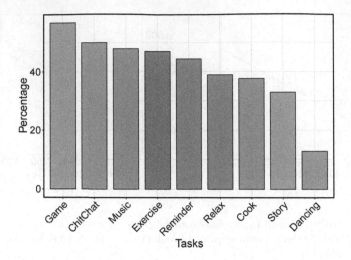

Fig. 4. Tasks that participants preferred to use a companion robot for. Percentage shows the percentage of participants who selected the task.

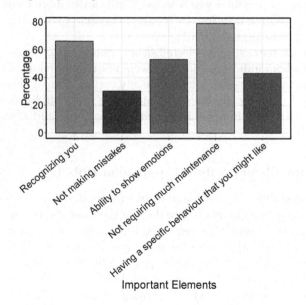

Fig. 5. Important elements of a companion robot as indicated by the participants. Percentage shows the percentage of participants who selected the element.

suggested that along with not requiring maintenance, social capabilities might be even more important than not making mistakes in a social companion robot. This confirmed H5.

In addition to these options, 22 participants selected "Other" and entered the elements that were important to them. Three of the inputs were about the application areas (i.e., playing guitar, fetching things, and doing chores/cooking), which reflects a misunderstanding of this question. Two others indicated that they were not interested in a robot regardless, so there were not any element that was important for them. One did not explain the choice of other and did not select any other element. The remaining others suggested additional elements. Two of them asked for the robot to be dynamic and helpful (which would also refer to a robot's functionality). Two others pointed out maintenance and safety as key elements: "safe around home and pets" and "easy to assemble, charge, and repair if needed". Seven addressed the communication capabilities of the robot (i.e., "natural conversation", "being able to communicate freely (not experience the same comprehension problems as with Alexa)", "doesn't not understand us" [sic], "sounding natural not robotic", "the ability to converse", "being able to react to a specific situation with some Randomnise" [sic], and "It is absolutely imperative that the ilusion of talking to something sentient and not just a bunch of lines of code be maintained, otherwise it is a tool, not a companion." [sic]). Furthermore, four participants emphasized the importance of other social capabilities of a companion robot (i.e., "Mimicking empathy and giving consolation", "a kind *personality*", "understand my mood", and "remembering me, getting to know me, building on a relationship") as key elements for a companion robot. Lastly, one participant indicated that "selecting gender" would be an important element.

4.4 Preferred Appearance of a Companion Robot

We also studied participants' appearance preferences for a companion robot. Both a human-like and an animal-like appearance were similarly preferred (110 versus 92 votes). Thirty two participants selected "Other" and proposed their own preferred appearance. 17 participants indicated robot-like or machine-like, with some giving more information (e.g., "A retro styled robot from the 1950s" and "robot like i.e. tv/movie like in appearance" [sic]). Further, one response indicated animal-like ("Anthropomorphic fox character") and two indicated that they would prefer no robot. Others suggestions included (a) any shape but human-like, (b) not similar to anything living, (c) in the form of a speaker or a box, (d) object-like, like a box, ball, or disk, (e) not like a life form. e.g., like a tennis ball or hockey puck, (f) the form should be dictated by the function of the robot, (g) the shape would not be important, and (h) not human but should have eyes.

4.5 Personality Traits and Adapting to COVID-19

Aside from the effects of the personality traits on perception of companion robots, Big 5 traits affected participants' general attitude towards the pandemic. Scoring high on the extroversion trait significantly increased being stressed as a result of COVID-19 ($t = 3.192, p < .01$), as reported by the participants, while scoring high on emotional stability significantly decreased participants' stress ($t = -5.800, p < .0001$). Also, those who reported to follow the rules better reported to have less stress about COVID-19 ($t = 4.147, p < .0001$). While not significant, the stress levels seemed to be higher in Study 2, as compared with the first study ($t = 1.909, p = .057$).

Furthermore, extroversion significantly and negatively affected following the social isolation rules ($t = -2.539, p < .05$), while agreeableness significantly increased following the rules ($t = 3.848, p < .001$). Also, conscientiousness did not affect how well people follow the social isolation rules ($t = -0.053, p = .957$). Finally, the results were different across two studies and participants reported to follow rules significantly more in study 2 as compared with study 1 ($t = 2.711, p < .01$).[5]

We also observed similar effects of Big 5 traits on participants' loneliness levels as was reported by Buecker et al. [9]: extroversion, agreeableness, and emotional stability significantly decreased loneliness. We did not find an effect of gender or age on loneliness. Further, we did not find an effect of study (i.e., when the study was conducted) on the loneliness levels and conscientiousness did not affect loneliness ($t = -0.072, p = .943$). Table 3 shows these results.

Table 3. Linear Regression model predicting loneliness based on participants' personality traits and the experience of immigration.

Covariate	Estimate	SE	t	Pr ($> |t|$)
Study2	0.091	0.563	0.161	0.872
FollowRules	−0.001	0.002	−0.925	0.356
Immigration	0.899	0.585	1.536	0.126
Extraversion	−0.829	0.224	−3.697	<.001
Emotionality	−1.315	0.234	−5.630	<.0001
Conscientiousness	−0.018	0.255	−0.072	0.943
Openness	−0.241	0.268	−0.899	0.370
Agreeableness	−0.635	0.257	−2.468	<.05

5   Discussion

"I think my perception has changed because I have never fully understood what it feels like to be isolated for such a long period. When thinking about social isolation I usually thought of people in remote areas or people who were in care homes without many visitors. Now it is easier to understand what people living alone must feel like and why having some sort of social interaction is important."[6]

---

[5] p-values were calculated through two linear models predicting stress and how much one follows rules based on participants' personality traits.

[6] Examples of participants' quotes related to their perception change.

"The COVID-19 pandemic has revealed to me that certain individuals are deeply distressed by isolation and the inability to socialize with others regularly or in the conventional way. If there is a tool available that can help others feel less isolated, I'm all for it."

"It was changed because recently it has been difficult to meet up with other people and socialize. This has put a strain on people's mental health, including mine. For this reason, I feel that a social robot would be an appropriate way to spend time. At this point, I am okay with spending time with anything that will keep me busy and interested."

There has been an ongoing debate regarding the benefits of using companion robots. While social robots are shown to be effective in reducing loneliness, concerns such as using companion robots may lead to neglect from family members, reduce human interactions, or replace humans and lead to loss of jobs have negatively affected society's attitude towards companion robots [16,52].

In this paper, we presented two studies conducted 8 months apart and hypothesized that COVID-19 could have changed society's perception of social robots, as during the self-isolation period people are more likely to experience social isolation and think about the consequences of social isolation, either due to the change they experienced themselves (RQ1), or thinking about others, such as older relatives who live alone or at a care center (RQ2). As a result, they may be able to see social robots as additions and complements, as opposed to replacements for human contact, which can lead to a more positive attitude towards social robots, and ultimately a higher acceptance of social companion robots in the future. Also, with loneliness being one of the situations that companion robots could help with, we asked if loneliness can increase one's tendency to purchase a social robot (RQ3).

Furthermore, to understand general preferences related to companion robots, we asked whether people have specific preferences towards the tasks designed for companion robots (RQ4), and if social elements of companion robots (e.g., the ability to show emotions) are important to them, and how this importance compares to other elements such as a robot's technical accuracy (RQ5). Finally, as it can be informative for designing social companion robots during pandemics, we asked whether people's personality (Big 5) can affect their behaviour during a pandemic and their attitude towards social robots (RQ6).

Two studies were conducted to ensure that the results were robust and did not depend on participants' level of experience with the pandemic (RQ7), as we hypothesized that the effects found will be long term.

The second study replicated results of the first study (H6 confirmed). Our results provided evidence about a change of perception of the benefits of social companion robots, and suggested that any change experienced during COVID-19 (negative or positive) affected perception of social companion robots (H1 confirmed), as well as the reported likelihood of buying a companion robot (H3 confirmed). While it was impossible to measure perception retrospectively, before and during the pandemic to compare the differences, we relied on participants' self-reported perception change. This change was in fact significantly different between those whose lives were not affected and those whose lives were affected by COVID-19.

We also noticed that those who had an older relative that either lived alone or at a care center had a significantly higher perception change (H2 confirmed). Similar to experiencing a change in the lifestyle, having an older relative who lives alone or is at a care center during the pandemic [7] can emphasize the benefits of social robots during situations where social contact is impossible, and that might explain this change on the attitude towards companion robots. Thus, experiencing a pandemic like COVID-19 could have positively changed society's attitude towards social companion robots, by emphasizing their benefits in a situation where human contact was clearly not possible. It is important to note that while our participants' ages ranged from 19 to 72 years, supporting that this perception change happened in both younger and older adults, future studies are needed to understand how this change would affect purchase of social robots for an older relative, and whether older relatives would be willing to accept and use social robots in these situations.

Other than this perception change, loneliness was another important factor that also increased the likelihood of buying a social companion robot (H4 confirmed). This is important as it can help adoption of social robots among those who have a higher level of loneliness and would benefit the most from the presence of a social companion robot. Loneliness was in fact previously reported to affect the perceived social presence of social agents, after people interacted with an agent [24]: loneliness led to feeling a higher social presence of the social agents and led to a more positive social response from the participants [24], which suggests that the benefits of social robots are experienced more by those who experience loneliness, who also, based on our study's findings, were more likely to adopt a social robot. Interestingly, openness trait of Big 5 personality had a negative effect on the tendency to purchase a social robot. This was unexpected as openness can also reflect one's openness to new experiences, and it is expected to positively affect the tendency to purchase a social robot. Future work is needed to understand why this effect was observed.

Our study also pointed out interesting and general findings on how people with different personalities adopted to COVID-19. Although we did not observe any effect of personality traits on participants' change of perception of social robots, personality traits affected participants' purchase tendency of social robots, stress levels, how much they followed rules in general, and their loneliness levels. All of these findings can be informative for the behaviour and functionality of a social companion robot during a pandemic. For example, these results suggest that extroverts could benefit highly from the presence of a companion robot during pandemics, especially one that can help reduce stress levels (e.g., by providing therapeutic support), and which could also possibly educate them and encourage them to follow social rules. Further, those with a lower emo-

---

[7] Note that visiting care centers by family members was prohibited during the time this study was conducted in Canada.

tional stability, extroversion, and agreeableness could benefit from the presence of a social robot that can reduce their loneliness.

Lastly, we provided a summary of participants' preferences towards tasks for a companion robot, its appearance, and the important elements/capabilities for such a robot. The results pointed out that a variety of tasks are preferred in general for a social companion robot, with dancing being the least preferred, and games being the most preferred. Among the important elements, "not making mistakes" was considered to be least important, and significantly less important as compared with some social aspects, such as recognizing the user and the robot's ability to show emotions (H5 confirmed). Further, maintenance and the ability to recognize one seemed to be the most important elements, selected significantly more than all other elements of a social robot. Regarding appearance, both animal-like and human-like appearances were equally preferred; a choice which we believe needs to be made based on the concrete tasks designed for a social robot and needs to be studied in the future work.

It is important to emphasize that it is not our intention to promote the replacement of human contact with social robots, but as the current pandemic is showing, social robots might play an important part in situations where direct human contact is prohibited (e.g., during pandemics) or impossible (e.g., for socially isolated older adults). While it was not the focus of our study, in addition to providing social communication and assistance, robots could even provide tactile contact for therapeutic purposes, which (while still mechanical in nature and lacking the nature of touching a biological, sentient being) has been shown to be beneficial [55].

6   Limitations and Future Work

Our studies had several limitations. First, we did not have data on people's attitude before and after COVID-19, we could only measure the change self-reported by the participants. Similarly, as the studies were conducted during the pandemic and during the period of self-isolation, we relied on participants' responses, and only loneliness and personality traits were measured through standard questionnaires (as opposed to direct questions). Furthermore, due to the strict rules on social distancing which were followed by the majority of people in Canada, participation was limited to Canada. Finally, our selection of options for appearance, tasks, and other robot elements were based on the existing literature, but more of those tasks and features could be explored. Also, in all of our multiple-choice questions we provided an option where the participants could input their preference beyond the existing selections. However, it is still possible that these results were affected by the provided choices and adding more options may change these results.

Future studies would be beneficial to understand how COVID-19 affected perception of social robots in other countries, and what can be learned from the perception change due to this pandemic to positively influence perception of social robots in other contexts and situations.

7 Conclusion

While social companion robots have been shown to have many benefits and can improve health and well-being, society's attitude towards them has not always been positive. In this study we asked how COVID-19 affected society's perception of social robot, as the pandemic was an example of a situation where social contact among humans could be impossible, and might have emphasized the benefits of using social companion robots as a "complement", as opposed to a "replacement" (which is commonly held believe and is a strong reason for negative attitudes towards social robots). The results of two studies conducted within 8 months of each other during the pandemic suggested that a change in one's life due to COVID-19 has changed the (self-reported) attitude towards social robots, as well as the tendency to purchase a social robot. These findings are promising, as a positive change in perception of social robots can increase their adoption, which would be especially advantageous for older adults who live alone or other socially isolated individuals, and can improve health and well-being.

Acknowledgements. This research was undertaken, in part, thanks to funding from the Canada 150 Research Chairs Program and the Network for Aging Research at the University of Waterloo. We thank Sami Alperen Akgun for his help with the implementation of the questionnaire.

References

1. Abdollahi, H., Mollahosseini, A., Lane, J.T., Mahoor, M.H.: In: A pilot study on using an intelligent life-like robot as a companion for elderly individuals with dementia and depression, pp. 541–546. IEEE (2017)
2. Alpass, F.M., Neville, S.: Loneliness, health and depression in older males. Aging Mental Health **7**(3), 212–216 (2003)
3. Armitage, R., Nellums, L.B.: Covid-19 and the consequences of isolating the elderly. Lancet Public Health **5**(5), e256 (2020)
4. Baisch, S., et al.: Acceptance of social robots by elder people: does psychosocial functioning matter? Int. J. Soc. Robot. **9**(2), 293–307 (2017)
5. Bennett, C.C., Sabanovic, S., Piatt, J.A., Nagata, S., Eldridge, L., Randall, N.: A robot a day keeps the blues away, pp. 536–540. IEEE (2017)
6. Bishop, L., van Maris, A., Dogramadzi, S., Zook, N.: Social robots: the influence of human and robot characteristics on acceptance. Paladyn J. Behav. Rob. **10**(1), 346–358 (2019)
7. Broadbent, E., Stafford, R., MacDonald, B.: Acceptance of healthcare robots for the older population: review and future directions. Int. J. Soc. Robot. **1**(4), 319 (2009)
8. Broadbent, E., et al.: Attitudes towards health-care robots in a retirement village. Australas. J. Ageing **31**(2), 115–120 (2012)
9. Buecker, S., Maes, M., Denissen, J.J., Luhmann, M.: Loneliness and the big five personality traits: a meta-analysis. Eur. J. Pers. **34**(1), 8–28 (2020)
10. Chandra, S., Dillenbourg, P., Paiva, A.: Children teach handwriting to a social robot with different learning competencies. Int. J. Soc. Rob., 1–28 (2019)

11. Dautenhahn, K.: Roles and functions of robots in human society-implications from research in autism therapy. Robotica 21, 443–452 (2003)
12. De Graaf, M., Allouch, S.B., Van Diik, J.: Why do they refuse to use my robot?: reasons for non-use derived from a long-term home study. In: 2017 12th ACM/IEEE International Conference on Human-Robot Interaction HRI, pp. 224–233. IEEE (2017)
13. Derek, M., Chan, J., Nejat, G.: A socially assistive robot for meal-time cognitive interventions. J. Med. Dev. **6**(1) (2012)
14. Douglas, M., Katikireddi, S.V., Taulbut, M., McKee, M., McCartney, G.: Mitigating the wider health effects of Covid-19 pandemic response. BMJ **369** (2020)
15. Gerst-Emerson, K., Jayawardhana, J.: Loneliness as a public health issue: the impact of loneliness on health care utilization among older adults. Am. J. Public Health **105**(5), 1013–1019 (2015)
16. Gnambs, T., Appel, M.: Are robots becoming unpopular? Changes in attitudes towards autonomous robotic systems in Europe. Comput. Hum. Behav. **93**, 53–61 (2019)
17. Goh, P.S., Sandars, J.: A vision of the use of technology in medical education after the Covid-19 pandemic. MedEdPublish **9** (2020)
18. Gosling, S.D., Rentfrow, P.J., Swann, W.B., Jr.: A very brief measure of the big-five personality domains. J. Res. Pers. **37**(6), 504–528 (2003)
19. de Graaf, M.M., Allouch, S.B., van Dijk, J.: Long-term acceptance of social robots in domestic environments: insights from a user's perspective. In: AAAI Spring Symposia (2016)
20. Hays, R.D., DiMatteo, M.R.: A short-form measure of loneliness. J. Pers. Assess. **51**(1), 69–81 (1987)
21. Heerink, M., Kröse, B., Evers, V., Wielinga, B.: The influence of social presence on acceptance of a companion robot by older people (2008)
22. Johnson, J.A.: Measuring thirty facets of the five factor model with a 120-item public domain inventory: Development of the IPIP-NEO-120. J. Res. Pers. **51**, 78–89 (2014)
23. Kim, J.S., Kwak, S.S., Kang, D., Choi, J.: What's in a name? effects of category labels on the consumers' acceptance of robotic products. In: In: Proceedings of the 2020 ACM/IEEE International Conference on Human-Robot Interaction, pp. 599–607 (2020)
24. Lee, K.M., Jung, Y., Kim, J., Kim, S.R.: Are physically embodied social agents better than disembodied social agents?: the effects of physical embodiment, tactile interaction, and people's loneliness in human-robot interaction. Int. J. Hum. Comput. Stud. **64**(10), 962–973 (2006)
25. Li, S., Xu, L., Yu, F., Peng, K.: Does trait loneliness predict rejection of social robots? The role of reduced attributions of unique humanness (exploring the effect of trait loneliness on anthropomorphism and acceptance of social robots). In: Proceedings of the 2020 ACM/IEEE International Conference on Human-Robot Interaction, pp. 271–280 (2020)
26. Mannion, A., et al.: Introducing the social robot Mario to people living with dementia in long term residential care: reflections. Int. J. Soc. Rob., 1–13 (2019)
27. Manyika, J., et al.: Jobs lost, jobs gained: workforce transitions in a time of automation. McKinsey Global Institute **150** (2017)
28. Moyle, W., Jones, C., Cooke, M., O'Dwyer, S., Sung, B., Drummond, S.: Connecting the person with dementia and family: a feasibility study of a telepresence robot. BMC Geriatr. **14**(1), 7 (2014)

29. Naneva, S., Gou, M.S., Webb, T.L., Prescott, T.J.: A systematic review of attitudes, anxiety, acceptance, and trust towards social robots. Int. J. Soc. Rob. **12**, 1179–1201 (2020). https://doi.org/10.1007/s12369-020-00659-4

30. Nomura, T., Kanda, T., Suzuki, T.: Experimental investigation into influence of negative attitudes toward robots on human-robot interaction. AI Soc. **20**(2), 138–150 (2006)

31. Nomura, T., Yamada, S., Kanda, T., Suzuki, T., Kato, K.: In: Influences of concerns toward emotional interaction into social acceptability of robots, pp. 231–232. IEEE (2009)

32. Odetti, L., et al.: Preliminary experiments on the acceptability of animaloid companion robots by older people with early dementia, pp. 1816–1819. IEEE (2007)

33. Paetzel, M., Perugia, G., Castellano, G.: The persistence of first impressions: the effect of repeated interactions on the perception of a social robot. In: Proceedings of the 2020 ACM/IEEE International Conference on Human-Robot Interaction, pp. 73–82 (2020)

34. Perugia, G., Doladeras, M.D., Mallofré, A.C., Rauterberg, M., Barakova, E.: Modelling engagement in dementia through behaviour. contribution for socially interactive robotics, pp. 1112–1117. IEEE (2017)

35. Picking, R., Pike, J.: Exploring the effects of interaction with a robot cat for dementia sufferers and their carers, pp. 209–210. IEEE (2017)

36. Poscia, A., et al.: Interventions targeting loneliness and social isolation among the older people: an update systematic review. Exp. Gerontol. **102**, 133–144 (2018)

37. Van der Putte, D., Boumans, R., Neerincx, M., Rikkert, M.O., de Mul, M.: A social robot for autonomous health data acquisition among hospitalized patients: an exploratory field study. In: 2019 14th ACM/IEEE International Conference on Human-Robot Interaction (HRI), pp. 658–659. IEEE (2019)

38. Robb, D.A., et al.: Robots in the danger zone: exploring public perception through engagement. In: Proceedings of the 2020 ACM/IEEE International Conference on Human-Robot Interaction, pp. 93–102 (2020)

39. Robins, B., Dautenhahn, K., Dickerson, P.: From isolation to communication: a case study evaluation of robot assisted play for children with autism with a minimally expressive humanoid robot, pp. 205–211. IEEE (2009)

40. Robins, B., Dautenhahn, K., Te Boekhorst, R., Billard, A.: Robotic assistants in therapy and education of children with autism: can a small humanoid robot help encourage social interaction skills? Univ. Access Inf. Soc. **4**(2), 105–120 (2005)

41. Šabanović, S., Bennett, C.C., Chang, W.L., Huber, L.: Paro robot affects diverse interaction modalities in group sensory therapy for older adults with dementia, pp. 1–6. IEEE (2013)

42. Santini, Z.I., et al.: Social disconnectedness, perceived isolation, and symptoms of depression and anxiety among older Americans (NSHAP): a longitudinal mediation analysis. Lancet Public Health **5**(1), e62–e70 (2020)

43. Scassellati, B., Vázquez, M.: The potential of socially assistive robots during infectious disease outbreaks. Science. Robotics **5**(44) (2020). https://doi.org/10.1126/scirobotics.abc9014. https://robotics.sciencemag.org/content/5/44/eabc9014

44. Share, P., Pender, J.: Preparing for a robot future? Social professions, social robotics and the challenges ahead. Irish J. Appl. Soc. Stud. **18**(1), 4 (2018)

45. Shibata, T.: Therapeutic seal robot as biofeedback medical device: qualitative and quantitative evaluations of robot therapy in dementia care. Proc. IEEE **100**(8), 2527–2538 (2012)

46. Smith, T.W., Ruiz, J.M.: Psychosocial influences on the development and course of coronary heart disease: current status and implications for research and practice. J. Consult. Clin. Psychol. **70**(3), 548 (2002)
47. Usher, K., Bhullar, N., Durkin, J., Gyamfi, N., Jackson, D.: Family violence and Covid-19: increased vulnerability and reduced options for support. Int. J. Mental Health Nurs. (2020)
48. Usher, K., Bhullar, N., Jackson, D.: Life in the pandemic: Social isolation and mental health. J. Clin. Nurs. (2020)
49. Van Bavel, J.J., et al.: Using social and behavioural science to support Covid-19 pandemic response. Nature Human. Behaviour, 1–12 (2020)
50. Wada, K., Shibata, T., Saito, T., Sakamoto, K., Tanie, K.: Psychological and social effects of one year robot assisted activity on elderly people at a health service facility for the aged, pp. 2785–2790. IEEE (2005)
51. Wada, K., Shibata, T., Saito, T., Tanie, K.: Robot assisted activity for elderly people and nurses at a day service center, vol. No. 02CH37292, vol. 2, pp. 1416–1421. IEEE (2002)
52. Wang, R.H., Sudhama, A., Begum, M., Huq, R., Mihailidis, A.: Robots to assist daily activities: views of older adults with Alzheimer's disease and their caregivers. Int. Psychogeriatr. **29**(1), 67–79 (2017)
53. Yang, G.Z., et al.: Combating Covid-19-the role of robotics in managing public health and infectious diseases (2020)
54. Zeng, Z., Chen, P.J., Lew, A.A.: From high-touch to high-tech: Covid-19 drives robotics adoption. Tourism Geograph., 1–11 (2020)
55. Šabanović, S., Bennett, C.C., Chang, W., Huber, L.: Paro robot affects diverse interaction modalities in group sensory therapy for older adults with dementia. In: 2013 IEEE 13th International Conference on Rehabilitation Robotics (ICORR), pp. 1–6 (2013)

Crowdsourcing Methods in HCI

BubbleVideo: Supporting Small Group Interactions in Online Conferences

Bill Rogers[1], Mark Apperley[1], and Masood Masoodian[2(✉)]

[1] Department of Computer Science, University of Waikato, Hamilton, New Zealand
{william.rogers,mark.apperley}@waikato.ac.nz
[2] School of Arts, Design and Architecture, Aalto University, Espoo, Finland
masood.masoodian@aalto.fi

Abstract. Increasing use of online conferencing systems, particularly over the past year, has highlighted problems in these systems, especially their poor support for small group interactions within larger meetings. These include clumsy small group formation (e.g., issues around joining and leaving existing groups), the difficulty of getting the correct level of audio isolation between groups, poor provision for shared editing of documents, as well as fatiguing aspects of video conferencing caused by presentation format and the necessity of remaining on camera view. This paper describes the motivation, design and implementation of a prototype online conferencing system, called *BubbleVideo*. Building on both virtual world and pure video paradigms, it implements an extensive 2D world with shared documents, in which users appear through real-time video, presented in "bubbles" that can be moved around. Users are given the possibility of deciding whether to join a group by viewing a conversation "leakage", which group members can share with outsiders.

Keywords: Online conferencing · Video conferencing · Group communication · Group interaction · Shared workspaces · Small groups

1 Introduction

Online conferencing is of great and increasing importance in many social, business and educational settings. Although growth in the use of online conferencing has been continuous over the past three decades, in more recent years there have been two waves of acceleration in its use: the global economic turn-down of 2008, and the COVID-19 pandemic starting in 2020. The first of these was driven by the need to reduce costs – particularly travel costs – and the second by the need to avoid physical group gatherings. In 2008, the poster child of online conferencing was Second Life [8], a massively multi-user computer game-like system in which people were represented by avatars – computer animated figures – that could be moved around in large simulated 3D worlds (see Fig. 1, left).

Between 2008 and 2020, improvements in the performance of computer systems and internet meant that real-time video communication became possible

© IFIP International Federation for Information Processing 2021
Published by Springer Nature Switzerland AG 2021
C. Ardito et al. (Eds.): INTERACT 2021, LNCS 12933, pp. 67–75, 2021.
https://doi.org/10.1007/978-3-030-85616-8_5

Fig. 1. Two alternative approaches to online conferencing, using avatars in Second Life (left) and video streams in Zoom (right).

for meetings involving 10's and even 100's of participants. One such conference system which provided support for a large number of participants is Zoom [21], which since 2020 has emerged as the most widely used platform for group meetings [11]. As such, the most commonly seen image of online conferences these days is with Zoom in its "Gallery" view, in which the screen is divided into a grid of separate video images – a grid of video talking heads (see Fig. 1, right).

In this paper we present a review of several current systems, chosen to show the range of variations and combinations of the above mentioned two approaches that have been developed. In addition to basic online conferencing features, we pay particular attention to support for smaller sub-group interactions, and identify some communication and interaction elements which are not yet supported by most existing systems. We then present a prototype conferencing tool, called *BubbleVideo*, which we have developed to support some of these elements.

2   Alternative Approaches to Online Conferencing

Online conferencing systems which aim to host a large group of participants need to not only provide the necessary communication channels – text chat, audio, and video – between the attendees, but also provide an environment in which the interactions between them takes place. Earlier systems, such as Second Life, provided minimum text chat and/or audio communication, in addition to a 2D or 3D space in which the participants could meet and share documents and workspaces. With the increase in speed and availability of high-bandwidth internet, real-time video communication has in more recent years been provided as a solution for all needs, while other interaction needs have largely been ignored [9,10]. Rather than seeing video communication as the ultimate solution, we would argue that both approaches have some clear benefits as well as disadvantages.

The main advantage of the Second Life-style conferencing systems was that their users were presented in a large 3D space – called the world – in which they could navigate – providing a "move to join" paradigm for choosing the groups in which they wished to participate. This 3D "world" modelled conventional physical conference meeting spaces, like conference presentation and meeting rooms. Detailed avatar models of participants were shown walking or seated. Avatar appearance could be roughly personalised, but their movement was generic. The ability to fully participate in meetings was limited by the clumsiness of avatar control and the lack of feedback from facial expressions and other non-verbal communication forms that are typical of real-life [3].

A review by Erikson et al. [5] of a large online conference conducted in Second Life showed that whilst the conference was generally successful, and many parts worked well, there were also aspects of the experience that participants found less than satisfactory. For instance, the avatars were not accurate images of the people they represented, and although this can be liberating in a social context – allowing people to experiment with their appearance – it was not helpful in a business context. In this case, attendees would have preferred a better match between their real and avatar appearance. Another issue was that although keynote presentations worked in the 3D world setting, they would have been better as simple video presentations, because sometimes conference attendees accidentally intruded on the stage during presentations.

Perhaps the most common problem was, however, related to social interactions. While such interactions worked when they were well organised or had a focus (e.g., for poster sessions), more open social situations where people formed ad-hoc small groups were less successful. The scale on which distance-based audio isolation worked was problematic, with the wide-scale that was used leading to passers-by feeling like eavesdroppers, and participants feeling that their sound carried too far and could disturb others. Finally, it was noted that moving about with a fellow participant was not well supported in Second Life.

Zoom-style video systems, on the other hand, work best for single-group conferences. The use of video provides clear identification of participants and permits considerable non-verbal communication, albeit mostly limited to facial expressions and head movements. In comparison to Second Life-style conferences, however, the ease with which people can form, join and leave sub-groupings is limited, and it is difficult or impossible for a participant to find out what is happening in groups other than the one in which they are taking part (e.g., in a breakout room). The inability to quickly form ad-hoc groups can, for instance, severely limit social interaction outside formal conference sessions [16].

The large number of Zoom meetings and conferences since 2020 have provided opportunities for study of personal experiences of video conference sessions [13, 20]. For instance, Bailenson [1] hypothesises four non-verbal reasons for the phenomenon of "Zoom Fatigue", to try to explain why people find continuous long Zoom video conferencing sessions tiring. His reasons are:

- *"Excessive amounts of close-up eye contact is highly intense."* A group of face images filling a screen, all seemingly staring at you "simulates a personal space that you normally experience when you're with somebody intimately".
- *"Seeing yourself during video chats constantly in real-time is fatiguing."* Bailensen likens the experience to constantly having a mirror showing your reflection, which can make people more self-conscious and self-critical.
- *"Video chats dramatically reduce our usual mobility."* In a social gathering people are able to stand and move around. Even in a meeting room people are free to look around, work with documents on the table, or talk to others.

– *"The cognitive load is much higher in video chats."* Bailenson refers to the changed nature of non-verbal communication, the need to be aware of "staying on camera", and limitations in the way we can gesture.

With growing popularity, particularly since the start of the current COVID-19 pandemic [12], there are now a large number of online conferencing systems available. Table 1 provides a summary of some of the systems we have examined, chosen to illustrate the variety of interaction features provided, particularly as related to small group interaction. Our review involved both reading documentation and in all cases directly experimenting with the systems.

The systems reviewed here vary in the way in which sub-groups can be formed, and in the degree to which groups' audio and video streams are isolated from each other. In those that support avatar navigation, entering and leaving groups can be divided into proximity-based or pre-defined location-based groups. The use of proximity offers the option of users moving near a group in order to find out what is being discussed by them, without actually joining the group – i.e., to receive some "leaked" content. Most proximity-based systems allow group members to see other people approaching their group – although full 3D modelling as occurs in Second Life and Virbela leaves open the possibility of being "sneaked up on from behind". Systems with location-based audio isolation require users to join before learning anything about a group's conversation. None of the systems reviewed here appeared to be good at providing information about group conversations to outsiders, or in providing an easy way of insiders inviting outsiders into a group.

Documents can be shared in many of the systems we reviewed. The most common method is through screen sharing, in which the shares are either shown as part of the environment (e.g., on virtual screens), or as additional video streams. None of the systems appears to strongly support collaboratively editable documents (e.g., as shared workspaces). However, some systems such as Zoom permit remote users to control shared screens, or provide whiteboard-like tools editable by all group members.

3 Requirements for Small Group Interaction

Our requirement gathering for an online conferencing system that would support small group communication and interaction started with an earlier prototype aimed at providing a 2D space for social gatherings during online conferences [16]. In addition, our experience of teaching online using existing conferencing systems during 2020-21 led us to widen the scope of its potential uses to include provisions for smaller group communication and interaction in online teaching, as well as other settings such as conferences and meetings. In particular, we wanted to support not only larger group communication and interaction (e.g., during a classroom lecture or a conference presentation), but also during smaller group activities such as a conference workshop or in-class group sessions.

Our experience of conducting such small group workshop-type activities using systems such as Zoom and Discord found them difficult or less than satisfactory

Table 1. Summary of the reviewed online conferencing systems.

Virbela [19]: Users navigate personalised avatars in a detailed 3D space. Audio is localised in pre-arranged spaces (e.g., theatres and poster areas).

An education system similar to Second Life. Groups defined by proximity, or pre-defined rooms/areas with audio isolation. Entry and exit is easy. Shared video and documents in presentation mode on simulated screens.

Rambly [14]: A 2D top-down world with person-like sprites used as avatars. Audio only. Supports proximity-limited audio.

Groups are proximity-based and it is easy to enter or leave them. No provision for document sharing.

Cozy Room [2]: A 2.5D world of connected spaces (shown as orange border in the image) using icons (yellow ball) as avatars. Audio only. Audio isolated in each space.

Groups easy to enter and exit. Real-time creation and decoration of spaces is supported. Avatars have eyes that move to follow the mouse, giving a potential to invite bystanders into a group by looking at them. No provision for document sharing.

Remo [15]: Groups and navigable space are represented as an array of 'tables'. Users join a table to share audio and video, isolated from other tables.

Combined video conferencing and avatar navigation. Groups pre-defined, with easy navigation in and out. Screen sharing is possible using video streams(video displays can be enlarged).

Spacial Chat [17]: The user's video image is used like an avatar for navigation in a single unified interface. Pre-arranged group areas with isolated audio communication.

Easy navigation in and out of group areas. Screen sharing is possible on in-world "screens".

Topia [18]: A sketch-style world providing focus areas for proximity-limited audio and video meetings. Abstract avatars are used for navigation.

Groups are proximity-based and limited in size (max 9). Navigation in and out of groups is easy. Although video and audio is limited to group members, it is possible to see the avatars of other groups that are nearby. Screen sharing is possible using video streams.

Gather [6]: A 2D top-down navigable world in which users have sprite avatars. Proximity limited audio and video windows along the screen top.

Groups formed by proximity. Easy to navigate in and out. Screen sharing allows access to documents, presented as enlarged video streams.

VMX [3]: A 3D meeting room, in which each user's video is projected on the face of an avatar animated by users body movement in real time (heads are see-through from behind).

Only one small group is supported but the system is interesting because of strong gesture and body position support.

Discord [4]: It was initially an audio and chat-based system structured in channels, which has now been extended to include video.

Depending on permission settings, any user can set up channels to support groups. Moving between channels is quick and easy, by clicking on a channel name in the list. Screen sharing is possible using video streams.

to use. For instance, the person in charge of a Zoom session has the responsibility of creating groups, and usually also assigning members to them. In Discord, channels are much better for this purpose, but still need to be created. Once the groups are formed in either of these systems, there is no way of maintaining an overview of their progress, other than visiting each one individually – which is slow to do in Zoom and somewhat intrusive in Discord.

Based on our own experiences and the review of existing systems, we defined the following requirements for a new prototype virtual gathering space which would support small group interactions and communication within larger gatherings. For the current prototype we decided to omit any provision of "host" control, and giving group participants equal rights. However, this might not be ideal in all situations (e.g., a teacher may need some controls in a class situation).

1. Use of real-time video rather than avatars to represent participants.
2. Support the "move to join" group formation paradigm, where a large space is provided and participants are free to form, join and leave groups.
3. Constrain audio within groups for private conversations, but also allow for overriding public audio across all groups for announcements or presentation.
4. Allowing side conversations in a setting where there is a principal speaker, without losing the main conversation.
5. Being able to share pre-prepared documents or live documents external to the conferencing system.
6. Provide support for collaborative editing of shared documents.
7. Allow people to move together in the conference space while maintaining a private conversation.
8. Provide a shared view of all the groups, so that each participant can see how people are grouped.
9. Help participants to know when it might be interesting or appropriate to join an existing group conversation.
10. Make it possible for people in a conversation group to be aware of others near by, but outside, their group who might be invited to join them.

4   *BubbleVideo* Prototype

The meeting paradigm implemented in *BubbleVideo* is that of a conversation pit – i.e., like a large floor space. By walking around this space (using arrow keys, like a video game) a user may find (or create) a small group pit – an area to gather around and have a shared audio/video conversation, and perhaps share documents with everyone in the group to read or edit – as shown in Fig. 2. By providing a single large space, *BubbleVideo* allows freedom of navigation over that space. Rather than moving avatars, users move their own small real-time video streams, which appear inside small "bubbles" on the floor space. This has the advantage of not separating movement from video conferencing – a single unified navigation/communication experience. Video bubbles are optionally tagged with users' names. The system provides for "zooming in" to get reasonably large video bubbles for more focused personal interaction – but the default

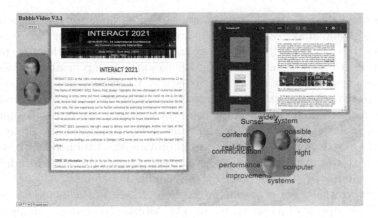

Fig. 2. *BubbleVideo* with two groups of participants (top left and bottom right), each sharing a document. The bottom right group is "leaking" their conversation.

is small images (110 by 90 pixels). To compensate for the small size, the system automatically centralizes and maximizes users' faces in their own video bubble, regardless of the actual wider video camera feeds. This improves the likelihood of faces being visible without users having to constantly try to keep on camera, giving them less reason to look at their own video. Video bubbles are also part of a larger screen space, where each user's location as well as other content such as shared documents are important. We hope that these factors will reduce the impact of the "array of staring faces", and the "intense eye contact" which both contribute to fatigue.

While audio conversations are by default global – initially all users receive audio from all other participants – users can however form audio bubbles in which their conversation can be fully or partially private. Both ad-hoc and round table-style audio bubbles are supported. In the ad-hoc form, an audio bubble is created when one user bumps their video bubble into another's and pauses for a moment. Once an audio bubble is formed by two users (grey areas around groups in Fig. 2), others can join by simply moving into the group's bubble. Moving video bubbles away from each other immediately removes the group's shared audio bubble. Round table-style audio bubbles can be added from the conference settings dialog, and remain displayed on the floor space until explicitly removed. Users can navigate into table-style audio bubbles, as with ad-hoc bubbles. All audio bubbles resize automatically to accommodate their users as they join or leave. In addition, table-style bubble repel each other to maintain some separation. Users' positions in an audio bubble gently animate to avoid overlap. Users in an audio bubble can converse with each other, and also hear audio from outside their bubble. This makes it possible to establish a small private conversation between people who might also be listening to a (global) speaker from outside, if there is someone talking in the bigger space.

Although audio bubbles have the option of full privacy, in some situations such as a social gathering (e.g., a cocktail party [16]) small group conversations do not necessarily need to be private, and are often open for outsiders to join. As such, a group may want people nearby to overhear all or, more usually, part of what is being said. Others may take advantage of overhearing parts of conversations to help them decide whether to join a group or not. *Bubble Video* also allows group member to see who is nearby when they are inside an audio bubble. We hypothesize that small video bubbles in an active context will lead people to behave more like normal conversations in real-world – keeping eye contact by looking at video bubbles for some of the time, and gazing around at other times – reducing fatigue and also improving the likelihood of passers-by being noticed and maybe invited to join. Passers-by might in turn indicate an interest in joining by standing nearby and looking hopeful.

To support this form of social interaction, *Bubble Video* includes a mechanism to allow aspects of a conversation to be "overheard" outside an audio bubble. When enabled by group members, this continuously runs automatic speech recognition on participants' audio streams, and extracts a randomized cloud of significant words to display around the group's audio bubble (see Fig. 2 bottom right). Despite some speech recognition errors, the system "leaks" a sense of conversation topic, but only a general sense. The number of words tends to be quite high and they are presented in random arrangement, so it is usually difficult to see what exactly was being said. Our hypothesis is that the system hits an acceptable balance between privacy and useful "leakage".

Finally, *Bubble Video* provides two forms of group shared workshpaces: screen shares and document shares, which can be presented in the navigation space (see Fig. 2). Participants can move their video bubbles close to a shared workspace window – and form their group audio bubble next to it – or position their video bubbles elsewhere. A screen share can be used as a presentation, in which case, viewers can gather nearby and listen to the presenter. Document share, on the other hand, enables concurrent editing by group participants. The current implementation supports direct embedding of Google Docs [7] in the navigation space, to allow group participants to co-edit shared documents. This makes it possible to have all the shared editing and viewing options provided by Google Docs, supported by group interactions inside audio bubbles formed around them.

5   Conclusions

This paper presented *Bubble Video* online conferencing prototype. Although we have used the system ourselves for discussions formulating this co-authored paper, our only other evaluation has thus far been limited to some informal tests of dynamic grouping with 14 participants. Overall it has functioned well and supported its initial design requirements. The remaining research questions are, how would participants make use of the grouping mechanisms, and how well does the leakage system work in providing conversation information and not violating privacy? A workshop style classroom trial is planned to test grouping, and conversation leakage will be evaluated using a word guessing game. The questions of supporting dynamic ad-hoc conversations will be tested in a "party" gathering.

References

1. Bailenson, J.N.: Nonverbal overload: a theoretical argument for the causes of zoom fatigue. Technol. Mind Behav. **2**(1) (2021). https://doi.org/10.1037/tmb0000030
2. CozyRoom: CozyRoom (2021). https://cozyroom.xyz. Accessed 01 June 2021
3. Dean, J., Apperley, M., Rogers, B.: Refining personal and social presence in virtual meetings. In: Proceedings of the Fifteenth Australasian User Interface Conference - Volume 150. AUIC 2014, pp. 67–75. Australian Computer Society, Inc. (2014)
4. Discord: Discord (2021). https://discord.com/. Accessed 01 June 2021
5. Erickson, T., Shami, N.S., Kellogg, W.A., Levine, D.W.: Synchronous interaction among hundreds: an evaluation of a conference in an avatar-based virtual environment. In: Proceedings of the SIGCHI Conference on Human Factors in Computing Systems. CHI 2011, pp. 503–512. Association for Computing Machinery, New York, NY, USA (2011). https://doi.org/10.1145/1978942.1979013
6. Gather Presence Inc.: Gather (2021). https://gather.town/. Accessed 01 June 2021
7. Google: Google Docs (2021), https://www.google.com/docs/about/. Accessed 01 June 2021
8. Linden Research Inc: Second Life (2021). https://secondlife.com/. Accessed 01 June 2021
9. Masoodian, M., Apperley, M.: The effect of group size and communication modes in CSCW environments. In: Proceedings Sixth Australian Conference on Computer-Human Interaction. OzCHI 1996, pp. 42–49 (1996). https://doi.org/10.1109/OZCHI.1996.559986
10. Masoodian, M., Apperley, M.: User perceptions of human-to-human communication modes in CSCW environments. In: Proceedings of the World Conference on Educational Multimedia and Hypermedia. ED-MEDIA '95, pp. 430–435. Association for the Advancement of Computing in Education (1995)
11. Molla, R.: The pandemic was great for Zoom. What happens when there's a vaccine? (2020). https://www.vox.com/recode/21726260/zoom-microsoft-teams-video-conferencing-post-pandemic-coronavirus. Accessed 01 June 2021
12. Oeppen, R., Shaw, G., Brennan, P.: Human factors recognition at virtual meetings and video conferencing: how to get the best performance from yourself and others. Br. J. Oral Maxillofacial Surg. **58**, 643–646 (2020). https://doi.org/10.1016/j.bjoms.2020.04.046
13. Ramachandran, V.: Stanford researchers identify four causes for 'Zoom fatigue' and their simple fixes (2021). https://news.stanford.edu/2021/02/23/four-causes-zoom-fatigue-solutions/. Accessed 01 June 2021
14. Rambly: Rambly (2021). https://rambly.app/. Accessed 01 June 2021
15. Remo.co Virtual Events and Office space. Remo (2021). https://remo.co/. Accessed 01 June 2021
16. Rogers, B., Masoodian, M., Apperley, M.: A virtual cocktail party: supporting informal social interactions in a virtual conference. In: Proceedings of the International Conference on Advanced Visual Interfaces. AVI 2018. Association for Computing Machinery, New York, NY, USA (2018). https://doi.org/10.1145/3206505.3206569
17. SpatialChat Ltd.: SpatialChat (2021). https://spatial.chat/. Accessed 01 June 2021
18. Topia: Topia (2021). https://topia.io/. Accessed 01 June 2021
19. Virbela: Virbela (2021). https://www.virbela.com/. Accessed 01 June 2021
20. WIRED: A mission to make virtual parties actually fun (2021). https://www.wired.com/story/zoom-parties-proximity-chat/. Accessed 01 June 2021
21. Zoom Video Communications Inc: Zoom (2021). https://zoom.us/. Accessed 01 June 2021

Comparing Performance Models
for Bivariate Pointing Through
a Crowdsourced Experiment

Shota Yamanaka[✉]

Yahoo Japan Corporation, Tokyo, Japan
syamanak@yahoo-corp.jp

Abstract. Evaluation of a novel user-performance model's fitness requires comparison with baseline models, yet it is often time consuming and involves much effort by researchers to collect data from many participants. Crowdsourcing has recently been used for evaluating novel interaction techniques, but its potential for model comparison studies has not been investigated in detail. In this study, we evaluated four existing Fitts' law models for rectangular targets, as though one of them was a proposed novel model. We recruited 210 crowd workers, who performed 94,080 clicks in total, and confirmed that the result for the best-fit model was consistent with previous studies. We also analyzed whether this conclusion would change depending on the sample size, but even when we randomly sampled data from five workers for 10,000 iterations, the best-fit model changed only once (0.01%). We have thus demonstrated a case in which crowdsourcing is beneficial for comparing performance models.

Keywords: Performance modeling · Fitts' law · Crowdsourcing

1 Introduction

It has recently become common for researchers to employ workers through crowdsourcing services for user experiments on graphical user interfaces (GUIs) [8,12,21,25,34]. However, those works focused mainly on designing better GUIs and evaluating novel interaction techniques in comparison with baseline methods. In this paper, we explore the potential utility of crowdsourced experiments to evaluate user performance models. Deriving a novel model to predict operation times on GUIs is a common topic in the human-computer interaction (HCI) field, but model evaluation is typically conducted in lab-based experiments with 10 or 20 university students, i.e., a limited subset of all computer users. If we instead used crowdsourcing for model comparison, it would save time for researchers and improve the evaluation validity because of the large number and diversity of the participants.

It is unclear, however, that we can use crowdsourcing as an alternative to lab-based experiments. For example, crowd workers use different mice, displays,

© IFIP International Federation for Information Processing 2021
Published by Springer Nature Switzerland AG 2021
C. Ardito et al. (Eds.): INTERACT 2021, LNCS 12933, pp. 76–92, 2021.
https://doi.org/10.1007/978-3-030-85616-8_6

operating systems (OSs), and so on. Also, it is known that there are many digital and non-digital distractors that can break workers' focus [17]. Even so, can crowdsourced experiments give the same conclusions on model evaluation as lab-based experiments? To investigate this, we replicated a model-comparison experiment that was previously conducted through lab-based experiments; i.e., the answer on the best model is already known. This enabled us to examine whether we could reach the same conclusion obtained in the lab-based experiments.

Specifically, we examined a bivariate (rectangular) target pointing task, which is modeled by modified versions of Fitts' law [13]. Because Fitts' law tasks have a well-structured methodology, are easy to conduct in desktop environments, and take a short time (typically less than 10 min), they are suitable for crowdsourced user experiments. Also, several formulations have been proposed for bivariate pointing tasks, but Accot and Zhai's weighted Euclidean model [2] is already considered the best-fit model; thus, we could determine whether a crowdsourced experiment would lead to the same conclusion on the best model. In other words, if Accot and Zhai's model were "our proposed novel model" and we identified it as the best in a crowdsourced experiment, we could conclude that our finding on the best model was consistent with the lab-based finding.

Our contributions are as follows.

- We conducted a crowdsourced mouse-pointing experiment with rectangular targets. In total, we recorded 94,080 clicks performed by 210 crowd workers. In line with previous studies, we confirmed that Accot and Zhai's model showed the best fit (adjusted $R^2 = 0.9631$).
- We simulated how the number of participants, N_P, affected the conclusion on the best-fit model. By randomly sampling worker data for N_P values from 5 to 100 (interval: 5) and testing the model fitness over 100 iterations, we found that the best model never changed. Because the model fitness had larger variability when the N_P was smaller, we also performed this simulation with $N_P = 5$ over 10,000 iterations. Even in that case, the best-fit model changed only once (i.e., with a 0.01% chance), which showed the robustness of crowdsourced model comparison even for a small sample size, at least in one case (bivariate pointing).

2 Related Work

2.1 Fitts' Law and Modified Versions for Bivariate Pointing

Fitts' law expresses the notion that the movement time MT to point to a target is related to the index of difficulty in bits, ID, as follows [13]:

$$MT = a + b \cdot ID, \tag{1}$$

where a and b are empirical regression constants. The Shannon formulation of the ID [22] is widely used in HCI:

$$ID = \log_2 \left(\frac{A}{W} + 1 \right), \tag{2}$$

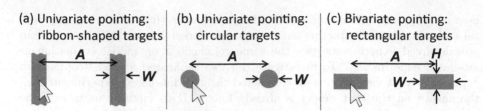

(a) Univariate pointing: ribbon-shaped targets

(b) Univariate pointing: circular targets

(c) Bivariate pointing: rectangular targets

Fig. 1. Pointing tasks with different target shapes.

where the distance between the target centers is A, and the target size (or width) is W. As shown in Fig. 1a, a traditional Fitts' law task has two ribbon-shaped targets; thus, participants do not need to pay attention to the cursor's y-axis movements. It is also common to use circular targets, which constrain the y-axis movements, as shown in Fig. 1b. In both (a) and (b), the target shape is defined by its width W alone; i.e., the target is univariate. In contrast, more realistic targets such as buttons and icons have another dimension, the height H; i.e., they are bivariate targets, as shown in Fig. 1c.

Crossman proposed the first model to predict the MT for such rectangular targets, which used another empirical regression constant c [9]:

$$MT = a + b \cdot \log_2\left(\frac{A}{W} + 1\right) + c \cdot \log_2\left(\frac{A}{H} + 1\right). \tag{3}$$

To make the regression expression clearer, we modify this model as follows:

$$MT = a + b \cdot \left[\log_2\left(\frac{A}{W} + 1\right) + c' \cdot \log_2\left(\frac{A}{H} + 1\right)\right], \tag{4}$$

where $c' = c/b$ (b cannot be zero). Crossman's original formulation did not include the "+1" factors. For fair comparison with other models, however, we consistently include these "+1" factors, as in Accot and Zhai's work [2]. This decision does not affect our conclusion because it has little effect on model fitness [16, 27].

MacKenzie and Buxton [23] and Hoffmann and Sheikh [19] independently proposed the same model using the smaller of W and H:

$$MT = a + b \cdot \log_2\left(\frac{A}{\min(W, H)} + 1\right). \tag{5}$$

This model indicates that the time is solely affected by the more difficult dimension. Accot and Zhai proposed another successful model for bivariate pointing, called the weighted Euclidean model:

$$MT = a + b \cdot \log_2\left(\sqrt{\left(\frac{A}{W}\right)^2 + c \cdot \left(\frac{A}{H}\right)^2} + 1\right), \tag{6}$$

where c is a weight for the target height with respect to the width. Hoffmann et al. identified this model as the best for bivariate pointing with a physical stylus [18], while Accot and Zhai used a mouse.

There are other variations for bivariate pointing, such as integrating the cursor's movement angle factor θ [4,23,36,38]. To limit our focus in this study, and to limit the task time for crowd workers, our experiment used only single-axis movements. This choice is consistent with previous studies [2,9,18,19].

2.2 Crowdsourced Studies on GUI Tasks and Model Evaluations

There have been reports on the consistency between lab-based and crowdsourced experiments involving GUI operations. For menu selection and target pointing tasks in desktop environments, Komarov et al. found that crowdsourced and lab-based experiments gave the same findings on user performance, such as the finding that novel techniques were better than baseline operations [21]. Yamanaka et al. tested the effects of target margins on touch-pointing tasks, and they reported that the same effects were consistently found in crowdsourced and lab-based experiments. For example, in both kinds of experiments, wider margins decreased the MT but increased the error rate [34]. In contrast, by using more powerful statistical analysis methods and recruiting many more participants for lab-based experiments, Findlater et al. showed that crowd workers had significantly shorter average task completion times and higher average error rates in both mouse- and touch-pointing tasks [12]. Thus, they cautioned against assuming that crowdsourced data from GUI performance experiments directly reflects lab-based data.

As for Fitts' law fitness analyses, Findlater et al. reported that crowd workers had average values of $r = 0.926$ with mice and $r = 0.898$ with touchscreens [12]. Schwab et al. conducted a crowdsourced scrolling task in desktop and mobile environments [28]. The results showed that Fitts' law fit the operation times with $R^2 = 0.983$ and 0.972 for the desktop and mobile cases, respectively (note that scrolling operations follow Fitts' law well [39]). Overall, these reports suggest that Fitts' law is valid for crowdsourced data, regardless of the operation style.

To our knowledge, the only literature on using crowdsourcing to determine a best-fit model was the work by Goldberg et al. [15][1]. They implemented Fitts' law tasks in an applet on their website and let visitors to the site perform the tasks. More than 5,000 visitors performed 78,410 clicks in total. Their focus was on whether the best-fit model would change depending on the A/W ratio. For example, when A/W was less than 5, Meyer et al.'s model ($ID = \sqrt{A/W}$) [26] was significantly better, while for harder tasks, the Shannon formulation (Eq. 2) was better.

There are several differences in focus between our work and Goldberg et al.'s work. First, they were interested in how model fitness differences depend on the task difficulty. This is important for understanding user behaviors in pointing tasks [14,26], but typically, model fitness is evaluated in terms of the regression expression for all A/W data points. Also, they mainly compared Meyer et al.'s square-

---

[1] We found this previous work as part of a Ph.D. thesis by one of these authors (Faridani) [11]. He defined this Fitts' law study as a crowdsourced task, and thus we introduce it here.

root-based model with the Shannon (logarithmic) model, which can be mathe-matically approximated [27]. Because their comparison cannot clearly reveal the effectiveness of crowdsourced model-comparison experiments, it is not applicable to our purpose in this study. Moreover, their participants were unpaid volunteers, and thus they called their study an "uncontrolled user study." In comparison, we paid our workers and thus assumed they were motivated to follow our experimental controls (i.e., instructions). Therefore, our results are more relevant for researchers who use crowdsourcing services such as Amazon MTurk.

In summary, no previous studies are directly related to our research question of how useful crowdsourced user experiments are for comparing novel perfor-mance models with baselines. If we can demonstrate the potential of crowd-sourced model comparison, at least for one example task (bivariate pointing), it will enable future researchers to investigate novel performance models with less recruitment effort, more diversity of participants, and less time-consuming data collection; this is our motivation for this work.

3   Experiment

We conducted a pointing experiment with rectangular targets by using *Yahoo! Crowdsourcing*[2]. The experimental system was developed with the Hot Soup Processor programming language (version 3.5). The crowd workers were asked to download and run an executable file from a URL on the recruitment page.

3.1   Task, Design, and Procedure

The task was to click a red target that had width W and height H. The study was a 4×7 within-subjects design: four W values (30, 40, 60, and 90 pixels) and seven H values (10, 20, 30, 40, 60, 100, and 200 pixels). The target distance was fixed to 640 pixels to limit the number of task condition combinations. Using only one A value is consistent with previous studies on bivariate pointing [6,9,19]. A *session* consisted of 21 cyclic clicks back and forth between the left and right targets with a fixed $W \times H$ condition. Each participant completed 28 ($= 4_W \times 7_H$) sessions.

The first target was on the left side. If the participant clicked the target, the red target and white nontarget rectangles switched colors, as illustrated in Fig. 2a. If the participant missed the target, it flashed yellow, and the participant had to keep trying until he or she successfully clicked it. We did not give auditory feedback for success or failure, as not all the participants would have been able to hear sound during the task. After completing 21 successful clicks, the participant saw the results of the session and a message to take a break, as shown in Fig. 2b.

After finishing 28 sessions, the participants completed a questionnaire on their age (numeric), gender (free-form to allow nonbinary or arbitrary answers), handedness (left or right), Windows version (free-form), input device (free-form),

---

[2] https://crowdsourcing.yahoo.co.jp.

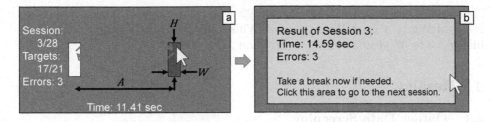

Fig. 2. (a) In the task, participants clicked alternately on each target when it was red. (b) At the end of a session, the results and a message to take a break were shown.

and history of PC use (numeric in years). The questionnaire also included a free-form response for comments on the task and their impressions.

To measure the central tendency of each participant's performance, it is recommended to require 15 to 25 clicks under each condition [30]. Thus, we treated the first five clicks as practice and the remaining 16 clicks (8 clicks on each target) as data. The order of the 28 $W \times H$ conditions was randomized. In total, we recorded $4_W \times 7_H \times 16_{clicks} \times 210_{workers} = 94{,}080$ data points.

3.2 Participants and Recruitment

We recruited workers who used Windows Vista or a later version to run our system. We used the "white list" option in the crowdsourcing platform to screen newly created accounts and prevent multiple entries. This option enabled us to offer the task only to workers who were considered reliable from their previous task history; however, criteria such as the approval rate were not available on the platform.

In the recruitment page, we asked the workers to use a mouse if possible. We made this request because, in our data analysis, we randomly selected a number of participants (e.g., 10) to examine the model fitness. If different devices were used (e.g., six mice, two touchpads, and two trackballs), we might have wondered if a poor fit was due to the device differences. Nevertheless, to avoid a possible false report that all the workers used mice, we did not limit them to using mice. Instead, we specified that any device was acceptable and then removed the non-mouse users from the analysis.

Once a worker accepted the task, he or she was asked to read the online instructions, which stated that the worker should perform the task as rapidly and accurately as possible. After a worker finished all 28 sessions and completed the questionnaire, the log data was exported to a csv file. The worker uploaded the file to a server and then received a payment of JPY 100 ($\approx$ USD 0.96). The main pointing task typically took 8 or 9 min to complete, and thus the effective hourly payment was approximately JPY 700 ($\approx$ USD 6.7).

In total, 225 workers completed the task, including 210 mouse users. The mouse users' demographics were as follows. Age: 20 to 64 years, with $M = 43.5$ and $SD = 8.70$. Gender: 160 male, 47 female, and 3 chose not to answer.

Handedness: 18 were left-handed and 192 were right-handed. Windows version: 26 used Win7, 4 used Win8, 4 used Win8.1, and 176 used Win10. PC usage history: 3 to 47 years, with $M = 21.0$ and $SD = 6.86$.

4   Results

4.1   Outlier Data Screening

Following previous studies [12,24], we removed spatial trial-level outliers if (1) the distance of the first click position was shorter than $A/2$ or (2) the click position of the x-coordinate was more than $2W$ away from the target center. We also applied the latter criterion to the y-coordinate: trials in which the click position was more than $2H$ away from the target center were removed.

To detect trial-level temporal outliers, we used a robust means of outlier detection called the inter-quartile range (IQR) method [10]. The IQR is defined as the difference between the third and first quartiles of the MT. Trials in which the MT was more than $3IQR$ higher than the third quartile or more than $3IQR$ lower than the first quartile were removed. This calculation was run for each session.

For participant-level outliers, we calculated the mean MT across all 28 conditions ($4_W \times 7_H$) for each participant. Then, using each participant's mean MT, we again applied the IQR method. Note that the trial- and participant-level outliers were independently detected and removed.

As a result, among the 94,080 trials, we found 1,043 trial-level outliers (1.11%). We also found one participant-level outlier worker. While the other participants' mean MT was 838 ms, this worker's mean MT was 1,487 ms, and nine of the worker's trials had $MT > 3,000$ ms. Accordingly, all 448 ($= 16_{\text{clicks}} \times 4_W \times 7_H$) data points for this worker were removed. He or she also had trial-level outliers (i.e., there were overlaps); as a result, 1,487 data points were removed in total (1.58%).

4.2   Analyses of Dependent Variables

After the outliers were removed, 92,593 data points (98.4%) were analyzed. The dependent variables were the error-free MT and the error rate ER. Hereafter, any MT value represents error-free data.

Movement Time. The Shapiro-Wilk test ($\alpha = 0.05$) showed that among the $4_W \times 7_H \times 209_{\text{workers}} = 5852$ conditions, 4983 MT data points passed the normality test (85.2%). Hence, to meet the normality assumption, we log-transformed the data before applying repeated-measures ANOVA. We used Bonferroni's p-value adjustment method for pairwise comparisons. For the F statistic, the degrees of freedom were corrected using the Greenhouse-Geisser method when Mauchly's sphericity assumption was violated ($\alpha = 0.05$).

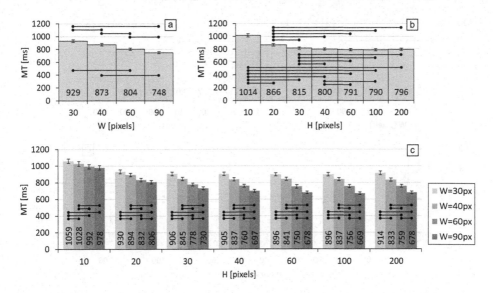

Fig. 3. (a, b) Main effects and (c) interaction for the MT. The error bars show 95% CIs. The horizontal bars show significant differences ($p < 0.05$ at least).

We found significant main effects of W ($F_{2.540,528.243} = 1876.778$, $p < 0.001$, $\eta_p^2 = 0.900$) and H ($F_{3.247,675.285} = 851.453$, $p < 0.001$, $\eta_p^2 = 0.704$) on MT. A significant interaction was found for $W \times H$ ($F_{13.603,2829.404} = 52.468$, $p < 0.001$, $\eta_p^2 = 0.201$). As the W increased, the MT decreased, and all pairwise tests (six combinations) showed significant differences (Fig. 3a). In contrast, the effect of H on MT plateaued gradually, and the pairwise tests for $H \geq 60$ showed no significant differences (Fig. 3b).

As for the interaction effect, for the largest H (200 pixels), the effect of W on MT was more clearly observed, as seen in Fig. 3c; this means that the effect of W was dominant. As the H decreased, however, the MT differences among the four W values were reduced, because H was dominant. For example, the largest difference for $H = 10$ pixels was $1059 - 978 = 81$ ms (7.6%), while that for $H = 200$ pixels was $914 - 678 = 236$ ms (26%). This result demonstrates that we should integrate the interaction effect of $W \times H$ to predict the MT accurately.

Error Rate. Error-rate data are typically nonparametric; thus, we used a nonparametric ANOVA with the *Aligned Rank Transform* [31] and Tukey's p-value adjustment method for pairwise tests. We found significant main effects of W ($F_{3,624} = 15.146$, $p < 0.001$, $\eta_p^2 = 0.068$) and H ($F_{6,1248} = 49.095$, $p < 0.001$, $\eta_p^2 = 0.191$) on ER. A significant interaction was found for $W \times H$ ($F_{18,3744} = 3.670$, $p < 0.001$, $\eta_p^2 = 0.017$). As the W increased, the MT gradually decreased (Fig. 4a), while for the H, the ER for 10 pixels was remarkably high, as seen in (b). For the interaction effect (c), when the H was small (10 or 20 pixels), the pairwise

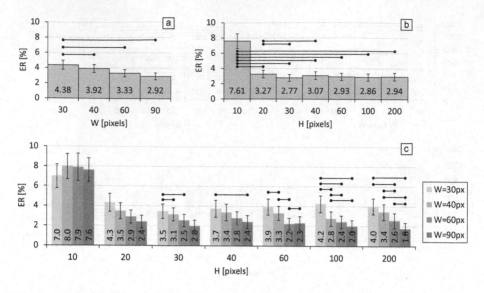

Fig. 4. (a, b) Main effects and (c) interaction for the ER. The error bars show 95% CIs. The horizontal bars show significant differences ($p < 0.05$ at least).

tests for W showed no effects, which indicates the dominance of H. Then, as the H increased, it lost the effect to impose errors; thus, the W had the dominant effect on ER.

4.3 Canonical Analysis

In addition to the ANOVAs, we ran a canonical analysis to examine how $\{W, H\}$ affected the two dependent variables of $\{MT, ER\}$ concurrently. We used the CCA function provided by the sklearn.cross_decomposition library in Python. The Pearson's r values for the first and second dimensions were 0.8974 and 0.4238, respectively. For the independent variables, the canonical loadings were $[0.9962, 0.0873]$, $[-0.0873, 0.9962]$. Thus, W had a stronger effect on the dependent variables than H; this is consistent with previous studies [2,18]. For the dependent variables, the canonical loadings were $[-0.9385, 0.4091]$, $[-0.5869, -0.8096]$. Thus, MT was affected by the independent variables more sensitively than ER. As shown in Fig. 4a–b, while the $H = 10$ pixels condition is an exception, W and H did not largely change the ER.

4.4 Model Fitness

Figure 5 summarizes the results of model fitness for the four candidate models. Because the numbers of free parameters in the models (a, b, and c) are different, it was necessary to use the *adjusted* R^2 rather than R^2. In addition, to compare the model fitness more statistically, the figure shows the Akaike information

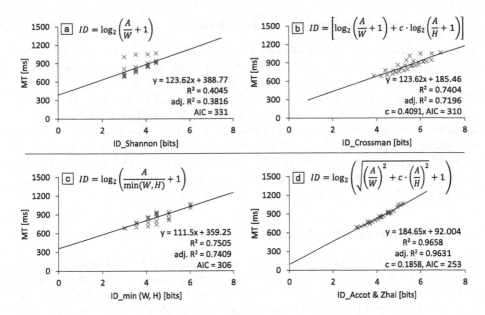

Fig. 5. Regression results for the four candidate models: (a) Shannon from Eq. 2, (b) Crossman from Eq. 4, (c) "min(W, H)" from Eq. 5, and (d) weighted Euclidean from Eq. 6.

criterion (AIC) values [3]. The AIC enabled us to determine comparatively better models in terms of the number of parameters, via the following brief rule of thumb: (a) a model with a lower AIC value is better, and the one with the minimum AIC ($AIC_{minimum}$) is thus the best; (b) a model with $AIC \leq$ ($AIC_{minimum} + 2$) is comparable with the better models; and (c) a model with $AIC \geq$ ($AIC_{minimum} + 10$) can be safely rejected [7]. To simplify the discussion in this paper, we consider an AIC difference greater than 10 to be significant.

As shown in Fig. 5a, the baseline model (Shannon) could not capture the fact that the MT depended on the H, because it considers only the W. The data points' vertical spread shows that the H significantly affected the MT. The modified Crossman and "min(W, H)" models (Fig. 5b and c, respectively) showed improved model fitness. The points spread farther horizontally, and more points thus lay on the regression lines as compared with the Shannon model. The adjusted R^2 values increased from 0.38 to at least 0.7, and the AIC values significantly decreased from 331 to 310 or lower.

Among the four candidates, Accot and Zhai's model showed the best fit for both the adjusted R^2 and AIC values (0.9631 and 253, respectively). All the points lay close to the regression line, and we could thus visually confirm that the MT can be predicted most accurately with this model.

4.5   Answers to the Free-Form Questionnaire

Among the 210 workers, 15 mentioned the effects of target size on task difficulty, e.g., "Small bars were difficult to click." Also, two workers explicitly mentioned the target height: "Horizontally long bars were more difficult to click than vertically long ones," which clearly indicates that the effect of H on task performance was dominant rather than W. Five workers stated that "It was easier to click horizontally long buttons" and one of them stated that "The frequency of clicking outside targets was lower for horizontally long bars," which indicates that a larger W had a positive effect on lowering the error rate. This result partially supports the result that the weight for W was heavier than H in model fitting (i.e., in Fig. 5d, the weight for W was 1 vs. 0.1858 for H).

4.6   Discussion on Model Fitness

Through this experiment, we confirmed that our crowdsourced data gave the same conclusion obtained in lab-based experiments. However, this result might have depended on the large number of participants: for example, even if some participants ignored the instructions [12] or did multiple tasks [17], we can compress such noisy data after recruiting over 200 workers. This easy recruitment is an advantage of crowdsourced user experiments, but it means that researchers might have to pay a high cost to obtain less noisy data. If we could reach the same conclusion with a much lower number of workers, such as 10% of the total here, it would also demonstrate the utility of crowdsourcing services. However, it is currently unclear how the sample size N_P affects the conclusion on model fitness. To assess this issue, we ran the simulation study described in the next section.

5   Simulation of Sample Size Effect on Model Fitness

Through this simulation, we analyzed how the number of participants, N_P, affects the model fitness and the conclusion on the best-fit model. We randomly selected N_P participants' data from the 210 crowd workers and computed the model fitness in terms of the adjusted R^2 and AIC. To handle the randomness, we repeated the simulation over 100 iterations for a single N_P value. Then, we computed the average and SD of the adjusted R^2 and AIC for the 100 iterations[3].

Figure 6 shows the results of this simulation, in which we varied the N_P from 5 to 100 with an interval of 5 (i.e., $20_{N_P} \times 100_{\text{iterations}} = 2000$ simulation trials). Regardless of the N_P, Accot and Zhai's model (green lines) was the best in terms of both the adjusted R^2 and the AIC. In addition, we could visually confirm that the mean adjusted R^2 values became stable after the N_P reached

---

[3] The simulation included data from the outlier worker detected in the analysis of the main experiment, because that worker's status as an outlier depends on the other sampled workers' results.

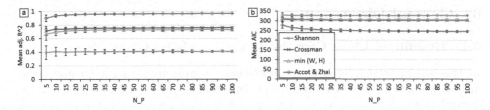

Fig. 6. Model fitness in terms of the (a) adjusted R^2 and (b) AIC, depending on the sample size. Each point shows the $Mean \pm 1SD$ obtained through 100 iterations. (In addition to the mean and SD, we computed the [min, max] values and 95% CIs [lower, upper] of the adjusted R^2 and AIC. The 95% CI was used for estimating the true value, but our goal here is to discuss how the sample size affects the mean and the variability of model fitness; thus, we show the $Mean \pm 1SD$ in this figure.)

approximately 20 or 25 for all the model candidates. This was also true for the AIC result. Throughout the 2000 simulation trials, Accot and Zhai's model showed the lowest AIC values, and the difference from the second-best model was always greater than 10; i.e., Accot and Zhai's model was consistently and significantly the best.

According to Fig. 6, as the N_P decreased, the variabilities in the adjusted R^2 and AIC increased (larger error bars). Thus, we assumed the possibility that one of the other three candidates could become the best-fit model. To examine this assumption, we ran the simulation again with $N_P = 5$ over 10,000 iterations. The results showed only one trial in which Accot and Zhai's model had a lower adjusted R^2 value than the $min(W, H)$ model: 0.559 vs. 0.592, respectively. For the AIC, however, there was no significant difference: 308 vs. 305. In contrast, in 9,998 simulation trials, Accot and Zhai's model was significantly the best model according to the AIC.

In conclusion, note that it would have been possible to observe the "opposite" conclusion from lab-based experiments, in which Accot and Zhai's model is not the best, but the probability of that situation was only 0.01%. Also, as the N_P increases, this probability should approach zero according to our simulation, which showed that the variabilities in model fitness became quite small.

Ideally, we would try all combinations of selecting $N_P = 5$ participants' data among the 210 crowd workers. However, our simulation of only 10,000 iterations took approximately 28 min; testing the $_{210}C_5 = 3,244,032,792$ combinations for this case would take 17 years, which is not feasible. Also, the simulation took longer times with larger N_P values for various reasons, such as random selection, averaging of more MT values, detection of outlier workers, and nonlinear regressions; thus, we tested only the remarkable case of the greatest variability in model fitness.

6   General Discussion

6.1   Benefits of Using Crowdsourcing for Model Comparison

In this study, we explored the potential of crowdsourcing for GUI operation model evaluation studies in desktop environments. As an example of a fundamental and well-structured experiment, a Fitts' law task with bivariate targets was used. The results obtained from 210 crowd workers showed that the best fit was achieved by the weighted Euclidean model proposed by Accot and Zhai (Eq. 6): adjusted $R^2 = 0.9631$ and $AIC = 253$. This conclusion on the best model was consistent with previous studies [2, 18].

Although comparison of GUI operation models through crowdsourcing is not common in HCI research, we have demonstrated its effectiveness, at least for one example (bivariate pointing). This is a motivating result for future studies on evaluating novel user-performance models. Also, according to a follow-up simulation, our conclusion on the best-fit model would not have changed in most cases, even if we had conducted this crowdsourced experiment with only five workers. An experiment that size would cost only JPY 500 ($\approx$ USD 4.8), thus enabling easy model fitness comparison at low cost. Furthermore, as the sample size increased, we observed a more robust, stable model fitness (i.e., less variability in the adjusted R^2 and AIC). Hence, if researchers can pay more to recruit more workers (e.g., $N_P = 100$) to improve the reliability of the data, such large model fitness studies can easily be performed through crowdsourcing, while lab-based experiments of that size are comparatively difficult.

6.2   Limitations and Future Work

Our claims are limited to the task we chose and its design. We emphasized the usefulness of crowdsourced user experiments for model comparison, but we only tested GUI operation models with mice. Even within the scope of Fitts' law tasks, we purposely limited the task design to horizontal movements and a fixed target distance so that the parameters W and H could be reasonably varied. We will need further studies on the applicability to other kinds of models such as cognitive ones and other input devices such as touchscreens.

Another possible limitation of our data analysis is that we used a single criterion for outlier detection, particularly for spatial outliers. While our criterion was based on $2W$ and $2H$ (see Sect. 4.1), some previous studies have used different criteria, e.g., $8W$ [37]. Thus, we ran a pseudo-ablation study: the click position of the x-coordinate was more than NW away from the target center (and also for the y-axis), where N ranged from 1 to 10 (the severest outlier criterion to the most relaxed one, respectively). As a result, among the 94,080 trials, we found 1,142 trial-level outliers (1.214%) when $N = 1$. This changed to 1,031 outliers (1.096%) when $N = 10$. This 0.1-point difference did not affect our conclusion. For example, Accot and Zhai's model showed adjusted $R^2 = 0.9729$ and 0.9728 for $N = 1$ and 10, respectively. This additional analysis demonstrates that our outlier detection criteria do not change our main claim.

A crowdsourcing-specific limitation for GUI tasks is that we cannot check if workers really follow the given instruction. For example, a previous study has mentioned that an experimenter could not check whether workers tapped a target with their thumb as instructed (e.g., some workers might have used their index finger when tapping a small target) [34]. Taking this into consideration, we cannot recommend measuring Fitts' law fitness and computing the throughput for comparing the performance of various devices such as mouse vs. trackball [30] because some workers might not use the specified device and the data reliability is thus questionable.

As a more important argument, we tested four model candidates and compared their model fitness as though our proposed model was Accot and Zhai's weighted Euclidean model. Because the results of lab-based experiments are already known (i.e., the finding that Accot and Zhai's model is the best), this study design enabled us to examine whether the crowdsourced user experiment gave the same conclusion. However, if future researchers conduct crowdsourced user experiments to evaluate their novel models with respect to baselines, it is unknown whether the conclusion on the best-fit model will be the same as in lab-based experiments. In this case, there will be no choice but to believe the best model as-is.

Still, such results obtained by crowdsourcing would motivate further lab-based experiments if more controlled conditions (e.g., the same device settings and no interruptions) and reliable participants who follow instructions are needed. Therefore, crowdsourced and lab-based experiments have different characteristics, and our purpose in this paper is not to state a binary claim on which choice is better. Rather, we seek to open up a new possibility of using crowdsourcing as a tool for HCI studies, particularly for human motor performance modeling.

In this study, we focused on a mouse pointing task. Other potential examples to use crowdsourcing for model evaluation include the steering law [1] and its refined versions for other path conditions [29,32,33], and Fitts' law for finger touching [5] and its refined versions [20,35]. Findlater et al. found that Fitts' law held well for touchscreens [12], and thus it is promising to use crowdsourcing for evaluating new models on touchscreen interactions. To demonstrate this generalizability to other tasks, more experiments under different conditions are required.

7   Conclusion

We conducted a crowdsourced user experiment to compare model fitness on a bivariate Fitts' law task. By analyzing the data obtained from 210 crowd workers, we found that the conclusion on the best model was consistent with previous studies. In addition, even when we randomly selected a limited number of workers from 5 to 100, we consistently reached the same conclusion. Although the model fitness variability was comparatively large when the random sample size was small, when we analyzed data from five randomly chosen participants over 10,000 iterations, the best-fit model changed only once, without a significant difference from the second-best model. Thus, we empirically demonstrated the robustness of data obtained through a crowdsourced model-comparison experiment, at least for our task of bivariate pointing. This work will contribute to research on novel GUI operation models, and it will motivate us to conduct further studies on exploring other applicable tasks.

References

1. Accot, J., Zhai, S.: Beyond Fitts' law: models for trajectory-based HCI tasks. In: Proceedings of the SIGCHI Conference on Human Factors in Computing Systems (CHI 1997), pp. 295–302 (1997). https://doi.org/10.1145/258549.258760
2. Accot, J., Zhai, S.: Refining Fitts' law models for bivariate pointing. In: Proceedings of the SIGCHI Conference on Human Factors in Computing Systems, CHI 2003, pp. 193–200. ACM, New York (2003). https://doi.org/10.1145/642611.642646. http://doi.acm.org/10.1145/642611.642646
3. Akaike, H.: A new look at the statistical model identification. IEEE Trans. Autom. Control **19**(6), 716–723 (1974). https://doi.org/10.1109/TAC.1974.1100705
4. Appert, C., Chapuis, O., Beaudouin-Lafon, M.: Evaluation of pointing performance on screen edges. In: Proceedings of the Working Conference on Advanced Visual Interfaces, AVI 2008, pp. 119–126. ACM, New York (2008). https://doi.org/10.1145/1385569.1385590. http://doi.acm.org/10.1145/1385569.1385590
5. Bi, X., Li, Y., Zhai, S.: Ffitts law: modeling finger touch with Fitts' law. In: Proceedings of the SIGCHI Conference on Human Factors in Computing Systems, CHI 2013, pp. 1363–1372. ACM, New York (2013). https://doi.org/10.1145/2470654.2466180. http://doi.acm.org/10.1145/2470654.2466180
6. Bohan, M., Longstaff, M., Van Gemmert, A., Rand, M., Stelmach, G.: Effects of target height and width on 2D pointing movement duration and kinematics. Motor Control **7**, 278–289 (2003)
7. Burnham, K.P., Anderson, D.R.: Model Selection and Multimodel Inference: A Practical Information-Theoretic Approach. Springer, New York (2003). https://doi.org/10.1007/b97636
8. Cockburn, A., Lewis, B., Quinn, P., Gutwin, C.: Framing effects influence interface feature decisions, pp. 1–11. Association for Computing Machinery, New York (2020). https://doi.org/10.1145/3313831.3376496
9. Crossman, E.R.: The measurement of perceptual load in manual operations. University of Birmingham, Ph.D. thesis (1956)
10. Devore, J.L.: Probability and Statistics for Engineering and the Sciences, 8th edn. Brooks/Cole, January 2011. ISBN-13 978-0-538-73352-6
11. Faridani, S.: Models and algorithms for crowdsourcing discovery. Ph.D. thesis, USA (2012)
12. Findlater, L., Zhang, J., Froehlich, J.E., Moffatt, K.: Differences in crowdsourced vs. lab-based mobile and desktop input performance data. In: Proceedings of the 2017 CHI Conference on Human Factors in Computing Systems, CHI 2017, pp. 6813–6824. ACM, New York (2017). https://doi.org/10.1145/3025453.3025820. http://doi.acm.org/10.1145/3025453.3025820

13. Fitts, P.M.: The information capacity of the human motor system in controlling the amplitude of movement. J. Exp. Psychol. **47**(6), 381–391 (1954). https://doi.org/10.1037/h0055392
14. Gan, K.C., Hoffmann, E.R.: Geometrical conditions for ballistic and visually controlled movements. Ergonomics **31**(5), 829–839 (1988). https://doi.org/10.1080/00140138808966724
15. Goldberg, K.Y., Faridani, S., Alterovitz, R.: Two large open-access datasets for Fitts' law of human motion and a succinct derivation of the square-root variant. IEEE Trans. Hum.-Mach. Syst. **45**(1), 62–73 (2015). https://doi.org/10.1109/THMS.2014.2360281
16. Gori, J., Rioul, O., Guiard, Y.: Speed-accuracy tradeoff: a formal information-theoretic transmission scheme (Fitts). ACM Trans. Comput.-Hum. Interact. **25**(5) (2018). https://doi.org/10.1145/3231595
17. Gould, S.J.J., Cox, A.L., Brumby, D.P.: Diminished control in crowdsourcing: an investigation of crowdworker multitasking behavior. ACM Trans. Comput.-Hum. Interact. **23**(3) (2016). https://doi.org/10.1145/2928269
18. Hoffmann, E.R., Drury, C.G., Romanowski, C.J.: Performance in one-, two- and three-dimensional terminal aiming tasks. Ergonomics **54**(12), 1175–1185 (2011)
19. Hoffmann, E.R., Sheikh, I.H.: Effect of varying target height in a Fitts' movement task. Ergonomics **37**(6), 1071–1088 (1994). https://doi.org/10.1080/00140139408963719
20. Ko, Y.J., Zhao, H., Kim, Y., Ramakrishnan, I., Zhai, S., Bi, X.: Modeling two dimensional touch pointing. In: Proceedings of the 33rd Annual ACM Symposium on User Interface Software and Technology, UIST 2020, pp. 858–868. Association for Computing Machinery, New York (2020). https://doi.org/10.1145/3379337.3415871
21. Komarov, S., Reinecke, K., Gajos, K.Z.: Crowdsourcing performance evaluations of user interfaces. In: Proceedings of the SIGCHI Conference on Human Factors in Computing Systems, CHI 2013, pp. 207–216. ACM, New York (2013). https://doi.org/10.1145/2470654.2470684. http://doi.acm.org/10.1145/2470654.2470684
22. MacKenzie, I.S.: Fitts' law as a research and design tool in human-computer interaction. Hum.-Comput. Interact. **7**(1), 91–139 (1992). https://doi.org/10.1207/s15327051hci0701_3
23. MacKenzie, I.S., Buxton, W.: Extending Fitts' law to two-dimensional tasks. In: Proceedings of the SIGCHI Conference on Human Factors in Computing Systems, CHI 1992, pp. 219–226. ACM, New York (1992). https://doi.org/10.1145/142750.142794. http://doi.acm.org/10.1145/142750.142794
24. MacKenzie, I.S., Isokoski, P.: Fitts' throughput and the speed-accuracy tradeoff. In: Proceedings of the SIGCHI Conference on Human Factors in Computing Systems, CHI 2008, pp. 1633–1636. ACM, New York (2008). https://doi.org/10.1145/1357054.1357308
25. Matejka, J., Glueck, M., Grossman, T., Fitzmaurice, G.: The effect of visual appearance on the performance of continuous sliders and visual analogue scales. In: Proceedings of the 2016 CHI Conference on Human Factors in Computing Systems, CHI 2016, pp. 5421–5432. Association for Computing Machinery, New York (2016). https://doi.org/10.1145/2858036.2858063
26. Meyer, D.E., Abrams, R.A., Kornblum, S., Wright, C.E., Keith Smith, J.E.: Optimality in human motor performance: ideal control of rapid aimed movements. Psychol. Rev. **95**(3), 340–370 (1988). https://doi.org/10.1037/0033-295x.95.3.340
27. Rioul, O., Guiard, Y.: Power vs. logarithmic model of Fitts' law: a mathematical analysis. Math. Soc. Sci. **2012**, 85–96 (2012). https://doi.org/10.4000/msh.12317

28. Schwab, M., Hao, S., Vitek, O., Tompkin, J., Huang, J., Borkin, M.A.: Evaluating pan and zoom timelines and sliders. In: Proceedings of the 2019 CHI Conference on Human Factors in Computing Systems, CHI 2019, pp. 1–12. Association for Computing Machinery, New York (2019). https://doi.org/10.1145/3290605.3300786

29. Senanayake, R., Hoffmann, E.R., Goonetilleke, R.S.: A model for combined targeting and tracking tasks in computer applications. Exp. Brain Res. **231**(3), 367–379 (2013). https://doi.org/10.1007/s00221-013-3700-4

30. Soukoreff, R.W., MacKenzie, I.S.: Towards a standard for pointing device evaluation, perspectives on 27 years of Fitts' law research in HCI. Int. J. Hum. Comput. Stud. **61**(6), 751–789 (2004). https://doi.org/10.1016/j.ijhcs.2004.09.001

31. Wobbrock, J.O., Findlater, L., Gergle, D., Higgins, J.J.: The aligned rank transform for nonparametric factorial analyses using only anova procedures. In: Proceedings of the SIGCHI Conference on Human Factors in Computing Systems, CHI 2011, pp. 143–146. ACM, New York (2011). https://doi.org/10.1145/1978942.1978963. http://doi.acm.org/10.1145/1978942.1978963

32. Yamanaka, S.: Steering performance with error-accepting delays. In: Proceedings of the 2019 CHI Conference on Human Factors in Computing Systems, CHI 2019, pp. 570:1–570:9. ACM, New York (2019). https://doi.org/10.1145/3290605.3300800. http://doi.acm.org/10.1145/3290605.3300800

33. Yamanaka, S., Miyashita, H.: Modeling the steering time difference between narrowing and widening tunnels. In: Proceedings of the 2016 CHI Conference on Human Factors in Computing Systems, CHI 2016, pp. 1846–1856. ACM, New York (2016). https://doi.org/10.1145/2858036.2858037. http://doi.acm.org/10.1145/2858036.2858037

34. Yamanaka, S., Shimono, H., Miyashita, H.: Towards more practical spacing for smartphone touch GUI objects accompanied by distractors. In: Proceedings of the 2019 ACM International Conference on Interactive Surfaces and Spaces, ISS 2019, pp. 157–169. Association for Computing Machinery, New York (2019). https://doi.org/10.1145/3343055.3359698

35. Yamanaka, S., Usuba, H.: Calibration methods of touch-point ambiguity for finger-Fitts law (2021). https://arxiv.org/abs/2101.05244

36. Yang, H., Xu, X.: Bias towards regular configuration in 2D pointing. In: Proceedings of the SIGCHI Conference on Human Factors in Computing Systems, CHI 2010, pp. 1391–1400. ACM, New York (2010). https://doi.org/10.1145/1753326.1753536. http://doi.acm.org/10.1145/1753326.1753536

37. Zhai, S., Kong, J., Ren, X.: Speed-accuracy tradeoff in Fitts' law tasks: on the equivalency of actual and nominal pointing precision. Int. J. Hum. Comput. Stud. **61**(6), 823–856 (2004). https://doi.org/10.1016/j.ijhcs.2004.09.007

38. Zhang, X., Zha, H., Feng, W.: Extending Fitts' law to account for the effects of movement direction on 2D pointing. In: Proceedings of the SIGCHI Conference on Human Factors in Computing Systems, CHI 2012, pp. 3185–3194. ACM, New York (2012). https://doi.org/10.1145/2207676.2208737. http://doi.acm.org/10.1145/2207676.2208737

39. Zhao, J., Soukoreff, R.W., Ren, X., Balakrishnan, R.: A model of scrolling on touch-sensitive displays. Int. J. Hum.-Comput. Stud. **72**(12), 805–821 (2014)

Older Adults' Motivation and Engagement with Diverse Crowdsourcing Citizen Science Tasks

Kinga Skorupska[1](✉)[iD], Anna Jaskulska[2][iD], Rafał Masłyk[1][iD], Julia Paluch[1][iD], Radosław Nielek[1][iD], and Wiesław Kopeć[1][iD]

[1] Polish-Japanese Acaemy of Information Technology, Warsaw, Poland
kinga.skorupska@pja.edu.pl
[2] Kobo Association, Warsaw, Poland

Abstract. In this exploratory study we evaluated the engagement, performance and preferences of older adults who interacted with different citizen science tasks. Out of 40 projects recently active on the Zooniverse platform we selected top ones to be represented by 8 diverse, yet standardized, microtasks, 2 in each category of image, audio, text and pattern recognition. Next, 33 older adults performed these microtasks at home and evaluated each task right after its completion to, finally, share what could encourage them to engage with such tasks in their free time. Based on the results we draw preliminary conclusions regarding older adults' motivations for engaging with such crowdsourcing tasks and suggest some guidelines for task design while discussing interesting avenues for further inquiry in the area of crowdsourcing for older adults.

Keywords: Crowdsourcing · Older adults · Citizen science · Motivation

1 Introduction and Related Works

The area of crowdsourcing for older adults is both underappreciated and underexplored and developing sustainable solutions for older adults is still challenging [13,14]. This may be due to multiple barriers both specific to the required ICT-skills [1] and the nature of crowdsourcing microtasks. Older adults differ from the younger generation in their online behavior and decision-making [9] and they seem more selective when choosing their engagements [5], which, alongside their generally lower ICT skills, may explain how little interest they expressed in the Mechanical Turk platform populated by tedious and repetitive tasks [3] and lacking a suitable motivation to participate in crowdsourcing, as tasks are not challenging, fun or easily relatable. This is in line with research placing the average age of crowd workers at around 20–30 years [15,24]. On the other hand, crowd-volunteering tasks, often called citizen science tasks, such as the ones found on the Zooniverse platform [26] can appeal to a more balanced representation of

© IFIP International Federation for Information Processing 2021
Published by Springer Nature Switzerland AG 2021
C. Ardito et al. (Eds.): INTERACT 2021, LNCS 12933, pp. 93–103, 2021.
https://doi.org/10.1007/978-3-030-85616-8_7

contributors, as about 15% of the platform contributors self-report as retired.[1] There are also some crowdsourcing systems designed specifically for older adults which mitigate technology barriers, as in Hettiachchi et al. [10] and tap into their knowledge and skills, such as tagging historical photos as in Yu et al. [29], proofreading, as in Itoko et al. [12] and Kobayashi et al. [17], or both as in Skorupska et al. [28] They often rely on motivations that are pro-social, as in Kobayashi et al. [15] and also social, as in Seong et al. [25] which is a trademark of Zooniverse. The Zooniverse platform allows crowd workers to support science projects at a larger scale by solving difficult tasks thanks to the impressive potential of such contributions [2] on a diverse crowdsourcing landscape of Zooniverse (https://www.zooniverse.org), which is why we have chosen this platform a to serve as the basis for this research. So, there is an opportunity to tap into the potential of older adults as crowd workers with a lot to offer and time on their hands - especially that their share in the society is increasing, and in 2019, "more than one fifth of the EU-27 population was aged 65 and over" [6].

The question whether crowdsourcing tasks are effective in keeping older adults cognitively engaged is relevant, as volunteering activities [22] in general may increase older adults' well-being [23], improve their mental and physical health [21] and can be seen as a protective factor for their psychological well-being [7,8], potentially delaying the onset of age-related issues [19]. Therefore, in this study we want to gain insights into older adults' motivation and engagement with online citizen science tasks and uncover some guidelines for designing and presenting crowdsourcing citizen science tasks to this group. In designing our research we took care to uniformly present the wide-range of real crowd-volunteering tasks often appearing in citizen science projects. Only after older adults have completed each task we asked them how to improve it, and finally what would motivate them to engage with such tasks in the future.

2   Methods

In this study 33 older adults were asked to complete and evaluate 8 diverse, but standardized citizen science tasks at home, in an unsupervised environment. The study consisted of a short socio-demographic survey including questions about the participants' age, sex, education, activity, ICT-use, and crowdsourcing preferences based on Seong et al. [25]. These questions were followed by a set of 8 different tasks chosen based on expert knowledge of the research team, localized into Polish and presented in an uniform way, broken into 4 pages - each page for a different type of a task. There were two tasks (one easier, and one more difficult/abstract) in each category of **image recognition (PIC)** for tasks T1 and T2, **audio recognition (AUD)** for tasks T3 and T4, **document transcription (DOC)** for tasks T5 and T6 and **pattern recognition (PAT)** for tasks T7 and T8, visible in Fig. 1 in order. The tasks were selected out of 40 community-chosen projects active on the Zooniverse platform in the

---

[1] Survey results were presented in a post: https://blog.zooniverse.org/2015/03/05/who-are-the-zooniverse-community-we-asked-them/.

2019-20 academic year and spotlit in the publication "Into the Zooniverse Vol. II",[2] published on the 17th of November 2020.

The final standardized tasks were as follows:

Fig. 1. Visual overview of the tasks; T1–T8 from the left to the right.

- **T1.** Recognizing animal silhouettes - multiple choice of animal silhouettes, including human visible, no animal and other (representing MichiganZoomIn)
- **T2.** Recognizing cat fur types on cat images - multiple choice with abstract images of a cat pelts with fur patterns (similar to image recognition tasks)
- **T3.** Recognizing radio programs (97 s-long recording) - checkboxes and a follow-up open answer about specifics (representing Vintage Cuban Radio)
- **T4.** Recognizing local urban sounds (10 s-long recording) - checkboxes with pre-defined answers and an other option (representing Sounds of NYC)
- **T5.** Transcribing key information from a hand-written birth certificate of a person born in 1887 - 4 open short answer questions about the dates, name, and the location (representing tasks such as Every Name Counts)
- **T6.** Transcribing a longer (346 characters) typewritten text on a specific subject - 1 open long answer question (representing tasks relying on longer transcription of typewritten documents)
- **T7.** Recognizing Aurora Borealis patterns (6s-long recording) - multiple choice question with names of patterns and colours (representing Aurora Zoo)
- **T8.** Recognizing eye elements in eye pictures on a coordinate grid: two drop-down questions about coordinates and one multiple choice on the visibility of veins. (based on Eye for Diabetes; image by Mikael Häggström [11])

There was a short standardized introduction to each task explaining its importance and purpose, as not to bias the participants with the quality of the project presentation, which can vary considerably between projects. Then, the participants performed each example microtask. After each task we asked the participants to judge, on a 3-point scale, its: **attractiveness, importance, ease of**

---

[2] The book is available for download here: https://blog.zooniverse.org/2020/11/17/into-the-zooniverse-vol-ii-now-available/.

performing it, engagement, and **if they would like to perform similar tasks in the future** and to suggest ways in which each task could be improved. The study protocol was positively evaluated by our ethics committee. The study itself was built in Google Forms and it took between 20–35 min to complete, depending on the amount of feedback given after each task and the ICT proficiency of the participants. Finally, after completing all tasks the participants were asked what could encourage them to engage in such tasks in general and whether they have done similar tasks in the past. The suggestions of motivating factors were inspired by an article by Campo et al. [4] as well as a wide body of research on crowdsourcing and volunteering.

3 Results and Discussion

3.1 Participants

There were 33 participants who completed and evaluated the chosen crowdsourcing tasks between Dec. 2020 and Feb. 2021. They were recruited from among the participants of our Living Lab [18] via e-mail as unpaid volunteers as we did not want to interfere with their motivation with a financial incentive. 22 participants were in the 60–69 age group, and 10 in the 70–79 group and 1 in 80+ group.[3] All of them were based in Poland, Polish and all but 6 of them came from larger cities (over 200k) and 21 of the participants had higher education. In Table 1 we can see the results concerning volunteering motivation before performing tasks for our 33 participants contrasted with results by Seong et al. [25].

Table 1. Motivations of volunteer participants before the volunteer experience.

	What would encourage you to engage with online or offline volunteer projects? n = 33		Values older adults wanted from game experience [25] n = 12	
	No. of P.	% of P.	No. of P.	% of P.
Physical improvement	10	30.3%	3	25.0%
Cognitive improvement	15	45.5%	4	33.3%
Opportunity to learn something new	26	78.8%	5	41.7%
Opportunity to communicate and interact with people	14	42.4%	8	66.7%
Opportunity to participate and contribute to society	11	33.3%	4	33.3%
None of the above	4	12.1%	–	–

Our participants use the following devices: 28 use a smartphone, 25 a laptop, 18 a desktop PC, 13 a tablet, 8 a SmartTV while 4 a smartwatch or a smartband and 2 a VR headset. They are also avid Internet users as 28 of them use the Internet either a few times a day or every day, and only 5 a few times a week

---

[3] We have chosen to use multiple choice for age groups as not to bias the participants with an assumption that the research was targeted at older adults.

or less often. As such, our participant group would be a good target for online volunteering and crowdsourcing tasks. Yet, after having completed the study 28 participants reported that they have never done similar tasks before, 3 of them said they did similar tasks at work and 2 did such tasks while volunteering.

3.2 Performance and Feedback

Image Recognition Tasks. In **T1** 26 participants correctly identified the animal silhouette, 4 pointed to other silhouettes, 1 answered that there was no animal present while 2 more chose the "other" option where they have given in one case each: the name of the animal, the more detailed description of the animal. After completion 2 participants suggested to have a video instead - and 2 others wished the task was more challenging, while 1 complained the question was imprecise. Additionally, 1 person wished there were more animals to spot and "better hidden". In **T2** there was less agreement with 13 people choosing pattern 3, and 7 each voting for patterns 1 and 2, 2 for pattern 4, 3 saying it is "hard to tell" and 1 deciding it was some "other" pattern. The suggestions were to have "a different view of the cat in the picture" (1), a "couple of different pictures" (2) and comments appeared that "if someone does not like cats nothing can improve this task", but also "I liked it, even more so, because I like cats".

Audio Recognition Tasks. In both **T3** and **T4** our participants had no trouble listening to the recordings. In both tasks the majority of participants successfully identified the key audio elements (in T3: "many male voices" (31) in T4: "bells" (28) and "traffic" (25)). In T4 about half identified other elements ("birds singing", "people talking", "music"), while only one person noticed "barking", and one indicated "there was nothing specific" in the recording. Additionally, over half of the participants (18) chose to provide additional comment about the exact content of the radio recording from **T3**. For two people the **T3** recording was too short, for another too long and one wished it was accompanied by visuals. The feedback for **T4** was to have a longer recording (5), 1 person also wished for "more variety, to make it more difficult, but also more interesting" and to show a visual connected to the sound. One participant admitted that they "heard birds singing only upon the second hearing" but they were not sure.

Document Transcription Tasks. Both transcription tasks were done very well. In **T5** only one participant decided that the text of the birth certificate was "intelligible" and only in 1 out of 4 places, while two people provided only the first name of the person. Among the others there is almost perfect agreement about what the text says with a varying level of detail for the name of the place and date notation. Additionally, one person provided a full transcription of the document, even though the task did not require it. Appearing suggestions were to have more information about the person in the birth certificate (2), to have more similar documents (1) and the participant suggesting it said that they have "transcribed 247 pieces of disappearing poetry before" and are experienced and now working on transcribing "very difficult historical letters". Another participant suggested to have documents related to the participants' own personal history (1). In **T6** most people (22) provided a complete transcription of the 346-character long text, on top of the transcription one person commented "(placing this dot here is incorrect - transcriber's comment)", while 3 wrote that the text was legible, and 6 provided an incomplete transcription, of these 2 added that the text was legible. Additionally, 2 wrote that it was intelligible. Two people wished for a more challenging text with a harder to read font, and one said other types of content interest them, other appearing comment was "For those who have not been involved in reading old manuscripts and other documents, this is a remarkably interesting activity (...) engaging and motivating, others will put it off or give up. I like it, it draws you in" while another participant mentioned that "such tasks require patience, they are not for everybody".

Pattern Recognition Tasks. In **T7** the count of choices was 12, 7, 6, 3, 3 for the dominant aurora pattern, while one person said that it is "hard to tell" and one person saw no aurora in the video. When asked about the colour 30 people agreed it was green, and over half added other colours (yellow, violet blue and pink). Here four people suggested to have a longer video, especially that "one would like to look longer, as we don't have that here and it is very interesting". In **T8** all participants (33) correctly identified the section coordinates with the described features; 26 said that the veins are clearly visible, 7 claiming to the contrary. One participant suggested that a longer analysis would improve this task, one more expressed that they are not sure where the macula of the retina was, and another wished for an analysis of some other organ.

Summary. Overall, the older adults from our study in most cases provided high quality contributions with no training. Only T2 and T7 proved to be somewhat challenging and with these participants asked for more data. Many wished for other tasks to be more challenging (harder font (T6), more audio variety (T4), more and better hidden animals (T1), longer analysis (T8)) and the "easy" dimension had the weakest correlations with willingness to do similar tasks in the future. It seems that older adults would not mind, and even preferred it, if the tasks posed more of a challenge (e.g. T5 vs T6), especially if it would allow them to learn something interesting. They also wished for the shorter tasks to be extended, either by additional data (T1, T2) steps (T8) or longer duration (T7, T3, T4), not only because they enjoyed them and wanted to learn more, but also to allow them to provide higher quality contributions by adding more data to verify their choices. It seems therefore, that microtasks, designed to be brief for efficiency, could be extended and elaborated upon to increase the contributors' satisfaction, especially if they rely on image, video or audio data.

3.3   Evaluation of Tasks

Participants rated T8 the highest, while T2 the lowest. They distributed most points in the category "I would do similar tasks" (380) followed by "easy" (370),

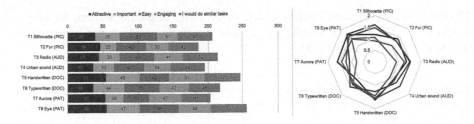

Fig. 2. Left: Total points awarded by our participants after the completion of each task. Right: Average scores for the same tasks.

"attractive" (363), "engaging" (328) and "important" (283). Our participants, once exposed to each task, reported a high willingness to engage with similar tasks (with an average of 1.44 out of 2) suggesting, that older adults would engage with such tasks more, if they were made more easily available to them (Fig. 2).

As seen in Fig. 3 the correlations with the willingness to do similar tasks in the future are either positive, or close to zero, while the strongest correlation is with the visual or thematic "attractiveness" of the task. It was also slightly important whether the task was "engaging" or "important", especially if it was not found to be "attractive" and to a lesser extent if it was "easy". This suggests that older adults' main motivation is rather intrinsic, connected to their own interest in the task, which of course is moderated by other variables.

Correlation r <-1,1>; r = 0 no correlation; r < 0 negative correlation; r > 0 positive correlation	I would do similar tasks and								Interpretation of |r|
	Attractive		**Important**		**Easy**		**Engaging**		
Correlation	Pearson	Spearman	Pearson	Spearman	Pearson	Spearman	Pearson	Spearman	
T1 Recognizing animal silhouettes (PIC)	0,5995	0,5653	0,5017	0,4315	0,2400	0,2712	0,3315	0,3424	> 0.9 – very strong colleration
T2 Recognizing cat fur types (PIC)	0,4282	0,4334	0,2965	0,2662	0,5141	0,4796	0,1354	0,1633	0.7 – 0.9 – strong correlation
T3 Recognizing messages on the radio (AUD)	0,6936	0,6091	0,3993	0,4078	0,2764	0,3475	0,2550	0,1958	0.4 – 0.7 – moderate correlation
T4 Recognizing local urban sounds (AUD)	0,2602	0,2351	0,4840	0,4699	0,0845	0,0989	0,6205	0,5937	0.2 – 0.4 – weak correlation
T5 Transcribing handwritten birth certificate (DOC)	0,7965	0,8077	0,0904	0,0680	0,2342	0,2651	0,2876	0,3369	< 0.2 – no linear relationship
T6 Transcribing a longer typewritten text (DOC)	0,3871	0,3253	0,2745	0,2485	0,2926	0,3476	0,1861	0,1832	
T7 Recognizing Aurora Borealis patterns (PAT)	0,4612	0,5438	-0,2336	0,2386	0,2895	0,2967	0,3967	0,3686	
T8 Recognizing eye elements (PAT)	0,3433	0,3146	0,5323	0,4415	0,0675	0,1200	0,6632	0,6731	
Arithmetic mean	0,4987	0,4793	0,3515	0,3215	0,2499	0,2783	0,3595	0,3571	
Standard Deviation	0,1835	0,1885	0,1540	0,1391	0,1388	0,1242	0,1923	0,1891	
Variance	0,0337	0,0355	0,0237	0,0194	0,0193	0,0154	0,0370	0,0358	

Fig. 3. Correlation matrix for the dimension "I would do similar tasks" and other dimensions, from older adults' evaluation of the tasks right after performing them.

3.4 Motivation

After having completed all of the tasks, the participants chose learning something new and information about the purpose of performing these tasks as the prevailing motivators. They would also like to receive feedback on their performance and to have detailed tutorials. Detailed results are reported in Table 2. Moreover, the ability to perform these tasks using interfaces (smartphone, Smart TV or audio) other than a computer screen was judged as not particularly important, however, this may be due to lack of familiarity with them for audio and

TV devices, as there are studies which successfully implement them for crowd-sourcing [10, 27] and the challenge of small-screen interaction for smartphones [16] which is still relevant [20].

Table 2. Answers to "Which of these elements would encourage you to perform tasks similar to the sample tasks in this survey?" asked after completing all of the tasks.

	No. of P.	% of P.
The opportunity to learn something interesting while performing these tasks	24	72.7%
More knowledge about the purpose of performing these tasks	24	72.7%
Receiving feedback on the use and usefulness of the tasks performed	21	63.6%
A short training to make sure I do the tasks well	17	51.5%
More interesting topic of tasks	9	27.3%
Online support and contact with other people performing these tasks	9	27.3%
Tasks suited to my skills	9	27.3%
Training and personal meetings for those performing the tasks	7	21.2%
Statistics showing the number of already completed tasks	7	21.2%
The ability to perform these tasks on the TV screen with the remote control	6	18.2%
Thanks from the researchers	6	18.2%
Ability to perform these tasks on a smartphone	5	15.1%
Ability to perform these tasks using the voice interface	0	0.0%
"None of the above" and "Other (own answer)"	0	0.0%

4   Conclusions

In this exploratory research we have verified that crowdsourcing microtasks, especially those appearing in citizen science projects, can be well-suited for some groups of older adults - both in terms of the quality of older adults' contributions and their motivation. Yet, even among older adults with average and higher ICT skills - sufficient to contribute to such projects, such as the participants in our sample, the awareness of the existence of such crowdsourcing projects is quite low, as such citizen science tasks are not easily found and sampled. Older adults as a group often overlooked as potential contributors to larger scale crowdsourcing projects due to their often lower willingness to engage online and the perception of their ICT skills. However, the older adults in our study who received no compensation, provided high quality contributions with little training and were open to continue volunteering online.

To increase participation, and thus the representation of this age group's voice in citizen science, we suggest that crowdsourcing tasks ought to be advertised in line with older adults' preferences. These are related to the way in which completing these tasks may benefit, first, them individually, and then, the society as a whole. Based on our research, crowdsourcing microtasks' presentation should focus on the aspect of learning something interesting (which was confirmed by an arithmetic mean correlation of 0.47 for "I would do similar tasks" and "Attractive, thematically or visually"), rather than the aspect of being able to utilize ones' existing skills and knowledge. The contributors should also be provided with a high awareness of the tasks' purpose and ought to be made aware of the usefulness of their individual contributions to reassure the participants that it was time well spent. The tasks could also be more elaborate, to provide an appropriate challenge and increase immersion. Hence, in future research we would also like to examine a wider range of tasks of increasing complexity and duration, as well as the effects of engaging in crowdsourcing on participant's physical, mental or cognitive well-being in further comparative longitudinal research with larger groups of participants of all ages.

References

1. Aula, A.: Learning to use computers at a later age. In: HCI and the Older Population, pp. 3–5. University of Glasgow, Leeds (2004)
2. Barber, S.T.: The ZOONIVERSE is expanding: crowdsourced solutions to the hidden collections problem and the rise of the revolutionary cataloging interface. J. Libr. Metadata **18**(2), 85–111 (2018). https://doi.org/10.1080/19386389.2018.1489449
3. Brewer, R., Morris, M.R., Piper, A.M.: Why would anybody do this?: understanding older adults' motivations and challenges in crowd work. In: Proceedings of the 2016 CHI Conference on Human Factors in Computing Systems, pp. 2246–2257. ACM (2016)
4. Campo, S.A., Khan, V.J., Papangelis, K., Markopoulos, P.: Community heuristics for user interface evaluation of crowdsourcing platforms. Future Gener. Comput. Syst. **95**, 775–789 (2019)
5. Djoub, Z.: ICT education and motivating elderly people. Ariadna; cultura, educación y tecnología. **1**, 88–92 (2013)
6. Population structure and ageing. https://ec.europa.eu/eurostat/statistics-explained/index.php
7. Greenfield, E.A., Marks, N.F.: Formal volunteering as a protective factor for older adults' psychological well-being. J. Gerontol. Ser. B Psychol. Sci. Soc. Sci. **59**(5), S258–S264 (2004)
8. Hao, Y.: Productive activities and psychological well-being among older adults. J. Gerontol. Ser. B Psychol. Sci. Soc. Sci. **63**(2), S64–S72 (2008)
9. von Helversen, B., Abramczuk, K., Kopeć, W., Nielek, R.: Influence of consumer reviews on online purchasing decisions in older and younger adults. Decis. Support Syst. **113**, 1–10 (2018)
10. Hettiachchi, D., et al.: "Hi! I am the crowd tasker" crowdsourcing through digital voice assistants. In: Proceedings of the 2020 CHI Conference on Human Factors in Computing Systems, . CHI 2020, pp. 1–14. Association for Computing Machinery, New York (2020). https://doi.org/10.1145/3313831.3376320
11. Häggström, M.: Medical gallery of mikael häggström 2014, July 2014. https://en.wikiversity.org/
12. Itoko, T., Arita, S., Kobayashi, M., Takagi, H.: Involving senior workers in crowdsourced proofreading. In: Stephanidis, C., Antona, M. (eds.) UAHCI 2014. LNCS, vol. 8515, pp. 106–117. Springer, Cham (2014). https://doi.org/10.1007/978-3-319-07446-7_11
13. Knowles, B., Hanson, V.L.: Older adults' deployment of 'distrust'. ACM Trans. Comput.-Hum. Interact. **25**(4), 21:1–21:25 (2018). https://doi.org/10.1145/3196490

14. Knowles, B., Hanson, V.L.: The wisdom of older technology (non)users. Commun. ACM **61**(3), 72–77 (2018)
15. Kobayashi, M., Arita, S., Itoko, T., Saito, S., Takagi, H.: Motivating multi-generational crowd workers in social-purpose work. In: Proceedings of the 18th ACM Conference on Computer Supported Cooperative Work & Social Computing, pp. 1813–1824. ACM (2015)
16. Kobayashi, M., Hiyama, A., Miura, T., Asakawa, C., Hirose, M., Ifukube, T.: Elderly user evaluation of mobile touchscreen interactions. In: Campos, P., Graham, N., Jorge, J., Nunes, N., Palanque, P., Winckler, M. (eds.) INTERACT 2011. LNCS, vol. 6946, pp. 83–99. Springer, Heidelberg (2011). https://doi.org/10.1007/978-3-642-23774-4_9
17. Kobayashi, M., Ishihara, T., Itoko, T., Takagi, H., Asakawa, C.: Age-based task specialization for crowdsourced proofreading. In: Stephanidis, C., Antona, M. (eds.) UAHCI 2013. LNCS, vol. 8010, pp. 104–112. Springer, Heidelberg (2013). https://doi.org/10.1007/978-3-642-39191-0_12
18. Kopeć, W., Skorupska, K., Jaskulska, A., Abramczuk, K., Nielek, R., Wierzbicki, A.: LivingLab PJAIT: towards better urban participation of seniors. In: Proceedings of the International Conference on Web Intelligence, WI 2017, pp. 1085–1092. ACM, New York (2017). https://doi.org/10.1145/3106426.3109040
19. Kötteritzsch, A., Koch, M., Lemân, F.: Adaptive training for older adults based on dynamic diagnosis of mild cognitive impairments and dementia. In: Pecchia, L., Chen, L.L., Nugent, C., Bravo, J. (eds.) IWAAL 2014. LNCS, vol. 8868, pp. 364–368. Springer, Cham (2014). https://doi.org/10.1007/978-3-319-13105-4_52
20. Kowalski, J., et al.: Older adults and voice interaction: a pilot study with google home. In: Extended Abstracts of the 2019 CHI Conference on Human Factors in Computing Systems, CHI EA 2019, pp. 187:1–187:6. ACM, New York (2019). https://doi.org/10.1145/3290607.3312973
21. Lum, T.Y., Lightfoot, E.: The effects of volunteering on the physical and mental health of older people. Res. Aging **27**(1), 31–55 (2005)
22. Morrow-Howell, N.: Volunteering in later life: research frontiers. J. Gerontol. Ser. B Psychol. Sci. Soc. Sci. **65**(4), 461–469 (2010)
23. Morrow-Howell, N., Hinterlong, J., Rozario, P.A., Tang, F.: Effects of volunteering on the well-being of older adults. J. Gerontol. Ser. B Psychol. Sci. Soc. Sci. **58**(3), S137–S145 (2003)
24. Ross, J., Irani, L., Silberman, M.S., Zaldivar, A., Tomlinson, B.: Who are the crowdworkers? Shifting demographics in mechanical Turk. In: CHI 2010 Extended Abstracts on Human Factors in Computing Systems, CHI EA 2010, pp. 2863–2872. Association for Computing Machinery, New York (2010). https://doi.org/10.1145/1753846.1753873
25. Seong, E., Kim, S.: Designing a crowdsourcing system for the elderly: a gamified approach to speech collection. In: Extended Abstracts of the 2020 CHI Conference on Human Factors in Computing Systems, CHI EA 2020, pp. 1–9. Association for Computing Machinery, New York (2020). https://doi.org/10.1145/3334480.3382999
26. Simpson, R., Page, K.R., De Roure, D.: Zooniverse: observing the world's largest citizen science platform. In: Proceedings of the 23rd International Conference on World Wide Web, WWW 2014 Companion, pp. 1049–1054. Association for Computing Machinery, New York (2014). https://doi.org/10.1145/2567948.2579215

27. Skorupska, K., Núñez, M., Kopeć, W., Nielek, R.: Older adults and crowdsourcing: android tv app for evaluating TEDx subtitle quality. In: Proceedings of the ACM on Human-Computer Interaction, vol. 2(CSCW), pp. 159:1–159:23 (2018). https://doi.org/10.1145/3274428
28. Skorupska, K., Núñez, M., Kopeć, W., Nielek, R.: A comparative study of younger and older adults' interaction with a crowdsourcing android TV app for detecting errors in TEDx video subtitles. In: Lamas, D., Loizides, F., Nacke, L., Petrie, H., Winckler, M., Zaphiris, P. (eds.) INTERACT 2019. LNCS, vol. 11748, pp. 455–464. Springer, Cham (2019). https://doi.org/10.1007/978-3-030-29387-1_25
29. Yu, H., et al.: Productive aging through intelligent personalized crowdsourcing. In: 30th AAAI Conference on Artificial Intelligence (AAAI 2016) (2016)

Quality Assessment of Crowdwork via Eye Gaze: Towards Adaptive Personalized Crowdsourcing

Md. Rabiul Islam[1(✉)], Shun Nawa[1], Andrew Vargo[1], Motoi Iwata[1],
Masaki Matsubara[2], Atsuyuki Morishima[2], and Koichi Kise[1]

[1] Osaka Prefecture University, Sakai, Japan
dd104006@edu.osakafu-u.ac.jp, {nawa,awv}@m.cs.osakafu-u.ac.jp,
{iwata,kise}@cs.osakafu-u.ac.jp
[2] University of Tsukuba, Tsukuba, Japan
{masaki,mori}@slis.tsukuba.ac.jp

Abstract. A significant challenge for creating efficient and fair crowdsourcing platforms is in rapid assessment of the quality of crowdwork. If a crowdworker lacks the skill, motivation, or understanding to provide adequate quality task completion, this reduces the efficacy of a platform. While this would seem like only a problem for task providers, the reality is that the burden of this problem is increasingly leveraged on crowdworkers. For example, task providers may not pay crowdworkers for their work after the evaluation of the task results has been completed. In this paper, we propose methods for quickly evaluating the quality of crowdwork using eye gaze information by estimating the correct answer rate. We find that the method with features generated by self-supervised learning (SSL) provides the most efficient result with a mean absolute error of 0.09. The results exhibit the potential of using eye gaze information to facilitate adaptive personalized crowdsourcing platforms.

Keywords: Crowdsourcing · Eye gaze · Self-supervised learning · Machine learning

1 Introduction

Crowdsourcing is widely employed as a way to achieve tasks that can be more efficiently done by human intelligence. Starting from simple labeling microtasks, researchers have broadened the scope of crowdsourcing to include tasks that require complex input [2] or creativity [5,21]. Crowdsourcing has long been discussed as a polemic topic in that research often focuses on how crowdworkers are exploited by task-providers and platforms [18,23] or focuses on how to improve task efficiency [12] and mitigate spam crowdworkers [17]. To make a fruitful society, it is necessary to prepare crowdsourcing environments that are beneficial to not only task-providers but to crowdworkers as well.

© IFIP International Federation for Information Processing 2021
Published by Springer Nature Switzerland AG 2021
C. Ardito et al. (Eds.): INTERACT 2021, LNCS 12933, pp. 104–113, 2021.
https://doi.org/10.1007/978-3-030-85616-8_8

A key to realize such environments is to introduce more precise quality assessment methods. Currently, the assessment is primarily to evaluate "crowdworkers" to distinguish high-skill workers from low-skill and spam ones [6,15]. Once a crowdworker is classified as low-skill or spam, it is not possible to receive rewards from the work. Although spam workers deserve to receive nothing, it is not fair for low-skill workers; they should receive rewards in response to the quality of output, e.g., the number of correctly answered tasks. Generally speaking, the performance of crowdworkers depends on many factors, including the tasks themselves, personal skills and psychosomatic aspects of workers' behaviors, and their computing and living environments [4,30]. Thus, it is more reasonable and fairer to assess the quality of not crowdworkers but each piece of crowdwork. Moreover, evaluation of crowdwork allows us to adaptively change task allocation, if low performance is due to the currently assigned task. In other words, quality assessment of crowdwork is mandatory to realize adaptive personalized crowdsourcing.

In this paper, we employ crowdworkers' eye gaze for quality assessment on tasks. It has been known that the eye gaze is influenced by confidence on an answer to a task [27], and the confidence is correlated with the correctness of the answer [10]. Thus, we can estimate the quality of crowdwork by analyzing the eye gaze. We use multiple-choice questions (MCQs) as the task and propose two different ways of feature extraction from the eye gaze: handcrafted and self-supervised learning (SSL). The findings are promising. For a large number of the tasks performed, the proposed methods, especially SSL, can estimate the performance with roughly half the error-rate as compared to a baseline estimator.

2   Related Work

Quality control has been a central issue for crowdsourcing. Quality in crowdsourcing is classified into three categories: quality model, quality assessment, and quality assurance [4]. In this work, we are looking at quality assessment. In particular, we limit our focus to computer-based methods that do not rely on evaluation by humans.

A fundamental goal of quality assessment is to identify spam crowdworkers or malicious behaviors for removal [6]. A simple way of conducting a quality assessment is using ground truth where, with known answers, we can estimate the quality of work by measuring the accuracy of the tasks [14]. However, preparing a ground truth for enough tasks is usually expensive. Another way is to evaluate the agreement in output across crowdworkers. This is also expensive because enough answers must be collected for each task. A more sophisticated way is based on crowdworkers' behavior called "fingerprinting," such as mouse usage and screen scrolling [24]. More advanced methods include ranking crowdworkers using a measure of spammers [22]. Besides, researchers have proposed time-series model [13] and cognitive abilities based model [9] to estimate quality.

Another vital point is the use of computational models. In addition to simple matching with the ground truth, game theory [20], probabilistic modeling and the EM algorithm [22], the log-normal model [28], and traditional machine learning

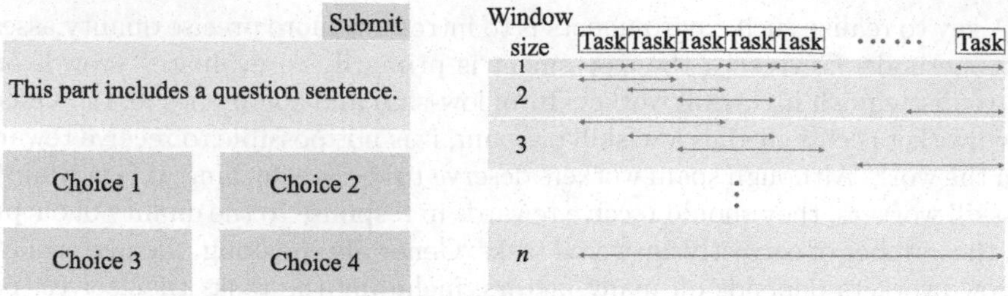

(a) The crowdworker is asked to select the correct choice (b) We employed a window to cover a sequence of performed tasks

Fig. 1. (a) MCQ format and (b) window format employed in our method.

methods such as decision trees [16] have been used. To the best of our knowledge, deep learning has not yet been well employed as a tool for crowdsourcing since it generally requires a large number of task outputs with ground truth.

The technology called SSL [1,19] is a paradigm to cope with the lack of labeled data issue (details in Subsect. 3.2). The SSL has been applied in many domains [7,29], and recently to the human activity recognition task with sensor data [8,25]. In this paper, we attempt to apply the SSL technology developed to analyze eye gaze data [11] for quality assessment of crowdwork. It is important to analyze eye gaze data since it conveys vital behavioral [28], attention [26] and confidence [27] information about the user.

3 Proposed Methods

In this work, we propose methods for the quality assessment of crowdwork by estimating the correct answer rate using eye gaze information. Crowdwork involves numerous tasks; answering MCQs, labeling pictures, solving math equations, and similar. Among all, we chose the answering MCQs since MCQs present the correct and incorrect answers. Figure 1a shows the MCQs format. The eye gaze is recorded while answering MCQs on the computer screen by an eye-tracker. Finally, we propose two methods; the first one is based on handcrafted features, and the second one is based on features generated by using the SSL, where the latter eliminates the handcrafted feature engineering.

3.1 Method with Handcrafted Features

This method consists of two stages: feature extraction and estimation of the correct answer rate.

Feature Extraction. The reading behavior is characterized by a sequence of fixations and saccades [27]. Fixations appear when the gaze pauses in a point, and saccades correspond to the jumps of the gaze between fixations. We extract

Table 1. List of the selected features.

Method	No.	Feature
Handcrafted	$f1$	Number of fixations on the question
	$f2$	Number of fixations on choices
	$f3$	Number of saccades on the question
	$f4$	Number of saccades between the question and choices
	$f5$	Answering time
	$f6$	Self-confidence on the answer
Automatic generation	$f256$	Feature vector generated by SSL

features for the eye gaze data for which we want to estimate the correct answer rate by detecting fixations applying the Buscher algorithm [3] and then extract other features. Table 1 shows the six ($f1$ to $f6$) selected and extracted features.

We employ a window to cover a number of sequential tasks performed, as shown in Fig. 1b, where the number of tasks included in the window is a parameter ranging from 1 to n (all tasks). We slide the window with the step of one task. Features for describing a window is just a concatenation of features from each task. For example, let f_{ij} be a feature j from the task i. Then, for example, the feature vector representing the window of size 2 including the task (i) and $(i + 1)$ is $(f_{(i)1}, ..., f_{(i)k},\ f_{(i+1)1}, ..., f_{(i+1)k})$.

Estimation. The feature vectors representing windows are then used to estimate the correct answer rate by employing the Support Vector Regression (SVR).

3.2 Method with Features Generated by Self-supervised Learning

This method also consists of two stages: feature extraction and estimation of the correct answer rate.

Feature Extraction. We propose an SSL method for automatic feature generation, as shown in Fig. 2, that consists of self-supervised pre-training, correctness estimation, and feature extraction stages. To handle eye gaze for this purpose, it is problematic that the size of eye gaze data varies from MCQ to MCQ. To cope with this issue, we convert the eye gaze data by plotting graphically, as shown in Fig. 3a. The red circles are eye gaze points and the x-axis belongs to the horizontal direction of Fig. 3a. The details are as follows.

The first stage is self-supervised pre-training, upper part of Fig. 2, by solving the pretext task, automatically applied to a large collection of unlabeled data. As shown in Fig. 3b to 3d, we consider three image transformations; reflection about y-axis and reflection about x-axis and 45° anti-clockwise rotation to format the pretext task. For each eye gaze image, we randomly applied one transformation or not transformed and solved a four-class classification task.

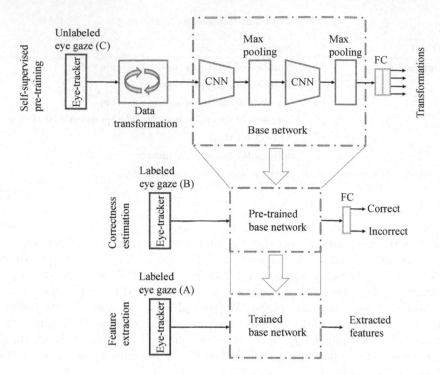

Fig. 2. The proposed method for automatic features generation using SSL. (Color figure online)

The red box in the upper part of Fig. 2 shows the base network, including two CNN blocks and a 2D max-pooling layer after each CNN block. Each CNN block consists of two 2D CNN layers. For the first and second CNN blocks, layers have 8 and 16 units, respectively. The kernel size of CNN layers is 3×3. Finally, we add a classifier consisting of two Fully Connected (FC) layers with 36 units for both. We use ReLU, softmax function, and SGD as the activation function, output layer, and optimizer, respectively. The input image size is $64 \times 64 \times 3$.

The second stage, middle part of Fig. 2, is the correctness estimation done by replacing the FC layers of the pre-trained network with an FC layer with 64 units and fine-tuning by using a labeled eye gaze dataset. The estimation of correctness is a binary classification; the answer is correct or incorrect.

In the third stage, lower part of Fig. 2, we extract features by collecting output at the end of the base network for the dataset we want to estimate the correct answer rate. The final feature vector length is 256 for each task, denoted as $f256$ in Table 1. We format windows in the way described in Subsect. 3.1.

Estimation. The feature vectors representing windows are then used to estimate the correct answer rate using SVR in the same way as described in Subsect. 3.1.

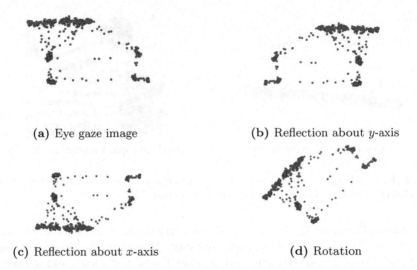

(a) Eye gaze image

(b) Reflection about y-axis

(c) Reflection about x-axis

(d) Rotation

Fig. 3. Eye gaze images, (a) actual eye gaze image with no transformation applied, and (b) to (d) are transformed copies of (a).

4   Datasets

We use three datasets: labeled dataset A, labeled dataset B, and unlabeled dataset C. We did not impose restrictions in data recording sans the task directions, so that datasets are considered "in-the-wild." Data were recorded using the Tobii 4C pro upgraded eye-tracker, as shown in Fig. 4a, a sampling rate 90 Hz. We asked participants to read and answer MCQs in the format shown in Fig. 1a on a computer screen as shown in Fig. 4b. An eye-tracker fixed at the bottom of the screen records the participants' eye gaze. We used MCQs centered on four-choice English questions. Although this is not a typical crowdsourcing task since correct answers are known, it is useful for building a ground truth. All of the datasets were recorded with proper ethical clearance. The details of the datasets are as follows.

Labeled Dataset A. We recruited ten native Japanese university students and worked voluntarily. Each participant read and answered four-choice English grammatical questions on a computer screen. After answering each MCQ, the correctness of the answer is stored automatically, which constitutes the label of the dataset. In total, we collected 2,974 labeled samples.

Labeled Dataset B. We recruited 20 native Japanese university students to participate. Participants were paid 10 USD per hour for up to 4 h. We followed the same experimental procedure as above with a set of four-choice English grammatical questions. In total, 8,218 labeled samples were collected.

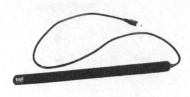

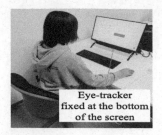

Eye-tracker
fixed at the bottom
of the screen

(a) Tobii 4C eye-tracker   (b) Participant answering MCQs

Fig. 4. Data collection environment, (a) eye-tracker used for data recording and (b) participants' eye gaze being recorded while answering MCQs.

Unlabeled Dataset C. We recorded this dataset following the previous methods for four-choice English vocabulary questions; however, the answers remained unlabeled. We recruited 80 native Japanese high school students and worked voluntarily. In total, 57,460 unlabeled samples were collected.

5   Experiments

5.1   Experimental Conditions

The aim of our experiments is to estimate the correct answer rate using SVR, which can then be used to assess the quality of crowdwork. We used labeled dataset A for the estimation of the correct answer rate. Unlabeled dataset C and labeled dataset B are used for self-supervised pre-training and correctness estimation training, respectively, in the SSL method.

We employed the following three sets for the experiment using handcrafted features: (1) only the feature $f5$, i.e., answering time, (2) $f1$–$f4$, i.e., eye gaze features, and (3) $f5$ and $f6$, i.e., answering time and self-confidence as described in Table 1. Besides, using the feature vector generated by SSL, $f256$, we conducted one experiment. In addition to the above experiments, we employed a baseline estimator defined as, $c = \frac{1}{n}\sum_1^n c_n$ where c_n is the correct answer rate of the nth window of the training dataset.

We conducted all correct answer rate estimation experiments in a participant independent way (leave one participant out cross-validation). As an evaluation metric, we used an absolute error that is calculated as $|c_t - c_p|$ where c_t and c_p are the true and predicted correct answer rate, respectively, for a window. We changed the window size from one to the maximum possible size of 102.

5.2   Results

Figure 5 shows the experimental results. It describes the change of mean absolute error in estimating the correct answer rate with the window size. For smaller windows, the mean absolute error decreases sharply for all methods, although it is relatively high. This indicates that the quality assessment by estimating the

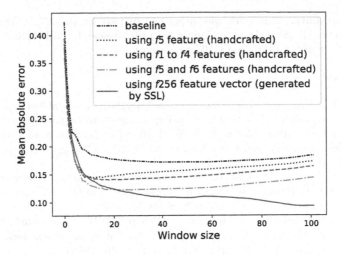

Fig. 5. Result of the correct answer rate estimation experiments.

correct answer rate is not an easy task by just taking into account the behavior for a short period of time. However, for larger windows, the tendency is different. As compared with the baseline, all proposed methods worked better. Among all handcrafted features, the use of $f5$ and $f6$ produced the best result. This is because self-confidence includes rich information about the correctness [10, 27], though it requires additional efforts by crowdworkers to declare the self-confidence for each task. The best performance was obtained by using the feature vector generated by SSL. At the largest window, the mean absolute error was 0.09. Note that in the feature vector generated by SSL, we do not include self-confidence manually so that they are easier to employ.

The best proposed method offers an absolute error around 0.1, which is 50% less than the baseline. This shows the advantage of using eye gaze information for quality assessment. We consider that the results show a new possibility of quality assessment using eye gaze—a richer fingerprint of crowdsourcing tasks.

6   Conclusion and Future Work

In this paper, we presented machine learning methods for the quality assessment of crowdwork by using eye gaze data, answering time, and self-confidence. The results are promising, especially with the SSL, and show the possibility that biometric data can be used to evaluate work quickly. With this, personalized adaptive crowdwork that is based on individual tasks is feasible. In the future, further experimentation on different types of tasks need to be conducted in order to gauge the suitability of the method and decouple it from burdensome tasks such as confidence labeling. Another important area that needs special focus is on leverage this technology for good, benefiting both crowdworkers and task-providers. This means developing platforms with clear ethical guidelines and regulations to ensure crowdworkers' rights.

Acknowledgments. This work was supported in part by the JST CREST (Grant No. JPMJCR16E1), JSPS Grant-in-Aid for Scientific Research (20H04213, 20KK0235), Grand challenge of the iLDi, and OPU Keyproject.

References

1. Amis, G.P., Carpenter, G.A.: Self-supervised ARTMAP. Neural Netw. **23**(2) (2010)
2. Baba, Y., Kashima, H.: Statistical quality estimation for general crowdsourcing tasks. In: Proceedings of the 19th ACM SIGKDD International Conference on Knowledge Discovery and Data Mining, KDD 2013, Chicago, USA, pp. 554–562. ACM (2013)
3. Buscher, G., Dengel, A., Elst, L. V.: Eye movements as implicit relevance feedback. In: CHI 2008 Extended Abstracts on Human Factors in Computing Systems, CHI EA 2008, Florence, Italy, pp. 2991–2996. ACM (2008)
4. Daniel, F., Kucherbaev, P., Cappiello, C., Benatallah, B., Allahbakhsh, M.: Quality control in crowdsourcing: a survey of quality attributes, assessment techniques, and assurance actions. ACM Comput. Surv. **51**(1), 1–40 (2018)
5. Dontcheva, M., Morris, R.R., Brandt, J.R., Gerber, E.M.: Combining crowdsourcing and learning to improve engagement and performance. In: Proceedings of the SIGCHI Conference on Human Factors in Computing Systems, CHI 2014, Toronto, Ontario, Canada, pp. 3379–3388. ACM (2014)
6. Gadiraju, U., Kawase, R., Dietze, S., Demartini, G.: Understanding malicious behavior in crowdsourcing platforms: the case of online surveys. In: Proceedings of the 33rd Annual ACM Conference on Human Factors in Computing Systems, CHI 2015, Seoul, Republic of Korea, pp. 1631–1640. ACM (2015)
7. Gidaris, S., Singh, P., Komodakis, N.: Unsupervised representation learning by predicting image rotations. CoRR, arXiv.abs/1803.07728 (2018)
8. Haresamudram, H., et al.: Masked reconstruction based self-supervision for human activity recognition. In: Proceedings of the 2020 International Symposium on Wearable Computers, ISWC 2020, Virtual Event, Mexico, pp. 45–49. ACM (2020)
9. Hettiachchi, D., van Berkel, N., Hosio, S., Kostakos, V., Goncalves, J.: Effect of cognitive abilities on crowdsourcing task performance. In: Lamas, D., Loizides, F., Nacke, L., Petrie, H., Winckler, M., Zaphiris, P. (eds.) INTERACT 2019. LNCS, vol. 11746, pp. 442–464. Springer, Cham (2019). https://doi.org/10.1007/978-3-030-29381-9_28
10. Ishimaru, S., Maruichi, T., Dengel, A., Kise, K.: Confidence-aware learning assistant. arXiv:2102.07312 (2021)
11. Islam, M.R., et al.: Self-supervised deep learning for reading activity classification. arXiv preprint arXiv:2012.03598 (2020)
12. Jiang, H., Matsubara, S.: Efficient task decomposition in crowdsourcing. In: Dam, H.K., Pitt, J., Xu, Y., Governatori, G., Ito, T. (eds.) PRIMA 2014. LNCS (LNAI), vol. 8861, pp. 65–73. Springer, Cham (2014). https://doi.org/10.1007/978-3-319-13191-7_6
13. Jung, H., Park, Y., Lease, M.: Predicting next label quality: a time-series model of crowdwork. In: AAAI Conference on Human Computation and Crowdsourcing. Association for the Advancement of Artificial Intelligence, Pittsburg, USA (2014)
14. Kazai, G., Kamps, J., Koolen, M., Milic-Frayling, N.: Crowdsourcing for book search evaluation: impact of hit design on comparative system ranking. In: Proceedings of the 34th International ACM SIGIR Conference on Research and Development in Information Retrieval, SIGIR 2011, Beijing, China, pp. 205–214. ACM (2011)
15. Kazai, G., Kamps, J., Milic-Frayling, N.: Worker types and personality traits in crowdsourcing relevance labels. In: Proceedings of the 20th ACM International

Conference on Information and Knowledge Management, CIKM 2011, Glasgow, Scotland, UK, pp. 1941–1944. ACM (2011)

16. Kazai, G., Zitouni, I.: Quality management in crowdsourcing using gold judges behavior. In: Proceedings of the Ninth ACM International Conference on Search and Data Mining, WSDM 2016, San Francisco, USA, pp. 267–276. ACM (2016)

17. Kuang, L., Zhang, H., Shi, R., Liao, Z., Yang, X.: A spam worker detection approach based on heterogeneous network embedding in crowdsourcing platforms. Comput. Netw. **183**, 107587 (2020)

18. Kwek, A.: Crowdsourced research: vulnerability, autonomy, and exploitation. Ethics Hum. Res. **42**(1), 22–35 (2020)

19. Liu, X., Weijer, J.V.D., Bagdanov, A.D.: Exploiting unlabeled data in CNNs by self-supervised learning to rank. IEEE Trans. Pattern Anal. Mach. Intell. **41**(8), 1862–1878 (2019)

20. Moshfeghi, Y., Huertas-Rosero, A.F., Jose, J.M.: Identifying careless workers in crowdsourcing platforms: a game theory approach. In: Proceedings of the 39th International ACM SIGIR Conference on Research and Development in Information Retrieval, SIGIR 2016, Pisa, Italy, pp. 857–860. ACM (2016)

21. Oppenlaender, J., Milland, K., Visuri, A., Ipeirotis, P., Hosio, S.: Creativity on paid crowdsourcing platforms. In: Proceedings of 2020 CHI Conference on Human Factors in Computing Systems, CHI 2020, Honolulu, USA, pp. 1–14. ACM (2020)

22. Raykar, V.C., Yu, S.: Eliminating spammers and ranking annotators for crowdsourced labeling tasks. JMLR **13**(16), 491–518 (2012)

23. Ross, J., Irani, L., Silberman, M. S., Zaldivar, A., Tomlinson, B.: Who are the crowdworkers? Shifting demographics in mechanical Turk. In: CHI 2010 Extended Abstracts on Human Factors in Computing Systems, CHI EA 2010, Atlanta, Georgia, USA, pp. 2863–2872. ACM (2010)

24. Rzeszotarski, J.M., Kittur, A.: Instrumenting the crowd: using implicit behavioral measures to predict task performance. In: Proceedings of the 24th Annual ACM Symposium on User Interface Software and Technology, UIST 2011, Santa Barbara, California, USA, pp. 13–22. ACM (2011)

25. Saeed, A., Ozcelebi, T., Lukkien, J.: Multi-task self-supervised learning for human activity detection. In: Proceedings of the ACM on Interactive, Mobile, Wearable and Ubiquitous Technologies, vol. 3, no. 2, p. 30 (2019)

26. Tsai, M., Hou, H., Lai, M., Liu, W., Yang, F.: Visual attention for solving multiple-choice science problem: an eye-tracking analysis. Comput. Educ. **58**(1), 375–385 (2012)

27. Yamada, K., Kise, K., Augereau, O.: Estimation of confidence based on eye gaze: an application to multiple-choice questions. In: Proceedings of the 2017 ACM International Joint Conference on Pervasive and Ubiquitous Computing and Proceedings of the 2017 ACM International Symposium on Wearable Computers, UbiComp 2017, Maui, Hawaii, pp. 217–220. ACM (2017)

28. Yuasa, S., et al.: Towards quality assessment of crowdworker output based on behavioral data. In: 2019 IEEE International Conference on Big Data, Los Angeles, USA, pp. 4659–4661. IEEE (2019)

29. Zeng, A., Yu, K., Song, S., Suo, D., Walker, E., Rodriguez, A., Xiao, J.: Multiview self-supervised deep learning for 6D pose estimation in the Amazon Picking Challenge. In: 2017 IEEE International Conference on Robotics and Automation (ICRA), Singapore, Singapore, pp. 1383–1386. IEEE (2017)

30. Zhuang, M., Gadiraju, U.: In what mood are you today? An analysis of crowd workers' mood, performance and engagement. In: Proceedings of the 10th ACM Conference on Web Science, WebSci 2019, Boston, Massachusetts, USA, pp. 373–382. ACM (2019)

Design for Automotive Interfaces

Designing for a Convenient In-Car Passenger Experience: A Repertory Grid Study

Melanie Berger[1,2](✉) ⓘ, Bastian Pfleging[1] ⓘ, and Regina Bernhaupt[1,2]

[1] Eindhoven University of Technology, Eindhoven, The Netherlands
{m.berger,b.pfleging,r.bernhaupt}@tue.nl
[2] ruwido austria GmbH, Neumarkt, Austria

Fig. 1. In a repertory grid study, we identified major factors of a convenient car ride: Our results show the importance of physical space, shared controls, the ability to view the landscape, communication, and personalization (from left to right).

Abstract. The driving experience has become one of the central decision factors when buying a car. In current manually driven cars, this experience is to a large extent influenced by driver-based infotainment functionalities. With the advent of rear-seat infotainment systems, manufacturers started to not only look at the driver's perspective but also focus on passenger experiences. But passenger experiences can go beyond traditional aspects of user experience as they also include aspects of coziness and comfort in the context of riding, which we describe as passenger convenience. While insights about the design space and passenger's needs are central when designing for an advanced level of passenger convenience, the body of knowledge in this area is limited. Therefore, we present the results from a repertory grid study (n = 32) where we investigated what makes a passenger ride in a manually driven car convenient. Based on three predefined and three participant-selected riding situations we accounted for common patterns and individual differences. The results confirm the importance of well-being, physical comfort, and safety. The interviews unveil that passengers strive for access to in-vehicle systems, the possibility to act as a co-driver, and the support for the integration of external technology, connectivity, and personalization. Based on our findings, we extracted a set of design recommendations to consider when designing automotive systems with passenger convenience and experience in mind.

Keywords: Automotive user interfaces · In-car experience · Riding experience · Passenger convenience

© IFIP International Federation for Information Processing 2021
Published by Springer Nature Switzerland AG 2021
C. Ardito et al. (Eds.): INTERACT 2021, LNCS 12933, pp. 117–139, 2021.
https://doi.org/10.1007/978-3-030-85616-8_9

1 Introduction

Beyond arriving safely at a destination, the unique selling point of a car is more and more defined around the in-car experience [3]. Due to the technical innovations during the past century, a modern car provides a high-tech interactive space [37]. Thus, the design of automotive user interfaces plays an important role when it comes to in-car experiences [3]. Looking at research in industry and academia, we see a focus on driver-based systems and functionality innovation, as driving safely has a top priority [7, 41]. However, with an average occupation of 1.67 people per ride in the United States [42], we see that 56% of all car rides are with at least one additional passenger [12], e.g., a family member, colleague, or friend. We investigate what exemplifies a "good experience" in riding in a manual car, and how we can enhance passenger experience to be more convenient. In this context, understanding manual car rides from a passenger perspective are essential. Looking at the literature, only little is known about passenger's needs. Inbar and Tractinsky [30] report the necessity of having access to trip-related data, while a few articles show the importance of observing the surroundings [37, 46] and having the opportunity to assist the driver [26, 45]. However, it is important to get deeper insights into the design space and the passengers' values to be able to design for a better convenient in-car passenger experience.

Therefore, we broadly explore the design space of passenger-based in-car applications by answering the open research question: "Which factors do account for a convenient passenger experience in a manual car"? Convenience is defined as a feeling of coziness, contentedness, comfort, and relaxation within a specific situation as this reflects the overall setting, surroundings, and contextual factors in a more detailed manner [51]. Hence, it helps us to get deeper insights into passenger's needs beyond traditional user experience (UX) dimensions. To answer our research question and to identify the important aspects that make a ride convenient, we conducted a repertory grid study (n = 32). Based on this interviewing technique, we elicited factors that contribute positively to a convenient passenger experience by focusing on participant's personal constructs about different (predefined and participant-specific) riding situations.

With our study, we first contribute to the general understanding of what makes the passenger experience in a manually driven car convenient, and second, we provide design recommendations with a focus on short-term product or service innovations that enable their incorporation into current (market-ready) cars. More precisely, we outline factors and their relationships that constitute to passenger convenience. Besides conforming common-sense assumptions like the importance of well-being, physical comfort, and safety, we discovered novel factors such as the need for shared functionalities between drivers and passengers and dedicated passenger applications. Figure 1 outlines such situations and scenarios that influence a convenient passenger experience. We translated our insights and findings into a set of design recommendations that focus especially on the design of technology-driven features and products that can easily be brought into current cars or enable to be applied on top of existing in-car services. Besides that, these recommendations systematically outline important aspects that should be considered during the design phase of the next generation of manually driven cars.

2 Related Work

In this chapter, we give an overview of prior work in the domain of passenger experiences and provide insights related to repertory grid studies.

2.1 Passenger Convenience

The ISO standard 9241-210 on human-centered design defines the user experience (UX) as "user's perceptions and responses that result from the use and/or anticipated use of a system, product, or service" [31] where the user's perceptions and responses comprise of user emotions, beliefs, preferences, perceptions, comfort, behaviors, and accomplishments. Thus, in the context of the car, the factors of driving comfort and more broadly well-being play an important role.

The Oxford dictionary describes comfort as a "state of physical and material well-being, with freedom from pain and trouble, and satisfaction of bodily needs" [44]. Depending on the mode of transportation and over time, different definitions for comfort have evolved. According to Looze et al. [36], a common denominator of these definitions is that comfort is a personal and subjective construct; it is the passenger's reaction to the environment, and it is affected by different (e.g., physical, physiological, psychological) factors. However, subjective well-being goes beyond traditional comfort aspects such as reaction to the environment as it also includes evaluations of oneself [17]. With this regard, well-being and comfort have been investigated generically for vehicles (e.g., [16]) and in specific domains, including airplanes [1, 49, 54] and trains [29, 48]. However, given that the latter are modes of public transportation, we expect them to only be applicable to some extent to the more private space of manually driven cars. In the automotive domain, the investigation of well-being refers mainly to automated driving. Elbanhawi et al. [19] therefore propose a theoretical framework to estimate comfort regarding path planning for automated vehicles. Sauer et al. collected qualitative and quantitative feedback on passenger well-being in automated cars using the MDBF questionnaire [50]. Regarding that, our study fills the gap by not only understanding the effects of well-being and comfort but also by identifying additional factors that contribute to a positive riding experience.

One additional factor that can influence passenger's experience is the feeling described with the Danish word "hygge" or with the German word "Gemütlichkeit". These words do not unambiguously translate into the English language. We use the term convenience to describe this feeling. In general, the perceived level of convenience refers to a feeling of coziness, contentedness, comfort, and relaxation within a specific situation. As an example, a single soft chair in a restaurant might be considered as cozy and improving UX. But the overall scene, sitting on that chair for dinner, surrounded by close friends with favorite music in the background is described as convenient (DE: "gemütlich"). Regarding product design, Shove defines convenience as the opportunity to create quality time [51]. More precisely, it refers to a product or service that helps users to finish a task more efficiently compared to traditional ways (e.g., the invention of the washing machine makes washing more convenient compared to manual washing) [51]. So, a convenient product is easily accessible, easy to use, and provides a high level of usability, by helping users within a specific context by finishing tasks efficiently and with satisfaction [20, 51].

2.2 Supporting Passenger Experience

Regarding in-car passenger experience, Inbar and Tractinsky [30] reported, that entertainment, as well as infotainment-oriented services, play an important role. Mentioned key factors are the access to trip-related information and the possibility to interact with the in-car system [30]. Based on that, Berger et al. [4] and Matsumura and Kirk [37] evaluated these factors based on an interactive car window that supports the in-car experience due to contextual information adaptation [37]. Another work from Berger et al. [5] shows, based on a passenger-oriented in-vehicle infotainment system (IVIS), that watching movies and looking for points of interests are equally important in terms of user experience (UX). A cultural probing study by Oswald et al. unveiled that front-seat passengers want to have entertainment services (TV and movies), communication platforms, and support for work-related tasks in future cars [42]. In addition to individual entertainment and information content, passengers enjoy collaborating during a ride, by playing different multi-player games [40] or sharing information with other occupants [42]. Pfleging et al. report watching out of the window as the most frequently performed task by passengers [46]. However, passenger experience is also about co-experience and goes beyond the need for entertainment services. While co-experience is defined by Forlizzi and Battarbee [21] as creating UX during social interaction with a product or service, in the specific context of driving this refers to the act of being a co-driver. Co-driver activities are mainly about assisting the driver in a specific form like setting up the navigation or helping to keep the focus on the traffic situation [26, 45]. Research shows that such collaborations can reduce the driver's workload and minimizes the level of driver distraction [14, 35]. However, the traffic situation, as well as the relationship between the driver and passenger, influence the passenger's likelihood of being a co-driver [26, 37]. In addition, passengers often need to prevent themselves from getting motion sick which limits their ability to assist the driver as well [11].

Through current literature, we see that research rather focused on individual factors than on investigating the overall factors that constitute a positive passenger experience. With our repertory grid study, we fill this gap and identify the essential factors that relate to a convenient passenger ride through user elicitation.

2.3 Repertory Grid Methodology

The repertory grid methodology is an interviewing method for eliciting people's ideas or opinions about a specific topic, expressed by their own terminology [6]. This allows getting a detailed and personal overview of user's opinions, in our case related to a convenient passenger experience. The strength of this method lies in uncovering customers' hidden needs as the method bases on Kelly's Personal Construct Theory [33]. This theory assumes that the way people act is defined by the meaning they attach to situations or objects, so-called elements. During repertory grid interviews participants rate those elements based on a set of constructs (opposing word pairs), either supplied by the participants themselves or pre-determined by the interviewer. Those constructs can then be analyzed to see how people think about elements and how the elements are related to each other [6]. Pre-defined elements and constructs result in a matrix that demonstrates the connection between a specific element and constructs [2]. In the case of non-fixed elements and constructs, the repertory grid method allows exploring a broader topic by investigating constructs (e.g., users, design space) based on people's opinions [18]. Within the HCI community, the repertory grid methodology has been applied in various domains. The most common ones are to get feedback on design ideas [28], or to understand people (e.g., [15, 32, 53]), and to explore the design space of a specific context (e.g., [23, 27, 34]). For instance, Gkouskos et al. conducted repertory grid interviews based on future vehicle concepts to identify driver needs for future transportation design [23]. Kawak et al. [34] and Hassenzahl et al. [27] used such interviews to create design spaces based on physical products the participants interacted with. In addition to the exploration of design spaces, repertory grids have also been applied across national backgrounds [53] and age groups [15].

3   Method Choice and Study

Previous literature about convenient riding experiences is scarce. Besides that, there is no systematic or structured framework for an interview that encompasses the breadth of this topic and at the same time achieves the necessary depth. Therefore, we applied the repertory grid interviewing technique because it is a structured approach to explore a design space from a user's perspective by collecting both qualitative and quantitative data [2, 25]. As it considers user's perceptions, needs, beliefs, and attitudes [27] it enabled us to get detailed insights into the aspects of a convenient passenger experience. More precisely, the repertory grid aims to provide insights into the important factors of a convenient car ride by people's personal constructs which they associate with their individual experiences. In the following subsection, we explain the research setup and the experimental procedure.

3.1   Elements and Constructs

The important dimensions for repertory grids are the elements that need to be judged, in our case the situations the participants remembered being a passenger (see also Table 1). During the interview, those elements/situations are used to elicit participants' personal constructs [2] – contrasting word pairs that describe participant's individual riding experiences based on the elements (e.g., long-distance trip vs. short distance trip).

Elements. The proposed numbers of different elements/situations for a repertory grid are typically between 6 and 10 elements [2]. Those elements can either be provided (pre-defined) by the researchers to compare elements/situations or defined by the participant during the interview to deeply discover the design space [2]. We followed the full repertory grid approach with a combination of pre-defined and participant-defined elements as described by Edwards et al. [18]. Therefore, we predefined three most frequent situations of being a passenger (see elements 4–6 in Table 1), while three additional elements (elements 1–3) had to be defined by each participant at the beginning of the interview. We asked the participants to come up with situations in which they could remember being a passenger. The description of an element/situation had to cover the reason for the trip, the distance, and with whom they were driving.

Constructs. Constructs are typically word pairs describing opposites (e.g., easy to use - difficult to use). These word pairs are in our experiment elicited through the participants during the interview by comparing elements/situations [2, 18]. This enabled us to explore participant's individual passenger experiences based on their own words and phrases. After the investigation of the constructs, the participants rated each construct on a 7-point Likert scale how important they consider each construct regarding a convenient passenger ride (1 = not important at all; 7 = highly important).

3.2 Participants

We conducted 32 interviews in German or English with participants living in Austria (22), Germany (5), the Netherlands (4), and France (1). The participants' ages ranged from 22 years to 77 years ($M = 42.37$ years, $SD = 15.42$ years, 17 males, 15 female). Our participants reported a variety of experiences in traveling as a passenger, ranging from several times a day (2) to several times a week, at least once a week (10), several times a month (9), once a month (4), and less than once a month (5). In addition, we asked the participants whom they travel with most frequently: 16 participants indicated that they travel with their partner, while other categories named were either family related: parents (5), kids (3), cousin (1), sibling (1); or with people close: friends (3), colleagues (2) or roommates (1). None of the participants was referring to ride-sharing or paid rides (e.g., taxi or Uber).

Table 1. The defined elements (=situations) for the repertory grid study

Nr.	Element
1	*Self-defined by the participant*
2	*Self-defined by the participant*
3	*Self-defined by the participant*
4	Short distance ride (<30 km) with your mother/father
5	Long-distance ride (>30 km) with your best friend
6	Your most convenient passenger experience imaginable

3.3 Procedure

We conducted the interviews either in person or online via Microsoft Teams[1] (the interviews were conducted in June 2020, after the end of the first European Covid-19 lockdown). At the beginning of the experiment, the experimenter introduced the participants

---

[1] Microsoft Teams: https://www.microsoft.com/en-us/microsoft-365/microsoft-teams/group-chat-software, last accessed: 2020/09/12.

to the purpose of the study and explained the repertory grid method. This especially concerned the definition and usage of elements and the procedure of generating constructs. Once the consent form was signed, the experimenter shared the repertory grid document. After an initial trial of adding and judging an example on the repertory grid, the study started following the steps listed in Table 2.

Table 2. Description of the four steps followed to elicit participants' personal constructs.

| | 1 | 2 | | 3 | 4 |
		2.1	2.2		
Step	Definition of the remaining three elements/situations	Selecting three out of six elements from the elements list	Generation of constructs (contrasting word pairs) based on the three selected elements	Defining the pole of each construct (word pairs) which contributed positively to passenger convenience.	Assessing the importance of how each construct contributes to convenience.
Description	The participant needs to think of three additional situations (elements) where he/she can remember being a passenger.	The experimenter selects three out of six elements from Table 1. These elements are used in step 2.2 to elicit the participant's personal constructs.	The participant needs to produce as many constructs as possible which describe two of the three selected elements (situations) from step 2.1. This means the statements define how two of the elements are alike but different from the third (triading).	The participant had to state for every construct generated in step 2.2, which pole contributes positively to his/her convenient passenger experience	The participant had to rate the constructs on a 7-point Likert scale from 1 (negative pole) to 7 (positive pole)
Output example	Three additional elements for the elements list: • Riding with my best friend from Germany to Italy for vacation (see also Table 1) • Visiting my grandma (40km) with my brother and my family • Going shopping with my boyfriend (20km)	Possible, random selection: • Riding with my best friend from Germany to Italy for vacation (see also Table 1) • Visiting my grandma (40km) with my brother and my family • short distance ride (<30km) with your mother/father	Example constructs out of the comparison of the three, selected elements in 2.1: *Used a navigation system vs. no navigation system was used* The part "used a navigation system" refers to the vacation ride while "no vacation system refers to the family rides.	Example construct from step 2.2: *Used a navigation system vs. no navigation system was used* ➜ Positive pole: used a navigation system ➜ Negative pole: no navigation system was used	Positive pole vs. negative pole from step 2: Used a navigation system vs. no navigation system used ➜ rated with 7 means, that it is perceived highly convenient if a navigation system is used.
Responsibility	Participant	Experimenter	Participant	Participant	Experimenter

As a first step, participants had to produce the three remaining elements - the situations in which they remembered being a passenger. The second step was the elicitation of the word pairs – so-called constructs. This step is based on triadic comparisons of elements [18] which means, the experimenter chooses three elements out of the defined six elements from Table 1 (step 2.1). The participant was asked to think about personal constructs that differentiate two of the elements from the third. This means, the participant had to come up with contrasting word pairs (constructs) which describe how two elements are alike but different from the third (e.g., using a navigation system vs. no navigation system was used, step 2.2.). Step 2.2 of defining constructs based on three elements was repeated until the participant could not think of any new ones. In case a construct was unclear for the researcher, the laddering technique was applied [6]: It allows to get more detailed information about the context and meaning of a construct by asking follow-up questions. To avoid leading the participant in any specific direction the laddering questions were limited to ask the participant about the exact meaning or a more detailed explanation of the construct.

After eliciting the constructs, the participant had to state which pole of the construct contributes positively to convenience (step 3) (e.g., either the pole of "using a navigation system" or the pole of "no navigation system was used"). To get quantitative insights into how strong each construct contributes to participants' most convenient passenger experience, we asked the participant to rate each construct on a 7-point Likert scale (1 = not important at all; 7 = highly important) (step 4) [47].

For each participant, we conducted three rounds of comparing elements/situations which incorporates steps 2, 3, and 4. In the first round, the experimenter randomly[2] chose 3 out of the elements 1–5 mentioned in Table 1. In the second round, the experimenter picked the two so far unused elements (from elements 1–5) and a random element from the first round. To understand what makes the most convenient passenger ride, element 6 (most convenient passenger experience) was chosen in the last round, it was complemented by two other randomly selected elements from Table 1.

Once the rating process was completed, participants answered demographic questions related to their age, gender, the frequency of being a passenger, and with whom they ride most often. At the end of each interview, the researcher checked if all constructs were rated. On average, sessions lasted one hour. The overall study was audio-recorded and was approved by the local ethics board.

3.4 Analysis of the Interview Results

We analyzed the interview results which incorporate the constructs and their ratings qualitatively and quantitatively.

Qualitative Analysis. We conducted a qualitative content analysis [38] based on inductive, thematic free coding to categorize the collected word-pairs (constructs). First, two researchers speaking the local dialect of the participants translated the word-pairs from German to English. As a next step, both construct poles have been assigned to one or multiple codes. This was done iteratively by combining similar codes to an overarching category which resulted in a hierarchical code structure with 3 levels (main, sub & sub-sub categories). The researchers performed these steps on a common agreement basis. We chose this approach to enable discussion of the meaning of the word pairs that were in the local regional dialect and how to categorize them accordingly. The same approach was used for the seven participants answering in English. Overall, the coding, with a series of iterations, resulted in 9 categories with subcategories (min: 3, max: 11) and sub-subcategories (min: 3, max: 11). Table 3 provides an overview of all categories including sub-categories.

---

[2] Google random number generator: https://bit.ly/32lNUIP, last accessed: 2020/09/12.

Quantitative Analysis. For the quantitative data analysis, we made use of the constructs rating and the mentioned frequency of categories. Therefore, we first analyzed the frequency of the sub-(sub) categories that have been mentioned by at least 50% of the participants (see Table 4). In addition, we also analyzed the rating of the constructs per category. We especially investigated the extreme rated (highest/lowest rated) constructs (see Table 5) to spot important but possibly rarely mentioned convenience aspects, as suggested by Fransella et al. [22]. This gave us the possibility to clearly define the aspects that make a passenger experience convenient.Besides that, we were interested in the relationship between the convenient categories/sub-categories and their strength of its connection. Therefore, we correlated the frequencies of the categories by calculating the 2-sided Spearman's rank order.

4 Results

In our study the research question "Which factors account for a convenient passenger experience in a manual car?" was central. To explain our findings, we first give an overview of the overall elicited constructs and their categories, and second, we capture the key factors per category that relate to a convenient passenger experience both qualitatively and quantitatively. Whenever specific constructs (i.e., contrasting word pairs) are mentioned in the subsequent text, the first item always refers to the participant's positive, convenient pole, i.e., the aspect that positively contributes to a convenient ride.

4.1 Overview About the Elicited Constructs

Overall, we elicited 1520 constructs, with an average of $M = 47.5$ ($SD = 15.8$) constructs per participant (min: 9, max: 83). Based on common agreement coding, two researchers grouped these constructs into *nine overarching convenient categories* with sub-categories and sub-subcategories (see Table 3). In this section, we provide a general overview of the main categories, while the next subsection will focus on the convenience aspects of the passenger experience.

Most of the constructs refer to *Technology & Equipment* (510 constructs) which incorporates the importance of accessible and controllable functions – mainly provided by the car itself. This is also about devices and goods passengers bring into the car (e.g., smartphone, food & drinks, clothes). The second most frequently mentioned category defines the passengers' *Physical Comfort* (451 constructs). It addresses the value of the sitting position, seat comfort, temperature regulation, and the condition of the car itself (e.g., serviced car). Another 211 constructs relate to passengers' *Well-being*, more precisely to positive emotions, feelings, moods, and outlines the importance of avoiding motion sickness. 181 constructs align to the *Trip* itself. Especially to the type of trip (e.g., leisure trip, shopping trip), the overall trip characteristics (e.g., a fun ride, an exciting trip), and its time and duration. Mentioned responses describing the communication of the occupants, the perceived togetherness as well as the relationship between people in the car relate to the *Social* category (154 constructs). The remaining constructs refer to the *Outside Environment* (128 constructs), *Safety* (78 constructs, driving safety and personal safety), *Driving Behavior* (74 constructs), and being a *Co-Driver* (35). Some of these categories strongly relate to each other. For instance, there is a significant positive correlation between *Well-being* and *Physical Comfort* ($r_s = .630, p = .0001$). Besides, there are significant positive correlations between *Technology & Equipment* and *Physical Comfort* ($r_s = .715, p = .0000$) as well as between *Safety* and *Driving Behavior* ($r_s = .637, p = .0001$). *Well-being* also shows a strong positive relationship with the *Social* Situation in the car ($r_s = .481, p = .0053$), the *Outside Environment* ($r_s = .475, p = .0060$) and Safety ($r_s = .449, p = .0099$). Between all other categories, there could no relationships be observed.

Table 3. The nine overall identified categories including sub-categories and example construct that participants associate with a convenient passenger experience – derived through the qualitative content analysis.

Category	#	Description	Sub-Categories	Example constructs (positive pole / negative pole)
Availability of Technology & Equipment	510	This category refers to the technology and equipment that is available in the car, either provided by the car itself or brought in by the passenger.	Infotainment, Entertainment, External Items (e.g., mobile phone, food & drinks), In-car technology-based Equipment, non-technology-based Equipment, Personalization & Recommendation	• Access to movies, Netflix, and Prime / No access to movies. • To have your own climate control / Not having an own climate control.
Physical Comfort	451	This category concerns the overall physical comfort provided by the car	Sitting position, Seat, Air & Climate, Space & Storage, Car Condition, Noise Scenery, Sound, Light Condition, Cleanness	• Sitting in the front / Sitting in the back. • Can stretch out the feet / Cannot stretch the feet out. • No smoking while driving / Smoking while driving. • Do not detect possible non-functioning of the car / To detect possible non-functioning of the car.
Well-being	211	This category refers to the passenger personally. It specifically concerns the feelings, and the perception passengers encounter during a ride.	Mood, Feelings, Emotions, Personal focus, Trust, Motion Sickness	• To be relaxed / Uncertainty • Trust in driver / No trust in the driver. • To be lost in thoughts / To be concentrated on the route. • No motion sickness / Motion sickness.
Trip	181	This category specifically concerns how the procedure of the trip looks like. It refers mainly to the type of the trip, the characteristics, and the travel time and distance	Trip Type, Stops & Places, Destination, Navigation, Trip Distance, Time, Trip-Planning, Schedule, Frequency of Travels, Trip Costs, Trip Characteristics	• Take spontaneous breaks / Mandatory breaks. • A leisure trip / A business trip. • Adventure ride / Shopping trip. • It is enjoyable / It is unpleasant.
Social	154	This category refers to the social situation inside the car. This often describes the communication between people in the car and the perceived togetherness.	Driver feelings, Relationship to the driver, Conversations in the Car, Relationship to other Passengers, Togetherness, Amount of People in the Car, Respect & Tradition, Social Connection with the outside world, Atmosphere in the Car	• Chat with the driver / Be quiet. • Play video games together / Everyone on specific screen playing different games. • Driving with people I love (friends, family) / Driving with people I hate.
Outside Environment	128	This category concerns everything that goes on outside the car. It specifically refers to the observation of traffic and landscape.	Road & Traffic, Situational Awareness & Overview, Landscape View, Seasons & Weather	• Avoid traffic jams / Standing in a traffic jam. • More overview of traffic / No overview of the traffic. • Nice location and view / Ugly city.
Safety	78	This category concerns what passengers associate with safety and what they need to feel safe.	Feeling safe, Driver focus, Safety in general, Accidents / Breakdowns, Actions in case of Emergencies, Injuries	• A safe feeling / To feel unsafe. • Car is safe and functional / The car is not so safe and functional. • To not have breakdowns / To have a breakdown.
Driving Behavior	74	This category refers to the perceived driving style and speed level.	Driving Style, Speed Level, Perception of the ride	• Comfortable driving style / Terrible driving style. • Lower speed level / Higher speed level
Co-Driver	34	This category concerns how passengers assist and alert the driver.	To (not) take over driving tasks, Alert the driver, Assist the driver	• To look for a parking space / No search for a parking space • Support the driver by navigating / Not supporting the driver by navigating

4.2 Passengers' Most Convenient Ride

To identify the important aspects that make a ride as a passenger convenient, we looked first at the preferred construct poles of the most frequently occurred sub-categories/sub-subcategories which are at least mentioned by 50% of our 32 participants. These 18 categories are listed in Table 4. Secondly, we analyzed the overall extreme ratings of constructs per main category (highest rating = 7; lowest rating = 1) to identify their importance, as suggested by Fransella et al. [22] (see Table 5).

Technology and Equipment: Overall, most constructs refer to the category of *Technology & Equipment*. When it comes to the passenger's most convenient ride, the level of entertainment, especially provided by personalized *Audio Content* (30/32 participants) (e.g., "Good music with a beat vs. Bad choice of music", P33) plays an important role. Currently, this is mainly achieved by connecting Bluetooth music devices (e.g., smartphone) to the infotainment system (e.g., "Own Bluetooth music vs. Radio", P14). In addition, passengers want to have access to the in-car infotainment system to manually *Control* it (e.g., "Controlling the music vs. Not being able to change the music ", P13).

Table 4. The most frequently mentioned categories which make a convenient passenger experience including the description of the preferred pole and the non-preferred pole of the construct. The categories highlighted in green are mentioned by over 90% of the participants, the blue ones by over 70%, the yellow ones by 60%, and the orange ones by at least 50%.

Code	Description of the preferred construct pole	Description of the non-preferred construct pole	Participants	Number of Constructs	Main Category
Sitting Position	Sitting in the front	Sitting in the back	96,87%	183	Physical Comfort
Audio Content	Listening to personalized audio content, while having the possibility to select or skip a specific song.	Listening to commercial, non-preferred audio content while selecting or skipping a song is not possible.	93,75%	103	Technology & Equipment
Conversations in the Car	Having conversations about fun and non-private topics with others in the car, preferable with the driver.	Having less conversations or no conversations at all. In case of conversations – talking about private, personal topics.	93,75%	94	Social
Feelings	Overall positive feelings a passenger perceives during the ride (e.g., comfortable, relaxed, safe)	Overall negative feelings a passenger perceives during a ride (e.g., stress, discomfort, unsafe)	90,62%	151	Well-being
Landscape View	To have a good and enjoyable landscape view	To have a non-enjoyable or restricted landscape view	81,24%	53	Outside Environment
Seat	An adjustable, comfortable seat	A non-adjustable, dis-comfortable seat	78,13%	64	Physical Comfort
Controllability	To have the ability to control (in-car) functions	To have restricted or limited ability to control (in-car) functions	75%	79	Technology & Equipment
Physical Space	Availability of physical space	Lack of physical space	75%	55	Physical Comfort
Air Conditioning	To have automatic air conditioning with climate zones	To have no air conditioning or manual air conditioning (without climate zones)	68,75%	36	Physical Comfort / Technology & Equipment
Driving Style	The driver drives with a reasonable driving style	The driver drives with an inappropriate driving style	68,75%	46	Driving Behavior
Trip Characteristics	The trip is joyful & exited	The trip is not enjoyable and stressful	68,75%	45	Trip
Information Access	Access to trip-related information and news	No / limited access to trip related information and news	62,5%	62	Technology & Equipment
Navigation System	The availability and usage of a navigation System	No navigation system is available or used	62,5%	37	Technology & Equipment
Situational Awareness & Overview	To have a good overview of the outside environment to stay situationally aware	To have a limited or restricted overview of the outside environment. Situational awareness is not given	62,5%	39	Outside Environment
Trip Type	To be on a private, voluntary, leisure Trip	To be on a mandatory, business trip	56,25%	35	Trip
Being a Co-Driver	To be able to alert or assist the driver	Limited ability or no ability at all to alert or assist the driver	56,25%	36	Co-Driver
Stops & Places	Make additional stops and breaks	Do not make additional stops and breaks	53,13%	24	Trip
Togetherness	Having a higher feeling of togetherness (with people in the car)	Having a lower feeling of togetherness (with people in the car)	50%	22	Social

Table 5. Overview of the extreme-rated (most important/least important) constructs per main category. Among the 1520 elicited constructs, 30 (1,97%) constructs were rated as least important and 475 constructs (31,25%) were rated as most important. The two highest average score ratings and the two highest proportion of most important constructs are highlighted in green.

Category	Number of constructs rated with highest value = 7	Proportion of constructs rated with 7	Number of constructs rated with lowest value = 1	Proportion of constructs rated with 1	Average rating	Number of different constructs
Technology & Equipment	118	23.14%	20	3.92%	5.48	510
Physical Comfort	147	32.59%	4	0.89%	5.69	451
Well-being	124	58.76%	1	0.47%	6.25	211
Trip	57	31.50%	2	1.10%	5.56	181
Social	29	18.83%	7	4.54%	5.01	154
Outside Environment	35	27.34%	1	0.78%	5.43	128
Safety	45	57.69%	0	0%	6.23	78
Driving Behaviour	36	48.65%	0	0%	6.00	74
Co-Driver	7	20.59%	3	8.82%	5.00	34

This refers to manually adjusting the music or to change the temperature as shown by significant positive correlations between *Control & Audio Content* ($r_s = .732, p = .0000$) and *Control & Air Conditioning* ($r_s = .639, p = .0001$). In addition, the infotainment system is perceived as convenient to retrieve information, especially through the integrated *Navigation System* (strong positive relationship between *Information Access & Navigation System*; $r_s = .488, p = .0047$). In general, *Information Access* is appreciated by 20/32 participants as they value staying informed about the outside world, the car, and the trip progress.

Physical Comfort: Passengers also strive for a high level of physical comfort to experience the most convenient ride. This incorporates having as much *Physical Space* as possible, especially more legroom to avoid being cramped in the car ("Can stretch legs vs. Cannot stretch legs", P17). In addition, convenience in terms of *Physical Comfort* refers to individual temperature regulations ("Individual climate zones (per seat) vs. single climate zone", P10) and to an adjustable, ergonomic *Seat*. These factors reflected the preference of 31/32 participants to sit at the front. Additional reasons for this are a better view out of the windows towards the landscape (mentioned by 11 participants), a better overview of the traffic & driving situation (mentioned by 17 participants), the possibility to interact with in-car systems (mentioned by 16 participants) and the availability of more physical space (mentioned by 17 participants). Quantitative results in addition unveil, that there is a strong positive relationship between the *Sitting Position* and the possibility to *Control* an in-car system ($r_s = .408, p = .0206$) as well as between the *Sitting Position* and the *Air Conditioning*. This reflects, that some functions are better or only usable from the front passenger's seat.

Well-Being: The *Well-being* of passengers has the highest priority as this category received the highest proportion of most important rated constructs (58.76%) and the highest average rating score (6.25, see also Table 5). The main aspects that refer to a high level of convenience are the possibility to relax (44 constructs by 19 participants), to feel comfortable (23 constructs by 15 participants), and the need to feel safe (34 constructs by 16 participants). Besides, *Well-being* shows a strong positive relationship with the categories *Trip Characteristics* ($r_s = .494, p = .0041$), the *Landscape View* (r_s

$= .503, p = .0033)$ and the *Physical Comfort* $(r_s = .481, p = .0053)$. This means, that these factors have an impact on passengers' perceived *Well-being*.

Trip: The feeling of convenience is also influenced by the characteristics of the trip itself. Participants mentioned that a convenient passenger experience is about a joyful and exciting trip rather than a stressful trip (e.g., "Relaxed trip vs. Stressful trip", P8). It is also rather a private, voluntary leisure ride without time pressure (e.g., "No time pressure vs. Time pressure", P1; "Leisure, private trip vs. Professional trip", P33) than a business trip. Therefore, adding additional *Stops & Breaks* to discover new places or taking time to go to a restaurant on a journey contribute to a positive experience, (e.g., "Spontaneous breaks vs. Mandatory breaks", P28). This is in line with the quantitative observation which shows a strong positive relationship between the *Landscape View* and the *Trip Type* $(r_s = .488, p = .0047)$.

Social: Constructs that relate to the social aspects in the car highlight the importance of having *Conversations* and staying connected with others. 19 of 32 participants mentioned that having general conversations contribute to their most convenient passenger ride. Another 15 participants appreciate to especially talk about fun and non-private topics (e.g., "Fun talk vs. Serious talk", P1). Besides, the factor *Togetherness*, more precisely the contact with others by having group conversations or playing games together is a convenience factor (e.g., "Communicate with others in the car vs. Silence", P9; "To play verbal games vs. Don't play verbal games", P3). In terms of the social situation in the car, results show a strong negative relationship between *Conversations* and the *Number of People* in the car $(r_s = -.490, p = .0044)$ which can be described by the difficulty to talk with people in the front when sitting in the back (e.g., "Can hear what people in the front tell when sitting in the front vs. Cannot hear what people in the front tell when sitting in the back", P1).

Outside Environment: Our data unveil the importance of the *Outside Environment* to experience a convenient ride as 127 out of the 128 constructs received high ratings. The convenience of the outside environment mainly refers to have a scenic view to enjoy the landscape (26 of 32 participants). This means, that passengers prefer to drive along panoramic roads to be able to explore new areas (e.g., "Explore new places vs. Drive along known places", P20; "[take a] panoramic road vs. [take the] shortest route", P26). This is again qualitative measurable by a strong relationship between the *Landscape View* & the *Trip Type* $(r_s = .488, p = .0047)$. Besides watching the beautiful scenery, participants mentioned the need to observe both the traffic and driving situation to stay situationally aware (e.g., "Better overview of the driving situation/Less overview of the driving situation", P2).

Safety: Only 78 constructs relate to the overreaching category of passenger's *Safety* (personal safety and driving safety), as safety might be considered a prerequisite. It is likely that participants thought there is no need to explicitly mention such aspects. However, over 50% of the mentioned constructs related to *Safety* were rated as most important which results in the second-highest average rating score of 6.23. This means that *Safety*, can have a strong impact on the perceived level of convenience. Especially the condition of the car itself (e.g., "A serviced car vs. A non-serviced car", P17) to avoid breakdowns and the available driving assistant functions are mentioned aspects that constitute to a convenient experience (e.g., "Driver assistance systems for relaxation as a passenger vs. No driver assistance system", P29). Also, our data shows the dependencies that other categories have on *Safety:* For instance, the overall *Safety* situation has a statistically strong relationship to the level of *Trust towards the driver* ($r_s = .455, p = .0089$) and how *safe a passenger feels* ($r_s = .509, p = .0029$).

Driving Behavior: With a high mean rating of 6 (see Table 5), *Driving Behavior* constitutes as well to a convenient passenger experience. 22 of our 32 participants mainly refer to a reasonable *Driving Style* which incorporates anticipatory driving (e.g., "anticipatory driving style vs. quick braking and tailgating", P14) and proactive braking (e.g., "Proactive baking vs. abrupt braking", P28). The analysis of the relations unveils that there is a significant positive correlation between *Driving Style* and *Driver's Focus* (the driver focusing on the driving task – category Safety) ($r_s = .638, p = .0001$). In addition, over 50% (17/32) of the participants mentioned that they prefer a reasonable speed level relative to the road condition and traffic situation.

Co-Driver: *Being a Co-driver* and having the possibility to assist or alert the driver

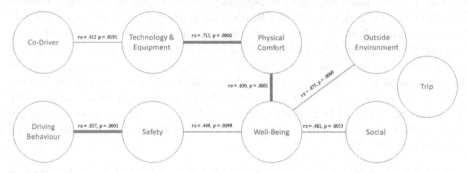

Fig. 2. The relationships between the nine overarching categories: significant, positive correlations are highlighted in dark green while strong, positive relations are demonstrated in light green. (Color figure online)

makes the ride more convenient for 18 participants. However, the level of importance of this category compared to the other ones is rather low as demonstrated in Table 5 by the average rating (5.0) and the proportion of least important rated constructs (8.82%). Nevertheless, over 50% of participants referred to co-driver tasks when talking about convenience. Such tasks are mainly about supporting the navigation and being responsible for music (e.g., "Support with navigation vs. Do not support with navigation", P8). This can also be observed by the strong positive correlations that *Being a Co-Driver* has with *Control* ($r_s = .488, p = .0047$), *Audio Content* ($r_s = .488, p = .0047$) and the *Navigation System* ($r_s = .503, p = .0033$). Another reported convenience aspect is the possibility to stay aware of the situation to be able to alert the driver in case dangerous situations occur (e.g., "To warn the driver about situations vs. No control over what the driver is doing", P13).

To summarize our results, the passenger's most convenient ride is a combination of nine overreaching factors that do relate to and influence each other. The overall relationships between those are visualized in Fig. 2.

5 Discussion and Design Recommendations for a Convenient In-Car Passenger Experience

For users of cars common-sense proffers several attributes of in-car experiences that contribute to a pleasant and convenient passenger experience. However, in the lack of a systematic study to evaluate whether these assumptions hold, our repertory grid study attempted to both generate novel insights on passenger convenience but also to validate the common-sense driven observations. The insights from our study confirm several of these assumptions but also reveal novel insights on other aspects of passenger experiences in cars that lead to a feeling of convenience.

Overall, our results confirm the assumption that well-being, physical comfort, and safety are the main factors for a convenient in-car passenger experience. To ensure that passengers perceive a ride as safe and convenient, the relationship to all occupants and the trust towards the driver is important. Regarding technological equipment, we give insights into the importance of information seeking, personalization, recommendations, and connectivity for passengers' external devices. In the following, we discuss our findings and summarize them in the form of design recommendations.

These design recommendations result from in-depth discussion and brainstorming of the authors, based on the identified categories. The focus lies especially on short-term product or service innovations that enable integration into current cars. In addition, they outline important aspects for the next generation of manually driven cars which should be considered by future in-vehicle interface designers.

Enable (Shared) Control of Functions. Our results show that controlling in-car systems evidently is a basic need that does not refer to the driver only. For a convenient experience, 75% of our participants think that controlling a device and having access to settings and functions is essential. Overall, passengers want to be able to change things by themselves, instead of relying on others. An established example of this fact is the invention of air conditioning with separate climate zones that enable individual access and controllability [55]. Besides that, we see the trend of dedicated rear-seat infotainment systems that give backseat passengers access to the internet and media-based services [9]. Other researchers investigated infotainment systems that provide especially passengers with information about points of interests [5, 37]. In addition, the positive correlation between the categories *Control & Navigation System* and *Control & Air Conditioning* unveils that driver-based functionalities are frequently used by and important for passengers, too. However, current infotainment systems still neglect passengers since the design focuses mainly on the driver [39, 41]. Thus, we see a clear need for future designers and developers to better integrate the passenger's role and needs when investigating in-car control functions.

> To enable a convenient passenger experience, future cars should be equipped with more passenger-dedicated services that align with passengers' need for controllability and access to functions. A key factor for a more convenient passenger experience is the ability to share control of functions between driver and passenger.

Allow for Connectivity and Technology and Support Personalization. Our results provide deep insights into the convenience aspects of the interactive in-car space. Regarding technological services, our data unveil the necessity of entertainment features as most constructs refer to this category. This is in line with previous suggestions by Meschtscherjakov et al. [41] and it confirms the importance of the investigations related to video and gaming services (e.g., [5, 40]). It also shows that entertainment services that are currently provided in mainly luxury cars are appreciated (e.g., [9]). Besides that, 30 of 32 participants report the importance of services that personalize and recommend content based on their preferences (e.g., audio content). Personalization in this case is not limited to entertainment. It also refers to route choices (e.g., panoramic road, route along sights) and physical aspects like individual temperatures. Looking at current cars we see already different ways of personalization like the seat that automatically adjusts to the driver or the pre-selection of the favorite radio channel when starting the car [7]. However, these features rather focus on the driver than on passengers. In addition, passenger convenience refers to the possibility to connect personal devices with the in-car environment. This was especially expressed by connecting the smartphone via Bluetooth to the in-car radio system ("Own Bluetooth music vs. Radio", P14). While current cars offer a basic integration of external devices (especially smartphone ↔ infotainment system), this integration is mostly limited to one device (owned by the driver) [8, 41]. However, passengers also bring their personal devices into the car and want to use them during a ride on a regular basis [37].

> To enhance passenger convenience, designers need to focus on improving and extending entertainment features and support the connectivity to personal devices beyond the driver's phone. Besides that, a higher level of personalization for both entertainment and physical aspects is needed to enhance passengers' convenience.

Design for Co-driving Experiences in the Car. Over 56% of the participants reported that being involved in the driving situation by acting as a co-driver contributes to a convenient riding experience. Reported co-driver episodes relate mainly to support activities like programming the navigation system or alerting the driver in case of dangerous situations, rather than on direct driving-related tasks (e.g., steering the car). Therefore, passengers prefer to sit in the front to be able to best contribute to the ride. This is to some extent in line with previous findings of co-driver activities by Meschtscherjakov et al. [41] and Gridling et al. [26]. Besides that, research shows that co-driving activities help the driver to minimize workload and to reduce distraction [14, 35]. With this regard, we see the need to design for a higher level of co-driving experience to relieve the driver and to enhance passengers riding experience.

> As co-driver activities reduce driver distraction and enhance passenger convenience, it is essential to design with the co-driving experience in mind. Therefore, future driving supportive services should be usable by front seat as well as by back seat passengers to best support convenient riding experiences.

Design for Engagement with the Surrounding and Creation of Memories. The out-side environment has a major impact on passengers' perceived convenience as this was reported by 81% of our participants. This especially refers to the landscape view and the possibility to observe sites through the window. Thus, our data confirm the need for contextual interfaces to support riding experience [30] and demonstrate the importance of past investigations that show information about the surrounding attractions (e.g., [5, 37]). Besides that, the creation of memories is important to experience a highly conve-nient ride. Therefore, it is advised to guide users through new areas and to recommend unusual routes or panoramic roads. Another aspect lies in the possibility to engage with the surroundings. Thus, we see an enormous potential for new innovations and techno-logical developments that should be extended to the use by passengers (e.g., augmented reality or virtual reality interfaces and systems [39]).

> To design for the most convenient ride, the integration of contextual information is key. Thus, we see the potential of creating positive memories through the engage-ment with the outside world and by recommending panoramic roads or routes with a high density of sites.

Design for Well-Being and Comfort. Overall, we confirm the assumption that well-being is a main factor of passenger's perceived convenience. Overall, the results are in line with Wilfinger et al. [56] who report that well-being combines the perception of feeling comfortable and relaxed, especially during long trips. Designing for a high level of comfort and well-being relates mainly to our assumptions about comfort qualities of the car like avoiding motion-sickness, supporting safety, providing an ergonomic seat, and guarantee enough physical space. Besides that, our data unveil that passenger's comfort and well-being are highly influenced by the level of trust towards the driver, the overall physical comfort, the outside environment, and the social situation in the car. Thus, it correlates highly with other design recommendations. However, the possibility to relax and feel comfortable depends on physical comforts such as an ergonomic and adjustable seat, a perfect temperature, and the right perception of space. Looking at current cars, an adjustable seat for front-seat passengers is standard, while also additional comfort functions like an integrated seat massage are already established in luxury lines (e.g., BMW 7 series[3]). Nevertheless, we still see a huge design potential for in-car experiences that can contribute to passenger's well-being and comfort, especially when it comes to the integration of external devices like body-posture support systems or wearables.

> Well-being and comfort are essential requirements when it comes to passengers' most convenient rides. While the design for these factors is already established, a huge potential still lies in integrating external devices that improve well-being in order to increase the riding experience.

---

[3] BMW   7:   http://content.bmwusa.com/microsite/7series_2013/com/en/newvehicles/7series/ sedan/2012/showroom/convenience/driving_comfort.html#t=l, last accessed: 2021/01/26.

Support Social Connectedness within the Car. When designing with passengers in mind it is important to consider the social situation within the car to allow passengers to experience a convenient ride. As our data shows, 93.75% of the participants like to have conversations when riding. This seems obvious and has already been discussed in the literature [41, 56]. However, recent technological considerations like in-car virtual reality applications focus more on the individual passenger than on the group interaction [39]. Besides that, we found that a convenient ride is rather a leisure or vacation ride with friends or family members than a business trip with colleagues or less known people. This confirms mentioned riding situations in literature that passengers prefer [30]. During rides with loved ones, our results unveil that passengers strive for a feeling of togetherness. This is to some extent in line with the need for relatedness to people inside/outside the car and by using the time to catch up with family-related things as reported by Gkouskos et al. [24]. Thus, the aspect of social connectedness is essential for perceived passenger convenience. This also incorporates the ability to allow for better communication between the front and the back as previously investigated with the integration of several microphones and speakers [52]. But activities that contribute to social connectedness can go beyond traditional conversations. Desired features, therefore, range from in-car games [40] to sharing information with other occupants [5, 42] or to support group decisions (e.g., shared music playlist). Thus, we see a clear need to explore the design space to support the feeling of togetherness through future in-vehicle systems in more detail.

> When riding with familiar people, there is a clear need to enhance the feeling of togetherness by allowing group decisions and information sharing. Thus, the development of future in-vehicle systems that support social connectedness is essential to establish a convenient passenger experience.

Information Access is Important for Convenient User Experiences. Passengers want to stay connected with the outside world, but they also want to explicitly connect with the activity or ride they are currently undertaking. Overall, trip-related information to enhance passenger experience was already proposed by Inbar & Tractinsky [30]. However, 20 of 32 participants unveil the need to receive information beyond the time of arrival, speed level, or traffic jams. This especially refers to information about the direct surroundings and having access to both local and global news. First attempts have already been made by showing reduced information about attractions [5]. While current rear-seat infotainment systems with access to the Internet are already established [9], we still see the need to investigate the integration of information access based on passenger's needs and preferences. This means to better embed information-based service to the in-car infrastructure and to selectively deciding what information to display when and how, to best support passenger's convenience.

> Information about the ride and the outside world is important to the support riding experience. Therefore, future in-car applications should selectively provide access to information, based on passenger preferences and needs.

Consider Passenger Safety Perception. While safety received fewer constructs compared to other categories, over 57.7% of the mentioned ones were rated with the highest possible importance value of 7. Thus, our results confirm the assumptions of the need to arrive safely without any major troubles like breakdowns or accidents and outline the importance of safety perception. However, the subjective feeling of being safe does not only refer to the driving situation but also depends on the relationship with the driver, as already reported by Inbar and Tractinsky [30]. Also, our data unveil that this feeling gets influenced by passenger's level of trust towards the driver as they wish for a responsible driving style and a speed level that aligns well with the road and traffic situation. In addition, the use of driving assistance systems (ADAS) does not only impact drivers' experiences [24] as our data shows. The use of an ADAS, like (adaptive) cruise control, is highly appreciated by passengers as it improves their convenience level positively. Therefore, we envision to better inform passengers about the status of such assistive systems to enhance their safety feeling as well as their level of trust towards the driver.

> The overall feeling of safety has highest priority for passengers and impacts their convenient riding experience centrally. Therefore, to improve the passengers' safety perception future vehicle concepts should a) aim for a higher level of trust between the passenger and the driver and b) better inform the passenger about the use and status of ADAS features.

Our design recommendations outline important factors when it comes to the design of technology-driven features and products that can easily be brought into current cars or that can be applied on top of existing in-car services. All recommendations were derived from the nine investigated convenience factors that we combined with findings from prior work in this field. Our results are possibly limited by the choice of our method: As the repertory grid method allows to explore a topic in depth, both qualitatively and quantitatively, it does not allow to identify hierarchical relationships of constructs mentioned after each other. Given the explorative nature, where each participant may produce different constructs which contribute to convenience, the frequencies do not provide a ground truth across all participants but indicate the importance of certain topics. In addition, we are aware that the employed convenience sampling to find our participants might influence our findings. Nevertheless, the sample represents participants from diverse age groups and is nearly gender-balanced. As our results are indicative for Europe, they may not fully generalize beyond Europe. Besides that, another limitation of any method involving users (and no domain experts) is that participants rather think about their daily lives, and we therefore might miss visionary aspects for future concepts. However, we do not see this as a true limitation, as our goal was to explore the design space from a user's perspective, and in addition, the automotive industry typically designs for evolution rather than using disruptive approaches leading to a revolution.

6   Conclusion

By means of a repertory grid study we investigated aspects that constitute to passengers' convenient riding experience in a human-driven car. Our interviews extend prior work,verify common-sense assumptions, and we unveil what aspects designers should focus on when designing in-car applications with the passenger in mind, especially when it comes to innovations that allow for easy integration into current cars. The interviews provided broad and deep insights into qualitative aspects that constitute a convenient riding experience. We condensed this information into a set of eight design recommendations that give an overview of the design space and provide future developers and designers with directions to best support passenger experiences. Beyond the assumptions of basic needs for well-being, physical comfort, and safety, passengers highly value access to in-vehicle systems. More precisely this relates to the possibility for shared control and an extensive integration of external devices, connectivity, and personalization. We, therefore, see the need for designing the co-driving experience, i.e., the creation of a shared experience when using in-vehicle systems during a joint ride with a passenger. Contradicting with concepts that advertise personal virtual reality experiences in cars [38], the interviews revealed that social connectedness is another essential aspect that constitutes to passenger's most convenient ride. Thus, the key for the next generation of in-car user interfaces will be the ability to make the whole journey for everyone in the car a shared experience. By enabling everyone to participate in this experience actively if they wish to or to enhance the journey with the ability to create shared memories seems promising. We conducted the interviews in central Europe, which is one of the core markets for automotive manufacturers. While future research should investigate whether cultural differences exist in other markets, we see our work as an essential starting point for the design of a shared user experience for manual car rides and in-car technology that takes driver and passengers into account. While revolutionary design and inventions are much desired, the industry is mostly bound to gradual improvements, for instance, to comply with safety and security requirements. Following the task-artifact cycle [11], which proposes continuous adaptations of existing systems to (changed) user needs, our findings match this approach of evolutionary design and suggest incremental improvements in future vehicles.

References

1. Ahmadpour, N., Lindgaard, G., Robert, J., Pownall, B.: The thematic structure of passenger comfort experience and its relationship to the context features in the aircraft cabin. Ergonomics **57**, 801–815 (2014). https://doi.org/10.1080/00140139.2014.899632
2. Baxter, D., Goffin, K., Szwejczewski, M.: The repertory grid technique as a customer insight method. Res. Technol. Manage. **57**, 35–42 (2014)
3. Bengler, K.: Driver and driving experience in cars. In: Meixner, G., Müller, C. (eds.) Automotive User Interfaces. HIS, pp. 79–94. Springer, Cham (2017). https://doi.org/10.1007/978-3-319-49448-7_3
4. Berger, M., Dandekar, A., Bernhaupt, R., Pfleging, B.: An AR-enabled interactive car door to extend in-car infotainment systems for rear seat passengers. In: Extended Abstracts CHI EA 2021, Article 404. ACM (2021). https://doi.org/10.1145/3411763.3451589
5. Berger, M., Bernhaupt, R., Pfleging, B.: A tactile interaction concept for in-car passenger infotainment systems. In: 11th International Conference on Automotive User Interfaces and Interactive Vehicular Applications: Adjunct Proceedings, Utrecht, pp. 109–114. ACM (2019). https://doi.org/10.1145/3349263.3351914

6. Bernard, T., Flitman, A.: Using repertory grid analysis to gather qualitative data for information systems research. In: 15th Australasian Conference on Information Systems, pp. 1–12. ACIS (2002)
7. BMW Driver Profiles. https://www.bmw.ca/en/topics/experience/connected-drive/a-to-z.html. Accessed 26 Jan 2021
8. BMW Mobile Office. http://content.bmwusa.com/microsite/7series_2013/com/en/newveh icles/7series/sedan/2012/showroom/convenience/bluetooth-office.html#t=l. Accessed 26 Jan 2021
9. BMW 7 series rear-seat entertainment. http://content.bmwusa.com/microsite/7series_2013/com/en/newvehicles/7series/sedan/2012/showroom/interior-design/rear-entertainment.htm l#t=l. Accessed 26 Jan 2021
10. Boll, S., Kun, A., Fröhlich, P., Foley, J.: Automotive user interface research moves into fast lane. In: Extended Abstracts CHI EA 2013, pp. 2525–2528. ACM (2013). https://doi.org/10.1145/2468356.2468821
11. Bos, J.: Less sickness with more motion and/or mental distraction. J. Vestib. Res. Equilib. Orientat. **25**, 23–33 (2015). https://doi.org/10.3233/VES-150541
12. BTS 2001 national household travel survey. https://www.bts.gov/archive/publications/highli ghts_of_the_2001_national_household_travel_survey/section_02. Accessed 15 Sept 2020
13. Carroll, J., Kellogg, W., Rosson, M.: The Task-Artifact Cycle, pp. 74–102. Cambridge University Press, USA (1991)
14. Charlton, S., Starkey, N.: Co-driving: passenger actions and distractions. Accid. Anal. Prev. **144**, 105624 (2020). https://doi.org/10.1016/j.aap.2020.105624
15. Clauss, T., Döppe, S.: Why do urban travellers select multimodal travel options: a repertory grid analysis. Transp. Res. Part A Policy Pract. **93**, 93–116 (2016). https://doi.org/10.1016/j.tra.2016.08.021
16. da Silva, M.: Measurements of comfort in vehicles. Meas. Sci. Technol. **13**, R41–R60 (2002). https://doi.org/10.1088/0957-0233/13/6/201
17. Diener, E., Oishi, S., Lucas, R.: Subjective well-being: the science of happiness and life satisfaction. In: Lopes, S., Snyder, C. (eds.) The Oxford Handbook of Positive Psychology. Oxford University Press, Oxford (2002)
18. Edwards, H., McDonald, S., Young, S.: The repertory grid technique: its place in empirical software engineering research. Inf. Softw. Technol. **51**, 785–798 (2009). https://doi.org/10.1016/j.infsof.2008.08.008
19. Elbanhawi, M., Simic, M., Jazar, R.: In the passenger seat: investigating ride comfort measures in autonomous cars. IEEE Intell. Transp. Syst. Mag. **7**, 4–17 (2015). https://doi.org/10.1109/MITS.2015.2405571
20. International Organization for Standardization. 2018. ISO 9241-20, Ergonomics of human-system interaction – Part 11: Usability: Definitions and concepts. https://www.iso.org/obp/ui/#iso:std:63500:en
21. Forlizzi J., Battarbee, K.: Understanding experience in interactive systems. In: Proceedings of the 5th Conference on Designing Interactive Systems: Processes, Practices, Methods, and Techniques, Cambridge, pp. 261–268. ACM (2004). https://doi.org/10.1145/1013115.101 3152
22. Fransella, F., Bell, R., Bannister, D.: A Manual for Repertory Grid Technique, 2nd edn. Wiley, Hoboken (2004)
23. Gkouskos, D., Normark, C., Lundgren, S.: What drivers really want: investigating dimensions in automobile user needs. Int. J. Des. **8**, 59–71 (2014)
24. Gkouskos, D., Pettersson, I., Karlsson, M., Chen, F.: Exploring user experience in the wild: facets of the modern car. In: Marcus, A. (ed.) DUXU 2015. LNCS, vol. 9188, pp. 450–461. Springer, Cham (2015). https://doi.org/10.1007/978-3-319-20889-3_42

25. Goffin, K., Micheli, P., Koners, U., Szwejczewski, M.: Benefits and limitations of using the repertory grid technique in management research. Acad. Manage. Proc. **2012**, 11080 (2012). https://doi.org/10.5465/AMBPP.2012.11080abstract
26. Gridling, N., Meschtscherjakov, A., Tscheligi, M.: I need help! Exploring collaboration in the car. In: Proceedings of the ACM 2012 Conference on Computer Supported Cooperative Work Companion, Seattle, pp. 87–90. ACM (2012). https://doi.org/10.1145/2141512.2141549
27. Hassenzahl, M., Wessler, R.: Capturing design space from a user perspective: the repertory grid technique revisited. Int. J. Hum. Comput. Interact. **12**, 441–459 (2000). https://doi.org/10.1080/10447318.2000.9669070
28. Holst, J., Hedman, J., Kjeldsen, M., Tan, F.: Payment instrument characteristics: a repertory grid analysis. In: Americas Conference on Information Systems, AMCIS (2015)
29. Huang, W., Shuai, B.: A methodology for calculating the passenger comfort benefits of railway travel. J. Mod. Transp. **26**(2), 107–118 (2018). https://doi.org/10.1007/s40534-018-0157-y
30. Inbar, O., Tractinsky, N.: Make a trip an experience: sharing in-car information with passengers. In: Extended Abstracts on Human Factors in Computing Systems, Vancouver. ACM (2011). https://doi.org/10.1145/1979742.1979755
31. International Organization for Standardization. Ergonomics of Human-System Interaction – Part 210: Human-Centred Design for Interactive Systems (2019)
32. Kawaf, F., Tagg, S.: The construction of online shopping experience: a repertory grid approach. Comput. Hum. Behav. **72**, 222–232 (2017). https://doi.org/10.1016/j.chb.2017.02.055
33. Kelly, G.: A theory of Personality: The Psychology of Personal Constructs. W. W. Norton, Oxford (1963)
34. Kwak, M., Hornbæk, K., Markopoulos, P., Bruns, M.: The design space of shape-changing interfaces. In: Proceedings of the 2014 Conference on Designing Interactive Systems. ACM (2014). https://doi.org/10.1145/2598510.2598573
35. Lee, C., Abdel-Aty, M.: Presence of passengers: does it increase or reduce driver's crash potential? Accid. Anal. Prev. **40**(5), 1703–1712 (2008). https://doi.org/10.1016/j.aap.2008.06.006
36. De Looze, M., Kuijt-Evers, L., Van Dieen, J.: Sitting comfort and discomfort and the relationships with objective measures. Ergonomics **46**(10), 985–997 (2003). https://doi.org/10.1080/0014013031000121977
37. Matsumura, K., Kirk, D.: On active passengering: supporting in-car experiences. In: Proceedings of the ACM on Interactive, Mobile, Wearable and Ubiquitous Technologies, vol. 1, no. 4, p. 154 (2018). https://doi.org/10.1145/3161176
38. Mayring, P.: Qualitative content analysis. Analysis **1**(2), FQS (2000)
39. McGill, M., Brewster, S.: Virtual reality passenger experiences. In: Proceedings of the 11th International Conference on Automotive User Interfaces and Interactive Vehicular Applications: Adjunct Proceedings, Utrecht. ACM (2019). https://doi.org/10.1145/3349263.3351330
40. Meschtscherjakov, A., et al.: Active corners: collaborative in-car interaction design. In: Proceedings of the 2016 ACM Conference on Designing Interactive Systems. ACM (2016). https://doi.org/10.1145/2901790.2901872
41. Meschtscherjakov, A., Wilfinger, D., Gridling, N., Neureiter, N., Tscheligi, M.: Capture the car! Qualitative in-situ methods to grasp the automotive context. In: Proceedings of the 3rd International Conference on Automotive User Interfaces and Interactive Vehicular Applications, Salzburg. ACM (2011). https://doi.org/10.1145/2381416.2381434
42. NHTS. https://nhts.ornl.gov/. Accessed 12 Sept 2020
43. Osswald, S., Sundström, P., Tscheligi, M.: The front seat passenger: how to transfer qualitative findings into design. Int. J. Veh. Technol. **2013**(07), 1687–5702 (2013). https://doi.org/10.1155/2013/972570

44. Oxford English Directory: comfort. https://www-oed-com.emedien.ub.uni-muenchen.de/view/Entry/36890?rskey=rmo0x3&result=1. Accessed 11 Sept 2020

45. Perterer, N., Sundström, P., Meschtscherjakov, A., Wilfinger, D., Tscheligi, M.: Come drive with me: an ethnographicstudy of driver-passenger pairs to inform future in-car assistance. In: Proceedings of the 2013 Conference on Computer Supported Cooperative Work, San Antonio. ACM (2013). https://doi.org/10.1145/2441776.2441952

46. Pfleging, B., Rang, M., Broy, N.: Investigating user needs for non-driving-related activities during automated driving. In: Proceedings of the 15th International Conference on Mobile and Ubiquitous Multimedia, Rovaniemi. ACM (2016). https://doi.org/10.1145/3012709.3012735

47. Pike, S.: The use of repertory grid analysis and importance-performance analysis to identify determinant attributes of universities. J. Mark. High. Educ. **14**(2), 1–18 (2005). https://doi.org/10.1300/J050v14n02_01

48. Pradhan, S., Samantaray, A., Bhattarcharyya, R.: Evaluation of ride comfort in a railway passenger vehicle with integrated vehicle and human body bond graph model. In: ASME International Mechanical Engineering Congress and Exposition, vol. 12 (2017). https://doi.org/10.1115/IMECE2017-71288

49. Richards, L., Jacobson, I., Kuhlthau, A.: What the passenger contributes to passenger comfort. Appl. Ergon. **9**(3), 137–142 (1978). https://doi.org/10.1016/0003-6870(78)90003-0

50. Sauer, V., Mertens, A., Heitland, J., Nitsch, V.: Exploring the concept of passenger well-being in the context of automated driving. Int. J. Hum. Factors Ergon. **6**(3), 227–248 (2019). https://doi.org/10.1504/IJHFE.2019.104594

51. Shove, E.: Converging conventions of comfort, cleanliness and convenience. J. Consum. Policy **26**(12), 395–418 (2003). https://doi.org/10.1023/A:1026362829781

52. Tai, G., Kern, D., Schmidt, A.: Bridging the communication gap: a driver-passenger video link. In: Wandke, H., Kain, S., Struve, D. (eds.) Mensch & Computer 2009: Grenzenlos frei!?, pp. 73–82. Oldenbourg Verlag, München (2009). https://doi.org/10.1524/9783486598551.73

53. Tomico, O., Karapanos, E., Lévy, P., Mizutani, N., Yamanaka, T.: The repertory grid technique as a method for the study of cultural differences. Int. J. Des. **3**(3), 55–63 (2009)

54. Vink, P., Bazley, C., Kamp, I., Blok, M.: Possibilities to improve the aircraft interior comfort experience. Appl. Ergon. **43**(2), 354–359 (2012). https://doi.org/10.1016/j.apergo.2011.06.011

55. Volkswagen 4-zone electronic air conditioning. https://www.volkswagen.co.uk/technology/comfort/air-conditioning-and-climate-control. Accessed 26 Jan 2021

56. Wilfinger, D., Meschtscherjakov, A., Murer, M., Osswald, S., Tscheligi, M.: Are we there yet? A probing study to inform design for the rear seat of family cars. In: Campos, P., Graham, N., Jorge, J., Nunes, N., Palanque, P., Winckler, M. (eds.) INTERACT 2011. LNCS, vol. 6947, pp. 657–674. Springer, Heidelberg (2011). https://doi.org/10.1007/978-3-642-23771-3_48

Exploring Application Opportunities for Smart Vehicles in the Continuous Interaction Space Inside and Outside the Vehicle

Laura-Bianca Bilius[1], Radu-Daniel Vatavu[1(✉)], and Nicolai Marquardt[2]

[1] MintViz Lab — MANSiD Research Center, Ştefan cel Mare University of Suceava, 720229 Suceava, Romania
{laura.bilius,radu.vatavu}@usm.ro
[2] University College London, London, UK
n.marquardt@ucl.ac.uk

Abstract. We describe applications that implement interactions between the driver and their smart vehicle in a *continuous interaction space* characterized by the physical distance to the vehicle and by the smart devices that implement those interactions. Specifically, we demonstrate the principles of smart vehicle proxemics with smart rings, smartwatches, smartphones, and other devices employed to interact with the in-vehicle infotainment system while the driver traverses five distinctly identifiable zones, from inside the vehicle to the personal, proximal, distant, and covert zone outside the vehicle. We present engineering details of our applications that capitalize on standardized web technology (HTML, CSS, JavaScript), communication protocols (WebSocket), and data formats (JSON) and, thus, enable straightforward extension to accommodate other smart devices for new interactions with smart vehicles. We also point to future opportunities for designing interactions from a distance and function of the distance between the driver and their vehicle.

Keywords: Smart vehicles · Connected vehicles · Proxemic interactions · Smart ring · Smartwatch · Wearables · Engineering interactive systems

1 Introduction

Smart vehicles embed a variety of sensing and processing systems to enable interactions with the driver and the passengers, but also with a variety of entities around the vehicle, such as other vehicles, buildings, road infrastructure, and pedestrians [22]. Prior work on interacting with smart vehicles has focused almost entirely on in-vehicle input [5,8] and proposed a variety of gesture, voice, eye gaze, and multimedia input techniques for applications inside the vehicle.

© IFIP International Federation for Information Processing 2021
Published by Springer Nature Switzerland AG 2021
C. Ardito et al. (Eds.): INTERACT 2021, LNCS 12933, pp. 140–149, 2021.
https://doi.org/10.1007/978-3-030-85616-8_10

Recent work [6] has brought a new perspective in this landscape by formalizing outside-the-vehicle interactions, where drivers interact with vehicles from a distance.

In this paper, we explore interactions with the vehicle performed outside the vehicle from the perspective of a *continuous interaction space*. Within this continuous space, drivers interact fluently with their vehicle as they approach and enter the vehicle or as they exit the vehicle and walk away, while the in-vehicle system and the drivers' mobile and wearable devices are aware of and effectively exploit the physical distance between the driver and the vehicle. To demonstrate the opportunities of this continuum, we present several interactions with a smart vehicle, e.g., *implicit interaction*, when data from the vehicle is stored on an NFC ring worn by the driver, and *explicit interaction* when the driver remotely connects using their smartphone to the in-vehicle infotainment system to resume music playing from the vehicle's playlist. We present the engineering details of four web-based applications designed for a smart ring, smartwatch, smartphone, and a desktop computer. By interpreting interactions with the vehicle as occurring in a continuous space defined by both the physical distance to the vehicle and the smart devices to implement those interactions, new opportunities open for designing rich user experiences for drivers when outside their vehicles.

2   Related Work

We synthesize prior work addressing interactions inside the vehicle, and we connect to the scientific literature on proxemic interactions and, especially, its recent application to smart vehicles [6] enabling outside-the-vehicle interactions.

2.1   Interactions with Smart Vehicles

In-vehicle interactions have been studied to a large extent, and many techniques have been proposed to increase driving safety and journey comfort. These include techniques based on gestures [9], voice input [2], eye gaze [23], and multimodal interactions [8]; see Bilius and Vatavu's [4] overview of input modalities for media consumption inside the vehicle. Each modality comes with specific benefits for drivers. For instance, gesture-based interfaces informed by elicitation studies [9] should be highly intuitive to drivers as they capitalize on gestures reflective of users' behaviors and mental models for interacting inside the vehicle; voice input enables drivers to keep their hands on the steering wheel and eyes on the road [2]; finger-augmentation devices, such as smart rings, open the possibility to interact with the vehicle by transferring controls from the steering wheel to the fingers [10]; and multimodal input techniques enable switching between various input modalities according to the specific context on the road and driver's preferences [8]. While these interactions have been proposed for the space inside the vehicle, a recent work [6] has shown that interactions outside the vehicle are equally relevant for drivers, and formalized such interactions with the proxemics theory [12]. We discuss this direction next from the perspective of a timeline of milestones in proxemic interactions and autonomous and smart vehicles.

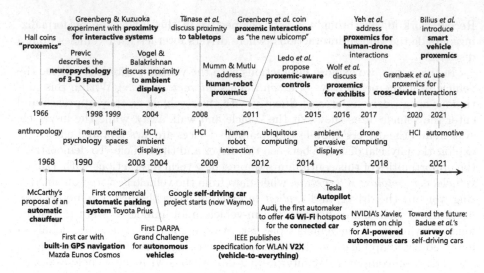

Fig. 1. A timeline of proxemic interactions (top) and autonomous vehicles (bottom) representing the recent context in which we position our work and contributions.

2.2   Proxemic Interactions and Smart Vehicles

The concept, principles, and tools of proxemic interaction [3,12,18] enable the design and engineering of interactive computing systems that employ the relative distance and orientation of users and other objects from the physical environment to adapt and react accordingly. Figure 1, top shows a timeline of investigations on proxemic interactions and applications to various areas—informed by Hall's [14] seminal proxemics theory, Previc's [21] neuropsychology of 3D space, and Greenberg and Kuzuoka's [11] original experiments with digital and physical surrogates as mediators for human interaction. Notable applications have targeted ambient displays [28], tabletops [27], robots [20], drones [30], smart homes [17], museum exhibits [29], and cross-device input [13]. The most recent application of proxemic interaction has addressed smart vehicles to enable interactions outside the vehicle [6]. Figure 1, bottom complements this timeline with milestones of research on autonomous and smart vehicles, from McCarthy's [19] vision of an automatic chauffeur at the onsets of AI to the Vehicle-to-Everything (V2X) specification [22], 4G Wi-Fi for vehicles [16], and self-driving cars [7].

At the intersection of proxemic interactions and smart vehicles, Bilius et al. [6] introduced the smart vehicle proxemics framework with a conceptual space for formalizing interactions outside the vehicle according to (i) the physical distance between the driver and the vehicle, (ii) the paradigm to interact with the vehicle, and (iii) the driver's goal. The framework specifies five proximity zones with respect to the vehicle: *inside* the vehicle, *personal* (the driver is close to the vehicle that they can easily reach and touch it), *proximal* (the driver is close to the vehicle, but far enough so that they cannot touch it), *distant* (the driver is farther away, but the vehicle is still in their visual field), and *covert* (the driver cannot see their vehicle). The authors proposed the rough guidelines of 1 m, 10 m, and 100 m to delineate these zones in relation to operating ranges of Class 1, 2, and 3 Bluetooth communications, a technology commonly used in smartphones, smartwatches, smart bracelets, etc. However, the framework has remained theoretical and applications yet to be demonstrated. In this work, we demonstrate interactions for mobile and wearable devices in a continuous space that starts inside the vehicle and ends in the covert zone.

3   Applications in the Continuous Interaction Space Inside and Outside the Vehicle

We illustrate the smart vehicle proxemics framework [6] with concrete interactive applications for mobile and wearable devices. We demonstrate interactions that span across the continuous space that starts with the driver inside the vehicle and follows the driver as it departs from the vehicle. In this space, the goals of the driver change as a function of the distance to their car, and those goals are accomplished with different devices, e.g., a smart ring when near the vehicle or a desktop computer when the user is in the comfort of their home. To this end, we consider the following support story to introduce our applications:

"Mary and Emma are long time friends. One day, they plan a trip to a nearby city with many attractions. It takes them a while to get there by car, so the two decide to listen to music to make the time pass faster—the new album of their favorite band that Mary has already uploaded to the infotainment system of her car. After two hours, they arrive at their destination. Mary parks the car and, while locking the vehicle, she touches the door handle just briefly, which is enough for data from the vehicle to be transferred to the smart ring from her finger. While they both walk away from the car, Mary receives a notification on her smartwatch confirming that the car is locked and safe, which she acknowledges with a quick turn of the hand. After a few more steps, the smartwatch vibrates slower and slower to signal that its Bluetooth connection with the vehicle was lost as they continue to walk farther away. Later during the day, Mary uses an app on her smartphone to connect to the infotainment system of her car via a mobile Internet connection, and they resume listening to the song last playing in the car. Mary and Emma spend a wonderful day enjoying all the attractions of the city they are visiting. Returning to the parking lot, Mary has troubles remembering where she parked, so she touches her ring to the smartphone, which displays the map with the GPS location of the car stored on the ring when Mary locked the vehicle. A mere touch between the ring and the smartphone is enough for the smartphone to automatically launch the smart vehicle app from the many applications installed on Mary's phone. In the evening, they arrive back home. Emma asks Marry for a guest passcode to remotely connect to the infotainment system of Mary's car to download the music playlist they have enjoyed during the journey."

Fig. 2. Interaction with the smart vehicle in the personal zone: an NFC ring receives data from the vehicle when in contact with an active NFC component from the vehicle.

When in the *personal zone*, the driver is very close to their vehicle (at about 1 m) and, thus, interactions in this zone can be implemented with direct touch input. Also, this zone is usually traversed quickly while the driver enters or exists the vehicle, but even this brief period of time is enough for *implicit interactions*. For instance, when in the personal zone, data can be transferred between the vehicle and the driver's personal devices, such as the GPS location of the vehicle can be stored on the driver's ring when in contact with an active component from the vehicle; see Fig. 2 for an illustration where the OMNI NFC Ring[1] is worn by the user and a reader could be embedded in the door handle. We implemented an application for the OMNI Ring (NFC Type B, Infineon SLE78 security controller, Java Card OS, dual 16-bit core CPU, 80 kB user memory, and AES/TDES/RSA 2k/ECC 521 cryptography standards) in the form of an Android app that writes and reads the following data to/from the ring: vehicle id, GPS location, parking ticket info, and the IP address of the vehicle. The application runs on an Android device, which can be the infotainment system of the car, as illustrated in Fig. 2, to which an NFC reader/writer is connected. In our implementation, we employed a Samsung Tab A T555 device.[2]

The proximal zone is followed by the *personal zone* at an approximate distance of 10 m from the vehicle. In this zone, the driver approaches the vehicle or departs from it but, unlike in the personal zone, direct interactions by touching the vehicle are no longer possible. In this zone, Class 2 Bluetooth devices still operate[3] and can exchange information with the vehicle. In our example, Mary receives a notification on her smartwatch a few seconds after she has locked the car, comforting her that the car is indeed safely locked; see Fig. 3 for an illustration of this scenario. The smartwatch is preferred to deliver such notifica-

---

[1] https://store.nfcring.com/products/omni?variant=30878229987373.

[2] https://www.samsung.com/au/support/model/SM-T555NZWAXSA.

[3] Typical range of operation of 10m; see a Bluetooth rang estimator here: https://www.bluetooth.com/learn-about-bluetooth/key-attributes/range.

Fig. 3. Interaction with the vehicle in the proximal zone: the smartwatch delivers a notification from the vehicle, letting the driver know that the vehicle is locked and safe.

Fig. 4. Interaction with the vehicle in the distant zone: a smartphone app enables transfer of data from the vehicle as the driver approaches or walks away from their car.

tions compared to a smartphone since it is readily available on the user's wrist and the interaction for consuming the notification is brief. We implemented a Tizen web application for the Samsung Watch3[4] (Dual-Core 1.15 GHz CPU, 1 GB RAM) using HTML, CSS, and JavaScript that communicates full-duplex via the WebSocket protocol with the tablet device from the vehicle representing the in-vehicle infotainment system. Notifications are sent from the infotainment system to the watch and acknowledged by the user with a simple arm movement.

The *distant zone* continues after the proximal zone, up to a distance of about 100 m around the vehicle [6]. Just like in the proximal zone, the driver can visually locate their vehicle. However, the larger distance creates the need for

---

[4] https://www.samsung.com/us/mobile/wearables/smartwatches/galaxy-watch3-45mm-mystic-silver-bluetooth-sm-r840nzsaxar/.

Fig. 5. Interaction with the smart vehicle in the covert zone: the user connects to the in-vehicle infotainment system with a remote desktop application.

new communication channels and devices. Examples include Class 1 Bluetooth devices that operate at a typical range of 100 m and mobile Internet connections provided by a wireless carrier. In our story, Mary connects to her vehicle to synchronize data and resume playing music from the car on her smartphone; see Fig. 4 for an illustration. In our implementation, a node.js web server handles communications with client applications requesting data via the WebSocket protocol. An Android app, running on the smartphone, acts as the client enabling Mary to resume listening to the music from the vehicle and to synchronize the playlist from the smartphone with that from the vehicle.

The *covert zone* is primarily characterized by the fact that the vehicle is no longer in view [6]. There is no fixed threshold in meters to demarcate the covert and distant zones, but typical applications in this zone assume that the user has access to desktop computers, such as in an office or at home. In our scenario, Emma wishes to access the playlist from Mary's car and asks for a guest passcode to connect to the in-vehicle infotainment system. Figure 5 illustrates this use case scenario, where we employed the AnyDesk[5] application to connect to the tablet device located in the vehicle from a desktop computer. In our implementation, the data stored on the ring also contains the IP address of the vehicle and Mary can simply touch Emma's smartphone to transfer this information.

4   Discussion

We presented interactions with a smart vehicle while the driver is outside the vehicle and at various distances from the vehicle in order to demonstrate the opportunities outlined by the smart vehicle proxemics framework [6]. These interactions employed convenient devices to minimize the effort and maximize the effectiveness of communicating with the vehicle when in various proximity zones around the vehicle. Although intended to be simple, our applications

---

[5] The fast remote desktop application - AnyDesk, https://anydesk.com/en.

demonstrate the opportunities for designing interactions outside the vehicle in a continuous space characterized by the combination between physical distance and a variety of devices to mediate those interactions. Moreover, since all the communications with the vehicle are handled via standardized web protocols and data formats, it is easy to extend our applications towards new devices and platforms, e.g., smartglasses [1], augmented reality [25], specialized software architecture [26], etc., and achieve new functionalities. For instance, other scenarios in the *personal zone* could use NFC tags embedded in jewellery [24], tattoos [15], or key rings,[6] and the information stored by those tags could address a variety of other applications, e.g., information about the technical state and inspection of the vehicle, consumption statistics, travel history, vehicle safety and location, etc.; see [6] for a study examining drivers' preferences for information to obtain from their vehicle while close to the vehicle. Other scenarios in the *proximal zone* could show the expiry time of the parking ticket as a reminder to the driver walking away from the vehicle or the inside temperature of the car when the driver is in the *distant zone* and approaching the vehicle, so that the driver could already make the appropriate setting for the air conditioning and heating system before reaching their car. Our web-based implementations can handle flexible associations between devices and the in-vehicle system and, thus, support the fluency of interacting in the continuous space inside and outside the vehicle.

5 Conclusion

We presented application opportunities for interacting with smart vehicles enabled by mobile and wearable devices employed fluently by the user according to the physical distance to the vehicle and their goals. To this end, we envisioned a continuous interaction space in which drivers move freely and interact with the vehicle as they depart or approach the vehicle. Our practical applications complement the theoretical discussion of the smart vehicle proxemics framework and demonstrate its practical usefulness with an illustrative scenario involving interactions with the smart vehicle when in various zones around the vehicle.

Acknowledgments. This work was supported by a grant of the Romanian Ministry of Research and Innovation, CCCDI-UEFISCDI, project PN-III-P1-1.2-PCCDI-2017-0917 (21PCCDI/2018), within PNCDI III.

References

1. Aiordăchioae, A., Vatavu, R.D., Popovici, D..M.: A design space for vehicular lifelogging to support creation of digital content in connected cars. In: Proceedings of the ACM Symposium on Engineering Interactive Computing Systems, EICS 2019, ACM, New York (2019). https://doi.org/10.1145/3319499.3328234

---

[6] https://www.hidglobal.com/sites/default/files/resource_files/hid-nfc-tags-and-solutions-wp-en.pdf.

2. Alvarez, I., Martin, A., Dunbar, J., Taiber, J., Wilson, D.M., Gilbert, J.E.: Voice interfaced vehicle user help. In: Proceedings of the 2nd International Conference on Automotive User Interfaces and Interactive Vehicular Applications, pp. 42–49. Automotive, UI 2010, ACM, New York (2010). https://doi.org/10.1145/1969773. 1969782
3. Ballendat, T., Marquardt, N., Greenberg, S.: Proxemic interaction: designing for a proximity and orientation-aware environment. In: Proceedings of the ACM International Conference on Interactive Tabletops and Surfaces, ITS 2010, pp. 121–130 (2010). https://doi.org/10.1145/1936652.1936676
4. Bilius, L.B., Vatavu, R.D.: A synopsis of input modalities for in-vehicle infotainment and consumption of interactive media. In: Proceedings of the ACM International Conference on Interactive Media Experiences, IMX 2020, pp. 195–199. ACM, New York (2020). https://doi.org/10.1145/3391614.3399400
5. Bilius, L.B., Vatavu, R.D.: A multistudy investigation of drivers and passengers' gesture and voice input preferences for in-vehicle interactions. J. Intell. Transp. Syst. (2020). https://doi.org/10.1080/15472450.2020.1846127
6. Bilius, L.B., Vatavu, R.D., Marquardt, N.: Smart vehicle proxemics: a conceptual framework operationalizing proxemics in the context of outside-the-vehicle interactions. In: Proceedings of the 18th International Conference on Human-Computer Interaction, Interact 2021 (2021). 22 pages
7. Claudine, B., et al.: Self-driving cars: a survey. Expert Syst. Appl. **165**, 113816 (2021). https://doi.org/10.1016/j.eswa.2020.113816
8. Detjen, H., Faltaous, S., Geisler, S., Schneegass, S.: User-defined voice and mid-air gesture commands for maneuver-based interventions in automated vehicles. In: Proceedings of Mensch Und Computer 2019, MuC 2019, pp. 341–348 (2019). https://doi.org/10.1145/3340764.3340798
9. Fariman, H.J., Alyamani, H.J., Kavakli, M., Hamey, L.: Designing a user-defined gesture vocabulary for an in-vehicle climate control system. In: Proceedings of the 28th Australian Conference on Computer-Human Interaction, OzCHI 2016, pp. 391–395. ACM (2016). https://doi.org/10.1145/3010915.3010955
10. Gheran, B.F., Vatavu, R.D.: From controls on the steering wheel to controls on the finger: using smart rings for in-vehicle interactions. In: Companion Publication of the 2020 ACM Designing Interactive Systems Conference, DIS 2020 (2020). https://doi.org/10.1145/3393914.3395851
11. Greenberg, S., Kuzuoka, H.: Using digital but physical surrogates to mediate awareness, communication and privacy in media spaces. Pers. Technol. **3**, 182–198 (1999). https://doi.org/10.1007/BF01540552
12. Greenberg, S., Marquardt, N., Ballendat, T., Diaz-Marino, R., Wang, M.: Proxemic interactions: the new ubicomp? Interactions **18**(1), 42–50 (2011). https://doi.org/10.1145/1897239.1897250
13. Grønbæk, J.E., Knudsen, M.S., O'Hara, K., Krogh, P.G., Vermeulen, J., Petersen, M.G.: Proxemics beyond proximity: designing for flexible social interaction through cross-device interaction. In: Proceedings of the 2020 CHI Conference on Human Factors in Computing Systems, CHI 2020, pp. 1–14 2020). https://doi.org/10.1145/3313831.3376379
14. Hall, E.T.: The Hidden Dimension. Doubleday, Garden City (1966)
15. Kao, C.H.L., Johns, P., Roseway, A., Czerwinski, M.: Tattio: fabrication of aesthetic and functional temporary tattoos. In: Proceedings of the 2016 CHI Conference Extended Abstracts on Human Factors in Computing Systems, CHI EA 2016, pp. 3699–3702 (2016). https://doi.org/10.1145/2851581.2890269

16. Khan, A., Qadeer, M., Ansari, J., Waheed, S.: 4g as a next generation wireless network. In: ICFCC, pp. 334–338 (2009). https://doi.org/10.1109/ICFCC.2009. 108
17. Ledo, D., Greenberg, S., Marquardt, N., Boring, S.: Proxemic-aware controls: designing remote controls for ubiquitous computing ecologies. In: Proceedings of MobileHCI 2015, pp. 187–198. ACM (2015). https://doi.org/10.1145/2785830. 2785871
18. Marquardt, N., Diaz-Marino, R., Boring, S., Greenberg, S.: The proximity toolkit: prototyping proxemic interactions in ubiquitous computing ecologies. In: Proceedings of the 24th Annual ACM Symposium on User Interface Software and Technology, UIST 2011, pp. 315–326 (2011). https://doi.org/10.1145/2047196.2047238
19. McCarthy, J.: Computer controlled cars (1968). http://jmc.stanford.edu/commentary/progress/cars.pdf
20. Mumm, J., Mutlu, B.: Human-robot proxemics: physical and psychological distancing in human-robot interaction. In: Proceedings of the 6th International Conference on Human-Robot Interaction, HRI 2011, pp. 331–338. ACM, New York (2011). https://doi.org/10.1145/1957656.1957786
21. Previc, F.: The neuropsychology of 3-D space. Psychol. Bull. **124**, 2 (1998)
22. Raza, N., Jabbar, S., Han, J., Han, K.: Social vehicle-to-everything (V2X) communication model for intelligent transportation systems based on 5G scenario. In: Proceedings of ICFNDS 2018, ACM (2018). https://doi.org/10.1145/3231053. 3231120
23. Roider, F., Rümelin, S., Pfleging, B., Gross, T.: The effects of situational demands on gaze, speech and gesture input in the vehicle. In: Proceedings of the 9th International Conference on Automotive User Interfaces and Interactive Vehicular Applications, Automotive, UI 2017, pp. 94–102. ACM (2017). https://doi.org/10.1145/ 3122986.3122999
24. Salmela, E., Vimm, I.: Digital Smart Jewelry: Next Revolution of Jewelry Industry?. Digital Transformation in Smart Manufacturing, IntechOpen (2018). https:// doi.org/10.5772/intechopen.71705
25. Schipor, O.A., Vatavu, R.D.: Empirical results for high-definition video and augmented reality content delivery in hyper-connected cars. Interact. Comput. **33**, 3–16 (2021). https://doi.org/10.1093/iwcomp/iwaa025
26. Schipor, O.A., Vatavu, R.D., Vanderdonckt, J.: Euphoria: a scalable, event-driven architecture for designing interactions across heterogeneous devices in smart environments. Inf. Softw. Technol. **109**, 43–59 (2019). https://doi.org/10.1016/j.infsof. 2019.01.006
27. Tanase, C., Vatavu, R.D., Pentiuc, S., Graur, A.: Detecting and tracking multiple users in the proximity of interactive tabletops. Adv. Electr. Comput. Eng. **8**, 61–64 (2008). https://doi.org/10.4316/aece.2008.02011
28. Vogel, D., Balakrishnan, R.: Interactive public ambient displays: transitioning from implicit to explicit, public to personal, interaction with multiple users. In: Proceedings of the 17th Annual ACM Symposium on User Interface Software and Technology, UIST 2004 (2004). https://doi.org/10.1145/1029632.1029656
29. Wolf, K., Abdelrahman, Y., Kubitza, T., Schmidt, A.: Proxemic zones of exhibits and their manipulation using floor projection. In: Proceedings of the 5th ACM International Symposium on Pervasive Displays, PerDis 2016, pp. 33–37. ACM (2016). https://doi.org/10.1145/2914920.2915012
30. Yeh, A., et al.: Exploring proxemics for human-drone interaction. In: Proceedings of the 5th International Conference on Human Agent Interaction, HAI 2017, pp. 81–88 (2017). https://doi.org/10.1145/3125739.3125773

Smart Vehicle Proxemics: A Conceptual Framework Operationalizing Proxemics in the Context of Outside-the-Vehicle Interactions

Laura-Bianca Bilius[1], Radu-Daniel Vatavu[1]([⊠]), and Nicolai Marquardt[2]

[1] MintViz Lab | MANSiD Research Center, Ştefan cel Mare University of Suceava, 720229 Suceava, Romania
{laura.bilius,radu.vatavu}@usm.ro
[2] University College London, London, UK
n.marquardt@ucl.ac.uk

Abstract. We introduce *smart vehicle proxemics*, a conceptual framework for interactive vehicular applications that operationalizes proxemics to *outside-the-vehicle interactions*. We identify four zones around the vehicle affording different kinds of interactions and discuss the corresponding conceptual space along three dimensions (physical distance, interaction paradigm, and goal). We study the dimensions of this framework and synthesize our findings regarding drivers' preferences for (i) information to obtain from their vehicles at a distance, (ii) system functions of their vehicles to control remotely, and (iii) devices (e.g., smartphones, smartglasses, smart key fobs) for interactions outside the vehicle. We discuss the positioning of smart vehicle proxemics in the context of proxemic interactions more generally, and expand on the dichotomy and complementarity of outside-the-vehicle and inside-the-vehicle interactions for new applications enabled by smart vehicle proxemics.

Keywords: Smart vehicles · Connected vehicles · Proxemic interactions · Conceptual space · Outside-the-vehicle interactions · Study

1 Introduction

Connected vehicles [20] can access online resources and services, integrate with the cloud and the Internet-of-Things [29], communicate with other connected vehicles and the road infrastructure [6], and interact with drivers' and passengers' personal smart devices [46,55] to enable safer and more comfortable car journeys and increased road safety [18]. Smart cars with embedded AI [30] further enrich the car traveling experience. In this context, interactions between drivers and their smart, connected vehicles need keeping pace with the advances in vehicular technology [18,20] towards a rich and rewarding user experience of driving.

© IFIP International Federation for Information Processing 2021
Published by Springer Nature Switzerland AG 2021
C. Ardito et al. (Eds.): INTERACT 2021, LNCS 12933, pp. 150–171, 2021.
https://doi.org/10.1007/978-3-030-85616-8_11

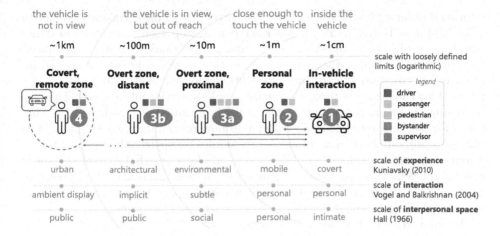

Fig. 1. An illustration of the smart vehicle proxemics framework with four distinct zones: ❶ inside the vehicle, ❷ personal interaction, ❸ overt interaction (proximal and distant), and ❹ interactions from the covert zone. While zones ❶ and ❹ have been studied before in the HCI and the intelligent transportation communities, interactions outside the vehicle corresponding to zones ❷ and ❸ have been mostly overlooked.

The HCI community has proposed a variety of interactive techniques, modalities, and devices to mediate inside-the-vehicle interactions—including voice input, mid-air gestures, haptic feedback, and others; see [8] for an overview. However, while much of the focus has been devoted to in-vehicle input [3,4,9,11,21,41,52], *the space outside the vehicle has been largely overlooked in terms of the opportunities it can bring for new interactive vehicular applications.* The most common interactions currently available to drivers when outside their vehicles are locking and unlocking the car and opening the trunk. Examples from the automotive industry include the Tesla key ring[1] and bracelet[2] leveraging NFC/RFID for remote access; the BMW Display Key,[3] with an integrated display, enables access to information about the vehicle from a distance; and smartphone apps[4] are available to assist with locating the car in a crowded parking lot. Recent work [24] has proposed integrating smart rings with smart vehicles for both inside and outside-the-vehicle interactions, e.g., the ring replaces steering wheel controls when inside the vehicle and, via a gesture, opens the trunk when outside, but such explorations are still at an incipient, mostly conceptual level.

In this context, there is an enticing practical opportunity for exploring complementing interactions with smart vehicles with a new design space dedicated to *outside-the-vehicle* interactions. To mitigate this kind of exploration, our work contributes a systematic categorization of the relevant design dimensions in the context of outside-the-vehicle interactions. We do this by leveraging notions of Edward Hall's Proxemics theory [28], which studies the nuances of people's inter-

---

[1] https://www.teslaring.com.
[2] https://www.teslawearable.com.
[3] https://www.bimmer-tech.net/blog/item/118-bmw-display-key.
[4] https://play.google.com/store/apps/details?id=com.elibera.android.findmycar.

actions at different levels of proximity, and correlates people's *physical* distance to *social* distance. Hall effectively categorized person-to-person interactions in structured zones—intimate, personal, social, and public—and his work has inspired the application in many other contexts. In particular, *proxemic interactions* [7, 26] identified key dimensions (distance, orientation, motion, identity, and space) most relevant for the design of proxemic-aware people-to-device interactions. This has been applied in many contexts, such as for large surfaces [5, 54], ambient displays [58, 59], and television [57]. Similar to how proxemics has been applied to ubicomp [26], our work operationalizes proxemics for smart vehicles, facilitating a more systematic exploration of interactive applications that exploit the space around the vehicle. In particular, we introduce a formalization of the interactive zones around the smart vehicle and a conceptual space for outside-the-vehicle interactions in the form of the *smart vehicle proxemics framework*.

In summary, our key contributions are:

1. We operationalize proxemics [28] for outside-the-vehicle interactions in the *smart vehicle proxemics framework*, and propose a four-zone proximity space for vehicles informed by proxemic interactions [7, 26]; see summary in Fig. 1.
2. As part of this framework, we formalize outside-the-vehicle interactions by introducing a conceptual space with three key dimensions: (1) the *distance* between the driver and their vehicle, (2) the *paradigm* to interact with the vehicle, and (3) the driver's *goal* that guides the interaction process.
3. We report results from a study with drivers to further explore these dimensions of the framework, in which we elicited 65 drivers about the type of information they would like to obtain and the system functions they would like to control for their vehicles from a distance, and we draw implications for outside-the-vehicle interactions in the context of smart vehicle proxemics.

2   Related Work

Much of the related work in automotive user interfaces (AutoUIs) has primarily focused on interactions designed for inside the vehicle [3, 4, 9, 11, 21, 41, 52]. Also, prior work from intelligent transportation systems has examined communications between pedestrians and vehicles in the context of autonomous driving cars and increasing road safety [22, 23, 36]. In this section, we synthesize this prior work, but also the relevant literature on proxemic interactions [7, 26, 27, 34, 63] that identified proximity zones around interactive systems, and which we apply in our context. But first, we discuss the concept of a smart vehicle and its recent modeling [49, 50] as a specific kind of a smart environment.

2.1   Smart, Connected Vehicles

A connected vehicle engages in communications with other vehicles, the road infrastructure, services from the cloud, and drivers' and passengers' smart devices to collect and generate data that improves its performance [20]. Services provided by connected vehicles include detection of driver fatigue and stress [20, 43], accident prevention [20, 38, 43, 56, 64], interaction with smart driving assistants

[16,20,38,43,56,64], parking assistance [20,43,56], traffic monitoring [20,43,56], integration with social networks [20,43], and media streaming inside the vehicle, including high-definition video and Augmented Reality (AR) content [50]. For example, Chirca *et al.* [17] introduced a valet parking system for fully autonomous vehicles; Liang *et al.* [36] examined a vehicular application scenario where traffic participants shared information about their speed, locations, and time of arrival to reduce delays in traffic; Wang *et al.* [60] addressed aspects of the security of the data collected by connected cars when integrated with cloud computing; and Aiordăchioae *et al.* [1] discussed vehicular lifelogging, where passengers document their car journeys with lifelogging technology, such as smartglasses.

Particularly relevant for our scope is Schipor and Vatavu's [49,50] modeling of the smart car as a specific kind of a smart environment [19]. Their work describes the goal of reusing available software architectures specifically designed for smart environments [51] in the context of smart cars, such as for the delivery of video and AR inside the vehicle [50]. Beyond this original goal, we argue that modeling the smart car as a specific kind of a smart environment allows reusing the design principles of ambient intelligence systems [47] and ambient media [44] for new interactive vehicular applications that connect to online services and resources.

2.2 Interactions Inside the Vehicle

Techniques based on car controls, touchscreens, mid-air gestures, voice, and multimodal input have been proposed for in-vehicle interactions towards increased road safety and a better user experience for drivers and passengers [3,4,41,52]; see Bilius and Vatavu [8] for a synopsis of input modalities for in-vehicle infotainment. For example, prior work has examined touch input on the steering wheel [3,4] and gestures in mid-air [11,37,41] so that drivers could keep their eyes on the road while interacting with their cars. Furthermore, voice input inside the vehicle has been addressed in terms of design guidelines [31,55] and technical aspects of speech recognition [2,53]. Bilius and Vatavu [9] reported a comparative analysis about drivers' and passengers' preferences for gesture and voice input inside the vehicle by employing questionnaires and the end-user elicitation method [61]. Multimodal input techniques that combine buttons and car controls, touch, gesture, and voice input offer increased flexibility that proves useful in many situations during driving [21,24]. Also, wearable devices have been recently considered for in-vehicle input, such as the opportunity of smart rings to complement and even replace the controls on the steering wheel [24].

2.3 Interacting with the Vehicle from a Distance

A large body of work exists on the communication between vehicles and pedestrians in the context of intelligent transportation systems to increase road safety. For example, Domeyer *et al.* [23] focused on vehicular cues to signal pedestrians when they can safely cross the street. Lee *et al.* [35] examined interactions in mixed traffic environments for cross-walking priority. Markkula *et al.* [39] proposed a taxonomy for the behavior of traffic participants including hand gestures, making eye contact, slowing down, using vehicle lights and body movements to express pedestrians' intentions to cross the street and drivers' intentions to give them priority, respectively. Dey and Terken [22] examined the importance of gestures and eye contact for the communication between pedestrians and drivers.

Remote control of the vehicle has been implemented by several car manufacturers. For instance, smart parking of the Volkswagen Touareg can be done from a smartphone app[5] and BMW cars enable drivers to connect to the in-vehicle infotainment system from the smartphone or the Display Key[6]. The Tesla key fob[7] summons the vehicle, the Tesla ring (see footnote 1) and bracelet (see footnote 2) lock/unlock the car, and a smartphone app[8] controls the air conditioning, lights, and engine. Although these devices are useful to remotely control the vehicle, their functionality seems to be only the beginning of the wider design space of out-of-vehicle interactions.

2.4 Proxemic Interactions

Edward Hall's Proxemics theory [28] studies people's implicit use of interpersonal space when interacting with others. Most importantly, Hall correlates personal distance to social distance, and structured people's interpersonal space into four explicit zones: the *intimate* zone up to 0.5 m, *personal* between 0.5 m and 1 m, *social* up to 4 m, and the *public* zone beyond 4 m. Beyond functioning as an analytical lens into people's implicit use of space, Proxemic theory has inspired work in ubiquitous computing environments to mediate people's interactions with technology. Proxemic interactions [26] draw inspiration from Hall's theory, and designed interactive systems that could sense the relative distance and orientation of users, and adapt and react accordingly to this information. For example, focusing on media spaces, Greenberg and Kuzuoka [25] designed digital and physical surrogates to mediate interactions between people. Addressing interactions with public ambient displays, Vogel and Balakrishnan [59] discussed how orientation and proximity to the display are indicators for the engagement with the display. Tănase *et al.* [54] designed an interactive tabletop system that detected and tracked users in its proximity by leveraging short-range distance sensors. By exploiting the proximity information, content was adapting to the location of the user, e.g., a PDF document could automatically rotate to be read correctly by the user moving around the tabletop. Later, Annett *et al.* [5] introduced a proximity-aware multi-touch tabletop with higher sensing resolution.

Considering the fine-grained nuances of proxemic theory and operationalizing it for person-to-device interactions have inspired the design of new types of interactions based on the distance, orientation, movement, identity, and location of entities in a smart environment [7,26,40]. For example, Mumm and Mutlu [42] studied proximity between humans and robots; Ledo *et al.* [34] proposed proxemic-aware controls for interactions employing a handheld device and surrounding appliances; proxemic interaction with museum exhibits was implemented by Wolf *et al.* [62] by

---

[5] https://play.google.com/store/apps/details?id=de.volkswagen.pap.

[6] https://www.bimmer-tech.net/blog/item/118-bmw-display-key.

[7] https://shop.tesla.com/search?searchTerm=KEYS.

[8] https://www.tesla.com/support/tesla-app.

leveraging video projections on the floor; Yeh *et al.* [63] studied proximity interactions for drones; and Grønbæk *et al.* [27] proposed cross-device techniques based on proximity to foster social interaction.

2.5   Summary

A considerable amount of work has been devoted to make in-vehicle input more efficient for drivers, while communication between vehicles and pedestrians has been examined in intelligent transportation systems to increase road safety. In this context of sustained innovations in smart vehicular technology, we are lacking a more systematic exploration of the opportunities offered by the interactive space *around* the vehicle, which prevents designs of new automotive UIs where drivers can interact with their vehicles not only from a distance, but adaptively according to the distance to their vehicles. Next, we formalize this space in the form of a smart vehicle proxemics framework for outside-the-vehicle interactions, and leverage proxemics theory to more systematically structure this space.

3   Smart Vehicle Proxemics Framework

We introduce the smart vehicle proxemics framework (Fig. 1) to structure the physical space around a smart vehicle in analogy with Hall's [28] zones of personal space and by drawing from the literature on proxemic interactions [7,26,40]. By applying proxemics as a lens to structure this space, we identified the following four distinct zones for smart vehicle proxemics:

❶ **In-vehicle interaction zone.** The driver is inside the vehicle and operates the car controls, touchscreens and the infotainment system, the steering wheel controls, etc. As discussed in Sect. 2, this interactive zone has been a particular research focus in the AutoUI community (e.g., [3,4,9,11,21,41,52]).

❷ **Personal interaction zone.** The driver is outside the vehicle, but close to the vehicle so that they could comfortably reach and touch it. We approximate the personal zone of about 1 m, roughly an arm's length.

❸ **Overt interaction zone.** The driver is outside the vehicle, but too far away to reach and touch the vehicle. This zone is characterized by the driver having a clear view of their car from a physical distance roughly between 1 m and 100 m, but these thresholds are by no means fixed ones. What is important is that a clear view of the vehicle is possible, which makes this zone "overt." In the overt zone, we distinguish between two subzones: *proximal interaction* near the vehicle, such as at less than 10 m away, and *distant interaction*, e.g., between 10 m and 100 m; see Fig. 1. In the proximal zone, the driver is very close to their vehicle: they have just exited the vehicle or are approaching it. In this zone, short-range communication devices start operating, such as Class-2 and Class-3 Bluetooth devices,[9] and voice input becomes feasible to

---

[9] Class-2 Bluetooth operates at a typical range of 10 m; Class-3 at about 1 m; see more details on the Bluetooth SIG page https://www.bluetooth.com/learn-about-bluetooth/key-attributes/range.

be picked up by sensors from the vehicle. In the distant zone, the driver is farther away, yet the vehicle is still in their field of view. In this zone, long-range Class-1 Bluetooth devices operate,[10] hand signaling can be picked up by high-resolution video cameras from the car, and smartphone apps can connect to the car via the Internet. Thus, distinct input modalities are available to drivers when either *proximal* or *distant* in the overt zone.

❹ **Covert interaction zone.** The driver is outside the vehicle but, unlike in the previous zones, the vehicle is covert from view. This zone covers large distances, where the driver is remote, e.g., at home. We use the threshold of 100 m as an approximation of this zone, but depending on the context the actual value of this distance is likely to vary. From this distance, Internet-based communication with the car is the norm, and different goals for inter-acting with the vehicle are expected compared to the previous zones, e.g., Is my car safe? Has my parking ticket expired? Where did I park? [29].

It is important to note that the physical limits of 1 m, 10 m, and 100 m are just an approximation of the thresholds to physically separate these four inter-action zones around the vehicle and, similar to the work in proxemics and prox-emic interactions [7, 26, 28], they are not static or fixed boundaries. The spatial thresholds of these zones are informed by spatial and technical constraints. For example, in the personal zone 1 m represents an arm's reach, and the visual acu-ity in the overt zone decreases with distance, e.g., between 10 m and 100 m. The overt zone distance thresholds also correlate to the operating ranges of Class 1, 2, and 3 Bluetooth devices, which is a technology commonly used in smartphones, smartwatches, bracelets, rings, etc. to interact with the vehicle. Moreover, these thresholds form a geometric progression with the common ratio 10 that connects directly to Kuniavsky's [33] *scales of experience* for ubicomp environments, from mobile (1 m) to environmental (10 m), architectural (100 m), and the urban scale (1 km). Figure 1 also shows correspondences between these zones and Vogel and Balakrishnan's [59] *scales of interaction*: our in-vehicle ❶ and personal ❷ zones, where the driver can reach and touch the car, are in direct correspondence with the personal interaction zone of an ambient display; our overt zone ❸, with its proximal and distant delineations, corresponds to Vogel and Balakrishnan's sub-tle and implicit interaction zones, respectively; while when the driver is in the covert zone ❹, the vehicle can be seen as situated in the city landscape ambient.

Given that interactions in zones ❷ and ❸ have not been well-explored in the scientific literature, we introduce a conceptual space to inform interaction design with the smart vehicle across these zones. Our conceptual space has three dimensions corresponding to the *interaction paradigm* chosen by or available to the driver depending on the physical *distance* from their vehicle and the driver's *goal* for initiating interaction with their vehicle (see Fig. 2):

1. **Distance.** These are the four spatial zones of our framework introduced above: in-vehicle, personal, overt (proximal and distant), and covert. The physical distance to the vehicle constrains the driver's options for possible interactions and devices, e.g., some Bluetooth devices operate within a limited range, such as 10 m, while others up to 100 m.

---

[10] Class-1 Bluetooth operates at a typical range of 100 m; see the link above.

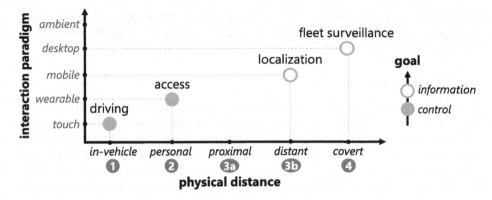

Fig. 2. Conceptual space for outside-the-vehicle interactions with three dimensions: distance to the vehicle, interaction paradigm, and the driver's goal. *Note:* several applications, e.g., fleet surveillance, car localization, etc., are highlighted in this space.

2. The **interaction paradigm** dimension includes the input modality, technique, and device employed to implement the interaction with the vehicle. Options range from touching the vehicle (i.e., when close to the car in the personal zone ❷) to using a Bluetooth mobile/wearable device (when near the car in the overt zone ❸) to using a desktop PC (e.g., to locate the car, open a live video stream from the car, etc.), or an ambient device when in zone ❹ (e.g., the Ambient Orb[11] could be used to gently inform—at the periphery of the user's attention—that the car insurance is about to expire).
3. **Goal of the interaction.** The goal impacts the type of interaction between drivers and vehicles, e.g., checking if the car is locked when near the vehicle ❸ *vs.* checking if the car is safe when not in direct view ❹.

Figure 2 illustrates our conceptual space and exemplifies various applications for outside-the-vehicle interaction. For example, fleet surveillance [48] is located at the intersection of the covert zone ❹, desktop PCs, and information seeking goals; access to the vehicle [13] is located at the intersection of the personal zone ❷, a mobile device, and seeking control; and localization of the vehicle [29] at the intersection of the overt distant zone ❸ with mobile applications with the goal of obtaining information about or from the vehicle. To validate the usefulness of these dimensions of the framework, in the next section we examine drivers' preferences for interactions to be performed outside the vehicle.

4   User Study: Understanding Drivers' Outside-of-Vehicle Interactions Across the Framework Dimensions

We conducted an exploratory study to understand drivers' needs and preferences for interacting with their vehicles from a distance, with a particular focus on

---

[11] https://ambientdevices.myshopify.com/products/stock-orb.

interactions across the dimensions of the framework. We implemented the study using an online questionnaire and addressing proximity zones ❷, ❸, and ❹ from Fig. 1 and the dimensions from our conceptual space from Fig. 2.

4.1 Participants

A total number of 65 drivers (46 male, 19 female), 19 to 54 years old ($M = 31.0$, $SD = 10.5$ years), participated in our study. We recruited participants via mailing lists, social networks, and from the student and staff body of our university. With one exception,[12] all of the participants had at least one year of driving experience. Participants' occupations and backgrounds were diverse including, in alphabetical order: administrator, cashier, construction worker, engineer, professional driver, economist, medical assistant, microbiologist, military personnel, professor, scientific researcher, sales consultant, software engineer, student, warehouse operative, and one participant was unemployed at the time of the study.

4.2 Task

Questions were grouped into the following four categories:

1. **Demographic information.** Participants filled out their age, gender, and professional occupation (or, in the case they were not employed at the time of their participation in the study, their field of education).
2. **Driving experience and driving habits.** Participants were asked to enter information about their driving experience, such as the number of years since they were driving, total mileage traveled in km, how frequently they were driving and for what purpose, and with whom they were regularly traveling.
3. **Use of computing devices.** We asked participants to indicate devices they were using on a regular basis by choosing from the following list (multiple selections were allowed): laptop computer, tablet, smartphone, smartwatch, smartglasses, smart ring, smart bracelet, wireless headphones, neural headset for brain-computer interfaces, and other. These categories of devices were informed by the scientific literature on in-vehicle input, but also by their prevalence (e.g., smartphones), emergence (e.g., smartwatches [55] and smartglasses [15]), and opportunities for the future of automotive driving assistance systems (e.g., neural headsets [14]).
4. **Preferences for outside-the-vehicle interactions.** Participants were asked to list the types of information they would like to obtain about or from their vehicles from various interaction zones (Fig. 1). Since in-vehicle interactions corresponding to zone ❶ have been studied in-depth in the literature, our questions focused on zones ❷, ❸, and ❹. Also, for each of these zones, we elicited participants about preferences for vehicle functions they would like to control from a distance. Finally, we asked participants about which devices they believed would be best suited to perform those interactions and rate the suitability of those devices using 5-point Likert scales with values ranging from 1 (not suitable at all) to 5 (very suitable).

---

[12] One participant had a driving experience of six months only.

4.3   Design

Our study was a 1×3 within-subjects design with the following variables:

1. PROXIMITY-ZONE, independent nominal variable with three conditions representing zones ❷, ❸, and ❹ (see Fig. 1). This variable corresponds to the *distance* dimension in our conceptual space illustrated in Fig. 2.
2. VEHICLE-FUNCTION, dependent variable with values collected as open-ended feedback representing functions that participants would like to control from outside the vehicle. Functions are located along the *goals* axis in our conceptual space from Fig. 2.
3. TYPE-OF-INFORMATION, dependent variable, with values collected as open-ended feedback representing information to obtain about the vehicle from outside the vehicle. Type of information is also located along the *goals* axis.
4. DEVICE, dependent nominal variable with the following conditions: (1) smartphone, (2) smartwatch, (3) smartglasses, (4) smart ring, (5) smart bracelet, (6) neural headset, (7) smart car keys, (8) smart clothes, (9) tablet, and (10) PC. These conditions represent various types of interactive devices that could be used to implement outside-the-vehicle interactions and correspond to the *interaction paradigm* dimension in our conceptual space from Fig. 2. Categories (1) to (8) apply for all the proximity zones, while categories (9) and (10) were available only for the questions referring to the covert zone ❹.

5   Results

We present results about the types of information that our drivers reported they would like to obtain about their vehicles or from their vehicles from a distance as well as preferences for vehicle functions to control from a distance. But first, we briefly present a characterization of our sample of participants to appreciate the generalizability of the results from our exploratory study.

5.1   Characterization of the Sample of Participants

The driving experience of our participants ranged between 6 months and 32 years with a mean of 7.6 years ($SD = 6.6$); see Fig. 3, left. Participants reported having traveled between 200 km and 2,000,000 km[13] with an average of 125.8 ($SD = 289.3$) thousands kilometers; see Fig. 3, right. Almost half of the participants (44.6%) reported driving everyday, a quarter (26.2%) almost daily, 13.8% once a week, and 15.4% only occasionally (less than once a week). The majority of our participants (73.8%) reported driving alone, but also with their families (69.2%) and friends (43.1%), and some (18.5%) with coworkers. The cars were used for various activities, such as for work (29.2%), commuting (72.3%), driving others (26.2%), making private trips (67.7%), shopping (84.6%), visiting family (80.0%), and for holiday travels (67.7%), respectively.

---

[13] A professional driver.

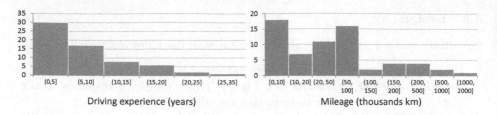

Fig. 3. Driving experience (left) and mileage (right) for our sample of drivers.

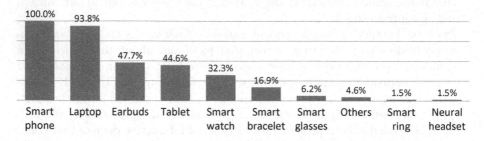

Fig. 4. Computing and personal devices used by our participants on a regular basis.

Figure 4 shows devices used on a regular basis by the drivers from our sample. All drivers reported smartphones (100%), nearly all reported laptop computers (93.8%), and about half used wireless headphones (47.7%) and tablets (44.6%) on a regular basis. One in three participants (32.3%) reported smartwatches, and one in six (16.9%) smart bracelets. Four participants had occasionally used smartglasses and one reported having used a smart ring and a neural headset.

This data reveals a diverse sample of participants with diverse driving experience and behavior and employing the vehicle for a variety of goals and needs, reflective of the diverse behavior of the driver population; see Kim and Tefft [32] for data from the AAA Foundation for Traffic Safety American Driving Survey. The results about devices used by our participants show the prevalence of smartphones, but also the emergence of new devices, such as smartwatches and bracelets, as representative upcoming categories of ubiquitous personal devices. The diversity observed in our sample is beneficial for the purpose of our exploratory study, enabling us to gain insights from a diversity of opinions.

5.2   Preferences for Information to Receive from the Vehicle at Different Proximity Zones

We collected a total number of 579 responses from our participants regarding the types of information they would like to obtain about or from their vehicles when in the proximity zones ❷, ❸, and ❹ (8.91 responses on average per participant and 2.96 responses on average per participant and proximity zone). Thematic grouping [12] of the responses revealed the following categories:

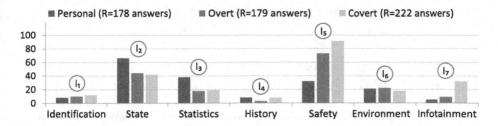

Fig. 5. Preferences for types of information to obtain from or about the vehicle from a distance. See the text for a description of information categories I_1 to I_7.

I_1. **Identification:** Information regarding vehicle identification, such as manufacturer and make, expiry date on the vehicle insurance, service schedule, vignette, the expiry date/time on the parking ticket, etc.

I_2. **State:** Information regarding the vehicle's technical state and inspection, its history of failures, the functional state of the on-board sensors and systems, tire pressure, engine temperature, battery level, etc.

I_3. **Statistics:** Information regarding consumption statistics, such as the car's fuel level, windshield fluid left available.

I_4. **History:** Information regarding the travel history of the vehicle, e.g., recent travels, last trip, total mileage, average speed.

I_5. **Safety:** Information regarding vehicle safety and security with respect to factors external to the vehicle, e.g., weather, break-in attempts, hand brake, the car being parked correctly, checking if the car is properly locked, etc.

I_6. **Environment:** Information about the in-vehicle environment, such as the inside temperature or the presence of personal objects, such as phone or wallet, that might have been forgotten inside the vehicle.

I_7. **Infotainment:** Information about the in-vehicle infotainment system, such as radio settings, music playlists, to do lists compiled and saved in the car.

Figure 5 shows the frequency of each thematic category I_1 to I_7 for each proximity zone, revealing several trends. For example, participants were more interested about the security and safety of their vehicles when in the covert zone ❹ (91 suggestions about safety), from where a direct view to their vehicle was not possible, rather than from the personal zone ❷ (32 preferences). Also, participants were more interested in obtaining technical information about their vehicles when near the vehicle in zone ❷ (66 suggestions) than when farther away (44 and 42 suggestions, respectively, for zones ❸ and ❹).

5.3 Preferences for Vehicle Functions to Control at Different Proximity Zones

We received 554 responses from our participants regarding vehicle functions they would like to control from a distance (8.52 responses on average per participant

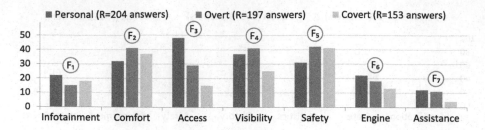

Fig. 6. Preferences for types of vehicle functions to control from a distance. See the text for a description of function categories F_1 to F_7.

and 2.84 on average per participant and proximity zone). Similar to before, we applied thematic grouping [12] and identified the following categories:

F_1. **Infotainment:** Control of the in-vehicle infotainment system, such as the audio, GPS, list of contacts, connecting to and screen sharing of the in-vehicle infotainment system, access to the video cameras installed in the vehicle.

F_2. **Comfort:** Control of functions for the comfort of passengers, such as seats heating, air conditioning, and the inside temperature.

F_3. **Access:** Access to the vehicle, e.g., opening the trunk, doors, windows.

F_4. **Visibility:** Visibility-related functions includes turning on/off headlights, hazard lights, wiping windows.

F_5. **Safety:** Control of functions about the safety and security of the vehicle, such as locking/unlocking the vehicle, setting the alarm, pulling the handbrake.

F_6. **Engine:** Engine control.

F_7. **Assistance:** Control of functions related to the driving assistance system, such as the parking assistant, summoning the car, driving assistance mode.

Figure 6 shows the frequency of each category for each proximity zone ❷, ❸, and ❹. Participants were more interested in controlling the vehicle security and safety systems when in the proximal zone ❸ (42 suggestions) rather than from the personal ❷ (31) or covert ❹ zones (41). They were also interested in access to the vehicle in zone ❷ (48 suggestions).

5.4   Preferences for Devices for Outside-the-Vehicle Interactions

Figure 7 shows participants' ratings of devices for outside-the-vehicle interactions. Results showed that the smartphone received the highest rating (M = 4.62 on a scale of 5), followed by the smart key (M = 4.12), smartwatch (M = 3.95), and smart bracelet (M = 3.40). The other devices from our list (see Sect. 4.3) received preference ratings below 3 (i.e., moderately suited). These results can be explained by the prevalence of touchscreens, the increasing availability of smartwatches that incorporate touchscreens, and the intuitive association between

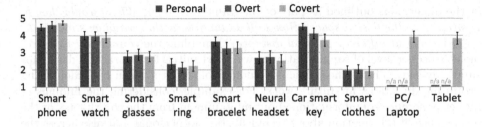

Fig. 7. Preferences for devices to implement outside-the-vehicle interactions.

controlling the vehicle and the car keys (for which some models[14] incorporate touchscreens as well). An interesting result concerns smartglasses and neural headsets that elicited some interest (2.82 and 2.65, respectively). For the covert zone ❹, for which the PC/laptop and tablet categories were available, ratings of their suitability were high (3.92 and 3.83, respectively).

6   Discussion

In this section, we reflect on the implications of our framework and findings for designing new interactions between drivers and their smart, connected vehicles when the drivers are outside the vehicle in various proximity zones. We also connect our findings to implications from prior work on proxemic interactions [7,26] regarding interactions in smart environments [27,34,62], discuss the dichotomy and complementarity of inside-the-vehicle and outside-the-vehicle interactions, and outline research directions towards pro-active proxemic-aware vehicles.

6.1   Using the Framework and Findings of Our Study to Inform Interaction Design for Smart Vehicles

Our framework and study findings provide different benefits and can be used in multiple ways to inform the design of novel outside-the-vehicle interactions. First, the framework can function as a guide to drive design decisions. By widening the focus on previously under-explored interactions outside of smart vehicles, and by articulating the key dimensions (e.g., explicit physical zones, relevant interaction paradigms), this unpacked design space can facilitate the exploration of novel techniques enriching the experience with smart vehicles. For example, practitioners can design different UI layouts for a car smartphone app showing just the relevant functions and hiding others based on the distance between the driver and their car. This design consideration can equally be applied to adaptive user interfaces for wearable devices that feature small screens, such as smartwatches. Second, the framework can also be applied as an analytical lens reflecting on existing interaction techniques for smart vehicles and re-evaluating them in light

---

[14] https://www.bimmer-tech.net/blog/item/118-bmw-display-key.

of the dimensions outlined as part of the framework (e.g., *Where would they be positioned in the design space? How well do the interaction paradigms match the requirements at different physical distance?*), enabling the community to examine at a deeper level of sophistication new opportunities for interaction design for smart vehicles. Third, the particular findings of our study can help identifying promising directions for future work. For example, considering the findings of higher preferences of information about infotainment from the covert zone, or the importance of information about technical state in personal, but also across the other zones, to design optimized interfaces. Fourth, the identified preferences of which devices to use for different outside-the-vehicle interactions showed a widespread spectrum across personal/wearable devices in all proximity zones (with only PC/laptop and tablet only matched to interactions at the covert proximity zone). We expect these results to foster more work at the intersection of wearable computing and automotive UIs, where drivers' personal devices turn into readily-available interfaces for controlling the car, such as emergent smartwatches [55], smartglasses [15], and smart rings [24], but also at the intersection of brain-computer interfaces and smart vehicles [14].

6.2   Smart Vehicle Proxemics as Part of Proxemic Interactions

Overall, we argued that smart vehicle proxemics closely relates to the concepts (and can be understood as a part) of proxemic interactions [7,26]. Operationalizing proxemics in interaction design allows us to better articulate important characteristics relevant for social interaction with devices. The overarching goal is to design proxemic-aware technology for vehicles that—similar to people's natural expectations and everyday use of proxemics—afford varying levels of information access and control of the vehicle that are finely tuned to the different proxemic distances. As the results of our study showed, these expectations are different depending on the distance to the vehicle. And similar to proxemic interactions studied in other contexts—such as interactions with large surfaces or robotics [27,34,42,62,63]—it is crucial to understand these distance margins not in a *binary* distinction of inside the vehicle and outside it, but rather as a practical means to operate within a continuous interactive space [10] that starts inside the vehicle, surrounds the driver departing their vehicle, and ends in the covert zone. Proxemics [7,26] functions well in this context as an effective first order approximation of this continuous space, and allowed us to define a framework to more thoroughly investigate the kinds of interactions that leverage the nuances of proxemics for smart vehicle interaction design. At the same time, we expect our framework to be expanded upon in the future with additional dimensions, complementary theories, toolkits, and new empirical findings.

6.3   The Dichotomy and Complementarity of Inside-the-Vehicle and Outside-the-Vehicle Interactions

The design of outside-the-vehicle interactions should be closely matched to any interactions inside the vehicle. In fact, as seen in our full spectrum of physical distance zones, "in-vehicle" is one end point of the continuous distance spectrum. Conceptually, interactions that begin somewhere in any of the other zones (e.g., personal, proximal, distant, or covert) are likely to relate to interactions within the vehicle, potentially at a later point in time. For example, notifications about remaining fuel level being low or about some aspect of the technical status of the vehicle can be delivered to the driver's smartwatch while they are approaching the vehicle and, when inside the vehicle, the driver can make a closer inspection of any issues already signaled to them. Or, interactions performed while inside the vehicle (e.g., stop the engine, pull up the handbrake) can continue while the driver exits the vehicle (e.g., lock the car) and departs from their car (e.g., the car streams statistics about the journey to the driver's smartphone). By looking at the four proximity zones as defining a continuum [10] that goes beyond the dichotomy of inside and outside-the-vehicle input, new opportunities emerge for designing interactions that span a wide range of physical distances, interaction paradigms, and goals. So while we argue that it is important to appropriately unpack the design space of outside-the-vehicle interactions, and that this focus and attention brings up potential for more refined interaction techniques in this space, it is important to emphasize that interactions likely have continuous trajectories across the physical distance zones. At the opposite end of this continuum, outside-the-vehicle interactions expose considerably lower safety concerns compared to interactions with the vehicle while driving, but they also create new potential security risks regarding the remote access to the vehicle by unauthorized individuals getting in the possession of the driver's mobile devices.

6.4   Pro-active Smart Vehicles and Proximity-Awareness

Many interaction techniques suggested within proxemic interactions require devices to have some kind of awareness of the physical distance of a person in relation to the device. This proximity-awareness is then often leveraged by the device to pro-actively initiate certain interactions, for example a whiteboard that reacts to a person's presence [59], or interactive controls that vary their functionality depending on a person's distance [34]. There is a potential to explore such pro-active, proximic-aware behaviors in the context of smart vehicles: knowing the exact distance of a driver to the car could be leveraged by a person's wearable devices (e.g., smartwatches, smart rings, glasses) or the car directly to best mitigate the information access or control functions. While such proximity-awareness could be based on Bluetooth standards, (See footnote 9) it could also involve other fine-grained hybrid sensing approaches, incorporating GPS and/or vision data from the car's integrated RGB or depth-sensing cameras. As part of future work, it would be interesting to identify the necessary granularity of such proxemic sensing necessary to best support different kinds of outside-of-vehicle interactions.

7   Conclusion

We introduced smart vehicle proxemics, a framework that structures interactive zones around the smart, connected vehicle and a corresponding conceptual space for outside-the-vehicle interactions. We also reported results from an exploratory user study conducted with drivers to uncover the types of information and system functions for vehicles to control from a distance. With these contributions, we are presenting the scientific community with the first theoretical examination and empirical insights regarding the opportunities offered by outside-the-vehicle interactions, when looking at the smart car as part of a proxemic-oriented smart environment [7,26].

Future work will look at other measures that are meaningful for smart vehicle proxemics, such as the orientation of the driver with respect to the vehicle, the driver's direction of movement (approaching or departing), relative distance and orientation of other vehicles, pedestrians, and road infrastructure in the context of the Social Vehicle-to-Everything (V2X) Communication Model [45] as well as incorporating drivers' and passengers' roles [9] into our framework, as already hinted in Fig. 1. Systematic exploration of proxemic interactions for smart vehicles will foster new designs of interactive techniques and devices, including modern key fobs with functionality that is contextualized and adapted to the physical distance to the vehicle.

Acknowledgments. This work was supported by a grant of the Romanian Ministry of Research and Innovation, CCCDI-UEFISCDI, project PN-III-P1-1.2-PCCDI-2017-0917 (21PCCDI/2018), within PNCDI III. The black and white "man" and "car" icons used in Fig. 1 were made by DinosoftLabs (https://www.flaticon.com/authors/dinosoftlabs, the "Insurance" icon pack) from https://www.flaticon.com, released free for personal and commercial purpose with attribution.

References

1. Aiordăchioae, A., Vatavu, R.D., Popovici, D.M.: A design space for vehicular lifelogging to support creation of digital content in connected cars. In: Proceedings of the ACM SIGCHI Symposium on Engineering Interactive Computing Systems, EICS 2019. ACM, New York (2019). https://doi.org/10.1145/3319499.3328234
2. Alvarez, I., Martin, A., Dunbar, J., Taiber, J., Wilson, D.M., Gilbert, J.E.: Voice interfaced vehicle user help. In: Proceedings of the 2nd International Conference on Automotive User Interfaces and Interactive Vehicular Applications, AutomotiveUI 2010, pp. 42–49. ACM, New York (2010). https://doi.org/10.1145/1969773.1969782
3. Angelini, L., et al.: Gesturing on the steering wheel: a user-elicited taxonomy. In: Proceedings of AutomotiveUI 2014, pp. 1–8. ACM, New York (2014). https://doi.org/10.1145/2667317.2667414
4. Angelini, L., et al.: Opportunistic synergy: a classifier fusion engine for microgesture recognition. In: Proceedings of AutomotiveUI 2013, pp. 30–37. ACM, New York (2013). https://doi.org/10.1145/2516540.2516563

5. Annett, M., Grossman, T., Wigdor, D., Fitzmaurice, G.: Medusa: a proximity-aware multi-touch tabletop. In: Proceedings of the 24th Annual ACM Symposium on User Interface Software and Technology, UIST 2011, pp. 337–346. ACM, New York (2011). https://doi.org/10.1145/2047196.2047240
6. Arena, F., Pau, G.: An overview of vehicular communications. Future Internet 11, 27 (2019). https://doi.org/10.3390/fi11020027
7. Ballendat, T., Marquardt, N., Greenberg, S.: Proxemic interaction: designing for a proximity and orientation-aware environment. In: ACM International Conference on Interactive Tabletops and Surfaces, ITS 2010, pp. 121–130. ACM, New York (2010). https://doi.org/10.1145/1936652.1936676
8. Bilius, L.B., Vatavu, R.D.: A synopsis of input modalities for in-vehicle infotainment and consumption of interactive media. In: Proceedings of the ACM International Conference on Interactive Media Experiences, IMX 2020, pp. 195–199. ACM, New York (2020). https://doi.org/10.1145/3391614.3399400
9. Bilius, L.B., Vatavu, R.D.: A multistudy investigation of drivers and passengers' gesture and voice input preferences for in-vehicle interactions. J. Intell. Transp. Syst. (2020). https://doi.org/10.1080/15472450.2020.1846127
10. Bilius, L.B., Vatavu, R.D., Marquardt, N.: Exploring application opportunities for smart vehicles in the continuous interaction space inside and outside the vehicle. In: Proceedings of the 18th International Conference on Human-Computer Interaction, INTERACT 2021, 10 p. (2021)
11. Brand, D., Büchele, K., Meschtscherjakov, A.: Pointing at the HUD: gesture interaction using a leap motion. In: Adjunct Proceedings of the 8th International Conference on Automotive User Interfaces and Interactive Vehicular Applications, AutomotiveUI 2016 Adjunct, pp. 167–172. ACM, New York (2016). https://doi.org/10.1145/3004323.3004343
12. Braun, V., Clarke, V.: Using thematic analysis in psychology. Qual. Res. Psychol. 3(2), 77–101 (2006). https://www.tandfonline.com/doi/abs/10.1191/1478088706qp063oa
13. Busold, C., et al.: Smart keys for cyber-cars: secure smartphone-based NFC-enabled car immobilizer. In: Proceedings of the 3rd ACM Conference on Data and Application Security and Privacy, pp. 233–242 (2013). https://doi.org/10.1145/2435349.2435382
14. Cernea, D., Olech, P.S., Ebert, A., Kerren, A.: Controlling in-vehicle systems with a commercial EEG headset: performance and cognitive load. OpenAccess Series in Informatics, vol. 27, pp. 113–122 (2012). https://doi.org/10.4230/OASIcs.VLUDS.2011.113
15. Chang, W.J., Chen, L.B., Chiou, Y.Z.: Design and implementation of a drowsiness-fatigue-detection system based on wearable smart glasses to increase road safety. IEEE Trans. Cons. Electronics (2018). https://doi.org/10.1109/TCE.2018.2872162
16. Chen, Y.L., Chen, Y.H., Chen, C.J., Wu, B.F.: Nighttime vehicle detection for driver assistance and autonomous vehicles. In: Proceedings of the International Conference on Pattern Recognition, vol. 1, pp. 687–690 (2006). https://doi.org/10.1109/ICPR.2006.858
17. Chirca, M., Chapuis, R., Debain, C., Lenain, R., Martin, G.: Autonomous valet parking system architecture. In: Proceedings of the IEEE 18th International Conference on Intelligent Transportation Systems (2015). https://doi.org/10.1109/ITSC.2015.421
18. Claudine, B., et al.: Self-driving cars: a survey. Expert Syst. Appl. 165, 113816 (2021). https://doi.org/10.1016/j.eswa.2020.113816

19. Cook, D., Das, S.: Smart Environments: Technology, Protocols & Applications (Wiley Series on Parallel & Distributed Computing). Wiley-Interscience, USA (2004)

20. Coppola, R., Morisio, M.: Connected car: technologies, issues, future trends. ACM Comput. Surv. **49**(3) (2016). https://doi.org/10.1145/2971482

21. Detjen, H., Faltaous, S., Geisler, S., Schneegass, S.: User-defined voice and mid-air gesture commands for maneuver-based interventions in automated vehicles. In: Proceedings of Mensch Und Computer 2019, MuC 2019, pp. 341–348. ACM, New York (2019). https://doi.org/10.1145/3340764.3340798

22. Dey, D., Terken, J.: Pedestrian interaction with vehicles: roles of explicit and implicit communication. In: Proceedings of the 9th International Conference on Automotive User Interfaces and Interactive Vehicular Applications, AutomotiveUI 2017, pp. 109–113. ACM, New York (2017). https://doi.org/10.1145/3122986.3123009

23. Domeyer, J., Dinparastdjadid, A., Lee, J., Douglas, G., Alsaid, A., Price, M.: Proxemics and kinesics in automated vehicle-pedestrian communication: representing ethnographic observations. Transp. Res. Rec. **2673** (2019). https://doi.org/10.1177/0361198119848413

24. Gheran, B.F., Vatavu, R.D.: From controls on the steering wheel to controls on the finger: using smart rings for in-vehicle interactions. In: Proceedings of DIS 2020 Companion (2020). https://doi.org/10.1145/3393914.3395851

25. Greenberg, S., Kuzuoka, H.: Using digital but physical surrogates to mediate awareness, communication and privacy in media spaces. Pers. Technol. **3**, 182–198 (1999). https://doi.org/10.1007/BF01540552

26. Greenberg, S., Marquardt, N., Ballendat, T., Diaz-Marino, R., Wang, M.: Proxemic interactions: the new ubicomp? Interactions **18**(1), 42–50 (2011). https://doi.org/10.1145/1897239.1897250

27. Grønbæk, J.E., Knudsen, M.S., O'Hara, K., Krogh, P.G., Vermeulen, J., Petersen, M.G.: Proxemics beyond proximity: designing for flexible social interaction through cross-device interaction. In: Proceedings of the Conference on Human Factors in Computing Systems, CHI 2020, pp. 1–14 (2020). https://doi.org/10.1145/3313831.3376379

28. Hall, E.T.: The Hidden Dimension. Doubleday, Garden City (1966)

29. He, W., Yan, G., Xu, L.: Developing vehicular data cloud services in the IoT environment. IEEE Trans. Ind. Inform. **10**, 1587–1595 (2014). https://doi.org/10.1109/TII.2014.2299233

30. Khayyam, H., Javadi, B., Jalili, M., Jazar, R.: Artificial intelligence and internet of things for autonomous vehicles. In: Jazar, R., Dai, L. (eds.) Nonlinear Approaches in Engineering Applications, pp. 39–68. Springer, Cham (2020). https://doi.org/10.1007/978-3-030-18963-1_2

31. Kim, J., Jeong, M., Lee, S.C.: "Why did this voice agent not understand me?": error recovery strategy for in-vehicle voice user interface. In: Proceedings of AutomotiveUI 2019, pp. 146–150. ACM (2019). https://doi.org/10.1145/3349263.3351513

32. Kim, W.A., V. Tefft, B.: American Driving Survey, 2014–2017 (Research Brief) (2019). https://aaafoundation.org/american-driving-survey-2014-2017/

33. Kuniavsky, M.: Smart Things: Ubiquitous Computing User Experience Design. Morgan Kaufmann (2010). https://www.elsevier.com/books/smart-things/kuniavsky/978-0-12-374899-7

34. Ledo, D., Greenberg, S., Marquardt, N., Boring, S.: Proxemic-aware controls: designing remote controls for ubiquitous computing ecologies. In: Proceedings of the 17th International Conference on Human-Computer Interaction with Mobile Devices and Services, MobileHCI 2015, pp. 187–198. ACM (2015). https://doi.org/10.1145/2785830.2785871

35. Lee, Y.M., et al.: Road users rarely use explicit communication when interacting in today's traffic: implications for automated vehicles. Cogn. Tech. Work (2020). https://doi.org/10.1007/s10111-020-00635-y

36. Liang, X., Guler, S.I., Gayah, V.: Traffic signal control optimization in a connected vehicle environment considering pedestrians. Transp. Res. Rec. **2674**(07) (2020). https://doi.org/10.1177/0361198120936268

37. Lin, H.: Using passenger elicitation for developing gesture design guidelines for adjusting highly automated vehicle dynamics. In: Proceedings of DIS 2019 Companion, pp. 97–100. ACM (2019). https://doi.org/10.1145/3301019.3324878

38. Lyu, N., Wen, J., Zhicheng, D., Wu, C.: Vehicle trajectory prediction and cut-in collision warning model in a connected vehicle environment. IEEE Trans. Intell. Transp. Syst. (2020). https://doi.org/10.1109/TITS.2020.3019050

39. Markkula, G., et al.: Defining interactions: a conceptual framework for understanding interactive behaviour in human and automated road traffic. Theor. Issues Ergon. Sci. **21**(6), 728–752 (2020). https://doi.org/10.1080/1463922X.2020.1736686

40. Marquardt, N., Diaz-Marino, R., Boring, S., Greenberg, S.: The proximity toolkit: prototyping proxemic interactions in ubiquitous computing ecologies. In: Proceedings of the 24th Annual ACM Symposium on User Interface Software and Technology, UIST 2011, pp. 315–326. ACM (2011). https://doi.org/10.1145/2047196.2047238

41. May, K.R., Gable, T.M., Walker, B.N.: Designing an in-vehicle air gesture set using elicitation methods. In: Proceedings of the 9th International Conference on Automotive User Interfaces and Interactive Vehicular Applications, AutomotiveUI 2017, pp. 74–83. ACM, New York (2017). https://doi.org/10.1145/3122986.3123015

42. Mumm, J., Mutlu, B.: Human-robot proxemics: physical and psychological distancing in human-robot interaction. In: Proceedings of the 6th International Conference on Human-Robot Interaction, pp. 331–338. ACM (2011). https://doi.org/10.1145/1957656.1957786

43. Nakrani, P.K.: Smart car technologies: a comprehensive study of the state of the art with analysis and trends. Master's thesis, Arizona State University (2015). https://repository.asu.edu/items/30030

44. Pogorelc, B., et al.: Semantic ambient media: from ambient advertising to ambient-assisted living. Multimedia Tools Appl. **58**(2), 399–425 (2012). https://doi.org/10.1007/s11042-011-0917-8

45. Raza, N., Jabbar, S., Han, J., Han, K.: Social vehicle-to-everything (V2X) communication model for intelligent transportation systems based on 5G scenario. In: Proceedings of the 2nd International Conference on Future Networks and Distributed Systems, ICFNDS 2018. ACM, New York (2018). https://doi.org/10.1145/3231053.3231120

46. Reininger, M., Miller, S., Zhuang, Y., Cappos, J.: A first look at vehicle data collection via smartphone sensors. In: Proceedings of the 2015 IEEE Sensors Applications Symposium (2015). https://doi.org/10.1109/SAS.2015.7133607

47. Sadri, F.: Ambient intelligence: a survey. ACM Comput. Surv. **43**(4) (2011). https://doi.org/10.1145/1978802.1978815

48. Saghaei, H.: Design and Implementation of a Fleet Management System Using Novel GPS/GLONASS Tracker and Web-Based Software (2016). https://arxiv.org/abs/1610.02667
49. Schipor, O.A., Vatavu, R.D.: Towards interactions with augmented reality systems in hyper-connected cars. In: Proceedings of the 2nd Workshop on Charting the Way Towards Methods and Tools for Advanced Interactive Systems. HCI Engineering 2019 (2019). http://ceur-ws.org/Vol-2503/paper1_12.pdf
50. Schipor, O.A., Vatavu, R.D.: Empirical results for high-definition video and augmented reality content delivery in hyper-connected cars. Interact. Comput. **33**, 3–16 (2021). https://doi.org/10.1093/iwcomp/iwaa025
51. Schipor, O.A., Vatavu, R.D., Vanderdonckt, J.: Euphoria: a scalable, event-driven architecture for designing interactions across heterogeneous devices in smart environments. Inf. Softw. Technol. **109**, 43–59 (2019). https://doi.org/10.1016/j.infsof.2019.01.006
52. Shakeri, G., Williamson, J.H., Brewster, S.: May the force be with you: ultrasound haptic feedback for mid-air gesture interaction in cars. In: Proceedings of the 10th International Conference on Automotive User Interfaces and Interactive Vehicular Applications, AutomotiveUI 2018, pp. 1–10. ACM (2018). https://doi.org/10.1145/3239060.3239081
53. Tamoto, A., Itou, K.: Voice authentication by text dependent single utterance for in-car environment. In: Proceedings of the 10th International Symposium on Information and Communication Technology, pp. 336–341 (2019). https://doi.org/10.1145/3368926.3369669
54. Tanase, C., Vatavu, R.D., Pentiuc, S., Graur, A.: Detecting and tracking multiple users in the proximity of interactive tabletops. Adv. Electr. Comput. Eng. **8** (2008). https://doi.org/10.4316/aece.2008.02011
55. Tombeng, M.T., Najoan, R., Karel, N.: Smart car: digital controlling system using android smartwatch voice recognition. In: 2018 6th International Conference on Cyber and IT Service Management, pp. 1–5 (2018). https://doi.org/10.1109/CITSM.2018.8674359
56. Uhlemann, E.: Introducing connected vehicles [connected vehicles]. Veh. Technol. Mag. **10** (2015). https://doi.org/10.1109/MVT.2015.2390920
57. Vatavu, R.D.: There's a world outside your TV: exploring interactions beyond the physical TV screen. In: Proceedings of the 11th Conference on Interactive TV and Video, EuroITV 2013, pp. 143–152 (2013). https://doi.org/10.1145/2465958.2465972
58. Vermeulen, J., Luyten, K., Coninx, K., Marquardt, N., Bird, J.: Proxemic flow: dynamic peripheral floor visualizations for revealing and mediating large surface interactions. In: INTERACT 2015 (2015). https://doi.org/10.1007/978-3-319-22723-8_22
59. Vogel, D., Balakrishnan, R.: Interactive public ambient displays: transitioning from implicit to explicit, public to personal, interaction with multiple users. In: Proceedings of the 17th Annual ACM Symposium on User Interface Software and Technology, UIST 2004, pp. 137–146 (2004). https://doi.org/10.1145/1029632.1029656
60. Wang, X., Shen, S., Bezzina, D., Sayer, J., Liu, H., Feng, Y.: Data infrastructure for connected vehicle applications. Transp. Res. Rec. **2674** (2020). https://doi.org/10.1177/0361198120912424
61. Wobbrock, J.O., Morris, M.R., Wilson, A.D.: User-defined gestures for surface computing. In: Proceedings of the SIGCHI Conference on Human Factors in Computing Systems, CHI 2009, pp. 1083–1092 (2009). https://doi.org/10.1145/1518701.1518866

62. Wolf, K., Abdelrahman, Y., Kubitza, T., Schmidt, A.: Proxemic zones of exhibits and their manipulation using floor projection. In: Proceedings of the 5th ACM International Symposium on PerDis 2016, pp. 33–37. ACM (2016). https://doi.org/10.1145/2914920.2915012

63. Yeh, A., et al.: Exploring proxemics for human-drone interaction. In: Proceedings of the 5th International Conference on Human Agent Interaction, HAI 2017, pp. 81–88. ACM (2017). https://doi.org/10.1145/3125739.3125773

64. Zhang, Z., Zhang, S., Jiao, S.: A vehicle lane-changing model based on connected vehicles. In: Proceedings of the 20th COTA International Conference of Transportation Professionals, pp. 3027–3038 (2020). https://dx.doi.org/10.1061/9780784482933.261

Design Methods

Advanced Kidney Disease Patient Portal: Implementation and Evaluation with Haemodialysis Patients

Ramsay Meiklem[1]([✉]) [iD], Karen Stevenson[2] [iD], Sabine Richarz[2,3] [iD],
David B. Kingsmore[2] [iD], Matt-Mouley Bouamrane[4] [iD], Mark Dunlop[1] [iD],
and Peter Thomson[2] [iD]

[1] Department of Computer and Information Sciences, University of Strathclyde, Glasgow, Scotland
{Ramsay.Meiklem,Mark.Dunlop}@strath.ac.uk
[2] Queen Elizabeth University Hospital, Glasgow, Scotland
{karen.stevenson2,Sabine.Richarz,David.Kingsmore,
Peter.Thomson}@ggc.scot.nhs.uk
[3] Universitätsspital Basel, Petersgraben 4, 4031 Basel, Switzerland
[4] Centre for Medical Informatics, Usher Institute, University of Edinburgh, Edinburgh, Scotland
Matt.Bouamrane@ed.ac.uk

Abstract. Patients on haemodialysis face complex care pathways, a high treatment burden and lower quality-of-life. Working with multidisciplinary domain experts, we have conducted several iterative development cycles to design, develop and evaluate a portal for patients on haemodialysis that can help them better understand and navigate their care pathways. A key functionality of the portal is to improve data and information sharing with clinicians, including on key aspects of quality-of-life through Patients Reported Outcome Measures. A case study was conducted with multidisciplinary experts and patients in the NHS Greater Glasgow and Clyde health board (Scotland), using interviews combined with the System Usability Scale (n = 26). Patients' feedback and system use observations were used to further refine the system design requirements and functionalities. Key lessons include: a wide preference for tablet-based input vs paper, identification of case-specific accessibility issues and situational impairment, benefits of self-completed digital data collection in overcoming such issues and promoting patient independence and privacy, with considerations for maintaining perceived value and engagement with such systems and when to offer alternatives.

Keywords: Chronic diseases · Patient portal · Co-design of digital health

1 Introduction

Chronic kidney disease (CKD) carries a substantial global health burden with high associated economic costs to health systems and substantial impact on quality-of-life

© IFIP International Federation for Information Processing 2021
Published by Springer Nature Switzerland AG 2021
C. Ardito et al. (Eds.): INTERACT 2021, LNCS 12933, pp. 175–196, 2021.
https://doi.org/10.1007/978-3-030-85616-8_12

(QoL) [1–3]. Treatment options and care trajectories for CKD patients are often complex and can vary widely between patients as well as over time. Haemodialysis treatment (HD) in particular places patients under a high treatment burden [1–3], with some studies highlighting that patients experience confusion, anxiety, frustration or dissatisfaction with their personal experiences of the disease and care trajectories as well as important fluctuations in their physical health [4].

Furthermore, the intense schedule of HD can also have substantial impact on families and social relationships [5]. One of the key decisions that is required is the choice of how HD is delivered – vascular access (VA). Most importantly, this key decision must be made at a time of illness, in a pressurized situation, potentially with limited time for professional input. Currently this is often delivered in an environment with time-limited consultations, paper-based generic information, and unstructured internet information. This is time-consuming, inefficient and can confuse patients. In addition, there is no routine mechanism to collect real-time patient experiences or outcomes.

Given the widely varying and unpredictable patient experience, it is not surprising that getting a reliable method of assessing and collecting patient-related outcome measures (PROMs) has proven difficult. PROMs focusing on Quality of Life (QoL) are clinically important as many of the key decisions regarding care are subjective and rely on patient input. Any additional support for patients to help them manage their care would be a major advance [4, 5]. Improving the integration of QoL into clinical care presents several hurdles. A fundamental requirement includes a mechanism for data collection that can be reliably used by patients during dialysis. There is little data in the HCI literature on how app-based technology for patient data collection compares to traditional paper, nor on how this can be evaluated in clinical situations where it is most required. In particular, patients on dialysis have particular accessibility limitations due to the impact of their underlying condition and intensive ongoing treatment (e.g. diabetes and reduced visual acuity) [6, 7]. Furthermore, collection during dialysis introduces situational impairments as patient movement is constrained. As such, multi-disciplinary research is required between haemodialysis clinicians and HCI designers.

Handheld tablet computers are promising data collection tools as they are lightweight and, in comparison to paper, support direct entry rather than requiring transcription hence have the potential for more reliable input. However, the design of a tablet solution for this population and environment is not clear and there are concerns with the introduction of shared devices such as transmission of infections amongst a vulnerable cohort. This design also poses an interesting case study as standard co-design methods are challenging when patients have considerable health issues and their treatment already entails a considerable lifestyle burden.

This paper reports on use of a tablet-based tool to support longitudinal developmental and validation studies of a novel QoL measure (the Vascular Access Specific Quality-of-Life, VASQoL) [8]. A set of design recommendations was developed from medical and HCI domain experts and a proof-of-concept portal proposed [9]. Previous literature and related work have emphasized that patient portal systems suffer if they do not meet the expectations and needs of stakeholders [10–12]. A multi-stakeholder co-design approach was performed including patients in design and evaluation, and aimed to answer the following research questions:

1. What are the benefits and disadvantages of digital tablet-based data collection over paper for the in-hospital HD population?
2. Is a two-stage approach in which the system is designed with multi-stakeholder co-design before testing with patients suitable?
3. What situational, accessibility and usability issues need to be considered for development of in-hospital systems for HD patients?

Previous research developed a set of design recommendations from multidisciplinary domain experts (comprised of medical, informatics and human computer interaction (HCI) academic experts) [9]. This paper reports the iterative development of a portal with a multidisciplinary group of experts followed by an in-hospital study with patients during dialysis. Qualitative feedback from patients and investigators' observations were collected and analyzed along with assessment of the usability of the system using the System Usability Scale (SUS) [13]. Given the lack of previous literature of usability studies in clinical settings with hemodialysis patients, it is currently not clear what the benefits and barriers to tablet-based data entry for patients are and how patients would respond to tablet-based entry compared to paper.

This paper presents the first case study of design and development of a portal conducted with a challenging user group in a hospital setting with the direct aim of supporting their clinical journey. The research contributions to the medical and HCI communities include:

- a novel technology in heterogeneous population, which warranted wider and deeper analysis;
- co-design approach produces a system which met needs and expectations, securing stakeholder interest;
- demonstrating engagement and activation of patient users;
- confirmed the benefits of digital data collection and considerations for alternatives where appropriate;
- identification of situational impairment and population accessibility issues.

2 Background

Haemodialysis (HD) is an intense, intermittent procedure typically performed three times a week, with sessions lasting four to five hours. A key limitation to HD is the mechanism to access the blood, their vascular access (VA). VA must allow regular cannulation with the insertion of needles to draw and return large volumes of blood via the dialysis machine. The three most common methods of VA are a fistula (surgical connection in the arm between the vein and artery, to be used for cannulation), a graft (plastic tube joining an artery and vein in the arm or leg, also used for cannulation), and a catheter or "line" (long plastic tube in the chest or groin, that hangs outside the skin which is connected to the machine). Each varies widely in the ease of insertion or creation, the practical use, the implications on regular lifestyle, and the frequency and severity of complications. Complications from VA are the leading cause of hospital admission and the leading modifiable cost of providing care for patients with kidney failure.

HD treatment is life-prolonging, but it is recognized it places a great burden upon the patient alongside their chronic condition. HD has been likened to an airplane flight, with busy periods at start and end of the activity with safety procedures, checks and actions to be completed [14], and a long period in between of restricted movement and activity. Outside of treatment, patients must manage their health, endure restrictions in diet, fluid intake, activities and monitor their vascular access for any irregularities or complications, alongside everyday life. Treatment can vary greatly based on patient characteristics and the options available, leading to dissatisfaction and frustration [4, 15].

To better understand and improve the patient experience and outcomes, routine collection of patient-related outcome measures (PROMs) via a patient portal was proposed in prior work [9]. Patient portal technologies previously deployed in clinical settings are discussed in the following section.

3 Related Work

There has been increasing recognition within the HCI (Human-Computer Interaction) literature that hospitalized patients are poorly served with supportive mechanisms such as facilitating patient-provider communication or accessing and managing health information. For example, one report highlights hospital patients wish to be engaged in tracking their health collaboratively with healthcare providers but lack the appropriate tools to do so [16]. Patient portals have been tried but have also occasionally failed to secure engagement from both patients and providers [10–12]. Research into patient engagement has shown patient characteristics (such as age, ethnicity, health literacy, etc.) strongly influence their interest and engagement [17], while the technology of patient portals itself presents barriers to engagement. Technology-related barriers in a frail population include a lack of experience or feeling uncomfortable using technology, difficulty accessing technology and a lack of trust in technology [12, 18]. It has been previously suggested that patients' preference for in-person communication and the lack of perceived need for patient portal use currently present the most important and unquantified barriers [18]. The patient-provider relationship is often discussed in the literature, as patients value this relationship and are often concerned systems that facilitate communication will replace or impact on it [11, 12, 16]. This is often met with the recommendation that the technology should always support the relationship and not replace it. It has been suggested that technology-based interventions can support dialysis patients, but there should also be availability of patient peer and provider support where technology is inappropriate for the individual [19]. Perhaps most importantly, some studies have suggested that patients do not necessarily perceive a need for patient portals [10, 11]. The failure of data input to influence clinical decision making can lead to disengagement from the technology. Conversely, when the features of the patient portal align with stakeholders' needs and functionalities, then engagement and endorsement can be sustained [11]. Without an objective assessment of these needs, there is a risk that systems' design will fail to meet user expectations [10].There are few design guidelines in this sphere in the literature, and thus any new work detailing functional and non-functional design requirements for patient portal systems is important both from an HCI and Medical Informatics perspective [9, 10].

Co-design is an effective methodology to gather design requirements. There are two common approaches – top-down and bottom-up. The typical top-down approach of adapting existing systems designed for healthcare providers results in systems inappropriate for inpatient use, a flaw that may be addressed by employing a bottom-up approach instead, where patients are the primary stakeholders [17]. Other studies demonstrate the benefit of capturing differences in goals and expectations between stakeholder groups [20] and producing a more widely accepted and person-centered system [21], with engagement from various stakeholders increasing over time. One extension of this is to utilize a multidisciplinary team of stakeholders, producing a system that requires fewer future redesigns and wide acceptability amongst stakeholders [21]. However, this theoretical approach has not been evaluated in a real-world setting. Co-design methodologies can also produce more person-centered systems, rather than an inappropriate "one size fits all" approach [19]. This was demonstrated in dialysis patients where the differences between individual patients meant no single solution or approach was sufficient. This is similar to other subpopulations of patients (i.e. elderly, low-income or those situationally impaired during treatment) who encounter accessibility issues in inappropriately designed systems [12, 19], which can often be remedied with design considerations and provision of alternatives e.g. audio output alongside text.

4   Methodology

This study followed a case study design [22], detailing the patient portal development and deployment within the context of a HD patient population. Case studies constitute an established research methodology within psychology and sociology but have been appropriated by other disciplines such as law, medicine, and political science. They are recognized as a qualitative approach where researchers explore one or more bounded systems (i.e. the case or context) over time [22]. A case study design was selected as the complexity of the case (i.e. a patient portal deployment with HD patients during treatment) warranted a deeper understanding and investigation, and the collection of various data from multiple sources allows for much richer design requirements and considerations for the system in question and others.

This study was completed in three parts. The first consisted in the iterative development of a patient portal with domain experts [9], collecting qualitative feedback to elucidate a refined set of design requirements. The second sought to evaluate the patient portal, through qualitative feedback from patients alongside a usability evaluation. Finally, the third part enlisted study coordinators to provide qualitative feedback based on their observations during the study.

These three parts are explained in detail in the following sections on participant recruitment, data collection and data analysis.

4.1   Recruitment of Participants

Expert Consultations. As part of this study, a multidisciplinary steering group (MSG) was convened, consisting of medical professionals and senior academics, with expertise in nephrology, vascular and transplant surgery, Medical Informatics and HCI. Seven domain experts provided feedback and further design requirements for the patient portal during thirty-three (n = 33) regular meetings between February 2019 and November 2020. Five experts were medical professionals, while the remaining two were senior academics with expertise in Medical Informatics and HCI. Medical experts were able to advise on what was required in practice and how to integrate the patient portal into routine care with patients. The academic experts provided expertise on system design, development, and implementation. The details of participants' expertise are provided in Table 1.

Table 1. Domain expert professions, expertise and sex

Profession/Expertise	Sex
Consultant, renal transplant surgery	F
Consultant, vascular and transplant surgery (associate professor)	M
Consultant nephrologist	M
Clinical research fellow	F
Dialysis nurse	F
Senior academic ('associate professor' level), medical informatics	M
Senior academic ('associate professor' level), mobile usability and Human-Computer Interaction	M

Patient Participants. Ethical approval for this study was provided by the University of Strathclyde Computer and Information Sciences departmental ethics committee (ID 1061) and the Greater Glasgow and Clyde (NHS GGC) health board (GN19RE634). Informed consent was obtained from all patients prior to participation.

A patient portal [9] was used to collect data for a validation study of a vascular access specific quality-of-life measure (VASQoL) [8] for patients requiring HD. This provided an opportunity to evaluate the system with patients in a clinical setting.

A quota sampling technique was employed for the recruitment of patients to complete digital questionnaires and cognitive interviews, with the intent to recruit a diverse population in terms of age, primary renal disease, vascular access history and mix of vascular access modalities. Inclusion criteria for the VASQoL study included (i) patients with chronic kidney disease and (ii) undergoing or about to undergo regular HD treatment.

Participants who met these inclusion criteria were approached and recruited from five regular dialysis units in the NHS GGC health board to participate in the study over a 6-week period. Patient participant numbers and characteristics are described below for both forms of evaluation.

Patient Usability Evaluation. A total of 26 out of 101 patients (25%) using the *Patient Portal* for quality-of-life data collection provided an SUS evaluation [13]. 35% were male (9/26) and patient ages ranged from 28 – 85, with 58% under 65 years of age (15/26). Half of patients (13/26) were in their first year receiving haemodialysis (HD) treatment, with two pre-HD and the remainder having received HD for over a year. There were 2 occurrences of incomplete data where patients did not provide their occupation, but otherwise the collected data was complete (Table 2).

Patient Comments and Semi-structured Interviews. Of the 26 participants in the SUS evaluation, just over half provided written feedback via a comment on the SUS form (14/26). An additional nineteen patients (n=19) were interviewed as part of the validation study and provided feedback on their experience using the *Patient Portal* as part of the validation study.

Researcher Interview. The clinical research fellow who conducted the study was also interviewed. The research fellow had ten years' experience of working with HD patients with some prior experience collecting data with traditional paper forms but no prior experience of working with a tablet device.

Table 2. SUS evaluation participant characteristics

Patient characteristics	Values	N (total = 26)
Sex	Male	9
	Female	17
Age	<65 years	15
	65+ years	11
Length of time on HD	Pre-HD	2
	<1 year on HD	13
	1+ years on HD	11
Occupation	Studying or working	6
	Retired	13
	Not working	5
	Unknown/Incomplete	2
SIMD (Scottish Index of Multiple Deprivation)	Level 1 (Most deprived)	5
	Level 2	10
	Level 3	4
	Level 4	4
	Level 5 (Least deprived)	3

4.2 Data Collection

MSG Group Sessions. The MSG met monthly in-person from February 2019, pausing in March 2020 as result of the COVID-19 pandemic, before continuing meetings fortnightly via Zoom from April 2020. A total of 33 meetings occurred in this period and meetings lasted between 60 to 90 min. During these meetings, the patient portal prototype was discussed and demonstrated, with participants able to view the system in-person or via a web app version prior to meetings. These sessions were audio recorded and transcribed, alongside contemporaneous notes which were summarized and distributed to all members of the group after each session. The continuous refinement of the *Patient Portal* ensured the system met the expectations of clinical expert stakeholders and aligned with clinical practices.

Patient Feedback and Evaluations. The *Patient Portal* was used to complete QoL measures regularly during their regular dialysis treatment. This required patients to access the *Patient Portal* via an Android application on one of two dedicated Samsung Galaxy Tab A tablets. The Android development environment was decided early in MSG meetings due to ease of app development and deployment, and the 10.1-inch screen size compromised screen size for viewing the interface and ease for patients holding the tablet with one hand. The clinical researchers delivered the devices to the patient during HD treatment and supported patients if required. Patients were required to complete the following three tasks:

(1)   update their vascular access modality and dialyzing status.
(2)   complete the QoL data collection.
(3)   log out and leave feedback if appropriate.

The three questionnaires (Short Form 36-Item Health Survey [23], EQ-5D-5L [24] and the VASQoL measure [8] under validation) were accessed via three separate buttons from the main menu, with only the relevant questionnaire accessible according to the scheduling of reporting. Other non-relevant questionnaires were made inaccessible until required (e.g. the SF-36 was not available if the latest submission was completed within 25 days of the current date, as the questionnaire is designed for monthly use). The data from the QoL questionnaires was not analyzed as part of this work.

Patients were asked to participate in the SUS evaluation upon completion of their final VASQoL study visit and final use of the patient portal, having used the portal up to four times over six weeks for QoL data collection. The SUS was used to measure system usability [13, 25] and the original questionnaire and questions were not modified. Paper questionnaires were chosen over digital ones to reduce the burden of participation for patients. The clinical researchers distributed the SUS to patients and aided with comprehension or acted as a scribe for participants where appropriate (e.g. writing arm being used for cannulation during dialysis, impaired vision, etc.).

Patients were also encouraged to record any comments or feedback they felt was important about the *Patient Portal* in a blank space below the SUS questions on the paper questionnaire.

Qualitative feedback was gathered from a separate cohort of patients as part of the VASQoL study. Data was collected by clinical researchers (two medical professionals with extensive experience of HD) thus avoiding patient contact with additional individuals outside those providing their treatment. Social distancing guidelines were adhered to throughout including limited access to hospital facilities during national restrictions in response to the COVID-19 pandemic. This also limited the number of patients they were able to recruit for SUS completion during HD sessions. However, it is widely accepted that the SUS measure is valid with smaller sample sizes (recommendations for at least twelve participants) [26].

Researcher Interview. The questions sought to elicit their experience working with patients and collecting patient data in paper and digital formats, alongside their views of the *Patient Portal* and their observations of patients' interactions with the *Patient Portal*. The 41-min interview was conducted remotely over Zoom, was audio recorded and subsequently transcribed.

4.3 Data Analysis

Thematic Analysis of Qualitative Data. Transcripts and notes from MSG meetings and patient and researcher interviews were analyzed using the health information systems quality assessment framework reported in [27], which is derived from DeLone and McLean's model of quality in information systems [28]. The model consists of six dimensions for ensuring information quality in health information systems, with potential issues, solutions and benefits provided for each: (1) eHealth information system quality, (2) information quality, (3) information usage, (4) user satisfaction, (5) individual impact and (6) organizational impact.

For example, the first dimension, eHealth information system quality is defined as the performance of information processing. Potential issues include a mismatch between system functionalities and clinical work processes or ambiguity of coding standards and errors or variability in assignment of codes. The proposed solutions to these issues are co-design of systems with stakeholders to closely match clinical practices (i.e. regular MSG meetings prior to deployment) and automated validity checks. The latter is a theme discussed in the following results section, highlighted by the clinical research fellow. Previous work within this setting [9] used this relevant framework in thematic analysis, and it was thus used to allow for consistency and comparison. The thematic analysis was completed in separate steps at each phase of the study. Transcriptions of meetings and interviews were indexed and coded before charting of codes in respect to the six dimensions detailed by the framework [27]. Finally, themes were synthesized from the charted codes, providing insight into the impact of the *Patient Portal* on treatment and patients and new or refined design requirements.

System Usability Scale (SUS) Quantitative Data. The SUS questionnaire [13] data was used to calculate an overall average usability score and averages for individual questions as well, to allow for insight into the different aspects of the SUS questionnaire and how patients responded to these in respect to the *Patient Portal*. For example, the second question "I found the system unnecessarily complex" is of relevance to a system that does not wish to impose further burden upon a high-treatment burden population such as HD patients.

5   Results

The results of this work are described as follows: (1) SUS scoring, (2) thematic analysis of patient and researcher interviews and (3) refined set of design requirements for the *Patient Portal*.

5.1   System Usability Scale (SUS) Scores

The overall average usability score was 86.9 (range 72.5 and 100 / 100) which can be considered as a "good" score [29]. Figure 1 shows average response score by question and is important to note for Fig. 1 that odd numbered questions (Q1, 3, 5, 7, 9) are scored low to high, with 5 being the highest score possible and 1 the lowest. The opposite is then true for even numbered questions (Q2, 4, 6, 8, 10). For example, Q3 has a very high average score of 4.8 and Q4 a low average score of 1.2 but this indicates that patients found the system easy to use and did not think they required support from a technical person (Q3 and Q4 respectively).

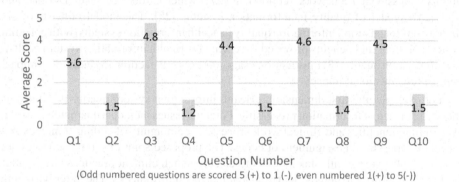

Fig. 1. Average score by question

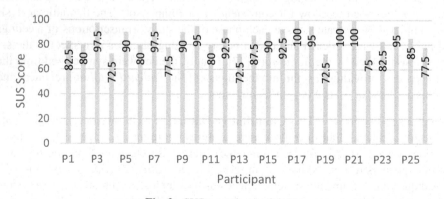

Fig. 2. SUS score by participant

Figure 2 shows SUS score by patient, with the minimum score of 72.5 placing the system in the "high" acceptability range as proposed by Bangor et al. [29]. While a small number of patients found the system presented a challenge and was considered "unnecessarily complex" (2/26 agreed or strongly agreed with statement Q2) or required prior learning before use (2/26 strongly agreed with Q10), the tablet-based system performed well and was of an acceptable standard to most patients, suggesting the co-design process was successful in producing a system which met the needs and expectations of stakeholders.

5.2 Thematic Analysis of Requirements for Patient Portal

Following the health information systems framework derived from DeLone and McLean [27, 28], design requirements were elicited from three sources: expert feedback in early iterative design phases, patient feedback via comments and interviews following study implementation and researcher observations during implementation. Findings are described according to the six dimensions of the framework.

T1: eHealth Information System Quality: Digital vs Paper. When asked during interviews if they would prefer paper alternatives to the digital *Patient Portal*, most patients preferred the tablet-hosted questionnaires (11/19) or had no preference (5/19), while three would have preferred paper. Both the researcher and patients noted the completion of the tablet-based questionnaires was easier and more feasible than using pen-and-paper during dialysis sessions. This is an important and previously unidentified observation as dialyzing with a fistula − particularly if in the dominant hand − makes writing difficult whilst receiving dialysis treatment but it did not limit the use of the *Patient Portal*. However, it was clear from both the patient and researcher interviews that traditional alternatives should be provided for those who may be inexperienced or unwilling to use technology. This suggests that while there are benefits to digital PROM data collection for this population, there is a need to provide traditional alternatives when appropriate [19, 30, 31].

> *"We had some trouble at the beginning but actually its quite good, a good thing to use it. I really liked it, I liked to work with the app or with the tablet."* – Researcher.

Overall, the interviews revealed patients found the *Patient Portal* to be usable. This reflects the results of the SUS evaluation, where scores indicated the *Patient Portal* was "easy to use" and patients did not think the support of a technical person was required to use the system. There was discussion amongst patients that it may be easier for younger and more experienced patients, but some inexperienced patients also praised the ease of use of the *Patient Portal*, as did the clinical researcher.

> *"I think it's easier to place a tablet on your legs and use a pen or stylus, even with your non-dominant hand, you can do that...So I think it's much more convenient to use a tablet, especially for the one-handed patients."* – Researcher.

> *"I personally would prefer to do it on the app [Patient Portal]. And for people who, if you are going to do the questionnaire for people who are on dialysis it is actually quite hard to write. Some people have their fistula in their dominant hand, I don't fortunately, but even just writing can be awkward but some people*

are a bit funny about computers. So I don't know, you maybe have to do a bit of both." – Interview P8.

T2: Information Quality. The researcher interviews revealed further benefits of the digital system over traditional data methods. Firstly, the validation processes of the *Patient Portal* reassured the researcher that any completed questionnaires were complete and automatically stored securely, mitigating the risk of missing or incomplete data from human error (i.e. incomplete questions only detected after participant has completed study or transcribing paper responses to digital formats).

"And the other thing is the feedback, if you miss a question, it doesn't store...- for paper forms, I won't realize until they missed a question or something..." – Researcher.

Secondly, there was also a common theme of independence amongst the patient comments provided, praising the ability to complete the quality-of-life questionnaires independently and provide honest responses. These comments suggest patients can be uncomfortable discussing their health and quality-of-life with others or feel unable to provide honest answers. Thus, the ability to self-complete the quality-of-life measures via the *Patient Portal* provided a "safe space", with no pressure from other individuals to respond in a certain manner. This positive feedback suggests that provision of systems like the *Patient Portal* encourage patient activation and engagement in their care, which would otherwise be difficult to achieve through purely direct communication with their healthcare team.

"I really enjoyed using the tablet system. I also preferred being on my own to do it so I could put honest answers." – SUS P3.

"I like being left to complete it. I feel I can be more honest than if I am asked a question directly." – SUS P6.

This important aspect of patient feeling better equipped to disclose sensitive information to a "computer" has also previously been highlighted in other work on computer-mediated patients' medical questionnaires [32–36].

T3: Information Usage: Perceived Value of Engagement. The theme of communication between patient and healthcare provider was identified in patient comments, with patients indicating they wished for staff to review their responses. However, while there was potential for the *Patient Portal* to support patient-provider communication, it was of little value to patients if their responses were not reviewed. These findings reflect those of Absolom et al. [30], where the perceived value of an intervention and collection of patient-reported outcome measure (PROM) data was doubted by patients when data was not referred to during clinical counters.

"Useful for nightshift or twilight shift to communicate with doctors - no use if nobody looks at it." – SUS P15.

"I would like the VA [vascular access] team to know my answers." – SUS P16.

While both this study and the VASQoL validation study did not utilize PROM data clinically, a clear sentiment was reported by patients that they only found benefit in reporting data through the *Patient Portal* where it is viewed and utilized by healthcare providers. This utilization of data will need to be visible in future implementations, through referral in discussions or other means to retain engagement from patients.

There were opposing comments, notably one patient felt "perfectly able" when communicating with healthcare providers and were the only participant to respond they strongly disagreed that they would like to use the system frequently. This suggests for patients who are confident in their ability to communicate and discuss their healthcare, interventions such as the *Patient Portal* are seen unnecessary and as a possible hinderance to their patient-provider relationship and communication.

"I feel I am perfectly able to communicate with nurses/doctors when I need to. I am also quite able to understand what is being said to me when discussing my health." – SUS P4.

T4: User Satisfaction: Physical Accessibility. Both patients and the researcher enjoyed using the system during the study. There were accessibility obstacles to overcome early on during the study, notably concerning patients' ability to utilize touchscreen input.

"What made a difference, a huge difference, is using like a pen [stylus]. They are not that precise without a pen. They sometimes miss a field." – Researcher.

"Awkward because in dominant hand but much easier than writing - difficult to add written comment with non-dominant hand - a voice recognition function could help with things." – SUS P14.

Considerations were made for these accessibility issues during the initial phase, as clinical experts provided this insight. Observations by the study coordinators highlighted the scale of the issue of touch input and HD patients. Decreased sensitivity or sense of pressure in patients' fingers, credited to carpal tunnel syndrome symptoms or neuropathy [6], appeared to result in incorrect gestures being registered and the system providing an incorrect response to the intended input (i.e. patients press on elements such as buttons for a longer length of time and the touch gesture is read as a "long press" instead of a click event). This caused frustration amongst patients and prevented them from completing the tasks required of them without difficulty. Immediate action was taken to remedy this by providing styluses alongside the tablet devices, which improved the touch input and accuracy of patients input.

Another common barrier was the impaired vision of patients, with the clinical research fellow required to support those unable to view the tablet and user interface clearly. Impaired vision can be common in this population, especially in diabetic or elderly patients receiving haemodialysis long-term [7].

"I totally underestimated, there are a lot of visually impaired patients." - Researcher.

Therefore, the addition of alternative output and input methods (e.g. text-to-speech and speech-to-text) should be considered and may also be well-received by other users i.e. those who experience issues with touch input.

T5: Individual Impact: Activating Patients. Patients highlighted how the *Patient Portal* and the quality-of-life questionnaires caused them to consider their healthcare and their role. There was a request for the addition of further information on how to leave comments following questionnaire completion and inclusion of a question to elicit patient preferences.

> *"Would like to be able to expand on other aspects of care or problems. Instructions of how to leave comments at the end."* – SUS P14.

> *"I think adding…asking a question that sticks in your head what is the preference of the dialysis patient. I mean, at the end of the day it doesn't fall into the preference because this is your lifeline. If this one fails you need to end up with this one."* – Interview P3.

The earlier theme of providing honest responses also supports this activation of patients, as they feel they can provide honest answers and engage with their health independently. There was a request for better explanation of some questions, which should be considered carefully in order to continue facilitating the independent completion of the questionnaires. This also connects back to the usability of the system, where the need for explanation of a question or instruction suggests the support of a technical individual is required and reduces system usability.

> *"I liked being able to fill it in and then have people ask me about it. I don't like bringing things up myself. I don't talk about it much."* – SUS P8.

> *"Most relevant to me are the health questions. Fill in the vascular access one if I have problems (haven't had with this line)."* – SUS P21.

T6: Organizational Impact: Facilitating PROM Collection. The *Patient Portal* proved to be an effective and usable method for collecting patient-reported outcome measure (PROM) data from patients, praised by both patients and researcher. There were benefits over paper data collection (e.g. accessibility for dialyzing patients, validation of data and reducing risk of human error) but considerations should be made for those who may not wish to engage with digital methods or are unable to. This population is typically older [37], and while there is an expectation that the prevalence and familiarity with technology will grow with time, this subpopulation of users should be supported, either through the accessibility of the system or by providing alternatives [19, 30, 31] e.g. pen-and-paper if requested or providing support through scribing.

> *"Like I said, there are some patients who just can't do it by themselves. They just have no experience."* – Researcher.

5.3 Formal Design Requirements

A set of formal design requirements was collated from all three sources: (1) iterative review and feedback from experts, (2) patient usability evaluations and interviews, and (3) researcher observations of the system implementation. They are classified as functional and non-functional, the former describing *what* a system will do and the latter *how* it does this [38]. These can also be understood as what makes the system *useful* and what makes it *usable*.

Expert feedback is described in four distinct phases which occurred during iterative development and feedback with the MSG: (1) Identification of Core Functionalities, (2) First Refinement, (3) Second Refinement and (4) Final Refinement. The first confirmed the essential functionalities and purpose of the *Patient Portal*. The second phase and third phases built upon this by incorporating elements to improve the user experience and improve performance of the system while the fourth the phase consisted of final refinements to ensure the system was ready for implementation ahead of the VASQoL study.

While most of the design requirements gathered from iterative development with experts were implemented, some functionalities were not included in the version of the *Patient Portal* used for hosting the QoL questionnaires for the VASQoL study and usability evaluation. The priority in development was to ensure core functionalities that were identified early were implemented robustly before the addition of later functionalities. For the VASQoL study, this required the quality-of-life questionnaire data collection and the accurate capture of clinical events and changes in vascular access as required of by the study. Others were not implemented due to feasibility and time-constraints, namely multiple language availability.

After the commencement of the VASQoL study, it became clear some emerging design requirements were of high priority and resolving these were critical to the patients' effective and continued use of the system. Early observations reported that dialysis patients struggled with touch gestures using the tablet devices, with a reduced sense of pressure or sensitivity in their fingers impacting their ability to tap buttons onscreen (i.e. too much pressure indicated a long-press gesture, highlighting the text of the button rather than registering a click event as intended).

To avoid interrupting the study and increasing frustration for patients, rubber-tipped styluses were acquired and provided alongside the tablets for the remainder of the study. Other modifications to reduce system complexity and patient frustration included the disabling of the user feedback functionality (which prompted patients during logging out to leave feedback) and modifying the size of the EQ5D5L user interface elements so all content was available onscreen regardless of, device screen orientation. In this case, patients were disorientated when navigation buttons were not visible in landscape orientation without scrolling (see Fig. 3). This may seem easily resolved by rotating the screen to the portrait orientation, but for a patient dialyzing with a fistula or graft, they are unable to both hold the tablet and touch the screen with one hand and rely on tablet being positioned upright to interact with it.

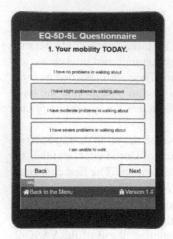
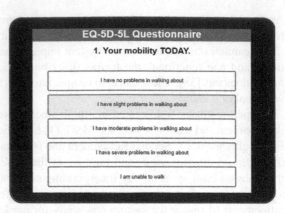

Fig. 3. Screenshots of EQ5D5L layout change on orientation, highlighting offscreen positioning of navigation buttons

Otherwise, the systems key functionalities and user interface elements remained unchanged for the duration of the study (Table 3).

Table 3. Formal design requirements and sources, in chronological order of identification. (Type: F = Functional, NF = Non-Functional).

Requirement description	Type	Source
Capture of SF-36, EQ5D-5L and vascular access quality-of-life questionnaires responses	F	Expert feedback (1)
Capture of clinical events (i.e. changes in vascular access and dialysis status)	F	Expert feedback (1)
User-reported feedback functionality	F	Expert feedback (1)
Patient information: provision and access to tailored patient information	F	Expert feedback (1)
User training or "demo mode"	F	Expert feedback (2)
Anonymity and security of patient data	NF	Expert feedback (2)
Multi-lingual options	NF	Expert feedback (2)
Handling network and data transfer issues	F	Expert feedback (2)
User progression visible during tasks	NF	Expert feedback (3)
Highly usable and accessible system, notably for user population typically older and living with chronic condition	NF	Expert feedback (3)

(*continued*)

Table 3. (*continued*)

Requirement description	Type	Source
Handles user error and provides adequate feedback	NF	Expert feedback (4)
Recording graft cannulation: selection of configuration and location	F	Expert feedback (4)
Recording graft cannulation: image quality consistently high	NF	Expert feedback (4)
Opportunity to review input before submission	F	Expert feedback (4)
Accounting for physical limitations i.e. reduced sense of touch/pressure in fingers, dominant hand unavailable, single-handed use	NF	Observations
Simplify and limit burden of completing tasks	NF	Observations
Adaptable and flexible user interface e.g. font-size, layout of elements, etc.	NF	Observations, Patient comments
Alternative input methods to text e.g. voice	F	Patient comments
Perceived value e.g. communicating with staff through responses, change in treatment as result of response review	NF	Observations, Patient comments
Able to be completed independently	NF	Patient comments

6 Discussion

We sought to produce a haemodialysis patient portal with the involvement of domain experts, building on a previous determined design [9, 17], and tested this with patients in a hospital setting. This study sought to determine if a two-phase multidisciplinary approach could produce a system appropriate for implementation into a real-world setting i.e. during HD treatment in a hospital environment. This was achieved by following a case study methodology, consisting of iterative developments closely supported by experts until the *Patient Portal* was robust enough to collect patient-reported outcomes and implement into clinical practice with patients. The system was evaluated with patients, achieving an above average SUS score and gathered rich design requirements from both patient feedback and investigator observations. The in-depth thematic analysis of qualitative data supplemented the quantitative SUS scores and the framework utilized in previous work with domain experts [9] proved to be suitable in this work.

The delivery of the QoL measures digitally via the *Patient Portal* benefitted most patients, overcoming situational impairment where traditional paper-and-pen question-naires would have been difficult to complete. The researcher also noted the validation of the digital data collection reduced human error and streamlined the process. However, observations also confirmed that younger patients were often more comfortable and adept at using the tablets than their older peers, with patients also aware others may simply chose not to engage with the technology due to personal preferences. While the growing prevalence of technology is often cited as an eventual solution to this issue [31, 39, 40], conventional alternatives should be provided alongside the digital options to prevent patients from becoming excluded from healthcare [19, 31].

A highly usable *Patient Portal* resulted in the engagement and activation of patients, promoting a sense of independence, and providing a private space for reporting their health and satisfaction with treatment. Interestingly patients reported that they felt they could be more honest via the tablet app than in a face-to-face conversation and felt it was a way to initiate discussion, confirming previous findings in the sphere of computer-mediated patient medical questionnaires research [32–36]. The perceived value of the system indicates it met the needs and expectations of patients [10] and was also a motivator for engagement for both patients (as demonstrated by their feedback) and clinicians [11], which has been difficult to secure with similar systems as noted in the section on related work.

While this work did not utilize patient data or influence treatment in any manner, it was clear from the patient feedback that the system will need to demonstrate this value or risk losing patient engagement, as made clear by patients' feedback. Systems such as the *Patient Portal* need to acknowledge patient input and demonstrate engagement from the other side, such as read receipts of submitted data, where an action in response may be delayed e.g. follow-up appointment with consultant. Implementation of functionalities such as this may reassure patients their input matters and prevent perceived value and engagement deteriorating.

The positive reception of the *Patient Portal* through implementation with HD patients showed clear support for future work in this field. This case study of the *Patient Portal* evaluation with HD patients during treatment identified unique accessibility issues within this user population. This included an example of situational impairment, already highlighted by Mishra et al. [16], which in turn can lead to patients preferring horizontal orientation for the tablet devices and identifying issues with the patient portal user interface. Considerations were made for such issues in selection of a suitable device and the design and layout of the user interface but still required refinement to improve the accessibility of the system with HD patients, such as adaptive layouts with orientation changes and use of a stylus to overcome touch sensitivity difficulties. While some actions were taken during the study to remedy this (e.g. the introduction of styluses), the *Patient Portal* will need to take these issues into consideration in future iterations, such as accounting for longer presses to achieve a click event or ensuring the shift in screen orientation does not result in additional actions to complete tasks (i.e. scrolling down to view offscreen buttons). Other condition-specific accessibility issues were also captured, including vision impairment which is common within this population. These findings will hopefully inform future work with this population and demonstrate the benefits of the in-depth analysis and description this case study has produced.

While we believe our methodology was appropriate and sufficient, this study has some limitations. The study was conducted under lockdown and other Covid-19 restrictions during the global pandemic in 2020 and great care had to be taken for patient safety as chronic kidney disease patients are classed as vulnerable [41]. This prevented a non-medical researcher attending the medical facilities, so data collection was reliant on healthcare professionals already working in the hospital. A single usability measure was employed as clinicians felt additional measures would have placed an excessive burden upon patients and the researchers during an already difficult period. The case study was conducted in only one setting, replication studies are planned as part of future development cycles.

Considerations for future work include further refinement of the existing system following this evaluation and implementation into routine practice, potentially at national and international levels. Most importantly, piloting this within a routine clinical setting such as monthly haemodialysis clinic reviews will be important as where there is lack of perceived value, the intervention is less likely to become normalized into routine practice [42, 43].

Further work with HD patients to address and resolve barriers to engagement and use of the *Patient Portal* is also required, notably those arising from situational impairment and condition-specific challenges, such as vision impairments and touch input difficulties. The design requirements elicited in this work will provide direction for further refinements of both this system and similar technologies.

Overall, the usability evaluation of the *Patient Portal* produced results indicating the system is usable and of "good" quality, with an average SUS score of 86.9. This score is supplemented with positive feedback from both patients and a clinical researcher familiar with the domain.

To our knowledge this work is novel and demonstrates the successful deployment and evaluation of a co-designed patient portal with a patient cohort marked by treatment and disease burden, comorbidity and age, within a clinical setting. This case study with HD patients using the *Patient Portal* during their regular dialysis treatment also provided an effective evaluation and yielded rich and important design requirements to consider, with data gathered from multiple sources. These insights and considerations are required to produce a system fit for purpose and accessible by its target end-users [44].

7   Conclusion

Our multi-stakeholder co-development method led to a functional application that facilitated completion of a digital PROM study that was usable by a comorbid population of patients, as evidenced by above-average SUS scores despite the challenging use environment. Researcher observation and patient interviews highlighted areas for review such as need for a stylus due to physical limitations with touch screen for this population and specific design issues such as their difficulty in rotating a tablet during hemodialysis. Patients overwhelmingly preferred tablet input over paper, primarily because of ease of entry and increased privacy. However, we identified a small group of patients who had a strong preference for paper. The study also highlighted the need for clinical apps to reassure users by demonstrating feedback and clinical responses to their input to maintain the perceived value of using the system. Our future work will include developing approaches for such feedback as well as addressing the accessibility issues raised and applying our lessons in development of care support apps for in-hospital patients.

Acknowledgements. This work was funded by a Strathclyde Centre for Doctoral Training (SCDT) Research Studentship in Digital Health and Analytics [45] (2018–2022). The authors would like to thank the dialysis nurses and patients for their participation in this work, while in the midst of a global pandemic. We would also like to thank Fabiano Pinatti (Aparecido F. P. de Carvalho) for his comments and improvement suggestions on earlier versions of this paper.

References

1. Hill, N.R., et al.: Global prevalence of chronic kidney disease–a systematic review and meta-analysis. PLoS ONE **11**(7), e0158765 (2016)
2. Fukuhara, S., et al.: Health-related quality of life among dialysis patients on three continents: the dialysis outcomes and practice patterns study. Kidney Int. **64**(5), 1903–1910 (2003). https://doi.org/10.1046/j.1523-1755.2003.00289.x
3. Cleary, J., Drennan, J.: Quality of life of patients on haemodialysis for end-stage renal disease. J. Adv. Nurs. **51**(6), 577–586 (2005). https://doi.org/10.1111/j.1365-2648.2005.03547.x
4. Oliver, S.W., et al.: A national appraisal of haemodialysis vascular access provision in Scotland. J. Vasc. Access **18**(2), 126–131 (2017)
5. Stenvinkel, P.: Chronic kidney disease: a public health priority and harbinger of premature cardiovascular disease. J. Intern. Med. **268**(5), 456–467 (2010). https://doi.org/10.1111/j.1365-2796.2010.02269.x
6. Fujita, K., Kimori, K., Nimura, A., Okawa, A., Ikuta, Y.: MRI analysis of carpal tunnel syndrome in hemodialysis patients versus non-hemodialysis patients: a multicenter case-control study. J. Orthop. Surg. Res. **14**(1), 1–7 (2019)
7. Gonda, A., Gault, H., Churchill, D., Hollomby, D.: Hemodialysis for methanol intoxication. Am. J. Med. **64**(5), 749–758 (1978)
8. Stevenson, K., et al.: Validation of a vascular access specific quality of life measure (VASQOL). Under Peer-Review
9. Bouamrane, M.M., et al.: Haemodialysis electronic patient portal: a design requirements analysis and feasibility study with domain experts. In: 2019 IEEE 32nd International Symposium on Computer-Based Medical Systems (CBMS), pp. 212–216 (2019)
10. Sadeghi, M., Thomassie, R., Sasangohar, F.: Objective assessment of patient portal requirements. In: Proceedings of the International Symposium on Human Factors and Ergonomics in Health Care, vol. 6, no. 1, p. 1. SAGE Publications, Los Angeles (2017)
11. Irizarry, T., Dabbs, A.D., Curran, C.R.: Patient portals and patient engagement: a state of the science review. J. Med. Internet Res. **17**(6), e148 (2015)
12. Latulipe, C., et al.: Design considerations for patient portal adoption by low-income, older adults. In: Proceedings of the 33rd Annual ACM Conference on Human Factors in Computing Systems, pp. 3859–3868 (2015)
13. Brooke, J.: SUS: a "quick and dirty' usability". Usability Eval. Ind. **189**, 4–7 (1996)
14. Noble, P.J.: Resilience ex machina: learning a complex medical device for haemodialysis self-treatment. In: Proceedings of the 33rd Annual ACM Conference on Human Factors in Computing Systems, pp. 4147–4150 (2015)
15. Murray, E., et al.: The first 365 days on haemodialysis: variation in the haemodialysis access journey and its associated burden. Nephrol. Dial. Transplant. **33**(7), 1244–1250 (2018)
16. Mishra, S.R., et al.: Supporting collaborative health tracking in the hospital: patients' perspectives. In: Proceedings of the 2018 CHI Conference on Human Factors in Computing Systems, pp. 1–14 (2018)
17. Haldar, S., Mishra, S.R., Khelifi, M., Pollack, A.H., Pratt, W.: Beyond the patient portal: supporting needs of hospitalized patients. In: Proceedings of the 2019 CHI Conference on Human Factors in Computing Systems, pp. 1–14 (2019)

18. Turner, K., Clary, A., Hong, Y.R., Tabriz, A.A., Shea, C.M.: Patient portal barriers and group differences: cross-sectional national survey study. J. Med. Internet Res. **22**(9), e18870 (2020)
19. Burgess, E.R., Reddy, M.C., Davenport, A., Laboi, P., Blandford, A.: "Tricky to get your head around" information work of people managing chronic kidney disease in the UK. In: Proceedings of the 2019 CHI Conference on Human Factors in Computing Systems, pp. 1–17 (2019)
20. Kuo, P.Y., et al.: Development of a checklist for the prevention of intradialytic hypotension in hemodialysis care: design considerations based on activity theory. In: Proceedings of the 2019 CHI Conference on Human Factors in Computing Systems, pp. 1–14 (2019)
21. Kildea, J., et al.: Design and development of a person-centered patient portal using participatory stakeholder co-design. J. Med. Internet Res. **21**(2), e11371 (2019)
22. Creswell, J.W.: Qualitative Inquiry and Research Design: Choosing Among Five Approaches. SAGE Publications, Thousand Oaks (2012)
23. Ware Jr, J.E.: SF-36 health survey (1999)
24. Herdman, M., et al.: Development and preliminary testing of the new five-level version of EQ-5D (EQ-5D-5L). Qual. Life Res. **20**(10), 1727–1736 (2011)
25. Brooke, J.: SUS: a retrospective. J. Usability Stud. **8**(2), 29–40 (2013)
26. Tullis, T.S., Stetson, J.N.: A comparison of questionnaires for assessing website usability. In: Usability Professional Association Conference, vol. 1, pp. 1–12 (2004)
27. Bouamrane, M.M., Mair, F., Tao, C.: An overview of electronic health information management systems quality assessment. In: Proceedings of the 2nd International Workshop on Managing Interoperability and Complexity in Health Systems, pp. 37–46 (2012)
28. DeLone, W.H., McLean, E.: R: Information systems success: the quest for the dependent variable. Inf. Syst. Res. **3**(1), 60–95 (1992)
29. Bangor, A., Kortum, P., Miller, J.: Determining what individual SUS scores mean: adding an adjective rating scale. J. Usability Stud. **4**(3), 114–123 (2009)
30. Absolom, K., Gibson, A., Velikova, G.: Engaging patients and clinicians in online reporting of adverse effects during chemotherapy for cancer: the eRAPID system (electronic patient self-reporting of adverse events: patient information and aDvice). Med. Care **57**, S59–S65 (2019)
31. Ashley, L., et al.: Integrating patient reported outcomes with clinical cancer registry data: a feasibility study of the electronic Patient-Reported Outcomes From Cancer Survivors (ePOCS) system. J. Med. Internet Res. **15**(10), e230 (2013)
32. Bachman, J.W.: The patient-computer interview: a neglected tool that can aid the clinician. Mayo Clin. Proc. **78**, 67–78 (2003)
33. Bouamrane, M.-M., Rector, A., Hurrell, M.: Using OWL ontologies for adaptive patient information modelling and preoperative clinical decision support. Knowl. Inf. Syst. **29**, 405–418 (2011)
34. Bouamrane, M.-M., Rector, A., Hurrell, M.: Development of an ontology for a preoperative risk assessment clinical decision support system. In: 22nd IEEE International Symposium on Computer-Based Medical Systems, pp. 1–6 (2009)
35. Bouamrane, M.-M., Rector, A., Hurrell, M.: Ontology-driven adaptive medical information collection system. In: An, A., Matwin, S., Raś, Z.W., Ślęzak, D. (eds.) ISMIS 2008. LNCS (LNAI), vol. 4994, pp. 574–584. Springer, Heidelberg (2008). https://doi.org/10.1007/978-3-540-68123-6_62
36. Bouamrane, M.-M., Rector, A., Hurrell, M.: Gathering precise patient medical history with an ontology-driven adaptive questionnaire. In: 21st IEEE International Symposium on Computer-Based Medical Systems, pp. 539–541 (2008)
37. Ronsberg, F., Isles, C., Simpson, K., Prescott, G.: Renal replacement therapy in the over-80s. Age Ageing **34**(2), 148–152 (2005)

38. Eckhardt, J., Vogelsang, A. and Fernández, D.M.: Are "non-functional" requirements really non-functional? An investigation of non-functional requirements in practice. In: Proceedings of the 38th International Conference on Software Engineering, pp. 832–842 (2016)
39. Basch, E., et al.: Patient online self-reporting of toxicity symptoms during chemotherapy. J. Clin. Oncol. **23**(15), 3552–3561 (2005)
40. Basch, E., et al.: Long-term toxicity monitoring via electronic patient-reported outcomes in patients receiving chemotherapy. J. Clin. Oncol. **25**(34), 5374–5380 (2007)
41. Bell, S., et al.: COVID-19 in patients undergoing chronic kidney replacement therapy and kidney transplant recipients in Scotland: findings and experience. BMC Nephrol. **21**(1), 1–12 (2020)
42. Jacobs, M., Johnson, J., Mynatt, E.D.: MyPath: investigating breast cancer patients' use of personalized health information. In: Proceedings of the ACM on Human-Computer Interaction, 2(CSCW), pp. 1–21 (2018)
43. Bouamrane, M.-M., Osbourne, J., Mair, F.S.: Understanding the implementation & integration of remote & tele-health services … an overview of normalization process theory. In: 2011 5th International Conference on Pervasive Computing Technologies for Healthcare (PervasiveHealth) and Workshops, pp. 300–307 (2011)
44. Aiyegbusi, O.L.: Key methodological considerations for usability testing of electronic patient-reported outcome (ePRO) systems. Qual. Life Res. **29**(2), 325–333 (2019). https://doi.org/10.1007/s11136-019-02329-z
45. https://pureportal.strath.ac.uk/en/projects/strathclyde-doctoral-training-centre-sdtc-in-digital-health-imple

Digital Work Environment Rounds – Systematic Inspections of Usability Supported by the Legislation

Jan Gulliksen(✉) 🆔

KTH Royal Institute of Technology, Stockholm, Sweden
gulliksen@kth.se

Abstract. Digital tools are an essential part of the work environment of many civil servants working at public authorities. They should therefore follow the prevalent work environment legislation. This paper describes a method to conduct digital work environment rounds to assess the usability of digitalized work to assess work environment risks and identify improvements. The methodology used is following a participatory action research project in collaboration between users, union representatives, managers and IT experts. The case presented in this paper describes the development of the digital work environment round in collaboration with a court in Sweden. It was based on an international standard in the making and collaboratively developed and adapted to the situation at the public authority. Based on this work the public authority has now decided to make this method a part of their annual systematic work environment management and other organizations are following in their tracks.

Keywords: Digital work environment · Digitalization · Usability · Work environment rounds

1 Introduction

Does your computer system prevent you from doing your work in an efficient way? Have you had the chance to influence the systems you use for your work? Would you consider your e-mail a work environment problem?

More or less everybody are using computers or other digital support systems as work tools today. According to Statistics Sweden [1] 78% of all working in Sweden uses a computer in their work. The share of females is slightly higher than men. 45% uses the computer more than half the working day. 58% of the PC users use computers more than half of the working day. 20% (for PC-users 25%) use computers more or less all the time. And the problems users experience in the use of computers are high and keep increasing: 35% of everybody working complain about pain in the upper part of the back or neck every week, 29% report that they every day are sitting still in their work more than two hours without a break and 7% in more than 4 h without a break. 40% experience such a stressful work that they do not have the time to talk with anybody or think about

© IFIP International Federation for Information Processing 2021
Published by Springer Nature Switzerland AG 2021
C. Ardito et al. (Eds.): INTERACT 2021, LNCS 12933, pp. 197–218, 2021.
https://doi.org/10.1007/978-3-030-85616-8_13

anything else than work during more than half the working day. 43% experience that they never or rarely are able to control when their tasks are supposed to be conducted.

How can we work in a systematic fashion to prevent usability problems to happen in the work setting and contribute to improving the digital work environments for everybody in an organization? Our hypothesis in this project was that this could be done, based on the systematic work environment management that is mandated through the legislation controlling labor.

The purpose of this paper is to show how the legislation can serve as a powerful tool and how systematic work environment management can leverage the union employer collaboration to improve the digital work environment. I will do that by demonstrating how the digital work environment round, by being supported by the legislation, can be a powerful way of improving the digital work environment for employees in an organization.

2 Theory and Related Work

In this theory and related work section I will go through the historical heritage of the work, from cooperative design methods through work environment related research. I will go through work environment legislation, systematic work environment management and digital work environment as a construct. The method of digital work environment rounds is introduced and related international standards work is presented.

2.1 Computer Supported Work and Cooperative Design

There is a lot of previous work done to develop our digital work environments by means of engaging directly with the user population, such as the Work-oriented design of computer artifacts [2], the concept of Cooperative design [3, 4] and Participatory Design (PD) [5]. Bødker has also in her recent work showed how the concept of participatory design can develop in the public sector with the increasing use of digital tools for work [6]. One of the reasons for the role that Scandinavian countries has played in developing the theories on cooperative design is its historically strong collaboration with trade unions and the union representatives.

In more recent approaches, Pilemalm [7] has provided an extensive overview of the development of PD over the years and shown that participatory design approaches may be redesigned for the public sector to better reflect contemporary needs for more user-centered activities. However, with the recent digital development in the work setting and the ever-increasing need of user engagement in the redesign of work and IT, there is a need to develop new ways of addressing the user perspective with a renewed interest in union collaboration and the need to focus the digital transformation not only in the collaborative design of the digital tools, but also on the redefinition of the work tasks and organization of the work. In this case study we have developed the approach to digital transformation grounded in the concept of digital work environments and union-employer collaboration to meet the needs to adhere to work environment legislation and the need to improve the development of the digital work environment.

2.2 Work Environment and Computer Systems Development and Use

There is not much research that has been conducted with the purpose of understanding the relationship between digital technologies and the work environment. Hoonakker [8] investigated the development and implementation of information and communication technology (ICT) and the impact it has had on the quality of working life and concludes that the recent development of the possibilities of collaborating through digital technologies has led to increasing demands from the work and unclear boundaries between work and leisure time. Bordi et al. [9] has also showed the increasing demands on communication that the digital technologies entail, resulting in a feeling of constant connectivity, an ever-increasing volume of digital communication, deteriorating quality of the contents of the communication, adaptation of new digital tools, technical problems and flexibility in communication may have an effect on the wellbeing, if it takes away the users feeling of autonomy and control. The relationship between the work environment and the usability of the computerized support tools have been clearly expressed in Sandblad et al. [10]. Many of the common usability problems may in a work setting lead to cognitive work environment problems. Work environment considerations have in the past been included in usability evaluations methods [11]. There is a need to develop mechanisms and routines that further supports the user in developing and growing its skills in the use of the systems and putting greater demands on the usability of the work supporting systems.

This study is based on a Socio-technical perspective emphasizing the importance of seeing the organization as a whole where technical and social functions are interacting and where both influences, and are influenced, by each other. The socio-technical values are based on the fact that the needs and rights of the employees must have as high priority as the changing technical and organizational structures in the system [12].

2.3 Relationship to Legislation: Case Swedish Work Environment Law

The national or international legislation can be a very powerful tool when it comes to ensuring a high-quality digital work environment. Legislation varies in different parts of the world but the worker rights are particularly strong in the Nordic countries. Nowhere else in the world the protection of the worker's rights and explicating the employer's responsibility for the work environment is as strong.

There is legislation in place to support high quality in the computerized work tools, even if they are rarely used to sue anybody. They are, however, strong when it comes to assuring strong support for the user perspective in the acquisition, adaptation installation and development of computerized work tools. According to the Swedish Work Environment Act [13] *"A work must be characterized by variation, social contact and cooperation, the connection between tasks, the opportunity for personal and professional development, self-determination and professional responsibility."* This means that Computer systems used in work settings should be designed to meet high quality criteria not only in the system design but in what it means for the design of the digital work tasks. This means that the organization need to ensure a working environment that does not expose workers to ill-health or accidents and which is satisfactory in view of the nature of work and the social and technological development of society; and to encourage employers and employees to work together to create a good working environment. Ensuring means that the work environment activities should be conducted in a systematic preventive way.

The Swedish Work Environment Authority has also issued regulations that, although they were derived a long time ago, still are valid for judging the digital work environments. The regulation Work with Display Units AFS [14] states that: *"Work with display units that are strongly controlled or tied physically or mentally or are unilaterally repeated may not normally occur. Systems and programs should be suitably designed with regard to tasks and users, be easy to use, be adaptable to the user's knowledge and experience level, provide feedback on the work performed, display information in a format and pace that is tailored to the user. And, special attention should be paid to ergonomic principles that apply to the ability to perceive, understand and process information. Control of the worker's work through the system must not be carried out without his knowledge."* This means that the quality of the systems needs to meet high criteria, both in terms of how they are designed and how they eventually are implemented in the work situation.

The Swedish Work Environment Law also states that *"The worker should be given the possibility to participate in the design of his/her own work situation and in changes and development that concerns the work."* This means that the law can be used not only to assure usable computer systems for work but a user-centered development processes to ensure the individual users' rights to be involved in the development.

2.4 Systematic Work Environment Management

Systematic work environment management (SWEM) is based on the fact that employers, employees and safety representatives map what risks of ill-health or accidents exist in the workplace and work together to counteract them. According to Swedish Work Environment Act, all employers must have SWEM (AFS 2001: 1) in place. SAM is normally conducted through a four-step survey in which workplace risks are 1) investigated, 2) assessed, 3) addressed and 4) followed up. This should also be done before changes in the business or organization, if a serious incident occurs in the workplace or if an employee is exposed to health risks or accidents. Risks that are detected must be assessed and prioritized and must always be documented in writing.

Systematic Work Environment Management in Sweden is also subject to evaluations. In an evaluation report published in 2003 [15] about 40% of employers claim that SWEM has been introduced in the workplace and is functioning well. 65% say that they have investigated the work environment and made an assessment of the risks, while 70% say that they have a 'good' (or 'very good') knowledge of SWEM. However, about 40% think that SWEM demands too much administration resources. No studies have been made yet on the use of SWEM for the digital work environment.

There are other countries that has similar arrangements for assessing the work environment, as for example the Risk Assessment Guidelines (APV) issued by the Danish Work Environment Authority [16].

2.5 Digital Work Environment

Digital work environment can be defined as *"the work environment, with its problems and possibilities of physical, psycho-social as well as cognitive nature that is the result of the digitalization of the tools and support systems"* [17]. This definition means emphasizes the importance of digital tools for the work environment and that the digital tools used in the professional role are a dominant part of the work environment of the employees. Robertson [18] on the other hand, defines digital work environment as a holistic set of tools, platforms and work environments delivered in a coherent, useful and productive way. He believes that the digital work environment should be considered holistic as it includes all systems, applications, connections and the physical workplace and by looking at these together, as a whole, one can take major steps to change how and where the work is done. Robertson further describes that the digital work environment should be coherent in order to coordinate tasks and projects, be useful by delivering simple and seamless user experiences that fit their workflow and productive by being structured to help employees perform their work tasks [18].

The digital work environment is a whole that includes both the technical systems used in the workplace and the context in which they are located. By looking at how people use information and communication technology in their particular context, you can get a holistic picture that includes both technical requirements and information on how the technical solution can best be used in the specific context [19]. The employer has the ultimate responsibility for ensuring that the digital work environment complies with the Work Environment Act, but according to Berg and Gustafsson [20] there is often no clear management and responsible problem owners for the digital work environment as a whole among organizations. They call for organizational coordination and a holistic view of the digital work environment to solve the problems that exist with the integration of the individual systems in the digital work environment. They believe that the individual parts of the digital work environment are often overlapping and conflict with each other because they are not developed or implemented with the specific organizational context in mind [20].

Williams et al. [21] has analyzed the concept of digital work environment in a literature review by categorizing selected research literature that addresses the concept into the three categories of organizational strategy and design, people and work, and technical platform. The first category, organizational strategy, looks at how a company's policies and strategies should be designed to promote the digital work environment. The second category, people and work, has been developed because the digital work environment should enable people to be productive in their work. Finally, the authors of this literature review believe that contemporary definitions of digital work environment have a heavy focus on the underlying digital technologies that a digital work environment can consist of, often in the form of an integrated platform that provides all the tools and functions an employee needs in their work [21].

Köffer [22] conducted a systematic review of the academic knowledge base on the digital workplace, and he identified stress and overload as one of four main research topics that affect the digital workplace. Previous research has shown that the support and training that the users may get reduce the perceived stress and overload from technology and also that a workplace culture that encourages employees to discuss and help each other on IT usage has positive effects. Changes in the digital work environment must take into account the individual differences. The circumstances surrounding the work, environment and personal characteristics of the employees affect how the digital work environment is experienced. Changes in the digital work environment that are based on the fact that employees are a homogeneous group with the same conditions and needs fail to deal with the challenges of a digital work environment. Therefore, many researchers propose a greater focus on individual solutions that fit the individual's preferences, tasks and approaches [22].

2.6 IT Protection Rounds

It-rounds – means that the hardware, software, equipment, overview, usability etc. are checked using a commonly agreed upon checklist. The concept of IT protection rounds started at Sahlgrenska university hospital where a group of colleagues started inspecting the effects of the digital work environments on the effects and outcomes of the work. It was unfortunately not subject to scientific studies but has been influential in Sweden as a point of reference. They developed a method called MedsITtning, a form of auscultation in which colleagues inspected the work of their fellow workers with a specific focus on the digital tools. Many organizations have developed corporate or union-based methods for IT protection rounds, but most of them are available in Swedish only, such as SuntArbetsliv [23], some provide general checklists, like Prevent [24].

2.7 Standardizing the IT Protection Round

The Swedish Technical committee SIS TK380 has developed a draft standard to systematize and further develop so-called IT protection rounds (IT rounds, innovation rounds, etc.), a practice that has emerged in parallel with the debate about the need to increase the influence of management personnel and users on how the interactive systems are designed, introduced and used. The usability round (as the standard has chosen to call what we refer to as digital work environment rounds) is a method where the users, within the framework of the systematic work environment management (SAM), identify usability deficiencies and improvement opportunities in interactive systems so that measures can be formulated in the short and long term. The purpose of the usability round is to improve the working environment and thereby help to increase the IT skills of the employees and the productivity of the organization.

The purpose of the usability round is to.

a) supplement the systematic work environment management with a method that focuses on the shortcomings and opportunities for improvement of the interactive systems

b) reduce the risk of cognitive and physical overload, thereby helping to reduce stress and absenteeism

c) increase and broaden the digital competence of the organization, thereby increasing the organization's efficiency, competitiveness and preparedness for the purchase and introduction of new systems

d) contribute to a people-centered business development and thereby increase the social and economic sustainability of the organization

e) contribute to increased efficiency and productivity and thus to the achievement of the organization's business objectives.

The standard has the preliminary title: "Ergonomics for information- and communication technology (ICT) – Testing by users of workplaces' interactive systems – The Usability round". It is based on the standard "SS-EN ISO 26800 Ergonomics - General guidelines, principles and concepts" [25] that describes the general guidelines for ergonomics and specify basic ergonomics principles and concepts applicable to the design and evaluation of tasks, jobs, products, tools, equipment, systems, organizations, services, facilities and environments. Furthermore, it is based on "SS-EN ISO 27500 The human-centered organization" [26] that explains to board members and management groups the values and beliefs that make an organization human-centered, important business and operational benefits that come with human-centered leadership and the policies they need to implement to achieve this. SS-EN ISO 27500 identifies the most important criteria that show that each principle has been met, the consequences for the organization if the relevant criteria are not met and what measures can be taken to reduce the risk thereof. Finally, it relates to "SS EN ISO 9241 Part 210 Ergonomics in human-system interaction - Part 210: User-centered design for interactive systems" [27] that describes six principles that all work with user-centered development should follow, i.e.;

a) the design is based on an explicit understanding of users, tasks and environments
b) users are involved throughout the design and development process
c) the design is driven and refined through user-centered evaluation
d) the process is iterative (it is repeated repeatedly)
e) the design encompasses the entire user experience
f) the design team has interdisciplinary knowledge and perspectives.

This work has made an attempt to apply the proposed standard and also worked to feedback the experiences from using the standard in the work to develop the standard.

3 Method

From an overall methodological point of view the project has applied an action-oriented research methodology in which researchers and the research subjects has collaborated in the development of the methodologies and specific research cases. To be able to critically examine and analyze the results we have closely adapted the quality criteria proposed by Klein and Myers [28].

3.1 Action Research

The project applied an action research methodology to adapt and implement a method to assess and correct the digital work environment in close collaboration with representatives from the organization. Action research is a research methodology that mixes reflection and observation with the actual activities undertaken in the project. It was coined by Kurt Lewin in 1946 [29] but has developed a lot since then. The researcher participates as an active change agent in the project and does thus work with the dual goals of managing the change in the organization at the same time as research on the case is conducted, hence the values and aspirations of the researcher also shapes the results. Action research is a cyclic process of planning, action, observation, reflection and redesign. The action research methodology is commonly used in other disciplines such as pedagogy, information systems or nursing, but not to the extent that one would expect within HCI. One of the few studies detailing how actions research would apply to HCI is conducted by Hayes [30].

3.2 Case Specific Details

This case was conducted in close collaboration with a court in Sweden, which is a form of public authority. There are more than 75 courts in Sweden and they serve under the Swedish National Courts administration that serves all courts with basic IT infrastructure and specific systems. One of their major impacts on the courts is the national case handling system Vera, that heavily influences the digital work environments at every court. Even if all courts are autonomous, they need the support of the National Courts administration.

3.3 Activities to Customize the Method to the Organization

The organization had during 2019–2020 identified its digital work environment as a strategic focus area for the development of the authority.

Pre-study and Townhall Meeting. With this strategy they invited to a staff townhall meeting to educate the entire staff on digital work environment. To manage a tailored townhall meeting we decided to conduct "speed field studies" (see Fig. 1), eight 30-min contextual observation-interview studies from all parts of the organization from judges to people working at the registrar. Even if the speed field studies were extremely short, they were conducted with a semi-structured observation interview technique in which a lot of information was possible to acquire. The author of this paper was given the assignment of conducting the education program, something that was done late 2019 and spurred a lot of interest from the organization. The support was immense, from the top management of the organization to the union representatives. The HR staff was instrumental in planning and facilitating the collaboration in such an excellent way and the open and engaged collaboration from everybody in the organization made it a success.

Fig. 1. Eight 30 min "speed field studies" were conducted to get a flavor of the digital work environment at the public authority.

Workshop to Adapt the Method to the Organization. Based on the successful pre-study it was decided to apply a method to adapt the ISO standardized approach to the organization in a sequence of steps. This was conducted during two workshop days involving two senior managers, one workplace safety staff, two HR representatives, one representative from the local IT department and one representative appointed by the union. The workshop was planned and conducted by the main author who also made all documentation in close collaboration with the workshop participants.

Part 1: What are the most common digital work environment problems you expect to find in the workplaces being investigated? All participants were given the task to brainstorm the most common and serious digital work environment problems that they would expect to find during the studies. This was done to safeguard the proposed method to be able to assess whether or not the method would be capable of identifying the major usability problems in the process. See more on Fig. 2.

Part 2: Review of the criteria list. Systematically the workshop participants worked through the proposed list of criteria from the suggested standard in a joint group discussion. The participants were asked to interpret the criteria, suggest how the wording could be contextualized to their business and discuss potential rewordings of the criteria to meet their needs. In the beginning the discussion was thorough and critical but the further throughout the document we came the more pragmatic the discussion became and the more the language was understood and contextualized.

Fig. 2. Brainstorming of potential work environment problems with all the representatives from the staff. Clustering of the problems based on similarity in scope and impact.

Part 3: Priority of the criteria. Early on we realized that the suggested list of criteria was too extensive and we needed to collapse and merge several of the criteria to make a tool that could be much easier to handle. Several of the criteria were also judged not to be relevant for the business at hand. All participants were asked to highlight which criteria they prioritize as the most important for being able to assess the digital work environment by marking each criterion with one dot. Everybody got the maximum of 15 dots to use. The question to ask was to choose which criteria they considered most relevant and not relevant to the organization (see Fig. 3).

Fig. 3. Choosing which criteria was the most important for the organization.

Part 4: Reorganizing the criteria. This task involved a card sorting activity in which the criteria were reorganized to make a better flow and more logical sequence and order of the criteria and categories. Below the criteria has been reordered to fit this logical flow.

Part 5: Matching the digital work environment problems with the criteria. Finally, the participants were asked to return to the digital work environment problems that had been identified in part 1 and group the underneath each category. In this way we would be able to see if there was any category underneath which no work environment problems were placed and to help us further sharpen the formulation of the criteria and the categories. All participants were asked to place "their" work environment problems on the respective criteria (see Fig. 4).

Fig. 4. Grouping the usability problems from part 1 under the reordered criteria and categories. The category on AI were judged to be out of the scope for this work activity and were therefore omitted from the categories. The organization also identified the need for an extra section on physical and social work environment problems.

Part 6: How do you assess the rating scale? Next step consisted of a discussion about the ranking scale of all criteria whether or not it was understandable, self-explanatory and sufficient for the task. The rating scale can be found in Fig. 5. The ranking scale proposed in the standard was said to be appropriate for the task and adopted the way it was presented. Minor changes were proposed for the criteria that was about judging times saved, for example.

Headline / question	1 Fully disagree	2	3	4	5	6 Fully agree	Don't know	Not relevant	Comments
Influence on work									
The computer support supports me in conducting my work									

Fig. 5. The proposed ranking scale with one example of a question to rank.

Part 7: Which people are most suitable for conducting the inspection? The final task was a discussion about which persons that would be the best suited to conduct the work environment rounds. There were concerns about the number of people conducting the rounds, that one does not want to overwhelm the interviewee, but at the same time a concern that all different skills present are needed to judge the work environment appropriately. There were also concerns about whether or not people would be willing to speak out freely in front of their boss, and therefore we chose to swap bosses so that the present boss was not the boss for that particular interviewee.

3.4 Digital Work Environment Rounds

Experiencing Digital Work Environment Rounds. During a trial period we conducted four digital work environment rounds in which four representatives from the organization participated (1 manager, 1 IT-representative, 1 representative from the work situation and 1 safety officer). The digital work environment rounds were observed by two researchers and one person from the organization's HR responsible for work environment issues and the research project officer from the organization. It was organized as a semi-structured self-organized observation interview (see Fig. 6).

Fig. 6. Digital work environment round conducted during the pilot tests.

Everybody took individual notes during the trial using the adapted checklist and all of these notes were collected. After the digital work environment rounds a short questionnaire was sent to the interviewee as well as a survey to make individual assessments of the questions in the questionnaire.

Assessment Meeting to Prioritize Findings and Decide on Actions and People in Charge. All the participants of the previous workshops were invited to a second workshop to go through and summarize all findings from the digital work environment rounds and the feedback collected from the participants. The staff together with the union representatives were gathered to discuss the results of the rounds and assess the power and efficiency of the method. The first step was to go through each criterium and look through everybody's collected notes and compare to the responses made by the interviewee in the survey. While going through them one of the participants documented the findings to arrive at a joint documentation. Attempts were made to discuss possible solutions to overcome the problems, but the fact that the interviewees need be involved to manage any good redesigns made it difficult to propose any final measures to overcome the problem, rather the problems were noted down for further investigations. We prioritized the actions and decide the way forward (including defining and distributing responsibilities). Finally, we evaluated the process and the results from the reviewers' point of view as well as the workers' experience of the round. We evaluated the result, the documentation and evaluated possible actions and the process for implementation. We discussed the reviewers' experience of the Usability Round and finally we discussed the possible integration of the method in the systematic work environment management at the organization.

4   Results

Generally, there are many bigger and smaller usability problems in everybody's work situation that people learn to live with and establish more or less inefficient work arounds to compensate from. Many workers report that there are from minor to severe usability problems that they are not reporting, because they do not have any experience that earlier reported problems have been corrected. And the expectation is not that the problem can or would be corrected. At the same time the experience reported from the IT department is that many of the existing usability problems could easily be corrected if they were only told about them. The earlier they would be informed about the problems the easier it would have been to correct them. Therefore, by allocating resources to correct problems and by introducing steps in the process to identify and prioritize these findings, many usability improvements could easily be made.

The general perception of conducting digital work environment rounds was positive and it was perceived as a useful and important addition to the existing methods in the organization to assess and correct the digital work environment. The fact that it was based on an ISO standard under production and the fact that the organization was an early adopter and pilot tester also contributed to the positive response towards the method.

4.1 Revised List of Criteria Adapted to the Organization

One of the major outcomes of the project was the revised checklist that was derived through the workshop with the representatives from the organization from management level to union representatives, from HR to IT. In comparison to the checklist presented in the ISO standard, this was significantly shortened by removing 30% of the questions and sometimes collapsing two criteria into one (see Fig. 7 and 8). The criteria were color coded with normal text and bold text to distinguish criteria with higher priority from normal.

Checklist usability round

Work place ____________________ **Worker** ____________________

Date ____________________ **Responsible for the protocol** ____________________

Digital work environment is the work environment, with its problems and opportunities of both physical, psycho-social and cognitive nature, which is the result of digitalisation of the work support system and tools. These may be deficiencies in IT support, inappropriate organization of work or deficiencies in knowledge or skills in order to manage the IT support. The purpose of the usability round is to identify the most common and / or most serious digital work environment problems with a view to proposing measures to rectify them through changes in IT support, changes in operations or through special training efforts. These measures will then be prioritized and a plan established for actions with clear responsibilities and deadlines.

This protocol summarizes the observations and assessments made in connection with the digital work environment at the workplace. Use the protocol as follows: Systematically review the questions in order. Ask the employee to evaluate each criterion according to the 6-degree scale and motivate the rating by exemplifying and showing cases that illustrate the criterion. You are encouraged to describe the problems so that others can understand them and also document by taking pictures. The documents will then be used by you during the assessment and prioritization meeting as everyone's assessments are reviewed.

Headline / question	1 Fully disagree	2	3	4	5	6 Fully agree	Don't know	Not relevant	Comments
Influence on work									
The IT support[1] supports me in conducting my work									
The IT support does not cause stress and strain in my work									
The IT support gives me good opportunities to follow up on my tasks and results									

Fig. 7. The revised protocol from the Digital work environment round derived from the workshop and revised after testing.

The protocol was also used as a survey of questions asking individuals to fill out the checklist as a survey. This was highly appreciated by those users that were a part of our test and they all filled it out without prioritizing between those with bold text and normal text. However, none of the users made use of the comment field, most likely since it was not expressed that this was mandatory in the survey.

1. Influence on work	4. Introduction and follow-up
The IT support[1] supports me in conducting my work	When introducing new IT or introduce major system changes, representatives from the business actively participated in the design of systems, routines and processes.
The IT support does not cause stress and strain in my work	I have gained enough information and knowledge to use the IT support effectively
The IT support gives me good opportunities to follow up on my tasks and results	There is continuous follow-up of my and other employees' needs and satisfaction with the IT support
The IT support helps me to do the job properly	The follow-ups lead to visible results or other feedback
The IT support contributes to my learning in my role and to the learning about the management of the software	I get the help I need from the local IT support and from the central support
The IT support gives me the flexibility to decide how I plan my work	We use data from the system for the purpose of analyzing and improving operations
The IT support facilitates my own planning of the work	The purpose of digitization is well known and well-rooted with the users
2. Technical design	5. Collaboration and communication
The IT support is easy to learn	The IT support gives greater control of the work and the opportunity to manage the workload
The IT support is easy to navigate in	The IT support facilitates collaboration within the business
The company-specific systems interact effectively with other computer programs I use	The IT support facilitates collaboration between different businesses
The IT support has the functionality that I need	The IT support facilitates collaboration with external players
3. Problems and disturbances	The IT support contributes to increased collaboration with individual parties and the public
How much time do you think you would save per day if IT support worked in the best possible way?	6. Usefulness for different stakeholders
How often are you delayed by the IT support?	Our digital solutions allow our department or group to use their resources efficiently
How often does the quality deteriorate because of disruptions in the IT support?	Our digital solutions mean that our department or group has high quality in product and delivery
On average, how much time do you think you save per day compared to before the introduction of IT support (or since you started using it yourself)?	Our digital solutions mean that we have more efficient resource management with the partner organizations as a whole (e.g. external players)
	Our digital solutions mean that the public and individual parties receive higher quality in product and delivery

Fig. 8. The revised checklist protocol from the Digital work environment round.

One important conclusion to draw is the importance of language and words. Careful attention needs to be paid on how to name things and the necessity of providing clear definitions of concepts used. It is also necessary to tailor the concepts to the general preunderstanding and language used in the organization.

4.2 Prioritized Findings from the Digital Work Environment Round

As a result of the discussion the major findings were grouped into three priority levels. And following is an attempt to generalize the findings.

Priority 1 – Vera. Emphasize the importance of modifying the general case handling system provided by the Swedish National Court Administration, to fit to the requirements posed by the local court (these have constantly been received less priority, given that the system has been designed for the general court and thus has severe usability problems for this particular court). The power of such an initiative may have a huge impact as usability problems pertaining to this system is so common and frequently causing severe problems both in quality and efficiency. The responsibility for driving this would be on the managers that could take the opportunity when the Swedish National Court Administration gets a new general manager. There are also great contacts into the organizations since one of the major business developers in the court moved to the central organization and is very familiar with the problem. It was difficult to give a time plan as this is such an important task and every achievement that brings closer to a new take on this system would be very beneficiary.

Priority 1 – Uniform working methods. For historical reasons the ways of working at the different departments at the court varies significantly, Previous management has grown independent ways of working, thus creating flexibility and power. However, over time this has gotten out of hand and has thus led to sub optimization, with loss in quality and efficiency and with a lacking consistency in the way that things are handled. The general view is that this can be dealt with in parallel to the aforementioned needs to improve the case handling system. It can be done by collecting routines and checklists, and by collecting the specific processes from each department to make the managers agree on a joint process for conducting the tasks in support of the general manager. This task requires a project group to work with it and it needs a management decision to support it. It could be dealt with during the first half of 2020.

Priority 2 – Collected instructions. This is low hanging fruit, and could be achieved within a short period of time. It is more about communication and an infrastructure to share the collected instructions, than actually developing something new. A person from IT could be in charge of the infrastructure and a person from the management must drive the actual change.

Priority 2 – Continuous follow-ups. A clearly expressed need to assess and follow up the digital work environment on a regular basis. Can be achieved by incorporating Digital Work Environment Rounds as a part of the Systematic Work Environment Management in the organization. The Systematic Work Environment Management Group in the organization will be in charge of the mission and as Digital Work Environment is a prioritized area, this can be achieved as soon as possible.

Priority 2 – Digital ambassadors. A role to be some form of superuser that could help spread innovative ways of working in the organization. There is a need to formalize the role, appoint one or two per department or per category of workers, establish a network of digital ambassadors for experience exchange. The managers are responsible and resources needs to be allocated for it to happen.

Priority 3 – Continuous knowledge exchange.

The strategy when choosing and prioritizing these activities was both to have an ambitious goal as this is a new activity for the organization and that it is necessary to show some results already from the start. The choice of activities was also to both prioritize long term initiatives that are important and quick fixes that can show a more or less immediate effect.

4.3   Assessing the Potential Time Savings if the System Would Work in an Optimal Fashion.

During the digital work environment rounds the interviewees were asked: "On average, how much time do you think you save per day compared to before the introduction of IT support[1] (or since you started using it yourself)?" When the interviewees were asked this question, it sparked a lot of discussion about the lacking functionality and usability of the system. The users spoke at length about their experiences with the system and why they needed to make use of cumbersome work arounds to manage their work, and many also noted that there was no point in complaining about it, since there is no mechanism to change based on comments received. The quantitative estimation of time savings to make ranged from 20 min per day to half of the working day. We heard testimonies saying that they could go from two to one person to handle the e-mail.

The second question: *"How often are you delayed by IT support disruptions?"* received answers ranging from less than once per day to up to 30 times per day. However, a comment in relations to the less frequent findings was that the interruptions could last for as much as up to 15 min.

The third question: *"How often does the quality of disruptions in IT support deteriorate?"* received answers ranging from never to 2 or 3 times per day and also comments about the interruptions lasting for a very long time and as frequent as once a week.

The fourth question: *"How much time do you think you would save per day if IT support worked in the best possible way?"* received answers ranging from 10 min per day up to 60 min per day.

In conclusion the potential gains from improving the digital work environments does not only mean that there is a potential for improved quality but also that there is a potential for increased efficiency leading to potential cost savings and possibilities for rationalizing the business. Seeing potential cost savings in addition to the improvements may help cost-justifying the efforts.

4.4   Assessing the Digital Work Environment Round from the User Perspective

The interviewees were very positive about their experience of having participated in the digital work environment rounds. Statements such as: *"I experienced that someone listened to me and it also gave me the opportunity to reflect on my digital work environment"* or *"the fact that someone actually turned to the experts working with the systems and asking our opinions"* shows the power of actually strengthening the user perspective and give the power to the users. One of the comments also constructively suggested an alternative approach in suggesting to hand out the questions beforehand for the users to be able to prepare and show more of the common problems that actually happens in practice. One of the interviewees is quite critical given how the observation interview

---

[1] For the study we used the concept of "IT support" to encompass the entire sociotechnical system of software, hardware and the organizational structure in which it is used. It should not be confused with the concept of support staff. Later on, the concept was changed to digital system, which in itself is an ambiguous concept as the interview subjects had troubles understanding it as the entire system rather than a particular computer application. Therefore, for this study the concept "IT support" was used to mark the entire sociotechnical system.

turned out, where she did not get a chance to actually show what it looks like and rather proposed a format more like could be expressed in an interview. Most likely the reason for this was that the pilot test for this particular person went a bit out of hand and the opportunity for actually making observations vanished.

4.5   Integrating the Digital Work Environment Round into the Systematic Work Environment Management

After the abovementioned activities to tailor the digital work environment rounds to the organization and the pilot test of the method the organization had its strategic meeting to decide on how to progress the integration of the method into the systematic work environment management in the organization. Based on the project a proposition was given to the management group of the organization on how to work in a systematic way with digital work environment in a more holistic perspective (individual, group and organization). The intention is to use the digital work environment round by first sending out the checklist broadly in the organization to gather more written comments before choosing a deepened interview with selected participants. As a complement the organization will use the Prevent union's IT stress survey to gather information on both individual, group and organization level based on identified risks to assess measures that needs to be taken on an organizational level and complement this with the Digital Work Environment Round on an individual level as a deepened investigation. This could be done for a specific identified part of the organization, on a particular software system or category of workers, or be used before and after to judge the introduction of a new IT support system. The organization believes that this will be an important asset in the systematic work environment management in the organization and they intend to follow up continuously.

5   Discussion

Digital work environment and digital work environment problems has received far too little attention in the research literature so far. Although there is a large number of studies focusing on developing usability evaluation methods for different types of contexts [31–34], not much has been anchored in the overall work environment legislation [13, 14] and developed as a part of the systematic work environment management mandated in the legislation. Also, the use of international standards [25–27] for the benefit of the development of the work tools, user skills and organization need to be further developed.

The purpose of this paper was to show how the legislation can serve as a powerful tool and how systematic work environment management can leverage the union employer collaboration to improve the digital work environment. I have demonstrated how the digital work environment round by being supported by the legislation could work as a powerful way of improving the digital work environment for employees in an organization. There is a high potential in working systematically on improving the digital work environment. Lacking functionality and usability of the IT systems contribute to building several work environment risks and hazards that may have a severe effect on the health and well-being of the employees, may bring large costs to the organization and may contribute to insufficient quality of the work. Issues relating to the user perspective when introducing new IT systems at work are rarely if at all considered in the acquisition, development, introduction and maintenance of the IT systems for work.

5.1   The Importance of Legislation

Making use of the fact that work environment is something mandated through the national legislation is an extremely powerful tool. Even if the law was authored way before computers were widely used for work, much of what is written clearly applies to the digital work environment, as shown above. In our development over the years, we have gone from viewing usability work as a part of the IT development, to usability work as an asset for the HR work in the organization to finally anchoring usability work as strategic work on a management level. The fact that digital work environment is finding its way into the legislation as a concept of its own has been an important contribution to the grounding of the work and thus the Swedish Work environment authority should consider bringing digital work environment in as a core part of the work environment legislation in the same way as Psychological and Social Work Environment was introduced a few years ago. The current regulation on "Work with Display Units" (In Swedish: AFS 1998:5 Arbete vid bildskärm) dates back to 1998 and is in urgent need of modernization and adaptation to the current situation.

5.2   Making Use of the Mandated Systematic Work Environment Management

As Sweden has a unique situation of great collaboration between the worker associations and employers and that this is mandated through the work environment act gives us a tool to be able to argue for systematic work to improve the usability, not only by arguing the benefit and potential financial gains it makes, but also since it is the law. The Swedish Work environment legislation safeguards systematic collaboration between employers and workers on every issue that may affect the worker's work environment and therefore it has a great potential to make use of the fact that everybody wants to obey the law as an argument for introducing systematic digital work environment rounds as a part of the work environment activities in the organization. However, so far, the systematic work environment management has more focused on social and organizational work conditions and not so much looked at the digital work situation. We thus need to develop and try out new tools focusing on assessing, prioritizing and mending digital work environment problems in a systematic manner.

5.3   The Importance of Standardization

International standards have contributed a lot to the opportunities for systematizing user-centered design work, usability and user experience work and overall ergonomics of the systems, however they are not sufficiently addressed in research. In this project we have had the opportunity to apply and text a forthcoming standard in practical development work and we have done so in collaboration with the editors of the standard, thus contributing to the development and credibility of the standard as such. It has really been a joint venture in which the standards development had an important role in the work at the public authority and the case contributed a lot to the development of the standard.

5.4 Contributions to HCI

This work contributes with an increased understanding of how to systematically apply HCI methods from a work environment perspective, grounded in standards [25–27] and legislation [13, 14]. It shows how cooperative or participatory approaches [2–7] may contribute to building deepened insights of the complex relations between digitalization as organizational development [17] and the power of actively involving users [35] addressing issues such as value-based design [36] and the development of the socio technical systems [12, 37]. Through this work a usable digital work environment can be required and developed to meet the overall work environment legislation in a systematic way.

Sweden has a unique situation in having a comprehensive work environment legislation. Up until now this legislation has mostly been used to assess and correct the physical, social and organizational work environment. But the law equally applies to the digital work environment. Providing usable technology for the work place often do not receive enough attention, investment and skills to help improve the situation to an acceptable one, despite the fact that it could make the organization more efficient and effective, improve the situation for the users and thus justify the costs for the investment. So, this is not a paper about another usability inspection method, it is about holistically approaching the root causes to why usability problems at the work place are not sufficiently dealt with and how the legislation can help improve the situation. Using the legislation as a vehicle to drive the development of more usable systems is what this case has explored and successfully shown that it can work.

Sweden has a unique opportunity to do this, due to its past history of participatory design, efficient union collaboration and unique workplace rights, that is a fact. But, many other countries could be able to make use of similar approaches and several countries are also showing an interest in doing so. That is why this is pioneering work in an area previously not researched. And that is why it has a potential interest to be implement in other countries as well. Even if Sweden has a unique situation, both when it comes to the union-employer collaboration to increase the quality of work and on the prevalent legislation, this case also could serve as an example on how other countries, organizations and employers can make use of the existing work environment legislation in the country to make sure that actual improvement work to safeguard a risk-free digital work environment actually happens.

6   Conclusion

In this paper we have demonstrated how Digital Work Environment Rounds can be integrated into the Systematic Work Environment Management by a case conducted within a Swedish Court. We have shown the importance of basing the work on the existing work environment legislation, by collaborating closely between union representatives and employers and by also contributing to the recently published Standard; the Usability

Round. We conclude that integrating Digital Work Environment Rounds in the systematic work environment routines at the workplace with support from the Work environment legislation has the potential of being a really powerful tool to assess and improve work with digital tools. However, for it to become successful there are several conditions that are necessary on an organizational level. These include, but are not limited to, the following:

- A high skill level and awareness throughout the organization.
- A willingness to make the necessary investments up front that may lead to gains further down the line.
- Strong support throughout the organization from management to the union representatives.

Also, there is a need to further develop the legislation and regulation to also explicitly cover digital work environments, to develop tools to assess and correct digital work environment problems and to make this a strategic goal for the organizations in their development work. Finally, there is a need for much more research to further understand and develop the methods and tools to increase the power and benefit of working with digital work environment rounds.

In this case we have shown how a digital work environment round can be incorporated in the systematic work environment management at a public authority, how this has worked to influence the standardization on the subject and shown as an exemplar that others can take after on how to conduct digital work environment rounds. Although this project is just about to end, several other requests to work towards integrating digital work environment in the systematic work environment management has been requested from several different organizations. This work is just the first step to launch a new standard way of improving our digital tools for work.

Acknowledgements. I would like to thank all the staff at Förvaltningsrätten i Göteborg (Administrative Court of Gothenburg) who took part in the case and provided support for this action research study. Their help and support were tremendous. They have also given their consent to being visible in the photographs from the study. I would also like to thank the Swedish Institute for Standardization (SIS) and particularly Åke Walldius, the editor of the Usability Round standard without whose input none of this would have been accomplished.

References

1. Statistics Sweden: Statistics Sweden. Statistical data base: the population of Sweden. Stockholm: SCB (2020)
2. Ehn, P.: Work-oriented design of computer artifacts (Doctoral dissertation, Arbetslivscentrum) (1988)
3. Greenbaum, J., Kyng, M. (eds.): Design at Work: Cooperative Design of Computer Systems. CRC Press, Boca Raton (2020)
4. Schuler, D., Namioka, A. (eds.): Participatory Design: Principles and Practices. CRC Press, Boca Raton (1993)

5. Bødker, S., Ehn, P., Sjögren, D., Sundblad, Y.: Co-operative design—perspectives on 20 years with 'the Scandinavian IT Design Model'. In: Proceedings of NordiCHI 2000, pp. 1–9, 22–24, October 2000. https://www.nordichi.net/Proceedings2000/Keynote/01CoOp.pdf

6. Bødker, S., Zander, P-O.M.: Participation in design between public sector and local communities. In: C&T 2015 Proceedings of the 7th International Conference on Communities and Technologies, pp. 49–58. Association for Computing Machinery (2015). https://doi.org/10.1145/2768545.2768546

7. Pilemalm, S.: Participatory design in emerging civic engagement initiatives in the new public sector: applying PD concepts in resource-scarce organizations. ACM Trans. Comput. Hum. Interact. (TOCHI) 25(1), 1–26 (2018)

8. Hoonakker, P.: Information and communication technology and quality of working life: Backgrounds, facts, and figures. In: The Impact of ICT on Quality of Working Life, pp. 9–23. Springer, Dordrecht. (2014). https://doi.org/10.1007/978-94-017-8854-0_2

9. Bordi, L., Okkonen, J., Mäkiniemi, J.P., Heikkilä-Tammi, K.: Communication in the digital work environment: implications for wellbeing at work (2018). https://tidsskrift.dk/njwls/article/view/105275

10. Sandblad, B., et al.: Work environment and computer systems development. Behav. Inf. Technol. 22(6), 375–387 (2003)

11. Åborg, C., Sandblad, B., Gulliksen, J., Lif, M.: Integrating work environment considerations into usability evaluation methods—the ADA approach. Interact. Comput. 15(3), 453–471 (2003)

12. Mumford, E.: The story of socio-technical design: reflections on its successes, failures and potential. Inf. Syst. J. 16, 317–342 (2006)

13. Arbetsmiljöverket: The Swedish Work Environment Act (Arbetsmiljölagen) English version available (1977). https://www.av.se/en/work-environment-work-and-inspections/acts-and-regulations-about-work-environment/the-work-environment-act/

14. Arbetsmiljöverket: AFS 1998:5 Work with display units, regulation (In Swedish: AFS 1998:5 Arbete vid bildskärm, föreskrifter). Only available in Swedish (1998). https://www.av.se/globalassets/filer/publikationer/foreskrifter/arbete-vid-bildskarm-foreskrifter-afs1998-5.pdf

15. Eurofound: Systematic work environment management in Sweden (2004). https://www.eurofound.europa.eu/publications/article/2004/systematic-work-environment-management-in-sweden

16. Arbejdstilsynet: Risk assessment (APV) WEA Guideline D.1.1–3 on Risk Assessment (APV) (2016). https://at.dk/en/regulations/guidelines/risk-assessment-apv-d-1-1-3/

17. Sandblad, B., Gulliksen, J., Lantz, A., Walldius, Å., Åborg, C.: Digitalization and the work environment (In Swedish: Digitaliseringen och arbetsmiljön). Studentlitteratur (2018)

18. Robertson, J.: A definition of the digital workplace… and a journey (2015). Accessed 27 Jan 2021. https://www.steptwo.com.au/papers/digital-Workplace-Definition/

19. Richter, A., Heinrich, P., Stocker, A., Schwabe, G.: Digital work design. Bus. Inf. Syst. Eng. 60(3), 259–264 (2018)

20. Berg, O., Gustafsson, H.: Digital workplace strategy & design: a step-by-step guide to an empowering employee experience. BoD-Books on Demand (2018)

21. Williams, S., P., Schubert, P. : Designs for the digital workplace. Proc. Comput. Sci. 138, 478–485 (2018)

22. Köffer, S.: Designing the digital workplace of the future–what scholars recommend to practitioners. In: Thirty Sixth International Conference on Information Systems, Fort Worth 2015 (2015)

23. Sunt Arbetsliv: Protection Round: Digital Work Environment (in Swedish: Skyddsrond: Digital Arbetsmiljö) (2021). https://arbetsmiljoutbildning.suntarbetsliv.se/wp-content/uploads/sites/2/2016/02/Modul2_Skyddsrond_Digital-arbetsmiljo-1.pdf. Accessed 27 Jan 2021

24. Prevent: Introduce the right IT (In Swedish: Inför rätt IT) (2021). https://www.prevent.se/infor-ratt-it/
25. International Organization for Standardization: ISO 26800:2011 Ergonomics — General approach, principles and concepts (2011). https://www.iso.org/standard/42885.html
26. International Organization for Standardization: ISO 27500:2016 The human-centred organization — Rationale and general principles (2016). https://www.iso.org/standard/64239.html
27. International Organization for Standardization: ISO 9241–210:2010 Ergonomics of human-system interaction — Part 210: Human-centred design for interactive systems (2019). https://www.iso.org/standard/77520.html
28. Klein, H.K., Myers, M.D.: A set of principles for conducting and evaluating interpretive field studies in information systems. MIS Q., 67–93 (1999)
29. Lewin, K.: Action research and minority problems. J. Soc. Issues 2(4), 34–46 (1946)
30. Hayes, G.R.: Knowing by doing: action research as an approach to HCI. In: Ways of Knowing in HCI, pp. 49–68. Springer, New York (2014). https://doi.org/10.1007/978-1-4939-0378-8_3
31. Gray, W.D., Salzman, M.C.: Damaged merchandise? A review of experiments that compare usability evaluation methods. Hum. Comput. Interact. 13(3), 203–261 (1998)
32. Hartson, H.R., Andre, T.S., Williges, R.C.: Criteria for evaluating usability evaluation methods. Int. J. Hum. Comput. Interact. 15(1), 145–181 (2003)
33. Hornbæk, K.: Dogmas in the assessment of usability evaluation methods. Behav. Inf. Technol. 29(1), 97–111 (2010)
34. John, B.E., Marks, S.J.: Tracking the effectiveness of usability evaluation methods. Behav. Inf. Technol. 16(4–5), 188–202 (1997)
35. Gulliksen, J., Göransson, B., Boivie, I., Blomkvist, S., Persson, J., Cajander, Å.: Key principles for user-centred systems design. Behav. Inf. Technol. 22(6), 397–409 (2003)
36. Friedman, B., Hendry, D.G.: Value Sensitive Design: Shaping Technology with Moral Imagination. MIT Press, Massachusetts (2019)
37. Trist, E.L.: The evolution of socio-technical systems, vol. 2. Ontario Quality of Working Life Centre, Toronto (1981)

Facilitating User Involvement in a Large IT Project: A Comparison of Facilitators' Perspectives on Process, Role and Personal Practice

Øivind Klungseth Zahlsen[1], Dag Svanæs[1,2], and Yngve Dahl[1(✉)]

[1] Department of Computer Science, Norwegian University of Science and Technology,
Trondheim, Norway
{oivind.k.zahlsen,dag.svanes,yngveda}@ntnu.no
[2] Digital Design Department, The IT University of Copenhagen, Copenhagen, Denmark

Abstract. Studies indicate that the way structured participatory design activities are facilitated significantly effects participation, power relations, and generated output. Although facilitation is always adapted to the conditions of each design project, the way facilitation is enacted primarily depends on the individual facilitator. It is assumed that enactment on an individual level is influenced by how the facilitator conceptualizes both user involvement and their own role. To address these issues, semi-structured interviews were conducted with three facilitators in the same development unit of a large-scale health IT project. The primary focuses were the individual facilitator's perspectives on the *design process*, their *role*, and their *practice* in the project. An in-depth qualitative content analysis of the transcribed interviews showed that the three facilitators held highly divergent perspectives on the facilitation of participatory design activities. Similarities were found between the facilitators' perspectives and how user involvement is understood in different system development traditions. Based on the findings, a reflective approach towards facilitation is proposed along with examples of possible co-reflection activities among facilitators.

Keywords: Facilitation · Participatory design · User involvement · Co-reflection · Large-scale IT systems

1 Introduction

User involvement is widely recognized as best-practice in the development of usable IT systems and is a fundamental principle in user-centered and participatory design (UCD and PD). In interaction design literature *user involvement* and *user participation* refer to activities in which users are actively involved in informing the design of products, systems, or services [1, 2]. Some of these activities, such as focus groups and co-design workshops, are structured activities that are typically managed or *facilitated* by a designer or other project associate. The person responsible for facilitating participatory design activities is commonly referred to as *facilitator*. Creating the right conditions for constructive user engagement in design-related questions is a central part of facilitation, as illustrated in [3–7].

© IFIP International Federation for Information Processing 2021
Published by Springer Nature Switzerland AG 2021
C. Ardito et al. (Eds.): INTERACT 2021, LNCS 12933, pp. 219–238, 2021.
https://doi.org/10.1007/978-3-030-85616-8_14

Despite the facilitator's central role in structured participatory design activities, there are relatively few design-related studies that have focused explicitly on the facilitator as a *practitioner* or facilitation as *practice*. Rejecting the idea of the PD practitioner as neutral or instrumental in the application of PD methods, Light and Akama [8] argued, "*We cannot know participative methods without the person or people enacting them*". In their opinion, a facilitator's enactment of participatory methods has strong implications both for the nature of participation and the output of participatory activities and processes. This could be studied empirically through detailed analysis of how facilitation is practiced (e.g., [8, 9]). However, to provide a better understanding of the conceptual ideas that may motivate practice, this study focuses on how facilitators of participatory activities in a large-scale IT project understand their own role. The implicit assumption is that attitude towards user participation and the understanding of one's role as a facilitator has a strong impact on how facilitation occurs.

Thus, putting the facilitator center stage raises an interesting question that is highly relevant for PD discourse: *How do facilitators of participatory design activities regard (i) the design process, (ii) the facilitator role, and (iii) their personal facilitation practice?*

To answer this question, a qualitative interview study of three facilitators working in a large health IT project in which the involvement of healthcare professionals (i.e., user representatives of the produced IT solution) is intended to take place across all project phases was conducted. This paper provides an in-depth analysis of the verbal accounts offered by the interview respondents with a special focus on their perspectives on the design process, the role of a facilitator, and their personal facilitation practices. Drawing on the analysis, this study argues that the facilitation of participatory design activities may be dependent on facilitators' individual perspectives on these three aspects. The key findings from this study are then used as a basis for recommending the adoption of co-reflective activities among facilitators to help foster conscious awareness regarding facilitation thinking and practice.

2   Background: Facilitation of Participatory Design Activities

Few design-related studies focus on the role of the facilitator. The studies described in this section cover what we consider the most relevant work in this regard.

One of the first investigations into the role of the facilitator in the context of participatory activities was conducted by Luck [10], who studied the relationship between facilitator expertise and opportunities for user engagement in an architectural project. Analyzing the spoken interaction between the facilitator and participants, the study found that more experienced facilitators tended to create richer opportunities for user engagement and that the development of such behaviors need to be honed through practice.

Light and Akama [8] investigated relations between context, facilitation, and outcomes in designing with communities in disaster mitigation. In particular, the study compared how facilitation took place in two different situations to engage with relevant concerns. The study brought attention to the ways in which facilitation style, scoping, structure, and control can affect participation as well as how facilitation practice needs to be considered in terms of the context in which it takes place. Seeing the facilitator's engagement with participants to involve an embodied knowing, the authors argued for a reorientation in PD towards participatory practice as opposed to participatory methods alone, i.e., a direction where the PD method and facilitator are no longer seen as detached.

Inspired in part by Donald Schön's [11] reflection-on-action theory, Dahl and Svanæs [9] brought attention to the often subtle and unforeseen ways in which facilitator actions (and non-actions) in participatory activities can influence the ways in which values become embedded in design solutions. They suggest that continuous introspective analyses and reflections may improve the facilitator's attentiveness to actions that may inadvertently impede participants who are disfavored vis-à-vis other partakers due to factors such as status, language, or eloquence.

There are also examples of studies that highlight the empathic qualities that facilitation of participatory activities may necessitate to understand users' perspectives in certain design contexts. Lindsay et al.'s [5] design work with people with dementia is a good example of how development of empathic relations with the user group led to strategic changes in the facilitator's interactions with participants in workshops.

All of the above studies acknowledge the strong impact of the individual facilitator on the ways that participatory activities are enacted. In terms of research methods, they all conducted detailed studies and analysis of facilitation practice. All studies were done in small or midsize projects, consequently not addressing the added challenges of user participation in large-scale projects [12–14].

To our knowledge, an in-depth investigation of the "mindsets" of facilitators of participatory activities has not been conducted before. This has motivated us to perform a qualitative study to unpack the views and perspectives that may lie behind the facilitation of participatory design activities. Our study thus complements the existing practice-oriented studies. The study is motivated by the assumption that enactment on an individual level is significantly influenced by how the facilitator conceptualizes both user involvement and their own role.

3   The Case

This interview study was conducted between January and March 2020 in the early phase of an ongoing electronic health record (EHR) system implementation project in which the respondents acted as facilitators of participatory activities related to a specific system module. A brief overview of the key characteristics of the project and their participatory activities is presented below.

3.1   The Project

The aim of the project is to implement a common EHR system for all primary and secondary healthcare services in Central Norway. The estimated cost of the project is EUR 270 million. The (current) post-contract part of the project is scheduled to last approximately four years and consists of seven distinct sequential phases. The following stakeholder organizations are part of the project:

- *Client Organizations*: The client organizations consist of the regional public health authority, the municipality of the region's administrative center, and primary care physician offices. Healthcare workers employed in the client organizations will be the users of the new EHR system.
- *Client Project Organization*: The client project organization is a joint-stock company owned by the client organizations. In addition to its permanent staff, the company has recruited more than 400 workers (domain experts) from the client organizations. These experts also act as user representatives. The company is mainly interested in implementing an EHR and a patient administrative system for the client organizations.
- *Developer Organization*: The EHR vendor is headquartered in the US and relocated 30 employees to Norway for the duration of the project. The vendor owns a configurable EHR system that can be customized according to the healthcare institution at which it is installed. The vendor's main interest is to deliver on the contractual commitments and securing a regional foothold in the national healthcare system.

While the project has a strong focus on the involvement of user representatives (primarily domain experts) in all its phases, the project does not focus on user *empowerment* as understood in the PD tradition [15, 16]. This is a procurement-through-tender project, meaning that the signed contract works as the overall requirement for the project and also regulates the legal relationships between the stakeholder organizations, the budget, and the overall time constraints. As stated by Bratteteig and Wagner [17], "*A PD project is embedded in a context that offers both constraints and opportunities for what and how to design.*" Implicit in the statement is a conceptualization of *participation* as a relative term, meaning that for a given project, participation may range from weak (or non-existent) to strong and that the level of participation may vary throughout the project. The current project is considered to be *participatory* mainly due to its ambition to give a large number of domain experts (user representatives) a say in the configuration of the new EHR system.

3.2 The Facilitated Participatory Activities

The project follows an implementation approach characterized by scheduled participatory activities (meetings) where invited project participants gather to decide on specific aspects related to the configuration of the EHR system. The participatory activities we studied as part of our investigation took place in the Specification phase (4 months), which followed the initial Preparatory phase. The activities typically include vendor representatives (e.g., activity facilitators and developers, with the latter only present via video conference from a different time zone), healthcare professionals with backgrounds relevant to the activity topic (domain experts), and client organization representatives responsible for tailoring the system. Most domain experts confer with their peers in their home organization between the participatory activities.

4 Methods

4.1 Interviews

Data for this study was collected via semi-structured narrative interviews with three facilitators working in the EHR implementation project described above. Each interview lasted between 30 and 60 min. An interview guide was developed that addressed the three topics relevant to the research question: design process, facilitator role, and facilitator practice.

All three interview respondents had responsibilities involving the facilitation of multi-stakeholder project meetings that aimed to inform the design of a specific EHR system module. Two of the respondents were US citizens employed in the developer organization who had moved to Norway to work at the project site for the duration of the project. The last respondent was a Norwegian employee in the client project organization. None of the respondents had received formal education in the facilitation of participatory design activities prior to the project. Two of the respondents were male, and one female. Their formal backgrounds were quite diverse, including international politics, computer science (human–computer interaction) and biology. Their work experience includes project management, software development in general and in relation to the health domain. To maintain respondent anonymity, we have not given specific background information for each respondent. For similar reasons, references to the gender of the respondents have been removed and replaced with gender-neutral terms (e.g., "he/she") throughout the paper.

4.2 Complementary Field Observations

To improve general understanding of the project and the project meetings prior to the interviews, and thereby provide a frame of reference for interpreting the respondents' feedback, complementary field observations were conducted at the project site. This involved both fly-on-the-wall observations of project meetings (typically 5–12 participants in size) and by being present at the project site in order to interact with project employees outside of meetings. Given the complementary role of the field observations, they have not been subject to systematic analysis. Getting access to the facilitators' perspectives on their own role, the design process and their practice required us to involve the facilitators in in-depth interviews as these are aspects that cannot be understood from simply observing facilitators in action.

4.3 Data Collection and Data Analysis

The interviews were video recorded, transcribed verbatim, and analyzed. The analysis of the transcribed interviews consisted of three steps; a deductive coding of the transcriptions, identification of those transcript excerpts considered most relevant to the research question, and a qualitative content analysis of the coded units in the transcript excerpts.

During the initial coding process the transcriptions were examined for meaningful units of text, or *phrases*, pertaining to the three main topics of relevance to the research question (process, role, and practice). Relevant phrases were then marked with one or more matching keywords or *codes* ("Process", "Role", and "Practice"). The coded phrases were then checked for consistency to ensure that the codes had been applied in a coherent manner.

After identifying the most relevant transcript excerpts with regards to the research question, a qualitative content analysis of the coded phrases contained within an excerpt was performed with a focus on the *inferred meaning* of the utterances. In contrast to semantic analysis, which is concerned only with the literal meaning of syntactic structures and their interrelations independent of context, latent (deep structure) qualitative content analysis addresses what is being communicated non-literally, i.e., the implicit meaning of utterances [18]. *Context* plays an important role in such an analysis as it provides a conceptual lens that can help infer meaning; context lends subtext to the meaning. The interpretations of the analysis were review several times by the authors, both individually and in plenary, to ensure a common understanding.

5   Results

This section presents the results of the qualitative content analysis described above. For each interview respondent, three selected transcript excerpts and the interpretations thereof (with codes) are presented in a tabular format. Each excerpt is divided into *phrases*, i.e., meaningful units of text (left column), with corresponding interpretations (right column). Square brackets with associated codes (e.g., *[role, process]*) appear in the interpretations to show how different phrases were coded. As with all semi-structured interviews, the exact order of questions posed to the respondents varied, but the list of topics covered was the same. The initial interview question associated with each excerpt is described in the top row of the relevant table.

5.1   Facilitator 1

Tables 1, 2 and 3 present the selected transcript excerpts from the interview with F1 and the interpretations thereof.

Table 1. Excerpt 1 with interpretations.

Initial question: *What is a good facilitator?*	
Phrase	Interpretation
I think a good facilitator, especially in these settings, will drive the meeting forward	[**role, process**] From the perspective of F1, ensuring progression in meetings, possibly relative to predefined goals or items on a meeting agenda, is a central responsibility of a facilitator
So, I think it's very… [pause]… it's a balance between moving the meeting forward [and] trying to make people speak up	[**role, process**] F1 also considers it part of the facilitator's responsibility to actively involve participants in discussions by encouraging them to express their views on relevant matters. However, F1 sees a potential trade-off between active involvement and progression in meetings
So, I think what I was trying to do [in the meeting] yesterday … when the [domain experts] were silent—[I was] trying to get them to say the things that I know they said to me earlier	[**practice**] F1 explains how he/she attempted to prevent inactivity during a meeting by asking participants a direct question

The interpretations provided in Table 1 regarding F1's views on the design process, the facilitator role, and personal facilitation practice can be summed up as follows:

- *Process*: The design process should actively involve participants in design-related questions; participants should be given the opportunity to present their perspectives to one another.
- *Role*: The facilitator of a participatory activity should ensure both that participants are given an opportunity to voice their opinions and that progression is being made.
- *Practice*: Asking users direct questions is one way to give participants an opportunity to present their views to others.

Table 2. Excerpt 2 with interpretations.

Initial question: *What would you say is your role in the meetings I have been in?*

Phrase	Interpretation
So, the meetings you [the interviewer] have been in particularly have been trying to get our developers and the [domain experts] here on the same page—and I'm kind of a bridge between them	[**process**] From F1's perspective, the meetings are aimed at creating a shared understanding between the US-based developers and the local domain experts [**role**] F1 sees himself/herself as an intermediary that helps the developers and domain experts understand one another
So, the developers have been talking to the [domain experts] for years in terms of making the plans, but I'm here living and breathing with the [domain experts] and so I have more of a pulse on what their emotions are	[**practice**] Through consistent in-person interaction with the domain experts as opposed to sporadic online discussions, F1 has developed a more intimate, and possibly empathic, relationship with the domain experts than the US-based developers. Through the development of such relations, F1 has gained an acute awareness of the needs of the domain experts and their feelings regarding design suggestions

The interpretations of F1's perspectives in Table 2 illustrate the following:

- *Process*: The participatory process should help form a shared understanding between the participants.
- *Role*: The facilitator is a mediator ("bridge") between participants that helps establish a shared understanding.
- *Practice*: In order to effectively act as a mediator, it is necessary to develop empathic relations with user representatives. Developing such relations requires close interaction over time.

Table 3. Excerpt 3 with interpretations.

Initial question: *What would you say is your role in the meetings I have been in?*

Phrase	Interpretation
And after the meeting time is when some importance, like emotions and feelings or understandings, are achieved	[**process**] The statement suggests that F1 considers non-verbal empathic aspects of communication to play an important role in aligning perspectives. The statement also implicitly suggests that F1 feels that the formal project meetings are an insufficient arena for establishing common ground
And that's the kind of thing that our developers, who are only ever on the phone, are never gonna get to be a part of until they come here to visit	[**process**] In terms of the intimacy characterizing the informal after-meetings, F1 believes that US-based developers, who are physically remote and only participate in meetings via video, are deprived of the ways in which alignment of understandings and establishment of common ground are achieved. The physical distance between the domain experts and the developers impedes qualitative aspects of interactions
I am in those little after-meetings and I did hear how they were saying, and I saw that look of panic on their face. I can message our developer and be like: "Not good (laugh), not good"	[**practice**] Elaborating on how he/she is able to act as a "bridge" between domain experts and developers, F1 explains that working closely with the domain experts attuned him/her towards their subtle non-verbal aspects of communication such as tone of voice and facial expressions

A summary of the key elements of the interpretations in Table 3 follows:

- *Process*: The structure or form of participatory activities affects how the participants interact and, consequently, the extent to which they are able to establish shared understandings.
- *Practice*: Being attentive to non-verbal aspects of participants' communication (both within and beyond scheduled project activities) and conveying responses from user representatives to the development team in a sincere manner are important for a facilitator.

Synthesizing F1's perspectives on the design process, the facilitator role, and personal facilitation practice (Tables 1, 2 and 3) leads to the following key characteristics:

- *Process*: The design process is an intimate group process that should help establish a shared understanding among participants.

- *Role*: The facilitator is a mediator, assisting participants in establishing a shared understanding. The facilitator should also ensure progress is made.
- *Practice*: To successfully fulfill the role, one needs to take steps to actively involve the participants in discussions, remain attentive to subtle aspects of their communication and responses (non-verbal and emotive aspects), and build empathic relations with user representatives over time.

5.2 Facilitator 2

Transcript excerpts from the interview with F2 and associated interpretations of these are presented in Tables 4, 5 and 6.

Table 4. Excerpt 4 with interpretations.

Initial question: *Can you tell me about group dynamics and how people are involved?*	
Phrase	Interpretation
There are 10 000 people at [the development organization], so, there might be somebody that actually knows more about something than the person you are talking to… and the culture [in the development organization] is that you pull that person in to make sure we have the best information possible	[**process**] F2 considers his/her colleagues in the development organization to be knowledge resources (i.e., that knowledge is contained within an individual) and that some individuals have more knowledge about a given topic than others. The typical way for a facilitator to optimize a meeting in the development organization is, according to F2, to ensure that the right persons, i.e., the optimal knowledge resources relative to the agenda of the meeting, are present. The knowledge of these resources can then be conveyed as information to other participants
The same thing will happen here at [the client project organization]. Sometimes we say: "We don't have the right person". We make sure we talk to this person, so we pull them in	[**practice**] F2 suggests that he/she will continue to follow a strategy similar to the one employed in the development organization when organizing meetings in the project, i.e., trying to ensure the optimal knowledge resources are present in meetings
I think more about: "Do we have the right people discussing this? […] what makes anything successful for the design of this project, is that you don't want any surprises at go-live	[**process**] F2 relates the constellation of knowledge resources in project meetings to the success (or failure) of the finial design solution and the overall project

The summary of the interpretations in Table 4 illustrate the following in terms of F2's perspectives on process and practice:

- *Process*: For design processes to result in a successful design, the optimal constellation of knowledge resources (user representatives and developers) relative to topics being discussed at any time needs to be present.

- *Practice*: The facilitator should work towards optimizing the constellation of knowledge resources present in specific participatory activities.

Table 5. Excerpt 5 with interpretations.

Initial question: *What is your role in the meetings that I observed?*

Phrase	Interpretation
Pretty much my role is to make sure we are prepared in those meetings because we sit in those meetings. But it's actually a lot of work to get done even before that meeting. For instance, I'll speak to [peer in the project organization], because [we]—[him/her] from [the project organization] and me from [the developer organization], technically—like, own the success of this. I will talk about what I mean by success in a bit, but we want to make sure: "Do we have the right agenda; do we have the right people?"	[role] As a facilitator, F2 puts particular emphasis on the preparation of meetings because he/she considers it both a personal responsibility and the responsibility of his/her Norwegian peer to make the meetings successful [practice] Together with his/her peer, F2 puts efforts into the preparations, particularly when it comes to optimizing the constellation of knowledge resources vis-a-vis the agenda of a meeting
Because what we never want to do is start a meeting and say: "What shall we talk about?" That usually doesn't get us like very far when we are trying to meet a deadline, because at the end of the day we are just trying get certain deadlines met. So that's what [peer in the project organization] and I am thinking about: "We have this deadline coming up. How do we get this deadline met?" And that's by making sure that this meeting we talk about this. In this meeting, we have the answers to this. In this meeting, we get information	[process] F2 considers thoroughly prepared meeting agendas to be important for a meeting to be productive and effectively inform design decisions. Productive meetings are considered a means to ensure that project deliverables are completed before scheduled deadlines. In order to reach project deadlines, project meetings need to provide answers to specific questions on the agenda that are relevant to the developers

The key takeaways from Table 5 are summarized below:

- *Process*: The participatory process should effectively help produce the highest quality answers to questions on the meeting agenda that drive the design process forward so that project deadlines can be met. Participatory activities are "information collection points" that should help developers determine how to proceed.
- *Role*: The facilitator is a preparer, one that "sets the stage" for participatory activities.
- *Practice*: Preparing participatory activities by ensuring that the optimal knowledge resources on matters relevant to the agenda are present is an important part of facilitation.

Table 6. Excerpt 6 with interpretations.

Initial question: *So, you are in a way steering what is going to be the product?*

Phrase	Interpretation
The way I see it, I'm making sure that the right people are talking to each other in the correct way. So, I may be managing it with [peer in client project organization] but at the end of the day, I'm not the one who is going to use the system. I'm not even the one who is going to build it. It's most important that the developers know what they are developing and agree that it makes sense. It's important that the operational people that we meet with—that we have involved, who are great—that it is going to work for them	[**role, process**] F2 sees himself/herself as less affected by the results of the design process than the developers and the domain experts because he/she only manages the preparations for the meetings [**process**] The developers understanding and agreeing to what they are designing and ensuring that the solution will fulfill the needs of the domain experts when it is employed in their daily work life is essential for the design process
So, what we often have a hard time with, I think, as humans in general, is [that] we all come from different backgrounds and are starting to speak the same language, especially with something as complex as software, medical software	[**process**] F2 regards the establishment of shared understandings between participants in the design process to be a key challenge, particularly in the context of developing medical software
And so my job is to make sure people are ready for that meeting and to keep them on the path where I think progress is	[**role**] F2 considers it is his/her responsibility to both prepare participants before the meetings and to ensure that the meetings evolve in ways he/she considers productive

The key takeaway points from the interpretations of F2's responses (Tables 4, 5 and 6) are as follows:

- *Process*: The design process is an information collection process in which the quality of collected information depends on the participating resources, i.e., the knowledge of those taking part.
- *Role*: The facilitator is a preparer (organizer) of activities related to the participatory process.
- *Practice*: Being a preparer involves taking steps to optimize the constellation of knowledge resources per activity, thereby maximizing the quality of the information transferred from domain experts to developers.

5.3 Facilitator 3

Transcript excerpts from the interviews with F3 and the corresponding interpretations are presented in Tables 7, 8 and 9.

Table 7. Excerpt 7 with interpretations.

Initial question: *Can you tell me about your facilitation and the methods you apply?*

Phrase	Interpretation
[A competent facilitator has] the ability to abstract—not everybody is equally good at it	[**role**] F3 considers the ability to think in abstract terms to be essential to the role of the facilitator
What I'm trying to say is that, as an enterprise architect [in the project], I know a little about everything but I'm not particularly good at anything. And that is perhaps the strength of having such a role; that you are not too deep into the details but have an overview, which in turn enables me to ask "silly questions" in quotation marks: "Is it really like that? Does it have to be that way or could we have done it differently?"— these kinds of open questions	[**role**] F3 feels that his/her skills as a facilitator are related to another role of his/hers within the project, that of enterprise architect [**practice, role**] The enterprise architect role has provided F3 with an overview of the project. This overview helps F3 take a more engaging role as facilitator by enabling him/her to ask questions in meetings that encourage discussions and reflection among participants, for example, concerning alternative solutions to design-related questions. This also implicitly suggests that F3 considers encouraging discussions among participants to be central to the facilitator role

The key elements of the interpretation of F3's perspectives are provided in Table 7.

- *Role*: Abstract thinking and maintaining an overview of the project are central to the facilitator role. The latter can especially help the in terms of creating opportunities for engagement and discussion, another key factor.
- *Practice*: Asking questions that promote discussions among participants helps facilitators fulfill their role.

Table 8. Excerpt 8 with interpretations.

Initial question: *What is your role in the meetings that I observed?*

Phrase	Interpretation
What I experienced in those meetings was that they [the participants] didn't understand one another. No! And I felt that we were not talking about the same thing. We have a different understanding of what the need is and different understandings of what the solution we will receive is going to be like	[**process**]: F3 describes how participants have "talked past" each other in a series of meetings without fully realizing it, resulting in a state of confusion. F3 considers this confusion to be an obstacle to a constructive design process. According to F3, a shared understanding between participants should comprise both user needs and ideas about the future solution
So that was when I talked to the process owner —I cannot remember who that was—and then I said: "We cannot continue on this course because then we will fail to hit the nail on the head"	[**role, practice**]: F3 feels that it is his/her responsibility to report the lack of a shared understanding between the participants to the project associate responsible for the module [**process**] F3 feels that the lack of a shared understanding could potentially compromise the end result

Key aspects of the interpretations provided in Table 8 are below.

- *Process*: Establishing a shared understanding between participants with respect to both user needs and the final product is essential for a constructive design process.
- *Role:* A facilitator needs to be mindful about challenges related to communication and understanding between participants.
- *Practice*: Reporting challenges related to a lack of a shared understanding between participants can potentially prevent the problem from escalating.

Table 9. Excerpt 9 with interpretations.

Initial question: *What is your role in the meetings that I observed?*

Phrase	Interpretation
So, my role there is to find roughly the right level of abstraction, describe the tasks using a form of language that makes it possible for others to understand, and to try to see things from different perspectives, and, yes, that's my job. I will not take control, but I will help them think in more general terms	[role] From F3's perspective, helping participants understand each other and see design issues from various perspectives are central facilitator responsibilities. Rather than seeing the facilitator as someone who leads a group, F3 considers his/her role to primarily involve encouraging holistic thinking among participants
And what's good about making a type of artifact—making something together? First, a joint ownership is established, because those who have been involved feel an ownership:"I have been involved in making this; I recognize myself in this." And then it becomes far easier to discuss	[Process, Practice] F3 highlights the value he/she sees in co-designed artifacts that emerge from participatory design activities. F3 considers such artefacts important in terms of establishing a shared ownership of the solution among participants, thereby increasing the likelihood of active engagement
When you're in a meeting where there are many interests you often end up with what I call "hobby-horse racing". Each actor is concerned with his own thing, riding his hobby-horse, and is unable to move forward in the discussion before having spoken out about things they are deeply passionate about: "Now you are at the start, now we're here. But, but, what you're concerned about now won't become relevant until towards the end"	[Process]: F3 considers individualistic thinking among meeting participants, i.e., only thinking in terms of how the solution might be beneficial (or harmful) from the individual domain expert's perspective (and the specific users he or she represents) to be counterproductive to the design process [Role, Practice] To ensure constructive meetings and avoid impeding the design process, F3 believes that it is important for the facilitator to manage discussions in such a way that issues that are important to specific user representatives are brought up at appropriate times

The interpretations of F3's perspectives (Table 9) can be summarized as follows.

- *Process*: The design process should promote strong commitment among all participants and should lead to a design solution that benefits all user groups. The design process should therefore help participants see beyond their individual needs and work towards a common good.
- *Role*: The facilitator should help establish a shared understanding between participants and encourage holistic (as opposed to individualistic) thinking among participants.

The facilitator needs to manage discussions in order to promote holistic thinking and constructive participatory activities.

- *Practice*: The use of artifacts that have been co-designed by participants is one way to help establish common ground. Careful sequencing of the topics to be discussed is an example of how participatory activities can be managed to encourage holistic thinking in the design process.

Synthesizing the interpretations of Facilitator 3's responses concerning process, role, and practice (Tables 7, 8 and 9) results in the following characteristics:

- *Process*: The design process is a managed collaborative process with the aim of designing for a common good.
- *Role*: The facilitator is a debate moderator that should encourage holistic (as opposed to individualistic) thinking among participants.
- *Practice*: Taking steps to encourage discussions and reflections by frequently asking critical questions but also sequencing topics to be discussed to avoid individualistic thinking are important aspects of the role.

6   Comparing the Facilitators' Perspectives

Having presented the analysis of the three facilitators' perspectives on the design process, the facilitator role, and personal facilitation practice, attention now turns to how the different viewpoints compare and contrast with one another. The synthesis of each facilitator's perspectives on the three aspects will be used as a basis for the discussion. A systematic overview of the syntheses is presented in Table 10 for clarity.

Table 10. Comparison of the facilitators' perspectives on process, role, and personal practice.

	Facilitator 1	Facilitator 2	Facilitator 3
Process	The design process is an intimate group process that should help establish a shared understanding among participants	The design process is an information collection process in which the quality of the collected information is closely linked to the knowledge resources involved	The design process is a managed collaborative process with the aim of designing for a common good
Role	The facilitator is primarily a mediator that assists participants in establishing a shared understanding	The facilitator is mainly a preparer (organizer) of activities related to the participatory process	The facilitator is a debate moderator that should encourage holistic thinking among participants
Practice	Being a mediator between participants requires the development of empathic relationships with user representatives, actively involving them in participatory activities, and remaining attentive to subtle aspects of their communication and responses	Being a preparer involves taking steps to optimize the constellation of knowledge resources per activity, thereby maximizing the quality of the information transfer from domain experts to developers	Being a debate moderator means encourage discussions and reflections through critical questions. It also involves sequencing topics to be discussed to avoid individualistic thinking

The intention here is not to rebuke or praise any of the facilitators' perspectives. Instead, the goal is emphasizing the conceptual differences and similarities within the various viewpoints. The conceptual difference will later be used as a foundation for discussing the key implications of these findings (Sect. 7).

6.1 Process

The analysis showed that facilitators conceptualized the design process differently. F1 regarded the process as an *intimate group process*, F2 described the process more as an *information collection process*, and F3 felt that the process was a *managed collaborative process*.

In comparing the three views, the most significant difference seemed to be between F1 and F3 on the one side and F2 on the other. Both F1 and F3 highlighted the forming of a shared understanding between participants to be a key component of the participatory process and regarded their active involvement in design-related questions to be central. These conceptualizations of the design process are in many ways aligned with the emancipatory and collective notions of PD in which knowledge and understanding is created through interaction between stakeholders [16].

F2, by contrast, describes the design process in terms of information. The individual activities in the process are *information collection points* where information relevant to further development is passed on from domain experts to developers. F2 sees knowledge primarily as residing *within* a person, as opposed to the more interactional perspective on knowledge creation expressed by F1 and F3. According to F2's assessment, the knowledge a person possesses can then be conveyed to others as information. This person-as-information perspective is particularly reflected in the way that F2 regards the ideal participatory design process as being dependent on having the optimal constellation of knowledge resources present. Such a constellation is seen to provide the qualified answers that developers need to continue developing the system and ensure that project deadlines are met.

One of the most significant differences in the perspectives of F1 and F3 in terms of the design process is related to how they conceptualize facilitator–participant interaction. While F1 highlights emotive aspects and the quality of participant interaction as central to a successful process, F3 puts more emphasis on the collaborative aspects and working towards a common goal.

While this study does not intend to label the three interviewed facilitators, the different conceptualizations of the design process outlined above reflect three distinct system development traditions to some degree. For example, F1's strong focus on developing empathic relations with participants is in line with principles of Empathic Design [19, 20]. F2's participants-as-information perspective reflects to some degree the positivistic notions of the requirements engineering phase as understood in Software Engineering [21]. Lastly, F3's holistic design thinking and goal to promote reflections in participants are similar to PD philosophy [16].

6.2 Role

The facilitators' views on the facilitator role also varied; their views on the role reflected their perspectives on the design process. F1, who regarded the design process to be an intimate group process, felt that her role was to act as a *bridge* or a *mediator* between different stakeholders taking part in meetings. F1 sees it as her responsibility to be able to interpret and convey user representatives' "true" responses to members of the developer organization and not simply to let emotions unfold.

F2, who emphasized that a successful design process is dependent on having the right knowledge resources (people) present in specific meetings, considers it a key facilitator responsibility to identify and recruit those knowledge resources. As such, F2 regarded the role of the facilitator to involve being a *preparer* or *organizer* of meetings.

Similarly to F1, F3 associated the facilitator role with actively helping participants communicate and understand each other. However, in contrast with F1, F3 highlights the need for a facilitator to help participants work towards a common goal, meaning that the facilitator needs to manage discussions, particularly when it comes to the question of which topics are appropriate to discuss when.

One key difference in the respondents' perspectives regarding the facilitator role concerns the participatory activity and the extent to which this requires management as it plays out. While F1 and F3 sees the facilitator role as active and attentive, F2 appears to view the facilitator as more passive. For F2, facilitation is mainly associated with preparation of participatory activities.

6.3 Practice

Similar to the close relationship found between each respondent's perspectives on the design process and the facilitator role, there is also a strong link in the role–practice relationship. For example, F1 and F3, who consider playing an active part in meetings to be part of a facilitator's responsibility, describe how they pose questions in a meeting with the goal of involving participants. F3's use of artifacts to help participants create common ground and mindful sequencing of topics for debate are other examples of an active facilitation style. F1 also describes how he/she invests time with domain experts beyond scheduled project meetings and the ways in which this helps her become better attuned to their responses.

F2 appears to be less concerned with taking an active part in meetings; his/her facilitation efforts primarily go into planning and organizing the meetings, i.e., recruiting the "right" people in regard to the meeting agenda.

7   Implications: Towards a Co-reflective Facilitation Practice

The respondents held distinctive perspectives and attitudes towards the design process, the facilitator role, and facilitation practice. As discussed earlier, some of the expressed viewpoints reflect notions of different system development traditions, such as Empathic Design, Software Engineering (requirements engineering phase), and PD. This illustrates how perspectives on user participation, even within related project activities and within the same development unit, may be based on conceptually different ideas. There is currently no empirical data to indicate the actual effects of this multi-paradigmatic thinking among co-facilitators on the outcome of the project. However, the distinct philosophies embedded in the aforementioned development traditions give reason to hypothesize that the implications on actual facilitation practice and generated output related participatory activities could be significant.

Having raised awareness towards the heterogenous perspectives that may exist between facilitators of participatory project activities, what are the main implications? With respect to IT projects, especially large-scale projects that are likely to involve several facilitators, we particularly recommend the adoption of a *reflective* approach towards facilitation—i.e., an approach that allows facilitators to exchange and compare perspectives on facilitation and discuss their experiences at regular intervals throughout the design process. Similar recommendations regarding reflective practices already exist in agile software development. Fowler and Highsmith [22] suggested in their 12th agile principle: *At regular intervals, the team reflects on how to become more effective, then tunes and adjusts its behavior accordingly. [...] we all recognize that we can't come up with the right process for every situation. So any agile team must refine and reflect as it goes along, constantly improving its practices in its local circumstances."* Various forms of co-reflection have also been employed as quality improvement strategies in teacher education [23] and nursing professional development [24]; the use of video-assisted reflective inquires is an example of such a strategy. To our knowledge, however, regular co-reflection activities on facilitation practice is far from standard.

The development of local communities of facilitation practice can help enhance facilitation skills in project stakeholder organizations. Rather than striving towards a uniform facilitation "mindset" and one way of practice, discussion and reflection should be goals in their own right. Highlighting the heterogenous circumstances under which facilitated participatory activities may occur, Light and Akama [8] warned against a "one-style-fits-all" approach, stating that there may be multiple meaningful rationales behind adopted facilitation practices. As such, it can be argued that having a conscious awareness towards one's facilitation thinking and practice is more important than adopting shared mindsets and practices among co-facilitators.

Inspired by best practice in agile software development [22], teacher education [23] and nursing professional development [24], the following list offers some suggestions to support reflection on the design process, the facilitator role, and facilitation practice to provide a concrete idea of how co-reflection among facilitators of participatory activities may be realized.

- *Design Process*: Discussions among co-facilitators, particularly in the planning phase or early stages of a project, concerning the motivation and goals of user involvement can be fruitful. Such discussion can help reveal different priorities and motivations among co-facilitators. Concretizing the different perspectives on user involvement embedded in various system development traditions, in form of a table that allows for comparison of key characteristics of the traditions, is one way that discussions related to the design process may be supported.
- *Role*: Practitioners could be offered the chance to present their personal views on the facilitator role to encourage reflection. This could be achieved by, for example,

allowing practitioners to first write down keywords or short phrases representing aspects they consider central to the role on post-it notes. Each facilitator could present and elaborate on the keywords they wrote down. The post-it notes from all participating practitioners could later be grouped according to thematical similarity and then used as a foundation for a discussion.

- *Practice*: The use of video footage from other facilitation practices as a basis for comparison and discussion is one way to foster practice-related reflections. Another alternative could be to employ role play, possibly in combination with video recording, where facilitation may be acted out in participatory design activities. Participants could switch between playing facilitators (i.e., their actual project role) and the users involved in the activities. These suggestions could also open up discussions concerning the consequences of practice, i.e., how different practices affect the output of the participatory activities.

An empirical investigation of the potential value of co-reflective activities, such as those proposed above, is beyond the scope of the current study. In order to become a standard practice in IT projects characterized by user involvement, the activities need to be planned in advance. In other words, resources (time and budget) need to be specifically allocated to such activities in the planning of the project.

8 Methodological Considerations

It seems appropriate to briefly highlight some methodological aspects that may have affected the presented analysis and findings before concluding.

First, while we found that the interview respondents conceptualized facilitation differently, it should be emphasized that we by no means consider our study exhaustive in terms of identifying facilitator "mindsets" nor has it been our objective to chart such a territory. Instead, the three distinct conceptualizations identified in this study should be considered no more than instances in a potentially multifaceted world of understandings. Considered from a natural science viewpoint, an in-depth qualitative study, such as the current one, can always be criticized for lack of generalizability. Maximizing generalizability, however, was never our intention. Rather, our emphasis has been on unpacking the unique personal experiences of the interviewed facilitators. With only three respondents, we cannot generalize to the whole population of facilitators concerning "mindsets", but as the three respondents showed very different perspectives, it is reasonable to conclude that the study indicates a high level of heterogeneity.

Second, we do not know the extent to which perspectives expressed by the facilitators who took part in the study affect the nature of their facilitation practice. We have relied exclusively on their verbal accounts. The distinctive ways that the respondents conceptualize facilitation, nevertheless, could suggest a similarly distinctive practice.

Third, the presented content analysis makes claims about phenomena based on interpretation of statements from the respondents. Such an analysis can easily raise validity issues due to the risk of potential misinterpretations. Measures taken to reduce this risk included complementary field observation aimed at improving our basis for valid interpretation as well as multiple individual and plenary reviews of the interpretations conducted by the authors.

9 Summary and Concluding Remarks

The current study investigated the ways in which facilitators of participatory activities in a large-scale health IT project understand the design process, the facilitator role, and their personal facilitation practice. The conceptual ideas embedded in the respondents' narratives were unpacked based on an in-depth qualitative content analysis of interview transcripts. It was discovered that many of the ideas pertained to different system development traditions such as Empathic Design, Software Engineering (requirements engineering phase), and PD.

While we consider our findings to be indicative rather than conclusive, they bring attention to a potential lack of systematic reflection among practitioners in terms of what it means to be a facilitator and what facilitation of participatory activities implies. We therefore proposed a co-reflective approach towards facilitation in individual projects and gave examples of possible co-reflection activities for facilitators.

This study hopes to contribute to the recognition of design facilitation as a practice and key methodological challenge for PD.

Acknowledgements. This study was conducted as part of the KonPas and PlatVel projects. Our special thanks go to the interview respondents for sharing their time, commitment, and viewpoints.

References

1. ISO 9241–210: Ergonomics of human-system interaction — Part 210: Human-centred design for interactive systems. International Organization for Standardization (2019)
2. Bjerknes, G., Bratteteig, T.: User participation and democracy: a discussion of Scandinavian research on systems development. Scand. J. Inf. Syst. **7**, 73–98 (1995)
3. Dahl, Y., Linander, H., Hanssen, G.K.: Co-designing interactive tabletop solutions for active patient involvement in audiological consultations. In: Proceedings of the 8th Nordic Conference on Human-Computer Interaction: Fun, Fast, Foundational, pp. 207–216. Association for Computing Machinery, Helsinki, Finland (2014)
4. Svanæs, D., Seland, G.: Putting the users center stage: role playing and low-fi prototyping enable end users to design mobile systems. In: Proceedings of the SIGCHI Conference on Human Factors in Computing Systems, pp. 479–486. ACM, Vienna, Austria (2004)
5. Lindsay, S., Brittain, K., Jackson, D., Ladha, C., Ladha, K., Olivier, P.: Empathy, participatory design and people with dementia. In: Proceedings of the SIGCHI Conference on Human Factors in Computing Systems, pp. 521–530 (2012)
6. Sahib, N.G., Stockman, T., Tombros, A., Metatla, O.: Participatory design with blind users: a scenario-based approach. In: Kotzé, P., Marsden, G., Lindgaard, G., Wesson, J., Winckler, M. (eds.) INTERACT 2013. LNCS, vol. 8117, pp. 685–701. Springer, Heidelberg (2013). https://doi.org/10.1007/978-3-642-40483-2_48
7. Cumbo, B.J., Eriksson, E., Iversen, O.S.: The "Least-Adult" role in participatory design with children. In: Proceedings of the 31st Australian Conference on Human-Computer-Interaction, pp. 73–84. Association for Computing Machinery, Fremantle, WA, Australia (2019)
8. Light, A., Akama, Y.: The human touch: participatory practice and the role of facilitation in designing with communities. In: Proceedings of the 12th Participatory Design Conference: Research Papers, vol. 1, pp. 61–70 (2012)

9. Dahl, Y., Svanæs, D.: Facilitating democracy: concerns from participatory design with asymmetric stakeholder relations in health care. In: Proceedings of the 2020 CHI Conference on Human Factors in Computing Systems, pp. 1–13. Association for Computing Machinery (2020)

10. Luck, R.: Learning to talk to users in participatory design situations. Des. Stud. **28**, 217–242 (2007)

11. Schön, D.A.: The reflective practitioner: How professionals think in action. Basic books (1984)

12. Dalsgaard, P., Eriksson, E.: Large-scale participation: a case study of a participatory approach to developing a new public library. In: Proceedings of the SIGCHI Conference on Human Factors in Computing Systems, pp. 399–408. Association for Computing Machinery (2013)

13. Pilemalm, S., Timpka, T.: Third generation participatory design in health informatics—making user participation applicable to large-scale information system projects. J. Biomed. Inform. **41**, 327–339 (2008)

14. Simonsen, J., Hertzum, M.: Participative design and the challenges of large-scale systems: extending the iterative PD approach. In: Proceedings of the Tenth Anniversary Conference on Participatory Design 2008, pp. 1–10. Indiana University, Bloomington, Indiana (2008)

15. Bødker, S., Kyng, M.: Participatory design that matters—facing the big issues. ACM Trans. Comput. Hum. Interact. (TOCHI) **25**, 1–31 (2018)

16. Robertson, T., Simonsen, J.: Participatory design: an introduction. In: Robertson, T., Simonsen, J. (eds.) Routledge International Handbook of Participatory Design. Routledge, London (2013)

17. Bratteteig, T., Wagner, I.: Unpacking the notion of participation in participatory design. Comput. Support. Cooper. Work (CSCW) **25**, 425–475 (2016)

18. Bengtsson, M.: How to plan and perform a qualitative study using content analysis. NursingPlus Open **2**, 8–14 (2016)

19. Wright, P., McCarthy, J.: Empathy and experience in HCI. In: Proceedings of the SIGCHI Conference on Human Factors in Computing Systems, pp. 637–646. Association for Computing Machinery, Florence, Italy (2008)

20. Postma, C., Zwartkruis-Pelgrim, E., Daemen, E., Du, J.: Challenges of doing empathic design: experiences from industry (2012)

21. Hinds, C.: The case against a positivist philosophy of requirements engineering. Require. Eng. **13**, 315–328 (2008)

22. Beck, K., et al.: Manifesto for agile software development (2001)

23. Tripp, T.R., Rich, P.J.: The influence of video analysis on the process of teacher change. Teach. Teach. Educ. **28**, 728–739 (2012)

24. Forbes, H., et al.: Use of videos to support teaching and learning of clinical skills in nursing education: a review. Nurse Educ. Today **42**, 53–56 (2016)

Focus, Structure, Reflection! Integrating User-Centred Design and Design Sprint

Virpi Roto[1]([✉]), Marta Larusdottir[2], Andrés Lucero[1], Jan Stage[3], and Ilja Šmorgun[4]

[1] Aalto University, 00076 Aalto, Finland
virpi.roto@aalto.fi, lucero@acm.org
[2] Reykjavik University, 101 Reykjavik, Iceland
marta@ru.is
[3] Aalborg University, 9100 Ålborg, Denmark
jans@cs.aau.dk
[4] Tallinn University, 10120 Tallinn, Estonia
ilja.smorgun@tlu.ee

Abstract. Google Design Sprint (GDS) is becoming a valued tool for interaction design practitioners today. Although GDS has some similarities to User-Centred Design (UCD), it does not study user needs before generating solutions. On the other hand, UCD provides little guidance on producing design solutions. We saw the two processes would nicely complement each other. This paper reports development of an intensive two-week interaction design course where UCD was combined with GDS. The feedback from 22 higher education students indicates how UCD helped them to keep the focus on the important things, and how the detailed structure of GDS process guided them fast forward. In the fast-paced Design Sprint, students need dedicated time for reflection. The contributions of this work include the course structure for teaching a User-Centred Design Sprint process, student feedback on the new process, and recommendations for teaching such a course.

Keywords: Interaction design · User-Centred Design · Design sprint · Higher education · Course development

1 Introduction

Human-Computer Interaction (HCI) education has been criticised for the lack of support for a creative design approach [6]. Since the centre of User-Centred Design (UCD) is on user needs, the actual craft of design receives too little attention [3]. When planning an intensive Interaction Design course, we wanted to combine the hallmark HCI method of UCD with a creative design method, aiming at a more balanced role between the user and the designer in the interaction design process [2].

At the time of developing the course, a design method called Google Design Sprint (GDS) [12] started to get more attention among interaction designers.

© IFIP International Federation for Information Processing 2021
Published by Springer Nature Switzerland AG 2021
C. Ardito et al. (Eds.): INTERACT 2021, LNCS 12933, pp. 239–258, 2021.
https://doi.org/10.1007/978-3-030-85616-8_15

GDS is an expedited design process for ideating, prototyping, and testing a design idea just in one week. This specific form of a design sprint was developed by Knapp while at Google, therefore it is also colloquially known as the Google Design Sprint [10]. GDS does not include UCD activities such as user interviews or observations to find out user needs in the early stages of the design sprint. This may be because in industry, knowledge on user needs accumulates over the years and today, many projects build on the previous knowledge of the users. But GDS includes user evaluations, which can be grouped as one of the core UCD methods, as the last activity of the design sprint. When designing for user groups and contexts that the designers are not familiar with, the User-Centred Design activities of interviewing and observing users are elementary to understand the contexts of use and user needs, and to verify that the users can adopt the new design as part of their practices [11].

In our previous work, we have tested teaching GDS and UCD on an intensive 2-week interaction design course. The first week was devoted to teaching the GDS process and the second week for UCD. This structure resulted in positive feedback from students but also revealed issues to be improved [15]. The students liked the fast pace of GDS and the structure that it provides to design work, but they missed clarifying the users' needs before starting the GDS process. The first edition of the course structure was not optimal.

Based on the above, there is need for research on integrating user-centred methods to creative design methods. There is also a need to study how to teach this integrated approach for students. Therefore, we defined two research questions to be answered in the present study.

RQ1: How can User-Centred Design and Design Sprint processes be integrated into a coherent structure in an intensive course?

RQ2: What should teachers pay special attention to in teaching User-Centred Design Sprint?

In this paper, we report the development of a structured design process that combines User-Centred Design (UCD) and Google Design Sprint (GDS) processes into a coherent User-Centred Design Sprint (UCD Sprint). The new design process was developed for and tested in the context of an intensive two-week course on interaction design in higher education. On this course, the basics of interaction design were taught through project-based learning.

The UCD Sprint has been developed along two editions of the course. After the first version of the course in 2018, we saw that it was important to improve the course structure so that students would do GDS after having conducted user research and thus gained understanding of user needs. We used the 2019 course as a case study to test a modified structure, where UCD process was combined with the GDS process in a more integrated way. We taught the new UCD Sprint for students with different backgrounds and gathered the student feedback on the course. The students acted as users of the new process, and their evaluation of the new course structure and content forms the main data set reported in this paper.

2 Related Research

In this section, we present the pieces of research that are closest to ours. We start by reporting studies around teaching UCD, then around teaching design sprints, and finally the works combining the two design approaches.

2.1 User-Centred Design and Design Sprints Education

The research literature on HCI includes an extensive number of references that present the rationale behind UCD or techniques that are relevant in a UCD process. Contrary to this, the literature on teaching of UCD is very limited, even though the number of developers skilled in UCD is critically important for the employment of UCD in software development organizations. One of the few exceptions focuses on the skills needed for UCD practitioners, arguing that UCD is a process that should yield a high level of utility and usability by developing good task flows and user interfaces. Therefore, UCD practitioners should have the knowledge and skills needed for considering and involving users [7].

There are also more specific descriptions of UCD courses. Greenberg [8] presents a complete course design. It is a general HCI course for university students, but it has a part on design with users. The main focus in this part is on evaluation, but the last element in this part is on involving users in the design process. There is not an overall method to guide the process and the application of the UCD techniques. Seffah and Andreevskaia [19] present the content of a course specifically on user-centred design for university students. In addition, they describe the approach behind the course through a list with 17 skills on design and evaluation that should be developed in a UCD course. Unfortunately, they neither outline the contents of the specific course nor any experiences from teaching it.

The literature mentioned above is mostly characterised by guidance on ways of teaching UCD, however, there is almost no evaluation of these teaching efforts. An early exception to this is a report from training workshops where the UCD process and related techniques were presented. The participants indicated that after a workshop, they felt more empowered to evaluate and design new systems [22]. An evaluation of teaching of UCD on elementary and secondary school level concluded that there was a clear lack of opportunities for pupils to experience user-centred approaches when undertaking tasks in classes on this topic [17]. The evaluation of a course for experienced practitioners provided experiences of different part of the contents of the course, but they are still on an overall level [13].

Culén [6] wanted to bring innovation and creativity to HCI education and used Design Thinking [5] for this purpose. She notes that while the overall Design Thinking process is similar to UCD, the role of research, requirements specification, questioning assumptions, the consideration of organizational issues, and the systematic exploration of design alternatives make the difference. Culén [6] reports an Interaction Design course within an HCI curriculum, which showed Design Thinking to foster innovation and creativity. This work is close to our attempt to combine UCD and GDS, since GDS is often seen as an implementation of Design Thinking in practice. However, while Culen aimed at bringing creativity to HCI education of non-designers, our aim was to develop a design process integrating UCD and design sprint to the education of interaction designers.

We have only found a few scholars investigating the topic of design sprints in education. [21] discuss design sprints in education and conclude that through the sprints, students can learn practical skills of avoiding fixation to the first idea of the solution, understanding the problem deeply because of its ambiguity, and collaborating with team members. They also list many values that design sprint can bring to design education. Encouraged by these works, our paper focuses on an unexplored topic of students' experiences of design sprint as a learning method, and especially of User-Centred Design Sprint.

2.2   Integrating UCD in Design Methods

Integration of UCD and design methods has been discussed to some extent. One of the first was [20] who discussed how UCD and software engineering could be integrated. They review a number of software life-cycle methods that involve a user-centred approach. There are other suggestions for integrating user-centred design into software development, but they are typically integrating UCD in established software engineering process models, e.g. [16].

A major stream of work has focused on the integration of UCD with agile software development approaches. Brhel et al. [1] provides an overview of this issue. Additionally, Cockton et al. [4] provide good insights into the challenges of integrating UCD in agile and conclude that both agile and UCD can learn from each other and from other approaches from design, engineering and business. Besides this focused area, there is very little literature on integration of UCD and design methods. The closest work, although not involving an interaction design method per se, is by Zhang and Joines [23] who integrate UCD and theory of innovation for problem solving.

In summary, the review of literature on teaching UCD and design sprints shows that both are used in education separately, but few publications disclose the course structure. The Design Sprint process is often described in detail elsewhere, e.g., GDS in Knapp [12]. We also studied existing works on integration of UCD activities with any kind of design method. We found publications that focused on the software development processes, but we were unable to find publications targeting the phase before the software development starts.

3   Course Development

To respond to the calls for teaching UCD with a creative design method [6] and for balancing the roles of the user and the designer in the interaction design process [3], we have developed an intensive Interaction Design course combining UCD with a design sprint. The design of the course was inspired by constructivist learning theories. They are often utilised in teaching interaction design in higher education where teams of students work on a design project and learn by doing [18]. Such project-based courses have shown to support students' deep learning, in contrast to surface learning of memorizing given pieces of information [1]. The course development is reported below.

3.1 Background of the Course

Over three years, we have developed a two-week summer course on interaction design for university-level students. We gave the course for the first time in 2017 at Tallinn University with 18 participants from four countries [14]. Since this edition did not include a design sprint, we do not discuss it in this paper. Based on the evaluation from the first edition, we redesigned the course to include GDS process, and provided it to a new group of 19 international students at Reykjavik University in 2018 [15]. This paper reports the third and last edition of the course, which was further developed based on the student feedback and held at Aalto University to a group of 24 international students in year 2019. The first two editions of the course were planned and delivered by four partner universities: Aalborg University, Aalto University, Reykjavik University and Tallinn University. Uppsala University joined the third edition of the course. Each year, five students from each country were chosen to participate.

In 2019, connected health was chosen as an interdisciplinary field, and we made an effort to recruit students from the related fields of design, engineering, computer science and medicine to the multidisciplinary teams. A total of 24 international students worked in five groups of four or five members on designing and evaluating an application prototype.

3.2 Course Structure

In teaching the course on interaction design, we wanted to find a structure where the UCD and GDS activities would form a coherent and balanced design process for a 2-week intensive course. Before describing our solution for the course structure, we briefly describe the process of UCD and GDS. The two processes are documented in detail in [11] and [12].

The standard process of UCD [11] starts by planning the design process, understanding and specifying the context of use, specifying the user requirements, producing design solutions, and evaluating the design. The UCD process is iterative, repeating the activities until the evaluation results satisfy the main goal of UCD, meeting the user requirements.

The goal of the GDS process is to solve big problems and test new ideas in just five days [12]. Before the sprint starts, an important challenge is defined, and small teams with diverse skills are recruited to join the one-week sprint. On Monday, a map of the problem is made by defining key questions, a long-term goal, and a target, thus building a foundation for the sprint week. On Tuesday, individuals follow a four-step process (i.e., notes, ideas, crazy 8, and solution sketch) to sketch out their own detailed, opinionated, and competing solutions. On Wednesday, the strongest solutions are selected using a structured five-step "Sticky Decision" method and fleshed out into a storyboard. On Thursday, between one and three realistic-looking prototypes of the solutions proposed in the storyboard are built, using tools like Keynote to create the facade for apps and websites, a 3D printer to quickly prototype hardware, or just build marketing materials. Finally on Friday, the prototype is tested with five target customers in one on one interviews or think-aloud sessions. While only some of the resulting solutions will work, going through such sprints provides clarity on what to do next to tackle the big important challenge.

On our course, the students used the first three days of the course for UCD activities with introductory sessions on the course theme (e-health), developing a design brief, collecting needs from potential users, analysing user data, and setting UX goals. On the first day, the students got an introduction to the challenges in digitization in healthcare digitalization. Students were asked to find an idea individually for a health-related software solution. After presenting the individual ideas to the team members, the teams decided on one idea to work further on during the course. The GDS process ran for 5 course days, from Thursday the first week to Wednesday the second week. The course concluded with UCD activities and wrap up during the last three days of the course. The course schedule is illustrated in Fig. 1.

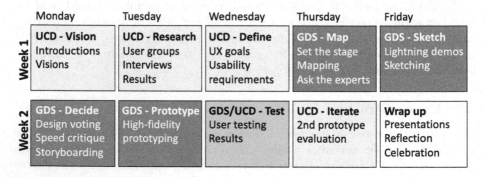

Fig. 1. Illustration of the course schedule.

The course schedule focused on combining UCD with the "by the book" GDS process during the two weeks. For the first three days, the focus was on UCD, so the students got an understanding of the problem they wanted to design for, the user needs, high-level usability requirements, user experience (UX) goals, documented in a design brief. The next two days were scheduled according to the first two days of GDS, by making a map, reflecting on the map by asking the experts and sketching the first ideas of the interaction design. During the second week, the first three days were according to the last 3 days of the GDS process: making a design solution, a storyboard, a hi-fi prototype and conducting user testing. The last Thursday focused on final evaluation and iterating the prototype.

On Friday, the students presented their design process and final outcomes, gave feedback, and celebrated the completion of the intensive course.

The changes in the course schedule in 2019 were triggered by student feedback from the 2018 edition of the course, where students expressed a need to be introduced to the context in which they would be designing, rather than immediately jumping into a Design Sprint. After extensive discussions within the teaching team, an understanding was reached that Design Sprints provide a very well-structured framework for quickly coming up with design solutions. However, if the idea for the solution, that will be the target of the design sprint, is brand new as in the course setting, the participants need to understand the users' needs prior to starting to design the software. Driven by the desire to combine the main concepts of UCD while also being able to "get something hands-on done" during a design sprint, we adjusted the course schedule from 2018 to 2019. An illustration of the course structure in 2018 and 2019 is shown in Fig. 2.

Week 1					**Week 2**				
2018 GDS Map	GDS Sketch	GDS Decide	GDS Prototype	GDS/UCD Test	UCD Define	UCD Research	UCD Iterate	UCD Iterate	Wrap up
2019 UCD Vision	UCD Research	UCD Define	GDS Map	GDS Sketch	GDS Decide	GDS Prototype	GDS/UCD Test	UCD Iterate	Wrap up

Fig. 2. Comparison of the course schedule in 2018 and 2019.

Another trigger for this change was the fatigue that we observed in the 2018 edition of the course, when after running a week-long design sprint and coming back after a weekend, there was a loss of energy and motivation within the student group to run the user-centred design methods after the design sprint, because they felt like that was not the right timing for those activities.

4   Methods

We used two data collection methods: a weekly Retrospective Hand technique and a final feedback questionnaire. For analysing the open-ended responses, we used Conventional Content Analysis method, and Mann-Whitney U test for comparing numeric ratings between the two editions of the course.

4.1   Data Collection

The data set was collected from students. Out of the 24 students, 12 were from computer science or similar technical fields, 4 from design, 1 from HCI, 4 from well-being or medical field, and 2 had experience in both medical and technical fields. Two students had to leave early on the last Friday, so we only had feedback from 22 students in the second week. All feedback was collected on paper, and the students returned the paper in a box to keep anonymity. The data collection methods will be explained in the following.

Retrospective Hand Technique. The students were given a blank A4 sheet of paper and asked to draw their right hand on the paper. In the space for the thumb, they were asked to write what was good on the course (hence the like finger), in the space for the index finger, they were asked to write anything they would like to point out, which could be either positive or negative. In the space for the middle finger, they were asked to write anything they think was not so good in the course, in the space for the ring finger they were asked to write what they take home from the course, and finally in the space for the pinkie, they were asked what they would like more of in the course. It took the students around 10 min to write the feedback they wanted.

Feedback Questionnaire. The Feedback Questionnaire consisted of three sections, of which this paper focuses on the questions regarding course structure and content. Section 1 contained evaluation on the following aspects of the course: 1. Course content, 2. Teaching methods, 3. Course structure, 4. Soft skills, 5. Learning environment, 6. Learning support, 7. Course administration, 8. Staff quality, 9. People, 10. Experience (overall course experience), 11. Feedback collection. Each aspect was explained with one sentence, for example Item 3, Course structure, was explained as: Structure and scheduling of the activities, days and the whole course. The students were asked to rate these aspects from 1 being "very bad" to 7 being "Very good" and 4 being "Neutral". The students were given the space to comment on each aspect. At the end of this section the students were asked to answer 6 questions about the questionnaire itself, results of which we do not report in this paper.

Section 2 contained two background questions on their expertise and if they planned to use these kinds of methods prior to the course. Section 2 also contained questions on 14 methods used in the course. The students were asked to rate if the method was thought provoking, was useful for the course and if they thought it would be useful in the future. The scale was 1 to 7, 1 = "Not at all", and 7 = "Extremely so". The students also answered two overall questions on the Google Design process as a whole and the user-centred design process as a whole.

Section 3 contained a evaluation of the pros and cons of the GDS process and the UCD activities. The students were asked to write three qualities with the two processes that they found good and three qualities that they found not so good. At the end of this section the students were asked particularly on the schedule of the UCD activities, i.e., if they found the 3 days of UCD activities in the beginning of the course to be short, about right, or too long. The same question was also asked about the 2 days of UCD activities at the end of the course.

4.2 Data Analysis

The qualitative data analysis covered student feedback from the Retrospective hand and Sects. 1 and 3 of the feedback questionnaire. The analysis followed the

Conventional Content Analysis by Hsieh & Shannon [10], although the student feedback was more lightweight and focused than typical data in content analysis. After converting the hand-written feedback to a digital table format, the section-specific analysis started by reading the responses of students for each feedback theme. When several topics were covered in one response, they were extracted as individual comments. Also, if the same student gave the same comment in multiple responses, they were combined into one. In this paper, we report the comments regarding the course content, structure, and teamwork. We leave out the comments regarding the course practicalities or teachers, due to the scope of this paper, the limited space, and the low value of case-specific details. The conventional content analysis started by open coding, i.e., one of the authors assigned initial codes for each individual comment. Another author used the initial codes to independently code the data. The two authors discussed the differing codes to gain a consensus and agreed on the final set of 24 unique codes for the Retrospective Hand data and 16 for the good and not so good aspects of UCD and GDS process. The most frequent and interesting codes from Sects. 1 and 3 of the questionnaire were further analysed, and they formed the three main categories of Focus, Structure, and Reflection. Finally, all student comments were re-checked to see if they contained new perspectives to the topics of the main categories.

The quantitative data from Sect. 2 in the questionnaire was analysed by calculating the means of the students' rating of each method. Since the data was ordinal and the sets of data were unrelated, we used the Mann-Whitney U test for the statistical comparisons of the means from 2018 and 2019. We compared the ratings of individual methods that were used in both course editions and the ratings of the UCD and the GDS processes as a whole. We use $p < 0.05$ and $p < 0.01$ as values for stating evidences of statistical differences in our findings.

5   Results

In this chapter, we shortly report the results from the different data collection methods. After the results from the Retrospective Hand, we report separately the quantitative and qualitative results of the feedback questionnaire.

5.1   Weekly Feedback on the Course

The Retrospective Hand technique was used to collect student feedback on the course as free-form comments. It was the only data collection method used twice, on both Fridays, which helped us to improve the course on the way and to receive feedback on the first week activities when it was still fresh in students' minds. The first week, 23 students, and the second week, 22 students returned their responses. Altogether 45 comments on week 1 and 43 on week 2 about the course content, structure, and teamwork were extracted for the conventional content analysis. The results of the analysis are depicted in Table 1.

Table 1. Coding of student comments about good and not so good aspects of the User-Centred Design Sprint.

	Good		Not so good	
Week 1	Fast process	10	Challenges in brainstorming	6
	Structured process	7	More real-life examples	4
	Time before GDS	3	Duration of lectures	4
	Lectures & Practice	2	Unclear structure	4
			Roles did not work	2
			Limited time	2
			Too much time	1
			Reflection	1
	Good in week 1, total	**22**	**Not so good in week 1, total**	**23**
Week 2	Prototyping	10	Limited time	7
	GDS process	6	Too much time	2
	User tests	6	More real-life examples	5
	Fast process	3	More lectures	2
			Roles did not work	2
	Good in week 2, total	**25**	**Not so good in week 2, total**	**18**

Both weeks, following the structured, fast-pace process attracted the highest number of positive comments (1st week: 17, 2nd week: 9). Most of these comments stated simply "GDS" or "the GDS process" without a reason for liking. Six students, one of whom was among those who spontaneously appreciated the fast pace of GDS, wanted more time for the interviews, brainstorming, data analysis, lectures, or to catch up. In contrast, there were 3 comments about too much time.

The comments regarding the UCD activities highlighted the user tests in the second week, which 6 students specifically mentioned as useful. In the first week, two students spontaneously commented that the activities before starting the sprint were good, and that "[we] are learning, so it's good to adapt first". However, the additional time for specifying the design brief before starting the GDS process was still not enough based on the comments of five students. One of them criticised: "We had to brainstorm on ideas before knowing the problem". Apparently, some teams worked more smoothly towards a joint idea, since a student reported idle time as a negative aspect in the first week: "Time allocated for the activities (some was too much)".

5.2   Feedback on the Methods Used

Data was gathered from students on the usage of 14 methods and the GDS and UCD process during the course in 2019. One student left this part of the questionnaire blank, so the results in this section are based on 21 students' ratings. The students were asked to rate three stages of the usage: a) if the method was thought provoking, (meaning that when getting introduced to the method it resulted them in getting new thoughts), b) if the methods was useful during the course and c) if they think it would be useful in their future job or studies. The students rated the methods on a scale from 1 to 7, where 1 was "not at all", and 7 was "extremely so". The same was done in 2018 for the methods used then, in total 13 methods [15]. Note that some methods were used only in 2018 and others only in 2019.

We acknowledge the difficulty in comparing two editions of a course, but to see if the new structure and order of using the methods made a difference for students, we compared the students' average ratings on the methods in 2018 and 2019 (Table 2). The ratings were compared with Mann-Whitney U test to check if there was evidence for significant differences. We mark the results with a statistical difference with asterisks, one for p ¡ 0.05 and two asterisks for p ¡ 0.01.

Table 2. The average rating of students of the UCD and GDS methods in 2018 and 2019 on scale from 1 to 7, with the highest ratings marked as bold.

	The Method was Thought Provoking		The Method was Useful for the Course		The Method will be Useful for Future Job or Studies	
	2018	2019	2018	2019	2018	2019
Making a map	5.94	4.71	6.06	6.38	6.00	6.00
Ask the experts	4.81	5.00	4.44	6.33**	5.63	**6.19**
Lighting demos	5.31	4.76	5.00	6.10*	5.00	5.95*
Sketching (incl. the crazy 8)	**6.38**	5.43	**6.63**	6.29	6.25	5.62
Voting on design solutions	5.00	5.33	6.13	6.33	5.56	6.14
Speed critique of the designs	5.63	5.10	6.00	6.19	5.44	5.81
Storyboard making	6.00	4.60*	6.31	6.05	6.38	5.80
Hi-fi prototyping	5.50	5.29	6.25	6.81	6.50	6.05
User evaluations of prototype	**6.38**	5.38	6.56	**6.76**	**6.63**	**6.19**
Stating usability goals	–	4.71	–	5.86	–	5.86
Stating UX goals	4.56	4.86	4.31	5.95**	5.00	5.90*
Storyboard evaluation	–	4.43	–	5.48	–	5.29
UX goals in storyboard evaluation	–	4.33	–	5.52	–	5.05
Evaluating against UX goals	4.63	–	4.50	–	5.13	–
Prototyping for the last evaluation	4.81	–	5.50	–	5.31	–
Summative evaluations in the end	5.19	5.00	5.06	6.24**	5.25	6.10*
Google Design sprint as a whole	6.69	5.48	6.75	6.76	6.63	6.24
User-centred design as a whole	5.06	5.29	5.13	6.62	5.40	6.43

The analysis shows that the students gave the Storyboard making method a significantly lower rating for thought-provokingness in 2019 than in 2018 (p = 0.023). The analysis shows evidence of statistical differences also in the ratings of how useful the methods were in the course for four methods: Asking the experts (p = 0.0012), Lightning demos (p = 0.012), Stating UX goals (p = 0.00024) and Summative evaluations in the end (p = 0.0034). The ratings were higher for all these four methods in 2019 than in 2018. The method of stating UX goals was used earlier in course in 2019 than 2018. This seems to be more natural and more useful for the students. The other three methods were used later, after having used UCD methods earlier in the course and this seems to give the students more confidence or willingness to use them. The statistical significance between years was found also when rating the method's usefulness in the future for Lightning demos (p = 0.029), Stating UX goals (p = 0.024) and Summative evaluations in the end (p = 0.047).

When the ratings from students on the whole GDS process from 2018 and 2019 are compared with a Mann-Whitney U tests we found no evidence of statistical differences between the 2018 and 2019 ratings. We also compared the ratings from students on the whole UCD process. There is no evidence of statistical difference in how thought provoking the UCD process is in 2018 and 2019.

On the contrary, there is strong evidence of statistical difference (p = 0.00022) that the students think the UCD process was more useful in the course in 2019 than in 2018. Additionally, there is evidence (P=0.011) that the students rate the usefulness of the UCD process for future jobs and studies higher in 2019 than in 2018. This indicates that the changes made on the course structure between 2019 and 2018 were appreciated by the students.

5.3   Feedback on the Processes as a Whole

In the last part of the questionnaire, the students were asked to list three good and three not so good aspects of both GDS and UCD. A total of 21 students contributed with a total of 181 comments. For unclear comments, the two authors returned back to individual responses to understand the context of the comment, so only 6 comments were ignored due to their unclear message, e.g., "Excellent" or "Research". Additionally, 10 comments were ignored since they were not about GDS or UCD, but about teaching e.g. "well taught" or "I'd like to have a bit more lectures", so the total number of comments included in this paper was 163. After the coding process described in 4.2, 16 codes emerged from the data, as shown in Table 3.

The left side of Table 3 lists the codes and the number of comments under each code, which emerged from the students' responses of 3 Good aspects of GDS or UCD, respectively. The codes and the number of comments on Not so good aspects of GDS and UCD are on the right. Some topics divided opinions, such as the Fast process on the good side and Limited time on the Not so good side, and Teamwork on both sides. GDS attracted almost a third more comments than UCD, 96 vs. 63.

Table 3. Coding of student comments about the good and not so good aspects of GDS and UCD.

	Good		Not so good	
GDS	Fast process	19	Limited time	15
	Structured process	12	Skills needed	7
	Facilitate design decisions	8	Teamwork	6
	Interesting/innovative	6	Slow process	5
	Prototyping	4	Detached from practice	3
	Teamwork	3	Activities/Products not useful	3
	User focus	3	Difficult activities	2
	User feedback	2	Design decisions	1
	Good in GDS, total	**54**	**Not so good in GDS, total**	**42**
UCD	Facilitate design decisions	14	Difficult activities	6
	User focus	12	Activities/Products not useful	5
	Testing/Evaluation	5	Slow process	4
	User feedback	4	Skills needed	3
	Interesting/innovative	3	Limited time	2
	Structured process	1	Design decisions	2
			Detached from practice	1
			Teamwork	1
	Good in UCD, total	**39**	**Not so good in UCD, total**	**24**

6   Discussion and Conclusions

This paper reports development of an intensive two-week interaction design course where UCD was combined with Google Design Sprint [12]. In this paper, we focus on the course structure and report feedback from the students, who also are the users of the new User-Centered Design Sprint process. The main contributions of this paper include 1) the course structure to teach User-Centred Design Sprint (Fig. 1), 2) the evaluation results of the new process (Tables 2 and 3), and 3) recommendations for teaching this kind of a course. Next, we will answer our two research questions by analysing the meaning of the results for the integrated UCD and GDS, and by sharing important remarks about teaching this kind of a course.

6.1   An Integrated UCD and GDS Process

We have tested two process structures of integrated UCD and GDS during the two editions of this Interaction Design course (Fig. 2). The change between 2018 and 2019 editions resulted in several statistically significant differences in students' ratings of the design methods. First, our results provide very strong evidence (p = 0,00022) on the new UCD process being more useful than the one used in 2018 both in the course and in the future (p = 0.011). This is very positive feedback on the changes we made to the design process. It is evident that the students found using the UCD process before and after using the GDS process more useful than doing all the UCD activities after the GDS activities like in 2018. The positive results could also be due to the similar structure of the UCD activities in the same way as the GDS activities, i.e., we kept the fast pace and the guided structure for the UCD activities similar to the GDS activities in 2019. This was not done to the same degree in the 2018 edition of the course.

The students rated Stating UX goals method on the third day in the course in 2019 much higher than stating those on the sixth day in 2018. There was a significant difference in the ratings for the method being useful in the course and in the future. Additionally, the students found the summative evaluation of the prototype in the end more useful in 2019 than in 2018. When conducting the method, the students gather quantitative data on the usability and the UX of their prototype. The method was used during the ninth day in both years. In 2019, the students had not done as many evaluations of their prototype before the summative evaluation as in 2018, which may be a reason for the difference. There is evidence that three GDS methods got higher ratings in 2019 than in 2018: storyboard making for being thought provoking, asking the experts for being useful in the course and lightning demos for being useful in the course and in the future. This may be because all these methods were used later in the course in 2019 than in 2018, so the students were more prepared to use those methods in a useful way.

The qualitative feedback supports and justifies the quantitative ratings about the new structure above. The content analysis of student comments show that the UCD activities in the beginning of the 2019 course were appreciated: "Time before sprint" and "Activities to prepare for the GDS" were mentioned by students in the What was good section of the first week feedback. Defining the target user group and conducting user interviews set the scene for the whole project: "[UCD] data are the roots of design". After the 3 days of UCD in the beginning, the students were ready to start the GDS process: "User interviews helped to set the tone for the GDS". For teachers, the new structure allowed to keep the same format and pace both for the UCD process and the GDS process throughout the course in 2019, focusing on one method at a time for a specific time slot. This shows in student feedback as a fluent overall design process: "Nice workflow" and "Flow of sprint".

The Retrospective Hand feedback (Table 1) provides us information on the process on weekly basis. The feedback on the integrated process shows that the integrated process worked well on both weeks. First week, 10 out of 22 positive comments were about the fast process, such as "tempo" or "speeds up the design process". The students were impressed how much they achieved during just one week: "achieve a lot in a short period". At the end of the second week, the students were not so happy with the results, since they did not have enough time to finalise the prototypes. While the goal of design sprints like GDS is to test an idea, not produce a high fidelity prototype, the students would have enjoyed spending more time on prototyping. This shows as the highest number of the positive comments on the second week being about prototyping (10), but the limited time did not allow it (7 negative comments).

Compared to GDS, UCD Sprint provides one additional day for prototyping and summative evaluation, i.e., another iteration round. The students seemed to appreciate this day, as the Summative evaluations method got high ratings for usefulness, and the qualitative feedback supports the rating, e.g., "summative evaluations where helpful". In the previous edition of the course, the weight was more on the iterative prototyping and evaluation. Back then, the first prototype was developed on the 5th day, two days earlier than in the new structure, and there were three iterations of prototype tests. The students thought the last summative evaluation was too much. On this class, we shifted the weight from prototyping towards UCD in the beginning of the course. The initial user studies eliminated the problem of a team working for one week on an idea that did not fly when users evaluated the prototype. Higher user relevance is an important benefit of allocating more time on UCD and less on prototyping.

Regarding the qualitative feedback on both GDS and UCD process (Table 3), the highest number of comments were coded under "Facilitating design decisions". This includes 22 positive comments about how both processes helped making decisions in the team. Seven of these comments mentioned the goals set for design, e.g., UCD "gives guiding stars (goals)" through user research based user experience and usability goals. GDS provided specific methods to facilitate decision making, of which students mentioned voting (3 comments, e.g., "democratic way of choosing ideas to develop further"), roles ("the use of decider and facilitator made most of the tasks easy") and storyboards ("creating storyboards was helpful to create common understanding between team members"). Also, some of the positive comments coded under "Fast process" were related to the need to decide and go on, from a timing perspective: "forced to move on and make decisions", "clocking the time", "pressure". The user research in the beginning and user feedback later in the process provide data to support decision making, so UCD provided a "good way to keep focus on important things". **Focus** is the first high-level theme we want to highlight. It was visible both in the guided structure that steered students to focus on one activity at a time, and in the above methods that provided focus to the fuzzy front-end phase of a design process. In conclusion, a clear focus expedites decision making and focus is what both user studies and GDS methods provide.

The new structure, where UCD activities took place before and after GDS, received significantly higher ratings from students than the structure in the first edition of the course, which started directly with GDS and UCD activities followed on the second week only. The structured process of GDS induced only positive comments, including "organized progression of ideation", "super nice to structure the process of finding out what to prototype", and "easy to follow". The comments under "Unclear structure" in the Retrospective Hand feedback were not about GDS but about teaching and will be discussed in the next section. Although there were more positive comments on the fast process than on the structured process, the teachers saw that it was the structure that enabled the fast process. Therefore, rather than the fast pace in itself, our second theme to highlight in teaching User-Centred Design Sprint is **structure**. There is a specific, granular structure in GDS, and we introduced a specific structure of UCD as well, as explained above. We conclude that when teaching GDS, emphasize the structure of the process rather than the speed. The strict timing can be relaxed, but the structure should stay the same. The teacher needs to find ways to handle the different pace of different teams, and this we will discuss in the next section.

As an answer to our first research question, how can UCD and Design Sprint methods be integrated into a coherent structure in an intensive course, we recommend reserving ample time for team building and user research before starting a Design Sprint, and an additional round of prototyping after it. During the fuzzy front-end of the design process, which User-Centred Design Sprint is targeting, activities that help to focus are important for efficient decision making. Examples of such activities include user interviews, voting, decider role, storyboards, and user evaluations. A predefined, detailed structure is the other important feature of User-Centred Design Sprint, which should not only cover GDS but also the UCD activities.

6.2   Recommendations for Teaching User-Centred Design Sprint

Teaching User-Centred Design Sprint is not only about optimizing the design process practised on the course. The two editions of the course have shown that teachers also need to handle a number of important challenges that may occur despite the smooth and fast overall process.

One such challenge was facilitation of teamwork. The Design Sprint process guidance is targeted for a single team, but a teacher needs to facilitate the work of several teams of students. This is a challenge both from the facilities perspective, as well as from the perspective of understanding how the teams are doing. Some teams seemed to work well, as 3 comments were positive to the teamwork: "allows professionals of different specialities to contribute" and "working with a team on ideation". Other students were more critical about the teamwork (7 comments): "depending too much on team dynamics", "needs disciplined team", and the most critical was "discussions were not fun, too many ideas and too many ego". To manage team dynamics, GDS provides the roles of decider and facilitator, but the Retrospective Hand feedback included 2 comments each week on the GDS roles not working. According to one comment, this was because the roles were decided before the students knew each other. Another reason was that students are not experienced to act as a facilitator or decider: "Because the roles holders did not manage to fulfil their roles the group did not manage to finish tasks on time". Thus, teaching User-Centred Design Sprint requires assistance on handling teamwork and team dynamics. We recommend doing this by paying special attention to the decider and facilitator roles.

There were mixed opinions about the pace of the design process that is enforced especially with GDS. Many students liked its fast pace, as emphasised above. Some students would have enjoyed even faster pace, and they commented that using five days for gaining the given outcome was too slow (9 comments altogether): "takes a long time", "could be done quicker". One student related the slow speed to teamwork by stating "without team support nothing moves ahead". On the other hand, the limited time was also emphasised as the main drawback, with 15 comments about difficulties due to the limited time for activities, e.g., "too fast", "stressful process", "time for prototyping is too short". In conclusion, even though some students seem impatient and want to move on, the teachers should be prepared to manage the different pace of the teams and individual students. Teachers should also consider relaxing the strict timing of activities with GDS if the students seem exhausted.

The fast pace of the intensive course leads us to our main finding on teaching, **reflection** activities. Two student comments at the end of the first week on what they would like more of, "Retrospect, what went well, where could do better" and "Not enough feedback/reflection on exercises" reminded us about the importance of reflection as part of the learning process. If the course simply follows the strict structure and timing of GDS, there is no time for reflection: "I sometimes need to reflect [for] a while, now it was not possible". Based on this feedback, we added a reflection discussion at the end of each day in the second week. The feedback collection in the end, the results of which we report now, was another important part of reflection. In conclusion, we recommend the teachers to arrange dedicated activities for proper reflection on what was learned.

Looking at the Retrospective Hand feedback, the students raised several challenges related to teaching, especially related to the lecture contents. Four students requested more real-life examples in week 1 and five are requesting that in week 2. Some students wanted more lectures, but longer lectures were criticised by some others. In an intensive course, there is little time to study additional materials, but one student suggested sharing materials (e.g., for prototyping) before the course.

In a class of students with different backgrounds, the teachers need to pay attention to the pedagogical aspects during the scheduled process: ensure all students learn, and the teams who finish quicker have something meaningful to do while waiting for others to finish. On the other hand, it seems difficult to reach a moment when all teams would agree that the idea chosen by the team is the right one to be developed. Since the objective of this intensive course is to learn to test ideas quickly in a user-centred way, the chosen idea for the exercise is not the main success criterion.

Two students in both weeks commented that the GDS roles did not work in their team. The reasons included 1) too early assignment of decider and facilitator, as the team members did not know each other to agree the most suitable one for the role, 2) rotating the roles on the 2nd week was "messy", 3) a Mediator role was missing, and 4) unclarity on the roles. These challenges may be alleviated by clarifying the roles, checking how the teamwork and the roles are working in each team, and reminding about the duties if the roles are rotated.

In line with the previous versions of this course, two students appreciated the balance between theory and practice. However, there was a contradiction in comments about too long lectures (on the 1st Wednesday, 2 students) and too few lectures (2 students). An important comment from the first week, although the only one at this point, was about the lack of retrospection after each phase, which we paid attention to during the 2nd week. Although there were only a few spontaneous comments about reflection in the feedback, pedagogically this was an important reminder about allocating ample time for reflection on a fast-paced course.

Finally, four students stated after week 1 that the structure of activities was unclear: "Hard to know where we are in the sprint", "Clarify the aim of the process". During the second week, we paid special attention to reminding where we are in the process, which seemed to help, as there were no such comments on week 2. Anyway, our recommendation for teachers is to be crystal clear about the phase of the process, e.g., having a slide of the whole process, or the day's structure, available when moving from one phase to the next.

To summarize the answer to our second research question, what should teachers pay special attention to in teaching User-Centred Design Sprint, we conclude that these specific points include facilitation of the teamwork, finding a pace for the sprint that serves all students, balancing theory and practice, providing examples outside the course work, reminding students about the structure and phase of the sprint frequently, and, last but not least, facilitating reflection on learning.

7   Limitations and Future Work

Our study shares the same general strengths and weaknesses as any case study in an educational context [9]. In our case, the quantitative data analysis compares two versions of the same course, between which there were many differences in the course structure, teaching facilities, students, some teachers, details of taught content, etc. We were most interested in student feedback on the course structure and content, which we could study by collecting feedback partly with the same methods.

The sample size of 21–23 students in the 2019 data collection can be considered small. However, we see it an adequate number of respondents in constructive education research that develops course content and leans on versatile qualitative data. The quantitative analysis confirmed several statistically significant differences between the two editions of the course. The total number of comments included in the qualitative data analysis was 251 (Retrospective Hand: 88; Key aspects of GDS and UCD: 163), which gave further evidence and reasoning behind the numerical results. However, since the qualitative feedback contains a small number of comments on one topic, we chose not to draw conclusions on the qualitative data between the two course editions.

Naturally, courses should be continuously improved regarding the course structure, content, and practical arrangements. Although some of the negative comments on our course criticise aspects that we cannot easily improve, such as the method characteristics or teamwork dynamics, the feedback collected point at many opportunities to address in the future work. For future research, it would be especially intriguing to study even more integrated UCD and a Design Sprint, where the Design Sprint would not be a separate module. Since the clear structure of GDS was appreciated by all students, defining a granular, guided and timed structure for the UCD activities would be worth further investigation.

Acknowledgements. We thank Nordplus for funding the series of courses, and the students for the permission to use the course feedback data for this publication. The first author was supported by Business Finland grant 81/31/2020.

References

1. Brhel, M., Meth, H., Maedche, A., Werder, K.: Exploring principles of user-centered agile software development: a literature review. Inf. Softw. Technol. **61** (2015). https://doi.org/10.1016/j.infsof.2015.01.004
2. Cockton, G.: Design isn't a shape and it hasn't got a centre: thinking big about post-centric interaction design. In: Proceedings of the International Conference on Multimedia, Interaction, Design and Innovation (2013). https://doi.org/10.1145/2500342.2500344
3. Cockton, G.: Worth-focused design, book 1: balance, integration, and generosity. Synth. Lect. Hum.-Centered Inform. **13**(2) (2020). https://doi.org/10.2200/S00992ED1V01Y202002HCI046
4. Cockton, G., Lárusdóttir, M., Gregory, P., Cajander, Å.: Integrating user-centred design in agile development. In: Cockton, G., Lárusdóttir, M., Gregory, P., Cajander, Å. (eds.) Integrating User-Centred Design in Agile Development. HIS, pp. 1–46. Springer, Cham (2016). https://doi.org/10.1007/978-3-319-32165-3_1
5. Cross, N.: Design Thinking: Understanding How Designers Think and Work. Berg Publishers (2011)
6. Culén, A.L.: HCI education: innovation, creativity and design thinking. In: International Conferences on Advances in Computer-Human Interactions, pp. 125–130 (2015)
7. Dayton, T.: Skills needed by user-centered design practitioners in real software development environments: report on the CHI'92 workshop. SIGCHI Bull (1993). https://doi.org/10.1145/155786.155790
8. Greenberg, S.: Teaching human computer interaction to programmers. Interactions **28**(2) (1996). https://doi.org/10.1145/226650.226651
9. Hodkinson, P., Hodkinson, H.: The strengths and limitations of case study research. In: Learning and Skills Development Agency Conference at Cambridge (2001)
10. Hsieh, H.F., Shannon, S.E.: Three approaches to qualitative content analysis. Qual. Health Res. **15**(9) (2005). https://doi.org/10.1177/1049732305276687
11. ISO: Ergonomics of human-system interaction (2010)
12. Knapp, J., Zeratsky, J., Kowitz, B.: Sprint: How to solve big problems and test new ideas in just five days. Simon and Schuster (2016)
13. Lai, J.Y., Yang, M.C.: Introducing user centered design to mid-career professionals: experiences to build upon. In: Proceedings of the International Association of Societies of Design Research, IASDR (2009)

14. Larusdottir, M., Roto, V., Stage, J., Lucero, A.: Get realistic! - UCD course design and evaluation. In: Bogdan, C., Kuusinen, K., Lárusdóttir, M.K., Palanque, P., Winckler, M. (eds.) HCSE 2018. LNCS, vol. 11262, pp. 15–30. Springer, Cham (2019). https://doi.org/10.1007/978-3-030-05909-5_2

15. Larusdottir, M., Roto, V., Stage, J., Lucero, A., Šmorgun, I.: Balance talking and doing! Using Google design sprint to enhance an intensive UCD course. In: Lamas, D., Loizides, F., Nacke, L., Petrie, H., Winckler, M., Zaphiris, P. (eds.) INTERACT 2019. LNCS, vol. 11747, pp. 95–113. Springer, Cham (2019). https://doi.org/10.1007/978-3-030-29384-0_6

16. Nebe, K., Zimmermann, D.: Aspects of integrating user centered design into software engineering processes. In: Jacko, J.A. (ed.) HCI 2007. LNCS, vol. 4550, pp. 194–203. Springer, Heidelberg (2007). https://doi.org/10.1007/978-3-540-73105-4_22

17. Nicholl, B., Hosking, I., Elton, E., Lee, Y., Bell, J., Clarkson, P.: Inclusive design in the key stage 3 classroom: an investigation of teachers' understanding and implementation of user-centred design principles in design and technology. Int. J. Technol. Des. Educ. **23**(4) (2013). https://doi.org/10.1007/s10798-012-9221-9

18. Schultz, N., Christensen H.P.: Seven-step problem-based learning in an interaction design course. Eur. J. Eng. Educ. **29**(4), 533–541 (2004)

19. Seffah, A., Andreevskaia, A.: Empowering software engineers in human-centered design. In: Proceedings of 25th International Conference on Software Engineering (2003)

20. Seffah, A., Gulliksen, J., Desmarais, M.C.: Human-Centered Software Engineering-Integrating Usability in the Software Development Lifecycle, vol. 8. Springer, Netherlands (2005). https://doi.org/10.1007/1-4020-4113-6

21. Thomas, J., Strickfaden, M.: From industrial design education to practice: creating discipline through design sprints. In: International Conference on Applied Human Factors and Ergonomics (2018). https://doi.org/10.1007/978-3-319-94601-6_13

22. Waller, A., Balandin, S.A., O'mara, D.A., Judson, A.D.: Training AAC users in user-centred design. In: Accessible Design in the Digital World Conference 2005 (2005)

23. Zhang, F., Joines, S.: User-centered design and theory of innovation: problem solving integration approach for ergonomic product design. In: Rebelo, F., Soares, M. (eds.) AHFE 2017. AISC, vol. 588, pp. 314–320. Springer, Cham (2018). https://doi.org/10.1007/978-3-319-60582-1_31

How HCI Interprets Service Design: A Systematic Literature Review

Christine Ee Ling Yap[1](✉), Jung-Joo Lee[1], and Virpi Roto[2]

[1] National University of Singapore, Singapore, Singapore
christine.yap@u.nus.edu, jjlee@nus.edu.sg
[2] Aalto University, Espoo, Finland
virpi.roto@aalto.fi

Abstract. The scope of Human-Computer Interaction (HCI) research is expanding with regard to the studied systems and stakeholders, and its impact areas. Service design has recently gained tractions in HCI as an approach to deal with these expansions. However, there has been confusion around the definitions and roles of service design in HCI, especially with its overlaps and differences with interaction design. To examine how HCI has adopted service design, this paper presents results from a systematic literature review on 52 papers from the most cited HCI publication venues. Our findings show that the adoption of service design concepts and methods in HCI has been sporadic over the past decade. The term service design has been interpreted as a variety of meanings. The most predominantly observed understandings include service design as a term for designing digital services instead of products, and as an approach providing a journey and system perspective to the design of social computing, Internet of Things, or other complex systems. Only a few studies adopted the fundamental logic of new value exchange or co-creation of systems from service design. We discuss the reasons behind the differing interpretations of service design by HCI and future opportunities for HCI to better benefit from service design.

Keywords: Service design · Systematic literature review · Multidisciplinary

1 Introduction

In recent years, Human-Computer Interaction (HCI) researchers have started to discuss service design as information technologies increasingly involve complex systems and multiple stakeholders, and the usage model for technologies becomes a service (e.g. Software as a Service – SaaS) [26, 28, 67, 79]. In 2019, the Encyclopedia of Human-Computer Interaction published a stand-alone chapter of service design by Zimmerman and Forlizzi [95]. In the past INTERACT conferences, albeit few, there has been a call to adopt service design approaches to design for more complex socio-technical systems [1, 20, 72]. Service design framing and approaches are called for to deal with the changes in the landscape of information technologies design, namely the change of the design context from end-users to multiple stakeholders, the change of design object from a

© IFIP International Federation for Information Processing 2021
Published by Springer Nature Switzerland AG 2021
C. Ardito et al. (Eds.): INTERACT 2021, LNCS 12933, pp. 259–280, 2021.
https://doi.org/10.1007/978-3-030-85616-8_16

single product to a system, and the change of the impact area towards a socio-economic system [28]. Previous research [26, 34, 95] argues that service design can offer a logic, approaches and tools to HCI to constructively respond to these changes. On the other hand, technology advancement has enabled the development of traditional services to new digital services, for example, by tapping on mobile technologies [15, 82], cloud computing and IoT [14, 64], social computing [31, 96], artificial intelligence [49] and autonomous systems [42, 52].

While the potentials of service design to HCI have been discussed, there are some concerns and confusions around the intersections between service design and HCI (e.g., see [27, 34, 45, 67]). For example, Roto et al. [67] addressed fuzziness in overlaps and differences between service design and user experience (UX) design. Lee [45] reports her observation that to HCI communities, service design might seem to deal more with business concerns than user concerns, which sets a distance from HCI to service design.

As a matter of fact, service design has grown across various research fields, including marketing and management, design, and information systems engineering. This results in varying perceptions and definitions of service design that co-exist, which makes its concept elusive [45, 92].

A few scholars in service design research observed that there has been a lack of clear understanding around concepts, theories and methodologies of service design due to its varying evolution paths and methodological traditions, which results in poor contextualization of service design by broader communities [62, 92]. Despite the current situation where the interest and confusion co-exist, there has been little research that systematically overviews how service design has been adopted and used in HCI research, to examine how HCI interprets service design and what elements of service design HCI views relevant and beneficial to adopt and by doing so identify limitations and future development directions.

Responding to these gaps, this research examines how HCI research has adopted and interpreted service design in its projects and discourses through a systematic literature review. The study focuses on the review of 83 publications from the top 20 HCI publication venues according to Google Scholar Metrics (refer to Appendix). The results identify different scopes of service design taken up by HCI projects, which imply multiple levels of service design contributions to HCI but also differing interpretations of what service design is. Based on the results, we discuss current limitations in how HCI adopts service design by identifying what is left behind in their uptakes, as well as new opportunity areas the current HCI projects have not fully tackled yet.

For our analytic sensitivity, we gained inspiration from Boehner et al.'s work [11], *How HCI Interprets the Probes*, which diagnosed dominating views and underlying tensions in HCI through the analysis of varying adoptions of the probes. With a similar analytic lens, we aim to shed light on underlying assumptions and tensions in HCI at the boundary with a new approach, in this case, service design with its origins and logic from marketing and management. In other words, our research focuses on *How HCI interprets service design*. In what follows, we begin by introducing the origins and varying scopes of service design, and its current appearance in HCI. Then we describe our findings from the literature review and discuss the underlying interpretations of service design in HCI.

2   Service Design and Its Adoption in HCI

Service design emerged in management and operations studies in the 1980s as a way to manage the quality of service and systematically approach its development [69]. In the early days, the object of design, "a service" is often distinguished with a product upon four characteristics, i.e., intangibility, heterogeneity, inseparability of production and consumption, and perishability [24, 93], often called IHIP framework [51]. The recognition of service design in design communities traces back to the 1990s, when designers started to correspond to the evolution of the service economy [12, 13, 55, 60, 63]. Researchers and practitioners in design have developed methods and strategies to approach this new object of design in a human-centered, creative and tangible way [63, 92]. Their work has been informed by various existing design approaches: for example, interaction design has informed the development of methods for designing service interfaces between users and service systems [68] and co-design has provided methods for stakeholder collaboration in service innovation (e.g., [35, 39]). In the early 2000s, service design has undergone a major shift by meeting the service-dominant logic (S-D logic) [75], from designing intangible service offerings to designing for a set of processes or platforms that facilitate value co-creation [43, 61]. S-D logic blurs the distinction between tangible goods and intangible offerings, as both work as mediums for value co-creation. This indicates that for service design informed by S-D logic, tangibility/intangibility is not a criterion that determines the object of service design versus product design.

   With the evolution of service design for the past few decades, there have been scholarly attempts to clarify concepts, methodologies and theoretical frameworks of service design (e.g. see [18, 34, 43, 54, 61, 68, 92]). As a crucial part of the clarification efforts, those studies offer a systematic conceptualization of multiple levels of service design. They mostly agree on the levels as follows, from the interaction level to the infra- and social- structure level [57, 61, 62]:

- First, service designers design for journey experiences of customers, where multiple touchpoints are orchestrated. A service design tool such as customer journey mapping supports this design activity.
- Secondly, service designers design for work processes of service co-production and delivery, by incorporating how employees and support systems should work together. A service design tool such as service blueprinting supports this design activity.
- Thirdly, service designers identify new and relevant stakeholders and design for new collaborative networks where values are co-created. A service design tool such as stakeholder mapping supports this design activity.
- Fourthly, with the development of new value exchange/co-creation models, service designers speculate on new socio-technical and economic models in the future, which often challenges existing structures and norms. Future casting and scenario methods support this design activity.

While there seems to be an exchange of methods between interaction design and service design [67, 68], the adoption of service design in HCI research has not been salient [67, 87]. More recently, a few studies aimed to "explore new opportunities at the intersection between HCI and service research" [78] and clarify their differences, discussing how the two fields could mutually benefit [9, 10, 19, 67, 79]. They discuss the benefits from engaging in service design in HCI research, especially for emerging technology landscapes such as SaaS, cloud and social computing, and IoT, and reinforce the need for "service framing" [28] to design IT systems [95]. As the advancement of these technologies introduces radical innovation to economic models, those researchers argue that service design can provide a logic, frameworks, and tools for HCI researchers to develop technological applications in line with new economic models. For example, the concepts of value co-creation in service design could "help HCI design teams to identify different types of value each stakeholder holds and wants, and design for interactions that can produce those values" [95]. However, they also address a challenge that designing for values for stakeholders is often considered outside the scopes of HCI research [95].

As service design has been developed across various domains, from marketing and management to design, there are multiple perspectives to defining what service design is and possibly due to that reason, service design has been poorly understood and con-textualized in other domains. In HCI, while there has been a growing interest, there is no clear picture of how HCI has engaged in service design in its research. The following sections of this paper explain the conduct of a systematic literature review to delve into this topic.

3   Systematic Literature Review

Our analysis is two-fold. First, we want to see the trends of design spaces and contribution areas that intersect between service design and HCI. To do so, we carried out quantitative analysis by looking at the technology enablers used, domains, and methods adopted by the papers. Secondly, we want to look at how HCI defines and perceives service design - its logic, scope, and capacity. For this second aim, we conducted an inductive content analysis [25] to identify themes that reflect the papers' understandings of service design.

3.1   Search Strategy

A systematic literature review was conducted and reported according to the PRISMA statement [58] to identify existing literature in HCI that adopt service design as a process, method, logic, or practice. We searched for the term "service design" in the top 20 publication venues in the field of HCI (according to Google Scholar metrics, as of July 2020, refer to Appendix). We restricted the search to papers with "service design" appearing in the title, abstract, or keyword, because our main goal is to analyze papers where service design plays a salient role.

3.2   Article Screening

All resulting papers from the top 20 HCI publication venues (n = 83) were screened to identify papers from the field of HCI that clearly convey how service design has informed or been adopted in the study. Figure 1 illustrates the screening procedure.

Exclusion Criteria. A total of 31 papers were categorized as *"excluded – irrelevant works or insufficient information"*), according to the criteria are as follows:

- "Service design" is mentioned without sufficient elaboration (e.g., listed as future work, listed in an abstract of a keynote, panel discussion or workshop proposals without elaboration showing how service design is adopted in its research setting) (n = 16)
- Papers from the field of Service/Software Engineering that only focus on how software is constructed (e.g., Service Oriented Architecture, RESTful service, SOAP (Simple Object Access Protocol)). (n = 2)
- Papers from the field of Service Marketing, Operations Management, or design communities that are not relevant to HCI adopting service design. (n = 6)
- Unintended keyword search results, where "service" and "design" were each of two separate parts in a sentence (e.g., "…public information service ‖ design principles…") (n = 4)
- Papers that did not cite any literature (n = 3)

Out of the remaining 52 papers, 21 papers were categorized as *"using 'service design' loosely"*, as these papers use the term "service design" loosely to just refer to designing digital services, without any link to service design as a distinct approach of design and research.

The remaining papers (n = 31) that show service design being adopted as a process, method, logic, or practice are categorized as *"adopting service design"*.

To account for inter-rater effects, after the first author screened all 83 papers, the second author randomly screened 20% of the papers. The first author and the second author resolved the discrepancies, then repeated the screening process until the inter-rater reliability, Cohen's unweighted kappa, was above 0.6. A final pool of 52 papers was shortlisted for in-depth analysis (31 papers categorized as *"adopting service design"* and 21 papers categorized as *"using 'service design' loosely"*, refer to the link in the appendix for the full list). The 21 papers categorized *as "using 'service design' loosely"* were included in the quantitative analysis for identifying the overall trends but were not included in our inductive content analysis [25], as these papers did not provide any insights related to how service design is engaged in.

3.3 Analysis

To overview patterns and trends of design spaces and contribution areas that intersect between service design and HCI, we first mapped the 52 papers (31 papers categorized as *"adopting service design"* and 21 papers categorized as *"using 'service design' loosely"*) according to the year published, service domain, technology enablers, design methods used, and region. We then delved into the varying scopes and perceptions of service design in HCI through inductive content analysis [25] of the 31 most relevant papers (categorized as *"adopting service design"*). The first and second author coded all papers separately, then held four meetings to discuss and resolve all coding discrepancies.

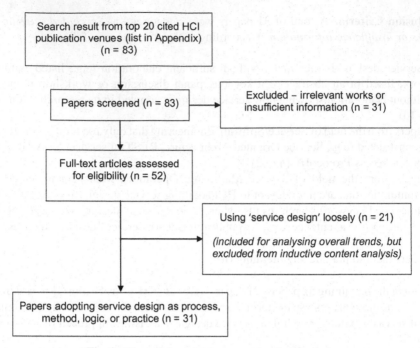

Fig. 1. The article screening procedure in this study.

4 Results

4.1 Overview of Service Design Adoptions

Number of HCI Papers Adopting Service Design over the Years. To see the frequency of occurrences of service design in HCI over the years, we firstly map all 83 papers where service design appears in the title, abstract or author keywords in the timeline. As seen in Fig. 2, the first appearance of the term "service design" in the title, abstract, or author keywords within the top 20 HCI publication venues was in 2004 [80], focusing on the visual appeal of user interface design, continued with a few till 2006. Out of the three earliest papers included from 2006, two papers [16, 40] were of student design competitions at CHI. Considering this, the adoption of service design in HCI starts to be salient only for the past 10 years, with the distribution of publications appearing to be quite sporadic. The years of 2012 and 2013 have the highest number of papers, with or without the 31 papers categorized as *"excluded - irrelevant works or insufficient information"*. They are, however, contributed by a few research teams publishing multiple papers from their projects (first team [36, 37], second team [88, 89, 96], third team [46–48], fourth team [33, 73, 83]), rather than indicate the increase of service design adoptions in HCI.

No Recognition of Service Design as a Distinct Design Approach. As mentioned in Sect. 3.2, there are 21 papers categorized as *"using 'service design' loosely"*. These papers use the term "service design" without referring to it as a distinct research field or practice. While having "service design" listed as an author keyword or an area of contribution, they did not project or build on any concepts or methods of service design as a distinct design approach or methodology but deal with digital services. These papers appear to perceive service design as a subset of interaction design where objects of design or final design outcomes are digital services rather than tangible products. For example, [70] only focuses on identifying the features of mobile service offerings for children (e.g., "low calling costs", "charge-free emergency numbers to parents"), [56] focuses on identifying the information architecture for an IT service request portal, and [23, 32, 80] evaluate the usability elements of user interfaces for digital solutions with-out any methods or logic of service design included. These papers adopt user-centered design and user experience design in designing digital solutions, but did not include the logic or approaches of service design in their literature review, methods, or design out-comes.

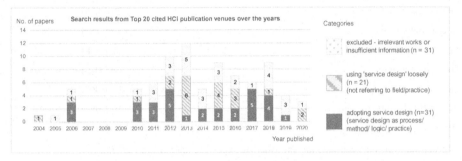

Fig. 2. Search result from the top 20 HCI publication venues over the years

Domains. Types of domains where service design was applied were analyzed for the 52 shortlisted papers (31 papers adopting service design +21 papers using "service design" loosely) to see the contribution domains that intersect between HCI and service design (Table 1). 14 papers (26.9%) do not specify any service domain, only reporting the studies on the computational technologies for digital services in general. The most commonly applied service domain is healthcare (10 papers, 19.2%), with the papers focusing on improving hospital services with technology [4, 85], general wellbeing [2, 40], or elderly healthcare [32]. Community service and transportation are the next most applied service domains (6 papers each, 11.5%). This finding is in line with that of service design communities, where service design is the most frequently used for healthcare and community sectors [55].

Technology Enablers. Types of technologies that are part of service concepts as touch-points or support systems were identified to see what kind of technology development service design is used for and vice versa, what kind of technologies enable the service concepts. Out of 52 papers, nine papers deploy more than one type of technology enablers in designing service encounter interactions (e.g., an autonomous vehicle, a chat-bot, and identification technology for an autonomous taxi service journey in [42]) and support systems (e.g. [86] use AI matching algorithms for a shared housing service, together with virtual reality for customer interaction). Mobile applications are the most frequently appeared technology enabler (e.g., see [2, 3, 15, 21, 32, 82], followed by interactive display (e.g., see [17, 21, 36–38, 76]. They serve as touchpoints for customers.

Table 1. Domains of service design applied in HCI.

Domain	Number of papers (%)*
Not specified *(focus on computational technologies for digital services in general)*	14 (26.9%)
Healthcare *(hospital systems/ equipment, vaccination program, diet recommendation, sports tracking, dementia care)*	10 (19.2%)
Community service *(engaging homeless individuals, distribution of donations, elderly welfare, refugee resettlement)*	6 (11.5%)
Transportation *(public transportation, ridesharing)*	6 (11.5%)
Food service *(food delivery, dining experience)*	5 (9.6%)
Logistics *(delivery drones)*	2 (3.8%)
Government service	2 (3.8%)
Social networking	2 (3.8%)
Finance *(mobile banking)*	1 (1.9%)
Housing service	1 (1.9%)
Retail	1 (1.9%)
Smart home environment	1 (1.9%)
Workplace	1 (1.9%)

* Percentage was calculated using (number of papers/52 shortlisted papers).

We also mapped the technology enablers over the years to identify possible trends (Fig. 3). While the usages of the different technology enablers are sporadic in the past decade, more recent studies for the past five years used service design for more advanced technologies such as artificial intelligence [42, 49, 85, 86], augmented/virtual reality [41, 86], drones [22, 52] etc. These studies use service design to envision future opportunities (e.g., algorithms for distributing donation) or visualize future operation models around those new technologies that do not exist yet [22, 52, 96]. There are more than a few papers that built new services based on technology networks, from ubiquitous computing [16, 38, 40] (a term referring to technology embedded environments in the mid-2000s), to social computing [31, 88, 89, 96], cloud computing [14], or IoT [64, 94]. Technologies that connect to digital platforms such as identification technology (e.g. RFID [16, 40], NFC [42]) and more recently QR code [82] were also used as they facilitate user's journey experience across various touchpoints. More conventional technologies such as 2G/3G mobile phones or web technologies that were identified after 2010 are used in service design projects for technologically marginalized communities (e.g. [5, 76]).

Methods Used. As adoption of methods indicates the adoption of practices [11], we also looked at what kinds of methods that are known as representative service design methods have been used in the 31 papers categorized as "adopting service design". Be-sides rather general design research methods, such as ethnographic observations, in-depth or focus group interviews, contextual inquiries, or prototypes; service blueprint (seven papers: [5, 41, 42, 50, 85, 86, 89]) and customer journey map (five papers: [15, 41, 42, 74, 90])

Technology enabler	2004	2005	2006	2007	2008	2009	2010	2011	2012	2013	2014	2015	2016	2017	2018	2019	2020	Total number of papers related*
Mobile application (tablet/ smartphone applications)									1	1		5						7
Interactive display (interactive tabletop surface, double screen/ touch panel display, public LED display)			1				1	1	1			1		1				6
Web technology (website, web portal)	1									2			1	1				5
Artificial intelligence (algorithms, machine learning, chatbot)												1	2		1			4
Social computing (crowdsourcing)						1	2		1									4
Identification technology (smart card, biometric, RFID/NFC)		2									1			1				4
Ubiquitous computing (term largely used in 2000s) (integration of computers into environmental objects in daily life)		3																3
Augmented reality/ Virtual reality								1					1	1				3
Robot						1		2										3
2G/3G mobile phone (non-smartphone)		1							1			1						3
Cloud computing									1			1						2
IoT											1		1					2
Wearable sensor										1			1					2
Drones									2									2
Autonomous vehicle														1				1
QR code												1						1

*Some papers have >1 technology enabler. This chart does not include studies that do not specify any technology enabler for service

Fig. 3. Technology enablers over the years

are the top two service design methods used in HCI papers. This finding matches with our qualitative analysis, where the adoption of service design in HCI mainly resides in creating a journey perspective and backstage processes. Some papers use service blueprint to map out and design new workflows enabled by new technology design (e.g. [5, 86]), whereas some use it unconventionally, for example, [50] use the service blueprint to map out the postural changes of a clinician while performing a series of work actions to redesign the clinician's chair. Two papers [82, 90] present system maps, and two other papers [15, 74] use stakeholder mapping to visualize the coordination, relationships or value exchange between organizations and users.

4.2 Qualitative Analysis

The inductive content analysis yielded 13 codes that were categorized under three high-level dimensions, D1 - scope of design, D2 - scope of actors, and D3 - mutually benefitting relations between HCI and service design. Dimension 1 (D1) tells us how the HCI papers view the scope of design for service design projects; D2 indicates the breadth of actors or level of a systemic perspective in terms of actors accounted for; D3 hints at the benefitting relations between HCI and service design, implying possible future directions for synergy. Each paper was coded multiple codes (e.g. [42] was coded C3, C4, C6, C11), hence the percentage of papers in Table 2 does not total up to 100%.

The following sections present five themes that depict the current status of service design adoptions in HCI.

Journey Perspective as the Most Frequently Adopted. As shown in Table 2, the most frequent code is C4: *includes journey/ end-to-end perspective* (18 papers, 58.1%). 10 of these papers [5, 15, 41, 42, 50, 74, 86, 89, 90] illustrate the journey perspective by employing the customer journey map or service blueprint (as mentioned in Sect. 4.1, sub-section "methods used"), while the other eight papers explain the user journey through written paragraphs or lists. Among the papers coded C4, the scope and granularity of

Table 2. The number of papers coded under the three dimensions, D1, D2, and D3.

Dimension (D)	Code (C)	Number of papers (%) *
D1: Scope of design	C4: Includes journey/ end-to-end perspective	18 (58.1%)
	C6: Including backstage work process	16 (51.6%)
	C7: Designing a collaborative network involving multiple stakeholders	14 (45.2%)
	C5: Service design for designing technological systems (technology-focused)	11 (35.5%)
	C2: Mainly focuses on UI/ UX/ usability/ features	9 (29.0%)
	C1: Focuses mainly on single touchpoint interaction design	8 (25.8%)
	C3: Consists of multiple touchpoints	7 (22.6%)
	C8: Value exchange / value co-creation among stakeholders	7 (22.6%)
	C9: Speculating future service systems (envisions future scenario to see the possibilities)	5 (16.1%)
D2: Scope of actors	C11: Considers multiple stakeholders	18 (58.1%)
	C10: Only focuses on end-users	10 (32.3%)
D3: Mutually benefitting relations	C12: Service design enabling new method/framework development for HCI	5 (16.1%)
	C13: HCI enabling new method/framework development for service design	1 (3.2%)

* Percentage is calculated by (no. of papers/ 31 included papers)

journey perspective vary. Some papers focus on mapping the detailed journey within a service encounter (e.g. [17, 40]), while some extend the journey perspective to include pre-service and post-service activities (e.g. [82, 86]). The former case papers focus on immediate contexts of interacting with technology, and the latter case papers include operation and management perspective, e.g., customer onboarding and retention, strategies for sustained use and development of the proposed technology systems [82]. While a journey mapping often includes user's interactions with multiple touch-points orchestrated in a service journey [91], more than a few papers use journey map-ping for a single product in our analysis: as seen in Table 2, only seven papers out of 18 papers coded C4, are coded C3: *consists of multiple touchpoints.* The journey map-ping appears to offer a new way to analyze the user's interaction with a single product, considering his/her various touchpoints with a single product over the course of inter-action (e.g., see [50]).

Expanded Design Space Including Backstage Processes and Stakeholder Collaborations. The next two most frequent codes in D1 are C6: *including backstage work process* (16 papers, 51.6%) and C7: *designing a collaborative network involving multiple stakeholders* (14 papers, 45.2%). Among the papers coded C6, [85, 89] analyze existing backstage workflows to identify problems or new design opportunities, [42, 46] simulate backend operations for user test, while [86] maps out the backstage workflow of the proposed service using a service blueprint. For the papers coded C7, the consideration of collaborative networks goes beyond multiple groups of "users" but include stakeholders who may influence the development and delivery of new services, such as government, policymakers, or community representatives (e.g., see [44, 49]).

11 papers (35.5%) were identified as adopting service design for designing technological systems beyond a single product (C5). These papers employ service design concepts and approaches in aligning multiple technological components with the needs of multiple stakeholders. For example, [52] uses co-design to develop the air traffic management system for logistic services using unmanned drones, [49] looks into the possibilities of a "fair" algorithm to prioritize donation services that involve complex user requirements, while [96] prototypes a crowdsourcing system to engage citizens in the co-production of public transportation services.

Although not many, 7 papers (22.6%) consider new value co-creation models enabled by technology platforms (C8: *value exchange/ value co-creation among stakeholders*). Especially, the papers dealing with crowdsourcing technologies [31, 96] or AI [86] explicate models of exchanges of values or resources in multiple-stakeholder collaborations. Some papers explicitly explain the notion of value co-creation based on customer competence [96] and co-design [89], while one paper illustrates a value exchange model through ecosystem mapping [82].

Informing New Interaction Design Strategies. While service design is used for the expanded design space as described above, more than a few papers using service design focus on a single product interaction. Nine (29%) focus more on evaluating UX or usability of the digital service in the study (C2), and eight (25.8%) focus on designing interactions of a single touchpoint (C1), half of which are also coded C2. While these papers deal with rather conventional design scopes in HCI, service design appears to inform new interaction design strategies to them. Some studies use the notion of service marketing to create "service interactions". For example, [47] proposes new human-robot interactions based on the notion of service breakdown and service recovery [7]. Other examples are [36, 37], where service design helped them to include "customers" of end-users in their design consideration.

Speculating the Infrastructural System of Future Technologies. A few recent papers use service design to speculate future service systems with emerging technologies (C9: *Speculating Future Service Systems*). For example, [22]'s speculative design of a community-owned drone delivery network and [52]'s co-design sessions to envision the future context for the unmanned air traffic management system. They design for and experiment with advanced technologies or "first-of-a-kind systems" [52], speculating what kind of infrastructural changes and issues the design of technologies may bring in terms of socio-cultural contexts. Speculating future scenarios has been a favorable research topic in HCI and interaction design [30, 59, 81]. While future speculations in the interaction design approach focus on relationships between humans and future technologies, and possible value conflicts and implications for socio-technical systems, service design seems to enable HCI research to systematically visualize the new infrastructure by incorporating multiple stakeholders roles (e.g. [22, 52]), value contributions and their implications in the system change (e.g. [88, 89, 96]). Those works are informed by the theories of service design, such as value co-creation, and the tools, such as stake-holder mapping and value-exchange modelling..

Mutually Benefitting Relations. D3 shows different ways service design and HCI can benefit from each other. Not only the papers show how service design is adopted in HCI, some works also show how two areas complement each other by borrowing and modifying methods and theoretical frameworks. Some used service design approaches to enable new methods or frameworks for HCI (C12). For example, [77] incorporates the concept of touchpoints and user journey to create a holistic user experience map of mobility and [41] develops an experience prototyping tool that incorporates a journey perspective and the physical environment (servicescape [6]). Vice versa, a subset of service design methods has been already informed by interaction design, for specifying user interactions with touchpoints. As such adoption of methods has already been part of the historical evolvement of service design, we did not code for this deliberately. However, we still found one paper that proposes a new framework of service design by incorporating the HCI concept of Technology Acceptance Model [4].

5   Discussion

Our systematic literature review reveals the sporadic adoptions of service design in HCI over the past decade. While HCI's interest in service design is arguably increasing, this research does not necessarily show that there is growth in service design literature in the most cited publication venues of HCI. While a mobile application is the most used technology platform, more recent studies use service design to deal with emerging technologies, such as AI, social computing, drones etc. Our inductive content analysis found that there are varying levels of understandings and adoptions of service design in the current HCI literature, in terms of the scopes of design and actors. In this section, we infer HCI's current understandings of service design based on the varying levels of adoptions and discuss future agendas by unpacking underlying tensions and what is left unexplored.

5.1   Varying Levels of Adoption

Out of the 52 papers in our analysis, 21 papers use the term service design loosely, without mentioning what kinds of concepts, processes or methods of service design have been used. Service design in those papers merely refers to the designing of digital services, arguably perceived as a subset of interaction design where the design objects focus on intangible services. Given that this is a considerable portion of the publications (40%), it could be inferred that service design is not fully recognized yet as a distinct design approach with its own logic, concepts and methodologies in HCI. Our goal is not to present this phenomenon as necessarily erroneous, but to highlight a poor definition of service design in HCI, which might hinder HCI researchers from fully benefitting from broader scopes and notions of service design.

Among the literature where service design plays a distinct role, our inductive content analysis shows varying scopes of service design work in HCI, ranging from end-user experience to backstage operation processes to future collaboration networks. In that spectrum, a customer journey appears to be the most prevalent design scope. There was also a considerable number of service design work (10 out 31 papers in the category "adopting service design") that only focuses on end-users, rather than considering multiple stakeholders which is often described as a distinct work scope of service design comparing to other fields of design. Those papers focusing on end-users use a journey perspective to design for a holistic experience of end-users around either a single product or user's seamless interaction across various touchpoints. These findings imply that end-users experience is a strong focus of the current service design work in HCI.

Service design considers not only the service users, but also the backstage service operations and the multiple stakeholders directly or indirectly involved in the service delivery. In the studied literature, we did find the expansion of design scopes engaging in backstage technology operations and multiple stakeholders. Service design helps these studies manifest the backstage work process to enable desirable user-technology interactions, identify possible pitfalls in actual operation scenarios and take into consideration socio-technical and political settings.

While more than a few studies consider or design for multiple stakeholder collaborations around technologies, the notions of value exchange and value creation, however, do not seem to be broadly taken up by HCI yet. There are a few studies that explicitly use value co-creation models to create a plausible collaborative system with crowdsourcing computing [88, 96] and designed new collaborative networks enabled by drone technology [22, 52], but they are found only in a limited number of research groups. On one hand, we acknowledge the limited number of studies that might come from the limited set of data in our study. On the other hand, this might also indicate that the notion of value co-creation might appear out of the scope of HCI to many HCI researchers, as addressed in Zimmerman and Forlizzi [95] and Lee [45]. HCI "tends to follow a product-centric design process, focusing on producing a thing – hardware and/or software" [95], and this product-centric view might have formed a challenge in adopting a broad notion of service design informed by S-D logic [75]. In addition, service design might appear to HCI to be associated with economic models or human resource management, as reflected from its vocabularies such as "customers" or "value exchanges". This 'business'-related connotation might have hindered HCI, which is deeply rooted in the user-centric mindset, from adopting service design more broadly and benefitting from its full potential [45, 66]. Based on this diagnosis on what is underexplored, the following subsection presents future opportunities between service design and HCI.

5.2 Future Agenda

While our findings reveal the potential of using service design for new technological systems, such as crowdsourcing technologies, social computing, AI, etc., we also found the HCI expansion towards service design has still remained in limited research groups, and there is no evident growth of such work over the past decade. As proposed by Zimmerman and Forlizzi [95] and Forlizzi [28], "service framing" [28] can provide HCI teams with a holistic lens to define a thoroughgoing design space when dealing with new technologies for complex systems and non-conventional actors in the design process, such as distributors or policymakers. The service framing can also enable them to design for new interactions based on the logic of value-in-use and value co-creation [75]. A few of the papers in our analysis did hint at these potentials. For example, [96]'s work on cloud computing for bus system shows co-creation of value by tapping on customer competence. [22] illustrates how service design can help to design for infrastructure for new technology by identifying new collaborative actors and mapping their resource (value) exchanges. Still, service framing would deserve more attention from those who study service design in HCI.

Service design can connect technological design with emerging forms of economy, such as shared economy and gig economy [45]. The notion of value co-creation and S-D logic [75] from service design, which goes beyond merely a method to design intangible services characterized into an IHIP model [51], holds innovative potentials for HCI to deal with those economic platforms. HCI has always been dealing with digital technologies and interfaces (which are nowadays often referred to as digital services). However, how those technologies are delivered have changed [95] from software inside physical products to a subscription model where multiple business stakeholders are involved and interacting with end-users. Service design and S-D logic help HCI researchers and design teams deal with this business model change as a new design material to continue providing positive user experiences. Designing for technological platforms, collaboration models and user experiences of subscription-based models (e.g. movie streaming [53], online games [71]) or peer-economy services (e.g. Waze [95]) is a good example. For this reason, Forlizzi [28] has proposed that the new economics may become a material for design in HCI, later echoed by Yoo et al. [87] and Lee [45]. Investigating the intersection of technologies and emerging economics through service design is a promising area for further research.

In addition, service design can be useful for value-sensitive design [29] and sustainable HCI [8, 65] due to its strengths in coordinating differing values of stakeholders and systems thinking. A few studies in our review demonstrate the potential for this in HCI. For example, Lee et al. [49] combine value-sensitive design and service design to explicate differing values of various stakeholders around donation allocation and propose an algorithm system that coordinates different wishes, needs and resources. In another work, Bisht and Mishra [5] demonstrate how service design contributes different models for technology-enabled financial services to be inclusive of the urban poor community. They called for a joint effort between policymakers, partner agencies, as well as researchers in the fields of information technology and services for financial inclusion initiatives in a developing economy [5]. Service design has been commonly used for social innovation projects [84] since systems thinking is in its nature. Therefore, HCI research that deals with complex social problems or aims at sustained change can lean to service design to unpack networked issues around the wicked problem.

We also believe that service design and HCI can mutually benefit from each other based on their overlapping interests, such as user experiences and social issues, and distinct expertise, e.g., value co-creation logic from service design and technological innovation from HCI. In the early days of service design, HCI provided a pool of methods and frameworks for user research, prototyping, and evaluation for service designers [78]. By doing so, HCI helped to bring attention to the experiences and emotions of customers in service encounters. As our literature review shows, HCI and interaction design have been adopting service design methods to deal with the expanded design spaces, and even led to the development of new methods in combination with computational technologies [41]. While service designers seem to be more conservative in choosing the technologies to use [95], the works like [22, 41, 86] in our literature review demonstrate the design of new types of services enabled by emerging technologies. HCI can push for technological advancement in the design for services through its strong technology orientation.

For the mutually benefitting relations and development, service design researchers' ongoing attempts at clarifying varying and multiple notions of service design will hopefully help HCI researchers to gain a clearer understanding of service design. Similarly, establishing more profound service design theories and methodologies (e.g. see [61, 68, 92]) will hopefully make it easier for HCI researchers and practitioners to engage in service design in their work. This will go beyond the narrow definition of service design that equals service design to the design of digital services. HCI researchers might embrace the increasing interplays between technology design and business models to be included in their design materials and research agenda [28, 45, 87]. For example, what kind of technological innovation can support and advance a shared economy? What kind of new value co-creation models are possible through the meaningful alignment of cloud computing technologies? These kinds of questions will open new, timely-relevant design vistas in HCI, which requires collaboration with various other disciplines, including service design.

6   Conclusion and Future Work

This paper presents the analysis on HCI's current understandings and adoptions of service design, by conducting a systematic literature review. HCI being a multidisciplinary field in its nature, clarification of understandings and benefits of new disciplines around HCI will help the field better collaborate with other disciplines and evolve. The systematic literature review conducted in this study is part of the ongoing clarification efforts.

According to the present literature review, service design work in HCI has not increased since the first years of 2004–2006, and the peak in publications in 2012–2013 is largely dependent on four research groups publishing in the top HCI venues. One reason behind the slow adoption may be the deeply rooted user-centered mindset of HCI. The most cited publications on service design come from management studies (e.g., [69, 75]) and for HCI, service design may seem too business-oriented. We discussed areas where HCI could benefit from adopting ideas from service design, such as systems thinking to handle the increasingly complex technology contexts in HCI, or value co-creation to create new collaborative networks in this complex context. On the other hand, service design would continue benefitting from adopting the HCI methods and frameworks for user research, prototyping, and evaluation. Service designers could also learn a lot about the opportunities provided by the interaction technologies.

Based on our findings, many HCI researchers do not recognize service design as a distinct design approach of its own. The service design term in many of the publications is used as a generic reference to designing digital services, rather than as a reference to a design approach including the core logic, concepts and methodologies of the service design community.

We proposed several topics to the future agenda of research to exploit the potential of closer collaboration between HCI and service design. We echo the calls for more research on service framing in designing ICT systems, and collaboration between service design and HCI in identifying new technological opportunities from systemic changes, such as the emerging economic models.

While we identified a set of patterns from the data set of this research, we acknowledge a shortcoming with the limited dataset from the top 20 HCI publication venues according to Google Scholar metrics, as of July 2020. We are currently expanding this research with a wider pool of the literature from Scopus to verify and further discuss our findings. With the methodological choice of a systematic literature review, our analysis only focuses on research projects and scholarly work. Analysis of how HCI practitioners use service design in their work would provide a more holistic picture to our research question – *how HCI interprets service design.*

Appendix

Top 20 HCI Publication Venues Used in This Study

Table 3. Top HCI publication venues as of July 2020 (Source: Google Scholar metrics)

	Publication Venue	h5-index *	h5-median #
1	Computer Human Interaction (CHI)	87	117
2	ACM Conference on Computer-Supported Cooperative Work & Social Computing	60	82
3	ACM Conference on Pervasive and Ubiquitous Computing (UbiComp)	57	84
4	ACM Symposium on User Interface Software and Technology (UIST)	46	69
5	IEEE Transactions on Affective Computing	42	71
6	ACM/IEEE International Conference on Human Robot Interaction	40	58

(*continued*)

Table 3. (*continued*)

	Publication Venue	h5-index *	h5-median #
7	International Journal of Human-Computer Studies	39	58
8	IEEE Transactions on Human-Machine Systems	36	54
9	Behaviour & Information Technology	36	47
10	Conference on Designing Interactive Systems (DIS)	33	46
11	International Conference on Multimodal Interfaces (ICMI)	33	46
12	International Journal of Human-Computer Interaction	31	47
13	ACM Transactions on Computer-Human Interaction (TOCHI)	30	48
14	HCI International	29	45
15	Mobile HCI	28	38
16	IEEE Transactions on Haptics	28	34
17	International Conference on Intelligent User Interfaces (IUI)	27	36
18	International ACM Conference on Assistive Technologies (Assets)	26	31
19	International Conference on Tangible, Embedded, and Embodied Interaction	25	35
20	International Conference on User Modeling, Adaptation and Personalization	25	33

* "h5-index is the h-index for articles published in the last 5 complete years. It is the largest number h such that h articles published in 2015–2019 have at least h citations each" (source: Google Scholar metrics).
# "h5-median for a publication is the median number of citations for the articles that make up its h5-index" (source: Google Scholar metrics).

The full list of all 83 papers and how they are categorized in this study can be found at https://www.notion.so/List-of-papers-in-used-in-systematic-literature-review-566010db676c402182595758e0d2fbb9.

References

1. Abdelnour-Nocera, J., Clemmensen, T.: Socio-technical HCI for ethical value exchange. In: Clemmensen, T., Rajamanickam, V., Dannenmann, P., Petrie, H., Winckler, M. (eds.) INTERACT 2017. LNCS, vol. 10774, pp. 148–159. Springer, Cham (2018). https://doi.org/10.1007/978-3-319-92081-8_15
2. Alhonsuo, M., Hapuli, J., Virtanen, L., Colley, A., Häkkilä, J.: Concepting wearables for ice-hockey youth. In: Proceedings of MobileHCI 2015, pp. 944–946. ACM (2015)
3. Bergvall-Kåreborn, B., Wiberg, M.: User driven service design and innovation platforms. In: Stephanidis, C. (ed.) HCI 2013. CCIS, vol. 373, pp. 3–7. Springer, Heidelberg (2013). https://doi.org/10.1007/978-3-642-39473-7_1

4. Bhandari, G., Snowdon, A.: Design of a patient-centric, service-oriented health care navigation system for a local health integration network. Behav. Inf. Technol. **31**(3), 275–285 (2012)
5. Bisht, S.S., Mishra, V.: ICT-driven financial inclusion initiatives for urban poor in a developing economy: implications for public policy. Behav. Inf. Technol. **35**(10), 817–832 (2016)
6. Bitner, M.J.: Servicescapes: the impact of physical surroundings on customers and employees. J. Mark. **56**(2), 57–71 (1992)
7. Bitner, M.J., Booms, B.H., Tetreault, M.S.: The service encounter: diagnosing favorable and unfavorable incidents. J. Mark. **54**(1), 71–84 (1990)
8. Blevis, E.: Sustainable interaction design: invention and disposal, renewal and reuse. In: Proceedings of CHI 2007, pp. 503–512. ACM (2007)
9. Blomberg, J., Evenson, S.: Service innovation and design. In: Proceedings of CHI EA 2006, pp. 28–31. ACM (2006)
10. Blomberg, J.: Participation frameworks in service design and delivery. In: Proceedings of PDC 2010, p. 299. ACM (2010)
11. Boehner, K., Vertesi, J., Sengers, P., Dourish, P.: How HCI interprets the probes. In: Proceedings of CHI 2007, pp. 1077–1086. ACM (2007)
12. Buchanan, R.: Design research and the new learning. Des. Issues **17**(4), 3–23 (2001)
13. Buchanan, R.: Wicked problems in design thinking. Des. Issues **8**, 5–21 (1992)
14. Burda, D., Teuteberg, F.: Exploring consumer preferences in cloud archiving – a student's perspective. Behav. Inf. Technol. **35**(2), 89–105 (2016)
15. Chakraborty, A., Hargude, A.N.: Dabbawala: introducing technology to the Dabbawalas of Mumbai. In: Proceedings of MobileHCI 2015, pp. 660–667. ACM (2015)
16. Chand, A., Gonzalez, M., Missig, J., Phanichphant, P., Sun, P.F.: Balance pass: service design for a healthy college lifestyle. In: CHI EA 2006, pp. 1813–1818. ACM (2006)
17. Chen, T.-H., Lin, H.-H., Yen, Y.-D.: Mojo iCuisine: the design and implementation of an interactive restaurant tabletop menu. In: Jacko, J.A. (ed.) HCI 2011. LNCS, vol. 6763, pp. 185–194. Springer, Heidelberg (2011). https://doi.org/10.1007/978-3-642-21616-9_21
18. Clatworthy, S.: Service innovation through touch-points: development of an in-novation toolkit for the first stages of new service development. Int. J. Des. **5**(2) (2011)
19. Colley, A., Häkkilä, J.: Service design methods for human computer interaction. In: Proceedings of MUM 2018, pp. 563–566. ACM (2018)
20. Colley, A., Marttila, H.: Introduction to service design for digital health. In: Bernhaupt, R., Dalvi, G., Joshi, A., K. Balkrishan, D., O'Neill, J., Winckler, M. (eds.) INTERACT 2017. LNCS, vol. 10516, pp. 395–398. Springer, Cham (2017). https://doi.org/10.1007/978-3-319-68059-0_38
21. Colley, A., Rantakari, J., Häkkilä, J.: Dual sided tablet supporting doctor-patient interaction. In: Proceedings of CSCW'15 Companion 2015, pp. 13–16. ACM (2015)
22. Davoli, L., Redström, J.: Materializing infrastructures for participatory hacking. In: Proceedings of DIS 2014, pp. 121–130. ACM (2014)
23. de Sá, M., Churchill, E.: Mobile augmented reality: exploring design and prototyping techniques. In: Proceedings of MOBILEHCI '2012, pp. 221–230. ACM (2012)
24. Edgett, S., Parkinson, S.: Marketing for service industries. Serv. Indust. J. **13**(3), 19–39 (1993)
25. Elo, S., Kyngäs, H.: The qualitative content analysis process. J. Adv. Nurs. **62**(1), 107–115 (2008)
26. Forlizzi, J., Zimmerman, J.: Promoting service design as a core practice in interaction design. In: 5th IASDR World Conference on Design Research 2013. IASDR Press (2013)
27. Forlizzi, J.: All look same? a comparison of experience design and service design. Interactions **17**(5), 60–62 (2010)
28. Forlizzi, J.: Moving beyond user-centered design. Interactions **25**(5), 22–23 (2018)

29. Friedman, B., Hendry, D.G.: Value Sensitive Design: Shaping Technology with Moral Imagination. MIT Press (2019)
30. Fry, T.: Design Futuring: Sustainability, ethics and New Practice. Berg, Oxford, UK (2009)
31. Fu, Z.: Design for public service application based on collective intelligence in China. In: RDURP 2011, pp. 3–6. ACM (2011)
32. Harrington, K., Fulton, P., Brown, M., Pinchin, J., Sharples, S.: Digital wellbeing assessments for people affected by dementia. In: Kurosu, M. (ed.) HCI 2015. LNCS, vol. 9171, pp. 409–418. Springer, Cham (2015). https://doi.org/10.1007/978-3-319-21006-3_39
33. Hayakawa, S., Ueda, Y., Go, K., Takahash, K., Yanagida, K., Yamazaki, K.: User research for experience vision. In: Kurosu, M. (ed.) HCI 2013. LNCS, vol. 8004, pp. 77–84. Springer, Heidelberg (2013). https://doi.org/10.1007/978-3-642-39232-0_9
34. Holmlid, S.: Interaction design and service design: expanding a comparison of design disciplines. In: Nordes 2007 (2007)
35. Hyvärinen, J., Lee, J.-J., Mattelmäki, T.: Fragile Liaisons: challenges in cross-organizational service networks and the role of design. Des. J. 18(2), 249–268 (2015)
36. Inbar, O., Tractinsky, N.: Interface-to-face: sharing information with customers in service encounters. In: CHI EA 2010, pp. 3415–3420. ACM (2010)
37. Inbar, O., Tractinsky, N.: Lowering the line of visibility: incidental users in service encounters. Behav. Inf. Technol. 31(3), 245–260 (2012)
38. Itoh, Y., et al.: Communication service design by interhuman interaction approach. In: CHI EA 2006, pp. 905–910. ACM (2006)
39. Kankainen, A., Vaajakallio, K., Kantola, V., Mattelmäki, T.: Storytelling group – a co-design method for service design. Behav. Inf. Technol. 31(3), 221–230 (2012)
40. Kim, E., Koh, B., Ng, J., Su, R.: myPyramid: increasing nutritional awareness. In: CHI EA 2006, pp. 1843–1848. ACM (2006)
41. Kim, H.-J., Kim, C.M., Nam, T.-J.: SketchStudio: experience prototyping with 2.5-dimensional animated design scenarios. In: Proceedings of DIS 2018, pp. 831–843. ACM (2018)
42. Kim, S., et al.: Autonomous taxi service design and user experience. Int. J. Hum.-Comput. Interact. 36(5), 429–448 (2019)
43. Kimbell, L.: Designing for service as one way of designing services. Int. J. Des. 5, 41–52 (2011)
44. Kotamraju, N.P., van der Geest, T.M.: The tension between user-centred design and e-government services. Behav. Inf. Technol. 31(3), 261–273 (2012)
45. Lee, J.J.: Service design and blind mice. Interactions 27(2), 20–21 (2020)
46. Lee, M.K., Forlizzi, J., Kiesler, S., Rybski, P., Antanitis, J., Savetsila, S.: Personalization in HRI: a longitudinal field experiment. In: Proceedings of HRI 2012, pp. 319–326. ACM (2012)
47. Lee, M.K., Kielser, S., Forlizzi, J., Srinivasa, S., Rybski, P.: Gracefully mitigating breakdowns in robotic services. In: Proceedings of HRI 2010, pp. 203–210. IEEE Press (2010)
48. Lee, M.K., Kiesler, S., Forlizzi, J., Rybski, P.: Ripple effects of an embedded social agent: a field study of a social robot in the workplace. In: Proceedings of CHI 2012, pp. 695–704. ACM (2012)
49. Lee, M.K., Kim, J.T., Lizarondo, L.: A human-centered approach to algorithmic services: considerations for fair and motivating smart community service management that allocates donations to non-profit organizations. In: CHI 2017, pp. 3365–3376. ACM (2017)
50. Liu, X., Qian, D., Wu, L., Xu, J.: Assessment of the working chair using affects the whole service process in b ultrasonic examination. In: Stephanidis, C. (ed.) HCI 2017. CCIS, vol. 713, pp. 540–547. Springer, Cham (2017). https://doi.org/10.1007/978-3-319-58750-9_75
51. Lovelock, C., Gummesson, E.: Whither services marketing? In: Search of a New Paradigm and Fresh Perspectives. Journal of Service Research 7(1), 20–41 (2004).

52. Lundberg, J., Arvola, M., Westin, C., Holmlid, S., Nordvall, M., Josefsson, B.: Cognitive work analysis in the conceptual design of first-of-a-kind systems – designing urban air traffic management. Behav. Inf. Technol. 37(9), 904–925 (2018)
53. Lusch, R., Nambisan, S.: Service innovation: a service-dominant logic perspective. MIS Q. 39, 155–175 (2015)
54. Mager, B.: Service design as an emerging field. In: Miettinen, S., Koivisto, M. (eds.) Designing Services with Innovative Methods. Otava Book Printing LTD, Keu-ruu, Finland (2009)
55. Mager, B.: Service Design Impact Report: Public Sector. Service Design Network, Cologne (2016). http://www.service-design-network.org/books-and-reports/impact-report-public-sector
56. Meckem, S., Carlson, J.L.: Using "rapid experimentation" to inform customer service experience design. In: CHI EA 2010, pp. 4553–4566. ACM (2010)
57. Meroni, A., Sangiorgi, D.: Design for Services. Gower (2011)
58. Moher, D., Liberati, A., Tetzlaff, J., Altman, D.G.: Preferred reporting items for systematic reviews and meta-analyses: the PRISMA statement. PLoS Med. 6(7), e1000097 (2009). https://doi.org/10.1371/journal.pmed.1000097
59. Nardi, B.: Designing for the future: but which one? Interactions 23(1), 26–33 (2016)
60. Pacenti, E., Sangiorgi, D.: Service Design research pioneers: an overview of Service Design research developed in Italy since the '90s. Swedish Des. Res. J. 1(10), 26–33 (2010)
61. Patrício, L., Fisk, R.P., Falcão e Cunha, J., Constantine, L.: Multilevel service design: from customer value constellation to service experience blueprinting. J. Serv. Res. 14(2), 180–200 (2011)
62. Patrício, L., Gustafsson, A., Fisk, R.: Upframing service design and innovation for research impact. J. Serv. Res. 21(1), 3–16 (2017)
63. Polaine, A., Reason, B., Løvlie, L.: Service Design: From Insight to Implementation. Rosenfeld Media (2013)
64. Rau, P.-L.P., Huang, E., Mao, M., Gao, Q., Feng, C., Zhang, Y.: Exploring interactive style and user experience design for social web of things of Chinese users: a case study in Beijing. Int. J. Hum Comput Stud. 80, 24–35 (2015)
65. Remy, C., et al.: Evaluation Beyond Usability: Validating Sustainable HCI Research. In: Proceedings of CHI 2018 2018, p. Paper 216. ACM (2018)
66. Roto, V., Lee, J. J., Law, F., Zimmerman, J.: The overlaps and boundaries between service design and user experience design. In Proceedings of DIS 2021, ACM (2021)
67. Roto, V., Lee, J. J., Mattelmäki, T., Zimmerman, J.: Experience design meets service design: method clash or marriage? In: CHI EA 2018, p. Paper W26. ACM (2018)
68. Secomandi, F., Snelders, D.: Interface design in services: a postphenomenological approach. Des. Issues 29(1), 3–13 (2013)
69. Shostack, L.G.: How to design a service. Eur. J. Mark. 16(1), 49–63 (1982)
70. Szóstek, A., Kwiatkowska, J., Górnicka, O.: The needs of early school children and their parents with respect to the design of mobile service offers. In: CHI EA 2013, pp. 2345–2346. ACM (2013)
71. Stenros, J., Sotamaa, O.: Commoditization of helping players play: rise of the service paradigm. In: DiGRA Conference 2009 (2009)
72. Teixeira, J., Patrício, L., Nunes, N.J., Nóbrega, L.: Customer experience modeling: designing interactions for service systems. In: Campos, P., Graham, N., Jorge, J., Nunes, N., Palanque, P., Winckler, M. (eds.) INTERACT 2011. LNCS, vol. 6949, pp. 136–143. Springer, Heidelberg (2011). https://doi.org/10.1007/978-3-642-23768-3_11
73. Ueda, Y., Go, K., Takahashi, K., Hayakawa, S., Yamazaki, K., Yanagida, K.: Structured scenario-based design method for experience vision. In: Kurosu, M. (ed.) HCI 2013. LNCS, vol. 8004, pp. 500–509. Springer, Heidelberg (2013). https://doi.org/10.1007/978-3-642-39232-0_54

74. V.S., S., Hirom, U., Lobo, S., Devkar, S., Doke, P., Pandey, N.: Participatory design of vaccination services with less-literate users. In: Stephanidis, C. (ed.) HCI 2017. CCIS, vol. 714, pp. 301–308. Springer, Cham (2017). https://doi.org/10.1007/978-3-319-58753-0_45
75. Vargo, S.L., Lusch, R.F.: Evolving to a new dominant logic for marketing. J. Mark. **68**(1), 1–17 (2004)
76. Vilaza, G.N., Mähönen, J., Hamon, C., Danilina, O.: StreetHeart: Empowering homeless through art and technology. In: CHI EA 2017, pp. 93–99. ACM (2017)
77. Wienken, T., Krömker, H.: Experience maps for mobility. In: Kurosu, M. (ed.) HCI 2018. LNCS, vol. 10902, pp. 615–627. Springer, Cham (2018). https://doi.org/10.1007/978-3-319-91244-8_47
78. Wild, P.J., van Dijk, G., Maiden, N.: New opportunities for services and human–computer interaction. Behav. Inf. Technol. **31**(3), 205–208 (2012)
79. Wild, P.J.: HCI and the analysis, design, and evaluation of services. In: BCS - HCI 2008, pp. 207–208. BCS Learning & Development Ltd. (2008)
80. Williams, D., Kelly, G., Anderson, L.: MSN 9: new user-centered desirability methods produce compelling visual design. In: CHI EA 2004, pp. 959–974. ACM (2004)
81. Wong, R.Y., Khovanskaya, V.: Speculative Design in HCI: from corporate imaginations to critical orientations. In: Filimowicz, M., Tzankova, V. (eds.) New Directions in Third Wave Human-Computer Interaction: Volume 2 - Methodologies. HIS, pp. 175–202. Springer, Cham (2018). https://doi.org/10.1007/978-3-319-73374-6_10
82. Wu, C.-C., Hong, S.-M., Huang, Y.-H.: GoodGuide: reconnecting the homeless and others. In: CHI EA 2015, pp. 55–60. ACM (2015)
83. Yamazaki, K., Go, K., Takahashi, K., Hayakawa, S., Ueda, Y., Yanagida, K.: Proposal for experience vision. In: Kurosu, M. (ed.) HCI 2013. LNCS, vol. 8004, pp. 137–145. Springer, Heidelberg (2013). https://doi.org/10.1007/978-3-642-39232-0_16
84. Yang, C.-F., Sung, T.-J.: Service design for social innovation through participatory action research. Int. J. Des. **10**, 21–36 (2016)
85. Yang, Q., Zimmerman, J., Steinfeld, A., Carey, L., Antaki, J.F.: Investigating the heart pump implant decision process: opportunities for decision support tools to help. In: CHI 2016, pp. 4477–4488. ACM (2016)
86. Yi, T., Rhim, J., Lee, I., Narangerel, A., Lee, J.-H.: Service design of intergeneration home-sharing system using VR-based simulation technology and optimal matching algorithms. In: Stephanidis, C. (ed.) HCI 2017. CCIS, vol. 714, pp. 95–100. Springer, Cham (2017). https://doi.org/10.1007/978-3-319-58753-0_15
87. Yoo, D., Ernest, A., Serholt, S., Eriksson, E., Dalsgaard, P.: Service design in HCI research: the extended value co-creation model. In: HTTF 2019, p. Article 17. ACM (2019)
88. Yoo, D., Zimmerman, J., Hirsch, T.: Probing bus stop for insights on transit co-design. In: CHI 2013, pp. 409–418. ACM (2013)
89. Yoo, D., Zimmerman, J., Steinfeld, A., Tomasic, A.: Understanding the space for co-design in riders' interactions with a transit service. In: Proceedings of CHI 2010, pp. 1797–1806. ACM (2010)
90. Yoo, J., Pan, Y.: Expanded customer journey map: interaction mapping framework based on scenario. In: Stephanidis, C. (ed.) HCI 2014. CCIS, vol. 435, pp. 550–555. Springer, Cham (2014). https://doi.org/10.1007/978-3-319-07854-0_96
91. Yu, E.: Looking into service representation tools through the multidimensional nature of service experience. Des. J. **22**(4), 437–461 (2019)
92. Yu, E.: Toward an integrative service design framework and future agendas. Des. Issues **36**(2), 41–57 (2020)
93. Zeithaml, V.A., Parasuraman, A., Berry, L.L.: Problems and strategies in services marketing. J. Mark. **49**(2), 33–46 (1985)

94. Zhao, S.: Research on future-oriented manager service design under the background of new retail. In: Stephanidis, C. (ed.) HCI 2018. CCIS, vol. 852, pp. 343–355. Springer, Cham (2018). https://doi.org/10.1007/978-3-319-92285-0_47
95. Zimmerman, J., Forlizzi, J.: Service design. In: The Encyclopedia of Human-Computer Interaction (2019)
96. Zimmerman, J., et al.: Field trial of Tiramisu: crowd-sourcing bus arrival times to spur co-design. In: Proceedings of CHI 2011, pp. 1677–1686. ACM (2011)

Sniff Before You Act: Exploration of Scent-Feature Associations for Designing Future Interactions

Giada Brianza[1]([⊠]) [iD], Patricia Cornelio[2]([⊠]) [iD], Emanuela Maggioni[2]([⊠]) [iD],
and Marianna Obrist[2]([⊠]) [iD]

[1] University of Sussex, Brighton, UK
g.brianza@sussex.ac.uk
[2] University College London, London, UK
{p.cornelio,m.maggioni,m.obrist}@ucl.ac.uk

Abstract. It has long been known that our sense of smell is a powerful one that affects emotions and behaviors. Recently, interest in the sense of smell has been growing exponentially in HCI. However, the potential of smell to inspire design is still underexplored. In this paper, we first investigated crossmodal correspondences between scents and selected features relevant for design (clustered in sensory, bodily, and qualitative features). Then, we created a set of cards (EssCards) to visually summarize the key findings to inspire designers. We carried out two preliminary design exploration sessions using the EssCards. Based on our findings, we discuss how to inspire and challenge design opportunities around the sense of smell and reflect upon applications for smell as inspirational material for designing future interactions and experiences.

Keywords: Sense of smell · Scents · Crossmodal correspondences · Cross-sensory associations · Multisensory design · Design interaction · Body image

1 Introduction

"Good design looks great, yes—but why shouldn't it also feel great, smell great and sound great" [33]. This is how the designer Lee Jinsop encourages design thinking that involves all five senses. In the past decades, the design of products and interactive systems has predominantly used limited sensory channels, with vision as a leading modality [11]. However, there is a growing awareness that the other senses also play an important role in making experiences more compelling [47]. Indeed, Schifferstein [46] has suggested that "designers who intentionally try to create specific experiences are more likely to succeed if they are aware of each sensory channel's contribution to the overall experience".

Electronic supplementary material The online version of this chapter (https://doi.org/10.1007/978-3-030-85616-8_17) contains supplementary material, which is available to authorized users.

While there are growing efforts in designing for all the senses in HCI [40, 48], we have only recently started to understand the vastness of the design opportunities, especially when it comes to our sense of smell. Compared to other modalities, smell plays an important role in our emotions and memories and can evoke more emotionally loaded and vivid experiences [25]. Despite increasing efforts in the area of design, smell is often considered as an "add-on", rather than a starting point for design. One reason for the sense of smell being considered a secondary sense [48] lies in its complexity to work with (e.g., control over scent stimuli, subjective variability). In this paper, we explore the role of smell as inspirational material for designing future interactions (see in Fig. 1).

Fig. 1. First, we asked participants to sniff and associate scents with features relevant for design (based on crossmodal correspondences). Then, we visualized the results through a set of cards (EssCards). Finally, we organized two preliminary design exploration sessions using the EssCards to ideate a multisensory garment.

As a first step in our investigation, we focused on the growing research in crossmodal correspondences, which refer to how "a sensory feature, or attribute, in one modality, can be matched (or associated) with a sensory feature in another sensory modality" [51]. We conducted a user study to explore crossmodal correspondences between different scents and selected sensory, bodily, and qualitative features, along with emotions, intensity, and verbal descriptors for each scent. We then summarized the key findings for each scent in a set of cards, called EssCards. The EssCards were designed with the aim of translating the findings into an accessible format that designers are familiar with and can use as inspiration for their design explorations. We organized two design exploration sessions to gain initial insights into the use of the EssCards in a design context. Based on our findings, we conclude by discussing emerging opportunities around designing future interactions based on smell.

Overall, the contribution of this work is three-fold. First, with our user study we revealed new insights into scent–feature associations (i.e., sensory, bodily, and qualitative features) advancing existing research on crossmodal correspondences to stimulate smell-inspired design. Second, we visualized our findings in the form of a set of cards (EssCards), as inspirational material for designers and anyone interested in the exploration of smell in the design of future interfaces. Our two design explorations exemplify possible uses of our study results using the EssCards. Third, we discuss future avenues for novel olfactory interaction and experience design.

Readers can find additional materials for each part of our work (from the scent–feature associations to the design explorations) in a dedicated Supplementary Material document that also includes the visualizations for all twelve EssCards.

2 Related Work

In this section, we review pertinent related work focused on the relevance of smell for HCI, multisensory design, and crossmodal correspondences (CCs) between scents and other senses and features relevant for design.

2.1 The Relevance of Smell in Design

Smell is a powerful sense that influences how we experience ourselves and the world around us [54, 56]. While smell is often considered a secondary sense [48], emerging research suggests that we use it more than we think. For example, previous work has shown that humans have scent-tracking abilities similar to dogs [42] and can detect emotions through the olfactory channel [59] (e.g., fear [14]). Moreover, prior studies show that scents not only regulate behavior [54] and evoke pleasant or unpleasant experiences [20], but also modulate mood [59], attention [29], stress [37], and memories [25].

Supported by this evidence, the sense of smell is gaining increasing attention in several design contexts. For example, in the context of wearable design [7, 22, 57], Essence [2] and Bioessence [1] are necklaces that release scents based on biometric or contextual data (e.g., heart rate and respiration). Most recently, Wang et al. [58] designed on-face olfactory wearable interfaces that are lightweight and can be adhered to the skin or attached to face accessories. These efforts are further extended towards multisensory design [46]. Most recently, Maggioni et al. [35] identified four key design features to guide smell-based experience design in HCI (i.e., chemical, emotional, spatial, and temporal features). This suggests that, in the imminent future, single-use case solutions and frameworks will become a rich ecosystem of smell-based applications and experience design. Those prior works demonstrate that smell is gaining increasing attention within HCI and the design community.

However, despite those efforts, smell is commonly considered as just an "add-on" to enhance and augment experiences, rather than inspirational material for designing future interactions and experiences. To guide smell-inspired design, we build upon the growing evidence in CC research, which has emerged from experimental psychology [51].

2.2 Smell and Crossmodal Correspondences

A growing body of research in experimental psychology and sensory science is showing that people exhibit consistent CCs between many stimulus-features in different sensory modalities. In this section, we provide an overview of previous work in CC research in relation to smell [52]. We have clustered the work according to the three features most relevant to the contribution made in this paper: sensory, bodily, and qualitative.

Smell and Sensory Features. Features including visual shapes, sound, temperature, and texture have previously been studied in relation to the sense of smell in CC re-search, and are recognized as relevant design targets in HCI [31].

Visual Shapes, Hanson-Vaux et al. [24] have found CCs between scents and visually displayed shapes. They presented participants with visual analogue scales (VAS) with spiky and rounded shapes as anchors and found that unpleasant and intense scents were associated with associated with spiky shapes, while scents rated as pleasant and less intense were associated with rounded shapes. Kaeppler et al. [28] corroborated the same associations following the "kiki-bouba" paradigm [50]. Moreover, Jezler et al. [27] focused their work on the effect of scented materials on participants' physical creations, showing that lemon-scented sculptures have a higher number of spikes than vanilla-scented sculptures..

Sound. Belkin et al. [5] asked participants to match auditory stimuli that varied in high or low pitch with scents from different categories (e.g., citrus, woody, floral). Their results suggest that scent–sound associations are due to fragrance type and pleasantness. Later, Crisinel et al. [12] studied CCs between scents, four different musical instrument samples, and varying pitches. Their results show consistent CCs between scents, pitches, and musical instruments. For example, fruity scents were consistently associated with high pitch.

Temperature. Wnuk et al. [61] examined scent–temperature associations in three cultures (Maniq, Thai, and Dutch). Participants matched fifteen scents to temperature by touching cups filled with hot or cold water. The results show that some scents are associated to temperature but that there is a cultural variation in those associations, arguing against their universality. Brianza et al. [10] used VAS to explore associations between three scents and "hot" and "cold" words visually displayed as anchors. However, no significant results were found. Furthermore, Krishna et al. [32] have explored whether the congruence between scents and temperature enhances haptic perception and product evaluation. They found an interaction effect between temperature and scents, i.e., the scent rated as cold led to significantly more positive evaluations of a cold gel-pack than the scent rated as warm, and vice versa.

Texture. Demattè et al. [16] have assessed scent-texture associations. Participants were asked to rate the softness of fabric swatches while presented with three scents. They showed that fabric swatches were judged softer in the presence of a pleasant scent compared to an unpleasant scent. Meanwhile, Krishna et al. [32] have explored associations of smell and texture in relation to gender (i.e., masculinity–femininity). They found mutual agreement on rating smooth paper as feminine and rough paper as masculine. Moreover, for the smooth paper, the feminine scent was perceived as more congruent than the masculine scent, and vice versa.

Smell and Bodily Features. Recently, it has been shown that the perception of our own body can be influenced by smell [10, 60], which becomes increasingly relevant in the wider context of wearable design [7, 22, 57]. From prior work, we have selected two relevant features that explore the relationship between smell and the body: body silhouettes (i.e., 2D body silhouettes, thin–thick) and gender (i.e., masculinity–femininity).

Body Silhouettes. Brianza et al. [10] have studied the concept of body image perception (BIP) through the VAS paradigm by exploring CCs between lemon and vanilla scents and 2D body silhouettes as a visual representation of different body types. They found associations between lemon scent and thin body silhouettes and between vanilla scent and thick body silhouettes. They also combined scents with sound to explore the relation between the same scents and the sound of participants' footsteps (increasing and decreasing pitch from low to high). They found that during the condition combining lemon scent and the sound of high-pitched footsteps, participants walked faster and felt lighter, in comparison with vanilla scent.

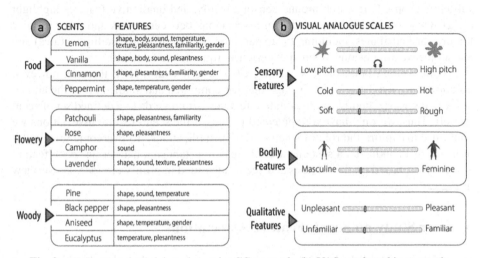

Fig. 2. (a) Scents selected, based on prior CC research. (b) VAS employed in our study.

Gender: Kaeppler et al. [28] have explored associations between scents and gender-related features (masculinity–femininity) to investigate color–scent correspondences for fragrances marketed as masculine, feminine, or neutral. They have revealed that the way people think of a fine fragrance (i.e., masculine or feminine) influences the color associated to the fragrance. Moreover, Krishna et al. [32] have used the association between masculinity and femininity and scents to determine a possible association be-tween smell and texture. They found that both scents and haptic experiences can have semantic associations in terms of gender, and the congruence of these semantic associations led to more positive perceptions.

Smell and Qualitative Features. Here, we review studies that account for the subjective experiences elicited by olfactory stimuli focused on two standard dimensions – pleasantness and familiarity. The perceived pleasantness and familiarity of an olfactory stimulus are mostly used to describe the subjective qualities of an odor [41].

Many studies have shown a variability in the ratings of those dimensions within and between participants for a given scent [18], and it has also been demonstrated that these dimensions are not independent [15]. Especially, a positive correlation between pleasantness and familiarity has been shown in prior literature [6, 18, 21, 45, 53]: the more familiar a scent is, the more pleasant it is rated. Indeed, studies previously cited for investigating different CCs also focused their research on familiarity with the scents [24, 28, 32, 63]. For example, in [12] it was found that the identification of the stimulus influences the ratings of familiarity and pleasantness: participants were better able to name the scents that they rated as more familiar. Correctly identified stimuli were also rated as more pleasant. This finding is in line with previous results concerning correlations between pleasantness and the familiarity ratings of scents (e.g., [18]).

Summary and Opportunity for Extending Scent–Feature Associations. The above subsections on CC research around sensory, bodily, and qualitative features highlight the growing interest and knowledge in associations between scents and other sensory features and attributes, including the expansion towards the body (bodily features) and the subjective dimensions of smell experiences (qualitative features).

While we can build on this existing CC research within HCI, there is, however, no comprehensive body of knowledge that has combined and studied all of the above-described sensory, bodily, and qualitative features with regards to a defined set of scent stimuli. Thus, we only have a fragmented picture of the scent–feature associations we could use to explore the role of smell in design applications. To overcome this limitation, we first conducted a systematic user study to establish a dataset on scent–feature associations, based on the features and scents identified in prior work (see an overview in Fig. 2).

3   User Study on Scent–Feature Associations

To enrich the established set of scent–feature associations that already exists in the literature to possibly inspire future design interactions, we designed a user study to investigate CCs between a selection of scents (see Fig. 2a) and a selection of features (see Fig. 2b) described in the previous section. Thus, we aimed to extend prior work and create a more comprehensive set of CCs between scents and different features.

3.1   Selection of Scents and Features

We selected twelve scents for our study, identified through the review of prior works on CCs (see Sect. 2.2). To facilitate future design choices, and influenced by the work of Belkin et al. [5] in which the stimuli were drawn from several fragrance categories (e.g., flowery, woody, citrusy), we wanted to cluster scents with similar features, as commonly done for other senses (e.g., environmental vs animal sounds, etc.).

We clustered each of the scents into one of three categories (i.e., food, flowery, and woody categories, with equal numbers of scents). Moreover, having more than one scent in each category enables the enrichment of personalization and customization in future design explorations (i.e., if one scent is disliked, another one from the same category can be selected). The scents of lemon, vanilla, cinnamon, and peppermint were clustered into food-related scents, while patchouli, rose, camphor, and lavender were grouped under flowery scents, and pine, black pepper, aniseed, and eucalyptus were clustered under woody scents. As scent stimuli, we used 100% undiluted natural essential oils from Holland and Barrett [3]. All the bottles containing the essential oils were anonymized for participants, and any link between the scents and their labels was removed.

It is worth noting that all the selected scents are considered pleasant. We did not consider unpleasant scents for this first attempt to explore the role of smell as inspirational material for designing future interactions and experiences. We wanted to create a pleasant initial experience to foster the potentials of smell in the wider context of multisensory design.

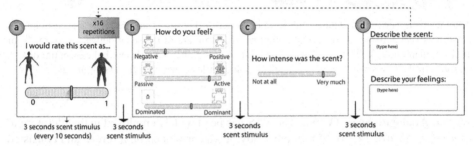

Fig. 3. Measures used: (a) example of VAS. (b) SAM for emotion assessment. (c) Intensity assessment. (d) Open questions. Scent stimuli were presented for 3 s, every 10 s during the presen-tation of the VAS (a), and for 3 s at the beginning of b–d.

Eight bipolar features were clustered in sensory, bodily, and qualitative features, as shown in Fig. 2b. As sensory features, we selected spiky versus rounded visual shapes [24, 27, 30], low- versus high-pitched sound [5, 12], cold versus hot temperature [32, 61], and soft versus rough texture [16, 32]. As bodily features, we selected thin versus thick body silhouettes [10] and masculine versus feminine gender [28, 32]. Finally, as qualitative features, we selected high versus low pleasantness [1, 7] and high versus low familiarity [24, 32].

3.2 Study Design

The study followed a within-participant design composed of two sessions that took place on two different days, in order not to overstimulate participants when presented with a total of twelve scents. In each of the two sessions, participants were presented with six of the twelve tested scents, counterbalanced across participants. Each session lasted 25 min and took place in a controlled study environment. Participants were provided with an information sheet and a consent form upon their arrival. The study was approved by the local university ethics committee. Below, we provide details on the measures used and the specific details on the study setup and procedure.

3.3 Measures

As shown in Fig. 3, for each of the twelve scents, we assessed (a) CCs through the use of visual analogue scales (VAS); (b) the main three emotion dimensions (valence, arousal, dominance) using self-assessment manikin (SAM) scales [9]; (c) intensity using a Likert scale; and (d) subjective descriptors through open question boxes.

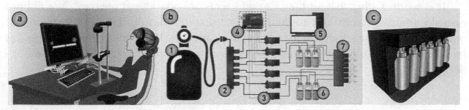

Fig. 4. (a) Experimental setup. The distance between the output nozzle and each participant's nose was kept constant at 1m using a chinrest. (b) Structure of the scent delivery system: 1. air tank, 2. manifolds, 3. electric valves, 4. Arduino board, 5. PC, 6. bottles with the essential oils, 7. output nozzle with six individual channels; (c) Six bottles containing the essential oils.

Visual Analogue Scale (VAS). The VAS has been widely employed in the literature to study CCs [5, 10, 24, 36, 55]. In our study, it was presented on a screen and consisted of continuous scales ranging from 0 to 1 (step size of 0.005). Shapes were represented with visual illustrations following the "kiki-bouba" paradigm [50] as shown in Fig. 2b. Similarly, body silhouettes were represented with body illustrations, following the study by Brianza et al. [10]. The remaining features were represented with words only (except for sound, we selected actual high-low pitch audio stimuli played via headphones) [10]. Participants were asked to enter their answers by positioning the mouse on the desired point on a slider. The eight bipolar features were presented twice in a counterbalanced order, resulting in sixteen repetitions in total (see Fig. 3a).

Emotion Assessment. Due to the important link between scents and emotions [20], we evaluated participants' emotional ratings for each scent using the 9-point SAM scale, commonly employed to study emotions [19, 36, 43] (see Fig. 3b). It consists of a standardized measurement technique that includes valence (from negative to positive), arousal (from passive to active), and dominance (from dominated to dominant).

Intensity Assessment. Since intensity has been shown to significantly influence smell perception [24, 28]), we used a 9-point Likert scale, as in [10], to rate the intensity ("How intense was the scent?") from 1 "not at all" to 9 "very much" (see Fig. 3c).

Qualitative Descriptions. To capture more qualitative insights about how the scent was perceived and the feelings towards the scent, we asked participants to answer two open questions at the end of the experiment, presented in random order: 1) "If you focus on the moment when you perceived the scent, how would you describe it?" and 2) "If you focus on the moment when you perceived the scent, how did it make you feel?". The aim was to capture subjective commonalities and differences among participants, following the work by Obrist et al. [41] suggesting that the way we describe a scent influences the overall smell experience.

3.4 Setup and Procedure

Participants sat in front of a desk while wearing headphones, as shown in Fig. 4a. We delivered the scent stimuli through a 3D-printed nozzle (with six independent channels for each scent) that was positioned at 1m distance from each participant's nose [10]. Throughout the study, participants were asked to place their chin on a chinrest to keep the distance consistent across trials and participants. The delivery device (shown in Fig. 4b–c) was developed to automatically deliver scents with time precision. The device is composed of six electrovalves that regulate the air passage (on–off) from a tank of compressed air (Fig. 4b). The tank supplies airflow through plastic pipes linked through electrovalves, which open six aluminum bottles that contain 2.5 ml of six undiluted natural essential oils (Fig. 4c). The delivery device was hidden from participants' view. The scent stimuli were automatically delivered throughout the experiment, using an Arduino board to control the delivery device. The scent was delivered every 10 s during the VAS task, three seconds (fixation cross on-screen) before the SAM task, and three seconds (fixation cross on-screen) before the open questions, as shown in Fig. 3. The pressure was constant at 1 Bar during the whole study.

3.5 Participants

We recruited twenty-one participants (10 male, 11 female, Mage = 27.96, SD = ±6.08). They reported having normal or corrected-to-normal vision and no olfactory impairments (e.g., allergies, cold, flu), tested by the Olfactory Assessment Test [39].

3.6 Results

Here, we present the results of our analysis of the collected data. First, we ran normality tests to check if any of our quantitative data violated the assumption of normality. In the Shapiro-Wilk test, skewness and kurtosis did not show any significant departure from normality. Then, it being a within-participants study, we ran several repeated measures analyses of variance (ANOVAs), which enabled exploration of the factor interactions across dependent variables. Below, we summarize our main results [49]. In addition, mean scores, standard deviations (SD), and significant pairwise comparisons of the full set of features for each scent are included in the Supplementary Material.

Scent–Feature Associations. With the data collected from the VAS, we ran a repeated-measures ANOVA. Sphericity was assumed for all the variables, apart from temperature and sound. We found no significant results for gender. However, we found statistically significant differences ($p < .05$) for the features listed below. Post hoc analysis, with Bonferroni correction was applied.

- Visual shapes: $F(11, 209) = 3.9, p < .001$
- Sound: $F(11, 209) = 3.67, p < .01$
- Temperature: $F(11, 209) = 3.33, p < .01$
- Texture: $F(11, 209) = 2.83, p < .01$
- Body silhouettes: $F(11, 209) = 5.12, p < .001$

- Pleasantness: $F(11,209) = 4.52, p < .001$
- Familiarity: $F(11,209) = 7.87, p < .001$

In summary, we found that peppermint and eucalyptus are the scents most significantly associated with a spiky shape, high-pitched sound, coldness, and a thin body silhouette. On the contrary, rose is the scent predominantly associated with a rounded shape, low-pitched sound, soft texture, and thick body silhouette. Concerning familiarity and pleasantness, lemon was rated as having high familiarity and high pleasantness. On the contrary, rose and pine were rated as having low familiarity and low pleasantness. Figure 5 shows the results on the scent–feature associations for the twelve different scents grouped by features.

Emotion Ratings of Scents. With the data collected from the SAM scale, we ran a repeated-measures ANOVA. Sphericity was assumed for all the variables. The results show a statistically significant effect ($p < .05$) for the features listed below. Post hoc analysis with Bonferroni correction were applied.

- Valence: $F(11,220) = 4.246, p < .001$
- Arousal: $F(11,220) = 2.267, p < .05$
- Dominance: $F(11,220) = 2.407, p < .01$

In summary, concerning valence, we found that peppermint and lemon were rated as significantly more positive than rose and pine. Concerning arousal, we found that peppermint, eucalyptus, lemon, camphor, and black pepper were rated as significantly more arousing than rose, lavender, vanilla, and patchouli. Concerning dominance, lemon was rated as more dominant than rose. Mean scores of emotion ratings are included in the Supplementary Material (Figures S2 and S3).

Intensity Ratings of Scents. With the data collected on perceived scent intensity using a 9-point Likert scale, we ran a repeated-measures ANOVA. Sphericity was assumed for the variable. The results showed a statistically significant effect ($p < .05$) for intensity, $F(11,220) = 16.357, p < .001$. Post hoc analysis, with Bonferroni correction, showed that the weakest scents were vanilla, rose, and patchouli, and the strongest scents were peppermint, eucalyptus, lavender, black pepper, and cinnamon. Mean scores of intensity ratings are included in the Supplementary Material (Figure S4).

Qualitative Descriptions of Scents. Scents are not always easy to describe and label [15, 41]. With the two open questions at the end of our experiment, we captured participants' descriptions and feelings elicited by the presented scents. Two researchers read through the responses individually first, and then together in order to identify commonalities and differences across participants. We noticed that scents rated as more familiar were described more coherently than unfamiliar scents. For example, lemon was always correctly identified ("lemon" or "citrus" labels) and, as personal feelings, described as "sweet", "pleasant", "nice", "fresh". When participants did not recognize the scent at all, the descriptions were more mixed and diverging. For example, patchouli was never correctly identified ("confused" or "strong") and in terms of feelings, it was described as "sharp" or "curious". To facilitate visual inspection, we created word clouds for each scent using the R word cloud package (see Fig. 6 as an example of a word cloud included in the EssCards).

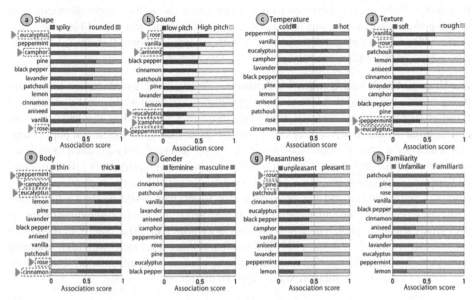

Fig. 5. Results on the associations between scents and bipolar sensory (a–d), bodily (e–f), and qualitative (g–f) features using the VAS scores. Dashed boxes and ▶ highlight the new scent–feature associations we identified in our study, thus extending existing literature on CCs.

3.7 Summary of Key Findings

Our results from the user study not only confirm previous associations between scents and other sensory features but also contribute new knowledge on CCs to the literature. Below, we summarize the new key findings for each of the three investigated groups of features, highlighted with dashed boxes in Fig. 5.

Findings on Smell and Sensory Features. Concerning scent-shape associations, our findings are in line with prior work [10, 24, 27, 28]. We also found new associations for the added scents. For example, rose was associated with rounded shapes while eucalyptus and camphor with spiky shapes. Concerning sound, we confirmed previously tested associations [10], but we further found that peppermint, camphor, and eucalyptus were associated with a high pitched sound, while rose and aniseed with a low pitched sound. With regards to the associations between scents and soft or rough textures, we did not confirm the findings of Dematte' et al. [16]. Indeed, our study showed strong associations between vanilla and rose and soft textures, and lemon and peppermint and rough textures. This could be due to the selection of pleasant scents only.

Findings on Smell and Bodily Features. We confirmed prior findings that link lemon with a thin body silhouette and vanilla with a thick body silhouette [10]. In addition, we found even stronger associations between peppermint, camphor, and eucalyptus and a thin body silhouette, and between rose and cinnamon and a thick body silhouette. For scent–gender associations, our findings were not significant, which could be due to the primary focus on scent–gender association without any additional features (as tested in [28, 32]). Further studies are needed to verify this assumption.

Findings on Smell and Qualitative Features. Finally, with regards to familiarity and pleasantness, we found that lemon and peppermint were rated as the most pleasant and familiar scents. On the contrary, rose and patchouli were rated as the least pleasant and familiar scents. With regards to the emotion assessment, we found that peppermint and lemon were rated as significantly more positive than rose and pine, even though we selected only pleasant scents. Concerning arousal, in line with prior work [10], we found that peppermint, lemon, and black pepper were rated as significantly more arousing than rose, lavender, vanilla, and patchouli. We also found new associations for the added scents (e.g., camphor and eucalyptus rated as high arousing). Concerning dominance, as previously shown in [10], lemon was rated as more dominant than rose. With regards to the intensity rating, as shown in [24, 28], we found that scents rated with high intensity were perceived as more familiar and pleasant (e.g., lemon and pepper-mint). Familiarity also played a role in the subjective descriptions participants provided.

4   EssCards and Design Explorations

The findings from our user study open up a range of future research directions to explore scent–feature associations. However, those results alone may not change the way designers approach scent–feature associations to create multisensory experiences. Hence, with the ambition to inspire the design of future interactions, we wanted to make our findings more engaging and accessible. Thus, we created the so-called EssCards – a set of cards that captures the key findings obtained in our user study. Below, we first describe the creation of the EssCards and then showcase their use in two design explorations.

4.1   Creation of the EssCards

To design the EssCards, we took inspiration from prior attempts to facilitate creativity through the use of design cards [23, 62]. The abstract frameworks into something more operational and tangible. As stated in [8], there are different types of design cards (e.g., exertion game design [38], tangible design [26], playful design [34]) but a common denominator is that they can facilitate design activity through keywords, pictures, and collaborative settings.

We adopted the card format as it is easy to use, printable, and easily shared and used online. Figure 6 shows an example EssCard for the scent of rose (the complete set of twelve cards is included in the Supplementary Material, section S.3). The EssCards set also includes an explanation card that describes the included data for first-time use. Each EssCard includes the following elements:

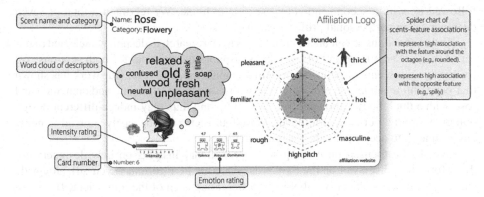

Fig. 6. Example of the EssCard for the rose scent, highlighting its main elements.

1. Scent name and category (food, flowery and woody).
2. Scent-specific generated word clouds based on participants' most frequently employed words to describe both the scent and the feelings associated with the scent
3. Intensity rating of the scent on a 9-point scale.
4. Emotion ratings of valence, arousal, and dominance for the scent (mean values of the 9-point SAM scale and the corresponding manikin for visual representation).
5. Spider chart of bipolar scent–feature associations for the scent, where "1" (outer layer of the chart) refers to a high association with the labelled feature (e.g., rounded) and "0" (in the center of the chart) refers to a high association with the opposite feature (e.g., spiky). In the shown example, we can see that rose is associated with a rounded shape (>0.5), thick body silhouette (>0.5), and low-pitched sound (<0.5).

To exemplify the possible use of the EssCards, we organized two exploratory design sessions – a group and an individual session. Both sessions are only meant to exemplify the possible use of the EssCards and collect some early-stage feedback from designers.

4.2 Design Explorations: Overall Approach and Design Brief

Using the EssCards, we organized two design exploration sessions to gain some initial insights into how scent–feature associations could inspire designers given a specific design brief (*"design a multisensory fashion garment that makes the wearers feel good about themselves"*). Below, we report a brief summary of both explorations to exemplify the possible use of our user study results in design. We do not provide detailed explanations of the design explorations and outcomes as these do not constitute the primary contribution of this paper, and further data collection is required. However, we hope to inspire through these initial explorations.

The original intention was to run in-person design workshops with designers. However, due to the COVID-19 pandemic and social distancing restrictions, we adapted our approach and moved the design explorations into an initial online group session, followed up with a second individual session at home. We recruited a total of seven designers from our personal professional network.

As these sessions are meant as initial steps from research to design, we selected a subset of the EssCards (four out of twelve) as inspirational material for both sessions. We focused on the scents of peppermint, lemon, cinnamon, and rose. Our work has shown that peppermint and lemon are associated with a thin body silhouette and cinnamon and rose with a thick body silhouette (see Sect. 3.6), and thus may induce different design outcomes around our brief. Moreover, those four scents can be easily sourced in home environments to accompany the design activities.

Overall, we focused on gaining some preliminary insights on how designers use the information displayed on the EssCards (shared in PDF format via email), alongside sniffing the scented objects (real objects representing each of the four selected).

4.3 Design Exploration – Group Session

The group session involved four designers (two male, two females, M age = 34.25, SD = ±8.42), all of whom, apart from one, had prior experience working with scents. The exploration consisted of two main parts: (1) a questionnaire to collect designers' educational and professional background, and (2) a two-hour online group session using Zoom as platform. The EssCards were shared via email before the group session. For the online group session, two subgroups were created. The designers were first invited to sniff the scented objects and focus on their own experiences and feelings for each of the scents. Then, they discussed and brainstormed ideas for the given design brief.

We collected comments and feedback, pictures of the scented objects, and design sketches made by the designers (see Fig. 7a–b). We noticed that the EssCards were consulted at the beginning without being explicitly reused again. This is in accordance with the study by Bornoe et al. [8], in which design cards were used as an initial source of inspiration and then put away for the rest of the design session.

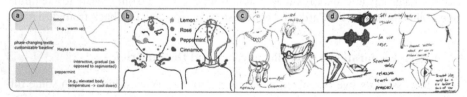

Fig. 7. Design outcomes from Group 1 (a) and Group 2 (b) during design exploration 1. Design outcomes from Designer 1 (c) and Designer 3 (b) during the individual design exploration 2.

In the final discussion with all designers, they all agreed that the EssCards would have been of great help during an in-person workshop as something tangible to work with ("I think if the workshop was not online, they could have helped just having them in hands") and they reported that having someone close by to share thoughts, comments, ideas with would have been nice. The affordances in an online design workshop were limited. Participants could have printed the EssCards, but it would not have been the same, as cards are often passed amongst designers to stimulate discussion and reflection.

However, despite this limitation, we can see traces of EssCard information in the designers' creations, such as in the use of scent–feature associations. For example, one group ideated a workout t-shirt made of fabrics with micro-capsules to spread scents based on wearers' body temperature during the workout ("...garments for workout made of phase changing material that you can program with temperature"). The designers described their approach as follows: "we are talking about lemon as a more uplifting and active scent and peppermint a bit more calming (..) so delivering lemon when the temperature increases and people are more active and peppermint to cool down, for stretching." (see Fig. 7a). Concerning the other group, the location of the devices on the body and the link between location, scent, and intensity of the scent flow (see Fig. 7b), can be seen as a reminder of the emotion and intensity data displayed in the EssCards (see Fig. 7b).

Based on our observations and designers' feedback, we further noticed that a key limitation was the online setting and the limited time available to define the problem, brainstorm, and create design ideas. Thus, we endeavor to adjust the setup and method to gain further insights on the use of the EssCards, this time using an individual design approach, carried out offline and spread over two weeks.

4.4 Design Exploration – Individual Session

Based on the lessons learnt from our first group exploration session, we refined our approach and gave designers more time to engage with the EssCards, scented objects, and design brief. The individual approach was chosen to enable an extended design exploration while still complying with the COVID-19 restrictions.

This second design exploration involved three designers (two male, one female, M age = 37.6, SD = ±8.31), who had no prior experience with working with scents. The exploration consisted of two main tasks (Sniff & Act) carried out at home by each individual:

- Task 1 (Sniff): We asked each designer to sniff the scented objects and complete online forms to collect their scent–feature associations through the same set of measures used in our user study (see Sect. 3.3). The aim of this task was to familiarize the designers with the scent–feature associations visualized in the EssCards.
- Task 2 (Act): We shared with the designers the set of four EssCards via email and they were given seven days to work on the design brief. They were invited to share any outcome from their design process and to annotate their design choices and thoughts. Once completed, we organized a final individual interview via Zoom.

The results from Task 1 matched the data visualized in the EssCards. Thus, we can confirm that the designers' scent–feature associations match our findings from the user study (described in Sect. 3.6).

Concerning Task 2, similar to the group session and prior work [8], all designers said that they used the EssCards at the beginning without explicitly reusing them again throughout the design session. As with the previous exploration, in the final interviews of the individual session the need for physical cards was confirmed. Each designer emphasized the usefulness of the cards as a physical object. However, we had to face constraints due to the continuous COVID-19 restrictions and remote design exploration. Future work can address this problem shipping to all participants a printed set of EssCards. Despite the limited use of the EssCards, we could again trace the information presented in the cards in the designers' outcomes, particularly in terms of shape and texture. For example, designers ideated goggles made of soft textile inspired by cinnamon, high heels with spiky shapes inspired by lemon, and rounded glasses inspired by rose (see Fig. 7c–d). All the sketches are included in Figures S8 and S9 in our Supplementary Material.

Overall, both the group and the individual design exploration sessions provided us with some initial opportunities to translate the findings of our user study into a design context. Despite the unusual setup in the form of online and remote design explorations, we received encouraging feedback from all designers on the use of scents and the EssCards, which opens new avenues for future interaction and experience design.

5   Discussion

Although recently designing olfactory interfaces and smell experiences has gained attention in the HCI community, there is still a lack of understanding of how smell can be used as a source of inspiration for designers. We focused on expanding the existing knowledge around CCs, running a user study to explore new scent–feature associations, and "translating" our findings into something that designers can easily engage with (Ess-Cards). Here, we discuss how we can think of scent–feature associations as inspirational material for designing future interactions and of the differences between "scent-inspired design" and "designing with scents".

5.1   Smell as Inspirational Material for Designing

It has long been known that the optimal design of products, systems, and experiences benefits from the broad consideration of all the senses [59]. Building on CC research allows us to think beyond single sensory stimulation and promotes the use of cross-sensory associations in design. Not only did we provide a detailed review of design features in relation to selected scents, but we also found novel scent–feature associations (see Sect. 3.7 for a summary of our findings).

We designed the EssCards to summarize and visualize the research findings. We observed that, in both design explorations, the use of the EssCards was limited to the beginning of the design activity. Hence, we can hypothesize that the EssCards are inspirational material during the design activity. Moreover, we noticed traces of the information represented in the cards within designers' outcomes, which makes us believe that they played an active role in the design explorations (e.g., high heels with spiky shapes inspired by lemon).

All designers mentioned that they would have liked to touch the cards and, if tangible, would have used them more. It remains to be studied how the physical use of the cards in in-person workshops would change the engagement as well as the outcomes.

Overall, we propose the EssCards as general profiles and summations of collected data on scent–feature associations and related emotion and intensity ratings that can be used to inspire designers easily and effectively.

5.2 Scent-Inspired Design and Designing with Scents

Based on previous work in HCI and on our observations in both design exploration sessions, we noticed two ways of thinking about scents: "scent-inspired design" and "designing with scents". While we are aiming to advocate the first with our work, the second is the dominant way of thinking about smell and design in HCI. Indeed, "designing with scents" reflects the approach when using the sense of smell as an "add-on" and involves the creation of wearable artefacts able to deliver scents (e.g., Essence [2]). An example collected from our design explorations is a t-shirt that delivers scents (see Fig. 7a). On the contrary, "scent-inspired design" is embedded in the creation of the Ess-Cards. While scents were not necessarily embedded in all the design outcomes collected from both design exploration sessions, they were present through characteristics of the outcomes based on the associations between the sensory features and scents. For example, rounded goggles inspired by cinnamon demonstrate the influence of scent–shape associations conveyed in the EssCards (see Fig. 7d). In other words, "scent-inspired design" does not need to result in the actual use and delivery of scents in the design outcome. Indeed, we imagine the use of the EssCards alongside with or even as a possible replacement of actual scents. Future work is needed to explore and compare designers' creations and experiences under different conditions with and without real scent stimulation.

It has been suggested that "smell is the Cinderella of our senses" [4] as it has acquired a poor reputation due to its subjectivity and difficulty to work with. However, increasing research is demonstrating the power of smell, and growing efforts are underway to establish the sense of smell in HCI for inspiring designers and designing olfactory interfaces. Our paper contributes to these efforts, showing that scent–feature associations can be a powerful source of inspiration as well as material to design with.

6 Limitations and Future Work

Despite the growing knowledge on the sense of smell in HCI, extended through our work, we also need to acknowledge limitations that require further investigation.

First, concerning the user study, we applied the VAS paradigm, visually presenting all the features with the exception of sound. We aim to conduct further studies with physical representations of the features, such as temperature (e.g., Peltier modules), texture (e.g., fabric swatches), or self-body representations (e.g., avatars in VR) to establish more fine-granular insights on scent–feature associations.

Second, digitalizing the set of cards allows us to add more information and, at the same time, designers to zoom in and out of the cards and enable a richer space of exploration. We also aim to improve the layout of the EssCards.

Third, future cross-cultural work could extend our findings on scent–feature associations to understand potential cultural differences around olfactory perception and scent–feature associations. Moreover, more qualitative data would be desirable to create a shared language around smell. We believe that the use of in-depth interview techniques such as micro-phenomenology can further enrich the EssCards information.

Fourth, it would be interesting to run more design explorations, in-person and online, with and without the EssCards and the scented objects, giving new design briefs. A set of EssCards can be shipped to designers to collect feedback on the layout, insights on the need of physicality, and discussion around their use during the design activity.

Fifth, although we explored how our EssCards can be applied in a design context, we believe that our results can also be used for other purposes to reach a broader HCI audience. For example, researchers could explore the use of the EssCards as an evaluation tool to engage with various categories of customers or as a teaching aid to share insights about multisensory and crossmodal association [13, 17, 44]. To facilitate these and other future explorations, including the study of further scent–feature associations, we have included a blank template of our EssCards in the Supplementary Material - section S.3.

7 Conclusion

Smell is a powerful sensory modality to inspire creativity and imagination, even though we are only starting to unlock its full potential. In this paper, we explored scent–feature associations relevant for designing future interactions and experiences. First, we ran a user study and established empirical evidence on novel scent–feature associations advancing existing knowledge on CCs. Second, we designed a visualization of our findings in form of a set of cards (EssCards). Then, we organized two preliminary design explorations to exemplify the use of the EssCards and obtain some initial feedback from designers. Finally, we discussed how future work can explore more systematically the role of smell in design practice.

Acknowledgments This work was supported by the European Research Council - ERC (grant number 638605). We would like to thank the participants and designers who took part in our research. Special thanks go to Dr Emeline Brule and Jesse Jesse Benjamin for providing valuable feedback on early drafts of our paper, and Rhiannon Armitage for the voice-over on our video.

European Research Council
Established by the European Commission

References

1. Amores, J., Hernandez, J., Dementyev, A., Wang, X., Maes, P.: Bioessence: a wearable olfactory display that monitors cardio-respiratory information to support mental wellbeing. In: 2018 Conference in Medicine and Biology Society (EMBC), pp. 5131–5134. IEEE (2018)
2. Amores, J., Maes, P.: Essence: olfactory interfaces for unconscious influence of mood and cognitive performance. In: CHI Conference on Human Factors in Computing Systems, pp. 28–34 (2017)
3. Barrett and H: https://www.hollandandbarrett.com/
4. Barwich, A.-S.: Smellosophy: What the Nose tells the Mind. Harvard Press (2020)
5. Belkin, K., Martin, R., Kemp, S.E., Gilbert, A.N.: Auditory pitch as a perceptual analogue to odor quality. Psychol. Sci. (1997). https://doi.org/10.1111/j.1467-9280.1997.tb00450.x
6. Bensafi, M., Rouby, C., Farget, V., Bertrand, B., Vigouroux, M., Holley, A.: Autonomic nervous system responses to odours: the role of pleasantness and arousal. Chem. Senses **27**(8), 703–709 (2002). https://doi.org/10.1093/chemse/27.8.703
7. Bonanni, L., Vaucelle, C., Lieberman, J., Zuckerman, O.: TapTap: a haptic wearable for asynchronous distributed touch therapy. CHI'06 Extended Abstracts. pp. 580–585 (2006)

8. Bornoe, N., Bruun, A., Stage, J.: Facilitating redesign with design cards: experiences with novice designers. In: Australian Conference on Computer-Human Interaction (2016)
9. Bradley, M.M., Lang, P.J.: Measuring emotion: the self-assessment manikin and the semantic differential. J. Behav. Ther. Exp. Psychiatry **25**(1), 49–59 (1994). https://doi.org/10.1016/0005-7916(94)90063-9
10. Brianza, G., Tajadura-Jiménez, A., Maggioni, E., Pittera, D., Bianchi-Berthouze, N., Obrist, M.: As light as your scent: effects of smell and sound on body image perception. In: Lamas, D., Loizides, F., Nacke, L., Petrie, H., Winckler, M., Zaphiris, P. (eds.) INTERACT 2019. LNCS, vol. 11749, pp. 179–202. Springer, Cham (2019). https://doi.org/10.1007/978-3-030-29390-1_10
11. Caon, M., Angelini, L., Abou Khaled, O., Mugellini, E., Matassa, A.: Towards multisensory storming. ACM Conference Companion Publication on Designing Interactive Systems (2018)
12. Crisinel, A.-S., Spence, C.: A fruity note: crossmodal associations between odors and musical notes. Chem. Senses (2012). https://doi.org/10.1093/chemse/bjr085
13. Darzentas, D., et al.: Card mapper: enabling data-driven reflections on ideation cards. In: Proceedings of the 2019 CHI Conference on Human Factors in Computing Systems, pp. 1–15 (2019)
14. De Groot, J.H., Semin, G.R., Smeets, M.A.: I can see, hear, and smell your fear: comparing olfactory and audiovisual media in fear communication. J. Exp. Psychol. Gen. (2014). https://doi.org/10.1037/a0033731
15. Delplanque, S., Grandjean, D., Chrea, C., Aymard, L., Cayeux, I., Le Calve, B., et al.: Emotional processing of odors: evidence for a nonlinear relation between pleasantness and familiarity evaluations. Chem. Senses (2008). https://doi.org/10.1093/chemse/bjn014
16. Dematte, M.L., Sanabria, D., Sugarman, R., Spence, C.: Cross-modal interactions between olfaction and touch. Chem. Senses (2006). https://doi.org/10.1093/chemse/bjj031
17. Deng, Y., Antle, A.N., Neustaedter, C.: Tango cards: a card-based design tool for informing the design of tangible learning games. In: Proceedings of the 2014 conference on Designing interactive systems, pp. 695–704 (2014)
18. Distel, H., Ayabe-Kanamura, S., Martínez-Gómez, M., Schicker, I., Kobayakawa, T., Saito, S., et al.: Perception of everyday odors—correlation between intensity, familiarity and strength of hedonic judgement. Chem. Senses (1999). https://doi.org/10.1093/chemse/24.2.191
19. Dmitrenko, D., Maggioni, E., Brianza, G., Holthausen, B.E., Walker, B.N., Obrist, M.: Caroma therapy: pleasant scents promote safer driving, better mood, and improved well-being in angry drivers. In: CHI Conference on Human Factors in Computing Systems (2020)
20. Ehrlichman, H., Bastone, L.: Olfaction and emotion. In: Serby, M.J., Chobor, K.L. (eds.) Science of olfaction, pp. 410–438. Springer New York, New York, NY (1992). https://doi.org/10.1007/978-1-4612-2836-3_15
21. Engen, T., Ross, B.M.: Long-term memory of odors with and without verbal descriptions. J. Exp. Psychol. (1973). https://doi.org/10.1037/h0035492
22. Ferrara, M.: Smart Experience in Fashion Design: A Speculative Analysis of Smart Material Systems Applications. Multidisciplinary Digital Publishing Institute, Arts (2019)
23. Halskov, K., Dalsgård, P.: Inspiration card workshops. Conference on Designing Interactive Systems (2006)
24. Hanson-Vaux, G., Crisinel, A.-S., Spence, C.: Smelling shapes: crossmodal correspondences between odors and shapes. Chem. Senses (2013). https://doi.org/10.1093/chemse/bjs087
25. Herz, R.S., Cupchik, G.C.: The emotional distinctiveness of odor-evoked memories. Chem. Senses (1995). https://doi.org/10.1093/chemse/20.5.517
26. Hornecker, E.: Creative idea exploration within the structure of a guiding framework: the card brainstorming game. In: Conference on Tangible, embedded, and embodied interaction, pp. 101–8 (2010)

27. Jezler, O., Gatti, E., Gilardi, M., Obrist, M.: Scented material: changing features of physical creations based on odors. In: Proceedings of the 2016 CHI Conference Extended Abstracts on Human Factors in Computing Systems, pp. 1677–1683 (2016)

28. Kaeppler, K.: Crossmodal associations between olfaction and vision: color and shape visualizations of odors. Chemosens. Percept. 11(2), 95–111 (2018). https://doi.org/10.1007/s12 078-018-9245-y

29. Keller, A.: Attention and olfactory consciousness. Front. Psychol. (2011). https://doi.org/10. 3389/fpsyg.2011.00380

30. Kilteni, K., Normand, J.-M., Sanchez-Vives, M.V., Slater, M.: Extending body space in immersive virtual reality: a very long arm illusion. PLoS ONE (2012). https://doi.org/10.1371/jou rnal.pone.0040867

31. Kortum P. HCI beyond the GUI: Design for Haptic, Speech, Olfactory, and Other Nontraditional Interfaces. Elsevier (2008)

32. Krishna, A., Elder, R.S., Caldara, C.: Feminine to smell but masculine to touch? Multisensory congruence and its effect on the aesthetic experience. J. Consum. Psychol. (2010). https://doi.org/10.1016/j.jcps.2010.06.010

33. Lee, J.: Design for all 5 senses. TED Talk (2013)

34. Lucero, A., Arrasvuori, J.: PLEX Cards: a source of inspiration when designing for playfulness. In: International Conference on Fun and Games, pp. 28–37 (2010)

35. Maggioni, E., Cobden, R., Dmitrenko, D., Hornbæk, K., Obrist, M.: SMELL SPACE: mapping out the olfactory design space for novel interactions. ACM Trans. Comput.-Hum. Interact. (2020). https://doi.org/10.1145/3402449

36. Metatla, O., Maggioni, E., Cullen, C., Obrist, M.: "Like Popcorn" crossmodal correspondences between scents, 3D shapes and emotions in children. In: CHI Conference on Human Factors in Computing Systems, pp. 1–13 (2019)

37. Motomura, N., Sakurai, A., Yotsuya, Y.: Reduction of mental stress with lavender odorant. Percept. Mot. Skills (2001). https://doi.org/10.2466/pms.2001.93.3.713

38. Mueller, F., Gibbs, M.R., Vetere, F., Edge, D.: Supporting the creative game design process with exertion cards. In: Conference on Human Factors in Computing Systems, pp. 2211–2220 (2014)

39. Nordin, S., Brämerson, A., Murphy, C., Bende, M.: A Scandinavian adaptation of the Multi-Clinic Smell and Taste Questionnaire: evaluation of questions about olfaction. Acta Otolaryngol. (2003). https://doi.org/10.1080/00016480310001411

40. Obrist, M., Ranasinghe, N., Spence, C.: Multisensory human–computer interaction. Int. J. Hum Comput Stud. (2017). https://doi.org/10.1016/j.ijhcs.2017.06.002

41. Obrist, M., Tuch, A.N., Hornbaek, K.: Opportunities for odor: experiences with smell and implications for technology. In: Conference on Human Factors in Computing Systems, pp. 2843–2852 (2014)

42. Porter, J., Craven, B., Khan, R.M., Chang, S.-J., Kang, I., Judkewitz, B., et al.: Mechanisms of scent-tracking in humans. Nat. Neurosci. (2007). https://doi.org/10.1038/nn1819

43. Rinaldi, L., Maggioni, E., Olivero, N., Maravita, A., Girelli, L.: Smelling the space around us: odor pleasantness shifts visuospatial attention in humans. Emotion (2018). https://doi.org/10.1037/emo0000335

44. Root, E., Heuten, W., Boll, S.: Maker Cards: Evaluating design cards for teaching physical computing to middle-school girls. Proc. Mensch Comput. 2019, 493–497 (2019)

45. Royet, J.-P., Koenig, O., Gregoire, M.-C., Cinotti, L., Lavenne, F., Bars, D.L., et al.: Functional anatomy of perceptual and semantic processing for odors. J. Cogn. Neurosci. (1999). https://doi.org/10.1162/089892999563166

46. Schifferstein, H.N.: Multi sensory design. In: Procedings of the Second Conference on Creativity and Innovation in Design, pp. 361–362 (2011)

47. Schifferstein, H.N.: The perceived importance of sensory modalities in product usage: a study of self-reports. Acta Physiol. (Oxf) (2006). https://doi.org/10.1016/j.actpsy.2005.06.004

48. Shepherd, G.M.: The human sense of smell: are we better than we think? PLoS Biol. (2004). https://doi.org/10.1371/journal.pbio.0020146

49. Sheskin, D.J.: Handbook of Parametric and Nonparametric Statistical Procedures. CRC Press (2000)

50. Shukla, A.: The Kiki-Bouba paradigm: where senses meet and greet. Indian J. Mental Health (2016). https://doi.org/10.30877/IJMH.3.3.2016.240-252.

51. Spence, C., Parise, C.V.: The cognitive neuroscience of crossmodal correspondences. i-Perception (2012). https://doi.org/10.1068/i0540ic.

52. Stevenson, R.J., Rich, A., Russell, A.: The nature and origin of cross-modal associations to odours. Perception (2012). https://doi.org/10.1068/p7223

53. Sulmont, C., Issanchou, S., Köster, E.: Selection of odorants for memory tests on the basis of familiarity, perceived complexity, pleasantness, similarity and identification. Chem. Senses **27**(4), 307–317 (2002). https://doi.org/10.1093/chemse/27.4.307

54. Trimmer, C., Mainland, J.: The Olfactory System. Conn's Translational Neuroscience. Elsevier (2017)

55. Van Doorn, G., Woods, A., Levitan, C.A., Wan, X., Velasco, C., Bernal-Torres, C., et al.: Does the shape of a cup influence coffee taste expectations? a cross-cultural, online study. Food Qual. Prefer. (2017). https://doi.org/10.1016/j.foodqual.2016.10.013

56. Von Hornbostel, E.M.: The unity of the senses. Psyche (1927)

57. von Radziewsky, L., Krüger, A., Löchtefeld, M.: Scarfy: augmenting human fashion behaviour with self-actuated clothes. Conference on Tangible, Embedded, and Embodied Interaction, pp. 313–316 (2015)

58. Wang, Y., Amores, J., Maes, P.: On-face olfactory interfaces. In: CHI Conference on Human Factors in Computing System, pp. 1–9 (2020)

59. Warrenburg, S.: Effects of fragrance on emotions: moods and physiology. Chem. Senses (2005). https://doi.org/10.1093/chemse/bjh208

60. Windlin, C., Ståhl, A., Sanches, P., Tsaknaki, V., Karpashevich, P., Balaam, M., et al. Soma bits-mediating technology to orchestrate bodily experiences. In: RTD 2019-Research through Design Conference 2019, the Science Centre, Delft, on 19th to 22nd March 2019 (2019)

61. Wnuk, E., De Valk, J.M., Huisman, J.L., Majid, A.: Hot and cold smells: odor-temperature associations across cultures. Front. Psychol. (2017). https://doi.org/10.3389/fpsyg.2017.01373

62. Wölfel, C., Merritt, T.: Method card design dimensions: a survey of card-based design tools. In: Kotzé, P., Marsden, G., Lindgaard, G., Wesson, J., Winckler, M. (eds.) INTERACT 2013. LNCS, vol. 8117, pp. 479–486. Springer, Heidelberg (2013). https://doi.org/10.1007/978-3-642-40483-2_34

63. Wright, P., Wallace, J., McCarthy, J.: Aesthetics and experience-centered design. ACM Trans. Comput.-Hum. Interact. (2008). https://doi.org/10.1145/1460355.1460360

Tales from the Materialverse: Comic-Based Narratives and Character Cut-Outs for Co-Design Fiction

Eleni Economidou[1](✉), Susanna Vogel[1], Nathalia Campreguer França[1],
Bernhard Maurer[2], and Manfred Tscheligi[1]

[1] University of Salzburg, Salzburg, Austria
{eleni.economidou,susanna.vogel,nathalia.campreguerfranca,
manfred.tscheligi}@sbg.ac.at
[2] Salzburg University of Applied Sciences, Salzburg, Austria
bernhard.maurer@fh-salzburg.ac.at

Abstract. Sequential art in the form of comics is a powerful and effective vehicle for graphic storytelling and communication, rendering it a suitable means for design fiction. Few, dispersed examples introduce comic-based design fictions in HCI research, yet little is reported on the design and implementation process or the use of paper cut-outs. In this paper, we present our process of crafting and implementing comics and character cut-outs for facilitating co-designing fictions. Our utopian visions, "Tales from the Materialverse", informed by our interest in future smart materials and their applications, were used as a provocative communication tool to mediate discussions and encourage critical thinking. Based on learnings derived from our process and an expert workshop, we propose suggestions for designing design fiction comics and cut-outs as an alternative co-design fiction approach.

Keywords: Comics · Design fiction · Co-design · Design tools

1 Introduction

Comics are an appealing and widespread entertainment medium of sequential art. Their visual language functions as a portal transporting the audience into a story [23], allowing for mental time travel to fictional worlds. Inherently, the comic format embraces the exaggeration element and facilitates identification with the main characters. When it comes to design fiction in HCI research - a technique where researchers employ imaginary narratives to explore fictional worlds, products, and concepts [23] - comics are under-explored. The limited examples (e.g., [21, 22]) present the final polished result, overlooking the process of conceptualising, designing, and implementing comics.

To fill this gap, we developed a co-design fiction approach based on comics. Our approach involves a design fiction comic booklet and character cut-outs

© IFIP International Federation for Information Processing 2021
Published by Springer Nature Switzerland AG 2021
C. Ardito et al. (Eds.): INTERACT 2021, LNCS 12933, pp. 302–311, 2021.
https://doi.org/10.1007/978-3-030-85616-8_18

designed in the context of a multidisciplinary research project on smart materials. As HCI researchers, our role in the project involves envisioning future smart material applications. Our design fictions act as a provocative means of future inquiry for evoking critical thinking and initiating discussions with our collaborators on the subject matter, with the ultimate aim to reach a common understanding and alignment. The booklet illustrates a fictional utopian narrative with an open ending. During a workshop, experts co-designed their ending to the story facilitated by the use of character cut-outs.

With this work, we contribute our comic-based design fictions and the process of designing and implementing them to the growing body of research on co-design fiction approaches. Through our suggestions, we envision broadening this design space and propagating the use of comic-based narratives and character cut-outs for facilitating co-creation in the context of design fiction.

In the subsequent section, we explicate the apt pairing of comics and design fiction by providing background into both areas. Next, we present our design fictions and the process of creating them. Further, we detail the expert workshop setup, procedure, and results. We conclude by formulating our lessons learnt from both the process and workshop insights as a series of suggestions for designing and implementing design fiction comics.

2 Background

Examples of traditional entertainment comics and visuals that depict visions of the future are recurrent and non-exhaustive. As early as the beginning of the 19th century Jean-Marc Côté and others depicted extravagant technology visions of the year 2000 [1], whereas more recently, examples such as the Ghost in the Shell manga series [20], depict technology-augmented humans with stories set in the near future. Over a decade ago, Marcus indicated that traditional entertainment comics started incorporating HCI-related concerns in their content, demonstrating awareness of HCI achievements and pitfalls [13]. Such works pinpoint the relevance of comic-based design fictions as a future inquiry for HCI.

2.1 Design Fiction Comics

In design fiction, comics are considered a suitable [23], yet under-represented medium. A prominent example we take inspiration from is work by Sturdee et al. [22], who made use of comics to explore their scenario of a digital empathy detector in a dating scenario. In their words, *"design fiction can be almost anything that creates a story world"* [22, p. 378], and indeed, other forms include diegetic prototypes [11], imaginary abstracts [3], and video sketches [18]. Other examples of participatory or co-design fictions approaches (e.g., [2]) do not involve comic-based scenarios.

In comparison to other visual narrative design fictions, such as live-action films [24] or short video clips [18], comics hold an advantage when it comes to creation time and hyperbole. Comics' visual language encourages the element of exaggeration [15], constructs an immersive environment, and allows the reader to identify with the fictional characters. Unlike films, comics are "permanent"; it is up to the reader to decide the pace at which information is consumed. In print form, comics afford a sense of ownership that digital means do not; Haughney noted that in studies participants tended to keep their comics' physical copy instead of dispersing it [9].

2.2 Comics in HCI Research

Design fiction aside, comics have been embraced in other areas of HCI research. Dykes et al. make use of them as a medium for illustrating their Research-through-Design (RtD) process [7], whereas Sturdee et al. present their alt-CHI provocation arguments in comic form [21]. Albeit the numerous examples, little reference exists on the comic's design process or the use of cut-outs.

When it comes to implementation, comics might not look dissimilar to story-boards [23], but they differ intent-wise; comics narrate a story and are a finished product, whereas storyboards are simply tools that guide product development. Instead of illustrations photostories utilise photographs to capture reality into stories. Rowland et al. make use of comics to showcase the potential of photostories implemented by both children and adults [19]. Comicboarding is a participatory design (PD) technique for co-creating or brainstorming [10,16], where comics are used as persona proxies so that children can share their ideas. Both photostories [19] and comicboarding [16] require an (experienced) artist to facilitate the process and convert participants' ideas into sequential art.

We situate our work in these design fiction examples and expand on the work by Sturdee and Lindley [23] on comics as a tool for inquiring the future. We do so by presenting and detailing our comic design process and showcasing how to implement comic-based co-design fiction sessions via paper cut-outs to elicit context-specific reactions and initiate discussions.

3   Our Design Process for Comic-Based Design Fictions

For our design fiction comics, we drew inspiration from McCloud's and Cohn's textbooks on comic creation [4,14,15] which divide the comic design process into narrative and illustration. Larson further splits the narrative part into three segments: ideation, plot development, and script [12], whereas the illustration part is divided into: art production (pencilling, inking, and colouring the illustrations), lettering (dialogue placed into speech balloons), and editorial (final checks). We opted for an episodic structure to explore diverse facets of the story world and to achieve flexibility in engaging with different stakeholders [8].

Narrative Design. Our narrative is shaped around the Materialverse; a future world presented through the eyes of a grandmother and her grandson. In contrast with traditional comic design practices where the starting point is the main storyline concept, our starting point (See Fig. 1) was an idea exploration based

Fig. 1. Our process of designing comic-based design fictions based on McCloud's textbooks [14, 15] and Larson's guide [12].

on preliminary non-fictional materials provided by our collaborators (i.e., wood-based 3D printing filament and translucent wood veneer). During the ideation, we defined sustainability-related values, such as circularity, which were translated into the first scenario ideas where we envisioned technology that has the ability to fulfil our visions. The narrative presented in this paper was based on this technology-based scenario and further outlined by crafting the characters. In hope for reader identification, we depicted an elderly person, 50 years in the future, conversing with a child. We added flashback elements from the past (the 2020s) into the story to underline the utopic facets of the story and add tension in the narrative, magnified by the two character's diverse perspectives. Once we defined the narrative, we created the plot structure and outlined the two characters' story-lines through narrative arcs (where peaks are followed by releases [4]). Deviating from established comic creation methods, we developed the story world as a worldbuilding practice [17], detailing its socio-technical assets (e.g., relations between citizens, objects, and technology, values, laws). We wrote the narrative's script collectively and divided the dialogue into pages with (a storyboard per page) based on the narrative arcs.

Comic Illustration. For the illustration part (Fig. 2), one of the authors translated the written script into digital illustrations, initially by outlining the main characters and their facial expressions and body language. We arranged the panels on each storyboard and placed characters in the panels accordingly. Afterwards, we cautiously drew future technology artefacts, elaborating on system functions and interaction possibilities. We proceeded with colouring, emphasising key elements of our story world. The dialogue was then positioned in each panel and, subsequently, speech and thought balloons were drawn around it. Finally, we reviewed the end result for spelling and other errors and combined all the comic pages, resulting in a six-page printed booklet.

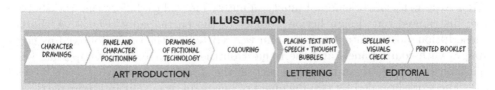

Fig. 2. Our process of illustrating our comic-based design fictions based on McCloud's textbooks [14, 15] and Larson's guide [12].

4 Tales from the Materialverse

Our fictional world is based on utopian circular economy visions situated in 2070, where all solid matter (i.e., metals, composites) could be 3D-printed and endure infinite life cycles. Contrasting the majority of design fictions, we opted for a utopian narrative; a hopeful scenario where people perform their best against all odds [5]. Albeit the utopian tone, we kept tension and conflict in the narrative to facilitate story climax and ensure engagement [8].

In the first episode of the Materialverse, the grandmother requests help in repairing her kettle with the MatterMix; a futuristic technological device that can manufacture or repair any device, or dismantle it into raw solid matter. We utilise the characters' dialogue to construe what changed from nowadays to 2070 and the eradicated concept of waste (See Fig. 3, left).

Fig. 3. Left: The comic's main characters, discussing the anachronistic notion of waste. **Right:** The last two panels of the comic booklet with a narrative peak ending.

In the second episode, the grandchild explains how to use the MatterMix, providing added clues on this new world, while the kettle gets repaired. For example, solid matter is viewed as a currency, used to construct technological devices and other material objects. Additionally, the knowledge around material science is open-sourced in a way that communities can collectively allocate materials where needed. The episode ends with a cliffhanger, a peak in the plot (i.e., the apex of narrative tension [4]) where the grandmother offers a 2 coin as a gratitude token and the grandson thanks her, while an empty thought balloon hovers above his head (Fig. 3, right).

5 Expert Workshop

To obtain qualitative feedback on the implemented comics, we recruited five HCI experts for a workshop of ninety minutes. Three days before the workshop, we distributed our design fiction booklet to the participants (Fig. 3). A short description of the context and the aim was written on the cover, followed by six pages with comic panels and the request on the last page of contemplating an ending, to provide them time to reflect on the story.

The workshop, led by two members of our team, was split into four parts: a short briefing of 5 min (introduction and consent), a 40-min feedback round on the design fiction booklet, a short (20 min) story-ending co-creation session, and a 25-min reflection part (discussing benefits and drawbacks of the approach and the use of paper cut-outs).

5.1 Feedback Round

The participants provided feedback, in a conversational manner, on the design fictions they had received. They addressed the comic's stylistic (e.g., wording, colouring, and depiction of future technology) and narrative elements (e.g., ending at a peak). Both the design and narrative were received positively, although the experts mentioned that some wording could be simplified or explained (e.g., protagonists, MatterMix), whereas selective colourisation confused one participant. In terms of narrative, the experts expressed that the booklet placed them into context and that the peak ending was intriguing.

5.2 Co-Design Session

Right after the feedback round, we split the group into two teams to co-create an ending to the story as they saw fit, in a 20-min. interval (Fig. 4, right). In anticipation of the participants facing difficulties in drawing the comic's characters, we prepared two sets of paper cut-outs (12 per set) of the main characters with different facial expressions and body language, beforehand (Fig. 4, left) to provide the same language form and facilitate the session. We suggested the use of the cut-outs and the whiteboard table surface installed at our research centre to draw speech or thought balloons or other objects. In each group, there was a member of our team observing and taking notes.

Two alternative endings were created; both teams made use of 5 or 6 of the provided cut-outs and 5 or 4 panels respectively. The experts drew speech balloons above the cut-outs to express the narrative of the ending verbally. Both teams drew the fictional technology presented in the booklets. Both endings depicted a similar narrative where the grandson reduces the coin into solid matter, yet one of them used humour for the release (the narrative's resolution) panels.

5.3 Reflection

In the final 25 min, we requested the two teams to read each other's story ending and discuss it as a reflection activity. We concluded the reflection with short feedback on the use of paper cut-outs. All the participants reported that they found the cut-outs helpful in completing the story; one of the experts specifically mentioned that the cut-outs *"takes(sic) away the fear of drawing, if you don't have confidence in your drawing skills"*. They suggested that different cut-outs could serve as inspiration. As Haughney noted [9], three experts requested to keep the comic booklets at the end of the workshop.

We compiled and classified our notes from the workshop and audio recording transcriptions into feedback on the comic design, the design fiction narrative, and reflections on the co-creation approach and the cut-outs. We formulated these findings into actionable elements, presented in the following suggestions.

Fig. 4. Left: Paper cut-outs assortment of the two main comic characters, used to support a co-speculation activity during the expert workshop. **Right:** Expert workshop, participants co-creating an alternative ending using comic character cut-outs.

6 Suggestions on Designing Design Fiction Comics

Based on insights from the experts' feedback, we propose a preliminary set of suggestions partitioned into stylistic, and design fiction elements of comic-based story worlds, and the implementation of character cut-outs.

Suggestions on Stylistic Elements of a Design Fiction Comic

- **Form matters:** Design a comic booklet or other tangible medium to facilitate the thought process of ending an episode. A tangible item may also trigger feelings of ownership and active engagement [6].
- **Style change assumes meaning:** Make use of the absence or presence of certain visual elements (e.g. colourisation and drawing style shifts) to indicate change in the plot and to highlight or draw attention to certain parts of the story.
- **Words and visuals are equal:** Visualise and name fictional technology cautiously as word choice affects interpretation and opens up discussions (e.g., on functionality), hindering dialogue on the rest of the content.
- **Visual simplicity:** Depict the characters or other entities simple enough so that they can be used as entities of a self-contained comic booklet or as character cut-outs, without compromising on the quality of the fiction.

Suggestions on Design Fiction Elements of a Comic Storyworld

- **Constructing believable characters:** Craft your design fiction characters as real people with believable backstories and convincing dialogue so that readers can empathise and identify with them. Keep tension between the characters for reader engagement [8]. Developing the story world extensively could further support this step.
- **Ambiguity before peaks as a stylistic element:** Use ambiguity elements in your design fiction narrative to allow for different interpretations [22]. In combination, introduce ambiguous objects right after a peak to offer a chance for questioning.
- **Capturing method:** Document the co-creation outcomes by using comparable means and have an observer in each team to take notes and photographs.

The set of cut-outs for completing the story facilitates comparison among the developed stories. Using a piece of paper as a working area instead of a whiteboard could be an alternative as Desjardins' et al. [6] showcase.

– **Boundaries for imagination:** Provide a fictional world in advance, to set the context and the right set of boundaries in which participants' imagination is free to develop their own story ending, instead of having a broad and open starting point. Another such boundary is the use of the character cut-outs.

Suggestions on the Use of Character Cut-Outs. Include enough depth and variation in the paper cut-outs to articulate how they would behave in a specific scene (e.g., via a range of different facial expressions and characters), as people inherently continue a story from a personal perspective. Through the paper cut-outs (Fig. 4, left) researchers and participants share the same language form and means to articulate ideas; a rather simple and low-technology technique for co-creation as it does not require an experienced artist to translate the participants' thoughts into visuals as in comicboarding [16]. Additional, object-based cut-outs could inspire and affect the completion of the story, providing guidance on other aspects of it (i.e., cut-outs depicting a technology artefact could guide or influence the participants in placing it in their story and exploring its functionality and interaction possibilities). However, the main character cut-outs were seen as more valuable for facilitating the completion of the story.

7   Conclusion and Future Work

In hope to open up the design space of comic-based co-design fiction, we presented our comics design process and suggestions for designing comic-based narratives and paper cut-outs as a tool for co-creating design fictions in a group setting. We found that the comics' narrative facilitated the co-design process in terms of communicating a fictional world, demonstrating how design fiction in a comic format can serve as a means of inquiry. In addition, the comic cut-outs provided support in co-designing an ending to the fictional story. In future work, we will make use of the design fiction outcomes for inspiration when designing future interactive systems. We see opportunities of implementing this approach as a co-design exercise in lieu of storyboarding, for establishing a common ground in multi-stakeholder workshops and initiating dialogue among participants.

The use of paper cut-outs provided support in co-designing an ending to the fictional story and seems promising as an idea-articulation means for co-designing fictions. Digitisation of this approach could be yet another step towards dislocated co-design fiction activities. Further implementation will be carried on in this direction and reported in future work.

Acknowledgements. We thank the HCI experts for their invaluable input and the reviewers for their constructive insights. This work is funded by the Federal government of Land Salzburg (WISS 2025) and EFRE (European Funds for Regional Development), AWS (Austria Wirtschafts Service) and Land Salzburg for the support in developing the Salzburg Center for Smart Materials (P1727558).

References

1. Asimov, I., Côté, J.M.: Futuredays : A Nineteenth-Century Vision of the Year 2000, 1st American edn. Holt, New York (1986)
2. Baumann, K., Caldwell, B., Bar, F., Stokes, B.: In: Participatory Design Fiction: Community Storytelling for Speculative Urban Technologies, pp. 1–1. ACM, Montreal, QC Canada (2018). https://doi.org/10.1145/3170427.3186601
3. Blythe, M.: Research through design fiction: narrative in real and imaginary abstracts. In: Proceedings of the 32nd Annual ACM Conference on Human Factors in Computing Systems (CHI 2014). pp. 703–712. ACM Press, Toronto (2014). https://doi.org/10.1145/2556288.2557098, http://dl.acm.org/citation.cfm?doid=2556288.2557098
4. Cohn, N.: The visual language of comics: introduction to the structure and cognition of sequential images. In: Bloomsbury Advances in Semiotics, Bloomsbury Academic, An imprint of Bloomsbury Publisher, London (2013)
5. David Johnson, B.: Utopia rising. Computer **47**(1), 87–89 (2014)
6. Desjardins, A., Key, C., Biggs, H.R., Aschenbeck, K.: Bespoke booklets: a method for situated co-speculation. In: Proceedings of the 2019 on Designing Interactive Systems Conference (DIS 2019), pp. 697–709. Association for Computing Machinery, New York (2019). https://doi.org/10.1145/3322276.3322311
7. Dykes, T., Wallace, J., Blythe, M., Thomas, J.: Paper street view: a guided tour of design and making using comics. In: Proceedings of the 2016 ACM Conference on Designing Interactive Systems (DIS 2016), pp. 334–346. ACM Press, Brisbane (2016). https://doi.org/10.1145/2901790.2901904
8. Hanna, J.R., Ashby, S.R.: From design fiction to future models of community building and civic engagement. In: Proceedings of the 9th Nordic Conference on Human-Computer (NordiCHI 2016), pp. 77:1–77:10. ACM, New York (2016). https://doi.org/10.1145/2971485.2993922
9. Haughney, E.: Using comics to communicate qualitative user research findings. In: Proceeding of the Twenty-Sixth Annual CHI Conference Extended Abstracts on Human Factors in Computing Systems (CHI 2008), p. 2209. ACM Press, Florence (2008). https://doi.org/10.1145/1358628.1358653
10. Hiniker, A., Sobel, K., Lee, B.: Co-designing with preschoolers using fictional inquiry and comicboarding, In: Proceedings of the 2017 CHI Conference on Human Factors in Computing Systempp (CHI 2017), pp. 5767–5772. ACM, Denver, May 2017. https://doi.org/10.1145/3025453.3025588
11. Kirby, D.: The future is now: diegetic prototypes and the role of popular films in generating real-world technological development. Soc. Stud. Sci. **40**(1), 41–70 (2010). https://doi.org/10.1177/0306312709338325
12. Larson, D.: Overview of the comic creation process (2014). https://www.makingcomics.com/2014/01/16/overview-comic-creation-process/
13. Marcus, A.: HCI goes mainstream in the comics. In: HCI and User-Experience Design: Fast-Forward to the Past, Present, and Future, pp. 265–269. Springer, London (2015), oCLC: 945966812. https://doi.org/10.1007/978-1-4471-6744-0
14. McCloud, S.: Understanding Comics: The Invisible Art. William Morrow, New York (1994)
15. McCloud, S.: Making Comics: Storytelling Secrets of Comics, Manga, and Graphic Novels. William Morrow, New York (2006)

16. Moraveji, N., Li, J., Ding, J., O'Kelley, P., Woolf, S.: In: Comicboarding: Using Comics as Proxies for Participatory Design with Children. ACM Press, San Jose, California, USA (2007). https://doi.org/10.1145/1240624.1240832
17. Fischer, N., Mehnert, W.: Building possible worlds: a speculation based framework to reflect on images of the future. J. Fut. Stud. **25**(3),(2021). https://doi.org/10.6531/JFS.202103_25(3).0003
18. Nicenboim, I., Giaccardi, E., Schouwenaar, M.: Everyday Entanglements of the Connected Home. ACM Press, Montreal (2018). https://doi.org/10.1145/3170427.3186596
19. Rowland, D., et al.: Sequential art for science and CHI. In: Extended Abstracts on Human Factors in Computing Systemsvol (CHI 2010), p. 2651. ACM Press, Atlanta (2010). https://doi.org/10.1145/1753846.1753848
20. Shirow, M., Schodt, F.L., Smith, T.: The Ghost in the Shell, 1st edn., p. oCLC: ocn567444265. Kodansha Comics, New York (2009)
21. Sturdee, M., Alexander, J., Coulton, P., Carpendale, S.: Sketch & The Lizard King: Supporting Image Inclusion in HCI Publishing, vol. 18, pp. 1–10. ACM Press, Montreal (2018). https://doi.org/10.1145/3170427.3188408
22. Sturdee, M., et al.: Design fiction: how to build a Voight-Kampff machine. In: Proceedings of the 2016 CHI Conference Extended Abstracts on Human Factors in Computing Systems (CHIEA 2016). pp. 375–386. ACM, New York (2016). https://doi.org/10.1145/2851581.2892574
23. Sturdee, M., Lindley, J.: Sketching & drawing as future inquiry in HCI. In: Proceedings of the Halfway to the Future Symposium 2019 on - HTTF 2019. pp. 1–10. ACM Press, Nottingham (2019). https://doi.org/10.1145/3363384.3363402
24. Superflux: Uninvited Guests (2015). http://www.superflux.in/work/uninvited-guests

Understanding the Role of Physical and Digital Techniques in the Initial Design Processes of Architecture

Emrecan Gulay[(✉)] [iD] and Andrés Lucero[(✉)] [iD]

Aalto University, Espoo, Finland
emrecan.gulay@aalto.fi, lucero@acm.org

Abstract. Architecture has been taking new turns with rapidly developing digital design and fabrication technologies. Consequently, establishing a link between physical and virtual design methods remains an open area for investigation. This paper explores the contemporary idea generation methods and the role of physical and digital design techniques in the initial design processes of architecture. We report our findings from interviews conducted with 14 participants consisting of experts and practitioners from the architecture field. Then, we discuss potential application areas of the results in the context of HCI research.

Keywords: Conceptual design · Physical model-making · Digital design

1 Introduction

The contemporary understanding of the architectural form led to departing from traditional design techniques (i.e., physical model-making, two-dimensional drafting, etc.) towards digital design and fabrication processes [28,29]. This transformation has changed architects' interactions with physical and digital design platforms. With the influence of nature-inspired movements and complex free-form geometries, parametric design tools and programming languages became increasingly prominent in architectural design processes [16]. *"Parametric design"* implies a rule-based digital design approach involving algorithmic thinking to model geometries in a programming environment [21]. Current digital design techniques enable architects to manage large amounts of data and handle complex design tasks. Despite their distinctive advantage, digital tools may not support material engagement [40] and the direct sensual information that the physical world affords. Norman [33] states that material properties, such as strength, stress, and texture, can only be experienced in the physical world. Digital and automated fabrication methods offer resources for realizing design ideas in the physical space. The term *"fabrication"* refers to the production process of physical prototypes out of digital 3D models or 2D vector drawings via

© IFIP International Federation for Information Processing 2021
Published by Springer Nature Switzerland AG 2021
C. Ardito et al. (Eds.): INTERACT 2021, LNCS 12933, pp. 312–329, 2021.
https://doi.org/10.1007/978-3-030-85616-8_19

subtractive or additive methods. Although fabrication techniques allow seamless design workflows, the divide between physical and digital platforms remains an open research area for architectural design processes.

Initial design processes play a critical role at the beginning of a project, and the impact of early decisions carries over to the construction stages. According to Rice and Purcell [41], initial design stages are where the seminal ideas and intentions are tested and laid down. During initial design processes, architects develop rough conceptual ideas by producing two-dimensional (2D) hand-drawn sketches, physical mock-up models, and three-dimensional (3D) digital visualizations. Architects also comprehend programmatic requirements, analyze the construction site, and generate building masses [22]. The later stages of design require detailed technical drawings and architectural documentation to communicate design ideas with people from various areas of expertise that operate within the same project [41]. Consequently, decisions made throughout the early stages can significantly impact design development as the ideas progress further. In this paper, we answer the following research questions;

1) What are the current idea generation practices in the initial stages of architectural design?

2) What roles do physical and digital design techniques play for architects while developing early design concepts and ideas?

Prior research within HCI and architecture domains explored the physical-digital integration and idea generation methods. With a specific focus on the initial design processes of architecture, our work explores the current idea generation methods and the role of physical and digital design techniques. We contribute to the existing research by providing up to date knowledge about the physical and digital design methods and the current situation in leading architectural offices/studios.

This paper is structured as follows. Our first section introduces the relevant literature within the areas of HCI and architecture. Next, we describe our methodology and interview processes. Then, we present the two main sections of the paper and report our findings regarding current ideation practices and the role of physical and digital techniques. Finally, we discuss the implications of our findings concerning the HCI community.

2   Related Work

We introduce relevant literature that focuses on physical-digital integration (TUIs and fabrication approaches), and idea generation processes in architecture (sketching and physical model-making).

2.1   Integrating Physical and Digital Design Methods (TUIs and Fabrication Approaches)

Integrating physical and digital design platforms has been explored within the HCI domain (i.e., tangible user interfaces and fabrication approaches). In the context of tangible user interfaces, Terrenghi et al. [48] studied the physical and digital media manipulation through a puzzle and an image sorting task. The study has revealed that digital interactions may not naturally encourage bimanual hand interactions that can be seen in the physical world. Earlier studies [42,43] with urban planners also identified a mismatch between the digital processes and the real-world outcomes. With a focus on landscape architecture, Ishii et al. [23] introduced a dynamic sculpting method enabling physical form-exploration and real-time digital feedback. Two tangible systems were designed and tested with clay [38] and sand materials. As part of the *metaDESK* [24] system, *activeLENS* allows touch-based interaction with the virtual information displayed on a screen. Äkesson and Mueller [2] explored real-time structural exploration by implementing a multi-touch display that enables physical manipulation of 2D geometries and a 3D form manipulation system utilizing a Leap Motion[1] sensor. These two implementations enhance initial concept development processes by combining physical interactions with real-time structural feedback. Sheng et al. [45] presented a physical proxy technique that employs a sponge as a physical input to sculpt 3D geometries on a computer screen. Scerbo and Bowman [44] explored physical interactions with the digital realm through commercial 3D motion tracking systems. Modelcraft framework [46] uses freehand annotations to extract data from physical models and feed them into the digital design platform during the initial design processes.

Prior HCI research introduced various fabrication approaches to address the separation between physical and digital design processes. *D-Coil* [36] is a hand-held fabrication approach that uses an additive wax coiling technique to bridge the gap between CAD models and physical artifacts. *MetaMorphe* [49], a digital fabrication framework, supports the manipulation and transformation of 3D static models into physical artifacts. *ShapeMe* [53] integrates physical architectural models with the 3D CAD modeling environment via a rapid inkjet printing technique. Willis et al. [54] established a real-time link between physical and digital design platforms with prototype devices that can convert touch and audio inputs to physical artifacts. Moreover, prototypes allowed designers to fabricate physical objects interactively and receive simultaneous digital feedback. Mueller et al. [32] presented an interactive and rapid fabrication system that reduces the need for physical assembly procedures. Ashbrook et al. [4] developed an augmented fabrication system for supporting novices to produce functional physical objects. Alongside the HCI domain, within the architectural discourse, Menges [31], Gramazio and Kohler [14], Oxman [34], and Iwamoto [25] have made important practice-oriented contributions with a focus on digital and automated fabrication approaches.

2.2 Idea Generation Methods in Architecture (Sketching and Model-Making)

This subsection reviews relevant research covering the techniques architects employ for expressing their ideas during the initial design processes.

---

[1] https://www.ultraleap.com/product/leap-motion-controller/.

Hand-drawn sketches play a critical role in the conceptual development phases of architecture, as in various other design disciplines. Goldschmidt [13] states that *"the generation of architectural form, by definition, is a creative activity."* Sketching with pen and paper supports creative processes by offering a platform to transfer and communicate design ideas. Goldschmidt [13] investigated sketching and the role of imagery in the context of architecture. The results showed that the ideation process that shifts between figure and concept is as systematic as other dialectic processes. Tversky [50,51] identified a link between the mental processes of designers and the order of their sketches. An in-depth review [50] of prior research confirmed that the order of drawing elements unveils the thinking structure underlying the design process. Perrone et al. [37] conducted interviews with architects to investigate the influence of preliminary drawings when designing architectural solutions. Furthermore, Rice and Purcell [41] studied the role of sketching in the early design stages of architecture from an educational viewpoint. Buxton [8] suggests that sketching is a way of *"exercising the imagination"*, and there may be different forms of sketching beyond pen and paper.

Besides two-dimensional freehand drawings, previous research also looks into physical modeling as a method for idea generation in the initial design processes. As Gedenryd [12] states, *"the writings of design theorists imply that the traditional method of design-by-drawing is too simple for the growing complexity of the man-made world."* Although two-dimensional sketches can facilitate complex design ideas, mock-up models support three-dimensional design exploration in a physical space. Gursoy and Ozkar [17] investigated model-making as a form of sketching by testing three different mediums *(sketches, physical models, and digital visualizations)* with architecture students. Moreover, Heimdal et al. [19] conducted experiments with architectural students and explored the potential of architectural models produced from textiles as tangible three-dimensional sketching tools. Knoll and Hechinger [27] introduced a comprehensive visual guide for building physical architectural models. Material engagement framework [40] is another contribution that addresses the relationship between the mind and materials. There are relevant works that focus on touch-based knowledge and haptic perception [18,26,30,39]. Digital tools have become prevalent in architecture. However, physical models retain their exploratory and tangible qualities for the initial design processes[14]. According to Dunn [11], if CAD alone had provided an adequate replacement for physical models, there would be no need for models produced using digital fabrication methods.

3   Methodology

In this paper, we present learnings, observations, and the visual data obtained from a total of 14 interviews conducted with seven experts (20 or more years of experience) and seven practitioners (between three to 20 years of experience) from leading architectural offices/studios in four countries. The first stage of the interviews took place in Finland. Then, we expanded our investigation in Switzerland, the United Kingdom, and Germany.

Initially, the study was planned as contextual inquiries to observe and comprehend how architects express and develop their ideas in the early design stages within their studio/work settings [6,20]. However, due to COVID 19 pandemic, we had to continue the study through virtual interview sessions. Before pandemic restrictions, we managed to conduct contextual interviews with three experts from three different companies in Finland. The contextual interview process (two hours in total) included an hour of participant observations followed by semi-structured interview sessions for covering relevant issues concerning our research questions. During the observation sessions, we collected photographs (i.e., sketches, conceptual drawings, physical models, 1:1 scale prototypes, digital visualizations) and drafted short field notes [10] without interrupting the participant's workflow. For the semi-structured interviews, fifteen questions have been prepared, with the addition of sub-questions, as a guide to utilize during the sessions. Hence, we did not follow a strict question order and conducted the interviews in a dialogue form. The rest of the interview sessions were conducted online (via Zoom and Microsoft Teams). Several participants shared images or sketches during the online sessions, and some participants sent them via e-mail after our discussions. Virtual interview sessions followed the same semi-structured format in a 45 to 60 min time frame.

The study aims to provide an up to date understanding of the early design stages and the role of physical and digital design methods in architecture. Therefore, while selecting participants, we focused on seven leading architectural practices that use cutting-edge digital design and construction methods and work with geometrically complex structures. We selected the participants based on publicly available portfolios and built projects. Through this selection process, we targeted to obtain relevant insights about the ongoing developments in architecture and the influence of digitalization on ideation processes. We reached out to participants via their work e-mail addresses. Before each session, participants were provided with an information sheet describing the study and the methodology. Alongside the information sheet, an informed consent form was sent to each participant. Participation was voluntary, and participants had the right to discontinue at any time without disclosing a reason.

Interviews were recorded and transcribed for data analysis. We used thematic analysis method [3,7] to comprehend emerging themes and relevant subjects. First, interview recordings and transcripts were transferred into ATLAS.ti, a qualitative data analysis software. Next, we found 11 main themes by going through transcripts, which included 42 sub-themes (codes). Codes were assigned to relevant sections of each transcript. Finally, we used the *"Smart Code"* tool to combine various themes and extract relevant quotes.

The following two sections present the interview outcomes by referring to participants' statements and relevant literature. We reference participants by using the letter P and a number (i.e., P3).

4   Current Idea Generation Methods in the Initial Design Processes of Architecture

For many architects, initial design stages are critical for exploring design solutions to fulfill programmatic requirements. Rice and Purcell [41] argue that conceptual stages are *"creative in the sense that the early expressions of thoughts and concepts need to give rise to spaces and forms often not seen before."* This section illustrates a variety of workflows and approaches architects adopt while developing initial design concepts.

4.1   Starting Points and Constraints

Physical and digital design techniques provide resources for early design exploration (sketching, physical modeling, digital visualizations). Although such design methods are widespread, architects do not always initiate the design process with blank papers or empty design spaces. One of the first questions we asked participants was their first starting point in an architectural project. The majority of the participants responded that before sketching up initial ideas, topology, scale, and surrounding areas of the project site needs to be comprehensively studied. P8 states, *"The initial task for the architect is to see how masses of the building can fit on the site to allow a proper site use."* Similarly, P3 says, *"You have to understand the program and also the site, the location, and the spirit of the place."* Statements gathered from participants imply that considering existing buildings and functional requirements is a significant first step in a new architectural project. During the early design stages, architects make many conscious and unconscious decisions. While making decisions, they also consider programmatic constraints. P9 elaborates, *"Well, you start with constraints because you are not on the moon or somewhere where there is nothing around you."* Other participants (P6, P2, P8, P9, P11, P14) also noted that their first starting point is understanding these limiting factors.

Participants who are fluent with digital design methods (P1, P5, P13) suggested that constraints and external factors can be seen as parameters that are components of a larger framework. P1 explains, *"If you have a strong concept and a structural framework, the logic behind that framework will make your design process very fluid."* Some participants emphasized that an architect's primary focus is to define parameters concerning the environmental, structural, social, economic impacts of the building. Such a parametric approach is essentially similar to the core logic of more conventional design approaches (P4, P8, P9). Remarks of P1, P5, and P13 indicate that modern parametric design tools have been influencing initial design approaches for some architects.

Several architects expressed different viewpoints towards parametric design thinking in the initial design processes. P8 and P4, who have more than 20 years of experience in the field, believe that architects also make visual decisions beyond parameters. P8 explains, *"We don't think much about the colors, textures, size or shape of windows at the beginning of the design. But, we think about how the building looks in the image of the city and the urban environment."*

Beyond parameters that address programmatic requirements, initial design processes of architecture may involve visual and spatial design decisions. As P4 states, *"Architects produce something to be seen, felt and touched. If you are making a physical object or a physical space, there's always an element of aesthetics."* P12 thinks that fixed parameters or visual inclinations will limit other potential outcomes: *"You just put some parameter, and something comes out. That is not an informed design."* Similar viewpoints (P2, P9) suggest that narrowing the process down to parametric definitions or a visual style may limit further design exploration.

4.2   Team Dynamic and Work Environment

By conducting three contextual inquiries and 11 online interviews, we gained insights into architects' team dynamics and work settings (Fig. 1) during idea generation processes. Conversations with participants unveiled that teamwork is a significant element of the initial design processes. Participants stated that they develop initial ideas as a team. For example, P5 describes how their team created early design concepts for a high rise project: *"We were three of us in the team. We sat around the table, and we developed maybe 10 to 20 initial concepts in half an hour."* Although each member can contribute individually during idea generation processes, final design decisions are made as a team. According to P3's description, architecture teams are led by a head designer. In some projects, specialists responsible for the restoration of old buildings can also be involved as decision-makers. The number of people in the group can vary (between three to eight architects) based on the project (i.e., commercial, residential, high-rise, etc.) P3 says, *"It's good to have a small team in the beginning. In our current project, we are three people. That's quite ideal."* 10 out of 14 participants agree that the team dynamic and workflow with the people involved in the project can influence initial design processes.

Fig. 1. Architects work with a variety of drawing equipment, computers, and material samples throughout the design processes.

In our contextual inquiries, we observed the participants and documented their work settings in three different architectural offices. Our observations and photographs show that there are individual and collective working areas. For instance, we observed a similar work setting in three of the offices we visited. Most architects utilize a large desk, or two desks, containing equipment for both digital and physical design processes. Computers, tracing papers, pens/pencils, material samples, and modeling tools are the types of equipment that can be found in architects' work-spaces. Some architectural offices work with physical models and 1:1 scale prototypes in separate workshop areas that contain digital fabrication machines. During the interview session, P8 stated, *"I think the physical modeling has its limitations. It takes more time to create them, but it also takes more time and space to transform, transport and store."* However, our observations show that architectural practices invest and create space for physical modeling despite limitations.

There are also architectural teams that prefer handling physical workflows and digital workflows separately. An executive of an architectural company (P7) explains, *"I see how much time and effort highly-trained architects show to keep up with the CAD development. My goal is to build our company in a way that we have a specific team of BIM (Building Information Modeling) experts."* Hence, a team of digital design experts could support architects for translating ideas into the software environment during the early design stages.

5   The Role of Physical and Digital Design Techniques While Developing Early Design Concepts

The previous section presented some of the core information obtained from the interview sessions. We looked into different initial design approaches and work settings. In this section, we focus on the role of physical and digital design techniques during the initial design stages.

5.1   Physical Design Techniques

Conversations with participants show that architects benefit from physical design skills by sketching and physical modeling. All participants stated that they use pen and paper sketching to express their initial design ideas. For instance, P1 elaborates, *"All of us start with the sketching. Even the offices working with just parameters and numeric factors of architecture start with sketches that you can see on their booklets."* Nevertheless, some participants noted that they mostly produce 2D sketches (i.e., plans, sections, elevations, etc.) but not 3D perspective drawings. P3 says, *"I don't do 3D sketches or perspectives by hand. During the (academic) studies we had quite a lot of drawing and artistic courses, but I don't draw like that so much anymore."* According to P5, sketching establishes a connection between the hand and the mind while creating spatial concepts. The participant (P5) adds that it is difficult to find a viable alternative to freehand sketching in the digital realm, and digital drawing tools are not offering the

Fig. 2. Example hand-drawn and computer-generated drawings documented during the observation sessions. Initial design sketches are translated into digital 3D models as the detail level increase.

convenience of a pen and paper. P2 suggests that the initial design phase requires a high level of abstraction, and a freehand sketch can provide information about designers' thinking process. Freehand sketching is one of the essential techniques to generate and develop ideas. Interviews reveal that most architects express their ideas through sketching with a pen and paper. Another interesting finding is that most of the sketches are transferred into the digital platforms as the ideas start to become more concrete (Fig. 2). P8 describes the process: *"I might put a tracing paper on top of the site plan and start sketching quickly. When I think I have something that looks good, I will go into the software and start building my massing model."* Several architects (P2, P4, P5, P8, P13, P14) reported similar workflows that shift from the physical form of drawing to a digital design environment.

Another essential design method is physical model making. Architects build physical models throughout the different stages of a design process (Fig. 3). P7 is one of the participants that utilize physical models for client meetings to display

Fig. 3. An example representational physical model that is built in a later stage of design.

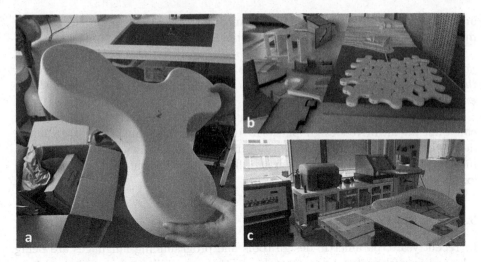

Fig. 4. a) 1:1 scale prototype produced for testing a curved structural system in early design stages, b) digital fabrication methods and traditional physical modeling techniques are being used in workshops, c) digital fabrication and physical model-making workshops include various tools for production and assembly.

their ideas in the physical realm. P7 says, *"The physical model is a strange thing. We bring our clients videos, cool rendered images. But if you show them a physical model, they go crazy. They can't stop looking and touching it."* In P7's case, physical modeling is used in later design stages to showcase and materialize the ideas created via CAD, 3D models, and sketches. However, physical models can also be employed as tangible design tools for structural exploration and form-finding (Fig. 4). As Gursoy and Ozkan [17] argue, physical modeling could be a three-dimensional way of sketching with materials during the initial design processes. P13 states, *"Hand-drawn sketches and physical models are exploratory tools. They can inform you in an early stage. If you are encountering problems already while doing small scale mockups, it is likely that the idea is not going to work."* Our conversations confirm that physical models are beneficial exploratory resources for architects, especially for creating complex non-linear structures. To exemplify, P2 is fluent with parametric design software and prefers a digital design workflow for architectural projects. P2 noted that one of their previous projects, a tensile structure made of wood plates, required extensive physical testing with models. Similarly, P1's team tested a curved windows system in a high-rise building via physical models before construction. P13 also benefited from physical models for their fiber-based complex structure: *"It is important to start this process with a small physical mock-up by taking the threads, making a scaffolding, and placing them on the scaffolding."* For some participants (P2, P4, P5, P6, P8), compared to 3D models on a computer screen, it is easier to understand the scale of a building through physical models. Furthermore, P10 and P14 suggest physical modeling is a more intuitive design approach than 3D modeling on a computer. P14 describes physical models:

"I think it is really about intuition, right? It is not this abstract thing that you are looking at. You are involved in it. It is like talking to the material rather than just talking to a block of geometry or a default material in the modeling environment."

Physical models form a link between the mind and materials [15], and they can offer an intuitive design platform to test, explore and materialize initial design ideas. Although there are various digital visualization and simulation techniques, physical models retain their significance for representation and structural exploration.

5.2   Digital Design Techniques

In recent years, parametric design tools and programming languages are being adopted by architectural practices due to their capability to generate and handle complex geometries. However, many architectural teams continue to use CAD and BIM (Building Information Modeling) software to produce 2D and 3D architectural drawings. Parametric design is mainly used for digital design exploration, whereas BIM is utilized in the later stages of a project to increase the efficiency of the construction process [21]. Moreover, CAD tools support producing 2D representations. Some of the most commonly used programs include ArchiCAD[2], AutoCAD[3], and Revit[4] for drafting (i.e., floor plans, sections, orthographic drawings, etc.) On the other hand, Rhino 3D[5], 3Ds Max[6], and Maya[7] are the software used for 3D modeling and photo-realistic rendering (i.e., V-ray[8]). Several participants (P2, P9, P10, P11, P12) utilize Rhino 3D in conjunction with Grasshopper plug-in, C Sharp, and Python frameworks. According to P3, 3D digital models provide valuable data during the initial design stages: *"Digital models are very informative for understanding the possibilities you have to use the space in 3D."* Experienced architects, P2, P3, P4, and P7, believe that digital design platforms are just tools that architects utilize for the initial design processes: *"We have to understand that digital tools are just tools for us, and they are developing all the time (P7)."* Nevertheless, some architects use computation to build dedicated design environments allowing a coherent design and fabrication logic. P9 explains through one of their projects: *"We set up tools that come from digital form-finding, but as importantly from the physical exploration based on how we want to control tolerances and aesthetics for specific fabrication strategies."* Therefore, beyond architectural drafting and representation, digital

---

[2] https://graphisoft.com/solutions/products/archicad.
[3] https://www.autodesk.com/products/autocad/overview.
[4] https://www.autodesk.com/products/revit.
[5] https://www.rhino3d.com/.
[6] https://www.autodesk.com/products/3ds-max.
[7] https://www.autodesk.com/products/maya.
[8] https://www.chaosgroup.com/.

techniques are employed to generate and manage an entire structural system from initiation to completion.

Advanced parametric techniques enable a flexible design environment where architects can create specific toolsets for projects by taking programmatic requirements and constraints into account during the initial design processes. However, participants also point out that digital methods should not be separating architecture from the physical realm. For example, P12 states, *"I am a very digital-oriented person. I believe we should be doing things digitally. But I think you cannot disconnect architecture and construction work or the physical building."* Furthermore, P9 describes the need for physical feedback through a specific case:

"Gravity. What you see on the computer is still a simulation, there is no gravity. When you are simulating gravity there is always an unknown because the outcome depends on your input and the assumptions that you make in the beginning. When you model the structure on your computer, you have perfect boundary conditions, perfect support, blocks that are contacting each other perfectly. But the reality is completely different."

P9 also notes that the simulation techniques they use are considerably advanced. Despite their capabilities, the cutting-edge parametric techniques and simulation engines may not provide sufficient information that the physical world affords. At this point, digital fabrication and automated construction technologies offer an integrated design workflow linking physical and digital processes. During our visits to architectural offices, we documented a workshop for building architectural models and 1:1 prototypes. In fabrication workshops, architects use various techniques (i.e., CNC milling, laser cutting, 3D printing, etc.) to transform digital models into physical prototypes. Apart from scale models, 1:1 prototypes inform both the early and later design stages by facilitating physical testing. P6 points, *"For us, prototyping is important to understand what type of solutions, even shapes are appropriate for a certain kind of fabrication strategy."* Custom computational resources allow the design and engineering of complex structural systems with the necessary fabrication data. Although a few participants point out (P2, P3, P8) that digital and physical design platforms complement one another, others think there is a divide between these realms. For instance, P6 illustrates,

"I see this in our team. People who are good with digital are often too disconnected from getting their hands dirty. That is why I keep saying that we have evolved towards a process where we want to make sure that we understand the system physically."

Participants described ideal digital workflows that can be developed in the future to facilitate intuitive initial design processes. As P4 reports, *"Maybe in the future digital drawing tools might be a way of incorporating hand drawings more into the design."* From a digital design perspective, P6 states, *"I believe we need to have a rule-based strategy. I would argue that computation can help us to discover exciting solutions, good designs starting from something that achieves and maintains a structural efficiency."* All participants expect that digital design techniques will become more prevalent in the future. P2 suggests that implementing artificial intelligence (AI) can provide efficiencies during the initial design processes. On the contrary, P8 believes that the parametric design and AI systems are not useful during the initial design stages. Several architects (P7, P9, P10, P11, P12, P13) emphasized the importance of an integrated physical and digital design process. As P12 elaborates, *"It would be quite nice if there is a feedback loop between what you are doing in the digital world and what is materialized."* Descriptions of the participants imply that an integrated design approach could support idea generation processes. Specifically, structural systems that utilize complex non-linear geometries require extensive physical testing. Connecting efficient digital frameworks with the physical design skills of architects could generate an intuitive design environment.

6   Discussion

In this paper, we presented our findings of the contextual inquiries and online interviews conducted with experts and practitioners within the field of architecture. The interviews uncovered some noteworthy points regarding initial design processes. In response to our first research question, the current idea generation practices in architecture mainly focus on developing a conceptual framework by analyzing the building site, physical conditions, topology, and scale. Although architects employ different approaches (parametric and visual) based on their computational or physical design skills, all participants initiate the process by comprehending the programmatic requirements and limitations. Therefore, constraints play a crucial role in the initial design processes. As prior research [13,41] and interview recordings suggest, initial design processes involve the creative input of the designer. Our results show that architects incorporate their creative inputs by considering constraints (i.e., construction methods, site, urban environment, etc.) instead of generating ideas in an unbounded design space. This finding could be a potential application area while developing tangible design tools for supporting architects. For example, tangible form manipulation methods (i.e., Song et al. [46], Sheng et al. [45], Ishii et al. [24]) could be expanded by focusing on the constraints in early architectural design processes. By considering the modern digital techniques, design constraints could also be explored as a part of fabrication frameworks (such as MetaMorphe [49], or ShapeMe [53].)

Another finding of the study is that even the participants that are fluent with digital tools utilize pen and paper sketching techniques while generating early design concepts. Consequently, participants use their manual design skills before benefiting from the efficiency of computation. To illustrate, P2 uses parametric design software and photo-realistic rendering tools to generate early design sketches. Although P2 mainly utilizes digital design software throughout the project development, the ideation process starts with freehand sketching. As the level of detail increases, hand-drawn conceptual drawings are translated into digital 3D models. Some participants also conduct testing via physical mockups or 1:1 scale models before establishing a computational framework for their designs. For instance, physical mock-up models play a central role in P10's non-linear structural systems. P2 and P3 tested the material behavior of complex structures by building scale models and 1:1 scale prototypes. Our findings indicate that architects extract information from sketches and physical mock-ups that they may not obtain from digitally generated models. Previous HCI studies [1,5,9,35,47] propose 2D and 3D sketching systems to enhance the initial design processes of architecture. We believe that these systems can be developed for promoting 3D and 2D explorations by incorporating various physical skill sets (i.e., drawing, model-making, assembling, etc.) of designers. One example is Rhino, a widely used 3D modeling software that integrates the Grasshopper plug-in and Python scripting language to generate intricate geometries. However, the software is still bound to a 2D graphical user interface and an abstract Cartesian design space. Consequently, participants prefer using physical models to discern the three-dimensionality of their initial designs. Implementing a tangible input (i.e., shape-aware materials [53]) or a proxy approach [45] into the Rhino would improve its current visual programming environment by allowing real-time intuitive physical and digital manipulations beyond a fixed coordinate system.

Architects work both with physical and digital design platforms in different stages of a project. Our second research question focuses on the role of these two platforms during idea generation: We learned that physical sketching and model-making are convenient methods to formulate, express, and test initial ideas, whereas digital processes support generating and managing complex architectural systems. One of the highlights of our investigation is the integration of physical and digital design methods. As in other design disciplines, the architectural design process progresses with iteration. From initiation to completion, architects develop their design ideas by taking the 1:1 scale performance and the construction site into account. Consequently, the feedback obtained from the physical realm is crucial for validating digital findings. Throughout the study, we documented physical 1:1 scale prototypes and mock-ups that architects use for materializing their ideas. Participants (P6, P9, P12) see physical prototypes as valuable resources for testing physical forces (i.e., gravity) that may not be precisely simulated in the digital realm, especially while working with non-linear geometries (P1, P2, P13). Observations and interviews also confirm that architectural practices continually invest in digital fabrication equipment and physical prototyping workshops. The results show that physical engagement with prototypes is becoming increasingly prominent despite the continuing digitalization in architecture. However, it is necessary to distinguish representational physical models from exploratory, structural test models or mock-ups. Detailed representation models are built for the client or public presentations, mainly in later design processes. On the contrary, exploratory physical models inform and impact the design process by providing data about the structural performance and material behavior. Participants pointed out a need for a more fluid initial design process that establishes a feedback loop between the physical and digital models. One method to achieve such a feedback loop could be through a bidirectional fabrication system (i.e., Weichel et al. [52]) by implementing 3D scanners to trace physical models in real-time.

We presented and discussed our findings from the interview sessions with architects. However, we acknowledge that there may be some limitations. For example, we conducted interviews in four different countries in Europe. The results may not represent the current situation in each part of the world. Despite the geographical limitation, this research can contribute to ongoing HCI research by adding up to date knowledge about the early design stages and the role of physical and digital design techniques.

7   Conclusion

This paper studies the current idea generation methods and the role of physical and digital design techniques with a focus on the initial design processes of architecture. Based on observations and semi-structured interviews, we presented and discussed the potential application areas of our findings. We contribute to the existing and ongoing research by providing up to date knowledge about physical-digital design workflows and the current situation in leading architectural practices. Our research can be adopted in the HCI domain to develop interactive systems and fabrication techniques to support architects during the initial design stages. By considering the feedback physical and digital platforms provide, intuitive tools, design workflows, and frameworks can be explored.

References

1. Abbasinejad, F., Joshi, P., Grimm, C., Amenta, N., Simons, L.: Surface patches for 3D sketching. In: Proceedings of the International Symposium on Sketch-Based Interfaces and Modeling, SBIM 2013, pp. 53–60. Association for Computing Machinery (2013). https://doi.org/10.1145/2487381.2487387
2. Akesson, D., Mueller, C.: Using 3D direct manipulation for real-time structural design exploration. Comput.-Aided Des. Appl. **15**, 1–10 (2018)
3. Aronson, J.: A pragmatic view of thematic analysis. Qual. Rep. **2**, 1–3 (1995) https://doi.org/10.46743/2160-3715/1995.2069
4. Ashbrook, D., Guo, S.S., Lambie, A.: Towards augmented fabrication: combining fabricated and existing objects. In: Proceedings of the 2016 CHI Conference Extended Abstracts on Human Factors in Computing Systems, CHI EA 2016, pp. 1510–1518. Association for Computing Machinery, New York (2016). https://doi.org/10.1145/2851581.2892509
5. Bellamy, R., et al.: Sketching tools for ideation (nier track). In: Proceedings of the 33rd International Conference on Software Engineering, ICSE 2011, pp. 808–811. Association for Computing Machinery (2011). https://doi.org/10.1145/1985793.1985909
6. Beyer, H., Holtzblatt, K.: Contextual Design: Defining Customer-Centered Systems. Morgan Kaufmann Publishers Inc., San Francisco (1997)
7. Braun, V., Clarke, V., Terry, G.: Thematic analysis, pp. 95–113. American Psychological Association (2014). https://doi.org/10.1007/978-1-137-29105-97

8. Buxton, B.: Sketching User Experience: Getting the Design Right and the Right Design. Morgan Kufmann (2007). https://doi.org/10.1016/B978-0-12-374037-3. X5043-3
9. Chen, X., Kang, S.B., Xu, Y.Q., Dorsey, J., Shum, H.Y.: Sketching reality: realistic interpretation of architectural designs. ACM Trans. Graph. **27**(2) (2008). https://doi.org/10.1145/1356682.1356684
10. DeWalt, K., DeWalt, B., Dewalt, B.: Participant Observation: A Guide for Fieldworkers. G - Reference, Information and Interdisciplinary Subjects Series, Rowman Littlefield Pub Incorporated (2002). https://books.google.fi/books?id=p1wcO3UNXQ4C
11. Dunn, N.: Architectural Modelmaking. Laurence King Publishing (2014). https://books.google.fi/books?id=2yN2oAEACAAJ
12. Gedenryd, H.: How designers work - making sense of authentic cognitive activities. Ph.D. thesis, Lund University (1998)
13. Goldschmidt, G.: The dialectics of sketching. Creativity Res. J. **4**, 123–143 (1991). https://doi.org/10.1080/10400419109534381
14. Gramazio, F., Kohler, M.: Made by Robots: Challenging Architecture at a Larger Scale. John Wiley Sons, Incorporated (2014)
15. Camilla, G.: Making sense through hands: design and craft practice analysed as embodied cognition. Ph.D. thesis, Aalto University (2017)
16. Gulay, E., Lucero, A.: Integrated workflows: generating feedback between digital and physical realms. In: Proceedings of the 2019 CHI Conference on Human Factors in Computing Systems, CHI 2019, pp. 1–15. Association for Computing Machinery (2019). https://doi.org/10.1145/3290605.3300290
17. Gursoy, B.: Is model-making sketching in design? In: Proceedings of the Design Research Society (DRS) Conference, Montreal, Canada (2010)
18. Hatwell, Y., Streri, A., Gentaz, E.: Touching for knowing: cognitive psychology of haptic manual perception. In: Advances in Consciousness Research. Touching for Knowing: Cognitive Psychology of Haptic Manual Perception, vol. 53 (2003). https://doi.org/10.1075/aicr.53
19. Heimdal, E., Lenau, T., O'Mahony, M.: Exploring textiles in architecture through tangible three-dimensional sketching tools. In: Paper presented at MAKING, Notodden, Norway (2012)
20. Holtzblatt, K., Beyer, H.: Contextual Design: Evolved. Synthesis Lectures on Human-Ce, Morgan Claypool (2014). https://books.google.fi/books?id=XHgDGwAACAAJ
21. Holzer, D.: BIM and parametric design in academia and practice: the changing context of knowledge acquisition and application in the digital age. Int. J. Archit. Comput. **13**(1), 65–82 (2015)
22. Huang, Y.S., Chang, W.S., Shih, S.G.: Building massing optimization in the conceptual design phase. Comput.-Aided Des. Appl. **12**(3), 344–354 (2015). https://doi.org/10.1080/16864360.2014.981465
23. Ishii, H., Ratti, C., Piper, B., Wang, Y., Biderman, A., Ben-Joseph, E.: Bringing clay and sand into digital design - continous tangible user interfaces. BT Technol. J. **22**(4), 287–299 (2004). https://doi.org/10.1023/B:BTTJ.0000047607.16164.16
24. Ishii, H., Ullmer, B.: Tangible bits: towards seamless interfaces between people, bits and atoms. In: Proceedings of the ACM SIGCHI Conference on Human Factors in Computing Systems, CHI 1997, pp. 234–241. Association for Computing Machinery (1997). https://doi.org/10.1145/258549.258715
25. Iwamoto, L.: Digital Fabrications, 1st edn. Princeton Architectural Press, New York (2013)

26. Jansen, Y., Dragicevic, P., Fekete, J.D.: Evaluating the efficiency of physical visualizations, pp. 2593–2602. Association for Computing Machinery (2013). https://doi.org/10.1145/2470654.2481359
27. Knoll, W., Hechinger, M.: Architectural Models: Construction Techniques. Journal Ross Publishing Architecture Series (2007). https://books.google.fi/books?id=wx8gudxqW60C
28. Kolarevic, B.: Architecture in the digital age: design and manufacturing. Nexus Netw. J. 6, 131–134 (2004). https://doi.org/10.1007/s00004-004-0025-4
29. Kotnik, T.: Experiment as Design Method Integrating the Methodology of the Natural Sciences in Architecture. Jovis, pp. 24–53 (2011)
30. Kuchler, S.: Materials and design. In: Clarke, A.J. (ed.) Design Anthropology, pp. 130–141. Springer, Vienna (2011). https://doi.org/10.1007/978-3-7091-0234-3_10
31. Menges, A.: Fusing the computational and the physical: towards a novel material culture. Archit. Des. 85(5), 8–15 (2015). https://doi.org/10.1002/ad.1947
32. Mueller, S., Kruck, B., Baudisch, P.: Laser origami: laser-cutting 3D objects. Interactions 21(2), 36–41 (2014). https://doi.org/10.1145/2567782
33. Norman, F.: Digital to analog: exploring digital processes of making. Int. J. Archit. Comput. 3, 191–202 (2005). https://doi.org/10.1260/1478077054214398
34. Oxman, R.: Digital architecture as a challenge for design pedagogy: theory, knowledge, models and medium. Des. Stud. 29(2), 99–120 (2008). https://doi.org/10.1016/j.destud.2007.12.003
35. Parakkat, A.D., Joshi, S.A., Pundarikaksha, U.B., Muthuganapathy, R.: Sketch and shade: an interactive assistant for sketching and shading. In: Proceedings of the Symposium on Sketch-Based Interfaces and Modeling. SBIM 2017. Association for Computing Machinery (2017). https://doi.org/10.1145/3092907.3122799
36. Peng, H., Zoran, A., Guimbretière, F.V.: D-Coil: A Hands-on Approach to Digital 3D Models Design, pp. 1807–1815. Association for Computing Machinery (2015). https://doi.org/10.1145/2702123.2702381
37. Perrone, R., Lima, A.G., Florio, W.: The sketches and the design process in architecture. Working papers in Art and Design, pp. 1–12 (2006)
38. Piper, B., Ratti, C., Ishii, H.: Illuminating clay: a 3-D tangible interface for landscape analysis. In: Conference on Human Factors in Computing Systems - Proceedings, pp. 355–362. Association for Computing Machinery, New York (2002)
39. Pohl, I.M., Loke, L.: Touch toolkit: a method to convey touch-based design knowledge and skills. In: Proceedings of the 8th International Conference on Tangible, Embedded and Embodied Interaction, TEI 2014, pp. 251–258. Association for Computing Machinery (2014). https://doi.org/10.1145/2540930.2540957
40. Poulsgaard, K.S., Malafouris, L.: Models, mathematics and materials in digital architecture. In: Cowley, S.J., Vallée-Tourangeau, F. (eds.) Cognition Beyond the Brain, pp. 283–304. Springer, Cham (2017). https://doi.org/10.1007/978-3-319-49115-8_14
41. Rice, S., Purcell, T.: The importance of early design sketches in architectural education. In: Proceedings of the 38th International Conference of Architectural Science Association ANZAScA. Architectural Science Association ANZAScA, Launceston, Tasmania (2004)
42. Russo, P., Lanzilotti, R., Costabile, M.F., Pettit, C.J.: Towards satisfying practitioners in using planning support systems. Comput. Environ. Urban Syst. 67, 9–20 (2018). https://doi.org/10.1016/2017.08.009
43. Russo, P., Lanzilotti, R., Costabile, M.F., Pettit, C.J.: Adoption and use of software in land use planning practice: a multiple-country study. Int. J. Hum.-Comput. Interact. 34(1), 57–72 (2018). https://doi.org/10.1080/10447318.2017.1327213

44. Scerbo, S., Bowman, D.: Design issues when using commodity gaming devices for virtual object manipulation. In: Proceedings of the International Conference on the Foundations of Digital Games, FDG 2012, pp. 294–295. Association for Computing Machinery (2012). https://doi.org/10.1145/2282338.2282406
45. Sheng, J., Balakrishnan, R., Singh, K.: An interface for virtual 3D sculpting via physical proxy. In: Proceedings of the 4th International Conference on Computer Graphics and Interactive Techniques in Australasia and Southeast Asia, GRAPHITE 2006, pp. 213–220. Association for Computing Machinery (2006). https://doi.org/10.1145/1174429.1174467
46. Song, H., Guimbretiere, F., Hu, C., Lipson, H.: Modelcraft: capturing freehand annotations and edits on physical 3D models. In: Proceedings of the 19th Annual ACM Symposium on User Interface Software and Technology, UIST 2006, pp. 13–22. Association for Computing Machinery (2006). https://doi.org/10.1145/1166253.1166258
47. Sun, Q., Lin, J., Fu, C.W., Kaijima, S., He, Y.: A Multi-Touch Interface for Fast Architectural Sketching and Massing, pp. 247–256. Association for Computing Machinery (2013)
48. Terrenghi, L., Kirk, D., Sellen, A., Izadi, S.: Affordances for manipulation of physical versus digital media on interactive surfaces. In: Proceedings of the SIGCHI Conference on Human Factors in Computing Systems, CHI 2007, pp. 1157–1166. Association for Computing Machinery (2007). https://doi.org/10.1145/1240624.1240799
49. Torres, C., Paulos, E.: Metamorphe: designing expressive 3D models for digital fabrication. In: Proceedings of the 2015 ACM SIGCHI Conference on Creativity and Cognition, CC 2015, pp. 73–82. Association for Computing Machinery (2015). https://doi.org/10.1145/2757226.2757235
50. Tversky, B.: What does drawing reveal about thinking? Visual and Spatial Reasoning in Design, pp. 1–7 (1999)
51. Tversky, B.: What do sketches say about thinking? Stanford University, pp. 1–4 (2002)
52. Weichel, C., Hardy, J., Alexander, J., Gellersen, H.: Reform: integrating physical and digital design through bidirectional fabrication. In: Proceedings of the ACM Symposium on User Interface Software Technology, UIST 2015, pp. 93–102. Association for Computing Machinery (2015). https://doi.org/10.1145/2807442.2807451
53. Wessely, M., Tsandilas, T., Mackay, W.E.: Shape-aware material: Interactive fabrication with shapeme. In: Proceedings of the 31st Annual ACM Symposium on User Interface Software and Technology, UIST 2018, pp. 127–139. Association for Computing Machinery (2018). https://doi.org/10.1145/3242587.3242619
54. Willis, K.D., Xu, C., Wu, K.J., Levin, G., Gross, M.D.: Interactive fabrication: new interfaces for digital fabrication. In: Proceedings of the Fifth International Conference on Tangible, Embedded, and Embodied Interaction, TEI 2011, pp. 69–72. Association for Computing Machinery (2010). https://doi.org/10.1145/1935701.1935716

Understanding Users Through Three Types of Personas

Lene Nielsen[1], Marta Larusdottir[2](✉), and Lars Bo Larsen[3]

[1] IT University, Copenhagen, Denmark
lene@itu.dk
[2] Reykjavik University, Reykjavik, Iceland
marta@ru.is
[3] Aalborg University, Aalborg, Denmark

Abstract. Personas is a suggested method to extend IT professionals' understanding of users and users' needs. A common advantage expressed is that personas extend the IT professionals' empathy for the users, but a disadvantage is that personas are typically defined at the start of a software project and gradually are forgotten, since there is little reference to the personas through the software development project. In this paper we report experiences of coaching IT professionals in defining agile user stories based on personas, called: Persona User Stories (PUS). The aim of these workshops, was to extend the usage of personas and thereby extend the IT professionals' understanding of their users. In a research project with three companies, we coached teams of IT professionals in three-hour workshops with 76 participants in total. The workshops were conducted at each company using personas already defined by the IT professionals. The persona descriptions were based on three types of information: (a) assumptions, (b) secondary research, and (c) data specific to a project. Our findings show that personas based on assumptions result in the participants questioning the description of the personas and having difficulties in understanding the personas. For making the persona user stories (PUS), the participants used themselves more often as a reference when working with the assumption based personas, than the participants using the other two types of personas.

Keywords: Personas · User stories · Persona user stories · Case study · Workshops · IT professionals

1 Introduction

Personas is a method that has been applied in the software industry for several years. One of the first to define the persona method was Alan Cooper [7] stating that personas are: "hypothetical archetypes of actual users" used during the software development process to represent the users, their needs and anticipated reactions to software being developed. Personas capture data in a form that enables empathy with different user groups [12, 22] and align user understandings internally in the organization [21].

© IFIP International Federation for Information Processing 2021
Published by Springer Nature Switzerland AG 2021
C. Ardito et al. (Eds.): INTERACT 2021, LNCS 12933, pp. 330–348, 2021.
https://doi.org/10.1007/978-3-030-85616-8_20

In this paper we study how personas can support IT professionals in defining user needs by using personas when describing agile user stories.

No standard definition exists of how to describe personas, but usually the personas are described by a fictive name and a description of goals, interests and preferences [23]. The description may also include a photograph, some text about a one-day experience and descriptions of life circumstances. A common advantage described of using personas in software development is that personas extend the IT professionals' empathy for the users, but a disadvantage is that personas are typically defined at the start of a software project and are gradually forgotten, since there is little reference to the personas through the software development project.

Interviewing is the most utilized method for the data gathering. It is labor-intensive to conduct the interviews and to analyze the data. Moreover, the interviews scale poorly and are thus costly [31]. Others have criticized that personas are not used that much during the software development and therefore there is even less reason to take on this time-consuming task. A study on the usage of UCD methods shows that personas are not frequently used by IT professionals even though the methods is quite highly ranked as being useful [16].

Especially in agile software development, IT professionals often describe user needs by defining user stories or epics, a quite common development process in the software industry. It is common to describe epics or user stories in one sentence, such as *"As a [user role], I want to [do some task] to [achieve a goal]"*, which is the most common format [6]. There is no difference between the format of an epic and a user story. The difference is that an epic is more comprehensive than a user story and it can be broken down into multiple user stories, while a user story is a small unit that cannot be broken down [4].

To investigate if IT professionals benefit from using personas while defining user needs, we conducted three workshops in three large companies in Denmark. The workshops used personas developed in advance by each company to define user needs by defining agile user stories based on the personas, called Persona User Stories (PUS).

In this paper we focus on the utilization of the personas based on three different types of personas: (1) personas based on hypothesis/assumptions of users; (2) personas based on secondary research with little domain-specific information, and finally (3) personas based on large amounts of data that is shown in the persona description. We wish to investigate how the usage of different types of personas affects IT professionals when writing Persona User Stories. For the sake of understanding the context within which the research takes place, we begin the paper by introducing background literature on personas and personas in agile development.

2   Related Work on Personas

In this section we will introduce related work on personas. We will introduce work on usage of personas in agile software development. We conclude this section by introducing related work on the relation to data from users in persona descriptions, personas based on assumptions and personas based on data from users, as this is important for the particular case.

2.1   Personas in Agile Development

It is complicated to incorporate a user perspective in agile software development. Personas have been suggested as a way of getting an understanding of users into agile development. They have typically been used as an up-front design method before the coding in agile software projects, referred to as sprint 0 [3], the result is a high-level specification [4]. It has been suggested to incorporate personas into the later process of coding, e.g. Cleland-Huang et al. [5] propose to create personas where each persona description has user stories with architecturally significant concerns. Hussain et al. [15] describe how personas can help guide the customer representative in the agile method XP (Extreme Programming) to identify user stories. Gothelf and Seiden [11] propose, in the Lean UX process, to divide the persona development into three small steps starting with proto-personas based on assumptions and develop these further with research to validate the initial assumptions. To incorporate the personas in the existing agile framework, several authors have suggested using personas for writing user stories [3, 6, 11]. Winter et al. [34] suggest a three-step model from defining personas, defining the context of use, to writing persona-driven user stories accompanied by a visual sketch of the use context. Similarly, Hudson proposes [14] to write user stories that are inspired by UML. Finally, a combination of personas and context of use for acceptance criteria in agile requirements has been suggested by Sedano et al. [32]. Common for the studies of personas in use, and in the specific environment of agile development, is that the studies do not look at how different persona descriptions perform when in use. We thus want to look at if the type of personas have implications for the understanding and utilization of personas while defining user stories.

2.2   Data Gathering for Personas

Over the years different paradigms have evolved that all are related to how much and the type of data that personas should be created upon. The origin of the persona method emphasized that personas should be abstracted from data and have a clear relation to data, whether qualitative or quantitative or a mix hereof [7, 12, 22]. Most often, personas are created using mixed methods, starting with secondary research, where research data is reviewed and interpreted but not gathered, and later using both qualitative research (e.g. interviews) and quantitative research (e.g. surveys) to gather data directly from users [12, 29]. The data used in the persona descriptions can be either specific to the domain that is designed for or more general collected to have many purposes.

Technology has developed since the introduction of personas and today it is much easier to incorporate big data, such as social media data for the creation of personas [1]. The personas based on quantitative data provides new opportunities to generate personas from social media and algorithms and machine learning libraries have made it possible to generate and automate the development process. The advantages are that the data is statistically valid and can be frequently updated [29].

Lastly, new paradigms have emerged that do not emphasize a relation to data, such as co-created personas and personas based on assumptions. Co-created personas reflect the users' daily lives as they are created by or together with the end users themselves [19]. In the next we will elaborate on personas based on assumptions.

2.3 Personas Based on Assumptions

The approach of using data was challenged with the arrival of methods such as assumption personas, ad hoc personas, and proto-personas [24, 26, 33]. Ad hoc personas [24], proto-personas [33], and provisional personas [10] are all hypothetical personas based on the design team's current assumptions about the user group. The assumptions are later to be tested through interactions with real users. The idea behind these sketches of personas is to make the assumptions explicit [11]. In the following, we coin assumption personas, ad hoc personas, provisional and proto-personas for 'assumption-based personas'. Assumption-based personas are, as the name suggests, based on the design team's assumptions and can be relatively easy to create. They are sketches of personas and give an overview of the team's suppositions and how these shape design decisions. They can be used to start the persona creation process [26]. Assumption-based personas are used when the time frame is tight [20, 27] or as a short-cut to being able to use methods such as scenarios [28]. They are often sketches, as illustrated by [11], and contain few selected information, such as a sketch of the persona, demographics, behavioral information, pain points and needs, and potential solutions [11]. Some development teams use them as an off-set for data-based personas [25, 32]. These personas can jump-start a persona process but have an inherent danger of not getting the real data. Companies might stick to their initial hypothesis, and they might build stereotypes that are never challenged with data [18].

In the following, we will distinguish between three types of personas. The first type is assumption-based (AB) personas, which are personas based on the design team's assumptions as mentioned above. The second type is personas based on secondary research, here called secondary research-based (SR) personas, and the third type is personas based on data explicitly gathered within a specific domain for a persona project, here called research-based (RB) personas. To our knowledge, no studies have reflected on what happens in the ideation phase when different types of data is reflected in the persona descriptions and if it affects the application of the persona method, in this case within user stories.

3 The Three Cases

In the study we performed three-hour long workshops in three large Danish companies (A, B and C) within shipping, insurance, and biotechnology. All the workshops were conducted by the same process. The aim of the workshops was to study if personas could be used to extend IT professionals' understanding of users by defining user stories. All the companies had predefined personas, which were of one of the following types in each company: (A) Assumption-based (AB) personas, based on hypothesis/assumptions of users; (B) Secondary-research (SR) personas based on secondary research with little domain-specific information, and (C) Research-based (RB) personas, which were data-driven personas based on large amounts of data that is shown in the persona description. In the following we describe the participants, the personas used in each workshop, and the workshop structure.

3.1 The Participants

We performed three workshops, one in each company A, B and C, with a total of 76 participants. All companies used an agile development process and reported that they used Scrum with their own modifications. The contact persons at each company had responded to an open invitation sent to a large number of people working within business, development, UX, and management. The contact persons recruited participants at their company. Most participants knew of each other, but some had not worked together before. The participants were most familiar with those with the same role. The roles of each participant can be seen in Table 1.

Table 1. An overview of the participants' roles

Participant role	Company A shipping	Company B insurance	Company C biotech
Business	7	10	9
IT development	9	3	3
UX	5	4	5
Management	3	3	5
Unknown		10	
Total	*24*	*30*	*22*

Table 1 provides an overview of the work areas of the participants in the three companies. The participants had different roles such as UX designer, developer, manager or business analyst (see Table 1). The participants were divided into groups of 4–6 members and each group was designed to have at least one participant from UX, business and agile development. The only deviation from this was company C where development is outsourced. Most of the participants were familiar with epics and user stories and could explain the concept to the other participants. As company C had outsourced development, the participants were less familiar with the concept of user stories and some groups struggled to understand what a user story is and the difference between an epic and a user story. The overview shows that the combination of participants' backgrounds are similar in the workshops in company B and C. However, in company A there were a higher number of people working within IT-development.

3.2   Persona Descriptions Used

All companies had newly developed personas that were presented to the participants at each workshop. All companies had developed the personas recently before the workshops. So most of the participants were new to the concept of defining personas and the persona descriptions used during the workshops. The companies had different numbers of personas. Company A had 2 assumption-based (AB) personas with a sketchy character; company B had 6 (SR) personas generated on secondary research with data not specific to the domain, while company C had 5 (RB) persona descriptions based on a large amount of qualitative and quantitative data that were visualized. An overview of the information in each type of the personas is given in Table 2.

Table 2. An overview of the personas in each company

	Company A	Company B	Company C
Number of personas	2	6	5
Domain	Shipping	Insurance	Biotech
Context	Based on hypothesis on customers	Based on internal secondary research of customers No domain specific information	Based on the company's employees worldwide. Domain specific information
Content	Demographics Technology use Needs and motivation concerning the domain	Demographics Personality Lifestyle Technology use and specific digital experience Attitude towards data security	Demographics Workday and way of working Technology use Frustrations Goals Preferences

In the following we will explain the differences of the persona types used in the three companies.

3.2.1   Assumption-Based (AB) Personas - Company A

Company A had developed two assumption-based (AB) personas with a short text in bullet form. The assumptions were based on hypotheses on customers of company A. The content included demographics, general knowledge, technology use of the persona, the persona needs and his/her motivation. One persona description is given in Fig. 1 (adjusted to keep anonymity).

Fig. 1. One persona assumption based persona description used in company A

3.2.2 Secondary Research (SR) Based Personas - Company B

Company B had developed six customer personas based on secondary research (SR) of previously collected data for other purposes. Here after we refer to those personas as SR personas. One example of a persona in company B can be seen on Fig. 2, (adjusted to keep the company's anonymity).

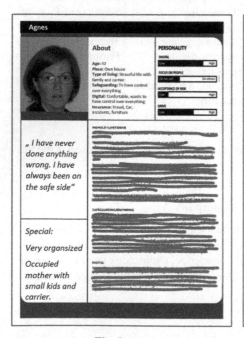

Fig. 2. Persona based on secondary research - company B.

The texts in the persona description were long and did not include attitude towards the specific domain of insurances. The content included demographics, personality, digital behavior, information channels and relation to the domain. Each persona was described on two pages.

3.2.3 Personas Based Data Specific to the Domain - Company C

Company C had developed five employee personas based on large amounts of data specific to the task. Here after we refer to those personas as research based (RB) personas. One example can be seen in Fig. 3, (adjusted to keep anonymity).

The information included visualizations of data. Beside the persona description, they had set up life-sized photostats of the personas in the office. The participants had seen the photo-stats, but not read the persona descriptions before the workshop. The content included demographics, workday, likely job roles, likely jobs, IT skills, frustrations, goals, and preferences. One of the personas can be seen on Fig. 3 (amended to keep company anonymization).

Fig. 3. Research Based Persona Used in Company C- Based on Domain Specifics

3.3 The Conduction of the Workshops

The workshops lasted three hours and fell into two parts. In the first part, the participants were asked to write user stories based on two different personas, which in company B and C were chosen from the pool of personas. These personas were picked to be very different in needs and attitudes towards the current IT system. The reason for picking two different personas was to make participants aware that they had more than one segment of users. The user stories were based on epics specific to current IT systems and defined before the workshops by the experimenters and the contact person in each company.

The schedule for the workshops was: Firstly, the participants got introduced to what would happen during the day and to the concept of personas for half an hour, then they got introduced to the particular personas at the company for half an hour. After the introductions the participants were instructed to write user stories based on a predefined epic. The tasks were carried out group-wise, where the tables in the room was moved around to accommodate 4–5 persons groups. These were predefined by the contact persons to assure the different roles (see Table 1). An example is given in Fig. 4.

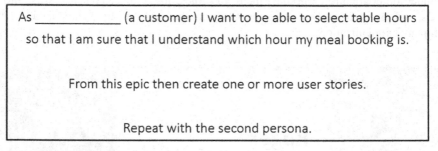

As _____ (a customer) I want to be able to select table hours so that I am sure that I understand which hour my meal booking is.

From this epic then create one or more user stories.

Repeat with the second persona.

Fig. 4. The epic from the workshop with company A (shipping).

The authors (who were also the facilitators of the workshops) gave a brief introduction to the concept of user stories. However, it was expected that the participants knew what a user story is or could be instructed by a developer, Scrum Master or Product Owner at the workshop. The participants had 15 min to write user stories for each of the two personas the team was handed. At the end of the workshop, a short plenary feedback session with discussions of the learnings was held. The participants provided user stories for both their appointed personas. In average, the group in company A and B wrote four stories per persona in the 15 min allotted. The groups in company C wrote, on average, three stories. This small variation might be explained in that the participants in company C had a harder time understanding the concept of epics and user stories and spent some time discussing what a user story is due to the lack of developers in the groups.

In the second part of the workshops, the participants were asked to write tasks to be used in a usability test with users. The tasks should be defined to evaluate the user stories created. The tasks were to be used during user testing of a prototype for achieving the user needs described in the user stories. This paper only reports from the first part of the workshops.

4   Method

In this section we will describe the data gathering and the data analysis. Data were gathered during the workshops. All group discussions during the group work and the plenary discussions during the workshops were audio-recorded and transcribed verbatim. Unfortunately, 2 group discussions were not recorded due to technical failures. The data collected are audio recordings of the group work sessions during the workshops, audio recorded comments from the plenary feedback sessions during the workshop and written documents that the participants delivered during the workshops. All in all, we have analyzed recordings from 13 group discussions (4 in company A and B, 5 in company C) lasting app. 30 min, and we report the findings in this paper. Similarly to Friess [9], we analyzed conversational turns, but we left out single words, such as OK and sounds that indicates agreement, disagreement or bewildering, such as Oh.

The 13 group discussion recordings lasted approximately seven hours and they were subsequently transcribed verbatim and have been analyzed in depth. The analysis started with open coding. To provide a stronger interpretive pattern, two researchers coded the same group discussion and from that created the foundation for the thematic units [13]. We have eliminated jokes, discussions of work and colleagues not related to the subject and single words, such as confirmations. The themes identified are: *understandings of contexts; understanding the task; reading the persona text aloud; design ideas; creating solutions; discussion of other services; discussions of user interactions; integration of facts into discussions; lacking data; references to own experiences; the persona in a scenario; comparing the two personas; interpretation of the persona*. We have primarily focused on the themes "*references to own experiences*"; "*lacking data*" and "*interpretation of the persona*". The authors have translated all quotations from Danish.

5   Findings on Personas in Each Company

In the following we report the findings on the interpretations on each type of persona. In the quotes, the three types of personas are in the following named as: (AB) for assumption-based personas; (SR) for secondary research-based personas; and (RB) for research-based personas. The number, e.g. G1, identify the group, so conversations from group 1 on assumption-based personas are marked: (AB)-G1. If more than one participant is quoted, they are numbered as Participant 1 and Participant 2.

5.1   Company A - Assumption Based (AB) Personas

Analysis of discussions shows that the negotiations around (AB) personas take a point of departure in an older persona. In this specific case, the participants cannot get income and travel behavior to match and **create a meaning**. To comprehend the information they invent a specific lifestyle. The conversion was as follows:

Participant 1: "It doesn't really make sense that he travels more than twice a year and that he has a moderate income [since he is so old]?
Participant 2: "Then he prioritizes travelling a lot. Maybe he has a small apartment?"
(AB)-G2.

Similarly, a participant from the same group, asks about the second persona:
"She travels by car to go on holidays, so she is probably driving to Germany and stuff like that, maybe Sweden?" (AB)-G2.

In the next quote, the participants try to narrow down the age of the persona's children as this is not mentioned in the description, where it is written she has two kids:
"Not that we can say how old the kids are. But I think also in, the kid... the kids are not 25, you mean." (AB)-G2.

These examples show that the participants do a lot of **interpretations** about the type of person that is described in the persona description.

One way of figuring out who the persona is, is to **refer to a type** of person rather than to the persona description, as seen in the next quotes from group 2:

Participant 1: "Yes, he is the type that wonders' why doesn't it say that I have got a table at the window. [Table] number 63, why can't I just choose that?" (AB)-G2.

And later in the conversation:

Participant 1: "But he is the type that doesn't have the latest browser version. He might not have the latest versions of different technologies."
Participant 2: "That's right. "
Participant 3:"He might still have Internet Explorer 8, because he is afraid of updating because it might cost money or something." (AB)-G2.

This conversion shows that both groups build up interpretations of who the user is, from guessing what type of person the persona is.

Participants had **difficulties in understanding the context**. One example is the following group discussion from group 3:

Participant 1: "But in the X restaurant you get free sodas, don't you?"
Participant 2: "No".
Participant 3: "It's 50kr. for the soda or something like that."
Participant 1: "I thought it was, what was it, a soft-drink machine?"
Participant2: "But you can buy a buffet, including a drink." (AB)-G3.

In this case, the participants struggle to figure out the setting of which route the persona takes and with this, which ship she is on and the meals on a specific ship. They end up spending time discussing the exact flow of having sodas with meals.

For the assumption based persona, the participants **draw on own experiences**, in this case their parents, to guess if the solution fits the age group.

One example can be seen from this conversation in group 5:

Participant 1:"At this age, judging by my parents, they are all about: 'Oh, let's try this new steak, because the other one, we had 67 times'.(....)"
Participant 2: "Maybe we shouldn't look too much on the age. Judging from my mom and dad - they're divorced and with their new partners. Dad likes to be very much in control, Mom likes to get out there and find something." (AB)-G5.

In summary the participants have to, in order to comprehend the information; invent information, interpretate the persona as a type, as they miss information, negotiate a context, and revert to draw on own experiences.

5.2   Company B - Secondary Research (SR) Personas

For the (SR) personas, the participants can relate to them, and one group feels that the female persona represents many customers to the company.

The group discuss a persona that has accepted not living together with her boyfriend, the information of how long the relationship has lasted and her attitude towards it, is not part of the persona description. To create a meaning, **they invent** a motivation. One participant states:

"She is just the type. They had a dream of living together, now 23 years have passed. 'We agree that this is fine as it is.' Why change something that isn't broke." (SR)-G4.

One way of figuring out who the persona is, is to **refer to a type** rather than to the persona description, as seen in the next quotes:

"Yes, she is the generation that is somewhat flighty" (SR)-G2.

In another group a participant remarks:

"I know she is a caricature. The quote is quite extreme: "I have never done anything wrong". No one would say that. But I think you can meet many, I am myself 42 years, many women here in [the company] that say this" (SR)-G5.

The participant also remarks:

"Overall, we have been pretty sensible in our lives, and we make good decisions. We are actually the same type" (SR)-G5.

Thus the participant is **validating information** with own experiences.

Participants showed signs of insecurity which was expressed by the participants as they **do not have data** on the personas:

"As it is now, we don't have, yes we know who Agnes is, but we don't have this kind of granulated data on her." (SR)-G4.

In summary, the participants invent information, refer to a type, validate information with own experiences, and show signs of lacking data. This occurred not as often as for the AB personas though.

5.3   Research Based (RB) Personas with Domain Specific Data

The (RB) personas are created based on the company's own workforce, which might be easier to relate to. The participants in this workshop also try to figure out who the persona is by **referring to a type** of person rather than to the persona description. One participant remarks:

"Isn't she the type that would like to have a basic tool?" (RB)-G3.

A participant from group 2 says:

"I think that Roger has a goal that it should run smoothly. If anybody in his team needs to be up to speed, then I think he will help them." (RB)-G2.

In the case of the RB persona, there is no mentioning of job roles, and this leaves the participants frustrated, and they **negotiate a job role** for the persona, as it is seen in the three quotes from three different groups.

One participant in group 5 says:

"It doesn't say anything here? It says he is away from his desk, but what about his phone, does he use that? It doesn't say. And it doesn't say anything about security, you can't have your phone with you in production – isn't it right." (RB)-G5.

A participant in group 4 says:

"If you have to come up with examples. One that works in Quality, who spends part of the time in the office, but also part walking around the site to see if production runs correctly. And it could be lab work or production work." (RB)-G4.

Finally a conversion from group 3 shows that participants struggle with this:

Participant 1: "Yes, he is around."
Participant 2: "No, on the contrary, he works factory."
Participant 3: "Yes he is factory… maybe a lab…"
Participant 1: "Yes that way he is around, but he is not someone who travels."
Participant 2: "No, he does not sit in front of the computer all day. He might be at storage, then he is out and about." (RB)-G3.

One of the many reasons for introducing RB personas in the biotech company was to break with the company's previous understanding of end-users as defined by job roles. As the examples above show it is not an easy task.

To understand the persona in known terms, some participants negotiated a specific role for the persona. In the example below the participant insists on talking about a production worker, despite the persona description mentioning multiple possible job roles for the persona. The participant remarks:

"He is a production man. I find the photo to be misleading. He should have a white lab coat on. He should be another age. I have this image, when I read it, of boys in white lab coats. He doesn't look 36. He should have white clogs on." (RB)-G5.

To change the internal understanding of employees seems to demand more than an introduction of personas.

The participants **draw on experiences** from their own family or colleague to guess if the solution fits the age group. In the first example, the persona is compared to the participant's nieces:

"Yes, I think it is one like Snap. What I really is puzzled about are my nieces, they take photos of their food all the time. What are they going to use that for? (…) My interpretation is, that he is in that category." (RB)-G5.

Another example of this is where some group members become aware of a shared implicit user that resembles one of the personas - and also many of their colleagues. One participant remarks:

"I think of Berit [a colleague] when I see her". (RB)-G5. The third example is from a comparison between the persona and many people from of the company: "What I want to say is, that I think that there are a lot of Susans [at our company] and I think that many of us have part of her in us. This, that we would like to see what happens and see the process, that's important. We don't like things where we can't see where we end." (RB)-G2.

Finally, the participants **compare own behavior** to the behavior of the personas, thus validating the persona:

"I have some of that Irene. We have Teams in our department, and some of what Irene likes, is the deadlines." (RB)-G2.

To sum up, the participants refer to a type, negotiate a job role, draw on own experiences, and validate by comparing to own behavior.

5.4 Summary of the Differences of the Personas in Each Company

In summary we have seen that for the Assumption based (AB) personas, these do not resemble the participants and the participants revert to stereotypical descriptions and negotiations when writing the personas user stories (PUS). Additionally we saw that there was little design relevant information in the descriptions, so the participants needed to interpret the user needs for the persona.

Contrary to this, the secondary research based (SR) personas resemble the participants, but they still have the tendency to revert to stereotypical descriptions and negotiations. Additionally, there is little design relevant information in these persona descriptions and we also saw that participants needed to interpret the user needs to some extent.

For the research based (RB) personas the personas also resembled the participants and there was more design relevant information in the descriptions, so the need for interpreting and guessing was less at that company.

6 Comparing and Discussing the Findings

From the analysis, we report from the thematic units identified from the themes in this section. The thematic units that are reported here are: requests for more data, discussing of the context of use, the participants use of own experiences, and finally, how much the participants refer to the written descriptions.

6.1 Requesting More Data

The references to lacking data vary for the three personas and between the groups in the company. In general, the groups working with the assumption-based (AB) persona are much more insecure, and they more often express a request for specific data. In contrast, the groups working with the research-based (RB) persona do not request more data. Looking at the discussion where participants lack data, there are different reasons for missing data. The discussions happen either when the participants feel insecure about the type of data they have and/or when they find that relevant data is missing.

There is a clear difference between the personas research based personas (DR) and RB) and the personas based on assumptions (AB), as the participants, in the latter, more often express a lack of specific information. With this lack, they need to revert to other sources of information, such as their own experiences, as seen in the next thematic unit; *references to own experiences*.

6.2   Reference to Own Experiences

When making the user stories, the participants refer to themselves, to colleagues, to family, or to knowledge from other sources to understand the persona better. In order to understand the persona, the participants draw on their personal and general knowledge of people they find is like the persona and they use their cognitive ability to categorize people into fixed types based on previous meetings with people and their cultural background [17]. This is tied to a lack of information in the description. Again there is a noteworthy difference between (AB) personas and (SR) and (RB) personas. The groups with assumption-based (AB) personas more often revert to talking about their own experiences, family or friends.

Common for both (SR) and (RB) personas is a comparison to colleagues, as in the example below. This is to be expected for the (RB) personas as the use context is of internal software. The lack of information creates a need for drawing on other sources of information. This is unavoidable as not everything can be represented in the persona description. However, the less information the description carry, the more the participants have to rely on their own experiences with the risk of creating stereotypes, as it especially is seen in the case of discussing age-related issues.

6.3   Describing the Context

The persona description can describe the context of use that is *where* the system will be used, *what* the goals and the user needs are for the usage, and even *what* technology will be used. This description is seen in the secondary research based (SR) persona where the context is in the home of the persona. It gets much more difficult to understand the context in the persona description when the context is on a ship (AB persona) or when the context is not clearly defined (RB persona).

The information about context, whether implicit or explicit, seems to play a role. The context is needed for the specificity of the user story. To understand the persona, the participants negotiate, with more or less success, where the use takes place. The importance of context is especially required when the surroundings are out of the ordinary (e.g. onboard a ship) or goes against an established way of looking at the persona (e.g. differentiate between employees based on job roles).

Company C is a special case as the organizational change to understand employees not from job roles, but from user needs, is not easy and the participants tries to revert to their shared understandings, from before the change.

6.4   Further Discussions of the Findings

This study is the first to compare different types of personas based on their data. There might be differences between the organizations and the participants that muddle the results. Furthermore, as already stated, the participants from company C were not as familiar with user stories as company A and B. Thus, in the future more rigorous evaluation studies are needed that let the same set of participants work with the same task, but different sets of personas. Especially research on the difference between using assumptions-based personas and data-based personas is needed.

Few studies have looked into the layout of the personas [21, 30]. In this case, the layout of the personas varied and future studies could look into which role the layout plays in connection to the different forms of personas and their usefulness.

Creating a user story is creating a specific instance of the user needs for that particular persona. A scenario is defined as including the context where the use takes place [2, 25] The persona description can indicate the context where the interaction takes place. This indication is seen in the secondary research based (SR) persona where the context is in the home of the persona. It gets much more difficult when the context is on a ship (AB persona) or when the context is not clearly defined (RB persona). In these two cases, the participants struggle to create a context. From the assumption-based persona, most participants do not have enough knowledge of the setting of use as they have not visited a cruise ship and need to create a shared understanding of how a restaurant works on board.

Empathy is defined as a complex imaginative process that includes a simulation of another person's situated psychological states [8] this requires access to information where it is possible to simulate. In the examples above, missing information or when the story is not comprehensive, the participants' makes information up with the purpose of creating a comprehensive story. Empathy benefits IT professionals when trying to understand the users' needs. In our study we can see that it is easier for IT professionals to gain empathy for users, when the personas are detailed and based on rich data, like the RB personas (e.g. in Fig. 3).

In summary, two conditions seem to influence how much the participants need to discuss and negotiate the persona in order to create a shared understanding: (1) if the persona resembles the participants, it is easier to understand and empathize with the persona (2) if there is more relevant information in the descriptions, it is easier to understand who the persona is. Thus the less the persona resembles the participants and the less design specific information, the more the participants revert to negotiations and stereotypical descriptions.

7 Conclusion

To our knowledge, no studies have compared the usage of different types of persona descriptions in industrial settings. This research contributes to an understanding of the perception of personas based on varying levels of data richness. The study shows that the foundational data have implications on the understanding and utilization of personas. The higher the data richness, the lesser the participants have to revert to their own experiences and guesses, and the more they can find the answers from reading the persona descriptions. However, it also shows that there is not much difference between secondary research-based and research-based personas. Secondary research can be considered as an easier way to create personas than collecting a large data sample while assumption-based personas seem to be more problematic when in use.

The discussions also show that the utilization of personas benefits from group work as the implicit assumptions become explicit, and the group members have to align their understandings. Many authors have promoted personas not built on data, such as proto-personas [11, 33] – sketches that later can be refined with more data. The industrial workshops with practitioners show that there is a correlation with the richness of data behind the persona descriptions, the relevance of the data, and how much designers and developers are forced to rely on their own experiences and how often they collectively have to create imaginative user stories. Furthermore, it also shows how insecure the project participants become on the solution when there are no facts to support it.

To summarize we have seen that the less data enriched assumption-based (AB) personas, make the participants guess and refer to own experiences more than in the data-enriched personas, even though the participants align their assumptions through group work.

Acknowledgement. This research is supported by Infinit – Network for digital innovation and new technology and Jeppe Emil Kjøller.

References

1. An, J., et al.: Imaginary people representing real numbers: generating personas from online social media data. ACM Trans. Web. **12**, 4 (2018). https://doi.org/10.1145/3265986
2. Aoyama, M.: Persona-and-scenario based requirements engineering for software embedded in digital consumer products. In: 13th IEEE International Conference on Requirements Engineering RE05 (2005)
3. Brown, D.: Agile User Experience Design: A Practitioner's Guide to Making It Work. Newnes, Oxford (2012)
4. Chamberlain, S., Sharp, H., Maiden, N.: Towards a framework for integrating agile development and user-centred design. In: Abrahamsson, P., Marchesi, M., Succi, G. (eds.) XP 2006. LNCS, vol. 4044, pp. 143–153. Springer, Heidelberg (2006). https://doi.org/10.1007/117741 29_15
5. Cleland-Huang, J., Czauderna, A., Keenan, E.: A persona-based approach for exploring architecturally significant requirements in agile projects. In: Doerr, J., Opdahl, A.L. (eds.) REFSQ 2013. LNCS, vol. 7830, pp. 18–33. Springer, Heidelberg (2013). https://doi.org/10.1007/978-3-642-37422-7_2
6. Cohn, M.: User Stories Applied. Pearson Education Incorporated, San Francisco (2004)
7. Cooper, A.: The Inmates Are Running the Asylum: Why High Tech Products Drive Us Crazy and How to Restore the Sanity, (vol. 2). Sams, Indianapolis (1999). https://doi.org/10.1007/978-3-322-99786-9_1.
8. Coplan, A.: Understanding empathy: its features and effects. In: Coplan, A., Goldie, P. (eds.) Empathy – Philosophical and Psychological Perspective. University Press, Oxford (2011)
9. Friess, E.: Personas and decision making in the design process: an ethnographic case study. In: Proceedings of the SIGCHI Conference on Human Factors in Computing Systems, pp. 1209–1218 (2012). https://doi.org/10.1145/2207676.2208572
10. Goodman, E., et al.: Observing the user experience: a practitioner's guide to user research (second edition). IEEE Trans. Prof. Commun. **6**(3), 260–261 (2013)
11. Gothelf, J., Seiden, J.: Lean UX: Applying Lean Principles to Improve User Experience. O'Reilly Media Inc, Sebastopol (2013)
12. Grudin, J., Pruitt, J.: Personas, participatory design and product development: an infrastructure for engagement. In: Proceeding of the PDC Conference, vol. 2, pp. 144–152 (2002)
13. Guba, E.G., Lincoln, Y.S.: Competing paradigms in qualitative research. In: Handbook of Qualitative Research, vol. 2, pp. 105, 163–194 (1994)

14. Hudson, W.: User stories don't help users. Interactions **20**, 50–53 (2013)
15. Hussain, Z., et al.: Agile user-centered design applied to a mobile multimedia streaming application. In: Holzinger, A. (ed.) USAB 2008. LNCS, vol. 5298, pp. 313–330. Springer, Heidelberg (2008). https://doi.org/10.1007/978-3-540-89350-9_22
16. Jia, Y., Larusdottir, M.K., Cajander, Å.: The usage of usability techniques in scrum projects. In: Winckler, M., Forbrig, P., Bernhaupt, R. (eds.) HCSE 2012. LNCS, vol. 7623, pp. 331–341. Springer, Heidelberg (2012). https://doi.org/10.1007/978-3-642-34347-6_25
17. Jung, H.Y.: The structures of the life-world. Northwestern University Press, Evanston, Illinois, pp. xxxvi, 335. $10.50 (1973). By Schutz, A., Luckmann, T. Translated from the German by Zaner, R.M., Tristram Engelhardt Jr, H. American Political Science Review. (1974). https://doi.org/10.2307/1959185
18. Liikkanen, L.A., et al.: Lean UX - the next generation of user-centered agile development? In: Proceedings of the NordiCHI 2014: The 8th Nordic Conference on Human-Computer Interaction: Fun, Fast, Foundational (2014)
19. Neate, T., et al.: Co-created personas: engaging and empowering users with diverse needs within the design process. In: Proceedings of the 2019 CHI Conference on Human Factors in Computing Systems - CHI '19, New York, New York, USA, pp. 1–12 (2019)
20. Newton, K., Riggs, M.J.: Everybody's talking but who's listening? Hearing the user's voice above the noise, with content strategy and design thinking. VALA2016: libraries, technology and the future (2016)
21. Nielsen, L., et al.: A template for design personas: analysis of 47 persona descriptions from Danish industries and organizations. Int. J. Sociotechnol. Knowl. Dev. **7**(1), 45–61 (2015). https://doi.org/10.4018/ijskd.2015010104
22. Nielsen, L.: Engaging personas and narrative scenarios. Ph.D. series 17, Copenhagen Business School (2004)
23. Nielsen, L.: Personas - user focused design (2019). https://doi.org/10.1007/978-1-4471-7427-1
24. Norman, D.: Ad-Hoc personas & empathetic focus. Jnd.Org. (2004)
25. Oderkirk, E., Jung, K.: From connect-exchange to ConnectX (2015)
26. Pruitt, J., Adlin, T.: The Persona Lifecycle: Keeping People in Mind Throughout Product Design. Morgan Kaufmann, Burlington (2006)
27. Bhattarai, R., Joyce, G., Dutta, S.: Information security application design: understanding your users. In: Tryfonas, T. (ed.) HAS 2016. LNCS, vol. 9750, pp. 103–113. Springer, Cham (2016). https://doi.org/10.1007/978-3-319-39381-0_10
28. Rooksby, J., Dimitrov, K.: Trustless education? A blockchain system for university grades. In: New Value Transactions Understanding and Designing for Distributed Autonomous Organisations Workshop at DIS 2017 (2017)
29. Salminen, J., et al.: A literature review of quantitative persona creation. In: Proceedings of the 2020 CHI Conference on Human Factors in Computing Systems, New York, NY, USA, April 2020, pp. 1–14 (2014)
30. Salminen, J., Guan, K., Nielsen, L., Jung, S.-G., Jansen, B.J.: A template for data-driven personas: analyzing 31 quantitatively oriented persona profiles. In: Yamamoto, S., Mori, H. (eds.) HCII 2020. LNCS, vol. 12184, pp. 125–144. Springer, Cham (2020). https://doi.org/10.1007/978-3-030-50020-7_8
31. Salminen, J., Jansen, B.J., An, J., Kwak, H., Jung, S.-G.: Automatic persona generation for online content creators: conceptual rationale and a research agenda. In: Personas - User Focused Design. HIS, pp. 135–160. Springer, London (2019). https://doi.org/10.1007/978-1-4471-7427-1_8
32. Sedano, T., et al.: The product backlog. In: Proceedings of the 41th International Conference on Software Engineering; ICSE'19 (2019)

33. Using Proto-Personas for Executive Alignment: (2012). https://uxmag.com/articles/using-proto-personas-for-executive-alignment
34. Winter, D., et al.: Persona driven agile development build up a vision with personas, sketches and persona driven user stories. In: Iberian Conference on Information Systems and Technologies (CISTI) (2012)

Designing for Smart Devices and IoT

Exploring Perceptions of a Localized Content-Sharing System Using Users-as-Beacons

Nazmus Sakib Miazi[1](✉), Heather Lipford[2], and Mohamed Shehab[2]

[1] Northeastern University, Boston, MA, USA
m.miazi@northeastern.edu
[2] The University of North Carolina at Charlotte, Charlotte, NC, USA
{richter,mshehab}@uncc.edu

Abstract. We envision a unique social interaction system, 'users-as-beacons' built upon Bluetooth Low Energy (BLE) beacon technology, that could provide potential privacy benefits. It leverages BLE to employ the user devices to act as mobile beacons. Its potential applications include community-based social networking, localized advertising, and instant reviewing. To evaluate the potential for this system and inform design, we conducted an exploratory interview study of 27 participants of a hypothetical localized content-creating system. Using a design prototype and multiple scenarios as prompts, we asked questions regarding users' perceptions of the potential benefits and challenges of a users-as-beacons system, focusing in particular on their privacy concerns and needs. Our results indicate that users do perceive the benefit of increased trustworthiness of user-beacons, but do not have expectations of greater location or behavioral tracking privacy. We highlight multiple design challenges of this system in supporting the trustworthy, relevant, and timely sharing of posts between people in a community.

Keywords: Bluetooth Low Energy · Beacons · Users-as-beacons · Internet of Things · Trust · Location privacy · Peer-interaction

1 Introduction

Bluetooth Low Energy (BLE) Beacon technology is primarily used for indoor location estimation and providing contextual information with low energy consumption and low-cost mobile beacons. BLE is widely adopted by a vast range of industries. For example, in 2016, 93% of U.S. baseball stadiums had been equipped with beacons to facilitate visitors finding seating locations, restrooms, and other facilities [1]. With over 90% of smartphones being BLE enabled [2], there are a variety of systems that potentially can be built on top of this technology. In fact, during the current Covid-19 pandemic, one of the privacy-preserving methods of contact tracing for limiting the spread of SARS-COV-2 infection is through BLE [3,4], utilizing its ability to detect proximity to other beacons without requiring GPS location. In this paper, we are exploring a potential use of beacons for a social system

© IFIP International Federation for Information Processing 2021
Published by Springer Nature Switzerland AG 2021
C. Ardito et al. (Eds.): INTERACT 2021, LNCS 12933, pp. 351–372, 2021.
https://doi.org/10.1007/978-3-030-85616-8_21

we refer to as 'users-as-beacons'. This system will leverage current BLE enabled smartphones by turning them into beacons themselves, which we refer to as a user-beacon. Combined with cloud integration, such a system can become a social web of information. This would enable a unique method of peer-to-peer interactions among users, with potential privacy and trust benefits.

In this platform, whenever user-beacons are within BLE range (100 m in the open, less indoors), they exchange their unique id's, allowing them to download each other's content from the cloud. We believe a users-as-beacons system can be deployed for a variety of social applications, including:

- *Community-based social network:* Users-as-beacons can be used for a localized social network, such as on a college campus, for circulating news and events throughout the community, or as a method of social posting within localized events and festivals.
- *Localized advertising platform for shopping areas:* If user-beacons are deployed throughout a shopping area, current offers, coupons, or other information from a shop can spread from one point to an entire area surrounding the store.
- *Crowdsourced localized platform for reviewing places:* Users-as-beacons can potentially be a localized instant review system for places such as restaurants, businesses, recreational facilities, and so on, similar to Google and Yelp but by crowd-sourcing from, and spreading to, users in a locality.

While a users-as-beacons system can offer functionality similar to existing social platforms or review sites, we believe it may provide several benefits, including

- *Trust:* We believe the platform will be particularly useful where a user would benefit from trusting the physical presence of another user. As the system would require a device to be physically present somewhere to be a user-beacon, faking a user-beacon would be a difficult task on a large scale.
- *Location privacy:* This platform enables an entirely localized method of user-to-user communication within Bluetooth range. Users need to be physically nearby another person, so users' locations do not need to be tracked or shared. Thus, the system may increase location privacy, as content can spread without the user-beacons sharing their GPS locations with the system or other people [5]. The system would also be resilient against GPS spoofing.
- *Localization and potential of peer-interaction:* This system provides a unique way of information dissemination, and thus allows potential peer-interaction among nearby users. Users may be able to directly meet and talk about a comment that they might think is helpful, which would make it more reliable and further increase trust. Yet, this potential for face-to-face interaction may raise privacy concerns and requirements for protecting one's identity.

Yet, similar to other social platforms this system will not be fully immune to adversaries, fake posts and location tracking. While requiring a beacon will make large-scale spoofing more difficult, there is no guarantee the beacon is connected to a real person. Moreover, the system could be more physically invasive since, depending on the implementation of the system, users could potentially be physically approached by others in proximity to them. Therefore, this kind of system will only be worth deploying if the benefits are valued by users when weighed against the potential privacy risks, all of which can be understood through use of the application. To investigate the potential of users-as-beacons applications and inform the design of such a platform, we conducted a formative study of user perceptions of envisioned applications of the system.

This paper explores the following research questions: (i) what privacy and trust benefits do users perceive of social users-as-beacons applications; (ii) what are users' expectations in how they would use such a system; and (iii) what are their privacy concerns or barriers to using such a system? We report the results of two versions of an exploratory interview study involving 27 participants from diverse backgrounds. The interviews were structured around a users-as-beacons design prototype [6] as well as several specific scenarios of the use of the system. Participants were asked about their perceptions in sharing and receiving content from people around them, their envisioned context and motivations of use, and their privacy concerns and expectations.

To summarize, the contributions of this paper are: (i) identifying the potential social applications of users-as-beacons involving mobile user-to-user communication; (ii) user perceptions of the potential benefits and use of a users-as-beacons review application; (iii) an understanding of the privacy concerns and expectations of being a user-beacon; and (iv) the design challenges and initial guidelines for implementing a privacy-preserving users-as-beacons prototype.

2 Application Example

One type of application we envision is a crowd-sourced, localized social platform, such as for sharing information at a festival. Figure 1 shows an example screenshot. In this scenario, 'Kim' visits a food festival and decides to share a picture of the food she likes. She takes a photo of her food and creates a post to share with others around her at the festival. The post's content is uploaded to the cloud. As Kim moves around the festival, her application advertises the ID of her user beacon using BLE to any other users she is near. Whenever she comes within BLE range of anyone else using the same app, their phones sense and store each other's BLE ID. Thus, the receiver can then see Kim's post. Receivers would have their

Fig. 1. Example of a 'users-as-beacons' app for creating crowd-sourced and localized posts in a festival.

own unique repositories of posts, depending on who has been encountered. There are a variety of features one could imagine in such a system, such as bookmarking and sorting posts, endorsing and forwarding posts, and customizing when the posts are shared and received.

3   Background

3.1   User Generated Content and Review Systems

In users-as-beacons applications, users become content creators, and share their content to their surroundings. Thus, research on user-generated content creation can inform the design of our proposed system. Hansen et al. [7] and Lawrence et al. [8] investigated the effectiveness of consumer-generated content and found that based on its realism, authenticity, and trustworthiness, user-generated content is much more effective than company-created content for advertising. Moreover, user-generated content can engage more people, and create a community of content creators [9–12]. Therefore, amalgamating with BLE to create a localized community of user-generated content creators has strong potential for building trustworthy social interaction.

One key type of user-generated contents that has been investigated are user reviews. Many platforms invest in incentives for reviewers, and sometimes even fake user reviews to appear competitive [13,14]. Much research has been done on how to identify and mitigate fake reviews in various review platforms, such as Yelp and Amazon. For any kind of review system, the reputation of the users and the reliability of their reviews are very important. [15–17].

One viable application of users-as-beacons is a localized review system similar to online review systems such as Yelp or Google reviews, but with reviews delivered based on physical presence that could potentially increase trust. In existing research, the user experience between the reviewers is often ignored, because there is little direct interaction possible. On the other hand, in a users-as-beacons system, physical interaction among the reviewers is much more likely to occur and could be seen as both beneficial and a cause for concern.

3.2   Data and Social Privacy in Mobile Systems

Users-as-beacons leverages users' capability of socializing with other users in a mobile environment. Unlike other social networking platforms, where it is imperative to manage one's personal information, in 'users-as-beacons' it is more important to maintain desired peer-interactions. There is a clear tension between reduced privacy risks by not allowing location-tracking, and increased reliability of contents, with potential loss of inter-personal privacy. Hence, it is essential to explore users' perceived comfort around others, as well as concerns regarding data dissemination, behavioral tracking, and privacy more generally.

In current social platforms, users are increasingly getting concerned about their data privacy, even while they are sharing significant amounts of information with other users [18–20]. As a result, we have seen the increased utilization of privacy settings and cautions about social interaction on popular platforms [21,22]. Behavioral tracking and targeted advertising on social sites are also important privacy concerns of many consumers [23–26]. As we explore social applications of user-beacons, we expect that similar privacy concerns will also be important factors in the design and adoption of such a system.

BLE technology is currently used to provide location-based services. While a users-as-beacons system is not dependent on estimating location and would not require the collection of location data, the system could still potentially infer location and users may still perceive the system as a location-based service. Users would still be sharing their proximity to surrounding user-beacons. Early studies found that location-based mobile services are often perceived as privacy intrusive, and users want granular control over location settings [27–29]. However, over time these concerns may fade, and people have become comfortable sharing their location with their friends and other users, provided that they have control over location sharing settings [30–32]. In contrast to sharing locations with friends, users remain concerned about sharing their locations with advertisers and third parties [33,34]. Yet, despite these concerns, many users regularly share their location with applications, perhaps due to their lack of awareness of the extent of location tracking [30]. We expect similar location concerns in users-as-beacons, which our study investigates.

Several frameworks have been developed to manage the security and privacy of BLE-based systems. Bello-Ogunu et al. developed a beacon privacy manager framework based on user-derived policies and their analysis showed that crowd-sourced privacy managers are effective for managing the privacy of BLE based systems [35]. There are different approaches to make BLE-sensing platforms more privacy-preserving by not allowing them to track the trajectory of users. For example, Higuchi et al. developed a *Anonycast* [36] to deliver precise location information to pedestrian's smartphones leveraging the crowd-tracking systems while keeping the users anonymous. Schulz et al. developed a security concept to prevent the possibility of requesting tracking and forgery in indoor location tracking beacons [37]. Gao et al. developed a privacy-preserving framework called TrPF [38] to preserve user privacy when the devices are deployed in a participatory sensing environment.

3.3 Proximity-Based Peer to Peer (P2P) Applications

Users-as-beacons is an example of a proximity-based peer to peer application, which have been previously investigated with other technologies. For example, Xing et al. developed a P2P proximity-based content sharing application using Wi-Fi [39]. Jung et al. developed a content sharing application to cooperatively download content from Bluetooth access points [40]. Shen et al. developed MobiUS, a collaborative video downloader application to watch high resolution videos over adjacent mobile devices [41]. And, Beach et al. developed WhozThat, a platform to share context-aware personal identification information to lower the barrier to social discourse [42].

However, none of these previous examples involve trusted reviews and social exchanges, particularly in a BLE-based interaction scenario. The only similar application scenario was introduced very recently with Covid-19 contact tracing. Several countries and organizations have created contact tracing systems to limit the spread of the SARS-COV-2 virus on top of BLE, as a decentralized, privacy-preserving proximity tracing system [3,4,43]. The privacy benefits of using BLE for contact tracing have made it reliable and effective. In this paper, we describe a more social use of this technology, which poses very different trade-offs between utility and privacy.

3.4 Users' Perceptions of BLE Beacons

Our idea of users-as-beacons is a system built on top of BLE beacons. Therefore, we now describe how people have already embraced this technology, as well as the privacy concerns and other challenges that have been raised. BLE beacon technology is especially useful for indoor settings, by enabling a plethora of location-based services [44,45]. While the technical implications of BLE beacons have been well researched, only a few researchers have examined users' perceptions and privacy needs around this technology. Thamm et al. [46] found that although 58% of the users have experience with Bluetooth, only 4% knew about BLE beacons. Also, even after explaining what BLE beacons are, 44% of the users did not agree to the use of beacons, mainly because of the fear of misuse of the collected data. Yao et al. identified several factors, including information flow and users knowledge about beacons system, that lead to people's conceptions of the technology and its privacy risks [45]. They suggested that user education is essential to reduce the likelihood of users overlooking real privacy problems, as well as mitigating unnecessary concerns. Bello-Ogunu et al. proposed a crowdsourced beacon rating system to allow users to define fine-grained policies for using particular beacons [47]. Although users-as-beacons is meant to be built upon BLE, the idea of having live user-beacons changes the privacy implications, with less potential for behavior and location tracking, yet increased potential for peer interaction and interpersonal privacy invasions. We seek to understand these perceptions in this paper.

4 Exploring User Perceptions

We conducted a user study with 27 participants to explore people's thoughts about a users-as-beacons system and its applications, factors they would consider in utilizing such a system, and their reactions to various situations unique to this system. We focused, in particular, on privacy concerns as compared to similar pervasive technologies. We chose a consumer generated advertising and review system as our example application domain to conduct the study, because this allows us to explore many different contexts of users' daily lives. We conducted an interview study, using a design prototype to enable participants to have a more concrete understanding of sharing and receiving posts or reviews (Fig. 2).

We also described several different scenarios that participants might face in using the system as a prompt for additional interview questions. These scenarios and the summary of the interview questions are described below.

Initially, the design prototype and scenarios centered around usage in shopping and advertising products. However, after conducting 13 interviews, we found that a significant portion of the participants saw greater potential in the use of a users-as-beacons system in other contexts such as restaurant review, social interaction, or event promotion. Thus, we redesigned the design prototype and study scenarios to explore the possibility of deploying the system in more social contexts. We then interviewed 14 additional participants. Each interview was conducted in an indoor lab setting and took approximately 40–45 min. At the beginning of each interview we described the functionality of a user-beacons system and our design prototype briefly to the participants. Both of the user study designs were approved by our university IRB.

4.1   User Study 1: Users-as-Beacons in a Shopping Area

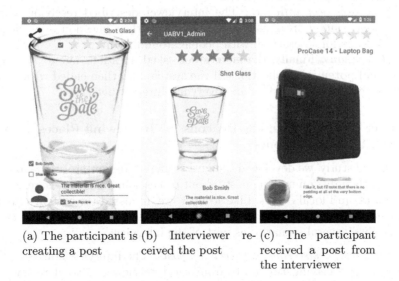

(a) The participant is creating a post   (b) Interviewer received the post   (c) The participant received a post from the interviewer

Fig. 2. Screen-shots of the design prototype built for conducting study 1.

– *Scenario one, signing up and creating posts:* We started the study by asking the participants to register themselves using our design prototype. Then we discussed a shopping mall scenario, asking the participant to select an example product and write and share a review. When the participant shared the post, the interviewer received it (Fig. 2b). Then the interviewer showed the participant the receiver's view and asked about their general perceptions of using such a system, and their opinion of sharing their personal information in the reviews.

– *Scenario two, receiving posts:* The participant then received a review from the interviewer (Fig. 2c), and was asked about their perceptions of receiving posts from those around them, their intentions about interacting with others, and their perceived motivations for making posts.

– *Scenario three, different places:* The interviewer described a daily life scenario where the user's device is beaconing throughout the day, in various contexts. The interviewer then asked about beaconing in different places and incentives that may impact usage decisions.

– *Scenario four, control over the system:* To understand the participant's reaction toward interacting with other users, we outlined a scenario where we gave the participant some controls to avoid the interaction by adding a short delay to a posted review. Participants then described their perceptions of that potential feature and its use and other kinds of desired controls in the system.

– *Scenario five, content types:* Here, the interviewer asked the participant to create a review of sensitive content (underwear), and then asked about the perceived comfort of sharing reviews of different kinds of content, along with the impact of potential incentives.

– *Scenario six, peer influence:* The interviewer described receiving a review of desired content from someone nearby and then questioned participants' expectations for interaction with people around them.

– *Final questions:* Finally, the interviewer asked questions about privacy concerns and potential applications of the system and then ended with a survey of demographics, education, and everyday Internet activities.

4.2   User Study 2: Users-as-Beacons for Reviewing Places, Services, and Localized Events

In the second study, we developed a slightly different design-prototype to investigate users' thoughts on making posts about places, small businesses, restaurants, social causes, and local events. Like study 1, we discussed the system's functionalities and demonstrated how the participant would receive and send reviews, and described several scenarios as part of the interview.

– *Scenario one, registering and receiving posts:* The interview started with the participant receiving two posts from the interviewer, a food review and a service recommendation. Then the interviewer asked the participant several questions related to receiving posts from people around them.

– *Scenario two, creating posts:* The participant used the design-prototype to create two posts, one for a small business and another to promote a social cause. Participants were then asked about their perceptions of reviewing different places, services, or social causes. They also answered questions regarding the different contexts in which they could envision using the system.

– *Scenario three, instant reviews:* The interviewer then described a restaurant scenario where the participant was having dinner and wanted to leave a review. The interviewer asked the participant several questions related to posting reviews and review timing.

– *Scenario four, reviewing small businesses:* The next scenario was about the participant hiring a pest control service. They were then asked about their opinion on reviewing small businesses, their motivation, and the factors they would consider in posting such reviews.
– *Scenario five, contextual controls and preferences:* Like the fourth scenario in the first interview, we described two social situations, then asked questions about interaction with others and participants' perceived needs for controls and preferences over potential interaction.
– *Final questions:* Like study 1, we asked general questions on overall perceptions, privacy, and suggested features and then ended with a survey of demographics, education, and everyday Internet activities.

4.3 Participant Recruitment and Demographics

We recruited 27 participants in total around our university campus, through our institutional research service, and recruiting posts through social media in neighborhood groups. We also utilized Snowball sampling, where initial participants suggested additional participants. After the interview session, each participant was compensated with a $10 gift card. Among the 27 participants, 11 of them were males, and 16 of them were females. Five of them were from the age range 18–24, 19 of them were from range 25–34, and 3 others were of the age 35 and above. The participants were from variety of occupations, including 13 students, physicians, administrators, health educators, and career advisers.

4.4 Analysis

This is an exploratory, formative study to understand the potential behaviors and concerns of users within a UaB system. Thus, we conducted inductive coding for each interview separately, and involved an additional coder for the 2nd interview who had not seen the first codebook. All interviews were transcribed for analysis. We first analyzed the 13 participants in Study 1. As a primary coder, the first author conducted inductive coding for three sample participants and discussed it with the other authors. The authors agreed on a codebook containing 15 codes. The primary coder then coded the remaining transcripts with the codebook. Based on initial results, we decided to conduct the second interview study before further analysis. This time two researchers independently coded three sample participants from the second study, comparing and merging their code books with discussion among all authors. An agreement was reached on the codebook and all codes for those 3 participants, resulting in a codebook of 19 separate codes. The two coders then coded all remaining participants independently with no further changes to the codebook. When coding was complete, the researchers discussed and resolved any disagreements. Disagreements were tracked, and inter-rater agreement was calculated at 96.47%.

The contexts and the scenarios were slightly different between the two studies; thus, the codebooks are slightly different from each other based on instant reviews, irrelevant reviews, irritating notifications, and writing reviews in different places. Overall, nine codes were the same between the two studies. Thus, as a final step, we grouped all the codes from both of the codebooks into higher-level categories to merge results for both of the studies altogether. While discussing the results, we enumerate the participants 1 to 13 for the first set of interviews and 21 to 34 for the second set of interviews.

4.5 Limitations

The limitations of our study are similar to other exploratory, qualitative studies. The sample size for each study was relatively small, with heavy student and university employee representation. Thus, participants were likely more educated than a general population, with views that may not match others from different populations or cultures outside of the United States. The system was also hypothetical, which means participants were discussing initial responses that may not accurately reflect later behavior with such a system. These responses may have also been more positive to be polite to the interviewer. Despite these biases, we believe our results provide valuable early feedback on the potential of this system, as well as inform the design of such a system.

5 Results

While the two interviews differed somewhat, many of the perceptions and reactions are similar across both studies. Thus, we describe our findings together, and only distinguish between the two versions as needed to further explain results or compare reactions if they differed. We regularly specify the number of participants while describing a specific perception in order to describe the prevalence of a sentiment in our sample. However, these numbers are not representative of a more general population. We also use generalized keywords with 'a few' describing 2–6 participants, 'some' as 7–13 participants, 'majority' as 14–16 participants, and 'most' as more than 17 participants.

5.1 Receiving Posts: Benefits and Trust

The most immediate reaction of participants to the notion of receiving posts from surrounding people was that it is not likely to be fake and instead would come from real people around them. For example, P30 said, " *I would prefer to trust the people close to me, or want to hear from people who are nearby me. This Beacon idea is appealing in that sense because I know that people around me are referencing that.*" And another example from P1: *"I may receive posts from my neighbors, right? I know them, so I would trust them..."* Thus, trust emerged as a key perception, and users reacted positively to the possibility of increased trust through this system. In order to trust the posts, they also expressed desire for users to not be anonymous so they could know where an opinion came from.

Participants also talked about the types of posts they would be most interested in. In study 1, most participants thought that the product reviews were useful to receive, but only in shopping areas, depending on time and context.

They agreed that the most useful posts to receive would be of restaurants and local places. P22 said, *"I would wanna receive reviews of food, restaurants, home services, probably Craigslist kind of things- sold things around me."* Participants also mentioned the usefulness of receiving discounts, as well as updates about nearby events.

However, many did not like the idea of promoting social causes. And, they wanted to receive service recommendations only when they needed them. All but three participants said that the relevance and context of the received posts are essential. Thus, most participants talked about customization features to filter the types of posts they are most interested in. A majority of the participants thought that receiving many instant notifications from others could be irritating. P2 said, *"Sometimes I see that people are saturated by posts. One of my concerns is that there is already a lot out there, I do not want any new system to add more."* And, P33 said, *"I think if I start to receive [posts] too much, like especially since I have the Apple watch and I have the notifications turned on. It buzzes all the time, and if I am in a meeting, I think people think that I must be really rude when I am looking at my watch."*

Some said that notifications can be very distracting to regular activities, even when they might actually be receiving relevant posts. Thus, the overall message was that the system would need to have different kinds of controls and preferences to filter and block notifications, and to customize or subscribe to different kinds of posts of interest.

5.2   Making Posts: Interests and Concerns

Participants were open to making posts if they liked the product or place and they trust the people around them. P21 said, *"Actually when I am sending my [post], I would think that it might help people around me."* Users compared this system to existing review platforms, such as Google or Yelp, and thought that this platform would be similarly useful. Similar to preferences for receiving different kinds of posts, participants stated that they would mostly make posts about restaurants and interesting places. They generally wanted to support small businesses as well, but only a few wanted to use it for social causes or services recommendations.

In many of the participants' opinions, making instant posts was a matter of discomfort. In study 2, when asked about writing a food review in a restaurant, 12 participants stated that they would not write a review while still in the restaurant, but later, when they are out of the area. One reason was that writing reviews requires time. *"What would be rather cool is that if this app knew that I ate at whatever the restaurant was, they send me a reminder later, saying, hey I know that you ate here yesterday, what do you think?"* P28. Participants also mentioned not writing a post immediately because of potential social interaction that might result. As P31 said, *"I would probably not want [to let people know] instantly. I think if I am sitting there at the restaurant, like, I do not want them to come and say, 'Oh I know who that was!' I am worried about probably restaurant management."*

The importance of social norms and network effects also emerged in how participants might react to such a system. As P6 said, *"For now, I have my concerns. But, if after a few years it becomes a trend, then I might not feel that way."* Participants also acknowledged that while it may feel strange at first to advertise certain products or places, that perception could change if that became more visible and normal. We asked participants about what incentives would motivate them to use such a users-as-beacons system. Most participants thought that cash back or redeemable points would be a good motivation. Even those with high concerns over negative peer-interaction would think twice if they get incentives. As P31 said, *"I am doing this study because I am getting a gift card, so any incentives are certainly gonna peak interest to an extent."*

In the second study, many participants thought that community feedback such as an upvote, downvote, or comments from the people around who read their posts would increase the appeal to make more posts. P31 commented, *"I think people, in general, like to see how many people are giving attention to them. So, just seeing how many people you have reached, I think it is motivational."* Others also thought that getting free items, such as a free cup of coffee or free donut can be a good motivation: *"I definitely think that would be cool; like Google has their opinion reward thing. For example, you go to a restaurant and get a free drink or something."* -P27

We wanted to know how the participants felt about sharing their personal information with other users nearby. All felt that it was acceptable to share their first name with the posts. However, most of the participants were cautious about sharing their full name, as that would identify them, and instead would prefer an alias. All but two were hesitant to share their photo. As P2 said, *"It's when you can match a name and a face, I could see potential privacy problems. So, [sharing] photo is a concern."*

Moreover, some were worried about trusting the peers to whom they are disclosing their information and thus desired anonymity. *"I might need the anonymity, because, you never know who is around, who is going to get it."* -P31. Five participants specifically mentioned concerns over being stalked and several others mentioned identify theft; as P12 said, *"It would also be a privacy issue if someone sees my photo and sees my name, I mean that is a lot of personal information, for predators or stalkers who can then easily get my photo and contact information."*

5.3   Interacting with Others: Comfort and Concerns

Twenty-three participants anticipated that people around them would come and talk to them about their posts. Seven of them felt some kind of discomfort in that, mainly because this was entirely a situation that they have never experienced. P7 said, *"It is kind of uncomfortable, because we never had this kind of experience before. Online reviews are different. Nobody knows the person who wrote it."* Some people felt discomfort because they were not comfortable talking to strangers. P28 suggested the virtual communication feature would be preferred, similar to existing review platforms, *"I would be fine if there is a way for someone to reply to my post, saying, hey, I have some questions about your review there. But, I would not want strangers to come and talk to me.".*

In study 1, we described an option to delay sharing a post in the shopping area to prevent unwanted interactions with others. Nine of the 13 participants in that study thought such a delay would be a good idea for various reasons, such as the sensitivity of the content, public exposure, and interference from store management. P2 said, *"If I really want to review a sensitive product, then delay might be a useful feature to have."*

Yet, eight participants were positive about potential interaction. Two of them were even delighted to interact with people. The participants thought that it is a new way of sharing thoughts and thus they can have a conversation with real users. P27 said, *"I would make friends out of it. There could be some negative experience, but that is probably less likely to happen."* A few participants, such as P10, took this model of real-time and localized communication as a new way of socialization. She said, *"There's this culture of fear, and so I might only share information with a privileged group, people who I am inside with. Whereas, I might be in a different world, want to share information with anyone and everyone because that might come from the place of trust and community and society. So, an app like this could start to change that kind of way of thinking..."*

In both versions of the study, we asked the participants about their opinions on beaconing in different contexts. In public places, 19 of the participants wanted to keep the devices' beacons open, particularly if they earned rewards for doing so. P33 said, *"It is like the Nextdoor app. I have the alerts turned on for that, and if there is something happens to my neighbors and they say something about it, I can help them... This could be a place where everybody can pay attention to their neighbors without having to physically do that. They could use the beaconing app, where they can feel the connection with their neighbors."*

Yet, participants were less sure about the need for beaconing with people in other contexts. For example, five participants did not want to keep beaconing in the workplace and expressed concerns about sharing too much private information with their colleagues. Only five participants were willing to keep beaconing at home; most felt that home is for family, and they wanted little to no intrusion there. As P31 said, *"I don't know if I would keep it on all the time in general. Whenever you are at the birthday party, you are spending time with the people around you. You don't want to be having them look at their phones just because you broadcasted something."* Several participants also argued that they can directly talk to the people they know instead of digitally posting something.

There was a common feeling against facing the establishment related to making posts about businesses, and that those in authority could interfere when a user is writing opinions. For example, three participants wanted to use the posting delay because of fear that store management might want to confront them if they post a negative review. P3 said, *"I think a delay would be a good idea if the manager would want to try to find you; if I fear that the manager might misbehave, they could be angry or something."* Interestingly, in the second study, the participants were also thinking about confronting the restaurant management when they made a food review post. And P31 said, *"I think if I am sitting there at the restaurant, I do not want them to know who that was. I am worried about probably the restaurant management."* Moreover, 7 participants were worried that store management might want to intervene in the system to promote their products. P8 said, *"I would question the reviews of their own employees. I know that many employees might try to push their products."*

5.4   Perceived Privacy in Users-as-Beacons

The participants expressed several privacy concerns perceived from our explanation of the system, many of which were the same threats found with the Internet and digital media. Participants were particularly concerned because, beyond just their posts, they were not sure what kind of information the app would need to prompt them to write such posts. Thus, behavioral tracking was a big concern (n = 11). P1 said, *"How the app knows what I already purchased? So, is it through my email? And are they then pulling purchase orders?"* And P29 said, *"Using one app leads to using another app. So they send information to each other, and then the next thing you know there is another ad, another service sending you the information. Phone number, email addresses, all these things are connected."* Yet, participants also discussed that existing applications and platforms already utilize such personal information, and thus they would also have similar levels of trust in reputable organizations. P31 said, *"We already know that Google is probably trading our identity, so, you know there are analytic and stuff on everything, on social media, Yelp, Instagram, Google reviews."* Thus, these privacy concerns were not related to the users-as-beacons concept itself, but merely using yet another social platform that may require access to personal information.

Not surprisingly, location tracking was a primary concern. P5 said, *"Also I can be tracked by the companies. They also know that I am around. That is a bit creepy."* P11 said, *"I would wonder about how my information is being used, not just from the users of the system, but also from the businesses. What are they doing with the information and the decisions are they making?"* Interestingly, one of the potential benefits of users-as-beacons is that the app would not need to accurately track location in order to work. Yet, users seemed to be expecting that their apps would know their location, even if not needed, and were thus not expecting any improvement in location privacy from this system. Surprisingly, some people wanted behavioral and location tracking to make the use of the system more convenient and receive tailored posts. P3 said, *"I would prefer a system that uses a location-based model that can automatically sort this thing out for me. I would like to receive the things related to where I am now. If I am a sender, I do not want to be a person who sends out-of-place things."*

As mentioned previously, a few of the participants were worried about their physical privacy and expressed their fear of being tracked by predators and stalkers. P10 said, *"If I am somewhere, using a beacon, someone can find me. I am worried about being tracked. People can track me easily if they follow my beacon.".* Others did not worry as much mainly because they already use several apps where they can turn the user location sharing off.

Despite perceiving that one benefit of a users-as-beacons system was the increased trustworthiness of the posts, the majority of participants were still concerned about spamming from fake users and bots. This was also tied to their desire to not be overwhelmed by too many irrelevant notifications. P11 said, *"Being spammed will be a concern, it might be overwhelming to receive so many, especially if you do not have any control."* Participants were also worried that, if they shared their full name along with their photos, it would become easy for spammers to create fake accounts using their identity, and use them to spam others who already trust those users. Thus, people were concerned about how their information would be managed and used, or misused.

These concerns are similar to many existing applications already in use, and thus users were often expressing a desire to remain in control of their information and identity in this novel application. As P8 said, *"I always put reviews somewhere and I put my name behind that, positive or negative. I don't mind that aspect, it's just the control I am worried about."* Participants also expressed a desire to control the audience of their posts, or block posts from other user-beacons. Thus, these issues overlap with needs and challenges of audience management in social media systems more generally.

Some participants also acknowledged that they would make a trade-off between the benefits and incentives received, and what they were willing to share. As with any privacy calculus, the nuanced context matters. For example, some participants were quite positive about supporting small businesses, and would not need many external incentives to express their opinions or share personal information. Thus, while the participants in the first study which focused on advertising products frequently mentioned the need for financial incentives, most of the participants in the second study were interested in using the system regardless of the incentives. And as mentioned in the previous sections, if such a system were to become widespread and normal behavior, then their privacy concerns would be lessened.

6   Discussion and Implications

In this paper, we introduced a potential social system that can be built on top of BLE beacon technology leveraging the ubiquity of BLE enabled smartphones. We envision this system as a privacy-preserving localized information dissemination system. The primary benefits include localized services without having to share the location through devices, limiting the vulnerability of GPS-spoofing, and potentially restricting the scope of having fake users, thus improving trust and maintaining reliable communication among the users. Moreover, this system will facilitate a localized information sharing system, which will enable potential peer-interactions. We explore user reactions to multiple types of posts, including social posts, product, places, and event reviews.

6.1 Feasibility and Applicability of the System

While overall response was relatively positive, users expressed a range of concerns that will need to be addressed for the successful development and deployment of such a system.

Trust: One of the most prominent user opinions of users-as-beacons was about the trustworthiness of the content in the system. In traditional systems, user-generated content is often considered more trustworthy than the contents generated by organizations and companies [7,8]. We have found a similar notion in our proposed platform, that enables users to create their own content. Users also seemed to understand the usefulness of a localized system such as this, perceiving that the platform would ensure the physical presence of user-beacons in their surroundings, ensuring the realism of posts in the system. Thus, users did perceive increased trust, and valued this benefit. This provides motivation that our proposed system is worth further development.

Location Privacy: Yet, while we tried to make sure that participants realized that their actual location was not needed by the system, users did not discuss location privacy benefits. Interestingly, some of the participants even wanted their location to be tracked in order to gain the benefits of tailored and relevant posts. So, even though location privacy is a potential benefit of the proposed system over related mobile applications, users did not perceive or value the privacy-preserving nature of users-as-beacons. In this case, the only benefit to the users would be the ability to function if GPS was disabled.

Localization and Potential of Peer-Interaction: We also talked about possible peer-interaction as this system is localized and has the potential to create a local social interaction system. It is highly possible for the users to directly meet people who post nearby and talk about those posts. The participants showed mixed reaction to this possibility. They have not experienced this type of interaction before. On the one hand, it is new and thus, participants were not entirely sure how they would feel about it. Some of them did not perceive it as a benefit, and were thus were worried about their identities being public. On the other hand, other participants appreciated the chance of interactions, as that might make the system reliable, and enjoyed the possibility of a new form of social interaction.

We believe the primary application domain for this kind of system would be a localized extension to current social interaction systems, with increased reliability. Based on our study, this system has potential in localized socialization, reviewing places, event advertising, and supporting businesses and events in particular locations. And, despite some concerns over the potential social interaction with strangers, participants felt that this type of system would be useful mostly in locally constrained areas, such as festivals and events, or restaurants and shopping areas, where posts would also be most relevant and people could trust their peers. Some participants also saw potential benefits in the interaction between community members that such a system could provide.

6.2   Design Challenges

We believe our exploratory study encourages us to continue to explore users as beacons, and our initial results highlight several key challenges that we will need to address through the design of such a system and research in greater depth.

Managing Trustworthiness: The biggest benefit the users perceived about the system is the trustworthiness of the contents. However, participants were still wary about sharing their personal information with the system and other user-beacons. Yet, the more users would share their personal information, the more trustworthy the contents become for receivers, and the more useful the entire system. Clearly, there is a tension between being able to know and trust those providing content in a users as beacons system, and a desire to restrict the sharing of personal information and remain private. Moreover, a user-beacon needs to be there to make posts, but it doesn't mean that it would always be a real person. It still can be faked, for example by a shop, even if it is comparatively harder than in current online systems. While this did not come up a lot in the interviews, users would need to understand this possibility in a real deployment. As with other novel technologies, users' comfort in sharing personal information may lessen over time, as they become more comfortable with how the system works and as they see others trusting the system. Therefore, it will be a challenge to provide users with sufficient awareness of others' access of their personal information and controls to restrict information sharing and maintain privacy, while still providing sufficient utility through trustworthy content.

Relevance and Timeliness: In both our design prototypes, we demonstrated how a post was delivered instantly to another user (the interviewer). Yet, we always envisioned that notifications would need to be delivered intelligently to reduce overload. On the one hand, users benefit from knowing about content in a timely manner, while users are nearby others who want to broadcast this content. Yet, participants' biggest concern was the annoyance of too many notifications, particularly of things that were not of interest to them. However, eliminating notifications and moving to a less synchronous delivery of content may also reduce the potential benefit of receiving content that is localized and the potential of user-poster interaction enabled by the system. Many also discussed how they wanted the posts they received to be contextually relevant to them, and mentioned different ideas for achieving that both through automatic tailoring and explicit user controls for filtering content, thus trading-off privacy for benefits. Therefore, a key challenge in this system will be to ensure the relevant and timely delivery of the content users receive with an acceptable level of trade-off between benefits and privacy, and investigating which methods can achieve these goals. This relevance may be achievable by restricting the system to very time- or location-constrained contexts, such as particular events.

Managing Peer-Interaction: Some participants were not at all comfortable with interacting with others as a result of making posts, yet others embraced the benefits of peer communication and were intrigued with the possibility of greater social interaction. Thus, another challenge is enabling users to manage their openness to such peer interactions, while maintaining comfort and privacy. In study 1 we mentioned one potential mechanism to participants, that of delaying delivery of a post to users. There are likely other novel mechanisms that we can explore to provide users with methods for managing their boundaries, and protecting themselves from intrusion.

6.3 Future Research Needs

While this initial investigation provided a range of user opinions, these will likely differ and depend on the details of a specific design and context of use. In addition to the challenges raised above, there are a number of additional issues we believe can be explored within this type of system.

User Privacy: In this study, users experienced a rather simple demonstration and a spoken description of the system, which might be insufficient to understand how the system works, without time for participants to become habituated to it. Future research needs to investigate how users respond over the long term to such a system, where do they find the most benefits and how does their privacy-behavior change over time? What concerns will arise as users repeatedly encounter the same people, in the same or different places? What positive and negative experiences will shape user behaviors, and lead to greater or reduced usage?

Within the Covid-19 contact tracing context, Reichert et al. [48], Bell et al. [49], and Tang et al. [50] discuss tools and techniques to prevent privacy threats from the perspectives of patients, potential patients, hospitals, and health professionals. Similar solutions would be needed for future social U-a-B applications, which may be functionally similar yet have different privacy trade-offs.

Incentives: We did question users about the potential incentives for using a users-as-beacons system. However, we did not examine this question deeply, and users for the most part answered based on experiences with online review platforms rather than more social platforms. Thus, we need to examine what incentives would be necessary and effective in motivating users to adopt and provide content to such a system. Examining this question can also provide insight into the key question of how users would trade off the benefits and incentives provided against their privacy concerns and needs.

Real Life Implementation: While we have outlined a users-as-beacons system abstractly in this paper, and implemented a basic system in our design prototype, there are many additional questions about how to best design and implement such a system for real world deployment. Designs are likely to differ based on the context and domain of use, including different solutions to the various challenges we raised above. We plan to further prototype a system using our university campus as a testbed for understanding the feasibility and use of users-as-beacons as a localized social interaction platform.

7   Conclusion

We believe that the widespread Bluetooth Low Energy technology provides an infrastructure on which to explore novel systems that may provide both interesting applications and privacy benefits to users. Our exploratory study shows that users do perceive some benefits in a users-as-beacons social system, namely trust and the potential for peer-interaction, yet did not value the increased location privacy and were more concerned about receiving content relevant to them. Our results also demonstrate that there are still many issues surrounding privacy and peer-to-peer interaction that need additional understanding and careful design in order to develop a successful system. We plan to use our results to design and deploy prototypes to examine these issues more deeply, providing insights into the incentives and privacy trade-offs in this novel mobile communication system.

References

1. Sterling, G.: Report: 93 percent of US baseball stadiums have deployed beacons - marketing land, August 2016. https://marketingland.com/report-93-percent-us-baseball-stadiums-deployed-beacons-186677. Accessed 22 Jan 2019
2. Smart industry — bluetooth technology website. https://www.bluetooth.com/markets/smart-industry. Accessed 15 Jan 2019
3. Decentralized privacy-preserving proximity tracing. https://github.com/DP-3T/documents. Accessed 2 June 2020
4. Bay, J., et al.: BlueTrace: a privacy-preserving protocol for community-driven contact tracing across borders. Government Technology Agency-Singapore, Technical Report (2020)
5. Kelley, P.G., Consolvo, S., Cranor, L.F., Jung, J., Sadeh, N., Wetherall, D.: A conundrum of permissions: installing applications on an android smartphone. In: Blyth, J., Dietrich, S., Camp, L.J. (eds.) FC 2012. LNCS, vol. 7398, pp. 68–79. Springer, Heidelberg (2012). https://doi.org/10.1007/978-3-642-34638-5_6
6. Sanders, E.B.-N., Stappers, P.J.: Probes, toolkits and prototypes: three approaches to making in codesigning. CoDesign **10**(1), 5–14 (2014)
7. Hansen, S.S., Lee, J.K., Lee, S.-Y.: Consumer-generated ads on YouTube: impacts of source credibility and need for cognition on attitudes, interactive behaviors, and eWOM. J. Electron. Commerce Res. **15**(3), 254 (2014)
8. Lawrence, B., Fournier, S., Brunel, F.: When companies don't make the ad: a multimethod inquiry into the differential effectiveness of Consumer-Generated advertising. J. Advert. **42**(4), 292–307 (2013)
9. Forman, C., Ghose, A., Wiesenfeld, B.: Examining the relationship between reviews and sales: the role of reviewer identity disclosure in electronic markets. Inf. Syst. Res. **19(3), 291–313**, 1 (2008)
10. Shih, H.-P., Lai, K.-H., Cheng, T.C.E.: Constraint-based and dedication-based mechanisms for encouraging online self-disclosure: is personalization the only thing that matters? Eur. J. Inf. Syst. **26**(4), 432–450 (2017)
11. Tawfiq, A., Richard, B.: The privacy paradox: the role of cognitive absorption in the social networking activity. In: ICIS 2015 Proceedings (2015). aisel.aisnet.org
12. Zwass, V.: Co-creation: toward a taxonomy and an integrated research perspective. Int. J. Electron. Commerce **8** (2014)

13. Banerjee, S., Bhattacharyya, S., Bose, I.: Whose online reviews to trust? Understanding reviewer trustworthiness and its impact on business. Decis. Support Syst. **96**, 17–26 (2017)
14. Luca, M., Zervas, G.: Fake it till you make it: reputation, competition, and yelp review fraud. Manage. Sci. **62**(12), 3412–3427 (2016)
15. Fayazi, A., Lee, K., Caverlee, J., Squicciarini, A.: Uncovering crowdsourced manipulation of online reviews. In: Proceedings of the 38th International ACM SIGIR Conference on Research and Development in Information Retrieval, SIGIR 2015, pp. 233–242. ACM, New York (2015)
16. Mathwick, C., Mosteller, J.: Online reviewer engagement: a typology based on reviewer motivations. J. Serv. Res. **20**(2), 204–218 (2017)
17. Zhang, D., Zhou, L., Kehoe, J.L., Kilic, I.Y.: What online reviewer behaviors really matter? Effects of verbal and nonverbal behaviors on detection of fake online reviews. J. Manag. Inf. Syst. **33**(2), 456–481 (2016)
18. Besmer, A., Watson, J., Lipford, H.R.: The impact of social navigation on privacy policy configuration. In: Proceedings of the Sixth Symposium on Usable Privacy and Security, SOUPS 2010, pp. 7:1–7:10. ACM, New York (2010)
19. Krasnova, H., Kolesnikova, E., Günther, O.: "It won't happen to me!": self-disclosure in online social networks **343**, 01 (2009)
20. Wang, Y., Norcie, G., Komanduri, S., Acquisti, A., Leon, P.G., Cranor, L.F.: "i regretted the minute i pressed share": a qualitative study of regrets on Facebook. In: Proceedings of the Seventh Symposium on Usable Privacy and Security, SOUPS 2011, pp. 10:1–10:16. ACM, New York (2011)
21. Johnson, M., Egelman, S., Bellovin, S.M.: Facebook and privacy: it's complicated. In: Proceedings of the Eighth Symposium on Usable Privacy and Security, SOUPS 2012, pp. 9:1–9:15. ACM, New York (2012)
22. Staddon, J., Huffaker, D., Brown, L., Sedley, A.: Are privacy concerns a turn-off?: Engagement and privacy in social networks. In: Proceedings of the Eighth Symposium on Usable Privacy and Security, SOUPS 2012, pp. 10:1–10:13. ACM, New York (2012)
23. Edmonds, R.: People don't want to trade privacy for targeted ads, January 2016. https://www.poynter.org/news/people-dont-want-trade-privacy-targeted-ads. Accessed 11 July 2017
24. (Catherine) Jai, T.-M., Burns, L.D., King, N.J.: The effect of behavioral tracking practices on consumers' shopping evaluations and repurchase intention toward trusted online retailers. Comput. Hum. Behav. **29**(3), 901–909 (2013)
25. Turow, J., Hennessy, M., Draper, N.A.: The tradeoff fallacy: how marketers are misrepresenting American consumers and opening them up to exploitation (2015)
26. Xu, H., (Robert) Luo, X., Carroll, J.M., Rosson, M.B.: The personalization privacy paradox: an exploratory study of decision making process for location-aware marketing. Decis. Support Syst. **51**(1), 42–52 (2011)
27. Consolvo, S., Smith, I.E., Matthews, T., LaMarca, A., Tabert, J., Powledge, P.: Location disclosure to social relations: why, when, & what people want to share. In: Proceedings of the SIGCHI Conference on Human Factors in Computing Systems, CHI 2005, pp. 81–90. ACM, New York (2005)
28. Iachello, G., et al.: Control, deception, and communication: evaluating the deployment of a location-enhanced messaging service. In: Beigl, M., Intille, S., Rekimoto, J., Tokuda, H. (eds.) UbiComp 2005. LNCS, vol. 3660, pp. 213–231. Springer, Heidelberg (2005). https://doi.org/10.1007/11551201_13
29. Sadeh, N., et al.: Understanding and capturing people's privacy policies in a mobile social networking application. Personal Ubiquitous Comput. **13**(6), 401–412 (2009)

30. Benisch, M., Kelley, P.G., Sadeh, N., Cranor, L.F.: Capturing location-privacy preferences: quantifying accuracy and user-burden tradeoffs. Personal Ubiquitous Comput. **15**(7), 679–694 (2011)
31. Patil, S., Norcie, G., Kapadia, A., Lee, A.J.: Reasons, rewards, regrets: privacy considerations in location sharing as an interactive practice. In: Proceedings of the Eighth Symposium on Usable Privacy and Security, SOUPS 2012, pp. 5:1–5:15. ACM, New York (2012)
32. Toch, E.: Empirical models of privacy in location sharing. In: Proceedings of the 12th ACM International Conference on Ubiquitous Computing, UbiComp 2010, pp. 129–138. ACM, New York (2010)
33. Fisher, D., Dorner, L., Wagner, D.: Short paper: location privacy: User behavior in the field. In: Proceedings of the Second ACM Workshop on Security and Privacy in Smartphones and Mobile Devices, SPSM 2012, pp. 51–56. ACM, New York (2012)
34. Kelley, P.G., Brewer, R., Mayer, Y., Cranor, L.F., Sadeh, N.: An investigation into Facebook friend grouping. In: Campos, P., Graham, N., Jorge, J., Nunes, N., Palanque, P., Winckler, M. (eds.) INTERACT 2011. LNCS, vol. 6948, pp. 216–233. Springer, Heidelberg (2011). https://doi.org/10.1007/978-3-642-23765-2_15
35. Bello-Ogunu, E., Shehab, M., Miazi, N.S.: Privacy is the best policy: a framework for BLE beacon privacy management. In: 2019 IEEE 43rd Annual Computer Software and Applications Conference (COMPSAC), vol. 1, pp. 823–832 (2019)
36. Higuchi, T., Martin, P., Chakraborty, S., Srivastava, M.: AnonyCast: privacy-preserving location distribution for anonymous crowd tracking systems. In: Proceedings of the 2015 ACM International Joint Conference on Pervasive and Ubiquitous Computing, UbiComp 2015, pp. 1119–1130. Association for Computing Machinery, New York (2015)
37. Schulz, T., Golatowski, F., Timmermann, D.: Secure privacy preserving information beacons for public transportation systems. In: 2016 IEEE International Conference on Pervasive Computing and Communication Workshops (PerCom Workshops), pp. 1–6 (2016)
38. Gao, S., Ma, J., Shi, W., Zhan, G., Sun, C.: TrPF: a trajectory privacy-preserving framework for participatory sensing. IEEE Trans. Inf. Forensics Secur. **8**(6), 874–887 (2013)
39. Xing, B., Seada, K., Venkatasubramanian, N.: Proximiter: enabling mobile proximity-based content sharing on portable devices. In: 2009 IEEE International Conference on Pervasive Computing and Communications, pp. 1–3 (2009)
40. Jung, S., Lee, U., Chang, A., Cho, D.-K., Gerla, M.: BlueTorrent: cooperative content sharing for Bluetooth users. Pervasive Mob. Comput. **3**(6), 609–634 (2007)
41. Shen, J., Li, Y., Peng, C., Zhang, Y.: MobiUS: a together-viewing mobile video experience. Mobisys'07 Best Demo Award, June 2007
42. Beach, A., et al.: WhozThat? Evolving an ecosystem for context-aware mobile social networks. IEEE Netw. **22**(4), 50–55 (2008)
43. Tracetogether. https://www.tracetogether.gov.sg/. Accessed 15 Mar 2020
44. Faragher, R.: An analysis of the accuracy of Bluetooth low energy for indoor positioning applications (2014)
45. Yao, Y., Huang, Y., Wang, Y.: Unpacking people's understandings of Bluetooth beacon systems-a location-based IoT technology. In: Proceedings of the 52nd Hawaii International Conference on System Sciences (2019)
46. Thamm, A., Anke, J., Haugk, S., Radic, D.: Towards the omni-channel: beacon-based services in retail. In: International Conference on Business Information Systems, vol. 255, pp. 181–192 (2016)

47. Bello-Ogunu, E., Shehab, M.: Crowdsourcing for context: regarding privacy in beacon encounters via contextual integrity. Proc. Privacy Enhancing Technol. **2016**(3), 83–95 (2016)
48. Reichert, L., Brack, S., Scheuermann, B.: Privacy-preserving contact tracing of Covid-19 patients. IACR Cryptol. ePrint Arch. **2020**, 375 (2020)
49. Bell, J., Butler, D., Hicks, C.: and Jon Crowcroft. Towards privacy preserving contact tracing, TraceSecure (2020)
50. Tang, Q.: Privacy-Preserving contact tracing: current solutions and open questions, April 2020

SENSATION: An Authoring Tool to Support Event–State Paradigm in End-User Development

Giuseppe Desolda[1]([envelope]), Francesco Greco[1], Francisco Guarnieri[2], Nicole Mariz[2], and Massimo Zancanaro[2,3]

[1] Computer Science Department, University of Bari Aldo Moro, Bari, Italy
{giuseppe.desolda,francesco.greco}@uniba.it
[2] Department of Psychology and Cognitive Science, University of Trento, Rovereto, Italy
{francisco.guarnieri,nicole.mariz}@studenti.unitn.it,
massimo.zancanaro@unitn.it
[3] Fondazione Bruno Kessler, Trento, Italy

Abstract. In this paper, we present the design and the evaluation of an authoring tool for End-User Development, which supports the definition of Trigger-Actions rules that combines events and states in the triggers. The possibility of using either states or events in triggers has already been discussed in the literature. However, it is recognized that the state/event distinction is difficult to manage for users. In this paper, we propose an authoring tool that provides explicit support for managing this distinction. We compare it with a state-of-the-art authoring tool that implements the classical event-event paradigm.

Keywords: End-User Development · Internet of Things · Trigger action programming

1 Introduction

Trigger-Action programming (TAP) is emerging as the most adopted paradigm for supporting end-users, particularly those without IT skills, in defining the behavior of *Internet-of-Things* devices and digital web services. TAP is a simplified form of the *Event Condition Action* (ECA), a common approach for rule-based systems, originally employed to manage databases [14] and control industrial processes [18]. However, when applied in the form of *Trigger-Action* rules for End-User Development (EUD), the *Condition* part is usually left out for the sake of simplicity, and the rules take the simple form of "*IF <a trigger occurs> THEN <an action is executed>*". This kind of rule has become popular on web services like IFTTT [16] and Zapier [29]. More advanced solutions propose the possibility to trigger a rule when different events co-occur or execute a chain of actions [10]. Some tools allow the specification of a condition but usually as

Electronic supplementary material The online version of this chapter (https://doi.org/10.1007/978-3-030-85616-8_22) contains supplementary material, which is available to authorized users.

part of a generic "IF" trigger, and it is usually not represented in the syntactic form of the rule (for example, [10, 14, 22]).

As noted by Brackenbury and colleagues [4], a source of confusion in the TAP paradigm derives from the fact that triggers indicate both instantaneous events or state, and users are not always able to understand the difference between the two [15, 28], causing inconsistencies, loops, and redundancies in the behaviors of the smart objects [7].

The work presented in this paper builds upon and extends the approach proposed by Huang and Cakmak [15], which recognizes the need to differentiate these two types of triggers. It also integrates the findings from Gallitto and colleagues [13] that argue how using different language forms may help the users better understand the semantic and operationalization of a set of rules. We discuss the design and an initial evaluation of an authoring tool, SENSATION, for the EUD of rules in a constrained form. It explicitly requires a single event that triggers the rule and conjunction of states in which the world is expected to be for the rule to be executed as a specific form of condition in the ECA approach. The proposed tool structures and guides the construction of a rule by contextual filtering the available choices regarding events and states.

2 Background and Related Work

Internet-of-Things (IoT) has now been established as one of the most widely used technologies in recent years, and recent forecasts tell that it will become even more pervasive in the next years. In 2019, around 26 billion devices were installed worldwide and, by the end of 2025, over 75 billion devices are expected[1]. This proliferation of technology brings several challenges, ranging from technical aspects to hardware miniaturization, energy consumption, security, cost, and aspects related to interaction with smart devices.

One of the most critical challenges concerns the possibility for non-technical users to customize the behavior of these devices to better satisfy their specific needs [12]. Customization might be required to personalize a single application's behavior (like a thermostat) or connect several IoT objects, each designed to solve a specific task, with the purpose to realize a more complex combined service. The need to create these combinations among devices is growing as the availability of smart objects increases.

Several Task Automation Systems (TAS) [9] have been proposed as web-based tools that allow users to compose smart objects' behavior through visual interfaces that support the TAP paradigm. Among the most popular there are IFTTT [16] and Zapier [29], EFESTO-5W [10], EFESTO-4SIE, [1, 2], Microsoft Flow [23], Mozilla's Things Gateway [24], SmartRules [26], NinjaBlocks [17].

Although the possibility of exploiting TAP for End-User Development has been widely demonstrated [5, 14, 15, 21], several critical aspects have been noted in the literature on the possibility for the users to understand and manage the potential complexity of rules. In this respect, explicit support for debugging has been proposed [7, 21, 25], and (semi-)automatic methods to prevent undesired effects have been experimented with [8]. Concerning other tools for rules with explicit conditions, a notable exception might

---

[1] https://financesonline.com/iot-trends/.

be the tool proposed by Troung and colleagues [27], which allows the syntactical spec-ification of the location ("WHERE") in which the event should take place in order for the action to be executed. Similarly, EFESTO-5W supports the specification of both temporal (WHEN) and spatial (WHERE) conditions in the trigger. Even if these TASs have much success due to their simplicity, many limitations result in ECA rule errors like inconsistencies, loops, and redundancies [7].

The need to differentiate events from states in TAP has been recognized as a source of possible misunderstanding by users. Brackenbury and colleagues [4] present ten pro-gramming bugs grouped in (1) bugs in control flow, (2) timing-related bugs, and (3) errors in user interpretation. They stated that one of the most important causes is the temporal aspect of triggers and actions [15, 28] since users are often confused when they had to distinguish triggers based on events (i.e., that occur in a specific moment in time) and states (i.e., that are true over a time span). This research focuses on the temporal aspect of triggers in TAP, proposing and evaluating a tool that provides explicit support for state/event distinction.

3   The SENSATION Tool

SENSATION (Smart EveNt and State AcTION rules) is a tool for the EUD of Trigger-Action rules designed to facilitate the distinction between events and state. Our starting point was that this distinction might be challenging to articulate by users but essential to recognize and reduce at least specific common bugs [4, 13–15].

Our first design assumption is that a constrained syntactic structure may help the user recognize the different roles of events and states in a rule [13, 15]. In the interface, this is implemented by structuring the rules on the form "DO <action> WHEN <event> WHILE <states specifications>".

The users might find it challenging to articulate the distinction between events and states [14, 15] (for example, between the event "the door is opening" and the state "the door is open"). Therefore, our second design assumption is that a filtering approach may alleviate the need to make such a distinction. In this respect, our interface structures the filling of the three parts of a rule by providing filtered access to actions, events, and state specifications. Figure 1 displays the main screen of the SENSATION interface. It has two principal areas: the top area that displays the three main parts of a rule, namely the action (called DO), the trigger event (called WHEN), and the state (called WHILE); and the bottom area in which the elements that can be chosen according to the specific part of the rule are listed.

SENSATION proposes a constrained process to construct triggering rules by which the user has to answer three questions: (1) what will be done? (2) what happens? (3) in which configuration of states should hold for the rule to trigger? The two final questions are meant to help the user to manage the distinction between events and states correctly.

Although the interface implicitly suggests starting from the action part, the user can decide whether to start from the event or the states. While one of the parts is selected, the specific elements are listed in the bottom area. The DO part can be filled with one action or a sequence of actions. The WHEN part has to be filled with exactly one event. The WHILE is optional; if present, it contains one or more state specifications. A video reporting an example of a rule created with SENSATION is available at this link https://youtu.be/_TOuFC8ghgI.

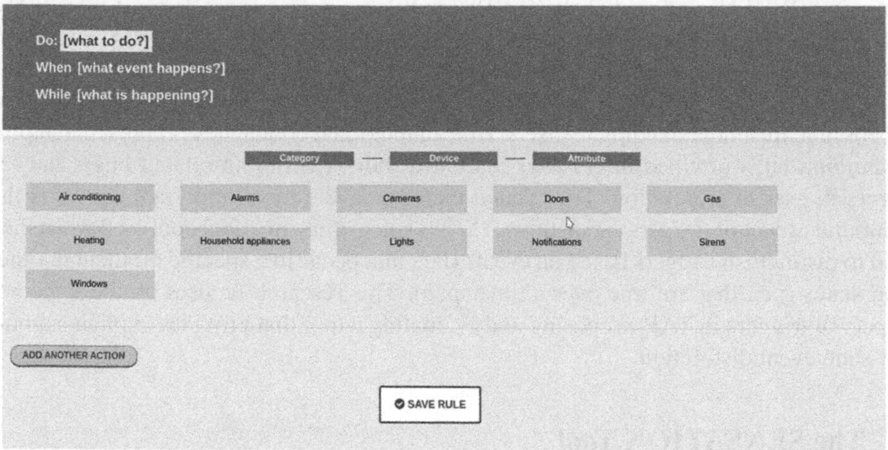

Fig. 1. The main screen of SENSATION where the users start the creation of rules by composing the DO (action), WHEN (event) and WHILE (the states). In the screen, the DO part is selected and the actual devices are listed: once selected the device, the tool will propose to select the specific actions available for that specific device.

4   The User Study

The study has been designed as a *within-subject* study with SENSATION as the experimental condition and EFESTO-5W [1, 2, 10] as a control condition. The study's main objective was to assess if the explicit support for choosing events and states in SENSATION improves accuracy in writing Trigger Action Rules with respect to the state-of-the-art TAP approaches.

From the SENSATION design assumptions, we posed the following hypothesis for the experimental study:

- *H1: SENSATION induces a more accurate definition of rules than EFESTO-5W, for those tasks in which the distinction between events and states is crucial (as discussed above);*
- *H2: the time to complete successful tasks with SENSATION should not be longer than with EFESTO-5W, despite it more strongly constrains the interaction.*
- *H3: the perceived usability of SENSATION is not lower than the usability of EFESTO-5W, despite it more strongly constrains the interaction.*

4.1   Materials

EFESTO-5W [10] has been selected as a control condition because *(i)* it outperforms popular tools like IFTTT [16]; *(ii)* it can be customized in term of smart devices and digital services to be used in the ECA rules; and (iii) it supports multiple events, states, and actions but without explicitly support the distinction between events and states.

Both SENSATION and EFESTO-5W have been configured with the same descriptions of smart devices, events and actions for a scenario of smart home control.

For the study, four tasks have been created. The first task requires a simple event/action rule: it has been used to provide a baseline between the two systems (we did not expect a difference in performance with this task). The other three tasks are based on the classes of bugs for TAP proposed by Brackenbury and colleagues [4]. The tasks have been proposed in the form of scenarios for which participants had to write the rules, (in both SENSATION and EFESTO-5W) to realize them (see Table 1).

Table 1. List of tasks in the form of scenarios and their rationale in the study

#	Task scenarios	Rationale for the tasks
T1	You want to have cameras record who is buzzing your home	Simple task that requires only one event and no states, it is used as a baseline to compare the systems
T2	It starts to rain but you are not at home (Via Roma 2, Milan) and you want to make sure that no water gets in through the windows	Medium difficulty task that may induce a *time window fallacy* bug
T3	With the alarm on, there must be no open windows	Difficult task that may induce a *flipped triggers* bug
T4	The camera detects that you are approaching the door of your house (via Roma 2, Milan) and you want the door to open automatically	Difficult task that may induce a *contradictory triggers* bug

4.2 Measures

For what concerns quantitative data, measures of performance and measures of perceived usability have been collected. The performance has been assessed by manually annotating the correct (referred to as "S" for success below) and the incorrect (referred to as "F" for failure) task execution. Furthermore, a task has been classified as partially corrected (referred to as "P") in those cases in which additional spurious elements are added (like more actions than requested or redundant states). Task time completion has also been recorded for successful and partially successful tasks. The SUS (System Usability Scale) questionnaire [6] has been used for measuring perceived usability, and the UMUX-Lite questionnaire [20] for user experience. Regarding qualitative data, the errors in the tasks have been analyzed and classified.

4.3 Participants and Procedure

Due to COVID-19 restrictions, the study had to be performed remotely. The tool *eGLU-Box PA* [11] has been used to perform the remote study. The participants have been recruited among the students at the University of Bari and at the University of Trento on a voluntary basis.

Forty (40) volunteers (14 females) were recruited. Their mean age was 21.7 years (SD = 3.46). All of them declared a good knowledge of IT technology (7.8/10, SD = 1.28), a medium experience with programming languages (4.8/10, SD = 4.81), a good experience with the use of IoT technology (6.2/10, SD = 2.0), and medium knowledge of tools for IoT configuration (5.1/10, SD = 2.28).

The participants received an email with a detailed description of the study and the specification of the required software and hardware (PC, microphone, a standard browser, and a stable internet connection), the link to the pre-questionnaire, and the link to start the test in eGLU-Box PA. The participants were free to decide when to do the study, but they were asked to start within few days from the reception of the email and complete it in one round.

The conditions and tasks were randomized among participants following a Latin-square design to avoid the carry-over effect. After the task execution, eGLU-Box PA administered the SUS [6] and UMUX-Lite questionnaires [20].

4.4 Results

Two participants experienced technical problems, and they are not included in the analysis, which therefore considers 38 participants.

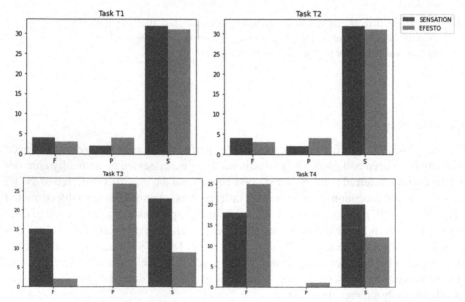

Fig. 2. Histograms depicting the distribution of successes (S), partial successes (P) and failures (F) for the 4 tasks in the two tools.

Analysis of Performance – Task Success (H1). Figure 2 shows the distribution of successes (S), partial successes (P), and failures (F) for the 4 tasks in the two systems. SENSATION seems to perform better than EFESTO in all tasks but the first one. In order to analyze the differences, we assigned a score of 2 to each successful task, a score of 1 to each partial successful task, and 0 to each failed task. Since the distributions are not normally distributed, we used the non-parametric Wilcoxon test, which also accounts for repeated measures.

Overall, SENSATION has a better performance rate with an average score of 1.19 (SD = 0.89) while EFESTO has an average score of 0.98 (SD = .97); the difference is statistically significant (Wilcoxon w = 550.0, p < 0.01).

Significant differences in the mean scores are found for task T2 (SENSATION $\bar{x}$ = 0.7, SD = 0.94; EFESTO $\bar{x}$ = 0.34, SD = 0.75; Wilcoxon w = 22.5, p < 0.05) and task T4 (SENSATION $\bar{x}$ = 1.05, std = 1.10, EFESTO $\bar{x}$ = 0.66, std = 0.94; Wilcoxon w = 6.0, p < 0.05).

The differences in task T1 and T3 are not statistically significant (for T1 SENSATION $\bar{x}$ = 1.74, SD = .64, EFESTO $\bar{x}$ = 1.74, SD = 0.60; Wilcoxon w = 10.5, p = 1.0; for T3: SENSATION $\bar{x}$ = 1.2, SD = 0.99, EFESTO $\bar{x}$ = 1.18, SD = 0.51; Wilcoxon w = 211.0, p = 0.876).

Qualitative Analysis of Errors (H1). In total, 130 errors have been detected and analyzed. As expected, the errors are not distributed evenly across tasks and participants. Task T1 had a minimal number of errors in both systems. These errors are usually related to the wrong choice of the event or the action. The most error-prone tasks are T2 (with 58 errors in total, 22 in SENSATION and 36 in EFESTO) and T4 (45 errors in total, 20 in SENSATION, and 25 in EFESTO). That is not surprising since both these tasks require a distinction between an event (respectively, the ringing of the bell and the detection of movement by the camera) and a state (the person's location). Task T3 is more complicated. This task required understanding the alarm both as an event and as a state. In EFESTO, the users made fewer errors (2 vs. 15 in SENSATION) but there a lot of partial successes (27 vs no partial successes in SENSATION) and fewer successes (9 vs. 23 in SENSATION). The most common type of error in SENSATION was the addition of unrelated events. In few cases, the participants confused the event with the action. In EFESTO, participants chose the wrong event or the wrong action. The partial successes were mainly due to the choice of either the event or the state related to the alarm but not both. Furthermore, this task has been perceived as ambiguous by many users. As a check, we tried the statistical tests on the performances described above without considering task T3. The results are comparable with a significant difference overall and for T2 and T4, and no significant difference for T1.

Analysis of Performance – Task Time (H2). For what concerns the time to completion (for successful and partially successful) tasks, SENSATION has an average time of 82 s (SD = 38.97) and EFESTO an average time of 97 s (SD = 52.49). Yet, there is a high variability (from a minimum of 20 s to a maximum of over 5 min: $\bar{x}$ = 89.5, SD = 52.49). Furthermore, the distributions are not normally distributed, and the variances are not equal. At the same time, the two samples are not independent. Therefore, none of the standard tests can be applied. Kruskal-Wallis test suggests that the means are not statistically different (w = 2.7, p = 0.097), while Welch test suggests a difference w = −2.13, p < 0.05 (it is worth noting that the Kruskal-Wallis' condition of independence is violated as well as the Welch's condition of normality).

Analysis of Perceived Usability (H3). The SUS scores highlighted that SENSATION had a good usability level with an average score of 70.6/100 (SD = 18.1) [3]. The high scores are also maintained in the two SUS subscales [19]: Usability has a mean score of 78.3 (SD = 16.4) and Learnability has a mean score of 80.9 (SD = 16.3).

EFESTO-5W, too, demonstrated high scores with a mean global SUS score of 77.2/100 (SD = 15.1); for the Usability subscale, the mean score is 72.2/100 (SD = 17.3) and for the Learnability scale, the mean score is 70.1/100 (SD = 22.2). Paired sample t-test revealed that there are no statistical significant differences between the two systems in term of SUS and its subscales ($t_{SUS\_GLOBAL}(37)$ = 1.819, p = 0.077; $t_{SUS\_USABILITY}(37)$ = 1.689, p = 0.099; $t_{SUS\_LEARNABILITY}(37)$ = 1.729, p = 0.092).

Similarly, the analysis of UMUX-Lite results revealed overall good UX of both EFESTO ($\bar{x}$ = 5.6, SD = 1.2) and SENSATION ($\bar{x}$ = 5.3, SD = 1.2), and even in this case, no differences emerged applying the paired sample t-test (t(37) = 1.108, p = 0.274).

5 Discussion and Conclusion

The study results indicate that the tasks have generally performed well both in EFESTO and in SENSATION. The simpler task T1, used a baseline, had a very high success score for both tools. The tasks T2 and T4, whose correct definition depended on an accurate distinction between events and states, had a better performance in SENSATION, as hypothesized (H1). That may suggest that the structured approach offered by SEN-SATION is effective in this respect. For time of execution, the statistical analysis may weakly suggest that SENSATION allowed a quicker completion of the tasks despite it more strongly constrains the interaction, as hypothesized (H2). Finally, both systems have a similar high score on usability, as hypothesized (H3).

Overall, we can claim that SENSATION provides effective support in managing the distinction between events and state without complicating the whole approach.

The study described has several limitations. In particular, task T3 raised some interpretation problems by users that make it difficult to properly analyze the performance. Although the results seemed to be robust even without considering it, this might impact the analysis of the users' experience. Furthermore, participants were just briefly exposed to both systems with minimal training. Therefore, the tasks had been kept simple. Longer and ecological studies with more meaningful tasks are needed.

As future work, we planned to refine SENSATION taking into account the limitations that emerged in this study. The new version of the tool will be also evaluated by performing a wider and deeper controlled experiment with more users and in different domains, as well as during a longitudinal study in real contexts.

Acknowledgment. This work is partially supported by the Italian Ministry of University and Research (MIUR) under grant PRIN 2017 "EMPATHY: EMpowering People in deAling with internet of THings ecosYstems."

References

1. Ardito, C., Desolda, G., Lanzilotti, R., Malizia, A., Matera, M.: Analysing trade-offs in frameworks for the design of smart environments. Behav. Inf. Technol. **39**(1), 47–71 (2019)
2. Ardito, C., et al.: User-defined semantics for the design of IoT systems enabling smart interactive experiences. Pers. Ubiquit. Comput. **24**(6), 781–796 (2020). https://doi.org/10.1007/s00779-020-01457-5
3. Bangor, A., Kortum, P., Miller, J.: The system usability scale (SUS): an empirical evaluation. Int. J. Hum.-Comput. Interact. **24**(6), 574–594 (2008)
4. Brackenbury, W., et al.: How users interpret bugs in trigger-action programming. In: Proceedings of the Human Factors in Computing Systems (CHI '19), Paper 552. Association for Computing Machinery (2019)
5. Brich, J., Walch, M., Rietzler, M., Weber, M., Schaub, F.: Exploring end user programming needs in home automation. ACM Trans. Comput.-Hum. Interact. **24**(2), 1–35, Article no. 11 (2017)
6. Brooke, J.: SUS-A quick and dirty usability scale. Usability Eval. Ind. **189**(194), 4–7 (1996)
7. Corno, F., Russis, L.D., Roffarello, A.M.: Empowering end users in debugging trigger-action rules. In: Proceedings of the Conference on Human Factors in Computing Systems (CHI '19), Paper 388. Association for Computing Machinery (2019)
8. Corno, F., Russis, L.D., Roffarello, A.M.: TAPrec: supporting the composition of trigger-action rules through dynamic recommendations. In: Proceedings of the International Conference on Intelligent User Interfaces (IUI '20), pp. 579–588. Association for Computing Machinery (2020)
9. Coronado, M., Iglesias, C.A.: Task automation services: automation for the masses. IEEE Internet Comput. **20**(1), 52–58 (2016)
10. Desolda, G., Ardito, C., Matera, M.: Empowering end users to customize their smart environments: model, composition paradigms and domain-specific tools. ACM Trans. Comput.-Hum. Interact. **24**(2), 52, Article no. 12 (2017)
11. Federici, S., et al.: Heuristic evaluation of eGLU-Box: a semi-automatic usability evaluation tool for public administrations. In: Kurosu, M. (ed.) HCII 2019. LNCS, vol. 11566, pp. 75–86. Springer, Cham (2019). https://doi.org/10.1007/978-3-030-22646-6_6
12. Fischer, G., Giaccardi, E., Ye, Y., Sutcliffe, A., Mehandjiev, N.: Meta-design: a manifesto for end-user development. Commun. ACM **47**(9), 33–37 (2004)
13. Gallitto, G., Treccani, B., Zancanaro, M.: If when is better than if (and while might help): on the importance of influencing mental models in EUD (a pilot study). In: Proceedings of the 1st International Workshop on Empowering People in Dealing with Internet of Things Ecosystems - Co-located with International Conference on Advanced Visual Interfaces (AVI 2020) (EMPATHY '20). CEUR-WS (2020)
14. Ghiani, G., Manca, M., Paternò, F., Santoro, C.: Personalization of context-dependent applications through trigger-action rules. ACM Trans. Comput.-Hum. Interact. **24**(2), 33, Article no. 14 (2017)
15. Huang, J., Cakmak, M.: Supporting mental model accuracy in trigger-action programming. In: Proceedings of the ACM International Joint Conference on Pervasive and Ubiquitous Computing, pp. 215–225. Association for Computing Machinery, Osaka, Japan (2015)
16. IFTTT Inc. IFTTT. https://ifttt.com/. Accessed 1 June 2019
17. Ninja Blocks Inc.: Ninja Blocks. https://github.com/ninjablocks. Accessed 10 Apr 2021
18. Bae, J., Bae, H., Kang, S.-H., Kim, Y.: Automatic control of workflow processes using ECA rules. IEEE Trans. Knowl. Data Eng. **16**(8), 1010–1023 (2004)
19. Lewis, J.R., Sauro, J.: The factor structure of the system usability scale. In: Kurosu, M. (ed.) HCD 2009. LNCS, vol. 5619, pp. 94–103. Springer, Heidelberg (2009). https://doi.org/10.1007/978-3-642-02806-9_12

20. Lewis, J.R., Utesch, B.S., Maher, D.E.: UMUX-LITE: when there's no time for the SUS. In: Proceedings of the Conference on Human Factors in Computing Systems (CHI '13), pp. 2099–2102. ACM, New York, NY, USA (2013)

21. Liang, C.-J.M., et al.: Systematically debugging IoT control system correctness for building automation. In: Proceedings of (BuildSys '16), pp. 133–142. Association for Computing Machinery (2016)

22. Metaxas, G., Markopoulos, P.: Natural contextual reasoning for end users. ACM Trans. Comput.-Hum. Interact. **24**(2), 1–36, Article no. 13 (2017)

23. Microsoft: Microsoft flow. https://flow.microsoft.com/. Accessed 28 Feb 2021

24. Mozilla: WebThings gateway. https://iot.mozilla.org/gateway/. Accessed 10 Apr 2021

25. Russis, L.D., Roffarello, A.M.: A debugging approach for trigger-action programming. In: Proceedings of the Extended Abstracts of the 2018 CHI Conference on Human Factors in Computing Systems. Paper LBW105. Association for Computing Machinery, Montreal QC, Canada (2018)

26. SmartThings. SmartRules. https://smartrulesapp.com/. Accessed 10 Apr 2021

27. Truong, K.N., Huang, E.M., Abowd, G.D.: CAMP: a magnetic poetry interface for end-user programming of capture applications for the home. In: Davies, N., Mynatt, E.D., Siio, I. (eds.) UbiComp 2004. LNCS, vol. 3205, pp. 143–160. Springer, Heidelberg (2004). https://doi.org/10.1007/978-3-540-30119-6_9

28. Ur, B., et al.: Trigger-action programming in the wild: an analysis of 200,000 IFTTT recipes. In: Proceedings of the SIGCHI Conference on Human Factors in Computing Systems (CHI '16), pp. 3227–3231. ACM, New York, NY, USA (2016)

29. Zapier Inc. Zapier. https://zapier.com/. Accessed 9 May 2021

The Controversy of Responsibility and Accountability When Maintaining Automatic External Defibrillators
Infrastructuring Lifesaving Technology with an IoT Solution

Oliver Rønn Christensen[1][✉], Signe Helbo Gregers Sørensen[1], Anne Stouby Persson[1], Anne Marie Kanstrup[1], and Adrienne Mannov[2]

[1] Department of Planning, Aalborg University, Aalborg, Denmark
{ochris16,shgs16,aperss16}@student.aau.dk, kanstrup@plan.aau.dk
[2] School of Culture and Society, Aarhus University, Aarhus, Denmark
mannov@cas.au.dk

Abstract. This paper contributes to HCI with a foundation for exploring ways in which an Internet of Things (IoT) solution can support the maintenance of public automated defibrillators (AEDs) sustainably. AED is a critical lifesaving technology installed in non-medical environments. The technology places enormous demands on public engagement for its use and maintenance. Insights into how medical technology is maintained in non-medical environments can complement current innovations in lifesaving technology. This ethnographic study investigates the complexity around an IoT solution to remedy breakdowns in the maintenance of AEDs in a Danish context. We conceptualize maintenance as infrastructuring and identify how the diverse field of actors around an AED entails technical but primarily social dimensions revealing a controversy of responsibility and accountability. This article recommends that when developing an IoT solution for maintaining AEDs, technical, social, political, and ethical dimensions should be considered to address responsibility and accountability issues.

Keywords: Health · Public automated external defibrillators · Ethnography · Infrastructure · IoT

1 Introduction

In 2018, there were 5,400 incidences of out-of-hospital cardiac arrest in Denmark [1]. Chances of surviving an out-of-hospital cardiac arrest diminish minute by minute without intervention, giving a survival rate that remains below 10% [2]. In the event of an out-of-hospital cardiac arrest, immediate cardiopulmonary resuscitation (CPR) and early defibrillation by an automated external defibrillator (AED) are the most critical interventions. These interventions show survival proportions between 50% [2] and 74% [3].

An AED is a transportable and automated defibrillator driven by a battery. It can analyze a person's heart rhythm and provide an electric shock if necessary by using gel

© IFIP International Federation for Information Processing 2021
Published by Springer Nature Switzerland AG 2021
C. Ardito et al. (Eds.): INTERACT 2021, LNCS 12933, pp. 383–401, 2021.
https://doi.org/10.1007/978-3-030-85616-8_23

pads [4]. The gel pads are durable for up to two years but must be changed if the AED has been used. The battery can last between three to five years, depending on the brand of the AED [5]. The AED can also indicate if a technical error has occurred by turning off a little green light [5]. While lifesaving technologies are most often under the auspices of hospitals, AEDs can be placed in a community (Fig. 1) as part of a public access defibrillation program. The American Heart Association and the European Resuscitation Council support several public access defibrillation programs that encourage laypersons to use AEDs outside a hospital context [2, 6].

Fig. 1. Automated external defibrillator.

For an AED to function as intended, it needs maintenance. AEDs need to be registered to be findable by a layperson [7, 8] and fully functional, with timely maintenance keeping the battery charged, sustaining the right cabinet temperature, and replacing dried-out gel pads [5, 8]. Studies from the United States [9, 10] and Singapore [8] and campaigns in Canada [11], the United States [12], and Denmark [7] raised awareness and educated the public about how to use and where to locate AEDs in case of an emergency [7]. However, these studies and campaigns do not focus on how and if the AEDs are fully functional over a more extended time. Therefore, when a layperson locates an AED in an emergency, a fully functional AED is not guaranteed [8]. In a Danish context, the owner is responsible for maintaining the AED, which in practice can be difficult for a layperson [13]. The lack of AED maintenance has been brought to both the Danish Parliament and Danish media attention several times [14]. In Denmark, where this study was conducted, no regulations are making the maintenance of AEDs compulsory, only a letter of recommendation from the Danish Health Authority stating that 1) all public sector owned AEDs must be registered on a free public online webpage, like Hjertestarter.dk, 2) there must be a standardized procedure when the AED has been used (e.g., registration of its location), and 3) a set procedure with an automatic electronic reminder that the AED needs maintenance [5]. Despite heightened focus on the awareness of maintaining AEDs, the controversy of who should maintain the AEDs and how remains.

In response to this controversy, a Danish non-governmental organization (NGO) has entered into a partnership with a Danish IoT Company to develop an Internet of Things (IoT) solution to help improve and support the maintenance of AEDs.[1] This IoT solution will become part of an insurance policy sold by the NGO to achieve fully functioning AEDs. The IoT solution aims to monitor AEDs in Denmark digitally, so errors in the AED can be detected and rectified. The NGO collaborates with a Danish IoT Company and a Danish Tele Company, which develops and provides the technical equipment. The development of this IoT solution was this study's point of departure, which led us to the broader investigation of the maintenance of AEDs in Denmark, opening the field to include an Administrative Organization and a Health Clinic. By analyzing the IoT solution and how it interacts with the other actors mentioned above, this study conceptualizes the maintenance of AEDs at an infrastructural level. This diverse field of actors shows that maintaining an AED does not just entail technical but also social dimensions. This diverse field inspired our theoretical perspectives on infrastructure and infrastructuring as an analytic lens to support an investigation of maintaining AEDs. As an AED is a public lifesaving technology, it places enormous demands on civic engagement. Understanding the complexity around an IoT solution is essential for future innovation of AEDs specifically and as a general insight into medical technology in non-medical environments.

While an infrastructure is conventionally considered a physical or technical foundation, Star and Ruhleder [15] proposed that infrastructure is socio-technical and relational. An infrastructure never stands apart from its designers, users, and people who maintain it [16]. The notion of infrastructuring emphasizes the processual qualities of creating and enacting infrastructures [17]. Maintaining AEDs in Denmark depends on public and civic engagement and voluntariness, with no compulsory regulations explained. Thus, the infrastructural circumstances regarding the responsibility can be arbitrary.

Given this socio-technical perspective, we argue that the infrastructuring of AED maintenance reveals a controversy of responsibility and accountability when the infrastructuring becomes connected and dependent upon multiple actors. In this paper, we differentiate between the notion of responsibility and accountability because responsibility is something that can be shared by various actors [42], and accountability is something only one actor can be attributed [40, 42]. We will further elaborate this in Sect. 2, 'Related Work.'

By investigating lifesaving technology outside the hospital setting, we further suggest that we can uncover why AED maintenance gets neglected by directing our attention to the infrastructural issues connected to AED maintenance. By adopting this infrastructural approach, we can explore how the proposed IoT solution could help sustainably maintain AEDs. In Sect. 5, we discuss why only focusing on the IoT solution as a technical dimension is problematic if wanting long-lasting upkeep and maintenance while critiquing the IoT technology as the answer to the controversy of responsibility and accountability. This study contributes to HCI by raising explicit attention to the discussion on responsibility and accountability in how AEDs are maintained and neglected.

---

[1] The name of the solution and names of the people involved have been pseudonymized.

2   Related Work

Previous research on AEDs in HCI has examined ways of technically optimizing AEDs by designing interactive systems with IoT-generated data [18, 19] and the training of laypersons [20, 21]. Furthermore, previous research on infrastructures of healthcare technology and IoT, primarily relates to medical applications such as fitness programs, health monitoring, and healthcare at home [22]. The research on infrastructure has attended to medication plans [23], electronic patient records [24], clinicians in hospitals [25], and how patients and caregivers make healthcare infrastructure work [16]. Research on infrastructuring and health information technology in the HCI literature presents a systematic perspective that supports a multifaceted approach. However, research on AEDs and infrastructuring is scarce, which means that researching AED maintenance with an IoT solution does not necessarily warrant an exclusive focus on the technical parts. It creates a space for investigating AED maintenance from a social, material, technical, political, and ethical perspective at the same time. For this study, exploring and analyzing the different perspectives in relation to each other enables a more holistic approach to an otherwise technical solution. As we discovered that the social and ethical concerns were vital, we realized that "maintenance" was not just technical. "Infrastructuring" helped us unpack the intertwining of the technical with the social and ethical and pointed us methodologically to ask about these connections [41].

As we will show, maintaining AEDs is a particular activity that needs social and technical infrastructure support. In studying infrastructuring, explicit attention to the ways people engage in the processes of infrastructure is required. Infrastructuring STS scholars Karasti and Blomberg (2018) argue that:

"The 'ing' terminology, including adapting, tailoring, appropriating, tuning, modifying, tweaking, making, fixing, monitoring, maintaining, repairing, hacking, vandalizing and instrumenting (…) shape infrastructures" [17].

Following this logic, we move beyond the hospital setting to the non-medical public, being "a particular configuration of individuals bound by common cause in confronting a shared issue" [26]. The issue in our case was out-of-hospital cardiac arrests. An infrastructure of volunteering [27] or infrastructuring civic engagement [28] may describe the AED as it is procured, used, and maintained by laypersons.

The social dimension of infrastructures makes them fundamentally relational, emerging in situ with organized practices and connected to particular activities [15]. Infrastructures are relational as they emerge in relation to other organized practices. They are not just stable objects of inquiry: "(…) the cook considers the water system as working infrastructure integral to preparing dinner, for the city planner it is a variable in a complex planning process, and for the plumber it is a target for repair" [17].

Just as infrastructures are relational, they are also connected. A relation depends on more than just itself. It requires other elements to be complete [17]. Star and Ruhleder [15] describe connectedness or scaling of infrastructures as reaching beyond a single event or a one-site practice. Connectedness as a characteristic of a phenomenon brings together things of different scales, extending the infrastructures' social, material, technical, and political dimensions [17]. Star [29] underlines the importance of these dimensions when looking into infrastructures. It especially emphasizes the ethical dimensions: "Perhaps most important of all, what values and ethical principles do we inscribe in the inner depths of the built information environment [the infrastructure]?" [29]. Therefore, attention to the social, technical, political, and ethical dimensions is valuable. They can reveal controversies in the infrastructuring of maintaining AEDs when the infrastructuring becomes connected to multiple actors.

In addition to being connected, infrastructures are emerging and in the making. The stability of infrastructures is relative and is an ongoing development process [30]. Karasti and Blomberg characterize the emerging quality of infrastructure formation as "temporal complexities full of ups and downs, false starts, disconnects, dead ends and failures" [17]. Therefore, actors developing an infrastructure need to do regular repairs, monitoring, and upkeep when it does not perform as planned.

The emerging qualities of infrastructuring when developing the IoT solution for maintaining AEDs also demand actors attending to the long-term sustainability of the IoT solution. This long-term perspective on developing infrastructures relates to Ribes and Finholt's focus on tensions between the short-term and the long-term vistas and their view of "the long now" [31]. The "now" of the IoT solution's development may inscribe tensions to long-term needs within the infrastructuring for maintaining AEDs.

Regarding infrastructuring of AED maintenance, recognizing differences in infrastructuring approaches is essential when understanding different actors' agendas. In this paper, infrastructuring AED maintenance is both seen through the lens of self-organized activities defined by individual willingness and an ad hoc approach, but also through the goal of creating a commercial IoT solution for maintaining AEDs. As described later in this paper, the tension between the different approaches of conceptualizing infrastructuring AED maintenance can cause controversies concerning responsibility and accountability.

Excellent and usable infrastructures disappear almost by definition: "the easier they are to use, the harder they are to see" [17]. By being out of the way, infrastructures gain their most significant effect when taken for granted and sometimes deliberately hidden [17]. However, making infrastructures invisible is an outcome of considerable work, effort, and investment [17]. The invisible becomes visible when the infrastructures break [15], which our study of maintaining AED will show. In healthcare infrastructure research, Gui and Chen [16] have shown that attending to breakdowns helps understand how patients and caregivers make healthcare infrastructure work. When infrastructures break down, the taken-for-granted logic and negotiations, needed to enable them to function, become visible. Therefore, attention to breakdowns that make infrastructures visible is relevant when looking into maintaining AEDs.

Scholarly work by Nissenbaum on accountability and responsibility [42] implies, "Responsibility, characteristically understood and traditionally analyzed in terms of a single individual, does not easily generalize to collective action" [42]. Going from self-organized maintenance to a commercially driven approach increases the number of actors involved, introducing more relations responsible for the maintenance to function. Nissenbaum draws on a moral-philosophical conceptual framework for understanding the interrelated concepts of liability, blame, and accountability in computerized systems [42]. This framework is used as a guideline when highlighting the increasing obscurity of accountability within computerized societies when, e.g., computerized systems are being built by "the hands of many" [42] or, in this study, connecting several actors in the development of an IoT solution to maintain AEDs. Nissenbaum emphasizes that labeling harm as accidents by the fault of the technology may produce further issues with the obscurity of accountability, highlighting that using "computers-as-scapegoats" may be tempting because "(…) computers present a curious challenge and temptation. As distinct from many other inanimate objects, computers perform tasks previously performed by humans in positions of responsibility. They calculate, decide, control, and remember" [42]. Holding computerized systems as "scapegoats" may, at first sight, be attractive, but as pointed out by Elish [40], that will not contribute to justice or serve the public good. Elish emphasizes the need for locating the responsible actor when a system fails and refers to the concept of 'moral crumple zones' deriving from 'crumple zones.' A crumple zone is intended to protect the human sitting in a car in case of an accident. The concept of a 'moral crumple zone' refers to cases where the aim is to protect a highly complex and automated system - the IoT solution for AEDs. However, the accountability for a fault often ends up being attributed to a human actor who had limited control of the failure in the automated and complex system. Thus, understanding the relational aspects of the different actors connected to maintaining AEDs may help untangle the obscurity presented by the many actors and differentiate between the social, technical, political, and ethical dimensions.

3 Methods

This section presents the ethnographic research methods used to investigate the infrastructuring of maintaining AEDs, constructed during our data collection.

3.1 Constructing the Field

We initiated our investigation by first contacting the Danish IoT Company that develops the hardware and software for the IoT solution. Here, Lucas, the CEO, a 'gatekeeper' [32], helped us extend our fieldwork to include the NGO that had initiated the IoT solution. The NGO pointed us to the Electrician Company responsible for installing the developed hardware on the AEDs. They also introduced us to the Medical Company that monitors the information in a software solution gathered from the hardware installed on the AEDs. To unfold the diversity of the infrastructuring of maintaining AEDs, we included a health clinic in possession of one AED and an administrative organization that owns and maintains 96 AEDs. As our fieldwork developed, so did our field. We ended up with our constructed field of informants being the IoT Company, NGO, Electrician Company, Medical Company, Health Clinic, and Administrative Organization (Fig. 2).

Ethnographically studying infrastructuring allows us to unfold the social, technical, political, and ethical dimensions present [17] within maintaining AEDs. Unfolding is a relational and situated job for ethnographers [33]. According to Karasti and Blomberg, we can understand the ethnographer's work as a fragmented process of creating options and possibilities when following connections and interactions between informants [17]. When studying the phenomenon, being the infrastructuring of maintaining AEDs, our field becomes constructed with this study's informants, the questions we ask, and how we understand the informants' answers. It is essential to be aware of the process of

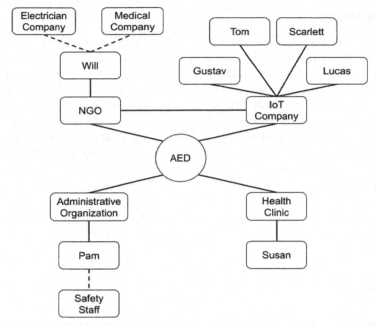

Fig. 2. The constructed field in this study. The fully marked lines indicate direct contact with our informants, and the dotted lines indicate actors mentioned by our informants.

constructing the field when seeking to unfold and understand the dynamics that consti-tute the phenomenon of infrastructuring [17]. In our case, it is the infrastructuring of maintaining AEDs. When engaging in a field where actors are not all in the same place, multi-sited ethnography [17] is useful as it brings the possibility of constructing the field by following connections of the phenomenon, being the infrastructuring of maintaining AEDs, as they arise.

3.2 Data and Materials

This study began in February 2020 and ran until June 2020, and the methods used to gather data derive from the anthropological discipline, being ethnographic methods. The methods include participant observations [34, 35] and interviews [36]. We conducted participant observations at the IoT Company at the start and at the end of the study, where we gained knowledge about the IoT Company. Furthermore, we met different employees, extending our insights into the diversity in the IoT Company's ongoing tasks. We carried out our unstructured interviews during the participant observations where we spoke with different employees involved in developing the hardware and software for the IoT solution. These observations and unstructured interviews provided us with knowledge about the various challenges of developing the IoT solution. In total, we conducted 14 interviews, both unstructured and semistructured [36], with a duration ranging from 10 min to two hours. We carried out the interviews with employees from the IoT Company, the NGO, the Administrative Organization, and the Health Clinic.

3.3 Data Analysis

In our analytical process, initial patterns related to the informants' experience with the infrastructural properties of maintaining AEDs emerged. Following the data, we used the software program NVivo to categorize and code [38] the detailed descriptions of the dialogues from the interviews and field notes. We conducted coding in two rounds. The first round was open coding [37], where we kept an open approach and looked for categories by marking excerpts with codes. Based on the open coding, we went to the second round, focused coding [37]. Here, we looked for patterns among the many identified categories to identify overarching themes. Using this study's theoretical framework of infrastructure and infrastructuring [17], analytical points emerged that constitute our findings by analyzing these overriding themes. This iterative process involved going back and forth between the inductive notions and patterns from the field [37, 38] and the deductive understandings [39] from the theoretical framework. Growing out of this coding process, we used a thematic narrative approach [37] to present our findings below.

4 Findings

Our thematic narrative approach converts our data into a coherent story, using excerpts, where the emerging themes from the coding process structure the narrative [37]. When unfolding the infrastructuring of maintaining AEDs, we noticed, through the work with our informants, that the social dimension of responsibility becomes a matter of accountability, which leads to controversy across organizational levels. Will, from the NGO, acknowledges the controversy of responsibility and accountability when maintaining AEDs. He pointed out that the person responsible for checking up on the AED and, e.g., calling electricians to fix errors, could end up feeling accountable for a fully functioning AED, with life and death as a potentiality. This feeling of accountability is one reason the NGO has initiated the development of an IoT solution. Will says:

> "We sell the IoT solution as part of an insurance policy. You get everything. We take care of everything, all maintenance for the customer; there will not be any unexpected bills. You get the whole package. This is safety. We are selling, taking the responsibility (...) If that person vanishes, there is no one taking care of the AED. With our future service agreement, this will not be the case. The AED will be cared for".

With the IoT solution, the NGO wants to take on the responsibility of accommodating the person who feels accountable for taking care of the AED. By taking the responsibility, they are ensuring that the AEDs will be maintained and stay fully functional. When we met Pam from the Administrative Organization, we found out that she is maintaining 96 AEDs. Pam is dedicated to maintaining the AEDs, but at the same time, she is what Will described as "that person" responsible for the maintenance, and if she "vanishes there is no one taking care of the AED". Pam said:

"I don't mind the responsibility, but it could be an advantage to have a technology that could support that the maintenance actually gets done. Right now, there are a lot of human factors that the maintenance depends upon".

In the next section, we follow Will, Pam, and Susan, as we unfold the relational infrastructural landscape of maintaining AEDs, leading to breakdowns, which draws our attention to the controversy of responsibility and accountability.

4.1 'The Wild West' of Infrastructuring

"As a private owner of an AED, you're not bound to anything. You can install an AED that does not work. Many people think that it is something that the State is accountable for, but that is not the case! There are no rules about this! You can install all the AEDs you like and then just remove the batteries. That's just how it is. It is the Wild West".

In this quotation, Will links the lack of Danish regulation and private AED owners' implicit accountability of maintaining AEDs to "the Wild West" – a state of lawlessness and low regulation with only the local sheriff trying to keep people safe. As a private AED owner, you cannot be held legally accountable for a non-functioning AED, which questions whether the purpose of the AED can be fulfilled in case of an emergency. With "the Wild West," there is plenty of room for breakdowns in the infrastructure of maintaining AEDs, which relates to the controversy of responsibility and accountability, as it questions who will maintain the AEDs. Susan, the receptionist at the Health Clinic, is also confused about who is responsible for maintaining AEDs. She said the following about who is responsible for their AED maintenance:

"Hmm, I'm not sure. Someone comes and changes the battery; I think it is in 2022. But I really don't know. We have it written on a note somewhere in the back office. It's a part of a Danish campaign."

Susan was not sure who was responsible for the maintenance, only that it was not the Health Clinic. She explained that she thought the maintenance was taken care of as part of the Danish campaign, wanting to distribute AEDs around the country. According to the Danish Health Authority, the responsibility of maintaining the AED relies on the actors that own the AED. Will explains how this is not always the case:

"(...) everyone can get an AED. Some owners invest in a service agreement having a firm do the check-up, but there are a lot of small firms selling it cheap. There is no control. Some firms have been in the media because they didn't live up to the signed agreement. Others do it [the maintaining] themselves."

When these relational infrastructures of maintaining AEDs become connected, reaching beyond just one actor, it becomes clear that the lawless dimension of "the Wild West" fuels the controversy of responsibility and accountability. Pam's, from the Administrative Organization, description about how she became acquainted with the AEDs and in charge of the maintenance relates to the mentioned controversy:

"The question was who is in charge of the maintenance. There is no law, no mandatory inspection. I couldn't find any regulation, but I needed to be sure the AEDs are taken care of."

It was unclear to Pam who was responsible for keeping their 96 AEDs fully functional. Pam only knew that the physical maintenance was provided by an electrician company once a year, as seen in Fig. 3. Implementing new regulations, making the AED owner legally accountable for a non-functioning AED, may seem to be an effective step to address the lawless"Wild West." However, such regulation could limit civic engagement in maintaining AEDs, as engaged people would feel hindered in acquiring AEDs. We will discuss this further in Sect. 5.1.

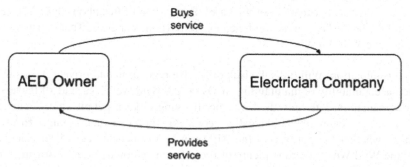

Fig. 3. Relationship of AED maintenance between the AED owner (*Administrative Organization*) and an Electrician Company.

4.2   Infrastructural Breakdowns

Breakdowns in the infrastructure of maintaining AEDs reveal the controversy of responsibility and accountability. Will described a breakdown, with an incident at a sports facility where an AED was not fully functioning and resulted in a man's death. More so, Will draws attention to breakdowns caused by poor design of the AED cabinet, leading to someone striping it together:

"People returning empty-handed because the AED is no longer there, or someone has stripped together the cabinet, making it impossible to reach the AED. Simply because the AED cabinet was poorly constructed, the battery has run flat, or the gel pads dried out, sometimes because the hard case has been opened or that there has not been a service check-up [maintenance] of the AED. All reasons for the AED not to function properly."

The technical dimension of the infrastructure for maintaining AEDs stands clear when such breakdowns happen, where the battery runs flat or gel pads dry out. Breakdowns in the relational infrastructure of maintaining AEDs is also something Pam from the Administrative Organization has experienced:

> "The AEDs kind of fell between two stools and got lost. The employee, who was very passionate about maintaining the AEDs, left his job, and no one knew, he was the one in charge of keeping an eye on the AEDs".

What Pam describes as "falling between two stools" is what we understand, as when the job of maintaining the AEDs was not taken over by other employees, when the former employee left. The responsibility of maintaining AEDs got lost, until Pam noticed it. This situation shows a breakdown in an invisible infrastructure created by the former employee. As Pam unravels this invisible infrastructure, she found that: "All emails about when to check up on the AEDs went into the former employee's mailbox." The former employee had put time and effort into the task of maintaining the AEDs. He followed the recommendation from the Danish Health Authority about an electronic reminder, creating a well-working infrastructure at the time. Because the infrastructure worked and was invisible, it was taken for granted when he left. Pam said:

> "When he left, it [emails] got lost. Somebody needs to get this reminder. Now, the emails go into our joint mailbox. We have 96 AEDs, I need to keep track of, so I created a local document on my computer, so I know what needs to be changed when."

These breakdowns in the relational infrastructures underline the unclearness about who is responsible for maintaining AEDs, which all relate to the controversy of responsibility and accountability. These breakdowns and the controversy speak to the need for a sheriff in "the Wild West." There is a need for someone to take on the responsibility of maintaining AEDs if they should continue to serve their purpose of being lifesaving technologies.

4.3 Breakdown Repair

> "(...) that's [maintenance of AEDs] Alpha and Omega. But there is no standardized procedure. Somebody must take responsibility for the maintenance. Management agreed to put them [the AEDs] up, but not the maintenance. You don't just install them. There are different types of maintenance, e.g., updates of different registers if the AEDs are moved around, doing the check-ups on AEDs, also making sure we have gel-pads in stock and keeping track of when to run a general status, which a company outside ours does. Management was like - that takes about five minutes - but it can't be done, it's unrealistic, it takes time. Someone has to feel passionate and have a true commitment when it comes to the maintenance of AEDs. We had that [refers to the former employee]."

Pam's initiative to avoid future breakdowns is by making a joint mailbox for electronic reminders and a personal, local document on her computer. In her local document, she decides on a fixed time, where all the batteries will be replaced. Pam tries to repair her experienced breakdown in the infrastructure of maintaining the AEDs. But the personal, local document makes the infrastructure fragile to future breakdowns, as she is the only person carrying the responsibility. Pam said that due to problems with her back, she needed to share the responsibility of maintaining the AEDs, prompting her to distribute the responsibility with the Safety Staff, a group of employees at the Administrative Organization. The distribution of the responsibility turned out to be a challenging task. Pam told how she used a lot of energy to make them see the importance of this task. The Safety Staff work day-to-day amongst the AEDs, making them able to detect if the AEDs send out alarms about errors, making the Safety Staff Pam's "sensors in the field." This was where Pam and the Safety Staff did not see eye to eye. As Pam said, "They didn't want to be held accountable if something wasn't working." Suddenly, the Safety Staff's work tasks were a matter of life and death, and they seemed uncomfortable with participating in the responsibility. "It's not rocket science, but there are just a lot of emotions at stake. It's not just about maintaining the AED," Pam continued. Here, Pam mentions that maintaining AEDs is not rocket science, meaning that it is not a difficult job, but the problem is that social dimensions get entangled. This draws our attention to the importance of the social and technical dimensions when maintaining AEDs. The problem is not just to distribute the responsibility. Still, the Safety Staff concerns the potentiality of them being held accountable for the AEDs and, consequently, accountable for someone's life. In this situation, the controversy of accountability and responsibility is apparent.

This section shows how Pam engages in developing an infrastructure for maintaining AEDs. Pam attempts to repair and avoid her experienced breakdowns and keep the AEDs from "falling between two stools." In this infrastructuring, Pam sees a need to distribute her responsibility of maintaining the AEDs to the Safety Staff, which leads to an unwanted feeling of being accountable.

Repairing with the IoT Solution
Just like Pam trying to repair and avoid breakdowns in AED maintenance, the NGO also takes responsibility for maintaining the AED by developing an IoT solution. As pointed out by Will in Sect. 1, 'Introduction,' the NGO wants to sell the IoT solution as part of an insurance policy, which is why they have collaborated with the IoT Company, developing the software and hardware.

Gustav, a hardware engineer at the IoT Company, showed us the hardware, which "consists of a monitoring unit and an optical eye" (Fig. 4). The monitoring unit is a white box installed in the AED cabinet connected to the "optical eye," the little black box at the end of the cord. The white box and the "optical eye" are designed to stay inside the cabinet. Gustav explained that they use magnets to make it easy for the Electrician Company to change the batteries in the monitoring unit: "If they are bolted into the cabinet, it takes too long." The IoT Company tries to avoid future breakdowns in the maintenance of the AEDs by a design that makes it easy to access the monitoring unit. In this way, the IoT Company inscribes the Electrician Company's work practices into a technical solution.

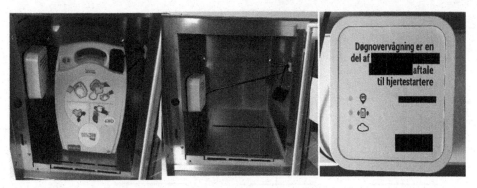

Fig. 4. Left: AED inside the cabinet. Middle: The monitoring unit and *"optical eye."* Right: The monitoring unit.

Once every hour, the monitoring unit and "optical eye" harvest data about temperature, humidity, GPS location, and its online connection. Internally, the monitoring unit and "optical eye" monitor the mentioned parameters every hour and then once a day, every 24 h, it sends these data to the Medical Company. The IoT solution functions as what Pam calls "sensors in the field." But when the social dimensions come into play, the controversy of responsibility and accountability remains.

> "The Medical Company will be given the screens [a dashboard]. They are in a better position to analyze the data. The Electrician Company is the one who is in charge of the practical stuff and needs to maintain the AEDs. The Electrician Company will be installing the monitoring units on the AEDs, but it will be the Medical Company that will monitor the AEDs. Then everybody does what they do best. We needed to feel comfortable in putting our trust in these companies in regard to the distribution of responsibility."

Here, Will introduces the Medical Company and the Electrician Company. These actors are involved in the infrastructuring of maintaining AEDs with the IoT solution. Just like Pam, Will distributes the responsibility of maintaining AEDs to the Medical Company and the Electrician Company, to ensure fully functioning AEDs and to accommodate people feeling accountable for maintaining AED. However, implied in this infrastructuring with the IoT solution is the controversy of responsibility and accountability. Will foresees that the NGO will be held accountable if the AEDs do not work and cannot save lives. Therefore, the NGO is dependent on reliable actors to distribute their responsibility amongst. The distribution of responsibility for maintaining AEDs among the Medical Company and the Electrician Company had been rearranged during the development of the IoT solution so that "everyone does what they do best," Will said. This reveals how the NGO seeks to distribute the responsibility of maintaining AEDs with the IoT solution (Fig. 5).

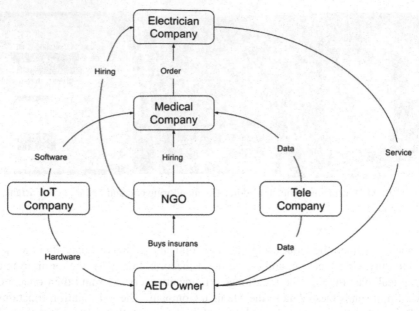

Fig. 5. Relationship between actors responsible for the IoT-driven maintenance of AEDs. (The Tele Company provides the means of communication for the AED data to travel from the AEDs to the Medical Company.)

5 Discussion

This study aimed to investigate the infrastructuring of maintaining AEDs. Unfolding the relational of the infrastructure of maintaining AEDs showed how the social, technical, political, and ethical dimensions are entangled herein. This study's informants experienced several breakdowns in the infrastructure, making them try to remedy these breakdowns with different solutions: a local document, a joint mailbox, and the IoT solution. These solutions aim to ensure that the AEDs are maintained, thus fully functioning and able to save lives, as an AED can be essential in the incidence of out-of-hospital cardiac arrest. However, this study revealed the controversy of responsibility and accountability when connecting the infrastructure of maintaining AEDs to other actors.

5.1 Civic Engagement in Lifesaving Technology

Investigating the infrastructuring of maintaining AEDs revealed several breakdowns, which resulted in AEDs not being able to fulfill their purpose as lifesaving technology (cf. Sect. '4.2 Infrastructural Breakdowns'). Social and political dimensions influenced these breakdowns, which show how the maintenance of AEDs is embedded into already existing structures and practices among this study's informants. The political dimension of AED maintenance showed us a landscape like "the Wild West," with no compulsory regulations, only recommendations (cf. Sect. '4.1 The Wild West of Infrastructuring'). A way to remedy these breakdowns could be to implement new regulations that would make the AED owner legally accountable for the AED maintenance. However, this could lead to civic engagement being minimized with the legal aspect as a judge. With less civic engagement, we take the risk of reducing the diffusion of publicly available lifesaving technology. The aim with the recommendations of AED maintenance relates to Korn and Voida's infrastructure of civic engagement, being "those socio-technical substrates that support civic activities [and] (…) enable and support local practices" [28], where the purpose is to engage people to act. The hope with only having recommendations is to engage people in maintaining their AEDs, so they are capable of saving lives, instead of implementing new regulations, forcing the owner to do the maintenance by holding them accountable. Both Pam and Will decided to engage in maintaining AEDs to remedy the experienced breakdowns. In their engagement, they seek to upscale and connect the infrastructure [15] of maintaining AEDs by distributing the responsibility with other actors. They sought to develop infrastructures of civic engagement. However, as the infrastructure got upscaled and connected [15] to other actors, tensions occurred. The social dimension of accountability became evident in the breakdowns (cf. Sect. 4.2 'Infrastructural Breakdowns') in the infrastructuring of maintaining AEDs. As Korn and Voida [28] put it:

"[These] moments of infrastructural breakdown can become moments of awareness, reflection, and questioning about the activities that infrastructures enable and the values inscribed in them" [28].

The social dimensions of accountability became entangled, and the task of maintaining the AEDs became a matter of life and death. This form of accountability speaks to a human-centered ethos, as humans watch the AED for humans. This raises the concern of who will participate in the responsibility of maintaining AEDs, and in the end, who will be held accountable for a fully functioning AED or, worse, a non-functioning AED.

5.2 Technological Repairs

"Perhaps most important of all, what values and ethical principles do we inscribe in the inner depths of the built information environment [the infrastructure]? We need new methods to understand this imbrication of infrastructure and human organization. One promising direction is to apply the tools of ethnography to this imbrication" [29].

In this quote, Star [29] underlines the importance and fruitfulness of applying ethnography to study infrastructures. By using the methods of ethnography, we saw how the social dimensions, or human organization [29], seem to be a struggle of coming to terms with the responsibility and accountability of maintaining AEDs (cf. Sect. '4.1 The Wild West of Infrastructuring' and '4.2 Infrastructural Breakdowns'). With the IoT solution, the aim is for the mentioned breakdowns to be remedied (cf. Sect. '4.3 Breakdown Repair'). A technical IoT solution, the "optical eye," is now watching over the AED. It tries to take on human-centered accountability with that of a technical one, leaving the IoT solution as the scapegoat. With 24-h feedback on the AED status regarding humidity, temperature, and GPS location, everybody should rest assured that the AEDs are taken care of. Even though the IoT solution distributes responsibility, accountability will still be attributed to humans, just as Elish describes with the moral crumple zone [40]. This relates to the importance of looking at technical and social dimensions when investigating infrastructure and infrastructuring, raised by Karasti and Blomberg [17]. There is a need to understand these dimensions when unfolding the relational infrastructure, as "[the infrastructure] is embedded in, sunk into, other structure, social arrangement and technologies. This emphasizes the dense, socio-technical imbrication of infrastructure" [17].

The IoT solution can assist in maintaining AEDs on a technical level. Still, the social and political dimensions of accommodating accountability by distributing responsibility, as part of the infrastructuring, are not done by the technology itself. The technological dimension, and more specifically the IoT solution, cannot be held accountable if an AED cannot serve its purpose as a lifesaving technology. Ethical reflections need to be considered when developing infrastructures [29]. Suppose accountability is inscribed in the IoT solution. In that case, it can be held accountable for not saving lives, leaving the technology as a scapegoat to blame, and excuse the owner for not maintaining his/her AED [42]. However, based on this study's findings, we believe that it will not be possible to hold the IoT solution accountable for not saving lives. As Nissenbaum pointed out, "computers perform functions previously performed by humans in positions of responsibility leading to the illusion of computers as moral agents capable of assuming responsibility" [42]. The IoT solution could help distribute the responsibility for maintaining AEDs. Human feelings of accountability become a driving force in taking care of lifesaving technology. Will seeks to accommodate feelings of accountability with a new technological solution but still claims the NGO will be held accountable.

5.3   A Sustainable Future for the IoT Solution

Studying the infrastructuring of maintaining AEDs has drawn our attention towards the importance of negotiating strategic goals. A working infrastructure needs regular repairs, monitoring, and upkeep [17]. In our case, the IoT solution is also a work-in-progress, where different actors have their strategies and goals. For the IoT Company, the hardware and software of the IoT solution are, in the future, set out to become connected to new customers in different cases with different demands. For the NGO, the goal is to maintain as many AEDs as possible, meaning the hardware and software of the IoT solution need adjustment to fit different brands of AEDs. This risk of diverging strategic goals relates to Ribes and Finholt's [31] emphasis on short and long-term vistas as a critical tension in an infrastructure. Designing an infrastructure for long-term maintenance of a lifesaving technology like the AED is a "varied compendium of work done today with an eye toward generating a sustainable future" [31], which Ribes and Finholt call "the long now." Ribes and Finholt describe how new technological platforms, like in the IoT solution in our study, often "do not match the extant needs of users, do not offer the functional stability that daily use demands, or lack the human resources to upgrade and maintain existing technology" [31]. Therefore, it is not enough for the two companies in our study to have one common goal of developing the IoT solution. They should have a joint responsibility to focus on a common sustainable future solution, where ongoing upkeep is in focus; otherwise, the IoT solution will only further lead to breakdowns in the infrastructure of maintaining AEDs.

6 Conclusion

In the case of out-of-hospital cardiac arrest, the use of an AED can be the difference between life and death. Thus, AEDs must be maintained to be fully functional and able to save lives. This study showed how a controversy of responsibility and accountability is present in the infrastructuring of maintaining AEDs. This controversy became clear as this study's informants experienced different breakdowns in the infrastructure of maintaining AEDs, which caused the AEDs not to function as intended. The maintenance of AEDs is not compulsory. Thus, the political foundation is unclear - "a Wild West" - only based on recommendations. Implementing new regulations, making AED maintenance compulsory, can be challenging as civic engagement can be minimized. With less civic engagement, we take the risk of reducing the diffusion of publicly available lifesaving technology. The informants in this study describe how they have initiated different solutions: the IoT solution and a local solution involving a local document and a joint mailbox to repair and overcome the experienced breakdowns in the infrastructure of maintaining AEDs. In these solutions, the aim is to accommodate the controversy of accountability by distributing the responsibility of maintaining AEDs. However, the social dimension of potentially being held accountable for the AED and being the scapegoat when scaling up and connecting the infrastructure of maintaining the AED to other actors became visible. The IoT solution can technically participate in distributing responsibility for maintaining AEDs, but actors cannot avoid the social dimension of accountability. Therefore, our recommendation is that socio-technical perspectives should be taken into account when doing infrastructuring and developing new infrastructures to address possible controversies of responsibility and accountability. Future research on developing IoT solutions for technologies installed in non-medical environments dependent on civic engagement should pay attention to technical, social, political, and ethical dimensions. Furthermore, future research should focus on the importance of a graphical user interface (GUI) for lifesaving technologies to accommodate public engagement.

Acknowledgements. The work presented in this paper did not receive any funding.

The authors of this paper would like to thank Seluxit (The IoT Company), The Danish Heart Association/Hjerteforeningen (The NGO), the Health Clinic, and the Administrative Organization for help with understanding the infrastructuring of maintaining AEDs.

References

1. Ringgren, K.B., et al.: Dansk Hjertestop Register. Technical report (2018). www.hjertestopre gister.dk
2. Baekgaard, J.S., Viereck, S., Møller, T.P., Ersbøll, A.K., Lippert, F., Folke, F.: The effects of public access defibrillation on survival after out-of-hospital cardiac arrest: a systematic review of observational studies. Circulation **136**(10), 954–965 (2017). https://doi.org/10.1161/CIR CULATIONAHA.117.029067. ISSN: 1524-4539
3. Agerskov, M., et al.: Public access defibrillation: great benefit and potential but infrequently used. Resuscitation **96**, 53–58 (2015). https://doi.org/10.1016/j.resuscitation.2015.07.021. ISSN: 1873-1570

4. Hjertevagt: ZOLL Hjertestarter – Hvem var opfinderen bag? https://hjertevagt.dk/artikler/zoll-hjerterstarter-hvem-var-opfinderen-bag/
5. Sundhedsstyrelsen: Hjertestartere (AED) placeret uden for sygehus. Technical report (2011). http://www.sundhedsstyrelsen.dk
6. Nielsen, A.M., Folke, F., Lippert, F.K., Rasmussen, L.S.: Use and benefits of public access defibrillation in a nation-wide network. Resuscitation **84**(4), 430–434 (2013). https://doi.org/10.1016/j.resuscitation.2012.11.008. ISSN: 0300-9572
7. TrygFonden: Du kan redde liv kampagnen får fornem hæder. https://hjertestarter.dk/find-hje rtestartere/tal-og-fakta-om-hjertestart/du-kan-redde-liv-kampagnen-faar-fornem-haeder
8. Bin Hussein, M.I.H., Fong, J.H., Lim, C.X., Lee, J.S., Tan, C.T., Ng, Y.Y.: Mobile application for crowdsourced gamification of automated external defibrillator (AED) locations. In: Proceedings of the 4th International Workshop on Multimedia for Personal Health & Health Care (HealthMedia 2019), pp. 24–31. Association for Computing Machinery, New York (2019). https://doi.org/10.1145/3347444.3356240
9. Merchant, R.M., et al.: A crowdsourcing innovation challenge to locate and map automated external defibrillators. Circ.: Cardiovasc. Qual. Outcomes **6**(2), 229–236 (2013). https://doi.org/10.1161/CIRCOUTCOMES.113.000140. ISSN: 1941-7713
10. Cummins, R.O., Ornato, J.P., Thies, W.H., Pepe, P.E.: Improving survival from sudden cardiac arrest: the "chain of survival" concept. A statement for health professionals from the Advanced Cardiac Life Support Subcommittee and the Emergency Cardiac Care Committee American Heart Association. Circulation **83**(5), 1832–1847 (1991). https://doi.org/10.1161/01.CIR.83.5.1832. ISSN: 0009-7322
11. Heart and Stroke Foundation. Your donation at work. https://www.heartandstroke.ca/what-we-do/our-impact/your-donation-at-work
12. American Heart Association. AED Implementation. https://cpr.heart.org/en/training-pro grams/aed-implementation
13. TrygFonden. FAQ – få svar på dine spørgsmål. https://hjertestarter.dk/harenhjertestarter/faa-hjaelp-til-hjertestarter
14. Jakobsen, K.N.: Minister om hjertestartere uden service: De skal kortlægges (2019). https://www.dr.dk/nyheder/penge/kontant/minister-om-hjertestartere-uden-service-de-skal-kortla egges
15. Star, S.L., Ruhleder, K.: Steps toward an ecology of infrastructure: design and access for large information spaces. Inf. Syst. Res. **7**(1), 111–134 (1996). https://doi.org/10.1287/isre.7.1.111. ISSN: 1047-7047
16. Gui, X., Chen, Y.: Making healthcare infrastructure work: unpacking the infrastructuring work of individuals. In: Conference on Human Factors in Computing Systems – Proceedings. Association for Computing Machinery (2019). https://doi.org/10.1145/3290605.3300688, ISBN: 9781450359702
17. Karasti, H., Blomberg, J.: Studying infrastructuring ethnographically. Comput. Supp. Coop. Work (CSCW) **27**(2), 233–265 (2017). https://doi.org/10.1007/s10606-017-9296-7. ISSN: 1573-7551
18. Ohta, S., et al.: Utilization of automated external defibrillators installed in commonly used areas of Japanese hospitals. Signa Vitae **8**(1), 21–24 (2013). https://doi.org/10.22514/SV81.052013.3. ISSN:1845-206X
19. Torney, H., Harvey, A., Finlay, D., Magee, J., Funston, R., Bond, R.R.: Eye-tracking analysis to compute the visual hierarchy of user interfaces on automated external defibrillators. BCS Learning & Development (2018). https://doi.org/10.14236/EWIC/HCI2018.42
20. Onan, A., Simsek, N.: Interprofessional education and social interaction: the use of automated external defibrillators in team-based basic life support. Health Inform. J. **25**(1), 139–148 (2019). https://doi.org/10.1177/1460458217704252. ISSN: 1741-2811

21. Bond, R.R., et al.: Using machine learning to predict if a profiled lay rescuer can successfully deliver a shock using a public access automated external defibrillator? Comput. Cardiol. **43**, 1181–1184 (2016). https://doi.org/10.22489/cinc.2016.343-521. ISBN: 9781509008964
22. Islam, S.R., Kwak, D., Kabir, M.H., Hossain, M., Kwak, K.S.: The Internet of Things for health care: a comprehensive survey. IEEE Access **3**, 678–708 (2015). https://doi.org/10.1109/ACCESS.2015.2437951. ISSN: 2169-3536
23. Bossen, C., Markussen, R.: Infrastructuring and ordering devices in health care: medication plans and practices on a hospital ward. Comput. Supp. Coop. Work **19**(6), 615–637 (2010). https://doi.org/10.1007/s10606-010-9131-x. ISSN: 0925-9724
24. Ulriksen, G.-H., Pedersen, R., Ellingsen, G.: Infrastructuring in healthcare through the OpenEHR architecture. Comput. Supp. Coop. Work (CSCW) **26**(1–2), 33–69 (2017). https://doi.org/10.1007/s10606-017-9269-x. ISSN: 1573-7551
25. Simonsen, J., Hertzum, M., Karasti, H.: Supporting clinicians in infrastructuring. Technical report (2015)
26. Dantec, C.A.L., Disalvo, C.: Infrastructuring and the formation of publics in participatory design. Soc. Stud. Sci. **43**(2), 241–264 (2013). https://doi.org/10.1177/0306312712471581
27. Voida, A., Yao, Z., Korn, M.: (Infra)structures of volunteering. In: Proceedings of the 18th ACM Conference on Computer Supported Cooperative Work and Social Computing, Vancouver, BC, Canada, pp. 1704–1716 (2015). ISBN: 9781450329224, https://doi.org/10.1145/2675133.2675153
28. Korn, M., Voida, A.: Creating friction: infrastructuring civic engagement in everyday life. In: Proceedings of the Fifth Decennial Aarhus Conference on Critical Alternatives, pp. 145–156. Aarhus University Library (2015). https://doi.org/10.7146/aahcc.v1i1.21198
29. Star, S.L.: Infrastructure and ethnographic practice. Scand. J. Inf. Sys. **14**(2), 107–122 (2002)
30. Star, S.L., Bowker, G.C.: How to infrastructure? In: Lievrouw, L.A., Livingstone, S. (eds.) The Handbook of New Media: Social Shaping and Consequences of ICTs, pp. 151–162. Sage, London (2002)
31. Ribes, D., Finholt, T.A.: The long now of infrastructure: articulating tensions in development. J. Assoc. Inf. Syst. **10**(5), 375–398 (2009)
32. O'Reilly, K.: Key informants and gatekeepers. In: Key Concepts in Ethnography, pp. 132–137. Loughborough University/Sage Publications Ltd (2009)
33. Haraway, D.: Situated knowledges: the science question in feminism and the privilege of partial perspective. Feminist Stud. **14**(3), 575–599 (1988)
34. Mogensen, H.O., Dalsgård, A.L.: At være til stede: deltagelse og observation. In: Antropologiske Projekter. En grundbog, pp. 163–179. Samfundslitteratur, Copenhagen (2018)
35. Spradley, J.: The developmental research sequence. In: Participant Observation, pp. 37–83. Cengage Inc, New York (1980)
36. Bernard, H.R.: Interviewing: unstructured and semistructured. In: Research Methods in Anthropology, chap. 9, pp. 210–250. Rowman and Littlefield, Lanham/AltaMira Press (2006)
37. Emerson, R.M., Fretz, R.I., Shaw, L.L.: Writing an ethnography. In: Writing Ethnographic Fieldnotes, chap. 7, pp. 201–242. University of Chicago Press, Chicago (2011)
38. Bundgaard, H., Mogensen, H.O.: Analyse: arbejdet med det etnografiske materiale. In: Antropologiske Projekter. En grundbog, 1st edn, chap. 4, pp. 73–91. Samfundslitteratur, Copenhagen (2018)
39. Sharp, H., Rogers, Y., Preece, J.: Data analysis, interpretation, and presentation. In: Interaction Design: Beyond Human-Computer Interaction, pp. 307–349. Wiley, Indianapolis (2019)
40. Elish, M.C.: Moral crumple zones: cautionary tales in human-robot interaction. Engag. Sci. Technol. Soc. **5**, 40–60 (2019)
41. Simonsen, J., Karasti, H., Hertzum, M.: Infrastructuring and participatory design: exploring infrastructural inversion as analytic, empirical and generative. Comput. Support. Coop. Work **29**(1), 115–151 (2020). https://doi.org/10.1007/s10606-019-09365-w
42. Nissenbaum, H.: Accountability in a computerized society. Sci. Eng. Ethics **2**, 25–42 (1996). https://doi.org/10.1007/BF02639315

Designing for the Elderly
and Accessibility

Improving the Language of Designing for Ageing

Elena Comincioli[1]([✉]), Alice Chirico[2], and Masood Masoodian[1]

[1] School of Arts, Design and Architecture, Aalto University, Espoo, Finland
{elena.comincioli,masood.masoodian}@aalto.fi
[2] Facoltà Lettere e Filosofia, Università Cattolica del Sacro Cuore di Milano, Milan, Italy
alice.chirico@unicatt.it

Abstract. In response to an increasingly ageing world population, the World Health Organization has recently proposed a new framework – called Healthy Ageing – to better cater to older adults' life needs and desires. This framework calls for transdisciplinary approaches to answer the challenges and opportunities posed by an ageing society. Following this framework, it is argued that the first step to accomplishing the goals of Healthy Ageing is to address the existing biases and stereotypes in the language used for addressing ageing issues. In this paper, we propose a series of linguistic guidelines that can help improve the lexicon used to talk about ageing in design research and practice, by countering many subconscious ageist biases and stereotypes. Ageism, especially in its implicit form, is a pervasive negative force that can affect not only design practitioners and researchers but also older adults, who often use ageist language to describe themselves. The proposed guidelines would also help the "false friends" of ageing people, who may be using apparently innocuous words, terminology, and remarks to refer to ageing, without perhaps realising the underlying ageist attitudes and stereotypes hidden in their used language. Overall, we aim to foster a change in design researchers' and practitioners' perspective on ageing, by paving the way for a transdisciplinary discourse on designing for ageing, which could then be further expanded and explored to eliminate ageism in design.

Keywords: Design for ageing · Ageism · Healthy ageing · Ageing population

1 Introduction

It is widely known that the world population is rapidly ageing. If we look at our social circles, we can often find someone we know who is over 100 years old, or at least past 90 [13]. This is because the life expectancy, especially in Western countries, is on the rise [63]. For researchers in many different fields investigating various aspects of ageing, this demographic change poses exciting opportunities due to ageing populations' specific characteristics. However, ageing is a complex topic that calls for researchers' efforts from different disciplines [60]. Beyond the domains of gerontology, medicine, and ageing studies, other fields such as psychology, human factors, ICT and design are also concerned with ageing.

© IFIP International Federation for Information Processing 2021
Published by Springer Nature Switzerland AG 2021
C. Ardito et al. (Eds.): INTERACT 2021, LNCS 12933, pp. 405–425, 2021.
https://doi.org/10.1007/978-3-030-85616-8_24

Interaction Design – a field grounded in human-centred approaches [55] – can also clearly contribute to further research in this area. Over the years, the relationships between various technologies and older adults (OA) have been investigated through a large number of proposed designs, interventions and case studies. In this context, the ageing-related factors have generally been considered from mainly two perspectives, ageing as: 1) *a source of problems which need to be solved*, or 2) *a natural process that can be positively targeted and improved*. It is important to note that in Interaction Design both of these perspectives carry several nuances. When ageing is seen from the first perspective, researchers primarily focus on the problems of socialisation (e.g. targeting social isolation), deficits (e.g. investigating the decline of specific abilities), health economics (e.g. investigating the care costs associated with ageing), or homogeneity (e.g. starting from a generalisation of the target audience) [55]. On the other hand, when ageing is seen from the second perspective, researchers tend to focus their attention on the lived individual experiences of older adults, and as such, the idea of what constitutes successful ageing is challenged and shaped, with older adults themselves being actively included in the design discourse and process [11, 16, 20, 21, 55].

Designing for older adults by taking this second perspective requires a transdisciplinary approach, with contributions from different fields, and involving older adults in the design process. The success of such an approach, however, is mostly dependent on the use of a shared language by those involved – often coming from divergent fields – which is devoid of any of the explicit or implicit stereotypes and biases towards ageing, generally found in most design approaches taken based on the first perspective. In this paper, we propose a series of linguistic guidelines that target many *implicit* ageist biases and stereotypes commonly used in design fields to talk about ageing. We base this approach on *Healthy Ageing*, as proposed by the World Health Organization [45, 60].

2   The Paradigm of Healthy Ageing

Healthy Ageing (HA) is one of the recurring terminologies present in many research articles investigating ageing. While this terminology has started to appear in research literature at least since the year 2000, its meaning has been evolving over the years, along with the evolution of the meaning of health itself. Although we all may have a personal understanding of what a healthy person is, or what a healthy diet or a healthy lifestyle might be, there is an ongoing debate aimed at better defining the meaning of health in a more rigorous way [50]. We can summarise this debate around health by looking at two alternative interpretations. The first of which revolves around the idea of *health as the absence of diseases*. The second one, most recently put forward by the World Health Organization (WHO), frames health as *"a state of complete physical, mental and social wellbeing and not merely the absence of disease or infirmity"* [59]. These two perspectives have strongly influenced the fields of HCI and Interaction Design. For instance, when the adjective "healthy" has been associated with the noun "ageing" following the first interpretation, it has been used to target a state of ageing without any diseases, infirmity, or frailty conditions, with the resulting technology only addressing such health-related aspects of ageing, and ignoring other needs of older adults.

WHO, on the other hand, proposes a broader form of HA by combining its own definition of health – mentioned above – with the concept of age, and urging society to make a shift in how we think, talk and act toward age [60]. WHO defines healthy ageing as *"the process of developing and maintaining the functional ability that enables wellbeing in older age"* [58]. In this definition, *functional abilities* are related to each individual's *intrinsic capacity*, the characteristics of the *environment* in which they live, and the results of the interactions between these three elements. In addition, *intrinsic capacity* is defined as *"all the mental and physical capacities that a person can draw on"* [58]. With the term *environment*, WHO encompasses all the levels from macro, to mezzo and micro: *"Environments include the home, community and broader society, and all the factors within them such as the built environment, people and their relationships, attitudes and values, health and social policies, the systems that support them and the services that they implement"* [58]. Based on these, HA aims at addressing **four challenges** that have emerged in recent years in the discourse of ageing research [58].

The **first challenge** in targeting healthy ageing is "Diversity in older age" [58], which refers to the idea that there is no such thing as a typical older person, and that age is an indicator which has little to do with the mental and physical abilities of a person (for instance, an older adult might have similar capacities to a person in her twenties) [13, 17, 58]. Based on this approach, as design researchers and practitioners, we need to consider the life experiences of individual older adults, because these experiences influence their needs and desires more than our preconceived notions of their age. It is also essential for designers to recognise that "As one grows older, one grows more like oneself" [10]. Therefore, we need to find new ways to investigate this target group and overcome the urge to simply cite statistics in defining older people. This, in turn, requires us to differentiate between, and separate, the generic older adults user group into more distinguishing subgroups – as several sociological approaches have already been doing [37].

When investigating a target audience, designers need to better understand those aspects of individuals which have been influenced by their personalities and their unique environments, in addition to those elements that are genuinely related to their older age [10]. However, it is essential to remember that older adults "are not a homogeneous group" [60]. Although it should also be noted that it would be rather difficult to get such finer detailed information about ageing people from currently available data sources on older populations. For instance, demographic data on older adults are limited or non-existent for 75% of the countries worldwide [60]. Even when such data is available, they often refer to older adults as a generic group of people – for example, those older than 60–65 years [60]. These kinds of data do not consider the infinite variations that make the lives of older adults different from each other. As a consequence, relying on most existing data can actually contribute to perpetuating ageist stereotypes, if they are used without considerations given to such variations. This is because most data sources are based on the idea that "Data must be disaggregated to understand better older adults' health status, social and economic contribution, and social capital" [60].

The **second challenge** in targeting HA is "Health Inequities" [58], which aims to address one of the most popular topics related to age – i.e. health. Looking at health from a perspective that goes beyond the idea of physical and mental limitations or health problems is crucial to recognising the role that the environment plays in each person's life. This "environment" includes the influences that come from one's family, gender, ethnicity, and the social context in which one is born and grows up. All these characteristics can influence, among other things, the individual's access to health services, and discriminations to which the individual might be subjected. This means that the diversity discussed above is not random [58], and when addressing health, we need to consider the personal perspective that we develop towards ourselves, and our own health perspectives can differ from the clinical definitions of health [9]. According to a study by Bowling [9], while many older adults consider themselves healthy and successfully ageing, most biomedical classifications do not in fact categorise them as such.

The **third challenge** in targeting HA is "A rapidly changing world" [58]. According to WHO, macro trends such as globalisation, technological innovations, urbanisation, social migration, and changing gender norms are all elements that need to be taken into consideration when researching the HA paradigm [58]. Technological solutions are clearly of interests to those involved in the fields of HCI and Interaction Design, who often investigate the relationships different technologies have with the ageing process. For instance, it has been noted that this coming decade "will provide opportunities to [...] harness technological, scientific, medical (including new treatments) assistive technologies and digital innovation that can foster Healthy Ageing" [60].

These three challenges are influenced by the **fourth underlying challenge** of "Outdated and ageist stereotypes" [58]. Ageist biases and stereotypes often portray older adults as frail or dependent, and therefore, as an economic burden on society. Unfortunately, these ideas are rather pervasive and can influence society at different levels, leading to discrimination, and affecting the development of policies and opportunities aimed at older people [58]. Combating ageism is also the key to better designing for Healthy Ageing. Ageism – considered as the discrimination against people based on their age [40] – poses a barrier to research and practice of design, development, and deployment of effective interventions, and related case studies and evaluations, because ageism "influences the way problems are framed, and the question asked, and the solution offered" [60]. This is why the primary concern raised by WHO when proposing the HA framework is the urgency to change how society thinks about age. As such, in 2020 WHO launched the Decade of Healthy Ageing [60], in a commitment to help its nation members to shift their approaches towards healthy ageing and overcome ageism.

3 Ageism

Facing ageism is sadly a common part of the lives of most ageing people [4]. Stereotypes and prejudices about old age are so pervasive in our modern world that even older adults themselves often have such views [17, 57]. Therefore, it is not surprising that many established negative norms of an ageist society can generally be very difficult to challenge or change [3, 13]. Nevertheless, this is something that needs to be done because ageism has a strong negative impact on older adults' mental and physical health, and can lead, for instance, to lower life expectancy, high blood pressure, reduced self-esteem, reduced risk-taking, and motivation [42, 43].

3.1 Ageism in Modern Society

One of the main problems with ageism is that it is very deceptive because "it can operate without conscious awareness, control, or intention to harm." [40]. Ageism in society is a form of implicit discrimination which is influenced by emotions and thoughts beyond the control, intention, and conscious awareness of the person experiencing it [40]. Furthermore, "Implicit bias can act as a barrier to inclusion and can reinforce stereotypes and prejudices. Our subtle, unconscious judgments of others can result in behaviours that promote separateness, such as not speaking directly to an individual or not making eye contact. Implicit biases are learned behaviours that are modelled by others, including family, peers and the media" [28]. Compared to other forms of more explicit or intentional discrimination – such as racism or sexism – implicit ageism is rarely sanctioned by society. Furthermore, the presence of benevolent ageism [14, 53] makes it difficult to understand when it is perpetuated. A clear example of how ageist perspectives can be tolerated and perpetuated is in using ageist birthday cards [24] – e.g. showing older adults wearing diapers.

At the root of discriminatory attitudes and beliefs, we can find a number of biases and stereotypes [25]. The difference between biases and stereotypes is that the former category represents a prejudice or preconceived opinion, while the latter consists in casting one's beliefs and expectations over a person or a group of people, regardless of their actual condition [25]. Stereotypes are characterised as static entities, whose original function is to provide the people who uphold them with a sense of order that helps them make sense of their world [30].

Ageist biases can be found at different levels in our society. At a macro level, we find evidence of an ageist perspective, for example, in the beauty industry, where the term anti-ageing is widely used [40] to portray ageing as something to be avoided – or at least controlled or delayed. At a micro level, we can find an example of ageism in our language when expressing discrimination and contempt towards old age and older adults [28].

As mentioned, ageism is different from other forms of discrimination – such as racism or heterosexism – because it is often "accepted and [is] normative for most cultures" [28]. From the ageist language perspective, discriminatory remarks can easily span between two opposite poles. On the one side, we have the expression of beliefs that are intended as positive, sometimes even as compliments, and on the other side, we have verbal humiliation, which can be unintentional or intentional and result in hostility or insults [28]. Biases can be expressed explicitly, in which case, those who are expressing them are aware of their judgments and the corresponding beliefs, and evaluate them as correct to some degree [23]. Usually, these kinds of biases are not socially tolerated though and, when stated, are considered non-politically correct. Ageist stereotypes generally belong to implicit or unconscious biases, representing social stereotypes associated with certain groups of people outside of one's conscious awareness [27]. Implicit biases are very common and widespread. As such, many ageist remarks are very subtle – often passing under the radar – and can be unknowingly activated and transmitted [40]. Furthermore, implicit biases are not easy to identify, not only by the person communicating them, but also difficult to notice by the person receiving the message [28].

3.2 The Underlying Causes of Ageism

One of the reasons behind the perpetuation of ageist beliefs is *gerontophobia* – i.e. the fear of ageing. Ageism and the perpetuation of stereotypes and biases can lead to people fearing their own ageing [28]. This, however, seems to be a natural thing to do for us as humans. To make sense of the world in which we live, we use social categorisations, identifying people with similar characteristics to ourselves "as part of our group (ingroup) or as different from those who constitute our group (outgroup)" [28]. Therefore, ageism can be externalised when the ingroup perpetuates it towards the outgroup, or internalised when it is inflicted by the ingroup upon itself [28].

In the case of ageism, there is also a paradox which we need to take into consideration that constitutes a unique characteristic of this form of discrimination. Jönson [32], underlines how, in the case of young people discriminating towards older adults, the perpetrators themselves will become part of the victimised group at some point in time in the future. In other words, the ingroup eventually becomes the outgroup. Realising that we are part of the outgroup can have drastic consequences in terms of our thinking and behaviour towards the outgroup. Pickering [47] describes the experience of us realising that we are part of an outgroup, by noting that "[...] imprisoned in an identity that harms you. You are both silenced and spoken for. You are seen but not recognised. You are defined but denied an identity you can call your own. Your identity is split, broken, dispersed into its adjected images, its alienated representations" [47]. This theory relies on the fact that we usually prefer our own ingroup members and discriminate against the outgroup members [28]. Bogardus [56] calls the distinction between one's own identity and other groups' identities as social distance – a mechanism that can be used to measure one's prejudices.

To better understand stereotypes, social psychologists have proposed the *stereotype content model* [26], according to which stereotypes have two dimensions: warmth and competence. The first dimension is used to judge strangers' intentions towards us – i.e., whether they intend to help or harm us – and the second dimension is used to judge their competence in carrying out their intentions. Social groups that do not compete with the ingroup are perceived as "warm" and those characterised by a lower status – for instance, due to economic or cultural reasons – are perceived as "incompetent" [26].

In ageism, stereotypes manifest themselves from a young age, with even children and teenagers expressing them [54]. According to Levy [41], ageist stereotypes operate from the society to individuals, and, during their lifespans, within the individuals themselves. This idea is best examined through the age stereotype embodiment theory, which shows how stereotypes are assimilated through the environment, including popular culture, everyday interactions, and social norms [41]. It is evident that the society we live in plays a crucial role in creating, perpetuating, and normalising ageist stereotypes. The media is full of examples in which older adults are made fun of – e.g. commercials showing older adults as unable to use technology, or engaging in sexual behaviour [19 , 28]. This type of continuous exposure to ageist stereotypes from a young age turns them into an effective part of our mental schema, both implicitly and explicitly, and thus creating internalised ageism [40]. This form of discrimination is then perpetuated by the ingroup – i.e. older adults themselves – against other members of their own ingroup. Examples of this can be found in people who do not want to be associated with peers of their age or resort to extreme measures – e.g. plastic surgery – to look like someone in a younger age group [28].

Furthermore, according to the attachment theory and its internal working model, mental representations of one's self, and fellow human beings, play an essential role in shaping our social relations, feelings, and thoughts [8]. Based on this theory, the way we construct our age identity is strongly related to social processes in which we engage with others – such as talking – and the quality of such interactions [61]. It is also worth noting that age identity is not something static. As such, we can decide to use multiple stereotypes associated with age to describe our age identity and experience, and we can adopt age norms that are associated with different ages – such as when an older adult identifies herself with a different age group when describing her personality [38].

3.3   The Role of Language in Addressing Ageism

WHO emphasises that the above mentioned challenges facing the HA framework can only be addressed through transdisciplinary approaches and a multiplicity of methods and perspectives. It further proposes that a research network should be established to create a common ground between researchers from different fields [60]. We believe that formulating a common ground is the much needed first step in creating dialogue, and developing "an approach that crosses traditional disciplinary borders and critically extends a disease-focused methodology" [34].

This radical change in perspective can be achieved by starting from the language we use to discuss age. "Language is the basis through which we communicate with each other. Through language, we share our thoughts, ideas, and emotions" [28]. While the language we use, and the way we think are closely related, the quest to understand if and how language influences the thinking process – and vice versa – is one of the oldest topics debated in research [62]. Here, we adopt the assumption proposed by Zlatev and Blomberg [62] that there is a direct relationship between language and thought, and it is, in fact, likely that language influences thoughts. We propose that if we consciously repeat the process of adopting a specific lexicon when referring to ageing and older people, we are then more likely to modify our way of thinking about ageing, or at least, critically question our existing false assumptions regarding ageing. This, in turn, will pave the way to a more precise and inclusive language on age [2], particularly in transdisciplinary research and practice settings.

Furthermore, it is understood that "Long-standing cultural practice can exert a powerful influence over even the most conscientious writer" [2]. Therefore, it is crucial that as design researchers and practitioners we should first recognise and identify possible ageist biases and stereotypes in our discourse, and modify how we talk and write about ageing and older adults in the design context.

In our quest to become more conscious of implicit ageist biases and stereotypes in our thinking and language, we should also be mindful of the pitfalls of becoming, what we refer to here as, *false friends* in our discourses regarding ageing. The term "false friends" is popular amongst the linguists who use it to identify words that look and sound similar in two different languages but differ significantly in their meanings. In our context, false friends refer to apparently innocuous words in discourse about ageing which reveal underlying implicit ageist attitudes and stereotypes. As such, false friends indicate the best of intentions from the person using a terminology, word, or phrase which is ultimately faulty in expressing the real intended meaning.

4   Common Ageist Biases and Stereotypes

We believe that because of the implicit nature of ageist biases and stereotypes in our modern societies, it is necessary to make conscious effort in better identifying them before we can attempt to eliminate them. This is also due to the fact that "people are often unable to identify the bias by typical means of introspection" [28]. In the following sections we have divided the most common ageist biases and stereotypes we have identified into three main categories, and provide some examples to describe them.

4.1   Generalisations and Assumptions About Ageing People

One of the main steps in most design research or practice projects is to identify and frame a question to be addressed. As design researchers or practitioners, we often follow our intuition that may or may not guide us towards a possible knowledge gap in need of investigation. However, when dealing with an ageing population, we have to be mindful that this "intuition" may have been strongly influenced by ideas that might be true only for a segment of an ageing population, but not necessarily for the entire group [5]. In fact, in worse case scenarios, our intuition might even be based on ageist assumptions and judgments [28], which might be far from actual reality.

Most ageist assumptions and judgments are similar to what Bell calls "stock stories" [6], in her case when dealing with the issue of racism. She defines these as stories or narratives which are widespread in our society, but are based on biased ideas that seem to make sense by being strongly grounded in so-called "common sense". In the case of racism, these are stories that narrate stereotypes, which are repeated when talking about certain topics, and are presented as justification for why racism is the way it is, and is not going to change. In the case of ageism, these stories are usually backed up by statistical data or facts that are found in governmental laws or institutional regulations – even though ageism is so pervasive that it influences not only individuals but also institutions and policies [9, 60]. The mechanism behind the creation of such stories is best illustrated by Krekula [38], who presents the case of retirement in Sweden as an example of how the law – that proposes 65 as the age of retirement – can be used as a proof that people over the age of 65 are of less value to society than those who are younger and are perceived as being still active in some form of paid employment.

Therefore, it is clear that one should stop perpetuating stock stories of ageing and avoid defining the target audience of design solutions solely based on the age criteria. This is in fact a common form of being false friends, influenced by demographic forecasts and classifications of ageing populations based on measurements which were perhaps relevant in the past but are no longer valid. In following the HA framework, it is important to find other means of classification of the target audience when designing for ageing people. For instance, in addition to age, it is important to consider the lived experiences of the target audience, their environments, and their functional and intrinsic capabilities [60].

The list below provides a few examples, to highlight some, but clearly not all, the stereotypes which can be included in this category of "stock stories".

Longevity is Hereditary. This stereotype describes the misconception that we will die at similar age to our parents, or will suffer from all the same health-related issues as them. If one comes from a family with perceived longevity traits, this misconception can create a "mortal hazard" and a false sense of immunity. In reality, longevity is strongly linked to our lifestyle, and our quality of life is directly influenced by the lifestyle choices we make during our lifespan and the environments in which we live [13]. For example, Type 2 Diabetes is more common in Western countries due to a low-fibre diet and less physical activities [13] than any specific genetic population characteristics.

Homogeneity of Age: This relates to the idea that all people who are in the 65+ demographic category share similar characteristics. Common stereotypes associated with older adults depict a group of people who are sexless, boring, and all the same [52]. In reality, ageing is very subjective [3]. The habits and the life experiences we have in our lives make us all age differently. For instance, if we look at a group of 70-year-olds carefully, we will soon realise how different they look compared to each other [3].

Loneliness: While this may seem like something to be associated with social isolation, in reality, there are many other dimensions to loneliness. Loneliness and social isolation can occur simultaneously, but there are also other factors that can cause loneliness.

Misery and loneliness is one of the variations of this stereotype, and relates to the assumption that older adults are usually not only lonely but also sad. A common stereotype is to imagine older adults as "sad, depressed, lonely, grouchy" [52]. According to Carstensen [13], there are actual facts proving this to be an ageist myth: 1) mental health generally improves with age – except for people living with dementia, 2) OA better manage their negative emotions, 3) OA have a better socio-emotional selectivity in deciding who to spend their time with, and 4) OA report higher levels of happiness.

Well-off Older Folks: This is about the idea of an elite group of older adults who spend all their time in constant vacation [19]. This not only creates false expectations in some older adults themselves, but also causes hate and discrimination by younger people who might be feeling jealousy towards the so-called richer older adults.

You Can't Learn New Things in Old Age: This is also known as "you can't teach an old dog new tricks". It is based on the idea that the more we age, the more difficult it becomes for us to learn new things. This stereotype depicts older adults as "unable to learn or change" [52]. While this stereotype is very pervasive, we would immediately notice how untrue it is if we only focused on its real meaning. In a recent article in The New Yorker, Talbot reviewed a series of books that talk about learning new skills in old age [51]. This demonstrates that it is not only possible to learn as we age, but the topic is so relevant that there is an entire range of popular literature emerging in this area.

4.2   Considering Ageing People as an Estranged Group of People

This category of stereotypes and biases is strongly influenced by the theory of ingroup/outgroup [28], as discussed earlier. The idea that older adults are a very distinct group of people – different from the rest of us – is false, due to the fact that we are all ageing and, if we are lucky, one day we will be able to consider ourselves as part of the older adult population [32]. Ageing is not something that happens after a certain age, but rather, it is a process that starts from the very moment we are born [3]. Framing older adults as different from "our" ingroup of "younger" people can lead to the creation and perpetuation of ageist stereotypes. Unfortunately, this is another difficult bias to tackle, as it is formed and reinforced by society during our entire lifespan [54]. A non-exhaustive list of stereotypes that fall under this category includes the following.

Intergenerational Conflict: This is tied to the idea that "the old benefit at the expense of the young" [3]. The media is often presenting an intergenerational conflict in which younger adults are resentful towards an elite of older adults who grew up during an economic boom and had an easier and more wealthy life – e.g. the idea of baby boomers versus millennials. In reality, according to McArthur Foundation, there is no clear evidence of such a conflict [3]. When asked, young people are not resentful towards the older adults of their own family or their community. The resentfulness is towards an abstract category called "elderly" or "boomers", the use of which dehumanises older adults as people. The real issue that we need to talk about is the fact that socioeconomic differences become even greater in old age. For older adults, there is a huge difference between who is wealthy and educated – e.g. those who live without frailty – and who are poor and struggling – e.g. those who often end up with disabilities and die earlier than expected [3, 13]. When discussing the ageing population, the most pressing issue is not the differences between the generations, but the socioeconomic differences within the same age group.

Older Adults are a Burden to Society: This stereotype perpetuates the idea that older adults consume the natural and economic resources of states and governments [3, 13]. It is based on the ideas that if people live longer, then in the future there will not be enough resources to support everyone, and that older people are the cause of overpopulation. The reality is that in those regions of the world where there is higher longevity, the population size has either stabilised or, in fact, declining – as is the case in many parts of Europe, for example.

Care in Old Age: This is based on the idea that when people grow old, they get sick and are in need of care more than when they were young. The truth is that the medical expenses are higher for everyone during the period before they die – be it at 18 or 81 [3]. The real question here is what we consider the "value of life", and the fact that we might value the life of an 18-year-old more than that of an 81-year-old – which itself is an ageist opinion endorsed by society.

Retirement: There are many stereotypes connected with retirement. The most common stereotype is based on the idea that there is somehow a direct financial link between people who are working and those who are retired. This idea is very popular in countries with a "pay as you go" pension model. In these countries, the media usually presents the link between the workforce and the pensioners, suggesting that the former is directly supporting the latter by "paying" for them. This concept is best summarised by the old-age dependency ratio, which calculates how many people aged 15–64 in a country are active and how many people over 65 are retired. However, most such calculations ignore the reality that many retired people are contributing to the economy and society in different ways – especially through informal economy, voluntary work, being caregivers, and staying socially active, not to mention that in a lot of instances pensioners offer support to their adult children and their families [60].

Retire Early to Create Space: Another popular stereotype associated with retirement is that older adults should retire early to provide employment opportunities for younger people. The reality is that if all the older adults retired early then, in many cases, there would be a shortage of skilled labour [13], and some companies might even go bankrupt – for example, consider the case of a German car manufacturer fighting to keep its ageing engineers with the right knowhow employed [17]. Furthermore, as mentioned above, the related notion of "well-off older folks" who can retire early influences older adults themselves greatly with other stereotypes such as "work hard, retire harder". Such notions perpetuate the belief that if people have worked all their lives, then they should be able to retire and go "on holiday" for the rest of their lives. The reality is that the idea of "holiday" retirement may have made sense when people had just ten years of life expectancy after their retirement at the age of 65 [13]. These days, however, the idea that after retirement one should not work does not make sense any longer. "You cannot think to work for 40 years and have enough money to support yourself for the next 40" [12]. In most developed countries, there is also a need for pension reforms and a societal change in how we view saving for retirement and our lives after retirement.

"Just Kill Me": This stereotype refers to the thought that someone might have when seeing an older adult who lives with debilitating or terminal physical or cognitive frailty. It is based on the idea that the life of such a person is not worth living. While this is largely a personal and moral issue, it is difficult to know how we might react if we were in a similar condition ourselves as individuals. More importantly, we cannot place a value on the life of such older adults, because that is ultimately ageist, insensitive, and offensive [19].

4.3   Certain Actions Should not Be Done by Ageing People

Some stereotypes are strongly influenced by the assumption that certain actions can be performed only at a certain age [28]. Krekula [38] presents the concept of "age coding" to explain how these assumptions are created, reinforced and normalised by society. These norms are based on the assumption that certain actions and behaviour are more appropriate at a certain age, and, as a consequence, individuals who feel that they belong to that age group choose to behave in the expected way to be accepted by society [38]. Krekula presents the case of a woman in her 80s, who states that she is not having intimate relationships with her partner because of her age. Such stereotypes are reinforced by phrases such as "you look old/young for your age" – which in this case is not a comment on our individual life but on the expectation of what our age means to the person saying it, or what that person imagines our age to represent [3].

The influence of ageist biases on our language can result in microaggressions towards older adults. Microaggressions are, for example, "[…] brief and everyday slights, insults, indignities and denigrating messages sent to people of colour by well-intentioned white people who are unaware of the hidden messages being communicated" [22]. This is an important point to remember, because often things we mean as compliments can, in fact, be harmful. A non-exhaustive list of stereotypes that fall under this category are discussed below.

I Do/Don't Feel My Age, or You Don't Look Your Age: This idea is perpetuated by what our society thinks we should or should not do at a certain age. This feeling can lead to internalisation of ageism when we do not feel we should be part of our ingroup because we behave differently [28]. Perhaps we should consider the fact that if many older people claim to be "younger" or "feeling young" because of what they are doing, then what they are doing should really be considered normal for their age [3].

Older Adults as Not Being Capable: This stereotype encompasses all the attitudes that are infantilising or patronising older adults. It is related to the tone and usage of specific words that strip older adults of their expertise, independence and abilities [19, 28].

Deficit Model of Ageing: Treating older adults as a category of people different from others is referred to as the "deficit model of ageing" [5]. It focuses the attention on the possible physical, mental and psychological fragility of the target audience. This approach is mainly present in clinical settings, and it influences other fields that rely on health definitions based on this idea. While this perspective might be valid from a clinical perspective, when applying the HA framework however, we also need to consider other factors, such as the subjective perception of age which can be different from medical classifications of age [9]. This perspective can be easily avoided if we imagine ourselves at a given older age – when we do so we rarely imagine living with deficits, on the contrary, we think that our lives will not be much different from what they are now [17]. A non-exhaustive list of words and stereotypes that fall under the deficit model of age are:

- "Feisty, spry, sweet, little, feeble, eccentric, senile, grandmotherly" [19]
- (Pronoun) is XX young!! [19]
- Inability to use new technologies, including computers and the Internet [19]
- Second childhood stereotype [19]
- Poor health, ill, disabled [52]
- Lack of mental sharpness failed memory, senile [52]
- Lack of vitality, loss of vigour, inevitable decline [52]

5   Addressing Ageism in Design Research Discourse

As discussed, ageist biases, stereotypes, and beliefs are so implicit in society that often design practitioners and researchers – even with the best of intentions – fail to recognise elements of ageism in their design discourse as well. When it comes to academic research in design areas, even the reviewers of related research publications tend to fail to identify – more than might be expected – such ageist language in their reviews.

In this section we provide some guidelines which we believe will assist researchers and practitioners in avoiding such biases and stereotypes in their design discourse. We have chosen some examples from published literature to highlight the implicit nature of such pitfalls. It is important to underline that in selecting our examples, we refer to studies in which researchers expressed high sensitivity toward the age-related topics presented in their publications. We did this to demonstrate that ageism is truly implicit, and as such, it can impact and influence even those with the best of intentions.

One of the most common false friends that we found under the category of *generalisations and assumptions about ageing people* is the representation of older adults as a homogenous group with a natural decline in cognitive and physical frailty issues [15, 49], or the selection of the target audience using a purely age-based demographic – identification of 65+ as older adults – resulting in groups of participants where numerous, and very different, cohorts are investigated in their entirety as a single homogenous group [39, 48].

For the category of *considering ageing people as an estranged group of people*, we found that the most common false friends made the biased and stereotyped assumption that all older adults are a group of people with the same unique characteristics different from the rest of the population [18, 35, 36], and as such, perpetuated the ingroup/outgroup dynamic between the researchers and their "older" age participants [15, 29, 30].

For the category of *certain actions should not be done by ageing people*, some of the false friends we found where those who used a paternalistic tone, or expressed surprise when older adults showed behaviour that are considered perfectly normal for other "younger" age groups [18]. Some of false friends also presented the idea that with age there is an inevitable decline that occurs, and that certain unavoidable disabilities and impairments emerge [1, 15, 29, 30, 36, 46]. As mentioned earlier, while such assumptions are true in some cases, they are by no means universal.

In what follows, we present a list of practical guidelines on the use of appropriate language in discourse regarding ageing and older adults. Language is strongly connected with society, and it is in continuous development [2, 31]. Therefore, this list is meant to be only a starting point, expected to be expanded and improved in the future.

5.1 Using a Person-First Language

To avoid ageist discrimination, it is important to keep in mind that the most important element when talking about ageing people or older adults is their individual "persons" and not their age [2]. We can start by asking ourselves questions such as: Is the person's age meaningful in our design context? If yes, why? If not, is the use of age triggered by ageist stereotypes and biases? [12] These questions can be a good first step in understanding if our intentions are well-motivated or formed by implicit ageist biases. If we realise that age is not such an important element, then we can proceed to refocus our research on what is important from ageing perspective. We should always consider that there is a distinction between age and problem – age alone cannot be the problem [31].

Avoiding a Patronising Tone: When talking about older adults and ageing people, often the problem is the tone used that can become patronising [12]. It is important to avoid the idea that some activities that are normal for a young cohort are a deviation from the norm for older adults. For instance, rather than describing an "active" 80-year-old person with surprise, if it is relevant to the study, it might be more useful to describe the "activities" that the 80-year-old person is pursuing [31, 33]. Similarly it is important to avoid using words such as *feisty, spry, sweet, little, feeble, eccentric, senile, grandmotherly* [33] when referring to older study participants – just as using such terms with younger participants would naturally be considered, for instance, sexist or demeaning.

Talking About Cognitive or Physical Frailties: In discussing such important issues, it is crucial to **consider the person first**. Many studies focus on how to overcome situations where people live with dementia or physical impairments. Following a person-centred approach in such studies requires these considerations:

- Avoiding phrases such as *"X suffer from …"* or *"X is affected by …"*, saying instead *"X lives with …"* [12]. This approach puts the emphasis on the person and keeps the human side at the centre of the conversation, thus avoiding the mistake of using a disease, a disability, or an impairment as the centre of one's identity [2].
- Avoiding words such as *demented* or *senile,* and instead using phrases such as *living with cognitive impairment* [12, 19].
- Avoiding words such as *dependent, incapable, needy*, and instead using terms such as *receiving assistance, needing …* [12, 31].
- Avoiding words that over-medicalise the participants or the target audience [12, 31].
- Considering the subjective self-perception of the participants. Even if there are statistics that might indicate health decline after a certain age threshold, this does not mean that all the people who are part of that demographic feel impaired or are living with bad health – on the contrary, many individuals' self-perception of their health might be of good due to their resilience [9, 31].

Talking About Retirement Houses and Care Homes: When talking about retirement houses and care homes, it is important to avoid reinforcing the stereotype of focusing on places or facilities, and instead focus on communities of people. In doing so, we *put people first* and reinforce the idea that these are *communities where people live* [12]. For instance, people who live in a retirement house can have fulfilling and often happy lives, rich in relationships, friendships and everyday activities. We must recognise this by using words that highlight this idea. Following this approach would require:

- Avoiding the use of terms such as *facility, old folks home, convalescent home, institution*, and instead preferring to the *community, senior living, assisted living* [12].
- Avoiding the use of words such as *units or beds*, and instead using terms such as *apartment, residence, home* [12].
- Avoiding the term *patients*, and instead using the term *residents* [12, 19]. It is important to keep in mind that the terminology used in a medical setting might not be appropriate in the field of design practice or research [31].

5.2 Using a Positive Language

To change how we think about ageing, we need to start focusing on words that describe ageing in a positive light, and as a natural fulfilling process. To do so requires the use of words that are characterised by a positive connotation [12], and avoiding the use of a resigned tone depicting ageing as an obstacle to overcome [2] or surrender to.

Highlighting Capabilities: Instead of using words such as *frail, declining, deteriorating, fragile, invisible, diminished, gone* which focus on the loss of capacity of self, it is important to use words that highlight capabilities, such as *engaged, adventurous, thriving, independent, capable, wellness* [12].

Focusing on Positive Stereotypes, If it is Not Possible to Think of Anything Better: When starting from the idea of ageing firmly grounded on the deficit model of ageing [5], it can be challenging to radically switch perspective. In such cases, the very first step might be to focus on the positive stereotypes associated with ageing [12]. However, this should be considered as just a temporary solution, since positive stereotypes can also easily result in paternalism towards older adults [14]. Nevertheless, it has been proved that positive or benevolent stereotypes can at least have immediate positive effects on the lives of older adults [40]. This approach requires the following:

- "Make[ing] sure that your language conveys that ageing is a normal part of the human experience and is separate from disease and disorder" [2].
- Avoiding the use of terms such *"a burden"* or *"drain on the system"* which devaluate, and instead focusing on words that value the older adults and their *wisdom, experience, contribution, guidance* [12].
- Avoiding the use of words such as *difficult, stubborn, non-compliant, cranky* that might highlight a negative character or attitude, and instead using words such *empowered, enabled, fulfilled, self-assured, confident, acceptance* that highlight the sense of self-worth [12].

5.3 Being Precise and Clear

It is important to be precise, and accurately depict the communities that are being targeted, and avoid assumptions based on stereotypes and generalisations [2, 12].

When in Doubt, Ask? Even When Sure, Ask Anyway! The design research participants or target audience should always be asked, of instance, what do they want to be called? do they prefer the term *older adults* or *older persons*? do they just want their names used instead? [12, 33] or what kind of community do they live in? However, when participants suggest using a term which might itself be based on stereotypes, it is better not to use it and use the most appropriate term instead [2].

5.4   Avoiding Ageist Concepts, Terms and Words

In addition to the issues discussed above, there are also many specific ageist concepts that are elicited by using specific words and terminology. Clearly the use of these types of words and terms should be avoided in design discourse. Below we provide a non-exhaustive list of such words and their associated concepts. However, as mentioned earlier, any such list is everchanging and is influenced by how society evolves and language transforms [31]. Some terms that might not be tinted today might be considered not acceptable tomorrow.

Avoiding the Use of "Old" as Negative, or "Young" as Positive: The word *old* may be used to indicate an undesirable state when associated with the concept of *old as negative*. This can be an opinion that is expressed by a third party – e.g. designer, researcher, media, caregiver – or expressed by the older adults themselves [28]. *I'm feeling old* is an example of the use of the word *old* as synonymous to *feeling bad*, with *no vitality* [3]. While the opposite concept of *young as positive* can be used independently from the concept of *old as negative*, the two are strongly related. The use of the word *young* is often the expression of the assumption that being, acting, or looking *younger* is preferable to being, acting and looking *older* [28].

As such, it essential to evaluate what we mean by the words *old* and *young*, and when necessary, find better terminology to express our intended meanings. When words such as *old* or *young* are used as adjectives describing a person's state, then they should not indicate an emotional state [3]. By removing the emotional value from a word, we can diminish its associated stigma. For instance, words such as *old* or *fat* can be used without reference to their original meanings, and by doing so, represent ideas that are extremely harmful and discriminatory – by adding biases and stigmas to the adjective *old* and the noun *fat,* they are transitioned into harmful emotions [3].

Avoiding the Use of Chronological Age: The first question we should ask ourselves when talking about older adults is "is age truly relevant here?". This can, however, be rather difficult to determine due to the pervasiveness of implicit ageism. One way of avoiding this could be to try to substitute the concept of *age* with *race*, and since race is less normed than age, it might become immediately clear if adding this detail can be considered redundant, or even worse, racist [33].

Consider that a cohort is made up of people that share the same year of birth. While this means that their lives might have been influenced by similar events and experiences – such as wars, cultures, etc. – these might have affected everyone in different ways [31]. Therefore, when describing chronological age, adjectives such as *old, elderly, aged,* and *ancient* should be avoided, and instead words such as *older, elder, ageing,* and *mature* should be used [12]. Similarly, terms such as *old person*, or *senior citizen*, can be avoided by using terms such as *older adult, elder, older people, older person, older individual, persons 65 years and older, and the older population* [2, 12]. More importantly, one should always question if it is crucial to refer to years, or if it might be better to refer to life stages [31].

Avoiding the Word Senior: The word *senior* is an example of a word that has been largely influenced by the development of society. While it was fine to use the word *senior* to describe a person a few years ago [33], these days is more acceptable to use it only when referring to non-human entities, such as a *seniors house* or a company that provides *senior housing* and services. Overall, the word *senior* should be entirely avoided when referring to people, as it is considered highly offensive [2, 12].

Avoiding the Word Elderly: *Elderly* is, arguably, the most ageist word one can use when talking about older adults. It is associated with an incredible amount of negative stereotypes – such as *frail, old, highly handicapped and disabled* – and it is a term that fuels the stigma on older adults [2, 33]. *Elderly* reinforces the idea of a homogenous group characterised by fragility and decline, and as such, its use should be avoided completely [33].

Avoiding the Terms Boomer and Baby Boomer: The terms *boomer* and *baby boomer* refer to a specific cohort of older adults, and therefore should be used just with this meaning and intention in mind [2, 33]. In recent years, however, these terms have been associated increasingly more with negative stereotypes on old age. For instance, they have been used when discussing intergenerational conflicts, describing a younger generation as *millennials* and an older generation as *boomer* [44]. *"Ok, boomer!"* is an example of how the term can be used to imply that someone is *out-of-touch*, has *outdated* or *conservative beliefs*, or is *delaying the progress* on societal matters, economic inequalities, or environmental issues [44].

Avoiding the Terms Middle-Aged and Midlife: As with the terms *boomer* or a *baby boomer*, the terms *middle-aged* and *midlife* should only be used to refer to a specific period during people's lifespan, and should never be used to identify people [33]. When talking about individuals, rather than using the term *middle-aged*, it is preferable to use *people in middle age* instead [31]. Furthermore, when using such terms, it is important to remember that as concepts their meanings have been changing as humans' life expectancy has been rising [33]. The International Council on Active Ageing [31] suggests using the following categories when needed: Middle Age (45–64), Young Old (65–74), Middle Old (75–84), Old Old (85–99), and Oldest Old (100+).

Avoiding Terms and Words That Have Political Implications: When discussing topics such as *care costs* or *health expenses*, it is important to be aware that using phrases such as *"the burden of population ageing"*, or *"this plan will save … on health spending"*, imply the belief that one group of society is more valuable than another [33]. Such terms are of course not neutral, and are expressions of particular political stances.

Avoiding The Term Anti-Ageing: This term is mainly used in the beauty industry and marketing. Its use is a clear example of how political correctness does not seem to apply to older adults, as might be the case with many other marginalised groups [31, 40]. Therefore, terms such as *anti-ageing* and *aged* or phrases such as *"they look good for their age"*, *"despite their age"*, *"even older adults can …"*, and *"they are active even at their age"* [31] should be avoided.

Avoiding The Term Senior Moment. The term *senior moment* has become very popular and relatively normalised, particularly in the US [7] to refer to a moment when an older adult might forget the name of a person, or experience some issues with memory. It is often used in a derogative tone, and the same stigma is not attached to younger people, who may also experience the same kind of temporary memory loss.

6 Conclusions

In this article we have examined the paradigm of Healthy Ageing as proposed by WHO – which calls for society to radically change the way we think, talk and act about aging. To achieve such a change, we have argued for modifying the lexicon we use to discuss ageing in design discourse in a more inclusive and bias-free manner. We have also presented guidelines for identifying implicit ageist stereotypes and biases in design research and practice, particularly when done by people with good intentions, to whom we refer to here as the *false friends*. Finally, to turn the false friends into true friends, we have provided practical guidelines on how to modify the lexicon used in discourse around issues related to ageing.

As design researchers and practitioners, we should also remember that society strongly influences ageist biases and stereotypes. Further work is still needed to identify how specific research fields can influence and improve our understanding of ageing. We believe that adopting the guidelines proposed here will help overcome implicit ageist biases, and influence other researchers and practitioners in their approach to ageing.

Acknowledgments. We would like to thank Professor Andrea Gaggioli for providing valuable feedback during the writing of this paper.

References

1. Alexandrakis, D., Chorianopoulos, K., Tselios, N.: Insights on older adults' attitudes and behavior through the participatory design of an online storytelling platform. In: Lamas, D., Loizides, F., Nacke, L., Petrie, H., Winckler, M., Zaphiris, P. (eds.) Human-Computer Interaction – INTERACT 2019. LNCS, vol. 11746, pp. 465–474. Springer, Cham (2019). https://doi.org/10.1007/978-3-030-29381-9_29
2. American Psychological Association: Publication Manual of the American Psychological Association (7th edn.) American Psychological Association (APA) (2020)
3. Applewhite, A.: This Chair Rocks: A Manifesto Against Ageism. Perfect Paperback (2016)
4. Ayalon, L., Tesch-Römer, C. (eds.): Contemporary perspectives on ageism. International Perspectives on Aging, vol. 19. Springer, Cham (2018). https://doi.org/10.1007/978-3-319-73820-8
5. Bangen, K.J., Meeks, T.W., Jeste, D.V.: Defining and assessing wisdom: a review of the literature. Am. J. Geriatr. Psychiatry **21**, 1254–1266 (2013). https://doi.org/10.1016/j.jagp.2012.11.020
6. Bell, L.A.: Storytelling for Social Justice. Connecting Narrative and the Arts in Antiracist Teaching. Routledge, New York/London (2010)
7. Bonnesen, J.L., Burgess, E.O.: Senior moments: the acceptability of an ageist phrase. J. Aging Stud. **18**, 123–142 (2004). https://doi.org/10.1016/j.jaging.2004.01.008

8. Bowlby, J.: The Making and Breaking of Affectional Bonds. Travistock Publications Limited, London/New York (1979)
9. Bowling, A.N.N.: Aspirations for older age in the 21st century: what is successful aging? Int. J. Aging Hum. Dev. **64**, 263–297 (2007)
10. Brody, E.M.: On being very, very old: an insider's perspective. Gerontologist **50**, 2–10 (2010). https://doi.org/10.1093/geront/gnp143
11. Burns, L., Masoodian, M.: Storytelling: a medium for co-design of health and well-being services for seniors. In: Clua, E., Roque, L., Lugmayr, A., Tuomi, P. (eds.) Entertainment Computing, vol. 11112, pp. 349–354. Springer, Cham (2018). https://doi.org/10.1007/978-3-319-99426-0_43
12. California Assisted Living Association: Elevate Aging Through Language: a Usage and Style Guide (2019)
13. Carstensen, L.L.: A Long Bright Future: Happiness, Health, and Financial Security in an Age of Increased Longevity. Public Affairs, New York (2011)
14. Cary, L.A., Chasteen, A.L., Remedios, J.: The ambivalent ageism scale: developing and validating a scale to measure benevolent and hostile ageism. Gerontologist **57**, e27–e36 (2017). https://doi.org/10.1093/geront/gnw118
15. Cogerino, C., Rosso, G., Bosi, I., Frisiello, A., Bazzani, M.: Multi-modal input devices for active and healthy ageing. In: 25th International Conference on Software, Telecommunications Computer Networks, SoftCOM 2017 (2017). https://doi.org/10.23919/SOFTCOM.2017.8115562
16. Comincioli, E., Masoodian, M.: A storytelling-based approach to designing for the needs of ageing people. In: Adjunct Proceeding, The 17th IFIP TC.13 International Conference on Human-Computer Interaction – INTERACT 2019, pp. 3–12 (2019)
17. Coughlin, J.F.: The Longevity Economy: Unlocking The World's Fastest-Growing, Most Misunderstood Market. Public Affairs, New York (2017)
18. D'Haeseleer, I., Gerling, K., Schreurs, D., Vanrumste, B., Vanden Abeele, V.: Ageing is not a disease: pitfalls for the acceptance of self-management health systems supporting healthy ageing. In: 21st International ACM SIGACCESS Conference on Computers and Accessibility, ASSETS 2019, pp. 286–298 (2019). https://doi.org/10.1145/3308561.3353794
19. Dahmen, N.S., Cozma, R.: Media Takes: On Aging. Styleguide for Journalism, Entertainment and Advertising. Internation Longevity Center – USA. Aging Services of California (2009)
20. Dankl, K.: Style, strategy and temporality: how to write an inclusive design brief? Des. J. **16**, 159–174 (2013). https://doi.org/10.2752/175630613X13584367984866
21. Dankl, K.: Design age: towards a participatory transformation of images of ageing. Des. Stud. **48**, 30–42 (2017). https://doi.org/10.1016/j.destud.2016.10.004
22. Sue, D.W.: Racial microaggressions in everyday life: is subtle bias harmless? Psychol. Today (2010). https://www.psychologytoday.com/us/blog/microaggressions-in-everyday-life/201010/racial-microaggressions-in-everyday-life
23. Devine, P.G.: Stereotypes and prejudice: their automatic and controlled components. J. Pers. Soc. Psychol. **56**, 5–18 (1989). https://doi.org/10.1037//0022-3514.56.1.5
24. Ellis, S.R., Morrison, T.G.: Stereotypes of ageing: messages promoted by age-specific paper birthday cards available in Canada. Int. J. Aging Hum. Dev. **61**, 57–73 (2005). https://doi.org/10.2190/ULUU-UN83-8W18-EP70
25. Fiske, S.T.: Social Beings: Core Motives in Social Psychology, 3rd edn. Wiley, New York (2014)
26. Fiske, S.T., Cuddy, A.J.C., Glick, P., Xu, J.: A model of (often mixed) stereotype content: competence and warmth respectively follow from perceived status and competition. J. Pers. Soc. Psychol. **82**, 878–902 (2002). https://doi.org/10.1037/0022-3514.82.6.878
27. Fiske, S.T., Taylor, S.E.: Social Cognition: From Brain to Culture, 3rd edn. Sage, London (2017)

28. Gendron, T.L., Welleford, E.A., Inker, J., White, J.T.: The language of ageism: why we need to use words carefully. Gerontologist **56**, 997–1006 (2016). https://doi.org/10.1093/geront/gnv066

29. Giakoumis, D., Segkouli, S., Votis, K., Paliokas, I., Altsitsiadis, E., Tzovaras, D.: Smart, personalized and adaptive ICT solutions for active, healthy and productive ageing with enhanced workability. In: ACM International Conference Proceeding Series, pp. 442–447 (2019).https://doi.org/10.1145/3316782.3322767

30. Helbostad, J.L., et al.: Mobile health applications to promote active and healthy ageing. Sensors (Switzerland) **17**, 1–13 (2017). https://doi.org/10.3390/s17030622

31. ICAA: ICAA's Guidelines for effective communication with older adults. International Council on Active Aging (2011)

32. Jönson, H.: We will be different! Ageism and the temporal construction of old age. Gerontologist **53**, 198–204 (2013). https://doi.org/10.1093/geront/gns066

33. Kleymann, P.: Words to age by: a brief glossary and tips on usage. Age Beat. Newsl. Journalists Exch. Aging (2007)

34. Kliegel, M., Iwarsson, S., Wahrendorf, M., Minicuci, N., Aartsen, M.J.: The European journal of ageing at the beginning of the decade of healthy ageing. Eur. J. Ageing **17**(1), 1–2 (2020). https://doi.org/10.1007/s10433-020-00557-8

35. Knowles, B, Rogers, Y, Waycott, J, Hanson, V.L., Piper, A.M., Davies, N.: HCI and aging: beyond accessibility. In: Proceedings of CHI Conference on Human Factors in Computing Systems Extended Abstracts, pp. 1–8 (2019). https://doi.org/10.1145/3290607.3299025

36. Kolasinska, A., Quadrio, G., Gaggi, O., Palazzi, C.E.: Technology and aging: users' preferences in wearable sensor networks. In: ACM International Conference Proceeding Series, pp. 153–158 (2018). https://doi.org/10.1145/3284869.3284884

37. Komp, K., Aartsen, M.: Old Age in Europe: A Textbook of Gerontology. Springer, Heidelberg (2013). https://doi.org/10.1007/978-94-007-6134-6

38. Krekula, C.: Age coding - on age-based practices of distinction. Int. J. Ageing Later Life **4**, 7–31 (2009). https://doi.org/10.3384/ijal.1652-8670.09427

39. Lee, H.R., Riek, L.D.: Reframing assistive robots to promote successful aging. ACM Trans. Hum.-Robot Interact. **7**, 1–23 (2018). https://doi.org/10.1145/3203303

40. Levy, B., Banaji, M.R.: Implicit agesim. In: Ageism. Stereotyping and Prejudice against Older Persons. MIT Press (2002)

41. Levy, B.R.: Stereotype embodiment: a psychosocial approach to aging. Curr. Dir. Psychol. Sci. **18**, 332–336 (2009)

42. Levy, B.R., Hausdorff, J.M., Hencke, R., Wei, J.Y.: Reducing cardiovascular stress with positive self-stereotypes of aging. J. Gerontol. Psychol. Sci. **55B**, 205–213 (2000)

43. Levy, B.R., Slade, M.D., Kunkel, S.R., Kasl, S.V.: Longevity increased by positive self-perceptions of aging. J. Pers. Soc. Psychol. **83**, 261–270 (2002). https://doi.org/10.1037//0022-3514.83.2.261

44. Meisner, B.A.: Are you ok, Boomer? Intensification of ageism and intergenerational tensions on social media amid COVID-19. Leis. Sci. 1–6 (2020) https://doi.org/10.1080/01490400.2020.1773983

45. Michel, J.-P., Leonardi, M., Martin, M., Prina, M.: WHO's report for the decade of healthy ageing 2021–30 sets the stage for globally comparable data on healthy ageing. Lancet Heal. Longev. **2**, e121–e122 (2021). https://doi.org/10.1016/s2666-7568(21)00002-7

46. Ordoñez Medina, O.E., et al.: Design implications for exergames with moderate activity to improve inter-joint angle for older adults. In: ACM International Conference Proceeding Series, pp. 1–8 (2019). https://doi.org/10.1145/3358961.3358964

47. Pickering, M.: Stereotyping: The Politics of Representation. Palgrave, London (2001)

48. Rodríguez, I., Karyda, M., Lucero, A., Herskovic, V.: Aestimo: a tangible kit to evaluate older adults' user experience. In: Lamas, D., Loizides, F., Nacke, L., Petrie, H., Winckler, M., Zaphiris, P. (eds.) Human-Computer Interaction – INTERACT 2019. LNCS, vol. 11746, pp. 13–32. Springer, Cham (2019). https://doi.org/10.1007/978-3-030-29381-9_2

49. Sarcar, S., et al.: Designing interactions for the ageing populations. In: Conference on Human Factors in Computing Systems - Proceedings 2018, pp. 1–5 (2018). https://doi.org/10.1145/3170427.3170607

50. Sholl, J., Rattan, S.I.S.: Explaining health across the sciences. Heal. Ageing Longev. **12**, 368 (2020). https://doi.org/10.1007/978-3-030-52663-4

51. Talbot, M.: Why It's Not Too Late to Learn New Skills. New Yorker, New York (2021)

52. Thornton, J.E.: Myths of aging or ageist stereotypes. Educ. Gerontol. **28**, 301–312 (2002). https://doi.org/10.1080/036012702753590415

53. Vale, M.T., Bisconti, T.L., Sublett, J.F.: Benevolent ageism: attitudes of overaccommodative behavior toward older women. J. Soc. Psychol. **160**, 548–558 (2020). https://doi.org/10.1080/00224545.2019.1695567

54. Vauclair, C.M., Borges Rodrigues, R., Marques, S., Esteves, C.S., Cunha, F., Gerardo, F.: Doddering but dear … even in the eyes of young children? Age stereotyping and prejudice in childhood and adolescence. Int. J. Psychol. **53**, 63–70 (2018). https://doi.org/10.1002/ijop.12430

55. Vines, J., Pritchard, G., Wright, P., Olivier, P., Brittain, K.: An age-old problem: examining the discourses of ageing in HCI and strategies for future research. Tochi **22**, 1–27 (2015). https://doi.org/10.1145/2696867

56. Vogt, W.: Bogardus social distance scale. Dict. Stat. Methodol. 2009 (2015). https://doi.org/10.4135/9781412983907.n197

57. Voss, P., Wolff, J.K., Rothermund, K.: Relations between views on ageing and perceived age discrimination: a domain-specific perspective. Eur. J. Ageing **14**(1), 5–15 (2016). https://doi.org/10.1007/s10433-016-0381-4

58. WHO Ageing and health. https://www.who.int/news-room/fact-sheets/detail/ageing-and-health. Accessed 2 Jan 2021

59. WHO: Constitution of the World Health Organization. World Health Organization (2006)

60. WHO: Decade of Healthy Ageing 2020–2030 (2020)

61. Ylänne-McEwen, V.: "Young at heart": discourses of age identity in travel agency interaction. Ageing Soc. **19**, 417–440 (1999). https://doi.org/10.1017/S0144686X99007436

62. Zlatev, J., Blomberg, J.: Language may indeed influence thought. Front. Psychol. **6**, 1–10 (2015). https://doi.org/10.3389/fpsyg.2015.01631

63. World Population Prospects - Population Division - United Nations. https://population.un.org/wpp/Graphs/DemographicProfiles/. Accessed 6 Aug 2021

Strategically Using Applied Machine Learning for Accessibility Documentation in the Built Environment

Marvin Lange[1], Reuben Kirkham[2], and Benjamin Tannert[3(✉)]

[1] University of Bremen, Bibliothekstr. 1, 28359 Bremen, Germany
`marvin4@uni-bremen.de`
[2] Monash University, Wellington Road, Clayton, VIC 3800, Australia
`reuben.kirkham@monash.edu`
[3] City University of Applied Sciences Bremen, Flughafenallee 10,
28199 Bremen, Germany
`benjamin.tannert@hs-bremen.de`

Abstract. There has been a considerable amount of research aimed at automating the documentation of accessibility in the built environment. Yet so far, there has been no fully automatic system that has been shown to reliably document surface quality barriers in the built environment in real-time. This is a mixed problem of HCI and applied machine learning, requiring the careful use of applied machine learning to address the real-world concern of practical documentation. To address this challenge, we offer a framework for designing applied machine learning approaches aimed at documenting the (in)accessibility of the built environment. This framework is designed to take into account the real-world picture, recognizing that the design of any accessibility documentation system has to take into account a range of factors that are not usually considered in machine learning research. We then apply this framework in a case study, illustrating an approach which can obtain a f-ratio of 0.952 in the best-case scenario.

Keywords: Accessibility · Built-Environment · Documentation

1 Introduction

According to the World Health Organization more than one billion people (15% of the global population) have a disability [9]. For many of these people, mobility remains challenging due to accessibility barriers in the built environment [16,35, 55]. For example, stepped surfaces are inaccessible to any wheelchair user, whilst inappropriate surfaces like cobblestones can be a barrier for most people with mobility impairments. Because of these accessibility barriers, many people with disabilities avoid or limit their travel outdoors, which often excludes them from wider society, employment opportunities and limiting their quality of life [31,66].

The mapping of inaccessibility in built environments is a form of empowerment in this context [66]. The provision of comprehensive documentation of

© IFIP International Federation for Information Processing 2021
Published by Springer Nature Switzerland AG 2021
C. Ardito et al. (Eds.): INTERACT 2021, LNCS 12933, pp. 426–448, 2021.
https://doi.org/10.1007/978-3-030-85616-8_25

(in)accessibility is potentially the cornerstone for a growing accessible built environment and the disposal of existing barriers [21]. There is an emerging program of research aimed at using technology to assist with making this documentation process more effective, be it via automatic approaches relying on a range of sensors such as acceleration sensors or depth cameras [37,40,58], direct inspections, done via crowdsourcing [8,32,67] or hybrid approaches that combine both methods [32,33].

At present, the necessary information about the accessibility of sidewalks is on one hand rarely available, and the limited information that is available is often unreliable or inaccurate [21]. Routing systems for wheelchair users regularly present routes containing unnecessary detours and/or inaccessible routes, when the shortest accessible route is needed [69,70]. Indeed, a cost benefit analysis even showed that existing systems in use are worse than using plain Google Maps [69]. One aspect that leads to these errors are missing information or misinformation about the type of surface [69,70]. This basic knowledge about the surface is very important both for people with disabilities but also for elderly people who have age related impairments [43].

We make two important contributions in this paper. First, we outline a decision-making framework for designing accessibility **documentation** systems (that could ultimately be used in a navigation or other system) based on a careful use of machine learning algorithms: the framework addresses the particular challenges that arise when addressing this unique context. This includes human rights and accessibility related considerations. Second, we then provide a proof-of-concept implementation of that framework to a particular scenario, applying it to the concern of surface classification in Europe. Our implementation has three distinguishing features (i) it involves a carefully chosen set of classes that can be practically recognized, (ii) it does not rely on inertial sensors or the motion of the person taking the records and (iii) focusses upon street segments, rather than trying to classify individual frames. Our evaluation shows that this approach is highly effective, obtaining an f-ratio of 0.952 in a best-case scenario.

2   Background

2.1   Benefits of Documenting Accessibility in the Built Environment

To understand the accessibility documentation problem, it is necessary to start with the purpose of documenting inaccessibility in the built environment. The overarching issue is one of human experience: the built environment has a multiplicity of physical barriers for people with disabilities. In some cases, this can have a serious negative impact on their day-to-day life, reducing mobility, access to the workplace, social opportunities and often increasing the level of care worker support that otherwise would not be needed if a location was accessible [16,23,60]. Effective documentation offers the following potential improvements on this situation:

Navigation and Route-Finding. Existing navigation tools do not presently provide a reliable or effective means for people with mobility impairments to traverse the built environment [69], with the result of considerable (and often distressing) inconvenience for many people with mobility impairments [30]. The problem is the absence of underlying data, with existing maps failing to provide reliable documentation of accessibility barriers [21], however the inaccessibility of a given system may also mean that some journeys are impossible [49]. A route-finding system would need to identify for a given user, in line with their unique requirements, what route to undertake, with sufficient accuracy as to offer better routes than existing routing tools. Notably, offering better routes than what has gone before might not be a high-bar in practice, not least because Google Maps for pedestrians is currently the best performing system, despite having no specialist features for computing accessible routes [69]: the simulations in [49] now provide strong evidence for the feasibility of such an approach. These limitations are perhaps unsurprising, given the limited amount of work that focusses on navigation for people with mobility impairments (compared to vision impairments) [26].

Determining Which Regions to Travel To. People with disabilities have the opportunity to make choices, such as where to go on holiday, or what parts of a city to explore. Accurate knowledge of the general level of (in)accessibility in a given location, and thus the relative risk of not being able to effectively access it are an important part of making an informed choice: either on where to travel, or whether support is needed (e.g., a relative, or a care worker). In effect, this would provide a broad-brush assessment of a location's level of accessibility, thus enabling a more informed choice, without having to rely upon a specialist travel agency (with the considerable expense and limited choice of locations this entails [13]), or paying for extra support (from a limited budget) 'just in case' there is a problem.

Determining and Influencing Change. Presently, planners lack effective details of the built environment so they can optimize which physical barriers to address [48]. Given limited public resources, better accessibility mapping would allow for the built environment to improve more rapidly, by more optimal targeting (and prioritization) of physical improvements, including maintenance work [23]. A general picture that allowed the comparison between municipalities and nation states would also enable more effective supervision of performance (by human rights NGO's, the UN and disability advocates alike) and thereby furthering Article 31 of the UN CRPD (which requires states to collect data to formulate and implement policies, as well as to demonstrate compliance with that convention) [2].

Measuring the Effect of the Built Environment. Fitness tracking has been recognized as an important concern, especially for people with mobility impairments [14]. Whilst it is now possible to effectively track the number of strokes with a fitness tracker [19], tracking *where* someone has been can provide more detailed performance information: this is because it is more (or less) effort to traverse different types of surfaces [55]. For someone learning how to use a manual wheelchair, this could also be an indication of rehabilitation progress and/or increased skill/confidence in using the chair: notably measuring real-world skill and performance is an important part of wheelchair skills training [44,45] (as well as separately, the assessment of disability benefits which focus on the level of functional impairment [74]). Separately, rough surfaces increase harmful whole-body vibration, with a long-term negative effect upon health [22, 76], so tracking the quality could also be useful for longitudinal healthcare studies of wheelchair users.

2.2   Existing Approaches Towards Documenting (In)Accessibility in the Built Environment

An Ideal Accessibility Measurement System. One way to understand the limitations of a measurement system is to compare it against an ideal system. An ideal system would *accurately* capture *all* relevant categories of accessibility information, be it the *presence or absence of the appropriate affordances* (such as dropped curbs [48], audible street crossings [10,46]) or the *quality of the surface* itself (e.g., does it contain trip hazards [15], or cause dam-aging whole-body vibration [13,65]). It should also capture *temporary or transient* barriers (e.g., a street that is partially obstructed for blind people because bins are placed on the street [12,60]), as well as an *up-to-date* picture of the environment itself. Finally, it should be *economically efficient* enough to ensure *complete coverage*, so that it can be used effectively in a navigation system [21,69].

Manual Expert-Driven Documentation. The most notable expert driven system is AccessAble (formerly known as Disabled Go) [1]. This involves a rigorous and expensive process of direct documentation by an expert of every feature in the built environment within a confined area (e.g., the local high street), performed by an expert assessor on behalf of the local authority. PhotoRoute [6] serves a similar, but discrete function: a venue can request a photo illustrated accessible route from an important landmark (e.g., a Train Station) to enable attendees to follow the most appropriate route. Whilst expert-driven systems are effective for the limited routes and locations that they actually cover, they have the limitation of sparse coverage caused by the underlying expense of adopting them (these exercises are notoriously "laborious and time consuming" [21]). The overall effect they simply do not scale to provide adequate coverage, with the exception of confined (but important) situations.

Semi-Automated and Crowdsourcing Approaches. There has been a considerable focus on crowdsourced approaches with the aim of obtaining scalability. Perhaps the most successful has been Project Sidewalk [67], which has managed to cover an entire urban area using Google Street View data, however, there were challenges with annotator accuracy in respect of certain data categories. Other semi-automated approaches have focused on accelerating the video-documentation of barriers in the town-planning setting, such as Wheelie-Map [48]. For providing landmarks for people with visual impairments, this has been successfully crowdsourced in the context of public transport [30].

Less-structured 'geocrowdsourcing' approaches have encountered significant problems in respect of their ability to accurately document barriers [54], whilst lacking effective user engagement and thus coverage [21]. A notable 'real world' exception is the widely used FixMyStreet [3], which is a *MySociety* project aimed at general problems in the local community, but also serves as a platform for reporting some accessibility related problems (e.g., potholes). At present, there is no crowdsourced or semi-automated system that works in real-time for obtaining standardized reports of inaccessibility, nor one that does not rely on Google Street View (which can be many years out of date and is effectively banned in many countries, e.g., Germany [54]).

Automated Approaches. In an ideal world, the most effective approach towards accessibility documentation would be an automated one, given the relatively lower cost. There are numerous works that claim to offer a viable system for using inertial sensors mounted on mobility aids (e.g., wheelchairs) to measure the accessibility of the built environment [38–40,51,77]. Unfortunately the evaluations that are said support these claims are based on 'toy problems' in respect of the data being collected in a laboratory rather than in the real world (meaning the findings are unlike to apply there [63]. Furthermore, they fail to use the appropriate leave-one-out metric of evaluation [29] (in some cases, participants were left out, but they all followed the same route, which is also a serious error). Another problem is that there are no performance metrics used that relate directly to problems in accessible navigation: typically F-scores or precision and recall of instances were used, which does not directly relate to problems of concern: whilst there are alternative metrics (e.g., as in [73]), these do not apply to accessible navigation.

In respect of work outside of inertial sensing, there has been some modest success. Some work has explored using aggregate GPS mapping to indicate where people have **not** gone [56,62], but that overlooks surface quality, and overlooks the subjective nature of accessibility barriers. Computer vision has been success-fully used to detect tactile paving [24], in hybrid approaches aimed at supporting annotation [32,33] and in identifying street crossings [10,11]. Deep learning approaches have been recently used to identify street features and accessibility barriers in the United States, yet there remains substantial challenges in respect of achieving sufficient accuracy for a navigation system, with an F-score of around 0.8 being the present state of the art [75].

3 A Practical Framework for Designing a Machine Learning Based Accessibility Documentation System

Automating accessibility documentation is in effect an applied machine learning problem. However, this problem has unusual and important qualities that present particular challenges, meaning it cannot be treated as a usual human activity recognition or documentation problem. For instance, there are substantial difficulties in determining what to classify (given the breadth of disabilities involved [26]), there are substantial 'grand challenges' (such as the need for economic efficiency) [21] and there is also the need to design documentation tools that are themselves accessible for disabled people. We distil the design challenge into five considerations that collectively constitute a **framework** for designing a machine learning approach in this setting. Whilst many of these observations are arguably routine (or even obvious), they all reflect concerns that are most often overlooked or not properly addressed (and which have important disability specific qualities), hence the need for this exercise.

3.1 Issue 1: What to Classify and How to Classify It?

Machine learning operates on the basis of data: a set of labelled data is used to train (and then test) an algorithm 'learned' through this process. In practice, this involves consistently annotating a dataset so that each item is labeled with one or more classes or categories. There is limited agreement amongst disabled people as to what constitutes an accessibility barrier or which barriers are most important [48], making such categorization controversial. This is especially so given that existing research on accessible navigation has been skewed away from certain groups [26], thus there is a need to ensure that a wider range of measures of potential inaccessibility are provided going forwards. The choice of categories also needs to work effectively from an engineering perspective, which is challenging enough at the best of times [59,64]. This means there is a need to carefully select and then justify an appropriate set of classes in respect of the challenging disability-specific scenario, whilst ensuring they are well defined enough to enable a robust division between testing and training data.

3.2 Issue 2: How to Measure Performance (and Success)?

Measuring performance involves dividing data into testing and training datasets, before training an algorithm on the training data, and then testing the resulting algorithm on the testing data. For this to be a fair comparison, there needs to be a proper division between testing and training data. In the scenario of activity classification, the widely used ten-fold random cross-validation is inappropriate due to the way it mixes these two categories together and inflates performance: instead, *a leave one out strategy* should be used to avoid this problem [29] With respect to inertial sensing for accessibility documentation, not using a leave one out approach has been shown to vastly inflate reported performance [53]: nevertheless, this inappropriate practice remains widely used.

In machine learning research, different algorithms are benchmarked using standardized datasets in order to compare their performance [68]. Yet, at present, there is no such dataset for accessibility recognition in the built environment (nor given the diversity of approaches, is one desirable or possible), representing another substantial problem, in that it is not possible to easily compare systems and works in this domain. Another issue in measuring performance is to use domain-appropriate metrics [73], that indicate the real world implications of the system if it were to be translated into practice: yet there are no domain-appropriate metrics for accessibility mapping. Activity recognition systems can be particularly prone to bias in respect of certain types of disabled people, in part due to limitations with testing and training data (and how this is evaluated), which is an issue that has only just begun to be addressed [25,51,72]. Thus measuring performance is one of the biggest concerns in designing an accessibility documentation system, especially as this determines what will be deployed in practice (especially when experiments are conducted in order to choose which approach to use, as is usual in machine learning research [18]).

3.3   Issue 3: What Measurement Apparatus to Use?

The choice of sensing apparatus underpins the design of a system: it is the source of information for classification. This involves deciding between what sensors to use (e.g., accelerometer, gyroscope, camera) and how/where to mount them, be it to a person, wheelchair or any other device that is capable of movement or being propelled. One important disability related challenge is the diversity of motion (arising from each individual mobility impairment): consideration has to also be given to the population who propel a device or to whom a sensor is attached. For example, different wheelchair users propel their chairs in different ways, and each wheelchair is highly customised to the specific anatomical requirements of its user [71], thus a source of variability that risks any algorithm not generalizing across wheelchair users, if it is dependent on how they move (approaches such as static cameras are less problematic in this regard). Thus, the wider concern of 'bias' and 'fairness' in AI, is also a prominent concern in respect of the choice of measurement apparatus [25,57,72]. Moreover, there is need to ensure that any means of affixing and operating the hardware is physically accessible in and of itself (typically commodity camera clamps have been used, which works well for manual wheelchair users, but might not be so effective in other circumstances [48]). The choice of measurement apparatus is therefore particularly complicated in respect of people with mobility impairments. As such, the choice of measurement apparatus must work practically for the people who have to use it (taking into account any relevant disabilities), as well as not depending on the characteristics of the individual user.

3.4   Issue 4: What (machine Learning) Algorithm to Use?

Machine learning involves representing data by a list of features, which is a set of numbers that describes each element to be classified. When deployed, these features are then fed into a classifier to produce a prediction, or label. There are multifarious ways of providing features, including statistical means and moments, as well as specialized functions and rules [28]: in some cases, as with neural net-works, the pixels of an image can be submitted directly as features to an input layer [61]. The machine learning algorithm will learn the appropriate decision rule based on the data provided via its feature representation. Thus, there are two choices to make: the first is the feature representation, whilst the second is the machine learning classifier itself (e.g., KNN, SVM), although in some cases (e.g., Deep Learning) these issues somewhat shade into each other. This combination can have practical issues, for example different features and classifiers are more robust to different types of error, whilst there can be considerable effects on battery life and speed of prediction depending on whether features are handcrafted and if certain forms of classifiers are used [34].

Typically, the choice of classifier is decided experimentally. The difficulty in respect of disability arises this way: given the variety of settings and different impairments types, there is a need to particularly emphasize the robustness of the algorithm to signal noise and the diversity of different approaches. This can also require using a care-fully constructed training/testing set that properly takes this into account. At the same time, there can be wider considerations that go beyond performance: for instance, there is a need in some cases to provide transparency of decision making, which itself varies across classifiers.

3.5 Issue 5: How to Address Legal and Economic Considerations?

A practical system for measuring the accessibility of the built environment has to work in the real world: the nature of disability poses challenges, this time from a societal perspective. For disability, the primary concern is an economic one, with accessibility mapping systems having wholly insufficient coverage due to the expense of measuring and documenting accessibility barriers [21]. So a successful system must have a clear economic model and roadmap that has sufficient cover-age: from a practical point of view, it should be suitably efficient and inexpensive to obtain the required data. Another consideration is legal: the main barrier is privacy concerns (a barrier that has tripped up systems such as Google Street View in many countries, especially in Europe, where there are human rights considerations). However, the law also presents opportunities, as it places obligations on organizations, potentially including providing supporting infrastructure [46] under disability human rights law. Designers should consider how to use legal obligations (especially the duty to make reasonable accommodations) to make it more likely that a system will be adopted. At the same time, access to information legislation and human rights law may also present design opportunities [47] – it is important to think more holistically about legislation, as even arcane provisions can serve as alternatives. Accordingly, there is need to have an economic model that also takes into account the wider legislative context – if a system is not able to lawfully and efficiently provide documentation, then it will probably be inadequate when used in practice.

4   Proof of Concept Case Study – Application of Our Framework

4.1   Scenario: People with Mobility Impairments in Europe

In what follows, we present a carefully chosen **example** that illustrates how our system might be applied to produce a useful system for some people with a mobility impairment. Choosing a scenario that is likely to demonstrate a real world impact mostly relates to *Issue 1* in our framework. Our scenario concerns a form of sensing that addresses surface types in the European Context. In Europe, there is a long-standing legacy of old areas, with cities including cobblestones, grass paths and legacy paving types. Compared to countries like the United States or Australia, European cities tend to have evolved organically to include a diverse variety of different path types within a small space: this is due to the fact that most cities were based on medieval structures and layouts [50]. The advantage of European style cities is that they have relatively short path segments, so it is not as critical for street features (e.g., curb-cuts) to always be in the right place, compared to US cities that have relatively large street blocks [50]. Moreover, the existence of relevant accessibility affordances is highly correlated with the surface type, because newer surfaces (e.g., asphalt) will normally involve the installation of accessibility features as they are replaced [32]. Taking a holistic view in line with [26], we focus on classifying surfaces, as classifying them into different types could substantially improve navigation for people with mobility impairments, without the difficulties of directly classifying specific street features.

4.2   Methodology

Data Collection. We mounted a modern smartphone via a commodity camera mount (similar to that used in [48]) on a rollator (or walker) (see Fig. 1). We chose a camera based approach given that inertial sensors are sensitive to individual users and have so far not shown promising performance for accessibility documentation. The smartphone was mounted at a height of 50cm at a 60° angle so that the surface could be directly observed, whilst ensuring that identifying pictures of individuals was not captured, in line with the approach of [48]. The advantage of this privacy sensitive approach is that we address an important concern in respect of *Issue 5* of the framework, as a system that does not meet this requirement might not be permitted in a range of circumstances (similar to the fact that Google StreetView is effectively banned in Germany). The camera covers a horizontal swath of about 1.15 m: this exceeds (by over 25%) the legal standard for barrier-free construction in Germany (DIN-18040) that says that the width of a path has to be 0.9 m for ease of access by wheelchair users. This field of view also minimizes the risk of capturing other objects, occlusions and other confounding information, thereby increasing the subsequent prediction quality [52].

The smartphone took a photograph every 800 ms, which were saved alongside their respective timestamp and GPS location. We traversed all of the available paths within a series of defined geographical regions in three cities, with a total path length of 36.22 km within an area of 1.641 km². The paths were traversed in 6 days by one person using a rollator. This approach was designed to ensure that the data collected was as naturalistic as possible while reflecting the variety of different surfaces, thus helping address an important concern associated with *Issue 2*. The relatively cheap nature of the hardware (around \$100) and the fact that data collection fits with ordinary day to day activities are intended to help address the economic concerns noted as being fundamental in *Issue 5*. For Bremen, the regions (see Fig. 3**I**) include the city centre (areas A and B), a suburb (C and D) and a university campus area (E and F), whilst we also collected smaller areas of different cities, namely Hamburg (see Fig. 3**II**) and Hannover (see Fig. 3**III**) to enable further experiments.

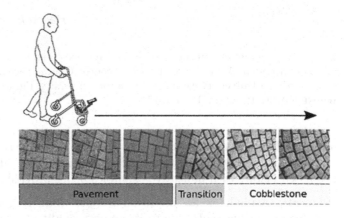

Fig. 1. The data collection apparatus, including the smartphone positioning

Fig. 2. An illustration of how transitions were identified and labelled in the collected data

Data Categorization. A key concern was to have easily annotatable categories that relate to the real concerns of people with disabilities. To address this part of *Issue 1*, the categories for the surfaces are a subset of those provided in OpenStreetMap, which is the pre-dominant open source mapping framework [27]. The advantage of using Open-StreetMap is that these categories are widely tested and used in practice (allowing them to be easily and consistently annotated), as well as having already been con-figured to be usable by people on the ground. Taking account of the framework for considering accessibility barriers in [58], these categories were carefully curated and merged to: (i) eliminate categories that were not present in the locale (e.g., snow, ice and salt), (ii) to ensure that the boundaries between categories that are well defined (so they can be effectively

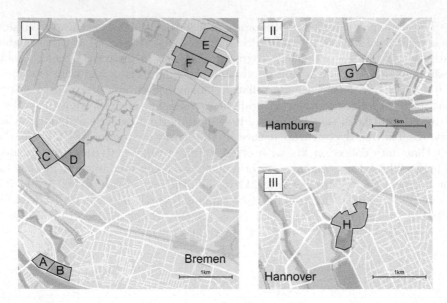

Fig. 3. Map of regions within the city that were explored for our evaluation. In Fig. 3(I) covering 'Bremen' A and B are in the city centre, C and D are in a suburb, whilst E and F are within a University campus of a major University. Figure 3(II) covers 'Hamburg', whilst Fig. 3(III) covers 'Hannover'.

annotated), merging where necessary and (iii) to ensure that only categories that are relevant to wheelchair accessibility were included. The resulting categories are listed below, with indicative examples being provided in Fig. 4:

Asphalt: Asphalt is an improved surface that is generally prioritised by wheelchair routing tools, due to its smooth quality (provided it is maintained) and the likelihood of other accessibility affordances being available (e.g., dropped curbs) [5,7].

Cobblestones: Cobblestones are an old form of paving, which is inaccessible to many wheelchair users and present a severe trip hazard [42]. In practice, they are to be avoided by any routing tool, if at all possible.

Ground/Unimproved: This is a path that is a dirt track, perhaps including gravel. Whilst this surface type is generally traversable (albeit uncomfortably [17,42]), there is a reduced likelihood of there being accessibility affordances, due to the unimproved nature of this path.

Grass: This is where there is no path at all, for example where someone has been directed through a park. This is a difficult surface for most wheelchair users to traverse [17], whilst also indicating that there no substantive path, thus meaning that accessibility affordances (for instances, markers for visually impaired people to aid navigation are less likely to be present, given the open nature of these spaces).

Pavement: Pavement (see Fig. 2) is an improved surface that is generally prioritised by wheelchair routing tools, due to its smooth quality (provided it is maintained) and the likelihood of other accessibility aid (e.g., dropped curbs). However, unlike asphalt, it can be an intrinsic trip hazard to wheelchair users (and ambulant people with gait or visual impairments), due to small variations in slab height [20].

We also annotated transitions between more than one category separately (in effect making them as a sixth class), with a transition being defined as the point where more than one different surface class was simultaneously visible to the camera. This process is illustrated in Fig. 2. More generally, the ground-truth labelling of the images was performed by the research team over a period of two working days. This could be done efficiently due to the fact that consecutive images often had the same surface (with a mean of 64.93 images being in a batch), allowing for a Panopticon [41] style approach to be used to speed up the annotation (but with frames, rather than videos).

Testing and Training Data. The choice of appropriate testing and training data specifically fits within *Issue 3*. We adopted two different types of leave one out approach for testing and training our approach:

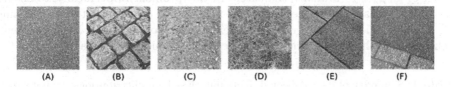

(A)   (B)   (C)   (D)   (E)   (F)

Fig. 4. Exemplars of different classes, from left to right: (A) Asphalt, (B) Cobblestones, (C) Ground/Unimproved, (D) Grass, (E) Pavement and (F) Transition.

Conservative: This is where areas geographically close together are not trained together. In practice this means testing areas A and B together (with areas C, D, E and F being the training data) and so on for areas C and D, and E and F. This makes three areas, S1 (equal to A and B), S2 (equal to C and D) and S3 (equal to E and F). The approach here is designed to be a 'worst-case-scenario' and is highly likely to understate recognition performance.

Leave One Region Out: In this case, we only leave one region out. For example, Region C would be trained on Regions A, B, D, E and F. This approach is designed to be in line with typical performance, if further training data were to be collected (for example in other cities).

By deliberately ensuring that the same area does not appear in both the testing and training data, we avoid the error that has been made in most previous works on accessibility mapping and thus ensure our algorithm generalizes to novel examples that it was not trained on.

The Machine Learning Algorithm. Recent developments in deep learning and in particular the use of Convolutional Neural Networks has led to substantial improvements in surface texture classification [52]. Addressing *Issue 4* requires adopting an approach which is already known to be effective for the problem at hand. We adopt one such approach, relying on the architecture of ResNet50 [36]: notably, ResNet approaches have already been used in other accessibility documentation scenarios [75]. This network architecture was retrained afresh on our dataset, with the only modification to this architecture being in the final layer, which was changed to have the correct number of output nodes. The images were cropped to a window of 480 by 480 pixels (the camera was positioned in portrait mode, with the bottom 160 rows being cropped). This was then interpolated to 224 by 224 pixels to be an appropriate resolution for ResNet50 implementation. We deliberately adopted a 'motion independent approach' to address the concern (per *Issues 2 and 3*) that machine learning algorithms are not well adapted to people with disabilities (and the fact that there re-mains a lack of metrics to evaluate the extent of this problem). Specifically, to ensure that our approach was independent of the motion of the rollator, each frame was trained independently of each other: we did not use any computer vision techniques (such as optical flow) that deal with sequences of images.

Table 1. Summary of data collected, including class label distributions, by individual frame. Regions A to F are all in Bremen.

Region	Asphalt	Cobblestone	Grass	Ground/ Unimproved	Pavement	Transition	Total (in Region)
A	0	1656	0	0	930	632	3218
B	44	577	0	1224	1696	423	3964
C	1017	47	0	0	3501	300	4865
D	78	132	662	4252	0	39	5163
E	1500	476	571	288	1940	161	4936
F	1249	785	807	730	2677	192	6440
G (Hamburg)	619	563	381	572	3034	227	5396
H (Hannover)	1136	1090	333	957	3612	211	7339
Total	5643	5326	2754	8023	17390	2185	41321

4.3   Results

Based on the real-world application of our framework we got results referring to the data collection and categorization but also for the performance of the trained system itself. The latter can be considered in relation to leave one out frames and conservative frames whereby both are investigated framewise and "streetwise". The first three results subsections focus on Bremen, whilst our final exercise compares the three cities.

Data Collection and Distribution. The eight regions A–H were all annotated, producing a total of 41321 individual frames. As can be seen in Table 1, there is skew in the class distribution, with certain types of surface being more common than others. The most common surface type was the pavement, followed by unimproved surfaces. Two of our analyses focus on within city performance and thus just 'Bremen', whilst we look at cross-city performance in Section *Cross-City Performance*.

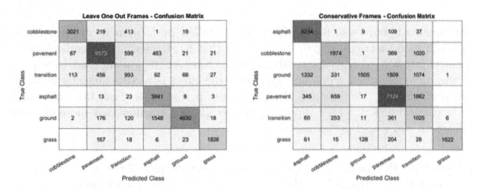

Fig. 5. . Confusion Matrices for both 'Conservative' and 'Leave one region out' on a *Frame* basis.

Framewise Performance. We report the raw performance per frame based on both approaches, conservative and leave one region out based on 'Bremen'. The conservative performance was a mean F1-score [28] of 0.621, whilst the leave-one-region-out mean F1-score was 0.802. The more detailed performance can be seen in the con-fusion matrices, Fig. 5, which shows that most relevant categories (asides transitions) were easily distinguishable, but with reduced performance in respect of certain categories, for example ground was regularly confused with asphalt and in the more conservative approach, with other categories.

Aggregated 'Streetwise' Performance. In practice, the concern is to identify whether streets contain problematic elements, rather than identifying each frame. Following [73], we therefore report results on a streetwise level using an aggregation process, addressing an important concern under *Issue 2* which hitherto has not been addressed in the context of accessible mapping. The conservative performance was a mean F1-score of 0.593, whilst the leave one region

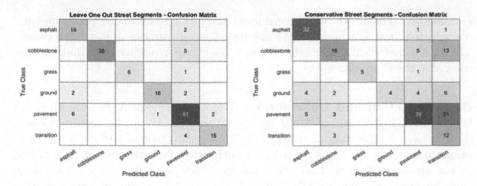

Fig. 6. Confusion Matrices for both 'Conservative' and 'Leave one region out' on a *Street* basis.

out mean F1-score was 0.871. The more detailed performance can be seen in the confusion matrices, Fig. 6, which shows that most relevant categories (asides transitions) were easily distinguishable in the leave one region out case. In respect of the more likely leave one out approach, the effect is to substantially increase the performance (there was a slight decrease in the other case, but this could be statistical noise), whilst reporting the results in a manner that more directly relates to real world performance.

Cross-City Performance. We present the performance of our approach where a system is only trained on data from other cities (so for example we would train on 'Hamburg' and 'Hannover' and test on 'Bremen'). This performance is poor, making it clear that some training data within a city is necessary. In respect of frame-wise performance, we obtain a mean F1-score of 0.495 for 'Bremen', 0.378 for 'Hamburg' and 0.378 for Hannover (Hannover was slightly higher, but rounding to three decimal places, we get the same value as for Hamburg). For streetwise performance (following the same process in *Aggregated 'Streetwise' Performance*), we obtain a mean F1-score of 0.487 for 'Bremen', 0.278 for 'Hamburg' and 0.333 for Hannover. In Fig. 7, we provide the confusion matrices illustrating more detailed performance.

5   Discussion

5.1   Real-World Surface Recognition Performance

Our framework was helpful in designing a practical system that obtained a high real-world performance. It is apparent from the results above that is possible to reliably recognize different surface types using our approach. The more conservative approach performed worse, as one would expect, partially because of the reduced volume of training data: however, even in this relatively extreme scenario, the performance would still improve upon existing tracking systems

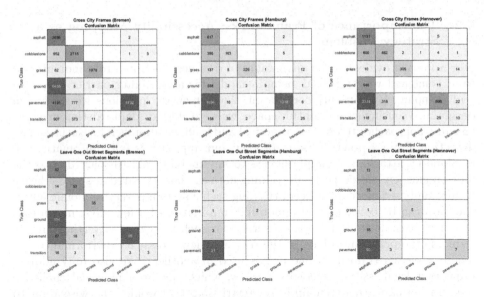

Fig. 7. Confusion Matrices for both 'Conservative' and 'Leave one region out' on a *Cross-City* basis.

(noting that none of these is any better than pedestrian routing tools [69]) and is substantially better than choosing a given route by chance.

The less conservative and more realistic (taking into account the considerations in [29]) approach of leave one region out yielded stronger performance and if this were to be real world performance, would lead to appreciably (rather than technically) better approaches for routing people with disabilities. Moreover, this approach is promising for other goals in addition to making more effective routing tools: for example, this approach would be sufficiently accurate to estimate the accessibility of a given city, or the distance travelled by someone on a rough surface.

In a real-world context, the decision to be taken really is a two-class problem – whether or not a path segment is accessible. As such, the general f-ratio across our six classes actually considerably understates performance in a navigation scenario. A more realistic approach would ignore the transitions (which could normally be identified using GPS and existing maps) and split the remaining classes. For example, doing this with asphalt and pavement being considered to be suitable surfaces and the rest be deemed unsuitable would lead to an f-ratio of 0.952 per street segment, if applied to the leave one out scenario. This would be adequate to produce an accuracy on a route of over 82%, if each route was assumed to be 4 path segments long and the accessibility of each segment independent from one another. However, this assumes that training data is collected from the same city in a sufficient volume to be adequate: training on one city and using it for another was shown to be infeasible (see Section Cross-City Performance) above, thus emphasizing the need for data to be quickly obtainable.

5.2   The Importance of Frameworks: Accessibility Mapping as a Strategy Problem

Our approach evidences the advantages of a camera mounted to a mobility aid (and combined with GPS) as being a model for accessibility barrier detection and mapping. By carefully considering the framework questions we set out in designing a sensing system in this space, we were able to adapt existing machine learning approaches to create a practical and realistic approach for surface class detection. From a practical point of view, our approach is fully automatic, can be done by attaching a simple device to any mobility aid (in part due to the motion independent design) and training data can be annotated at speed relative to motion-based systems. Indeed, training such a system is very economic, given the data can be collected and annotated in a matter of a few days, meaning it would be feasible to perform this exercise for each individual city (thus greatly reducing the practical impact of the relatively low 'cross-city' performance, i.e. where a system trained on one city is used in another). We also fully address important legal issues, especially privacy, which can be a practical challenge (e.g., in Germany, there remain heavy restrictions that would otherwise apply to street photography per the "Bundesverband Informationswirtschaft, Telekommunikation und neue Medien" [4]). At the same time, this work can be directly used in a specific setting: for instance, the documentation generated by the surface detection described in our case study might in turn be used in a navigation tool to reduce risk of falls in elderly people by reducing the probability they will need to follow a route containing an unimproved surface.

In effect, this work treats accessibility mapping as primarily a strategy problem, rather than a technical machine learning problem. It reflects the fact that there is a 'bigger' and more complex picture that is perhaps unique to accessibility sensing. In articulating these concerns and providing an exemplar of how to address them, we offer a clear road forwards in offering an automated approach, which we hope help resolve the wider challenge of inaccessibility in the built environment. Our approach of developing a set of practical principles that could be adopted more widely (rather than just focusing on one system) offers a means for addressing wider concerns about AI fairness with respect to people with disabilities, with the principles we have identified in respect of accessible navigation serving as a potential starting point for frameworks that apply to other settings.

5.3   Real World Performance

Our work is the only one so far to adopt a real-world approach towards assessment of performance, including in respect of appropriate metrics in line with [73]. This is an important consideration that should be taken up in this field: presently it is not possible to understand the performance of existing systems and thus to understand progress. The implications of this for our work is that we can reliably expect our results will generalize and thus have clearly illustrated the benefits of our camera centric approach for accessibility mapping.

We expect (and sincerely hope) that a renewed focus on performance metrics that more directly relate to the problem of accessible navigation will be something given an increased emphasis in this sphere. Going forwards, this would allow us to directly determine whether our work is more effective than others, as presently it is very difficult to compare real-world navigation performance as existing papers do not report 'street segment' performance.

5.4   Limitations

This work has clearly shown the advantage of a given strategy in documenting accessibility barriers in the built environment, yet we still have some important limitations. First, whilst we identify appropriate surface types, this does not address the need to identify broken surfaces (e.g., cracks in the pavement) and other trip hazards. Second, the dataset only contains pictures from a six-day period without influence of rain or seasons like snow. The third concern is motion-blur, which occurs where there are quick movements to pull the apparatus up a curb: addressing this may increase performance (e.g., using optical flow to give less weight to frames that include this). Fourth, future work may have a larger dataset available, potentially increasing performance further, likewise with any approach that combines multiple sources of information, as opposed purely our on-ground assessment process. Finally, we note that our framework itself should evolve, as we develop our knowledge of fairer machine learning approaches for people with disabilities, and better accessibility documentation systems.

6   Conclusion and Future Work

We have presented a new approach towards documenting accessibility barriers in the built environment and measuring the performance of a recognition system in this space, focusing on the practical problems faced by people with disabilities. This approach is pragmatic, reflecting that the problem of concern is an intersection of HCI concerns and applied machine learning. To explore this approach, we presented a case study, which implemented an instance of our framework in a fully automated pipeline that operates effectively in the navigation context. Future work could explore more instances of this approach, thereby helping to concrete this strategy for documenting barriers going forwards, as well as translating it to a real-world system.

References

1. Accessable. https://www.accessable.co.uk/. Accessed 31 Jan 2020
2. Convention on the rights of persons with disabilities (CRPD)—united nations enable. https://www.un.org/development/desa/disabilities/convention-on-the-rights-of-persons-with-disabilities.html. Accessed 27 Jan 2021
3. Fixmystreet. https://www.fixmystreet.com/. Accessed 18 Sept 2016
4. Machine learning und die transparenzanforderungen der ds-gvo, p. 44

5. Openrouteservice. https://www.openrouteservice.org
6. Photoroute. http://www.photoroute.com/. Accessed 14 Sept 2016
7. Routino. https://www.routino.org
8. Venues—axs map. https://www.axsmap.com/. Accessed 31 Jan 2020
9. World report on disability 2011 (2011)
10. Ahmetovic, D., Manduchi, R., Coughlan, J.M., Mascetti, S.: Zebra crossing spotter: automatic population of spatial databases for increased safety of blind travelers, pp. 251–258. ACM (2015)
11. Ahmetovic, D., Manduchi, R., Coughlan, J.M., Mascetti, S.: Mind your crossings: mining GIS imagery for crosswalk localization. ACM Trans. Access. Comput. (TACCESS) **9**(4), 11 (2017)
12. Atkin, R.: Sight line: designing better streets for people with low vision (2010)
13. Bowtell, J.: Assessing the value and market attractiveness of the accessible tourism industry in Europe: a focus on major travel and leisure companies. J. Tour. Futures **1**(3), 203–222 (2015)
14. Carrington, P., Chang, K., Mentis, H., Hurst, A.: "But, i don't take steps": examining the inaccessibility of fitness trackers for wheelchair athletes. ASSETS 2015, pp. 193–201. ACM, New York (2015). https://doi.org/10.1145/2700648.2809845
15. Chen, W.Y., et al.: Wheelchair-related accidents: relationship with wheelchair-using behavior in active community wheelchair users. Arch. Phys. Med. Rehabil. **92**(6), 892–898 (2011)
16. Clarke, P., Ailshire, J.A., Bader, M., Morenoff, J.D., House, J.S.: Mobility, disability and the urban built environment. Am. J. Epidemiol. **168**(5), 506–513 (2008)
17. Daveler, B., Salatin, B., Grindle, G.G., Candiotti, J., Wang, H., Cooper, R.A.: Participatory design and validation of mobility enhancement robotic wheelchair. J. Rehabil. Res. Dev. **52**(6), 739–750 (2015)
18. Drummond, C., Japkowicz, N.: Warning: Statistical benchmarking is addictive. kicking the habit in machine learning. J. Exp. Theoret. Artif. Intell. **22**, 67–80 (2010). https://doi.org/10.1080/09528130903010295
19. Fast-Company: How apple made the watch work for wheelchair users (2016). https://www.fastcompany.com/3061283/how-apple-made-the-watch-work-for-wheelchair-users
20. Fotios, S., Uttley, J.: Illuminance required to detect a pavement obstacle of critical size. Light. Res. Technol. **50**(3), 390–404 (2018)
21. Froehlich, J.E., et al.: Grand challenges in accessible maps. Interactions **26**, 78–81 (2019)
22. Garcia-Mendez, Y., Pearlman, J.L., Boninger, M.L., Cooper, R.A.: Health risks of vibration exposure to wheelchair users in the community. J. Spinal Cord Med. **36**(4), 365–375 (2013)
23. Gharebaghi, A., Mostafavi, M.A., Chavoshi, S., Edwards, G., Fougeyrollas, P.: The role of social factors in the accessibility of urban areas for people with motor disabilities. ISPRS Int. J. Geo-Inf. **7**(4), 131 (2018)
24. Ghilardi, M.C., Macedo, R.C., Manssour, I.H.: A new approach for automatic detection of tactile paving surfaces in sidewalks. Procedia Comput. Sci. **80**, 662–672 (2016)
25. Guo, A., Kamar, E., Vaughan, J.W., Wallach, H., Morris, M.R.: Toward fairness in AI for people with disabilities: a research roadmap. arXiv:1907.02227 [cs], August 2019

26. Gupta, M., et al.: Towards more universal wayfinding technologies: navigation preferences across disabilities. CHI 2020: CHI Conference on Human Factors in Computing Systems, pp. 1–13. ACM, Honolulu, April 2020. https://doi.org/10.1145/3313831.3376581. Accessed 27 Jan 2021
27. Haklay, M., Weber, P.: Openstreetmap: user-generated street maps. IEEE Pervasive Comput. **7**(4), 12–18 (2008). https://doi.org/10.1109/MPRV.2008.80. Event: IEEE Pervasive Computing
28. Hammerla, N.Y., Kirkham, R., Andras, P., Ploetz, T.: On preserving statistical characteristics of accelerometry data using their empirical cumulative distribution, pp. 65–68. ACM (2013)
29. Hammerla, N.Y., Plötz, T.: Let's (not) stick together: pairwise similarity biases cross-validation in activity recognition, pp. 1041–1051. ACM (2015)
30. Hara, K., et al.: Improving public transit accessibility for blind riders by crowdsourcing bus stop landmark locations with google street view: An extended analysis. ACM Trans. Access. Comput. (TACCESS) **6**(2), 5 (2015)
31. Hara, K., Chan, C., Froehlich, J.E.: The design of assistive location-based technologies for people with ambulatory disabilities: a formative study, pp. 1757–1768. ACM (2016)
32. Hara, K., Le, V., Froehlich, J.: Combining crowdsourcing and google street view to identify street-level accessibility problems, pp. 631–640. ACM (2013)
33. Hara, K., Sun, J., Moore, R., Jacobs, D., Froehlich, J.: Tohme: detecting curb ramps in google street view using crowdsourcing, computer vision, and machine learning, pp. 189–204. ACM (2014)
34. Haresamudram, H., Anderson, D.V., Plötz, T.: On the role of features in human activity recognition, pp. 78–88. ACM (2019)
35. Harpur, P.: Time to be heard: how advocates can use the convention on the rights of persons with disabilities to drive change. Technical report, Rochester, NY, April 2011. https://papers.ssrn.com/abstract=1804734. Accessed 27 Jan 2021
36. He, K., Zhang, X., Ren, S., Sun, J.: Deep residual learning for image recognition, pp. 770–778 (2016)
37. Holloway, C., Tyler, N.: A micro-level approach to measuring the accessibility of footways for wheelchair users using the capability model. Transp. Plan. Technol. **36**(7), 636–649 (2013). https://doi.org/10.1080/03081060.2013.845434
38. Iwasawa, Y., Nagamine, K., Yairi, I.E., Matsuo, Y.: Toward an automatic road accessibility information collecting and sharing based on human behavior sensing technologies of wheelchair users. Procedia Comput. Sci. **63**, 74–81 (2015)
39. Iwasawa, Y., Yairi, I.E.: Life-logging of wheelchair driving on web maps for visualizing potential accidents and incidents. In: Anthony, P., Ishizuka, M., Lukose, D. (eds.) PRICAI 2012. LNCS (LNAI), vol. 7458, pp. 157–169. Springer, Heidelberg (2012). https://doi.org/10.1007/978-3-642-32695-0_16
40. Iwasawa, Y., Yairi, I.E., Matsuo, Y.: Combining human action sensing of wheelchair users and machine learning for autonomous accessibility data collection. IEICE Trans. Inf. Syst. **99**(4), 1153–1161 (2016)
41. Jackson, D., Nicholson, J., Stoeckigt, G., Wrobel, R., Thieme, A., Olivier, P.: Panopticon: a parallel video overview system. In: Annual ACM Symposium on User Interface Software and Technology, UIST 2013, pp. 123–130, November 2013. https://doi.org/10.1145/2501988.2502038, https://research.monash.edu/en/publications/panopticon-a-parallel-video-overview-system. Accessed 01 Feb 2020
42. Kasemsuppakorn, P., Karimi, H.A.: Data requirements and a spatial database for personalized wheelchair navigation, pp. 31–34. Singapore Therapeutic, Assistive & Rehabilitative Technologies (START) Centre (2008)

43. Kerr, J., Rosenberg, D., Frank, L.: The role of the built environment in healthy aging: Community design, physical activity, and health among older adults. J. Plan. Lit. **27**(1), 43–60 (2012). https://doi.org/10.1177/0885412211415283

44. Kirby, R.L., et al.: Wheelchair skills capacity and performance of manual wheelchair users with spinal cord injury. Arch. Phys. Med. Rehabil. **97**(10), 1761–1769 (2016). https://doi.org/10.1016/j.apmr.2016.05.015

45. Kirby, R., Swuste, J., Dupuis, D.J., MacLeod, D.A., Monroe, R.: The wheelchair skills test: a pilot study of a new outcome measure. Arch. Phys. Med. Rehabil. **83**(1), 10–18 (2002). https://doi.org/10.1053/apmr.2002.26823

46. Kirkham, R.: Can disability discrimination law expand the availability of wearable computers? Computer **48**(6), 25–33 (2015)

47. Kirkham, R.: Using European human rights jurisprudence for incorporating values into design. In: Proceedings of the 2020 ACM Designing Interactive Systems Conference, pp. 115–128. Association for Computing Machinery, New York, July 2020. https://doi.org/10.1145/3357236.3395539. Accessed 26 Jan 2021

48. Kirkham, R., et al.: Wheeliemap: an exploratory system for qualitative reports of inaccessibility in the built environment, p. 38. ACM (2017)

49. Kirkham, R., Tannert, B.: Using computer simulations to investigate the potential performance of 'A to B' routing systems for people with mobility impairments. In: Mobile HCI 2021: ACM International Conference on Mobile Human-Computer Interaction (2021)

50. Koch, F.: Die europäische Stadt in Transformation: Stadtplanung und Stadtentwicklungspolitik im postsozialistischen Warschau. Stadt, Raum und Gesellschaft, VS Verlag für Sozialwissenschaften (2010). https://doi.org/10.1007/978-3-531-92109-9, https://www.springer.com/de/book/9783531170909

51. Kurauchi, Y., Abe, N., Konishi, H., Seshimo, H.: Barrier detection using sensor data from multiple modes of transportation with data augmentation, vol. 1, pp. 667–675. IEEE (2019)

52. Liu, L., Chen, J., Fieguth, P., Zhao, G., Chellappa, R., Pietikäinen, M.: From bow to CNN: two decades of texture representation for texture classification. Int. J. Comput. Vision **127**(1), 74–109 (2019)

53. Mascetti, S., Civitarese, G., El Malak, O., Bettini, C.: Smartwheels: detecting urban features for wheelchair users' navigation. Pervasive Mob. Comput. **62**, 101115 (2020)

54. Meinke, U.: Kamera-autos von google fahren wieder durchs ruhrgebiet. WAZ, June 2018. Accessed 01 Feb 2020

55. Meyers, A.R., Anderson, J.J., Miller, D.R., Shipp, K., Hoenig, H.: Barriers, facilitators, and access for wheelchair users: substantive and methodological lessons from a pilot study of environmental effects. Soc. Sci. Med. **55**(8), 1435–1446 (2002)

56. Mora, H., Gilart-Iglesias, V., Pérez-del Hoyo, R., Andújar-Montoya, M.: A comprehensive system for monitoring urban accessibility in smart cities. Sensors **17**(8), 1834 (2017)

57. Morris, M.R.: Ai and accessibility: a discussion of ethical considerations. Commun. ACM **63**(6), 35–37 (2020). https://doi.org/10.1145/3356727, arXiv: 1908.08939

58. Mourcou, Q., Fleury, A., Dupuy, P., Diot, B., Franco, C., Vuillerme, N.: Wegoto: a smartphone-based approach to assess and improve accessibility for wheelchair users. In: Annual International Conference of the IEEE Engineering in Medicine and Biology Society. IEEE Engineering in Medicine and Biology Society. Annual International Conference 2013, pp. 1194–1197 (2013). https://doi.org/10.1109/EMBC.2013.6609720, pMID: 24109907

59. Nguyen-Dinh, L.V., Waldburger, C., Roggen, D., Tröster, G.: Tagging human activities in video by crowdsourcing. ICMR 2013, pp. 263–270. Association for Computing Machinery, Dallas, April 2013. https://doi.org/10.1145/2461466.2461508. Accessed 30 Jan 2020

60. Norgate, S.H., et al.: Accessibility of urban spaces for visually impaired pedestrians. Municipal Engineer **165**(4), 231–237 (2012)

61. Ordóñez, F., Roggen, D.: Deep convolutional and LSTM recurrent neural networks for multimodal wearable activity recognition. Sensors **16**(1), 115 (2016)

62. Palazzi, C.E., Teodori, L., Roccetti, M.: Path 2.0: a participatory system for the generation of accessible routes, pp. 1707–1711. IEEE (2010)

63. Poppe, R., Rienks, R., van Dijk, B.: Evaluating the future of HCI: challenges for the evaluation of emerging applications. In: Huang, T.S., Nijholt, A., Pantic, M., Pentland, A. (eds.) Artifical Intelligence for Human Computing. LNCS (LNAI), vol. 4451, pp. 234–250. Springer, Heidelberg (2007). https://doi.org/10.1007/978-3-540-72348-6_12

64. Reyes-Ortiz, J.L., Oneto, L., Samà Monsonís, A., Parra, X., Anguita, D.: Transition-aware human activity recognition using smartphones. Neurocomputing **171** (2015). https://doi.org/10.1016/j.neucom.2015.07.085

65. Rice, M.T., et al.: Quality assessment and accessibility mapping in an image-based geocrowdsourcing testbed. Cartographica: Int. J. Geograph. Inf. Geovis. **53**(1), 1–14 (2018)

66. Rodger, S., Vines, J., McLaughlin, J.: Technology and the politics of mobility: evidence generation in accessible transport activism. CHI 2016, pp. 2417–2429. Association for Computing Machinery, San Jose, May 2016. https://doi.org/10.1145/2858036.2858146. Accessed 30 Jan 2020

67. Saha, M., et al.: Project sidewalk: a web-based crowdsourcing tool for collecting sidewalk accessibility data at scale. In: CHI 2019 (2019)

68. Stallkamp, J., Schlipsing, M., Salmen, J., Igel, C.: Man vs. computer: benchmarking machine learning algorithms for traffic sign recognition. Neural Netw. **32**, 323–332 (2012)

69. Tannert, B., Kirkham, R., Schöning, J.: Analyzing accessibility barriers using cost-benefit analysis to design reliable navigation services for wheelchair users. In: Lamas, D., Loizides, F., Nacke, L., Petrie, H., Winckler, M., Zaphiris, P. (eds.) INTERACT 2019. LNCS, vol. 11746, pp. 202–223. Springer, Cham (2019). https://doi.org/10.1007/978-3-030-29381-9_13

70. Tannert, B., Schöning, J.: Disabled, but at what cost?: an examination of wheelchair routing algorithms. MobileHCI 2018, pp. 46:1–46:7. ACM, New York (2018). https://doi.org/10.1145/3229434.3229458. Accessed 16 Oct 2018

71. Trefler, E., Taylor, S.: Prescription and positioning: evaluating the physically disabled individual for wheelchair seating. Prosthet. Orthot. Int. **15**(3), 217–224 (1991)

72. Trewin, S.: Ai fairness for people with disabilities: point of view. arXiv:1811.10670 [cs], November 2018

73. Ward, J.A., Lukowicz, P., Gellersen, H.W.: Performance metrics for activity recognition. ACM Trans. Intell. Syst. Technol. (TIST) **2**(1), 6 (2011)

74. Watson, C., Kirkham, R., Kharrufa, A.: Pip kit: an exploratory investigation into using lifelogging to support disability benefit claimants. CHI 2020: CHI Conference on Human Factors in Computing Systems, pp. 1–14. ACM, Honolulu, April 2020. https://doi.org/10.1145/3313831.3376215. Accessed 27 Jan 2021

75. Weld, G., Jang, E., Li, A., Zeng, A., Heimerl, K., Froehlich, J.E.: Deep learning for automatically detecting sidewalk accessibility problems using streetscape imagery, pp. 196–209 (2019)
76. Wolf, E., et al.: Vibration exposure of individuals using wheelchairs over sidewalk surfaces. Disabil. Rehabil. **27**(23), 1443–1449 (2005)
77. Yairi, I.E., et al.: Estimating spatiotemporal information from behavioral sensing data of wheelchair users by machine learning technologies. Information **10**(3), 114 (2019)

What Happens to My Instagram Account After I Die? Re-imagining Social Media as a Commemorative Space for Remembrance and Recovery

Soonho Kwon⑩, Eunsol Choi⑩, Minseok Kim⑩, Sunah Hwang⑩,
Dongwoo Kim⑩, and Younah Kang⁽⊠⁾

Yonsei University, Seoul, Republic of Korea
{harrykwon98,jupiteraca,minseokdaniel,yakang}@yonsei.ac.kr

Abstract. This research explores the relationship between social media and mortality, focusing on social media as a thanatosensitive technology that promotes death preparation and commemoration. Employing concepts from the Value-Sensitive Design approach, our research identifies three main stakeholders surrounding the online commemoration experience. As an exploratory study, we conducted in-depth interviews and observations (n = 9) to better understand key stakeholders' experiences in online and offline commemorations. After analyzing the qualitative data, we extracted design requirements that were used to create a conceptual commemorative system and a functioning prototype. An informal user testing (n = 6) yielded positive feedbacks on the new system for it offers the unique opportunity to reflect existence, prepare for death, and create a community of commemoration that helps memorialize the deceased and recover from grief. The study suggests that commemoration via social media aids in maintaining user volition, induces active and interactive participation, and allows for a continuation of the digital legacy. Such findings may help deepen the understanding of humans' perception of death and commemoration within the context of social media.

Keywords: Design Research · Death · Commemoration · Social Media · User Experience

1 Introduction

Death is perhaps the only experience that all humans go through. The human species has been trying to understand and explore the concept, preparation, and aftermath of death from many different perspectives. Scholars in the field of Human–Computer Interaction (HCI) have recently started to emphasize the importance of 'thanatosensitivity' to create and discuss designs that allow us to comprehend, reflect, and discuss mortality [1–3]. These attempts were often in the form of memorializing the deceased through technology such as digital family heirlooms, digital cemeteries, and digital gravestones [4–8].

© IFIP International Federation for Information Processing 2021
Published by Springer Nature Switzerland AG 2021
C. Ardito et al. (Eds.): INTERACT 2021, LNCS 12933, pp. 449–467, 2021.
https://doi.org/10.1007/978-3-030-85616-8_26

While they successfully opened up new schemes to reconcile the living and the dead, implementing such ideas into our everyday lives still seems quite out of reach, as it is difficult to have users prevalently using digital screens as their family tombstones or replacing their family heirloom with a USB stick. Preceding studies also lack the opportunity to address all involved parties and to incorporate their different values in a unanimous design space. Thus, in an attempt to imagine a thanatosensitive design solution that can easily be implemented in our lives, we conducted an empirical study from which value-sensitive design insights were drawn.

In this research, we identify three stakeholders surrounding the experience of death on social media: the to-be-dead, the after-death account manager, and the bereaved, and we incorporate their values in designing an online commemorative system. We hope to broaden horizons for researchers and designers in considering social media as an effective commemorative space in catering to users' various value priorities.

The contributions to our research include the following:

- Through an empirical study, we investigate how each of the three stakeholders perceives death and commemoration in digital space
- Based on the empirical study, we discuss how social media is/can be utilized as a death preparation and commemoration tool by establishing design requirements
- We suggest a new design system for death preparation and commemoration
- We evaluate the users' reactions to the newly proposed system on death and online commemoration

2 Background

2.1 Thanatosensitive Design

The term "thanatosensitivity" was first coined by Massami and Charise [2] to "recognize and actively engage with the facts of mortality, dying, and death in the creation of interactive systems." The HCI community has recognized the importance of the concept and urged people from diverse backgrounds to get involved with thanatosensitive design [3]. The concept initiated much research and many projects including Shoebox, an application that hands down the digital traces such as Gmail archives and YouTube videos of the deceased to the bereaved [9].

In discussing thanatosensitive designs, Bassett [10] suggests an interesting perspective of eternal life in the digital sphere. The research emphasized the users' desire to be remembered by the bereaved (or live eternally) and suggested the importance of investigating its impact on the bereaved. Similarly, Ellis Gray [11] emphasized the importance of recognizing the complicated relationship between the deceased and the remaining data traces of the deceased. The suggestions can be related to various works that discussed how the bereaved used social media technology to cope with close ones' deaths and the digital presence of the deceased [12–15]. Our research aims to expand these discussions by proposing the concept of commemoration through social media and establishing a series of guidelines and design requirements.

2.2 Social Media and Death

Existing studies on online commemoration discuss the possibility of utilizing network-based technologies to commemorate and prepare for death. Krysinska and Andriessen [16] analyzed how members of nuclear families often create online commemoration pages through memorialization services such as Faces of Suicide and Gone too Soon.

Relatedly, many researchers have turned their attention to social media to investigate its relationship with mortality. As introduced by Wagner [17], the incorporation of technological features within cultural norms seems necessary in expanding the collective nature and interactive privileges of social media. Popular social media platforms such as Facebook and Instagram both have memorial account conversion systems upon the account owner's death report. In the case of Facebook, contents that were posted by the deceased remain on the memorialized account based on the privacy settings. The bereaved are allowed to post writings or pictures to commemorate on the timeline, which are managed by the legacy contact assigned by the account owner before death.

Compared to Facebook, Instagram's commemorative services are somewhat limited. To report death, a family member must submit the account owner's birth and death certificate, and proof of authority under local law that one is the lawful representative of the deceased owner. After that, they can either to completely delete or memorialize the account from Instagram. Once memorialized, no one can log into the account, and posts remain visible to authorized viewers; in other words, nothing much changes.

The role of social media in relation to mortality includes the bereaved actively utilizing the deceased's accounts for news dissemination, preservation, and community [18]. It was also found that commemorating on Facebook allows for the bereaved to 'expand' the meaning of commemoration temporally, spatially, and socially [19].

2.3 Digital Volition

Barve and Bhalerao [11] suggest it is necessary to improve the user experience of the bereaved when using social media. Elliott [20] contends the importance of creating a fundamental solution for social media platforms on how to handle the account of the deceased and the remaining data, as most users are fairly young and are not likely to leave a will. Similarly, Maciel [21] stresses that digital legacy in the virtual world should concur with the 'volitive' element by the deceased, wherein the user may decide what will become of their account after death [22]. With the current problem, that digital life goes beyond the physical life and is limited due to software constraints, the study also claims for the need of a person 'in charge' for the remains. The aforementioned studies collectively assert the importance of digital 'volition'. Thus, designers are expected to identify the many actors involved [23] behind the tangible line of the system and take careful considerations when dealing with social media and interactions after death.

Our research will focus on the problems previously identified and propose a design solution that provides both a better commemorative experience by considering multiple stakeholders' values as well as a chance for the younger users of social media to ponder their death and decide on what will happen to their accounts after their demise.

2.4 Value-Sensitive Design

Value-Sensitive Design emphasizes how our technologies shape and deal with human values as a means to safely combine human values with technology. It aims to establish a solid, logical, and socially acknowledgeable structure based on morality and ethical values to build and incorporate any ideas. A central tenet of this design methodology is to discover and use stakeholders' core values into technologies during early-stage research and development [24]. Researchers first undergo extensive research to identify these stakeholders and their fundamental values, after which they conduct empirical investigations to carefully unravel the ethical implications and value-driven conflicts in a system. Finally, with the collective insights, the researchers institute grounded settings to reconcile the technical efficiencies and central values of the stakeholders [25].

In our research, we utilized the approach and perspective of the Value-Sensitive Design, identifying the key stakeholders as well as the values they deem important. While the widely acknowledged Value-Sensitive Design methodology aims to identify the possible ethical conflicts in an attempt to bridge them by design, the main focus of our approach lies in identifying and deeply analyzing the key values each stakeholder takes into account. The aim also lies in ultimately reducing the gap between user's social volition and technical constraints. Our research aspires to make sense of the interactions that take place on social media regarding death preparation and commemoration, finally creating a sensitively designed system based on the examined values.

3 Exploratory Study

3.1 Methods

As the first step of our research, we conducted an exploratory study to better understand users' perceptions on commemoration and death, as well as the purposes and behaviors of commemoration. We conducted in-depth interviews with three groups of stakeholders: the to-be-dead (or, all users), the bereaved, and the legacy contact, incorporating concepts of Value-Sensitive Design. A total of 9 social media users (specifically, Instagram, Facebook, and Twitter users) in their 20s were recruited through online survey distributed across Korean online university communities which was used to gain preliminary information on the participants such as their previous experience in social media usage and experience of losing their friend or family. Based on the information, we recruited interviewees from a fairly younger generation because social media was more likely to be a major part of their social lives, which was important for our purposes.

The specific criteria used for each stakeholder group are explained below along with the general questions and the tasks given during the interview. The hour-long sessions were conducted either online or offline and were recorded under consent. The recordings were later transcribed, and a six-phase thematic analysis was conducted, drawing themes to make sense of the qualitative data [26]. Based on the themes identified from the analysis, we tried to categorize the empirical values of commemoration and drew design considerations for social media-based commemoration services.

To-be-Dead (T1, T2, T3). Three social media users were recruited to represent the 'to-be-dead.' The interviews for the to-be-dead explored preferences for managing social media accounts after death. In this process, we aimed to identify how users wish to be remembered in an online environment. Additionally, there was an observation on the user behaviors of preparing for death on social media. We observed how users change their social media accounts to the scenario in which they have a limited amount of time left to live, thus identifying the key values in preparing for death on social media.

Bereaved (B1, B2, B3, B4, B5). Five interviewees, all of whom have had the experience of losing someone close to them, were recruited to represent the 'bereaved.' The interviews focused on their experience of processing death through various commemorative behaviors. We explored the purpose and motive of commemoration and the specific emotions, behaviors, and practices (both online and offline) that consist of them, identifying the key values in commemorative behaviors.

Legacy Contact (L1). One interviewee, who had the experience of running Facebook and Twitter memorial accounts for his deceased best friend, was recruited to represent the 'legacy contact.' As the culture of using Legacy Contact is still unfamiliar in Korean society, a limited demographic was used for the interview. In order to complement such limitation, the To-Be-Dead interviewees and the Bereaved interviewees were also asked several hypothetical questions on the concept of Legacy Contact to identify users' perception and potential needs as a Legacy Contact. We explored how the legacy contact manages the digital presence of the dead and investigated various aspects that consist of the legacy contact's user experience.

Records. Finally, various records were consulted to deepen our understanding of the values and insights discovered through the interviews. These records, which were in the form of writing, photographs, or music, were posted by the bereaved after the death of loved ones. The materials were willingly provided by the interviewees. These qualitative data were coded and used as additional material for the six-phase thematic analysis to create richer insights.

3.2 Findings

Below is the report of the interview findings based on the categories identified through thematic analysis.

Processing Death. The processing of death begins the moment the user receives an obituary. Most interviewees received the news through digital media such as social media postings, either directly (via announcements) or indirectly (via commemorative posts). General emotional responses to the death of a close one were denial, fear, sorrow, and regret. In most cases, the emotions in response to death were often emotionally exhausting and defined as something to be recovered from.

Purposes and Practices of Commemoration. The purpose of commemoration was twofold: to remember and to recover. Some interviewees focused on the idea of commemoration as a tool to remember and memorialize the deceased, while others found it to be a phase that helps the bereaved to overcome their pain. Following such purposes, interviewees reported multiple commemorative behaviors. Interviewees stated that the size or form of commemoration did not matter as long as these purposes were met. *"It doesn't have to be something big. Either alone, or together, thinking about the deceased, that is a commemoration"* (B3).

Commemorative behaviors often involve a medium, which can be an object, a place, or digital remains. Some interviewees shared their experience of going through objects that belonged to or were given by the deceased to remember them by. They also commemorate by visiting the places that they used to go to together, where the deceased is buried, or where the deceased passed away. These objects were not confined to the physical realm but included digital traces such as online conversations with the deceased or social media postings.

Commemorative Communities. An important part of commemoration was to form a community. These commemorative communities have two purposes: forming emotional solidarity and confirming the deceased's existence. As for the emotional solidarity, interviewees often reported the urge and experience of giving hands to the fellow bereaved to develop in them an emotional sense of belonging and engagement, along with the hope to receive one. *"I was worried about my mom. He was grandpa for me but for her, he was dad. So, I hugged her and asked her if she was okay"* (B1). Interviewees also found it reassuring to know that they were not the only ones who knew the deceased, preventing the denial of the deceased's existence by death. *"It was like confirming my own memory. This person knows him too…"* (B4).

Communities were found to break the barrier between online and offline spheres. The legacy contact interviewee remarked how he befriended the friends of the deceased at the funeral and still meets them to this day to remember the deceased. Other interviewees reported that online commemoration motivated them to attend offline funerals.

Online Commemoration: Pros and Cons. Interviewees recounted the positive aspects of online commemoration as easy participation and collective experience. Social media lowers the barrier for commemoration and provides a shared experience between the commemorating individuals. Yet, not many interviewees were positive toward online commemoration. Much of such rejection came from the notion of online space as being more casual than offline. Many interviewees claimed to have witnessed imprudent remarks and were concerned for the potential belittlement of death, such as disclosing private matters of the deceased and the bereaved. An additional source of negativity toward online commemoration was related to the sensitivity of the matter and the public nature of online space. Interviewees contended that sharing such private, sensitive, and potentially negative experiences in an online environment may be inappropriate. Additionally, an interviewee expressed opposition for its being a mere replica of offline commemoration. *"We saw a lot of online memorial services due to COVID-19 this year. You just drag a flower icon and place it with your mouse. It was… I don't know, I am negative toward those"* (B3).

Using Social Media After Death. Interviewees were interested in leaving a digital legacy for the bereaved to pick up and commemorate fond memories. When preparing for their death, they wished to organize data that can represent their identity on social media for others to utilize for commemoration, which is an example of digital volition.

There were concerns about no longer being able to control the account after death. Such apprehension was related to unwanted exposure, attacks from followers, identity thefts, and unauthorized access. In that context, the role of the legacy contact came to the fore. They wished their legacy contact to protect their accounts from being abused or bombarded with advertisements and vulgar contents, and to make announcements regarding their death and commemoration with minimal changes to the account. Users preferred to keep the contents intact and expected the legacy contact to not alter them. As for the legacy contact designation, users considered those with whom they can share their honest thoughts and emotions as candidates for their account management.

3.3 Insights and Discussion

Role of Writing and Community in Recovery. Most interviewees responded that social media commemoration often involves posting media. The act of posting consists of two aspects: writing and sharing. The bereaved goes further than simply writing to organize their thoughts and emotions by sharing it with the fellow bereaved. We identified two motives for posting which are closely related to the two purposes of commemoration: remembrance and recovery.

Sharing memories compiles individual memories into a collective memory that the community shares. Such community-based sharing activities remind us of the Western culture of funerals, at which close friends and family members publicly recite their loving memories of the deceased to the fellow bereaved. This allows for the member of the community to find the previously unknown sides of the deceased. *"I liked it the most when someone posted a picture that I have never seen (...) When his family member posted his pictures when he was young, it really felt good. It was like seeing a side of him I never knew" (B3).*

Additionally, by sharing their emotional experience, interviewees hoped to provide a sense of solidarity to the people who are going through similar difficulties. Such behaviors are closely related to the power of support groups in grievance procedures. Existing research emphasizes the importance of individuals' sharing their experience with peers who suffered from loss for quick recovery [27]. *"If someone is facing the same experience as I am, if that person reads what I wrote, that person might find his own way of going through with it" (B5).*

Aperiodic Space for Commemoration Separated from Daily Activities. Many interviewees used the phrase "returning to daily life" when they successfully recovered from the negative feelings caused by death. This suggests that while the bereaved are processing death, they consider themselves as being in an aperiodic space, separated from their daily place. The act of commemoration allows them to recover and return to their daily lives. This suggests the necessity of separated space solely dedicated to commemoration.

Figure 1 provides a recovery process model for the bereaved after the loss of their close ones. The arrows signify the unilateral events with accompanied emotions. The main finding derived from our interviews was that the incipient agony comes from the realization of the absence of the loved ones in his or her regular daily activities. Then feelings of voidness, denial, fear, sorrow, and regret follow, irrespective of the order of occurrence. Finally, the bereaved enters the phase of eventual recovery once they

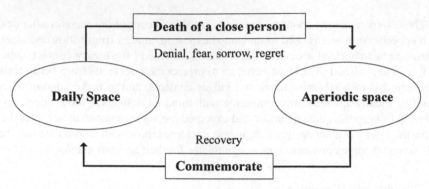

Fig. 1. Recovery process from negative emotions caused by death

have processed their feelings and emotions in an aperiodic space. This is identified as a space solely dedicated to mourning and commemoration that ultimately lessens their emotional distress. The significance is that they require a phase that is separate from 'daily' lives, while close enough to everyday space, to immediately return during and after the recovery. *"I think death, sorrow, and such topics are difficult to discuss in an offline daily environment. The fact that you have space to comfortably talk about those (issues) is positive"* (B4).

The separation is also important insofar as it prevents users from unwanted exposure to extreme sorrow caused by continuous exposure. *"(for the celebrity who recently passed away) I kept seeing commemorative posts on social media and it made me feel even sadder. The videos that commemorated them kept coming up which only aggravated my sorrow"* (B2).

Changing the Nature of the Account After Death. We observed that social media accounts were often regarded as the representation of one's identity in the digital space—a finding consistent with existing research [14, 28]. As the account owner posts his or her thoughts via different media, the account becomes a vessel that reflects the ever-changing identity of the owner. Yet, when the owner passes away, the digital identity is no longer updated and the use of the account changes; it turns into a space that shares the news regarding the deceased, memorialize the deceased and, above all, becomes an aperiodic space visited by the bereaved for commemoration. The overall findings reconfirm previous research [18], which discuss the role of the deceased's account as news dissemination, preservation, and community. The account also serves as a 'notification board' to share reasons for death or annual memorial services. Some interviewees drew a parallel between the act of creating a monument for the deceased and using their social media account. *"I think the essence of leaving something behind to commemorate someone will always be the same (…) we may only feel strange and unfamiliar since it is so new, but the act itself may not be so different in essence"* (B5).

4 Design Solution

4.1 Design Requirements

Our previous key findings included that the goal of commemoration is to recover from negative emotions and to remember the deceased, both done through posting media to share their sentiments with a community and perpetuate their memories. A 'space' that is familiar yet detached from everyday space, helps the users to remember and recover, given that the deceased's account itself can be a memorializing space. Social media can reconcile technology and cultural norms with collective interactions [17] and 'image-based' social media can aid collective remembrance through archives of memories in visual media and sharing them with a bereaved community, given its high-level simulated social presence among other forms [31]. Thus, we have selected Instagram, a photo and video based social media, to implant a structured commemorative space. Instagram is void of death preparations, or any other commemorative supports, suitable to design a system in which the users will encounter the chance to prepare for their death and commemorate for the first time. Following are our main design requirements and key values to be considered and incorporated, jointly shown in Table 1.

A SPACE to Recover and to Perpetuate the Memory. The system must provide a space solely dedicated to commemoration, separated from day-to-day Instagram experiences for an effective and healthy recovery of the bereaved. This space must aid the bereaved in forming a commemorative community. To do so, allowing them to post their thoughts and memories about the deceased is essential. Additionally, the system should go beyond mimicking the offline commemoration rituals, creating a system of sincerity. Also, we must keep in mind how private these experiences are and thus provide a private commemoration outlet for the bereaved.

A SYSTEM that Could Set Up the Commemorative Space Before Death. When creating such a space, the volition of the deceased must be of utmost priority. Thus, the system needs to ask the users what should happen to their accounts after their death. They should be able to decide whether or not they want to leave their digital identity behind after their death. Also, since users have different preferences based on their definitions of commemoration and privacy, options to finc-tune their commemorative space should be available.

A MANAGER to Run the Commemorative Space. After the death of the account owner, it is important to have a manager who supervises and leads the running of the commemorative space and secures the account from inappropriate activities. The managers should be provided with permissions and tools that aid them in performing the tasks assigned by the deceased to aptly execute the owner's volition, but only to an extent where they do not invade the owner's privacy. Additionally, these managers should have the authority to report the death of the account owner, mitigating the currently complex death-reporting system and securing the account from falling into the wrong hands.

Table 1. Design requirements and key values of the commemorative system for Instagram

System	Requirements	Features	Values
A SPACE to recover and to perpetuate the memory	Must be separated from day-to-day experience	Commemoration Account	Recovery
	Must aid in collective commemoration in a community	Commemorative postings made by the bereaved	Remembrance, Community
	Must allow the bereaved to commemorate privately	Direct Message (DM) to the Commemoration Account	Privacy
	Must be sincere and focused on the essence of commemoration	Do not simply mimic the offline commemoration rituals	Sincerity
A SYSTEM that could set up the commemorative space before death	Must prioritize the account owner's will	Commemoration Account setup system	Privacy
	Must provide options of deleting their digital presence		Volition
	Must provide options to fine-tune their commemorative space		
A MANAGER to run the commemorative space	Must be provided with the authority to run the commemorative space	Managing account for the Account Manager	Protection
	Must be able to know what the account owner wished the commemorative space to look like	Account Manager accepting process	Volition
	Must be able to report death of the account owner	Death reporting system	Security

4.2   Design Proposal and Prototype

Based on the design requirements, we propose a new conceptual commemorative system for Instagram. A functioning prototype of this system was created using Figma.

Encountering the Commemoration Account. Once the death of the account owner is reported to Instagram by the Account Manager, assuming that the owner wished to create a Commemoration Account, the original Instagram account is converted into a Commemoration Account. Here, the bereaved can use various features to remember the deceased and recover from emotional distress. The detailed and collective snapshots of how users see the Commemoration Account is provided in Fig. 2. The user interface on the very front page of the account presents the Commemoration Account indicators (Fig. 2-A). It first displays a pop-up to alert that this is a Commemoration Account to familiarize users with the system. To help the followers readily recognize the account's status as a Commemoration Account, the account is labeled 'Remembering.' Unique technical features such as 'Create a Commemoration Post' and 'Contact Manager' are easily seen and incorporated on the profile page.

(a)   (b)   (c)   (d)

Fig. 2. A Encountering the Commemoration Account (B) Notification when sending the Direct Message (C) Contacting the account's Account Manager (D) Posting a Commemoration Story

In the Commemoration Account, followers can directly post commemorative posts on the commemoration tab by tapping "Create a Commemoration Post." This allows followers to directly post feeds on the Commemoration Account to enable a more active and affluent commemorative interaction, ultimately creating a community of commemoration. Created posts are archived on a separate tab within the profile page.

The bereaved could also create a commemorative 'story' by tagging the Commemoration Account (Fig. 2-D). When someone tags a Commemoration Account in their story, they can choose to share it with the deceased's followers. If they choose to share it, the story will appear on the Commemoration Account. Followers can also send DMs to the deceased privately (Fig. 2-B). Through the button "Send a Message," they will be able to talk to the deceased or recall memories by looking at their previous conversations. A privacy notice will be provided to let followers know that this DM is private, meaning that it cannot be accessed by anyone else—not even the Account Manager. Additionally, followers can contact the Account Manager if needed (Fig. 2-C).

Setting Up the Commemoration Account. Commemoration Account setup process is required for the users to enact their volition before death. A brief and concise walkthrough is provided with a preview for the users to familiarize themselves with the concept of Commemoration Account. General settings are provided to select whether the users wish to leave their digital traces and to what extent. A more 'advanced' settings are provided during the customization section to accustom their detailed preferences to their account after death. Figure 3 provides the snapshots of each procedure to set up the Commemoration Account.

(a)   (b)   (c)   (d)

Fig. 3. A Commemoration Account Walkthrough (B) Commemoration Account Basic Settings (C) Commemoration Account Customization (Fine-Tuning) (D) Account Manager Assignment

The setup screen can be accessed by tapping on the pop-up that appears on other Commemoration Accounts, or through Instagram's account settings menu (Fig. 2-A). When the user enters the setup menu, he or she will go through a tutorial on how to set up the Commemoration Account (Fig. 3). Users can either delete the account or create a Commemoration Account after their death (Fig. 3-B). Should users choose to create a Commemoration Account after their death, they can allow or limit certain activities according to their preferences; for example, they can decide whether they wish to receive commemoration posts, stories, DMs, comments, and new followers (Fig. 3-C). Users can always revisit the setting to edit their preferences. They are also asked to assign an Account Manager, who will file their death report and run their Commemoration Account according to their will (Fig. 3-D). Users can precisely set the Account Manager options to allow or limit certain activities for the manager.

Managing Account for the Account Manager. The Account Manager is the legacy contact assigned by the account owner during his or her Commemoration Account setup. Provided that the Account Manager has accepted the request and filed the owner's death report, the Account Manager specialized account is generated so that he or she can switch between his or her account by clicking the profile. The Manager performs a series of tasks to run and manage the account for the bereaved under the volition of the account owner. Figure 4 displays the snapshots of the series of activities that can be performed by the Account Manager.

Once the account owner requests a user to become an Account Manager, a push notification is sent. Accordingly, the Manager goes through a brief guidance to what

(a)   (b)   (c)   (d)

Fig. 4. A Accepting the role of Account Manager (B) Posting of management-related stories (C) Managing Direct Messages and the list of Followers (D) Activity tab to alert general notifications as well as suspicious activities for the Account Manager to manage

the key roles and settings left for the Manager to perform are, under his or her own willingness. After the acceptance, a notification is sent to the owner, and the system directs the user to send a DM to the owner to express his or her thoughts and emotions, as well as to discuss further details (Fig. 4-A). When the Account Manager discovers the death of the account owner, he/she can report it to Instagram. Once the report goes through, the Commemoration Account is activated, and the Account Manager can log into the managing account (Fig. 4-D). We expect their roles to be about creating a safe and sincere commemoration platform for the bereaved and honoring the deceased. Block and report functions are also provided to help the manager efficiently run the account.

The manager is expected to respond to inquiries through the manager DM (Fig. 4-C). The manager DM is separated from the deceased's original DM, meaning that this function is solely dedicated to answering inquiries from the followers. The bereaved will be able to ask questions on diverse matters such as funeral events or how to commemorate in the Commemoration Account. Lastly, the Account Manager can utilize the story feature to deliver a wide range of content such as—but not limited to—general announcements, anniversaries, and any other information that is deemed important (Fig. 4-B). One story highlight—an Instagram feature that stores the stories after 24 h if the user wishes—can be generated to keep the important notices.

5 Evaluation

5.1 Methods

We conducted six user testing sessions on the newly proposed system, based on the three main systematic features. Six Instagram users in their 20s were recruited and were asked to use the prototype and were interviewed intensively before and after the task to investigate perception and acceptance. Each test was conducted online through Zoom and lasted between 60 and 90 min. The session was recorded and transcribed under consent for analysis. General aims and instructions for each feature are guided as below.

Setting up the Commemoration Account. We aimed to see how participants engage in learning the primary ways to access commemorative settings and set up a Commemoration Account. They were told to identify the entry point for the Commemoration Account setup and customize their account based on our system. They were also asked to assign an Account Manager and decide on his or her scope of responsibility.

Managing the account as an Account Manager. We aimed to explore how participants engage as Account Manager, from accepting the role to performing the given roles. Participants were asked to take a glance at what an Account Manager can do with the account and how it can altogether affect the commemorative interactions of Instagram and its environment.

Commemorating with the Commemoration Account. We aimed to discover how participants utilize different features of the Commemoration Account. They were given access to different ways of commemoration and were asked to widely utilize diverse options while voicing their impressions and thoughts aloud.

5.2 Results

We investigated the users' reactions to the system's concept as well as the comprehensive responses to each specific feature. Participants recognized the importance of the system and were positive about the idea of being able to decide what to happen to the account after death. They also found the proposed system suitable for commemoration since it allows them to share memories in a space dedicated to the deceased and helps recover from grief through the given commemorative features. Below are the detailed results of the user testing sessions investigated through thematic analysis [26].

Chance to Contemplate Death. The account setup process provided users with a unique opportunity to contemplate death. As the participants were in their 20s, they reported that they have rarely thought about their death let alone what would happen to their social media account after death. Going through the setup procedure for the Commemoration Account, they were given the chance to ponder their existential objectives and ideals. They asked themselves how they want to be remembered, how they want their friends and family to commemorate them, and who they trust the most to give the position of the Account Manager.

Volition Before Death. Participants were also satisfied with how detailed the setup process was. Since users are obviously unable to change the settings after their death, they desire to have control over even the most minute details. When it comes to designing their deaths, users do not appreciate the service making decisions for them.

The necessity of an Account Manager was highlighted when users deemed the function necessary, for they felt that someone must have the capacity and responsibility to ensure, as a safety measure, that the account is upheld. A participant said that *"someone has to have the wheel to ensure that the car keeps running as a safety measure" (P2).*

Varying Expectations on Account Manager's Role. Users' desires for the role of Account Manager vary vastly. Some users wish for theirs to actively lead the commemoration and hold events, while others wish for their Account Manager to simply look out for information abuses. Given individual disparities, participants emphasized the importance of communication between the Account Manager and the account owner. The function that enables their conversation is helpful since it also establishes the premise of manager authority and duties, while it could be improved via intuitive walkthrough of their duties and owner's volition. Some also expressed concerns about the feature of the Account Manager. They wondered what would happen if the Account Manager passed away or found themselves incapable of managing the account, as already addressed [21]. Additionally, some participants found it uneasy to have no other safety measures other than personal trust toward the Account Manager to run the account and to protect their digital identity.

Commemoration Account as an Aperiodic Space. Users wished for the Commemoration Account to be made very different in relation to the current Instagram profile page so that they could easily acknowledge that they are in a space of commemoration.

In anticipation of sorrow caused by continuous exposure to the Commemoration Account, they also wanted the option to mute it if needed. Such a reaction once again confirms the importance of creating a separate aperiodic space devoted to commemoration, parted from daily Instagram activities.

Space for Sharing. Users found the function of commemorative posting very intriguing. They expected that such participation will not only foster stronger emotional commemoration but also encourage interactions amongst the followers, creating a community of commemoration. Additionally, participants expressed the aptness of Instagram as a commemoration tool because it is a photo-based social media. Users expected that should someone wish to make a commemorative posting, they must upload a picture, which will provoke reminiscence for the fellow bereaved. A participant reported that Commemoration Account *"feels like an opportunity for users to share warm feelings and emotions, decreasing the fear and sorrow of death" (P1).*

6 Discussion

There exist valuable discussion points regarding the identified values of each stakeholder and their relationships with the qualities of social media. We discuss to what extent its role can make the online commemoration functional and effective, as well as the potential prerequisite to future studies.

6.1 Social Media—Apt Tool for Commemoration

This research unveiled the possibility of social media as an apt tool for death preparation and commemoration. As we utilize social media daily, we are archiving our identity and ingredients to be memorialized on our social media. This readily prepares a space that could be used for commemoration in the future. It also reaffirms the existing research that introduced the broader concept of hosting funerals through Instagram, creating a less formal and less institutionalized ritual [30].

It was also discovered that community and interpersonal relationships are key elements in commemoration. As social media is already a place where friends and family members establish, strengthen, and continue their relationships, it is an efficient tool to gather the bereaved together. Such findings are consistent with the previous report by Contentworks Agency [31], which identified a sense of belonging and love as one of the prime motivations for posting on social media.

6.2 'Living Forever' (Perpetual Communication)

Our finding also corresponds to the proposition of Moore, Magee, Gamreklidze, and Kowalewski [15], in which mourners use social media for immortality communication and connection with the deceased. As Bassett [10] argues, immortality is no longer an option confined to pharaohs or kings and is available for everyone through digital tools. Participants affirmed their desire to be remembered forever by the loving people and found our system an appropriate modern adaptation of realizing such a desire.

The users' desire went beyond perpetuating their existence to communicating with the people they cared for after they die. Surprisingly, four out of six user testing participants suggested the feature of 'scheduled posting' in which they create posts to be uploaded after their death. An interesting point is that this communication is technically one-way. Despite not being able to hear back, the users expected to send a final message (or multiple messages annually) to the bereaved and considered it a communication. In a way, they are communicating without their physical presence and only digitally. Further research is necessary on how the users perceive and define the concept of communicating with the dead, and on the root of the desire to communicate with the living.

6.3 Enriched Bonding and Mutual Respect

In reaching the goal of commemoration, personal relationships are significant. Users collectively memorialize the deceased by gathering fragmented memories that each member possesses and actively aiming to help others recover. Such behaviors could be linked to the concept of 'technospirituality', which contends that such spiritual bonding could take place in daily life among the bereaved [14]. This once again emphasizes the importance of social media as a link for friends and families [32].

In addition, the relationship between the account owner and the Account Manager is also found to be extremely important. The act of asking one to become an after-death Account Manager and accepting that role could potentially become a huge bonding experience in which two people show mutual trust and loyalty. Thus, the system needs to create an environment that encourages these two to communicate intensively. Further, as it is almost solely dependent on the goodwill of the Account Manager, we must not overlook the chance of an Account Manager not being available for the duties and should prepare safety measures to realize the volition safely and sincerely.

6.4 Memento Mori and Amor Fati

Discussing the topic of death using daily social media service provoked users to ponder diverse existential topics. Users were able to think about how they want to be remembered and commemorated, who will take care of the digital traces they leave behind, and to what extent they want to secure their existence. While death is an experience that all humans will experience, the majority of the research participants were fairly unfamiliar with discussing the topic of their death, let alone its stance and treatment in social media. On such a note, using daily technology to give the users a chance to think and plan their death is a new possibility for a thanatosensitive design. Designers and technicians should go further than simply developing functions after death, and instead aim to guide users to think about their existential reality, social volition and the moment they are living in through the topic of death.

While death and technology co-exist in our lives, many users fail to consciously acknowledge this reality. Thus, the system needs to surface these ideas to the users and encourage them to employ conscious choices about what will happen to their digital presence after their death. In doing so, the system promotes a greater degree of responsibility among users. Such discussion points are also in line with previous research on mortality and reflective design, as the reflection itself becomes a form of the design outcome and allows users to bring unconscious values and cultural norms to the surface and make choices consciously [33–35].

6.5 Limitations

There exists a number of limitations. The VSD methodology could have been further investigated prior to the exploratory study. While it did attempt to transcend technical constraints for a value-sensitive commemoration, the main purpose of our VSD approach was to mainly understand and incorporate the values of each stakeholder. Additionally, the present research was conducted on a narrow pool of participants that consisted of adults in their 20s living in the Republic of Korea. We involved a young group of people as the participants who have existing familiarity and adaptive ability with social media, but we also must acknowledge the results can drastically vary with different age groups. Death is also a topic that involves multiple perspectives and explanations in different cultures; thus, it is difficult to generalize the results of the study globally. An ethnographic and cross-cultural approach is prerequisite to future studies.

7 Conclusion

Our research empirically explored the topic of death and social media via assessing the potential of social media as a space for death preparation and commemoration. The findings suggest that social media is a prospective platform to memorialize one's identity and convalesce through the commemorative community. As the research was largely based on the conceptual and value-sensitive system design of an existing service, we were able to observe users' reactions in a realistic manner and provided a potential guideline to shape a novel culture of commemoration and death preparation.

At an age where technology is actively shaping our daily lives, we discussed how the universal experience of death could be mediated through the lens of technology and social media. We hope that our findings provide for a deeper understanding of human behaviors regarding the concept of death in the sphere of social media, ultimately helping to shape a more positive commemoration and death preparation experience.

References

1. Massami, M., Odom, W., Kirk, D., Banks, R.: HCI at the end of life: understanding death, dying, and the digital. In: CHI 2010 Extended Abstracts on Human Factors in Computing Systems, pp. 4477–4480 (2010). https://doi.org/10.1145/1753846.1754178
2. Massimi, M., Charise, A.: Dying, death, mortality: towards thanatosensitivity in HCI. In: CHI EA 2009: CHI 2009 Extended Abstracts on Human Factors in Computing Systems, pp. 22459–22468 (2009). https://doi.org/10.1145/1520340.1520349
3. Massimi, M., Moncur, W., Odom, W., Banks, R., Kirk, D.: Memento mori: technology design for the end of life. In: CHI 2012 Extended Abstracts on Human Factors in Computing Systems, pp. 2759–2762 (2012)
4. Gauler, M.: Digital Remains [Design Output]. Museum of Modern Arts, New York (2006)
5. Kirk, D., Banks, R.: On the design of technology heirlooms. In: SIMTech 2008 (2008)
6. Malkin, E.: Cemetery 2.0, November 2006. Dziga.Com. http://dziga.com/hyman-victor/
7. Uriu, D., Takahiro, O., Naohito, S., Naohito, O.: MASTABA: the household shrine in the future archived digital pictures. In: SIGGRAPH 2006: ACM SIGGRAPH 2006 Sketches, 151-es (2006). https://doi.org/10.1145/1179849.1180038
8. Häkkilä, J., Colley, A., Kalving, M.: Designing an interactive gravestone display. In: Proceedings of the 8th ACM International Symposium on Pervasive Displays, pp. 1–7, June 2019
9. Wiley, C., Wang, Y., Musselman, R., Krumm, B.: Connecting generations: preserving memories with thanatosensitive technologies. In: Stephanidis, C. (ed.) HCI 2011. CCIS, vol. 173, pp. 474–478. Springer, Heidelberg (2011). https://doi.org/10.1007/978-3-642-22098-2_95
10. Bassett, D.J.: Who wants to live forever? Living, dying and grieving in our digital society. Soc. Sci. 4(4), 1127–1139 (2015)
11. Ellis Gray, S.: Remains in the network: reconsidering thanatosensitive design in loss, Doctoral dissertation, Lancaster University (2015)
12. Barve, M., Bhalerao, J.V.: Discourse Centered Online Ethnography (DCOE) study to understand online mourning on Social Networking Sites (SNS) and Thanatosensitivity (2017)
13. Bovero, A., Tosi, C., Botto, R., Fonti, I., Torta, R.: Death and dying on the social network: an Italian survey. J. Soc. Work End-of-Life Palliative Care 16(3), 266–285 (2020)
14. Brubaker, J.R., Vertesi, J.: Death and the social network. In: Proceedings of the CHI Workshop on Death and the Digital, April 2010
15. Moore, J., Magee, S., Gamreklidze, E., Kowalewski, J.: Social media mourning: using grounded theory to explore how people grieve on social networking sites. Omega 79(3), 231–259 (2019)
16. Krysinska, K., Andriessen, K.: Online memorialization and grief after suicide. OMEGA—J. Death Dying 71(1), 19–47 (2015). https://doi.org/10.1177/0030222814568276

17. Wagner, A.J.M.: Do not click "Like" when somebody has died: the role of norms for mourning practices in social media. Social Media + Society (2018). https://doi.org/10.1177/205630511 7744392
18. Rossetto, K.R., Lannutti, P.J., Strauman, E.C.: Death on Facebook: examining the roles of social media communication for the bereaved. J. Soc. Personal Relat. **32**(7), 974–994 (2015)
19. Brubaker, J.R., Hayes, G.R., Dourish, P.: Beyond the grave: facebook as a site for the expansion of death and mourning. Inf. Soc. **29**(3), 152–163 (2013). https://doi.org/10.1080/01972243. 2013.777300
20. Elliott, A.: Death and social media implications for the young and will-less. Jurimetrics **55**, 381 (2014)
21. Maciel, C.: Issues of the social web interaction project faced with afterlife digital legacy. In: Proceedings of IHC+CLIHC 2011, pp. 2–12. ACM Press (2011)
22. de Toledo, T.J., Maciel, C., Muriana, L.M., de Souza, P.C., Pereira, V.C.: Identity and volition in Facebook digital memorials and the challenges of anticipating interaction. In: IHC 2019: Proceedings of the 18th Brazilian Symposium on Human Factors in Computing Systems, pp. 1–11 (2019). https://doi.org/10.1145/3357155.3358454
23. Jamison-Powell, S., Briggs, P., Lawson, S., Linehan, C., Windle, K., Gross, H.: "PS. I Love You" understanding the impact of posthumous digital messages. In: Proceedings of the 2016 CHI Conference on Human Factors in Computing Systems, pp. 2920–2932, May 2016
24. Umbrello, S.: Imaginative value sensitive design: using moral imagination theory to inform responsible technology design. Sci. Eng. Ethics **26**(2), 575–595 (2019). https://doi.org/10. 1007/s11948-019-00104-4
25. Friedman, B., Hendry, D.G.: Value Sensitive Design: Shaping Technology with Moral Imagination (The MIT Press) (Illustrated ed.). The MIT Press (2019)
26. Nowell, L.S., Norris, J.M., White, D.E., Moules, N.J.: Thematic analysis: striving to meet the trustworthiness criteria. Int. J. Qual. Methods **16**(1), 1609406917733847 (2017)
27. Forte, A.L., Hill, M., Pazder, R., Feudtner, C.: Bereavement care interventions: a systematic review. BMC Palliat. Care **3**(1), 3 (2004)
28. Braman, J., Dudley, A., Vincenti, G.: Death, social networks and virtual worlds: a look into the digital afterlife. In: 2011 Ninth International Conference on Software Engineering Research, Management and Applications, pp. 186–192. IEEE, August 2011
29. Pittman, M., Reich, B.: Social media and loneliness: why an instagram picture may be worth more than a thousand twitter words. Comput. Hum. Behav. **62**, 155–167 (2016). https://doi. org/10.1016/j.chb.2016.03.084
30. Gibbs, M., Meese, J., Arnold, M., Nansen, B., Carter, M.: # Funeral and Instagram: death, social media, and platform vernacular. Inf. Commun. Soc. **18**(3), 255–268 (2015)
31. Contentworks Agency: The Psychology of Social Sharing—Content-works Agency. Medium 24 October 2018. https://contentworks.medium.com/the-psychology-of-social-sharing-82b e5fe08436
32. Leaver, T.: Researching the ends of identity: birth and death on social media. Social Media + Society **1**(1), 2056305115578877 (2015)
33. Foong, P.S., Kera, D.: Applying Reflective Design to Digital Memorials. In: SIMTech 2008 (2008)
34. Kaptelinin, V.: Making the case for an existential perspective in HCI research on mortality and death. In: CHI EA 2016: Proceedings of the 2016 CHI Conference Extended Abstracts on Human Factors in Computing Systems, pp. 352–364 (2016). https://doi.org/10.1145/285 1581.2892585
35. Sengers, P., Boehner, K., David, S., Kaye, J.J.: Reflective design. In: Proceedings of the 4th Decennial Conference on Critical Computing: Between Sense and Sensibility, pp. 49–58, August 2005

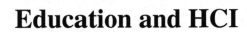

Education and HCI

Pepper as a Storyteller: Exploring the Effect of Human vs. Robot Voice on Children's Emotional Experience

Berardina De Carolis[1], Francesca D'Errico[2], and Veronica Rossano[1(✉)]

[1] Department of Computer Science, University of Bari Aldo Moro, Bari, Italy
{berardina.decarolis,veronica.rossano}@uniba.it
[2] For.Psi.Com Department, University of Bari Aldo Moro, Bari, Italy
francesca.derrico@uniba.it

Abstract. Social robots are autonomous entities able to engage humans at the emotional and social level. They are being used in several domains, especially in those where kids are the primary users (i.e., education, games, rehabilitation). The paper presents an experience in which the social robot Pepper is used as a storyteller. A storyteller robot should engage humans by combining its verbal and non-verbal behaviors and 'immerse' the user into the story. Therefore, to design an engaging and effective storytelling experience we started to address a first design issue: does a human voice have an advantage over a synthesized voice of the robot in this context? To this aim, two versions of the same story for kids from 8 to 9 y.o. have been developed. The social robot Pepper was used to tell the story in two modalities. In the first modality, Pepper storyteller was designed as a kind of audiobook in which the robot had just the role of a device, but the story was narrated by a human voice; in the second modality, Pepper was designed to tell the story using its own voice combined with non-verbal behaviors. The system has been tested in a real context and results show that Pepper's voice affected more positively the children's emotional experience, also by giving the children the perception that they learn more easily.

Keywords: Storytelling · Social robots · Educational technology

1 Introduction

Since childhood storytelling is one of the most appreciated activities by kids. Storytelling is a participatory and immersive experience that allows children to acquire language skills in a dynamic and entertaining way. In recent years, the educational power of storytelling has also been newly discovered. Storytelling was found to be a valuable tool for motivating students to listen, engaging them during lessons, improving reading skills, and as a springboard for beginning units and skill development [1].

Recently, several digital solutions have been applied to the domain of storytelling [2, 3] and each solution aims at enhancing the value of storytelling using the features of

C. Ardito et al. (Eds.): INTERACT 2021, LNCS 12933, pp. 471–480, 2021.
https://doi.org/10.1007/978-3-030-85616-8_27

the digital medium. Among these solutions, the most similar to the original experience of the human storytelling activity is the audiobook [4]. An audiobook allows hearing a human voice reading a story, and sometimes there are sound effects or background music to allow the users to have an emotional experience. The audiobooks are widely accepted and appreciated, but they are not an actual innovation, but they represent a traditional approach in which communication happens through a new device.

To contribute to this context, the research herein aims at investigating whether social robots can engage children in listening stories. Social robots are embodied, autonomous agents that communicate and interact with humans on a social and emotional level. They represent an emerging field of research focused on developing a social intelligence that aims to maintain the illusion of dealing with a human being [5]. Thanks to their ability to interact with humans naturally and familiarly, social robots are spreading more and more often into human life not only for entertainment purposes, but also to support users in their daily activities, or in teaching and educational settings [6, 7].

The paper presents a case study in which the social robot Pepper acts as a story-teller. The main aim of the study was to investigate the effect of the social interaction of this innovative device on children's emotional experience. The research questions will be: (RQ1) is there a difference in user's emotions comparing human voice and synthe-sized voice of the robot and (RQ2) is there a difference in user's experience in the two conditions?

To this aim, the story was implemented using two different approaches. In the first one, Pepper was used as a device to convey the story using a pre-recorded human voice, in this context Pepper acts as a sort of audiobook. In the second approach, Pepper tells the story using its own voice, slightly modified with appropriate pitch and speed variations. In both cases, the storytelling was enriched by typical Pepper's non-verbal behaviors. The paper presents a between-subjects study involving 34 children, 17 of them interact with Pepper which uses the human pre-recorded voice (Real), the others interact with Pepper which uses its own voice (Robot). Results show that children feel positive emotions and user-experience mainly in the Robot condition, pointing how voice signal can affect the perception of robot authenticity.

2 Related Works

Storytelling is the most ancient form to transfer knowledge from across the centuries. Telling stories has been successfully used to narrate experiences, teach social norms, past traditions, and so on. Stories provide a realistic and authentic opportunity to capture children's attention and help them listen and learn more actively than other forms of instruction [8]. Stories are not just for literary narratives but can be used to illustrate even the most complex and abstract concepts or subjects (e.g., math and science). According to Bruner [9], stories engage our thinking, emotions, and imagination all at once. As listeners, we participate in the story with both mind and body as we enter the narrative world and react to it. Stories help teachers reach novices in ways they cannot with other strategies.

When storytelling becomes digital, through new media and innovative technologies, it can be enriched with other communicative elements to enhance the user experience.

Digital storytelling has been shown to be a valuable tool to acquire content [10, 11], to enhance motivation and reflection for deep learning [12, 13].

In [14] digital storytelling has been applied to develop digital literacy skills in a higher educational context. Students were asked to design and develop a short self-introduction video using technological tools including cameras, microphones, and video editing software. The findings suggest that students acquired or improved their digital skills and communication skills, since thanks to digital storytelling they were able to communicate and express their ideas effectively using digital media. Similar findings are reported in [15] where digital storytelling helps secondary school students to enhance their writing skills.

The effectiveness of digital storytelling has been investigated also in the context of health professions education. The investigation of the literature in this context underlines that the creation and use of health professionals' digital stories can positively enhance learning [16]. Digital storytelling has been used also as a tool to foster reflection, in [17] some undergraduate students were asked to develop digital stories to reflect on their study abroad experiences. Findings show that the process of creating digital stories can promote deep reflection.

Robots as storytellers have a long tradition and their evolution has been in line with technological support. One of the first talking robots was launched on the market in 1959 by Mattel®, Chatty Cathy, a doll able to tell a story when a string was pulled. Recently, smart speakers, such as Alexa, are becoming popular digital storytellers.

In the research context, the trend is to imply social robots as a storyteller in order to investigate if beyond learning and motivational improvements there are more deep benefits in terms of emotional or evaluative processes and how they can affect their attitude.

Leite et al., for example, use socially assistive robots to help children build their emotional intelligence skills through interactive storytelling activities [18].

The results of the study on the influence of stories narrated either by a humanoid robot or by a human teacher suggest a positive effect of the expressive behavior in robot storytelling, whose efficacy is comparable to the human expressing the same behavior [19]. Social robotic storytellers have been used also to teach new vocabulary to children showing increased vocabulary learning [20].

In [21] a comparison between recorded voice of an actor with text-to-speech synthesis and the effect on the participants was investigated. The emotional reaction of the participant towards the story told was measured. The results were twofold, they found out that the physically embodied robot attracts the listener as compared to a virtual embodiment and that a human voice is preferable to the text-to-speech.

All these studies have in common the fact that social robots are a good tool for digital storytelling, and they have a positive impact on children's engagement and learning. The new issue herein investigated is that the robot, in this case, is used in this study to convey the human voice, like an audiobook, and to tell a story. The differences in children's emotions during the storytelling will be measured.

3 User Study

In order to design an engaging and effective storytelling experience we started to address a first design issue: does a human voice (Real) have an advantage over a synthesized voice of the Pepper robot (Robot) in this context? This section describes the user study designed for this purpose. In particular, the research questions the study was addressing are:

- RQ1: are the user's emotions (concentration, enjoyment, anger and feeling of learning) different in the two conditions: Real and Robot?
- RQ2: is the user's experience (pleasantness, clarity and easiness during the interaction) different in the two conditions: Real and Robot?

To answer these RQs different measures were collected to evaluate the general engagement in listening to the story, the experience with the robot, and the affective and evaluative elements that came into play during the story listening. A between-subject design was used to collect data, since two different groups of people tested each condition, so that each subject was only exposed to a single use of Pepper.

3.1 Equipment

The Robot. The robot used in this study is the Pepper, a semi-humanoid robot developed by SoftBank Robotics (formerly known as Aldebaran Robotics). It is an omnidirectional wheeled humanoid robot 1.21 m tall, with 17 joints and 20 degrees of freedom. The robot is equipped with several LEDs to signal and support communication. These are software-controlled to change colors and intensity. It is equipped with four directional microphones in its head that allow it to detect the origin of entries and thus to turn its face to whoever is talking. The microphones can eventually be used to analyze the voice tone and therefore interpret the emotional state of the interlocutor. A 3D camera and two HD cameras allow Pepper to recognize not only faces but also images and objects. The robot is equipped with 20 motors that allow it to move its head, back and arms. It has other accessories, such as six laser sensors, two ultrasonic sensors and three obstacle detectors.

The Story. The story used in this first experience is "Tu Sei la Regina delle Oasi Incantate" (in English "You are the Queen of Charmed Oases") [22] that in 1994 was published as a story game since it has different points in which the reader can choose what the heroine, the princess, can act in the story. Choices influence the story and its ending. Only in some cases the princess finds and rescues her prince, in other endings she fails the rescue mission. The interesting part of the story is that some choices have to be made simply by choosing to trust the characters you meet (should I trust the shadow I encountered in the garden?).

Fig. 1. Pepper robot during a storytelling session

The Questionnaires. Two questionnaires were used to collect data. The pre-test one, filled in before the activity, was aimed at collecting users' demographic data. It was composed of 6 questions: 2 measuring the confidence with a robot, and 4 measuring the confidence with stories. The post-test was composed of 14 questions, and it was aimed at measuring:

- Children's emotions: concentration, easiness, enjoyment, feeling able, feeling of learning.
- Children User Experience: pleasant to listen to, pleasant way of telling story, easy to play, easy to understand, Clear image.

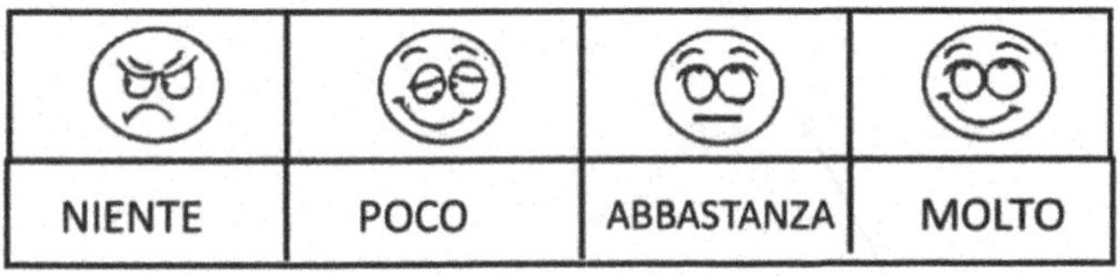

⊗	⊛	⊚	☺
NIENTE	POCO	ABBASTANZA	MOLTO

Fig. 2. An example of the emoticons used as answers (labels: Never, Little, Enough, High)

In both questionnaires, children have to express a score between 1 (very low) to 4 (very high). To help children the questions were very simple, and the answers were represented using emoticons (Fig. 2).

3.2 Participants and Procedure

The study involved 34 children, (balanced for gender, 52% males), aged from 8 to 9 y.o. attending the third grade of a primary school in Bari (Italy) (Fig. 1). Children were divided into two groups: in the first group Pepper uses a human pre-recorded voice (Real), in the second group Pepper uses its own voice (Robot). The voice of Pepper was manipulated by modifying the pitch and the speed parameters in order to follow the same intonation of the human voice during story narration. Before the activity, the pupils underwent a pre-test to collect demographic information and to measure trust and potential enjoyment in playing with the robots and fun in storytelling activities and the user's perceived enjoyment of listening to the stories.

Then the activities, using two different robots, Peppers, were carried out at the same time in two different rooms: in one room the group Real listened to Pepper using a pre-recorded human voice, and in the second room the group Robot listened to Pepper as storyteller. During the activity, only one pupil at a time was asked to interact with Pepper and make their own choices to reach the end. In this way, all pupils could interact with Pepper.

At the end of the game session, the participants were asked to evaluate their experience with Pepper as a storyteller by answering the post-test.

3.3 Results and Discussions

As mentioned above, our participants before the interaction with Pepper answered the questions aimed at measuring their general level of confidence in playing with robots and their enjoyment in listening to stories. The analysis of data reports that the involved children did not show significant gender differences but a general low confidence in playing with robots and a medium level of enjoyment in playing with robots and in listening to stories. The analysis reveals a significant difference between the means of playing with robots and the remaining ones [$F(1, 24) = 7.49$; $p < 0.05$] (Fig. 3).

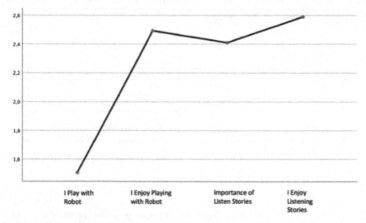

Fig. 3. Descriptive on level of confidence in robots and enjoyment in listening stories.

As to the experimental conditions (human voice vs robotic voice) an Anova repeated measures was performed, which revealed a within effect among the items of the children's emotions [F(1, 24) = 12.75; p < 0.000] especially considering the feeling of a positive sense of mastery - feeling able and feeling of having learned after the interaction with Pepper - and negative emotions ('anger') that is very low. Furthermore, including the experimental variable of voice type, children felt more positive emotions when interacted with a robotic voice than the human one [F(1, 24) = 3.98; p < 0.05], by feeling able, concentrated, at-ease, enjoyed and they also perceived to have learned more, maybe due to a kind of satisfied expectations. In the *Real* condition, with the human voice, children evaluated less positively their emotions since they feel a kind of violation of hearing a robotic voice, more coherently with Pepper (Fig. 4).

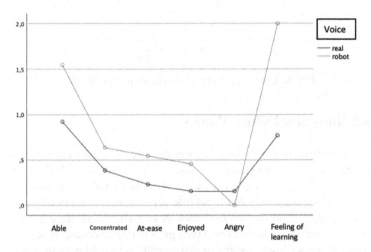

Fig. 4. Emotional experience of the children*type of voice (real or robot)

As regarding the user experience, emerged how children evaluate the interaction with Pepper pleasant to listen, easy to play and understand, pleasant also the way of telling stories, and image clarity, mainly when the voice of Pepper is robotic [F(1, 24) = 3.97; p < 0.05]; they evaluate a sense of pleasantness in listening to Pepper and this positive evaluate is also high in the story understanding (Fig. 5). This result is also in line with the previous one on the children's emotionality, and it shows a tendency to feel positive emotions and evaluations toward Pepper with 'robotic' features.

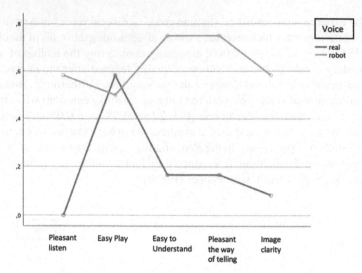

Fig. 5. User experience of the children*type of voice.

4 Conclusions and Future Works

As the first step of our research for assessing the effectiveness of using a social robot, Pepper in this case, as a storyteller the issue of investigating whether there was an advantage in using a human voice instead of the robot's voice was addressed. To this aim, the study carried out shows that robot interaction is best evaluated by children when the social signals [23] expressed by the robot are consistent with the expectations of the users, in this case, the use of the robotic voice goes in this direction. When Pepper uses a coherent voice there is a lower feeling of disorientation instead present when they listen to the human voice. On the contrary of the results reported in [21], in our sample, this effect is quite clear, even if the children involved do not have many opportunities to interact with the robots, as stated before the interaction with Pepper.

This might be due to the fact that the robot used in that experiment has a human-like face, while Pepper has a cute but still robotic appearance.

Our results are quite promising from a learning point of view, since the children's emotional state was positive and their level of engagement and mastery on the task (easy to play and easy to understand), mainly in the robotic voice condition.

In the future, more stories will also be implemented to measure the effects of Pepper storytellers on knowledge acquisition or persuasive processes. Moreover, future studies will also measure the long-term effect of using Pepper as a storyteller on the affective and cognitive aspects of the learning process [24] by having more and regular sessions with children, who will interact with a robot having differentiated stance - humble vs dominant [25] - toward the young users.

References

1. Groce, R.D.: An experiential study of elementary teachers with the storytelling process: Interdisciplinary benefits associated with teacher training and classroom integration. Read. Improv. **41**(2), 122–129 (2004)
2. Alexander, B.: The New Digital Storytelling: Creating Narratives with New Media--Revised and Updated Edition. ABC-CLIO (2017)
3. Syafryadin, H., Salniwati, A.R.A.P.: Digital storytelling implementation for enhancing students' speaking ability in various text genres. Int. J. Recent Technol. Eng. (IJRTE) **8**(4), 3147–3151 (2019)
4. Van Maas, S.: Opening the audiobook. Comp. Lit. **70**(3), 337–356 (2018)
5. Malerba, D., et al.: Advanced programming of intelligent social robots. J. e-Learn. Knowl. Soc. **15**(2), 13–26 (2019)
6. Westlund, J.M.K., Dickens, L., Jeong, S., Harris, P.L., DeSteno, D., Breazeal, C.L.: Children use non-verbal cues to learn new words from robots as well as people. Int. J. Child-Comput. Interact. **13**, 1–9 (2017)
7. Castellano, G., De Carolis, B., D'Errico, F., Macchiarulo, N., Rossano, V.: PeppeRecycle: improving children's attitude toward recycling by playing with a social robot. Int. J. Soc. Robot. **13**(1), 97–111 (2021). https://doi.org/10.1007/s12369-021-00754-0
8. Isbell, R., Sobol, J., Lindauer, L., Lowrance, A.: The effects of storytelling and story reading on the oral language complexity and story comprehension of young children. Early Child. Educ. J. **32**(3), 157–163 (2004). https://doi.org/10.1023/B:ECEJ.0000048967.94189.a3
9. Bruner, J.: Actual Minds, Possible Worlds. Harvard University Press, Cambridge (1986)
10. Robin, B.R.: Digital storytelling: a powerful technology tool for the 21st century classroom. Theory Pract. **47**(3), 220–228 (2008)
11. Rossano, V., Roselli, T.: Game-based learning as effective learning method: an application of digital storytelling. In: 2018 22nd International Conference Information Visualisation (IV), pp. 542–546. IEEE (2018)
12. Barrett, H.: Researching and evaluating digital storytelling as a deep learning tool. In: Professional of Society for Information Technology & Teacher Education International Conference, pp. 647–654. AACE (2006)
13. Smeda, N., Dakich, E., Sharda, N.: The effectiveness of digital storytelling in the classrooms: a comprehensive study. Smart Learn. Environ. **1**(1), 1–21 (2014). https://doi.org/10.1186/s40 561-014-0006-3
14. Chan, B.S.K., Churchill, D., Chiu, T.K.F.: Digital literacy learning in higher education through digital storytelling approach. J. Int. Educ. Res. (JIER) **13**(1), 1–16 (2017)
15. Rong, L.P., Noor, N.M.: Digital storytelling as a creative teaching method in promoting secondary school students' writing skills. Int. J. Interact. Mob. Technol. **13**(7), 10–11 (2019)
16. Moreau, K.A., Eady, K., Sikora, L., Horsley, T.: Digital storytelling in health professions education: a systematic review. BMC Med. Educ. **18**(1), 1–9 (2018)
17. Hamilton, A., Rubin, D., Tarrant, M., Gleason, M.: Digital storytelling as a tool for fostering reflection. Front. Interdisc. J. Study Abroad **31**(1), 59–73 (2019)
18. Leite, I., et al.: Emotional storytelling in the classroom: individual versus group interaction between children and robots. In: Proceedings of 10th ACM/IEEE International Conference on Human-Robot Interaction (HRI), pp. 75–82. IEEE (2015)
19. Conti, D., Di Nuovo, A., Cirasa, C., Di Nuovo, S.: A comparison of kindergarten storytelling by human and humanoid robot with different social behavior. In: Proceedings of the Companion of the 2017 ACM/IEEE International Conference on Human-Robot Interaction, pp. 97–98. ACM (2017)

20. Westlund, J.K., Breazeal, C.: The interplay of robot language level with children's language learning during storytelling. In: Proceedings of the 10th ACM/IEEE International Conference on Human-Robot Interaction - Extended Abstracts. ACM, pp. 65–66. ACM (2015)
21. Costa, S., Brunete, A., Bae, B.-C., Mavridis, N.: Emotional storytelling using virtual and robotic agents. Int. J. Humanoid Robot. **15**(3), 1850006 (2018)
22. Fabri, S., Pasini, M.: Tu sei la Regina delle Oasi Incantate. Giunti (1994)
23. Poggi, I., D'Errico, F.: Social signals: a framework in terms of goals and beliefs. Cogn. Process. **13**(2), 427–445 (2012). https://doi.org/10.1007/s10339-012-0512-6
24. D'Errico, F., Paciello, M., De Carolis, B., Vattani, A., Palestra, G., Anzivino, G.: Cognitive emotions in e-learning processes and their potential relationship with students' academic adjustment. J. Educ. Psychol. **10**(1), 89–111 (2018)
25. D'Errico, F., Poggi, I.: Tracking a leader's humility and its emotions from body, face and voice. In: Web Intelligence, vol. 17, no. 1, pp. 63–74. IOS Press (2019)

Reducing the UX Skill Gap Through Experiential Learning: Description and Initial Assessment of Collaborative Learning of Usability Experiences Program

Audrey Girouard[✉] [iD] and Jin Kang[iD]

School of Information Technology, Carleton University, Ottawa, ON, Canada
{audrey.girouard,jin.kang}@carleton.ca

Abstract. There exists discrepancy between the skills possessed by Human Computer Interaction (HCI) students and the expectations of user experience (UX) industry. This skill gap lowers HCI students' successful transition from academia to the field of UX. To reduce the skill gap, HCI educators have started to integrate experiential learning techniques into their teaching, ranging from workshops to service learning and industrial internships. In joining their efforts, we have created an innovative usability training known as Collaborative Learning of Usability Experiences (CLUE) for HCI students of all levels. In this paper, we detail CLUE's unique experiential training components—UX Internship, Short Courses, Workshops, and Knowledge Transfer—and we report the assessment of the program by evaluating our graduates' job placement and their academic achievement and also by examining our UX industry partners' evaluation of the program and student interns on five important UX skills.

Keywords: UX Education · Experiential Learning · Usability Training

1 Introduction

User experience (UX) professions are popular career paths for Human Computer Interaction (HCI) students [1–3]. This career trajectory makes sense as a wealth of skills and knowledge acquired by HCI students are fundamental to design, research, and develop user-centered products that are championed by service industries and governments [4]. To best prepare students for the workplace, HCI educators are putting immense effort to include experiential learning components in their courses and curriculum. Such effort is essential to bridge the gap between the actual skills possessed by HCI graduates and the expected skills in these graduates by hiring managers and employers (i.e., skill gap) [5, 6]. Hiring managers and employers have questioned the effectiveness of traditional teaching methods in preparing HCI students for the UX labour market [7] and this concern over skill gap has motivated them to rely on students' experiential learning involvement to judge their work-readiness [8].

© IFIP International Federation for Information Processing 2021
Published by Springer Nature Switzerland AG 2021
C. Ardito et al. (Eds.): INTERACT 2021, LNCS 12933, pp. 481–500, 2021.
https://doi.org/10.1007/978-3-030-85616-8_28

In this paper, we describe our own innovative training program to enhance HCI students' employability. The Collaborative Learning of Usability Experiences (CLUE) has four unique components, specifically UX Internship, Short Courses, Workshops, and Knowledge Transfer. In this training program, we attempt to decrease skill gap by giving HCI students the opportunity to work with leading UX experts and to expand their knowledge and skills on technical and professional skills, ranging from cutting-edge UX research and design tools, teamwork, communication, ethics, and programming. CLUE stands apart from the traditional "chalk and talk" method of teaching by incorporating various experiential learning techniques.

In what follows, we first provide relevant work on skill gap, experiential learning, and innovative HCI education. Then, we detail CLUE's four training components, outlining each component's learning objectives and activities. Next, we report the assessment of the program success in four different ways: (1) student job placement (2) industry and government partners' evaluation of student interns on core UX skills, (3) the quality of relationship with industry and government partners, and (4) student academic performance. The first two metrics can serve as evidence of successful skill gap reduction. If students have a competent range of employability skills expected by employers, they will receive job offers and positive skill evaluation from industrial partners. The last two metrics tell us whether the program has done well to maintain positive relationship with internship partners, which is crucial to sustain the program, and whether the program has influenced students' academic performance.

Our contribution lies at advancing the current state of HCI education by creating one cohesive experiential training program that enhances HCI students' UX skills and knowledge. We share the details of the program, so that it can become a point of reference to be implemented and modified for other HCI educators. We highlight the creative elements and structured training components of CLUE that have made the program successful over the past six years.

2   Related Work

We provide relevant work on skill gap, experiential learning, and innovative HCI education. Given the interdisciplinary nature HCI, in this paper, we define HCI students as those whose research focus center on understanding the interaction between human users and computer from diverse perspectives, including psychology, human factors, computer science, industrial design, information systems, and more.

2.1   Skill Gap in HCI Students

UX professions are red-hot professions of the 21st century [4]. The Nielson Norman Group has estimated their growth factor to be 100% from 2017 to 2050 [9] and CNN Business has estimated the growth factor of 19% for UX researcher and of 13% for UX designer for next 10 years [10]. Against this high demand for UX professions, HCI students are ideal candidates to meet this demand given their extensive training on user-centered research, design, and development [3]. However, hiring managers and employers have noted the lack of core UX technical and professional skills in new

HCI graduates. Radermacher and Walia [5] found that recruiters viewed written communication, oral communication, project management, and teamwork as most deficient knowledge in new computer science graduates. Gonzales and colleagues [6] conducted content analysis of UX job postings and compared required skills listed by recruiters and employers against actual academic training received by human factors graduate students. The result revealed that there was an overlap between the required skills and the received training (e.g., knowledge elicitation, tasks analysis), but there were also skills that were not being taught to students (e.g., visual design, basic programming).

The presence of skill gap can be attributed to many factors: faculty's limited understanding of which UX skills are needed in industry [11], faculty's emphasis on training teaching technical knowledge (e.g., prototyping and software development, research and evaluation methods) as opposed to professional skills [12], and a program's heavy reliance on traditional learning approaches. In these approaches, students passively absorb knowledge with limited interaction with teachers and peers and they do not apply their classroom knowledge to solve simulated and/or real usability problems [13].

Skill gap is concerning for all stakeholders—the student, the employer, and the university. From the student's perspective, they will have a hard time securing UX professions after graduation. Even after securing a position, they may fail to adjust in the professional working environment since they originally lack core UX skills. Given that employers expect new graduates to work effectively upon being hired with limited supervision [14], new HCI students may not have enough support to develop essential skills. From the employer's perspective, skill gap means new HCI graduates will significantly deter the organization's productivity, including slowing down the production of new products [15] and lowering the company sales performance [16]. From the university's perspective, skill gap means they have failed to educate the next body of UX professions, with the long-term consequence of hurting the economic development of the country [17]. Against this, experiential learning can help close skill gap and we will now discuss the core features of experiential learning.

2.2 Experiential Learning and Innovative HCI Curriculum

Experiential learning occurs when students learn by doing or learn from experiences [18]. In this learning, students are exposed to *concrete* experiences and they *reflect* on these experiences by noting the differences and similarities with their prior experiences. Then, students engage in *abstract conceptualization* where they make connections between old and new experiences and form a new set of theories and generalizations. Finally, students engage in *active experimentation* where they apply their theories to solve new problems. Recent years, HCI educators have increasingly incorporated experiential learning given its superiority in cultivating work-readiness skills in students than traditional classroom activities, including practical knowledge, understanding of the corporate culture, ability to take initiative and adapt to change, team work and project management skill [19], ability to cope with stress [20], being an empathetic [21] and creative thinker [22], and ability to manage unexpected events [23].

Experiential learning in HCI education comes in many different flavours, with each empowering students to be an active participant. Leshed [1] reported their Advanced HCI class at Cornell that combined traditional lectures with student-led workshops. Musabirov and colleagues [24] introduced two courses—User Centered Design and Information Systems Architecture—where students role-play as a designer or developer on usability projects to closely reflect the real working environment of UX. Murad and Munteanu [2] described a user experience design course in which students worked on client-facing projects to learn about agile software development. Lazar [25] described Web Design Course where Information Systems students designed websites for local communities. Among these different forms, industrial internship and service learning are viewed most effective to enhance students' employability [26, 27], as they immerse students completely in the professional working environment.

We now detail our own training program which has incorporated experiential learning techniques to prepare HCI graduate students for the UX labour market. Our program is similar to other HCI training programs; it exposes students to concrete experiences (e.g., workshops, internships) that initiate the cycle of reflection, concrete abstraction, and active experimentation. Yet our program is unique; it offers students with well-rounded exposure to different forms of experiential learning (vs. one), thereby strengthening each other's positive effect on students' development of work-readiness skills. Other usability training programs tend to focus on giving students with real UX projects and they do not offer structured training over a long period of time [28, 29].

3   Collaborative Learning of Usability Experiences (CLUE) Training Program

3.1   Program Overview

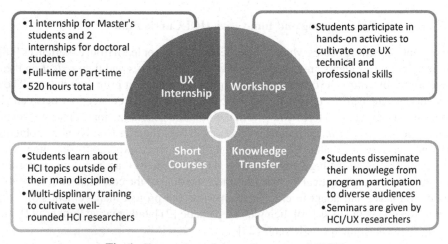

Fig. 1. Four major training components of CLUE

Collaborative Learning of Usability Experiences (CLUE) is a usability training program primarily dedicated to HCI graduate students. It also supports the growth of undergraduate and postdoctoral students by giving them the opportunities to conduct usability research with the program faculty. CLUE is led by Carleton University and supported by Queen's University and Ontario Tech University. It is funded by the National Sciences and Engineering Research Council of Canada (NSERC)'s CREATE program, which supports an innovative educational training program designed to prepare graduate students for careers in industry, government, and academia. There are four training components: UX Internship, Short Courses, Workshops, and Knowledge Transfer (Fig. 1). Each training component has been designed to teach students with technical and professions skills that meet the demands of UX industry.

Students learn about basic UX knowledge, methods, and concepts through Short Courses, Workshops, and Knowledge Transfer before they participate in internships. This order of program progression is crucial. Experiential learning theory, which is a widely adopted pedagogical framework in curriculum design, suggests learners need to face concrete knowledge before they can progress to other major learning stages [30].

Through UX Internship, students work with leading UX experts from industry and government. They apply theories, methods, and technologies from classes to address real usability problems. There are two structural factors that make internship accessible to graduate students. First, unlike co-op and other internship programs, CLUE offers students internship opportunities with its partners and thus it relieves them of the pressure of finding a host organization on their own. Students are easily discouraged from applying to internships because they do not know how find suitable host organizations [6, 31]. CLUE removes such accessibility barrier by partnering up with industry and government partners and make internship opportunities as accessible to many students as possible. Second, CLUE provides research assistantship to students while they complete internship and it removes students' concern for financial loss during internships and partners' financial burden.

Workshops and Short Courses prepare students for their internship. Workshops teach students professional and technical skills. Short Courses expose students to HCI topics that are outside of their major. For instance, graduate students of psychology can participate in a short course on programming while students of computer science can participate in a short course on design methods and prototype development. Lastly, Knowledge Transfer allows students to network and learn about effective communication in two ways: seminars and student-led presentations. Seminars bring together students, HCI communities, and the general public in one shared space. Students are financially supported to attend and present their research projects at local and top-tier international conferences. They also present their internship experiences to their peers. Table 1 lists the critical elements in CLUE.

Table 1. Critical elements in CLUE

Name of element	Brief description
New Student Orientation	New CLUE students learn about their responsibilities and available opportunities, including internship requirements, seminar/workshop/short courses attendance, and conference funding
UX Internship	The student participates in a full-time or part-time internship with the program's industry and government collaborators
Mid-placement Interview	The program coordinator meets the student and the mentor at the mid-point of their internship (2 months after the start for full-time internships and 4 months after the start for part-time internships)
End-of-Internship Report	The student completes a written end of internship report that provides an overview of their learning experiences, accomplishments, and suggestions to improve the program
End-of-Internship Presentation	The student gives presentation about lessons learned during internship
Seminar, Workshop, & Short Course	The student must attend 10 seminars and 3 workshops/short courses. Seminars last an hour while workshops and short courses last 2 to 3 h. They occur about 2 to 4 times per month
Symposium	This annual event invites all stakeholders of the program, specifically the faculty, students, and mentors, to learn about each other's profession, expertise, and research projects. The community is also invited
Student Handbook	This handbook details general program requirements and informs the student to keep learning journal and tips on receiving feedback. It also has a checklist that the student can use to check off their major milestones in meeting the program requirements
Industry Partner Handbook	This handbook provides an overview of placement procedure and tip on coaching and mentoring the student
End-of-Internship Feedback Survey	Industry and government partners evaluate student interns and the program after 2 weeks of internship completion
Internship Agreement	A document that details the host organization's mentor and legal responsibilities and it needs to be signed before internship
Website & Social Media	The program has a website that lists all events happening in each month and other important program information and its own YouTube channel housing past seminars and a LinkedIn group page that connects all CLUE students, partners, and faculty

3.2 Main Stakeholders

There are three main stakeholders in the program—students, industry and government partners, and faculty—and this section provides information about each stakeholder.

Program and Student Relationship. Graduate students who show strong interests in UX and academic and personal competencies can join the program with the support of their thesis advisors. Once joined, the program provides New Student Orientation to new students that outlines all the key elements of the program. For past six years, CLUE has trained over 96 students of diverse degree program and Table 2 provides the background of past and current CLUE students of all levels.

Table 2. CLUE student information

Level of studies	n	Program of studies	n	Program of studies	n
Bachelor's	17	Cognitive Science	7	Interactive Multimedia and Design & Industrial Design	7
Master's	51	Computer Science	13	Psychology	7
Doctoral	19	HCI	28	Serious Games	1
Postdoctoral	3	Information Technology	22	Design	5

Program and Partner Relationship. Initially, the program had already established partnerships with 33 industry and government partners. We have continuously fostered new partner connection is several ways: new partners came across the work of CLUE students and faculty at academic and professional conferences (e.g., CHI) and expressed interests in joining the program, graduated students introduced CLUE to their new workplace, and existing industry partners had moved to a different new organization and then initiated the relationship with their new organization.

There are three requirements to become the partner: (1) they had to be a UX expert on site to provide mentorship to the intern, (2) a physical working space allocated as their desk, on-site as part of a team environment (prior to the global pandemic), and (3) the ability to assist students in the contribution of their skills to work on projects relevant to the growth of the company. To further validate their eligibility, potential partners send their CVs and job opportunities for CLUE students to the program director.

Our industry and government partners have come from diverse sectors. Industry partners belonged to Design, Computer Software, Real Estate, Computer Games, Information Technology and Services, and Aviation and Aerospace industry; Government partners have belonged to departments in charge of researching aerospace, public safety, general government services, and immigration and citizenship. These partners are employed by organizations of varying sizes, ranging from startups (11–50 employees) to multinational corporations (over 350 thousand employees worldwide).

Program and Faculty Relationship. CLUE has recruited faculty across disciplines to design cross-disciplinary training program and the core faculty is composed Engineering & Design, Computer Science, Business, Arts, and Social sciences. Their representative areas of expertise are computer vision, tangible user interface, serious games, cognition, usable security, agile software development, and architectural denotation.

3.3   Training Component: UX Internship

Internship Preparation. Industry and government partners send job descriptions to the program director at the start of each internship cycle (Fall, Winter, Summer). These descriptions outline the responsibility and required qualifications and skills for a given position and they are posted on the CLUE website. Students decide on the timing of internship with their thesis supervisor and consider factors such as expected graduation and candidacy and course requirements. Through the validation of internship positions by the program direction and the discussion of appropriate internship placement with thesis advisors, students can ensure to meet their internship and academic learning goals. students prepare an application package: a cover letter, resume, and portfolio. The program coordinator sends the packages to the corresponding partners. next, industry and government partners contact potential candidates and conduct interviews. Then, students and partners rank each other and matched based on their preferences. After a successful match, students receive an internship placement letter that outlines all important deadlines, including the start and the end date, mid-placement interview, the end-of-internship presentation and report.

Internship Placement. Students are assigned with a mentor and a UX team. CLUE students take on diverse UX-related job positions, ranging from UX architect, Design Researcher, Human Factors Researcher, User Interface Designer, UX Programmer, and Business Intelligence Analyst. Table 3 provides examples of what our students have done in their internships. As some partners have limited experience with supervising graduate students, we take active approach to ensure good mentorship is provided. Our mid-placement interview reflects one approach. This interview ensures students and mentors are satisfied with their internship experience. The coordinator meets with each mentor and student independently to hear about any concerns and then all parties discuss as a group to resolve concerns. Our enforcement of the mid-placement interview and the program requirement that host organizations must provide a mentor ensures students will have meaningful learning experience. Over the past six years, we have offered 81 internships with 42 partners from 28 organizations.

Table 3. Illustrative examples of CLUE student internship

Students	Position	Internship responsibility
Student A	UX Designer	The student assisted launching a company's new online service: they created simple pen-and-pencil sketches and low- and high-fidelity prototypes of website using Balsamiq and Figma and defined user journey
Student B	UX Software Developer	The student assisted in developing tools for UI/UX artists that allow them to convert their Sketch scenes into UI for a game without needing to write any line of code
Student C	UX Specialist	The student redesigned the government's internal websites. They initiated ideation session using Trello Board, took charge of usability testing—recruiting participants, running testing, and analyzing data—and presented findings to UX team

Internship Termination. When internship is over, students share their internship experience with other CLUE students. In this 20-min presentation, students talk about what they have learned, be it technical or professional. In past, students have presented on topics including how to have an effective communication with software developers and how to navigate the communication ladder in the government. Students also submit the end-of-internship report 2 weeks after internship is over. This report outlines 5 components: (a) the kinds of work undertaken during internships, (b) relationship between work experiences to the student's academic studies, (c) the student's challenges and accomplishments, and (d) the strengths and weakness of the work experience, (e) suggestions to improve the experience, and (f) the contributions of the student to the work.

Training Component: Workshops, Short Courses, and Knowledge Transfer. Students are required to attend 10 seminars and 3 workshops/short courses. Table 4 summarizes the targeted technical and professional skills cultivated during workshops, short courses, and seminars. Also, students are financially supported to present their research projects at local and international conferences and they are supported to attend UX professional conferences, including CanUX and UXR Conference.

Table 4. Targeted skills for workshops, short courses, and knowledge transfer

Targeted technical & professional skills	Description	Examples of presented topics
Ethics	Students learn about being an ethical HCI researcher	Ethical challenges for HCI field, Ethical Conduct of Research Online Modules
Accessibility	Students learn about accessible design and research and websites and applications for legislation on accessibility	Inclusive research for people with disabilities, eAccesbility and accessible assistive technologies
Entrepreneurship	Students learn about the process of starting a business and commercialization	Thinking like an entrepreneurial researcher, the Business of game development
Intellectual Property	Students learn about, IP management, patents/trademarks, copyright, and licensing	Logistics involved in applying and owning patents
Research Thinking	Students see cutting-edge HCI research by HCI researchers/UX practitioners	Mobile device app development, designing deformable sensors, using crowdsourcing platform
Interpersonal Skills	Students learn interpersonal skills for workplace	UX project management of UX project, preparation for UX interview, cross-culture teamwork, and digital storytelling for children

4   Initial Assessment of CLUE

We examined past students' job placement and industry and government partners' evaluation of student interns. These metrics give us some evidence of whether the program has decreased the UX skill gap: past students' job placement after their graduation indicates students were successful in securing UX professions, supposedly due to their possession of core UX skills from participating in the program; industry and government partners' evaluation of student interns informs us whether internship has cultivated core UX skills, namely independence, self-reflectional capacity, teamwork, professionalism, and dependability [3]. We also examined students' academic achievements to see their overall growth as HCI researchers and our industry and government partners' program evaluation to get a glimpse on how the program should improve.

4.1   Student Job Placement and Academic Achievement

Our data show CLUE students have successfully secured UX professions (Table 5). We have had 90 students in the program: 47 have graduated from universities and 41 have not graduated yet. Focusing on the graduates, 39 out of 47 students have transitioned to UX roles and a half of their employers had connection to CLUE (Table 6); we do not have information on the remaining 8 students who have graduated. For those who went to pursue careers in universities, they became research associate and assistant/analyst.

Table 5. CLUE graduates' job placement

Position Title	n	Position Title	n
UX Researcher/ Design Researcher	16	Storytelling Developer	1
Unknown	8	Data Science Software Developer	1
UX Designer/ Interaction Designer	6	Human Factors Researcher	1
UX Specialist	2	UX Manager	1
Software Developer/Developer	3	Product Manager	1
Research Associate/Assistant/Analyst	4	IT Analyst and Developer	1
Engineering Specialist	1	UX Instructor	1

Table 6. Employer type and employer CLUE affiliation

Employer type	n	Employer CLUE affiliation	n
Industry	19	Yes	17
Government	16	No	22
University	3		
Self-employed	1		

CLUE students also show strong publication records (Table 6). As of spring 2021, we have witnessed 116 papers and posters published in journals and conferences and

30 awards and scholarships that recognized the student's outstanding academic achievement. Students presented and published at top-ranked HCI conferences (e.g., CHI, DIS, TEI). Majority students were first author and published their research projects on usability in collaboration with thesis supervisors, industry partners, and lab. The social connection that was formed at internship has presented a few of them with additional opportunity to work on research projects with industry partners (Table 7).

Table 7. Publication and academic achievement of CLUE students

Type of publication and awards	n	Examples of venues
Conference Presentations, Posters, & Demonstrations	105	Int. Symposium on Aviation Psychology, CHI Conference on Human Factors in Computing Systems, DIS Conference Designing Interactive Systems, Spatial User Interface Conference, International Symposium on Wearable Computers, Int. Conference on Cloud and Big Data Computing, Int. Conference on Information, Intelligence, Systems and Applications, CHI PLAY, TEI Int. Conference on tangible and Embedded Interaction
Journal Articles	11	Computers in Human Behaviour, IEEE Internet Computing, IEEE Pervasive, Games for Health Journal, Int. Journal of Child-Computer Interaction, Int. Journal of Cyber Behaviour and Psychology Learning
CLUE and local university presentations	68	End-of-Internship Presentation, Symposium, Graduate Colloquium, University Learning Forum, CAPCHI
Technical Reports and Non-refereed Articles	21	Research and Development Technical reports, Interactions Magazine
Awards and Scholarships	30	Provincial Scholarship, International Excellent Program, Provost Scholar Award, University A Senate Medal for Outstanding Academic Achievement for Master's work, Scholarship of Teaching and Learning, Best Paper Honourable Mention Award at DIS, Best Demonstration at ACM Spatial User Interface Conference, Postgraduate Scholarships

4.2 Industry and Government Partner Evaluation

We analyzed 22 industry and government partners' responses in the End-of-Internship Feedback survey using qualitative and quantitative approach and Table 8 presents the questions that were analyzed for this paper.

Table 8. Questions for industry partner

Questions asked	Question label
Q1. Would you recommend the student for future employment?	Employment Recommendation
Q2. Will you participate in CLUE again?	Partner Future Participation
Q3. The intern demonstrated an awareness of their strengths and weaknesses (1 = strongly disagree to 5 = strongly agree)	Self-reflectional Capacity
Q4. The intern demonstrated the ability to be an independent worker (1 = strongly disagree to 5 = strongly agree)	Independence
Q5. The intern worked effectively with others on team projects	Teamwork
Q6. The intern exhibited a professional attitude and behaviour (1 = strongly disagree to 5 = strongly agree)	Professionalism
Q7. The intern exhibited a sense of responsibility and dependability (1 = strongly disagree to 5 = strongly agree)	Dependability
Q8. Can you recommend actions that CLUE could initiate to better support you in your coach/mentor role?	Mentor Support
Q9. What additional support could CLUE provide to better maximize the usefulness of the program?	General Support
Q10. What additional preparation could interning student have had, prior to starting work, which would have increased the usefulness of the internship?	Student Preparation

Analysis of Quantitative and Binary Questions. For **Employment Recommendation,** we see that 24 students will be recommended for future employment, 4 students have received job offers from their internship organizations, 2 students were not given a clear answer, and 2 students received the response 'Maybe.' For **Partner Future Participation,** 20 of our partners expressed strong interest in participating in program again and only 2 partners said 'No.' Lastly, the partners positively evaluated the students on their independence, self-reflectional capacity, teamwork, professionalism, and dependability, with means for each skill nearing 5 (Fig. 2).

Analysis of Qualitative Questions. We conducted thematic analysis on the last three questions. For **Mentor Support,** we found three themes—**Information, Pre-Internship Preparation,** and **None.** Under **Information,** industry and government partners expressed they wanted better guidance on mentoring and clear learning outcomes

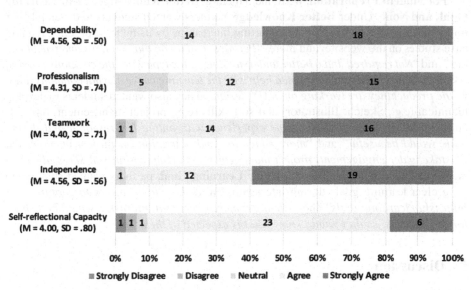

Fig. 2. Partner evaluation of CLUE students on core UX skills

for students during an internship: *"Clear guidelines on skills that CLUE interns should gain from* their *experience"* and *"It would be good to have the opportunity to hear about what other organizations are doing with the interns to learn from one another."* They also wanted important information to be placed at one place, *"Single trusted source with dates, and assessment/evaluation materials/links"* Under **Pre-Internship Preparation**, partners wanted a student to be prepared, skill-wise and mindset-wise: *"Foster a willingness to try, to fail, and to learn, a desire to push herself to try new things even with the risk of being wrong/bad and taking the feedback"* and *"It would be useful to have a list of 'transferable skills' that the interns are expected to be familiar with before they join."* Under **None**, partners were satisfied with current support and two partners especially appreciated the mid-placement interview: *"I think the current systems of midterm check in and end of term review works well"* and *"It's good that you have a check in period to ensure it's a mutually good fit for both mentor and student."*

For **General Support**, we found three themes: **Information, Other,** and **None**. Under **Information**, partners wanted to learn about how to evaluate a student, how other partners coached their students, and how students evaluated their internship experiences: *"Would be useful to see final deliverables from past CLUE internships in order to gauge how much students typically accomplish during their term"* and *"Invite students to provide feedback on their experience working with us."* Under **Other**, partners expressed they wanted the internship process to start earlier, to have more students involved from the two supporting universities, and prepare students to work in profession settings. Under **None**, partners were satisfied current support and liked CLUE's mid-placement interview.

For **Student Preparation**, we found 3 themes: **Better Knowledge, Clear Learning Goal, and None**. Under **Better Knowledge**, partners wanted students to develop better understanding of a company before starting internships by using their product, reading case studies on the website, and more: *"Perhaps read up on our products and tried them out"* and *"Not required, but a better understanding of the type work the company is doing – supply chain or electronics - would help with the learning curve of what company does, vs the product they are working on in UX design."* They also wanted students to develop technical (e.g., Sketch, Illustrator) and soft skills (e.g., project management, business culture): *"If anything perhaps some experience with online UX research and design tools would be useful"* and *"more education and activation on project management … stakeholder engagement, project management, communication soft skills always a nice baseline to build off."* Under **Clear Learning Goal**, partners wanted students to have clear learning goals during internship: *"Worksheet for students to capture their internship learning goals"* and *"Having a more structured internship would be helpful for the students, as they would know what is expected of them."*

5 Discussion

CLUE is an innovative usability training program for HCI graduate students, with providing additional support to undergraduate and graduate students. In this paper, we reported the critical elements and initial assessment of the program. CLUE is not the first usability training that has been created to enhance the employability of HCI students for the UX labour market: there are other likeminded HCI scholars and educators who have offered usability training in varying forms, ranging from student-led workshops to service learning [1, 24, 25]. However, it is the creative elements of CLUE (see Table 1) and the sheer scope of training that has been purposefully targeted to cultivate core UX skills that make the program most deserving of HCI educators and scholars' attention. In below section, we define the success of CLUE at three different levels and discuss recommendations and future work.

5.1 Defining the Success of CLUE

The success of CLUE can be assessed by asking three questions. First, we can ask, "Has the program decreased the UX skill gap by equipping students with core UX skills?" and we have some confidence to say the answer is 'Yes' based on our metrics. There are several program elements that are noteworthy. Prior to starting their internship, students actively participate in seminars, workshops, and short courses to develop baseline UX-specific professional and technical skills. While completing their internships, we can infer elements such as learning journal and mid-placement interview encouraged students to reflect on their weakness and strengths and learning goals, further fueling their motivation to refine their skills and do well on assigned UX projects. All these program elements operate together to push for the growth of students as UX professions and the evidence of decreased UX skill gap is most evident in our partners' positive evaluation of student interns on give important UX skills (see Fig. 2) and their willingness to recommend student interns for future employment. We believe our partners provided fair student assessment because they took on one student per term and they contextualized their assessment to the individual student.

In addition, we observed that almost half of our graduates secured a position at organizations affiliated with CLUE. Our anecdotal evidence indicates that students received job offers from the organizations that they interned at or they received job offers from the organizations with whom they only had met during the CLUE placement interview. This direct recruitment from the program is remarkable for two reasons: it shows CLUE students became attractive junior UX professionals who met partners' expectations and it shows CLUE's standing as a trustworthy program that trains students with employability UX skills.

Altogether, we believe reduction in the UX skill gap depends on both teaching methods and educational contents. CLUE's training components forces students to become active learners. For instance, in Workshops, students participate in group discussions and hands-on activities rather than passively receiving information. Students also learn about up-to-date UX knowledge on a monthly basis.

Second, we can ask "Has the program maintained positive relationship with industry and government partners?" and the answer is also 'Yes.' Our results indicate the mid-placement interview was an important element that contributed to partners' satisfaction with the program; this element was repeatedly mentioned in partners' responses to two open-ended questions (**Mentor Support** and **General Support**). Students are perceived as the key stakeholder in internships and thus HCI educators and scholars' efforts have been dedicated to making sure their experiences stay positive [32, 33]. However, it is our view that equal efforts should be placed to ensure satisfying partners' needs. In general, host organizations have two major needs when they host student interns: (1) students who are qualified and motivated to assist full-time employees and (2) students who can teach them new things and excite them with fresh ideas [29, 34]. Failure to satisfy partners' needs will inevitably lead to partner dissatisfaction, which in turn will influence their interaction with students and their willingness to continue the partnership with a program. Our mid-placement interview was a perfect venue to check mentors' needs fulfillment with students and the program and act accordingly.

There are other creative elements in CLUE that serves to enhance positive partner-program relationship: the program's financial support to students while they complete internship and the opportunities to form industry-industry and industry-faculty connections by attending seminars, workshops, and symposiums. Looking at the program as a whole, we have had 42 partners from 28 organizations since the beginning of the program and 17 organizations have repeatedly recruited CLUE students. For instance, one organization has hosted students for three years while another organization has hosted students for five years. This number adds to another line of evidence attesting to the success of CLUE in maintaining positive relationship with our partners.

Lastly, we want to highlight the possible positive spillover effect of internships to students' academic performance. We saw strong publication and scholarship records by CLUE students. One can assume the program's constant exposure of cutting-edge HCI research in seminars and workshops and numerous conferences have contributed to their academic achievement. This observation aligns with prior studies demonstrating the positive effect of internships on students' academic performance, including enhanced GPA

[35] and greater likelihood of completing university [36]. While the primary objective of CLUE is enhancing students' UX employability skills, this finding suggests the program can prepare students to pursue careers in academia.

In sum, we have defined the program success at three levels—decreased UX skill gap, maintenance of positive partner-program relationship, and improved academic performance—and demonstrated how various program's creative elements and scope of training make the program stand apart from other usability training.

5.2   Recommendations: Developing a Successful Usability Training Program

We make several recommendations to HCI scholars and educators on how they can create an effective usability training program. Our recommendations are based on CLUE's weaknesses that have been identified in the initial assessment and our reflections over the past six years in managing the program. We first outline a set of recommendations a program can consider for students.

1. **Refining New Student Orientation.** A program should explicitly tell students about why they should strive to produce good work at internship. Students have drastically different expectations and understanding about internships [27, 37] and it is possible that students do not make automatic connection between good internship performance and future job offer from host organizations. Helping students to make this explicit connection can motivate them to attend and participate in Seminars, Workshops, and Short Courses diligently, so that they feel ready for internships.

2. **Collaborating on Seminars, Workshops, and Short Courses Topics.** CLUE has successfully offered seminars, workshops, and short courses on skills that were mentioned by our partners (e.g., project management, communication). At the same time, partners have also mentioned a few tool-specific skills (e.g., Sketch, Illustrator) that students can benefit from learning prior to starting internship. First, a program can compile a list of these tools which students can familiarize themselves with tools through online and University resources. Second, we propose partners and a program to collaboratively create training topics and teach students with curated professional and technical skills that accurately reflect the current UX practices and technologies. This collaboration is especially useful if a program and its participating faculty have limited exposure to UX industry.

3. **Supporting Student Interaction.** CLUE offers training to students from three universities and there is a higher number of participating students from the leading University A. Prior to COVID-19, while students saw each other in-person at Symposiums and UX conferences, their interaction was typically limited with CLUE students who were also from their university. Even after COVID-19, establishing meaningful interaction between students from different universities has remained equally difficult, with reduced non-verbal cues and physical presence and warmth that characterize online meetings. A program can create a student-only online space (e.g., Slack) where all students can converse with each other about any topics.

We now outline a set of recommendations a program can consider for their industry and government partners:

1. **Providing Industry Partner Orientation.** Our industry and government partners repeatedly expressed the need for an improved coaching guide. This implies some of them did not find the current Industry Partner Handbook as enough resource to learn about being a good mentor. Instead of presenting partners with a text-based Industry Handbook, a program can consider providing an orientation at each internship cycle and invite industry and government mentors to have an open discussion on (a) what it means to be a mentor, (b) what are useful mentoring strategies, (c) how to set learning goals, and (d) how to evaluate student progress.
2. **Creating Information Package About Organization.** Some partners expressed students can develop better knowledge about their organization prior to starting internship. In addition to the job descriptions, host organizations can share the program with information package that outlines (a) the mission of the organization, (b) organization structure. (c) organization rules, policies, and expectations, (d) intern's responsibilities, and (e) links to their case studies and prior projects [38].
3. **Facilitating End-of-Placement Feedback Session for partners.** Our industry and government partners seldom received in-depth suggestions on how they can improve their role as the mentor and as the host organization. Questions such as, "did the student value the project that they worked on?" and "were my mentoring strategies effective to achieve their learning goals?" remain unanswered and unimproved for next incoming student interns. We suggest a program can consider the end-of-placement meeting or mediating a focus group where students share honest experiences with program partners.

5.3   Limitations and Future Directions

There are several limitations with our initial assessment of CLUE and these limitations open up exciting future directions. First, we examined the effect of the program on decreasing the UX skill gap by surveying students' job placement and partner's evaluation of students on five UX skills. Prior research has achieved the same objective by asking employers to evaluate their recently hired graduates on important skills [39, 40] in which they compared newly hired graduates against full-time employees. In contrary, our partners may have evaluated students' UX skills by comparing the student from their start and the end of internship (i.e., within-individual comparison) and this comparison may not necessarily inform us on how comparable students are against full-time UX employees. Furthermore, students' job placement can be attributed to factors unrelated to CLUE. Future researchers can adopt more standardized ways to assess the effect of a program on decreasing the UX skill gap by including comparison data. For instance, they can compare students who participated in a program versus those who did not participate in a program on employment rate or types of landing jobs.

Relatedly, our students' academic achievement can also be attributed to factors unrelated to CLUE. Future researchers can obtain comparison data that show changes in GPA throughout students' tenure in a program as stronger evidence.

Second, our assessment does not inform us how students found program's critical elements. We understand industry and government partners' appreciation of a specific program element (i.e., the mid-placement interview) and their desire for a new program element (e.g., a better coaching guide) through administering a survey with open-ended question. But the same assessment approach has not been adapted for students. Future researchers can consider conducting surveys or focus group with students to identify program elements that have facilitated their experiential learning journey.

Third, we did not report CLUE faculty's experience of the program. Prior research indicates that faculty who are involved in the internship program experience unique difficulties, including their time commitment and service not being recognized in tenure review [41] and their lack of clear guidance on how they should be serving the role as an internship program faculty [42]. At this point, we only have anecdotal stories to illustrate CLUE faculty's experiences with the program and we recommend future educators to incorporate more formal assessment approach to evaluate faculty's experience with their usability training program. Lastly, HCI educators and researchers should be cautious in generalizing our results to UX training programs that are in a different format than our program.

6 Conclusion

CLUE offers students a comprehensive learning experience and incorporated experiential learning technical in every training component. Our work has identified the details of the program, from initiating relationship with industry partners, type of evaluations to ensure the program success, type of targeted professional and technical skills provided. Thus, we invite other HCI educators and practitioners to use our training program as a point of reference as they design a curriculum to prepare graduate students for UX careers. In future, we plan to engage in more comprehensive assessment of the program by evaluating the experiences of all three stakeholders—students, industry partners, and faculty—and this assessment will add to our current understanding of the effectiveness of CLUE in bridging the UX skill gap.

Acknowledgement. This work was supported and funded by the National Sciences and Engineering Research Council of Canada (NSERC) through the Collaborative Learning in Usability Experiences CREATE grant (2015–465639).

References

1. Leshed, G.: Scaling student-run workshops in an advanced HCI course. In: Proceedings of EduCHI 2019 Symposium, Glasgow, UK (2019)
2. Murad, C., Munteanu, C.: Teaching for voice: the state of VUI design in HCI education. In: Proceedings of EduCHI 2019 Symposium, Glasgow, UK (2019)
3. Rosala, M., Krause, R.: User Experience Careers What a Career in UX Looks Like Today. https://www.nngroup.com/reports/user-experience-careers. Accessed 25 Jan 2021
4. Henneman, R.L., Ballay, L., Wagner, L.: The Master's degree in HCI at 20: issues and trends. In: Proceedings of Human Factors in Computing Systems (2016). https://doi.org/10.1145/2851581.2886441
5. Radermacher, A., Walia, G.: Gaps between industry expectations and the abilities of graduates. In: Proceedings of the 44th ACM Technical Symposium on Computer Science Education (2013). https://doi.org/10.1145/2445196.2445351

6. Gonzalez, C.A., Ghazizadeh, M., Smith, M.: Perspectives on the training of human factors students for the user experience industry. In: Proceedings of the Human Factors and Ergonomics Society (2014). https://doi.org/10.1177/1541931214581378
7. Brechner, E.: Things they would not teach me of in college: what Microsoft developers learn later. In: Proceedings of the Conference on Object-Oriented Programming Systems, Languages, and Applications, OOPSLA (2003). https://doi.org/10.1145/949344.949387
8. National Association of Colleges and Employers: Internship and Co-Op Hiring Make Gains in 2017. https://www.naceweb.org/job-market/internships/internship-and-co-op-hiring-make-gains-in-2017/. Accessed 01 Feb 2021
9. Nielson, J.: A 100-Year View of User Experience. https://www.nngroup.com/articles/100-years-ux/. Accessed 01 Feb 2021
10. Braverman, B.: Best Jobs in America. https://money.cnn.com/gallery/pf/2017/01/05/best-jobs-2017/index.html. Accessed 01 Feb 2021
11. McGill, M.M.: Defining the expectation gap: a comparison of industry needs and existing game development curriculum. In: Proceedings of the 4th International Conference on the Foundations of Digital Games (2009). https://doi.org/10.1145/1536513.1536542
12. Wilcox, L., DiSalvo, B., Henneman, D., Wang, Q.: Design in the HCI classroom: Setting a research agenda. In: Proceedings of the 2019 ACM Designing Interactive Systems Conference (2019). https://doi.org/10.1145/3322276.3322381
13. Roldan, W., et al.: Opportunities and challenges in involving users in project-based HCI education. In: Proceedings of the 2020 CHI Conference on Human Factors in Computing Systems, pp. 1–15 (2020). https://doi.org/10.1145/3313831.3376530
14. Andrews, J., Higson, H.: Graduate employability, "soft skills" versus "hard" business knowledge: A European study. High. Educ. Eur. 33, 411–422 (2008). https://doi.org/10.1080/03797720802522627
15. Tether, B., Mina, A., Consoli, D., Gagliardi, D.: A Literature Review on Skills and Innovation. How Does Successful Innovation Impact on the Demand for Skills and How Do Skills Drive Innovation? CRIC Report for The Department of Trade and Industry (2005)
16. Forth, J., Mason, G.: Information and communication technology (ICT) skill gaps and company-level performance: Evidence from the ICT professionals survey 2000–01 (2004)
17. Raza, S.A., Naqvi, S.A.: Quality of Pakistani University Graduates As Perceived By Employers : Implications for Faculty Development. J. Qual. Technol. Manag. 7 (2011)
18. Kolb, D.A.: Experiential learning: Experience as the source of learning and development. David A. Kolb, Prentice-Hall International, Hemel Hempstead, Herts., 1984. No. of pages: xiii + 256. J. Organ. Behav. 8 (1984)
19. Lee, S.: Increasing student learning: a comparison of students' perceptions of learning in the classroom environment and their industry-based experiential learning assignments. J. Teach. Travel Tour. 7 (2007). https://doi.org/10.1080/15313220802033310
20. Maelah, R., Mohamed, Z.M., Ramli, R., Aman, A.: Internship for accounting undergraduates: comparative insights from stakeholders. Educ. Train. 56 (2014). https://doi.org/10.1108/ET-09-2012-0088
21. Lundy, B.L.: Service learning in life-span developmental psychology: higher exam scores and increased empathy. Teach. Psychol. 34 (2007). https://doi.org/10.1080/00986280709336644
22. Kilgo, C.A., Ezell Sheets, J.K., Pascarella, E.T.: The link between high-impact practices and student learning: some longitudinal evidence. High. Educ. 69(4), 509–525 (2014). https://doi.org/10.1007/s10734-014-9788-z
23. Samura, M.: Examining undergraduate student outcomes from a community-engaged and inquiry-oriented capstone experience. Scholarsh. Pract. Undergrad. Res. 1 (2018). https://doi.org/10.18833/spur/1/3/15

24. Musabirov, I., Suvorova, A., Bulygin, D., Pavel Okopnyi, P.: Co-aligning UX & development courses: the case of MSc in information systems and HCI. In: The Proceedings of EduCHI 2019 Symposium (2019)
25. Lazar, J.: Using community-based service projects to enhance undergraduate HCI education: 10 years of experience. In: Proceedings of Human Factors in Computing Systems (CHI 2011) (2011). https://doi.org/10.1145/1979742.1979653
26. Ishengoma, E., Vaaland, T.I.: Can university-industry linkages stimulate student employability? Educ. Train. **58** (2016). https://doi.org/10.1108/ET-11-2014-0137
27. Raymond, M.A., McNabb, D.E., Matthaei, C.F.: Preparing graduates for the workforce: the role of business education. J. Educ. Bus. **68** (1993). https://doi.org/10.1080/08832323.1993.10117613
28. Talone, A.B., Basavaraj, P., Wisniewski, P.J.: Enhancing human-computer interaction and user experience education through a hybrid approach to experiential learning. In: Proceedings of the 18th Annual Conference on Information Technology Education, pp. 83–88 (2017). https://doi.org/10.1145/3125659.3125685
29. MacDonald, C.M., Rozaklis, L.: Assessing the implementation of authentic, client-facing student projects in user experience (UX) education: insights from multiple stakeholders. Proc. Assoc. Inf. Sci. Technol. **54**, 268–278 (2017). https://doi.org/10.1002/pra2.2017.14505401030
30. Kolb, D.A.: Experiential Learning: Experience as the Source of Learning and Development. Pearson Publishing (2015)
31. Kapoor, A., Gardner-McCune, C.: Barriers to securing industry internships in computing. In: Proceedings of the 22nd Australasian Computing Education Conference, Held in conjunction with Australasian Computer Science Week (2020). https://doi.org/10.1145/3373165.3373181
32. Maaravi, Y., Heller, B., Hochman, G., Kanat-Maymon, Y.: Internship not hardship: what makes interns in startup companies satisfied? J. Exp. Educ. 1–20 (2020). https://doi.org/10.1177/1053825920966351
33. Jaradat, G.M.: Internship training in computer science: exploring student satisfaction levels. Eval. Program Plann. 63 (2017). https://doi.org/10.1016/j.evalprogplan.2017.04.004
34. Scott, M., Richardson, S.: Preparing for practice: how internships and other practice-based learning exchanges benefit students, industry hosts and universities. AICCM Bull. **32**, 73–79 (2011). https://doi.org/10.1179/bac.2011.32.1.010
35. Knouse, S.B., Tanner, J.R., Harris, E.W.: The relation of college internships, college performance, and subsequent job opportunity. J. Employ. Couns. **36** (1999). https://doi.org/10.1002/j.2161-1920.1999.tb01007.x
36. Walker, R.: Business internships and their relationship with retention, academic performance, and degree completion (2011)
37. Michael Knemeyer, A., Murphy, P.R.: Logistics internships: employer and student perspectives. Int. J. Phys. Distrib. Logist. Manag. **32** (2002). https://doi.org/10.1108/09600030210421732
38. True, M.: Starting and maintaining a quality internship program. Glob. Internsh. Conf. (2002)
39. Cappel, J.J.: Entry-level IS job skills: a survey of employers. J. Comput. Inf. Syst. **42** (2001). https://doi.org/10.1080/08874417.2002.11647490
40. Abbasi, F.K., Ali, A., Bibi, N.: Analysis of skill gap for business graduates: managerial perspective from banking industry. Educ. Train. **60** (2018). https://doi.org/10.1108/ET-08-2017-0120
41. Gallagher, R.: What is it good for? (2007). https://www.the-scientist.com/editorial-old/tenure-what-is-it-good-for-46158. Accessed 01 Feb 2021
42. Tuberville, K.: A Case Study: Faculty Perceptions of the Challenges and Successes in Experiential Learning At A Public University. Ph.D thesis, 1–203 (2014)

What Students Do While You Are Teaching – Computer and Smartphone Use in Class and Its Implication on Learning

Carli Ochs[1(✉)] and Andreas Sonderegger[1,2]

[1] Department of Psychology, University of Fribourg, Fribourg, Switzerland
carli.ochs@unifr.ch
[2] Bussiness School, Bern University of Applied Sciences, Bern, Switzerland

Abstract. The presence of mobile devices (e.g., smartphones, tablets and computers) in the classroom gives students the possibility of doing off-task activities during lectures. The purpose of this mixed-method field study was to learn more about students' behaviors, reasons, and opinions regarding such activities and their consequences on learning. This study is one of few to take a holistic view on this topic by taking the use of all technical devices in class into account and assessing its consequences on learning objectively. This is important to gain a full picture concerning the consequences of off-task activities in class. Right after a lecture, bachelor students (N = 125) answered a survey containing questions on their usage of mobile devices during this last class. Furthermore, they took a test on the content of that lecture. Qualitative and quantitative analysis of data revealed that students spent an average of more than 19% of their time using a digital device for non-class purposes. Interestingly, this was not significantly linked with learning, although many students reported being aware of this behavior's potential negative consequences. But there was a significant negative link between the number of received notifications and learning. These results suggest that external interruptions have a stronger negative effect than internal interruptions, allowing us to make better recommendations on how to use electronic devices in the classroom.

Keywords: Digital distractions · Academic performance · Notifications

1 Introduction

The days of looking at a classroom filled with students holding a pen or pencil and yellow legal notepad are long gone. While a few students still enjoy taking handwritten notes, they often seem to be in the minority, while a diversity of devices is visible in classrooms; these might be laptops, smartphones, or tablets. The question hence arises whether these changes are for better or worse in terms of the student's learning.

Research has shown that technological devices can be useful to support learning (e.g., taking notes on a computer) [1]. However, these devices can also be a source of distraction [1–4]. Students can either be interrupted and distracted by their own usage

© IFIP International Federation for Information Processing 2021
Published by Springer Nature Switzerland AG 2021
C. Ardito et al. (Eds.): INTERACT 2021, LNCS 12933, pp. 501–520, 2021.
https://doi.org/10.1007/978-3-030-85616-8_29

but also through the usage of others (e.g., seeing content on fellow students' screens or receiving notifications), which may result in reduced attention in the classroom [1, 5]. Reduced attention might represent an important issue since attention seems to play an important role in learning and performance [6]. Research done on technological devices in the classroom has mainly shown a negative impact on learning when students use their devices for off-task activities [2, 7–9].

However, most of the research on distraction in the classroom focuses on a specific kind of use (e.g., texting, using social media) or on a particular device (e.g., laptop computer or smartphone). In addition, learning was assessed often only at the end of the term, allowing for the influence of different other variables (e.g., motivation, time spent studying) on learning performance [2, 10, 11]. Also, the objective assessment used in some studies (e.g., through an app) implies that the study's goal was disclosed to the students [11]. This might lead participants to behave differently and heavily impinge on the study's ecological validity.

In addition, due to rapidly growing technological advancements, user behavior has changed significantly in recent years (e.g., an always increasing number of students using laptops), which is why the collection of up-to-date data is of importance. In the following paper, we took a holistic approach to technology usage in the classroom. We assessed the kind of usage (e.g., social media or communication), the length and frequency of use (e.g., usage time, number of unlocks), and what devices were used (e.g., laptop or smartphone) directly after class. In addition, we evaluated how the use of technology in the classroom affected learning objectively and questioned the students on their opinion regarding technology use in class.

1.1 Technology-Induced Interruptions in Class

Technology in the classroom can be distracting in mainly two ways. Students can distract themselves by doing nonrelated course work activities on their technological devices. Such type of behavior is termed self-interruption [12]. Additionally, to self-interruption, individuals can be externally interrupted. External interruptions can come from other students but also from notifications [12]. Both types of distractions have been shown to have a negative impact on student's learning performance [2, 5].

Self-interruption in Class. When students self-interrupt from following the class to do something else, this activity is called an off-task activity [13]. Examples of such activities are online chatting, playing games, social media use, and working for a different class [14, 15]. Off-task activities have been shown to be problematic because they reduce the attentional resources available for following the class [6]. In this context, it has been shown that students who engage in off-task activities on their laptop or smartphone during lectures score lower on knowledge tests [2, 7, 8, 11]. However, when asked about the potential consequences of off-task activities, many students seem to think that they do not affect their performance [16]. Others were aware of potential negative consequences, but still engaged in them [16, 17]. Reasons given by students for using technology for off-task activities in class are boredom, the need to communicate with someone, and class-specific characteristics (e.g., number of students in the classroom, structure, and content of the course) [15]. Supporting these explanations are Tran et al.' [18] findings who reported that a trigger for smartphone usage during class was unoccupied moments (e.g., boredom).

In addition, it has been argued that self-interruption is often due to a fear of missing out (FOMO) [13, 19]. FOMO describes a belief that others might enjoy themselves without the concerned person and is characterized by the desire to remain constantly in touch with others to avoid the risk of missing out [20]. It has been shown that FOMO can cause people to check their phones on average every 30 min without an external trigger to make sure that they are not missing any notifications [19].

External Interruptions in Class. In addition to the negative consequences of technology-induced self-interruptions in class, students can be externally interrupted. One good example of an external interruption are notifications. Notifications are generally attended to very quickly [21, 22]. They are designed to attract attention and hence likely to distract [23]. Just the sound or vibration of a notification has been shown to have a negative impact on attention by impacting the cognitive load and attentional resources of the user [24, 25]. In addition, a notification can distract not only the users of a device but also others around them.

Notifications exist on all devices and are either automated messages from applications such as calendar reminders but can also come from people through email, messenger apps and video calls. Most often, notifications are not controlled by users, unless they explicitly disable them or enable a 'do not disturb function' on their technological device. While several studies addressing the impact of notifications on learning focused on the writing of text messages during class, empirical research regarding the disturbance caused by notifications in the classroom is to our knowledge rather scarce. Outside the educational field of research, studies have shown that constant interruptions by notifications impinge on work and even social life [21, 26]. Pielot and Rello [21] showed that users who switched off notifications for an entire day reported higher levels of productivity and lower levels of distraction as compared to a baseline day with notifications switched on.

The notification type with the highest affordance to react is the text message type [22]. Agrawal et al. [19] have shown that in 90% of the cases, individuals reply in the following 15 min after having received a text message. Text messaging has been shown to be a rather common off-task activity in class, with over 70% of students reporting texting during a lecture [15]. Addressing the link between texting and learning, Bowman et al. [27] reported that texting had a consequence on speed of reading but not on comprehension in a text comprehension test. Several other studies showed that texting during class had a negative effect on learning performance (e.g., total grade point average (GPA), or questions on a video recorded lecture that participants watched while they received texts) [3, 5, 28, 29]. Hence texting in class can be considered to be a substantial problem for learning.

Another external source of distraction to students can be their fellow students' off-task usage of technology [8]. Seeing fellow students engaging in off-task activities has been reported to be a trigger to engage oneself in such activities [13].

An important issue of off-task activities in class is that they come with higher costs than expected. Once distracted by an off-task activity, users often report feeling sucked in or losing control of their usage [30, 31]. This implies that students risk spending more time on their device than the original interruption would have taken. Meaning that just checking, or just reading a message might have a higher price than some users expect.

1.2 Present Study

In summary, students either self-interrupt their focus from the lecture by doing off-task activities or are externally interrupted by others' usage or by notifications appearing on their devices. Additional issues are that once interrupted, students tend to stay on their device longer than intended, and once they do decide to redirect their attention towards the course, this can also demand a certain amount of cognitive load [32].

This present mixed method survey study aims to determine how much time students spend on off-task activities during a typical 90-min university lecture, what kind of activities they perform, what devices they use to perform these activities, and what the impact on learning performance is. As hypotheses, we expect off-task activities to have a negative impact on learning. This effect is expected to be particularly pronounced if interruptions have an external source (e.g., notifications).

While previous studies addressing similar questions used different, eventually biased methodological approaches (e.g., regarding the assessment of learning and off-task activities), focused on one device (smartphone or computer) or a specific type of usage (texting), we chose a holistic approach to assess students' off-task activities and learning directly after the class. Taking a holistic approach is important to gain a full picture of student's activities in class as students that might partake in off-task activities on one device might not do so on the other.

2 Method

2.1 Participants

One hundred and twenty-five bachelor students (105 female, 18 male, 2 did not specify) of the University of Fribourg ranging from the age of 18 to 29 yrs ($M = 21.28$, $SD = 1.95$) were tested at the end of bachelor level lecture in different psychology method classes (introduction to psychological methods and introduction to psychological testing) taught by different lecturers.

An a priori sample size estimation following the minimally important difference approach [33, 34] revealed that for the detection of a change in the grade of a student based on the applied grading scheme (i.e. the decrease of the grade by one point, $d = 0.86$, was defined as minimal important difference), 64 participants would be required (assuming an error probability of $\alpha = .05$) to achieve a power of $1 - \beta = .95$ for the correlational analysis, and 74 participants for the analysis of variances [35].

2.2 Measures

Questions Regarding Computer Use and Smartphone Use. Participants were asked a series of questions on their computer and smartphone use during the lecture. These questions can be found in Table 1. Second order questions (e.g., 1a. How many notifications/messages did you receive on your computer, during this lecture?) were only presented if participants answered yes to the first order question (e.g., 1. Did you use your computer during this lecture?). Question 2.a, and 3.c left enough space to report up to 5 activities. At the end of the questionnaire (question 4) participants were asked to answer an open question about their opinion on the use of technology for off-task activities in the classroom.

Table 1. Questions regarding participants' computer and smartphone use during the lecture.

	Computer use	
1.	Did you use your computer during this lecture?	Yes*/No
1.a	How many notifications/messages did you receive on your computer, during this lecture?	
2.	Have you used your computer for activities other than those related to today's lecture?	Yes*/No
2.a	Which off-task activities did you do on your computer? Indicate the different activities and the estimated time you spent on doing them.	
	Activity: Estimated time:	
	Smartphone use	
3.	Did you use your smartphone during this lecture?	
		Yes*/No
3.a	How many times did you pick up your smartphone or clicked the Main/Home button?	
3.b	How many notifications did you receive during this lecture?	
3.c	Which off-task activities did you do on your smartphone? Indicate the different activities and the estimated time you spent on doing them.	
	Activity: Estimated time:	
	General opinion questions	
4.	What is your opinion on the use of smartphones and computers for non-study related activities during classes?	

Learning Score. Six multiple choice questions on the content of the specific topic of the class were asked. Questions were selected from previous exams and thus represented a valid assessment of learning performance. These questions were of K-prime 1/0 type; with four answer options, of which one or two could be correct (cf. Table 2). Students received a point if all the answering options were responded to correctly. Based on this test, a learning score was calculated. Since data analysis revealed that difficulty level and learning performance varied between the different classes, learning scores were standardized for each class (z-scores).

Table 2. Exam example question

1) Which statement(s) is/are correct?	
a)	Moderation bias implies that participants tend to choose the middle of the scale to answer questions.
b)	Moderation bias implies that participants tend to choose the extremes of a scale.
c)	One way to avoid moderation bias is to standardize the scores.
d)	One way to avoid moderation bias is to reverse the items.
2) The BOLD (Blood-Oxygenation-Level Dependent) effect is important for which psycho-physiological measurement method(s)?	
a)	EEG
b)	ECG
c)	fMRI
d)	fNIRS
3) Which statement(s) about advantages and disadvantages of EEG is/are false?	
a)	EEG has a very high spatial resolution
b)	EEG is tolerant with regard to movement
c)	EEG is non-invasive and quiet
d)	The signal-to-noise ratio in EEG is poor

3   Procedure

For all classes, no specific class policy regarding the use of technology in the classroom has been imposed. Participants were recruited at the end of lectures given by staff of the psychology department. Students were asked 20 min before the end of a lecture if they would be willing to participate. If they agreed, they stayed seated in the lecture hall and completed the online survey that lasted about 15 min.

Participants were informed of the theme of the questionnaire a first time orally and a second time in written form on the first page of the survey. Great importance was attached to emphasizing that the survey is anonymous and that students should answer as honestly as possible. After the participants had confirmed their informed consent, they answered the questionnaire, took the learning test and were allowed to leave.

4 Data analysis and Accuracy Evaluation

4.1 Analysis of Quantitative Data

Since the collected data met the requirements of parametric testing (normal distribution and homogeneity of variances), quantitative data was analysed using between-groups analysis of variance (ANOVA) and correlations (Pearson).

4.2 Analysis of Qualitative Data

Since two very different types of qualitative data were collected, two different methods of analysis were used. Firstly, ten categories of activities were inductively created from the data specifying off-task activities students adhered to during class. Then two coders proceeded to code each activity into the 10 different categories (cf. Table 2 in the results section). The inter-rater reliability was measured using Cohen's kappa and showed to be satisfactory ($k = .84$). The few differences in coding were then solved through discussion.

Secondly the open question (4., cf. Table 1) regarding students' opinions was analyzed using the inductive thematic analysis methodology [36]. After reading all of the students' answers, a set of preliminary codes were independently produced by both coders. These codes were then compared and discussed by the two coders. The coders then proceeded to code the data with these codes while regular meetings were organized to compare and discuss coding, as well as to make sure that the analysis was comprehensive, coherent, and reflecting the actual data. Following the coding of the data, emerging themes and sub-themes were identified and discussed between the two researchers. We did not measure inter-rater reliability for this analysis, because this would imply an unequivocally "true" way of interpreting data, which we believe is not possible for this type of dataset [36].

4.3 Accuracy Evaluation of Self-reports of Technology Use

Previous research has shown that participants' knowledge (e.g., telling participants that data of their usage behavior will be assessed) or guesswork about the objective of a study can influence their behavior [37]. Therefore, we decided not to log students' usage behavior to avoid influencing it. This implied that the data on usage behavior were collected subjectively after class. However, a recent meta-analysis has shown that self-reported data of media use are only moderately correlated with objective (logged) measurements [38]. Different cognitive processes such as memory biases are usually put forward as main reason for such moderate correlations [39, 40]. However, most studies analyzed in the above-mentioned meta-analysis compared self-report and objective data regarding the use of unspecific media types over a rather long period of time (e.g., days or even weeks). In contrast to this, use of technology was recorded in this study within a highly restricted timeframe (i.e., the previous 90 min) regarding very specific usage behaviors (i.e., off-task activities).

In order to gain a better knowledge of the reliability of such self-report data (i.e., specific, short-time usage behavior directly assessed after class), a separate study was conducted (N = 23) in which usage time and number of received notifications during a class were subjectively assessed as well as automatically logged. Analysis of these data is presented in Table 3, indicating a moderate to good reliability of self-report data [41]. This points out that the subjective assessment of usage data is reliable for such short-term evaluations as conducted in this piece of research.

Table 3. Results of interclass correlation (ICC) calculation using single-rating, absolute-agreement, 2-way mixed-effects model and Pearson correlations between self-report and log data.

	ICC	95% CI	F	r
Usage time	.76	.43 to .90	$F(22, 22) = 9.33, p < .000$	.83***
Number of notifications	.60	.30 to .83	$F(19, 19) = 5.42, p < .000$	.91***

***significant at the 0.01 level (2-tailed), CI = confidence interval

5   Results

5.1   Off-Task Activities and Notifications

Data analysis revealed that more than half of the students ($N = 71, 57\%$) used their computers and more than two thirds ($N = 89, 71\%$) their mobile phones for off-task activities during class, while a rather small number did not use any of their devices for off-task activities ($N = 16, 13\%$; see Table 4 for details).

Table 5 summarizes the activities reported by students (several activities could be mentioned for each device used in class). Interestingly, the most frequently mentioned activities are related to communication, e.g., writing or reading emails or text messages and the use of social networks. The use of WhatsApp might be considered in both of these categories (communication or social media)[1]. A closer look into the off-task activities as a function of device that was used revealed that the mobile phone was mainly used for communication and social media purposes (72.34%). In contrast, the most frequently mentioned activities for the computer were communication (23.5%, mainly emails) and the preparation for other classes (17.5%). The average time each student spent on off-task activities during a 90-min lecture (calculated based on the total number of participants) was 17.2 min ($SD = 19.0$) which represents 19.1% of the total time. About half of the

---

[1] There is a distinction between WhatsApp and other social media apps: WhatsApp is used primarily for communication while other social media apps offer other content. As for Facebook it is possible to make the distinction between Facebook and its messenger app, we would suggest coding the messenger app as communication and the social media app as social media when such a distinction is possible. In order to have the most fined grained analysis we chose to create a separate category for WhatsApp instead of coding it as social media or communication app.

time (8.56 min, $SD = 11.9$) was spent on the laptop computer and half (8.62 min, $SD = 15.14$) on the mobile phone.

Regarding the number of notifications students received during the class, data analysis revealed a mean value of 2.79 notifications ($SD = 6.53$) on the computer and 4.72 ($SD = 6.16$) notifications on the smartphone. For both, the measures ranged between 0 and 30 notifications.

Table 4. Use of computer and smartphone for off-task activities.

		Smartphone use		
		No (%)	Yes (%)	Total (%)
Computer use	No (%)	16 (13)	38 (30)	54 (43)
	Yes (%)	20 (16)	51 (41)	71 (57)
	Total (%)	36 (29)	89 (71)	125 (100)

Table 5. Evaluation of the mentioned off-task activities ordered by different categories (average time of use was calculated for students reporting this activity).

Activities	On computer		On mobile phone	
	No. of mentions (%)	Average time of use in min. (SD)	No. of mentions (%)	Average time of use in min. (SD)
WhatsApp	29 (14.5)	8 (5.9)	70 (37.2)	5 (4.2)
Social networks (e.g., Facebook, Instagram)	18 (9)	6.5 (4.2)	50 (26.6)	6 (5.2)
Communication (e.g., e-mail, text messages)	47 (23.5)	5 (4)	16 (8.5)	3 (5.1)
Other	27 (13.5)	12 (5.9)	26 (13.8)	10 (21.2)
Activities for another class	35 (17.5)	23.9 (34.7)	1 (0.5)	15
Planning/organisation	18 (9)	4 (2.5)	9 (4.8)	2 (2.1)
(Online) games	6 (3)	25 (18)	8 (4.3)	11 (9.3)
Magazine/news	8 (4)	12 (5.9)	5 (2.7)	10.3 (19.5)
Online shopping	9 (4.5)	8.3 (10.8)	1 (0.5)	5
Videos, Netflix, YouTube	3 (1.5)	17.3 (14.2)	2 (1.1)	30 (42.4)
Total	200	11.9 (19.8)	188	5.2 (11.2)

5.2 Learning Performance

With regard to the question whether non-lecture-related activities influence learning, visual inspection of the standardised learning scores (see Fig. 1) indicated slightly higher scores for participants who did not use their mobile phone and computer during class. Statistical analysis however revealed only a small and not significant main effect for computer use on the learning score, $F(1, 121) = 0.77, p = .38, \eta^2_p = .01$. Also smartphone use did not show a significant effect on students' learning score $F(1, 121) = 3.26$, $p = .073, \eta^2_p = .026$. The interaction of computer and smartphone use did not reach significance level either, $F(1, 121) = 0.31, p = .58, \eta^2_p = .00$.

Correlational analysis revealed that the standardised learning score did neither correlate with the time students spent on the smartphone nor with the time they spent on the computer for off-task activities (see Table 6). Interestingly, the only measure that was considerably correlated with learning was the number of smartphone notifications received during the lecture. The more smartphone notifications a student received, the lower was their learning score. In addition, the number of received notifications showed a significant correlation with the time students spent on their smartphone for non-lecture related activities. In a similar vein, the number of notifications received on the computer were correlated with time spent on the computer.

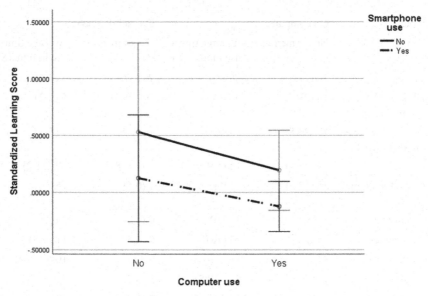

Fig. 1. Learning score (scale represents range of lowest and highest scores obtained) as a function of computer and smartphone use (errors bars representing 95% CI).

Table 6. Correlations (Pearsons's rho) between the various measures recorded in this study.

	Time on Computer	Time on Smartphone	Notifications on computer	Notifications on smartphone
	$n=125$	$n=130$	$n=94$	$n=90$
Learning Score (standardized)	-.05	-.05	-.10	-.21[*]
Time on Computer		-.03	.17[*]	.06
Time on Smartphone			-.01	.22[*]
Notifications on computer				.12

[*] p < .05,

5.3 Students' Opinions on the Use of Technology in Class

Qualitative analysis of students' answers to the open question regarding their opinion on the usage of technology for off-task activities in class revealed three main themes. These themes were consequences on learning and attention, judgement and reasons. All three themes and their subcomponents are described in the following sections.

Consequences on Learning and Attention. The theme "consequences on learning and attention" summarizes the negative consequences stemming from technology use for off-task activities in class. We identified four different types of negative effects based on students' comments: less attention/distraction, hindrance to learning, out of the loop and disturbing others. These negative effects can be found in Table 7 with their definition and an example of such a mention by a participant.

Table 7. Summary of the qualitative data analysis for the theme "detrimental effects"

Consequences on learning and attention	Definition	Example
Less attention/distraction	Distraction caused by technology/attention diverted from the course	P.10 "In general, I see such activities as a distraction to the lecture content. You can't have your attention on the lecture and your smartphone at the same time"
Hindrance to learning	Loss of information related to the course due to technology	P.29 "You should not use smartphones because you miss things"
Out of the loop	Loss of the thread of the course due to distraction caused by technology	P.112 "[…] the few minutes we spend looking at the phone makes us lose track of the class"
Disturbing others	People being disturbed due to other people's off-task activities	P.121 "Sometimes it can be annoying when someone in front of us does something else on their computer during class […]"

Judgement. The theme "judgment" summarizes any judgment given on the use of technology for off-task activities by a participant. We identified six different types of judgment: Individual responsibility, bad/to be avoided, no big deal, stay home, and lack of respect. These can be found in Table 8.

Table 8. Summary of the qualitative data analysis for the theme Judgement

Judgement	Definition	Example
Individual responsibility	Everyone is responsible for their own use and the possible consequences of such use	P.118 "Since we are all adults, it is up to each of us to decide how we want to use our time, whether we think we need to be attentive or not. [...]"
Bad/to be avoided	The use of technology for anything other than the course is bad or should be avoided during the course	P.101 "Should be avoided if something (important) is taught."
No big deal	The use of technology for off-task activities during the course is not a serious matter	P.16 "[...]. Personally, I don't think it's bad if you use your smartphone or computer for other things during class."
Useful/practical	Usefulness and convenience of the telephone or computer	P.43 "This can be handy to organize something happening later [...]"
Stay home	It is better to stay at home than to use your devices in class	P.108 "In my opinion one should concentrate mainly on the lecture, otherwise one can stay at home. [...]."
Lack of respect	Lack of respect for the professors	P.68 "I find it disrespectful to the person who teaches [...]."

Reasons. The theme "reasons" contains all explanations/justification put forward by students for using technology for off-task activities in class. We identified two subcategories of reasons: intentional reasons and unintentional reasons. Intentional reasons refer to descriptions of a clear goal or objective participants put forward to explain their usage of technology for an off-task activity. We identified two intentional reasons: to occupy oneself and important stuff (cf. Table 9). Reasons classified as unintentional reasons were descriptions with no clear objective or explanation for the off-task activity (e.g., usage because of habit, or because it is tempting). The four nonspecific reasons identified were accessibility, tempting, habit, and addictive.

Table 9. Summary of the qualitative data analysis for the theme Reasons

Intentional reasons	Definition	Example
To occupy oneself	Used to take a break, to keep busy, to pass the time	P.125 "[…] But sometimes, when the teacher is rambling on another subject, I often take the opportunity to look at my phone […]"
Important stuff	Used only for urgent or important personal matters	P.108 "[…] If you're expecting an important message, I think it's okay to use your smartphone for this"
Unintentional reasons	Definition	Example
Accessibility	Easy access to the telephone or computer (e.g., within arm's length/on the table)	P.130 "Having my computer/smartphone handy distracts my attention faster […]"
Tempting	Temptation to use the phone or computer for off-task activities	P.110 "[…]. In theory I wouldn't like to do something else, but it' s very tempting. […]"
Notifications	The display of notifications that can distract or tempt the person to use their devices for off-task activities	P. 33 "[…] especially when notifications are enabled. A notification attracts our attention and we don't pay attention to the course"
Habit	Use of technology by habit, automatic reflex	P. 96 "These are activities that I do out of habit"
Addictive	Difficult to prevent oneself from doing off-task activities on the computer or phone during lectures	P.50 "It's a harmful distraction. we do it anyway so it's addictive"

6   Discussion

Qualitative and quantitative analysis of the data revealed several interesting results. A large proportion of students engage in off-task activities during class. Taking a holistic approach, this study distinguished which devices were used for such activities. In this regard, data revealed that mobile phones were used more often for off-task activities compared to laptop computers. Furthermore, differences were found in the activities that the students performed with the devices. While mobile phones and laptop computers both were often used for communication purposes (i.e., messaging, and social media), students used their laptops during class interestingly quite often to prepare for other courses. A thematic analysis of the comments students formulated regarding their reasons and opinions with regard to off-task use of electronic devices during class revealed that there was a certain awareness of possible negative consequences of such activities on learning. Statistical analysis of learning scores revealed however that it was not the duration students engaged in off-task activities that considerably affected their learning performance but the number of notifications they received on their mobile phones.

6.1   What Students Do in Class

Results of this study reveal that the mobile phone was used by a large part of the students (72,3%) for purposes of communication and social media, during an average time of almost five minutes (in a 90-min class). Less often, students reported using their mobile phone for activities such as planning and organization, playing games, or reading news. These findings are in line results of another study showing that social media and communication are the most frequently used app types [17]. However, this other study focused on smartphone usage and did not assess typical computer use in class.

In general, the activities that students engaged in on their laptop computers varied somewhat more (as compared to the mobile phone). Although communication and social media were also often mentioned as off-task activities, this was the case only for 47% of the mentions and during over six minutes on average. Several students mentioned other activities such as preparing for another class, planning and organization, reading online magazines or news, online shopping, or even (online) gaming and streaming.

6.2   Students Opinion on What They Do in Class

The qualitative analysis of the students' answers to the questions about their opinion on off-task technologies in the classroom has revealed various interesting results. Firstly, the theme "consequences on learning and attention" shows that students seem to be aware that using technology for off-task activity may have a negative effect on learning. Additionally, students mentioned that off-task activities were distracting, and caused them to lose track of the course content. In line with findings of previous research [e.g., 12], students also noted that usage could be disturbing to fellow students and mentioned that off-task usage was only acceptable as long as it did not disturb others.

The belief that off-task activities are inappropriate in the classroom is also reflected in the theme "judgments", with mentions of off-task activities as being something bad or something that should be avoided. Some students took a more rigid stance by saying that there was no point in coming to a lecture if it was not to follow the class actively, and a few also mentioned that following off-task activities was a lack of respect towards the lecturer. However, some participants gave more moderate judgments. Some said that it was each student's individual responsibility to follow the class or not. Some students also mentioned that off-task activities were no big deal. Lastly, some students said they thought it would be very practical to do off-task activities because it would allow them to get organizational things done.

6.3   The Impact of What Students Do in Class on Learning

While many students seem to believe that off-task activities have a negative impact on learning, the analysis of the results of the learning test has shown that there is only a very small and non-significant link between time spent on off-task activities and learning performance. This seems at first to be a rather surprising result, also in view of the fact that it contradicts the results of previous research [e.g., 2, 7, 8]. However, the correlational analyses revealed that notifications are negatively linked with learning while usage time did not show an effect. This emphasizes the importance of notifications for the interplay between off-task activities and learning, corroborating results from previous research on texting in class [3, 5, 15, 29]. Those studies showed a negative link between notifications and learning, highlighting the detrimental effect of notifications in the classroom.

Several assumptions can be put forward to address these unexpected findings of a missing link between time on off-task activities and learning performance. For one, intentionality of actions might play an important role on the link between off-task activities and learning. It could be assumed that intentional shifts of attention from the class to off-task activities (i.e., to complete an assignment for another class while the professor is presenting an example for a theory the student has already understood) is less detrimental to learning compared to unintentional shifts of attention (i.e., provoked by a notification). This is because it could be assumed that intentional shifts of attention occur in situations during the lecture when a focus on the content is of lesser importance (e.g., the student has understood the topic or is bored). This is not the case for unintentional shifts of attention provoked by a notification, which can arrive at any moment during a lecture and divert the attention in phases of high importance for the understanding of the topic (e.g., when a concept is defined which is important for the understanding of the further development of the lecture). Below you can find an example of a student expressing what happens when receiving a notification:

P.33 "This is detrimental to the attention given to the lesson, especially when notifications are activated. A notification attracts our attention, and we don't pay attention to the course anymore."

However, notifications are not the only unintentional reason mentioned by students to use their devices for off-task activities. Students also mentioned their temptation, the accessibility, addiction to their devices and habit for use as unintentional reasons. All these motifs differ in one way from notifications: A notification is an external interruption. Contrary to the other unintentional reasons driving students to engage in an off-task activity, notifications are not an interruption coming from the student themself but from someone else.

Regarding the unexpectedly weak link between time spent on off-task activities and learning, the question arises as to why the results in this study differ from those presented in other work, where it has been shown that off-task activities are negatively linked with learning. Explanations may be found in differences in the methodological approach chosen in this piece of research. First, several studies reporting effects of off-task activities on learning followed an experimental design. In one study for example, students were asked to watch a lecture recorded on video. To simulate an off-task activity during a lecture, students were asked to either send a certain number of text messages or perform another task while following the recorded lecture [7, 8, 42]. In such an experimental setting, it is not the students' choice whether they pay attention to the class or not. The off-task activities represent therefore no self-interruptions, and they are also not intentional. Students are forced by an external reason (the instructions) to interrupt their learning task, which is very similar to the situation of being distracted by an external trigger such as a notification. In contrast, in the ecologically valid field study, unintentional and intentional shifts of attention can occur, which either can be triggered internally or externally. However, there have also been field studies in which a link between off-task activities and learning was shown. Most of these studies did not assess learning directly after the class but through a grade point average (GPA) score established at the end of a term [2, 10, 11]. Assessing learning at the end of the year is a considerable difference because it allows many other variables to influence the results. For example, it can be assumed that students who report to engage often in off-task activities are generally less motivated for the subject, which might influence their GPA performance.

6.4 Limitations

The results of this study must be interpreted taking into consideration several limitations. In this respect, it is worth mentioning the relatively small and homogeneous sample. Data was collected in five different psychology lectures for bachelor students (group sizes varied between 30 and 60 students) on different topics held by experienced lecturers who did not define specific rules regarding the use of technology during the class. In this context, it can be assumed that similar results might be obtained in comparable circumstances. For future research however, it might be interesting to test whether these results can be replicated for other study domains (e.g., medicine, engineering, economy), different types of courses (e.g., seminars, exercises), for different student groups (e.g., high school, undergraduate, Masters etc.), and in classes of different student numbers (e.g., results of a previous study showed that students' off-task use increased with class size [43]).

Another limitation might be the fact that students' off-task activities during the class were self-reports. Although we highlighted the anonymity of the survey as well as the importance of being honest, it cannot be excluded that social desirability could be a potential bias leading to an underestimation of the reported frequency of off-task activities. We are however not the first in this field to use self-reports to asses digital distraction in class [2, 16, 44]. Previous studies have also asked students to report on the frequency and duration of off-task activities in class. However, these studies ask for mean or typical use, and the ones that also looked at performance asked for overall GPA [2, 16, 44]. By asking students directly after a lecture about the usage and testing their knowledge, we reduce potential memory biases but also avoid potential cofounding variables such as motivation or time spent studying for exams. Non the less we are aware of potential biases due to inadequacies in estimating durations and frequencies of off-task technology use in class, although our preliminary study (cf., Sect. 4.3) showed that self-report data as collected in this study seem to be reliable. However, alternative methods of tracking this behavior (e.g., observation or automatic recording via pre-installed app) would not be possible without divulging the purpose of the study and thus significantly affect the observed behavior [45, 46]. After intensive consideration of the advantages and disadvantages of the various methodological options, we concluded that the chosen method was the best fit for the question at hand.

In terms of confounding variables, even in a controlled setting there is risk of them having an impact on results. We specifically tested for digital distraction, but participants might have been distracted by something else (e.g., a peer talking to them, daydreaming, or studying for another class with a printed document). In addition, it might have been interesting to assess the use of smartwatches in the classroom because such devices are becoming increasingly popular.

Lastly, previous research has shown that prior knowledge on the course topic might influence performance on the learning test [47, 48] or that the use of devices for off-task activities might be influenced by students' self-efficacy [48]. Therefore, it may be of interest to include such potentially confounding variables in future research.

6.5 Implications for HCI

The results reported in this ecologically valid piece of research open up exciting questions for future research. While notifications are a problem, they seem to be an easy fix; notifications can be disabled manually for each application or temporarily by another application. However, while these possibilities are already available, students don't seem to use them. For this reason, more research in this domain is important. Research either needs to focus on methods to make students more aware of the problem and how to fix it or on other alternative ways to reduce disturbance through notifications.

Some alternatives to reduce the impact of notifications have already been suggested [21, 49–51]. Such suggestions encompass, for example, to batch notifications, so users only receive them three times a day [49], as well as to only send notifications when the phone detects a break cue, something such as silence or a person standing up, that would suggest a break or a transition moment [50]. These types of suggestions should be tested in the specific context of the classroom.

7 Conclusions

To conclude, this study partially confirms results of previous research by suggesting that notifications are negatively linked with learning. In addition, it suggests that external interruptions have a stronger detrimental effect on learning than self-interruptions. This might be because students have less to no control over the interruption. When students self-interrupt, it is likely that this occurs not during the most crucial part of the class. Notifications however can divert a student's attention at every moment. So, you might not need to worry too much about your students using their devices for off-task activities during your class - just remind them to switch off notifications.

References

1. Anshari, M., Almunawar, M.N., Shahrill, M., Wicaksono, D.K., Huda, M.: Smartphones usage in the classrooms: Learning aid or interference? Educ. Inf. Technol. **22**(6), 3063–3079 (2017). https://doi.org/10.1007/s10639-017-9572-7
2. Bjornsen, C.A., Archer, K.J.: Relations between college students' cell phone use during class and grades. Sch. Teach. Learn. Psychol. **1**, 326–336 (2015). https://doi.org/10.1037/stl000 0045

3. Dietz, S., Henrich, C.: Texting as a distraction to learning in college students. Comput. Hum. Behav. **36**, 163–167 (2014). https://doi.org/10.1016/j.chb.2014.03.045
4. May, K.E., Elder, A.D.: Efficient, helpful, or distracting? A literature review of media multitasking in relation to academic performance. Int. J. Educ. Technol. High. Educ. **15**(1), 1–17 (2018). https://doi.org/10.1186/s41239-018-0096-z
5. Mendoza, J.S., Pody, B.C., Lee, S., Kim, M., McDonough, I.M.: The effect of cellphones on attention and learning: the influences of time, distraction, and nomophobia. Comput. Hum. Behav. **86**, 52–60 (2018). https://doi.org/10.1016/j.chb.2018.04.027
6. Randall, J.G., Oswald, F.L., Beier, M.E.: Mind-wandering, cognition, and performance: a theory-driven meta-analysis of attention regulation. Psychol. Bull. **140**, 1411–1431 (2014). https://doi.org/10.1037/a0037428
7. Kuznekoff, J.H., Munz, S., Titsworth, S.: Mobile phones in the classroom: examining the effects of texting, Twitter, and message content on student learning. Commun. Educ. **64**, 344–365 (2015). https://doi.org/10.1080/03634523.2015.1038727
8. Sana, F., Weston, T., Cepeda, N.J.: Laptop multitasking hinders classroom learning for both users and nearby peers. Comput. Educ. **62**, 24–31 (2013). https://doi.org/10.1016/j.compedu.2012.10.003
9. Aaron, L.S., Lipton, T.: digital distraction: shedding light on the 21st-century college classroom. J. Educ. Technol. Syst. **46**, 363–378 (2018). https://doi.org/10.1177/0047239517736876
10. Junco, R.: In-class multitasking and academic performance. Comput. Hum. Behav. **28**, 2236–2243 (2012). https://doi.org/10.1016/j.chb.2012.06.031
11. Ravizza, S.M., Uitvlugt, M.G., Fenn, K.M.: Logged in and zoned out: how laptop internet use relates to classroom learning. Psychol Sci. **28**, 171–180 (2017). https://doi.org/10.1177/0956797616677314
12. Dabbish, L., Mark, G.: Why do I keep interrupting myself?: environment, habit and self-interruption, 4 (2011)
13. Parry, D.A., le Roux, D.B.: Media multitasking and cognitive control: a systematic review of interventions. Comput. Hum. Behav. **92**, 316–327 (2019). https://doi.org/10.1016/j.chb.2018.11.031
14. Barak, M., Lipson, A., Lerman, S.: Wireless laptops as means for promoting active learning in large lecture halls. J. Res. Technol. Educ. **38**, 245–263 (2006). https://doi.org/10.1080/15391523.2006.10782459
15. Kornhauser, Z.G.C., Paul, A.L., Siedlecki, K.L.: An examination of students' use of technology for non-academic purposes in the college classroom. J. Teach. Learn. Technol. **5**, 1–15 (2016). https://doi.org/10.14434/jotlt.v5n1.13781
16. McCoy, B.: Digital distractions in the classroom phase II: student classroom use of digital devices for non-class related purposes. J. Media Educ. (2016)
17. Brennan, A., Dempsey, M.: The student voice: the students own views on smartphone usage and impact on their academic performance. Presented at the March 5 (2018). https://doi.org/10.21125/inted.2018.1836
18. Tran, J.A., Yang, K.S., Davis, K., Hiniker, A.: Modeling the engagement-disengagement cycle of compulsive phone use. In: Proceedings of the 2019 CHI Conference on Human Factors in Computing Systems - CHI 2019, Glasgow, Scotland, UK, pp. 1–14. ACM Press (2019). https://doi.org/10.1145/3290605.3300542
19. Agrawal, P., Sahana, H.S., De', R.: Digital distraction. In: Proceedings of the 10th International Conference on Theory and Practice of Electronic Governance - ICEGOV 2017, New Delhi AA, India, pp. 191–194. ACM Press (2017). https://doi.org/10.1145/3047273.3047328
20. Przybylski, A.K., Weinstein, N.: A large-scale test of the goldilocks hypothesis: quantifying the relations between digital-screen use and the mental well-being of adolescents. Psychol. Sci. (2017). https://doi.org/10.1177/0956797616678438

21. Pielot, M., Rello, L.: Productive, anxious, lonely: 24 hours without push notifications. In: Proceedings of the 19th International Conference on Human-Computer Interaction with Mobile Devices and Services - MobileHCI 2017, Vienna, Austria, pp. 1–11. ACM Press (2017). https://doi.org/10.1145/3098279.3098526

22. Sahami Shirazi, A., Henze, N., Dingler, T., Pielot, M., Weber, D., Schmidt, A.: Large-scale assessment of mobile notifications. In: Proceedings of the SIGCHI Conference on Human Factors in Computing Systems, Toronto, Ontario, Canada, pp. 3055–3064. Association for Computing Machinery (2014). https://doi.org/10.1145/2556288.2557189

23. Pielot, M., Vradi, A., Park, S.: Dismissed!: a detailed exploration of how mobile phone users handle push notifications. In: Proceedings of the 20th International Conference on Human-Computer Interaction with Mobile Devices and Services - MobileHCI 2018, Barcelona, Spain, pp. 1–11. ACM Press (2018). https://doi.org/10.1145/3229434.3229445

24. End, C.M., Worthman, S., Mathews, M.B., Wetterau, K.: Costly cell phones: the impact of cell phone rings on academic performance. Teach. Psychol. (2009). https://doi.org/10.1080/00986280903425912

25. Kushlev, K., Proulx, J., Dunn, E.W.: "Silence your phones": smartphone notifications increase inattention and hyperactivity symptoms. In: Proceedings of the 2016 CHI Conference on Human Factors in Computing Systems - CHI 2016, Santa Clara, California, US, pp. 1011–1020. ACM Press (2016). https://doi.org/10.1145/2858036.2858359

26. Mark, G., Czerwinski, M., Iqbal, S.T.: Effects of individual differences in blocking workplace distractions. In: Proceedings of the 2018 CHI Conference on Human Factors in Computing Systems - CHI 2018, Montreal QC, Canada, pp. 1–12. ACM Press (2018). https://doi.org/10.1145/3173574.3173666

27. Bowman, L.L., Levine, L.E., Waite, B.M., Gendron, M.: Can students really multitask? An experimental study of instant messaging while reading. Comput. Educ. 54, 927–931 (2010). https://doi.org/10.1016/j.compedu.2009.09.024

28. Froese, A.D., et al.: Effects of classroom cell phone use on expected and actual learning. Coll. Student J. 46, 323–332 (2012)

29. Larry D.R., Alex F.L.L. Mark, C., Nancy A.C.: An empirical examination of the educational impact of text message-induced task switching in the classroom: educational implications and strategies to enhance learning. Revista de Psicología Educativa. 17, 163–177 (2011). https://doi.org/10.5093/ed2011v17n2a4

30. Lukoff, K., Yu, C., Kientz, J., Hiniker, A.: What makes smartphone use meaningful or meaningless? In: Proceedings of the ACM on Interactive, Mobile, Wearable and Ubiquitous Technologies, vol. 2, pp. 1–26 (2018). https://doi.org/10.1145/3191754

31. Mutchler, L.A., Shim, J.P., Ormond, D.: Exploratory study on users' behavior: smartphone usage, 11 (2011)

32. Liefooghe, B., Barrouillet, P., Vandierendonck, A., Camos, V.: Working memory costs of task switching. J. Exp. Psychol. Learn. Mem. Cogn. 34, 478–494 (2008). https://doi.org/10.1037/0278-7393.34.3.478

33. Anderson, S.F.: Best (but oft forgotten) practices: sample size planning for powerful studies. Am. J. Clin. Nutr. 110, 280–295 (2019). https://doi.org/10.1093/ajcn/nqz058

34. Lakens, D.: Sample Size Justification (2021). https://psyarxiv.com/9d3yf/. https://doi.org/10.31234/osf.io/9d3yf

35. Faul, F., Erdfelder, E., Lang, A.-G., Buchner, A.: G*Power 3: a flexible statistical power analysis program for the social, behavioral, and biomedical sciences. Behav. Res. Methods 39, 175–191 (2007). https://doi.org/10.3758/BF03193146

36. Braun, V., Clarke, V.: Using thematic analysis in psychology. Qual. Res. Psychol. 3, 77–101 (2006). https://doi.org/10.1191/1478088706qp063oa

37. Ochs, C., Sauer, J.: Curtailing smartphone use: a field experiment (2020, submitted)

38. Parry, D.A., Davidson, B.I., Sewall, C.J.R., Fisher, J.T., Mieczkowski, H., Quintana, D.S.: A systematic review and meta-analysis of discrepancies between logged and self-reported digital media use. Nat. Hum. Behav. 1–13 (2021). https://doi.org/10.1038/s41562-021-011 17-5

39. Schwarz, N., Oyserman, D.: Asking questions about behavior: cognition, communication, and questionnaire construction. Am. J. Eval. **22**, 127–160 (2001). https://doi.org/10.1016/S1098-2140(01)00133-3

40. Jobe, J.B.: Cognitive psychology and self-reports: models and methods. Qual. Life Res. **12**, 219–227 (2003). https://doi.org/10.1023/A:1023279029852

41. Koo, T.K., Li, M.Y.: A guideline of selecting and reporting intraclass correlation coefficients for reliability research. J. Chiropractic Med. **15**, 155–163 (2016). https://doi.org/10.1016/j.jcm.2016.02.012

42. Flanigan, A.E., Babchuk, W.A.: Digital distraction in the classroom: exploring instructor perceptions and reactions. Teach. High. Educ. 1–19 (2020). https://doi.org/10.1080/13562517.2020.1724937

43. Zaza, C., Neiterman, E.: Does size matter? instructors' and students' perceptions of students' use of technology in the classroom. J. Inf. Technol. Educ. Res. **18**, 379–393 (2019)

44. Leysens, J.-L., le Roux, D.B., Parry, D.A.: Can i have your attention, please?: an empirical investigation of media multitasking during university lectures. In: Proceedings of the Annual Conference of the South African Institute of Computer Scientists and Information Technologists on - SAICSIT 2016, Johannesburg, South Africa, pp. 1–10. ACM Press (2016). https://doi.org/10.1145/2987491.2987498

45. Haynes, S.N., Horn, W.F.: Reactivity in behavioral observation: a review. Behav. Assess. **4**, 369–385 (1982)

46. Gittelsohn, J., Shankar, A., West Jr., K., Ram, R., Gnywali, T.: Estimating reactivity in direct observation studies of health behaviors. Hum. Organ. **56**, 182–189 (2008). https://doi.org/10.17730/humo.56.2.c7x0532q2u86m207

47. Beland, L.-P., Murphy, R.: Ill Communication: technology, distraction & student performance. Labour Econ. **41**, 61–76 (2016). https://doi.org/10.1016/j.labeco.2016.04.004

48. Lepp, A., Barkley, J.E., Karpinski, A.C.: The relationship between cell phone use and academic performance in a sample of U.S. college students. SAGE Open. **5**, 2158244015573169 (2015). https://doi.org/10.1177/2158244015573169

49. Fitz, N., Kushlev, K., Jagannathan, R., Lewis, T., Paliwal, D., Ariely, D.: Batching smartphone notifications can improve well-being. Comput. Hum. Behav. **101**, 84–94 (2019). https://doi.org/10.1016/j.chb.2019.07.016

50. Park, C., Lim, J., Kim, J., Lee, S.-J., Lee, D.: Don't bother me. I'm socializing!: a breakpoint-based smartphone notification system. In: Proceedings of the 2017 ACM Conference on Computer Supported Cooperative Work and Social Computing - CSCW 2017, Portland, Oregon, USA, pp. 541–554. ACM Press (2017). https://doi.org/10.1145/2998181.2998189

51. Shin, I., Seok, J., Lim, Y.: Ten-minute silence: a new notification UX of mobile instant messenger. In: Proceedings of the 2019 CHI Conference on Human Factors in Computing Systems, New York, NY, USA, pp. 442:1–442:13. ACM (2019). https://doi.org/10.1145/3290605.3300672

Experiencing Sound and Music Technologies

Experiences of Personal Sound Technologies

Stine S. Johansen[1]([envelope]) [iD], Peter Axel Nielsen[1] [iD], Kashmiri Stec[2] [iD],
and Jesper Kjeldskov[1] [iD]

[1] Aalborg University, Aalborg, Denmark
{stinesl,pan,jesper}cs.aau.dk
[2] Bang & Olufsen, Struer, Denmark
ksh@bang-olufsen.dk

Abstract. Listening to sound individually while in close proximity of
other people is increasingly enabled by a range of technologies. One still
in development is sound zone technology that aims to provide personal
sound without headphones or other wearable speakers. User-oriented
studies in the area of personal listening primarily emerge from the fields
of acoustics and sound engineering but are gaining increasing interest
within HCI research. In this paper, we present a study investigating the
experience of personal sound in relation to different types of situations
and personal sound technologies. Our findings show strategies for adjusting personal sound and social interaction, descriptions of sound quality
in relation to sound and situation types, and insights into participants'
experiences of awareness using personal sound technology. The paper
contributes with a thematic characterisation of this type of technology,
serving as a foundation for further studies. This furthermore initiates a
discussion on personal sound technology and soundscape composition in
how situation types affect which sounds to include or exclude, and when.

Keywords: Soundscape · Sound zone · Personal sound · Headphone

1 Introduction

In this paper, we are concerned with the experience of personal sound technologies. A number of technologies have been developed to provide users with
personal listening experiences. Some fit in or around the user's ears, some are
worn on the user's neck, and some are stationary speaker systems attached to
walls or ceilings. One type that is receiving increasing amounts of attention is
sound zone technology [1]. Sound zone technology poses new opportunities for
users to modify what they are listening to where they no longer have to wear
headphones as a prevention from disturbing other people or when wanting to listen to sound privately [12]. Previous work has shown that wearing headphones
has disadvantages such as decreasing the ease of social interaction and becoming uncomfortable when worn for an extended period of time [11]. Therefore,

© IFIP International Federation for Information Processing 2021
Published by Springer Nature Switzerland AG 2021
C. Ardito et al. (Eds.): INTERACT 2021, LNCS 12933, pp. 523–541, 2021.
https://doi.org/10.1007/978-3-030-85616-8_30

personal listening using sound zones presents an attractive alternative. In the vision for sound zones, multiple users inhabiting the same physical space can listen to sounds individually without interference between zones, meaning that users in one sound zone are not disturbed by sound from other sound zones [14]. From a user's perspective, this means that they can experience an individually controlled 'soundscape' within a shared space [12]. With soundscape, we refer to the entire acoustic environment as perceived by a person [13].

Previous research elaborates current usage patterns and points toward future wishes for personal sound technology [9]. The relation between an individual and the peripheral environment, including other people nearby, is usually the center of those discussions. Future technological development in this direction includes soundscape filtering strategies that are contextually adapted such as allowing certain kinds of interruptions and masking irrelevant information. An overlap can be seen between those suggested tools and sound zones; both are parts of a broader group that can be called personal sound technologies.

With this paper, we expand on what previous research has called the *phenomenon of personal sound curation* [9]; i.e., the modifications users can apply to their soundscape and a characterization of the resulting experience. We present findings from an investigation into how people use personal sound technologies in different situations, and how we can enable them to talk about the way the technology fits into their daily lives. While technical challenges still exist on the path towards physical spaces with multiple sound zones and limited interference between zones, other technologies enabling personal listening experiences exist and are increasing in variety. Examples include active noise cancellation (ANC) in headphones (such as Bose QC35 or the Sony WH-1000 series) and wearable speakers (such as Bose SoundWear Companion or Zulu Alpha). Currently, personal sound is achievable with these technologies, but at the expense of social interaction, listening in private, or avoiding disturbing other nearby persons. Sound zone technology poses a potential solution to this but with currently limited setups in labs, it is not yet possible to study how. Therefore, it is necessary to create a frame of reference for the experience of sound zone technology by other means to steer future research. We do this by providing a preliminary set of characteristics that describe that experience. Our findings furthermore show that these characteristics are experienced differently in different situations.

The outset of our study is three situations where participants are present in a physical space with personal and shared sound. While wanting a personal listening experience, the social aspects of the situation might change. This leads us to the research question: How are personal sound technologies experienced in various social situations with mixed personal and shared soundscapes?

In answering this, we make two main contributions. First, we provide insights into the experience of personal sound for different situations and sound types. Our findings show different strategies participants devise to deal with a complex soundscape, both for adjusting their own personal sound and for communicating with other participants. They also provide insights into qualities related to sound and situation types as well as participants' experience of awareness while using personal sound technologies. Second, we provide a set of future directions for conducting user studies related to personal listening experiences.

2   Related Work

In order to clarify the foundation on which we can investigate and characterize the experience of personal sound technology, we outline current work on personal sound technologies, including sound zones. Our general interest is to put sound zone technology into the broader frame of personal sound technology. We also outline existing research on the relation between soundscape and perceived situation appropriateness as a basis for understanding elements of situations that affect the experience of particular sounds. With this previous research, we distinguish between activities and situations. Multiple activities can co-occur in one situation.

2.1   Personal Sound

Within the field of sound studies, Bull analysed the use of the Walkman [2] as an early example of a music player that provided a private listening experience in public places. This was enabled by its portability. In more recent years, noise cancellation has enabled users to control their soundscape to a higher degree. Previous research shows that in order to do so, users employ a number of different strategies, such as adapting the physical fit of the technology or turning up the volume of the personal sound to drown out environmental noise [9]. These findings are based on focus group interviews conducted by showing staged video footage of a person using a set of headphones. The focus group then discussed their own use of similar technologies. In a model derived from the results, Haas et al. describe aspects of personal soundscape curation which includes *intervening conditions*. With this, they refer to social protocols and hierarchies, e.g., the effect of wearing headphones on how they are perceived by other people. Other studies are concerned with users' isolation from the outside world by for example exploring warning systems for headphones to prevent traffic accidents [18].

2.2   Sound Zones

In some cases, users do not want to wear headphones, or they are inhibited from doing so, but personal sound might still be desired. One example of this is a family sharing a living room, where the acoustic environment can become chaotic in the event of everyone engaging with their own activity such as playing a video game and listening to the radio. The family members might want to listen to only their own sound but still be able to interact with each other. Another example is museum exhibitions, where a guest might want to listen to the sound from one exhibit without disturbing other guests at other exhibits. At the same time, they also sometimes want to interact with others at the museum. To solve this, speaker systems where sound is directed towards a predefined area have been developed. These systems aim for total individual control of particular sounds. A system known as a parametric array uses ultrasound waves which become audible through nonlinear media [15]. Such systems, however, perform poorly for low-frequency reproduction of sound, so other methods for directing sound have been explored. One example is parabolic speakers, e.g., Focus Point FP6030 by Soundtube, where sound is played into a parabolic reflector aimed towards one or more target listeners. SpatialSound Wave by Fraunhofer IDMT is another related example where several sound objects can be positioned in a physical space to give a user the impression that they are in a wanted position in an acoustic scene.

While different methods for implementing sound zone systems have been proposed [8, 14], in conceptual terms, they aim for a similar result. The vision of sound zone technology, as it is currently framed, holds that users can position a number of sound zones in a physical space which allows them to share the space, listen to individual sounds and not wear headphones [1]. This suggests that might be expected in the future when the technology is commercialized, including a possibility for social interaction, low intrusiveness from other sound zones, and increased awareness of the peripheral environment. Awareness does not necessarily entail attention, meaning that sounds from the environment might not necessarily become intrusive. With sound zone systems, users can experience an acoustic environment as they would without headphones but still receive personal sound. In this way, the environment is made up of foreground and background sounds which users can shift their attention between. Different use cases for sound zone systems described in previous work [11] show differences in the way the resulting soundscape is composed. In some cases, users might want complete silence, such as when using noise cancelling headphones, and in other cases, they might want a private listening experience while also hearing the environment around them. In this way, sound zone technology can be viewed as varying forms of interventions into a soundscape [12].

2.3   Soundscape and Situations

We address the relation between personal sound and sound zones as outlined above with research on soundscape and, more specifically, how the experience relates to situations. We refer to the widely recognised definition of soundscape by Schafer as "...the auditory equivalent of a landscape" [16], while also acknowledging later clarifications of the definition that emphasize soundscape as something that is perceived by persons rather than only a physical phenomenon [4]. In other words, the understanding of soundscape behind the study presented here is the total acoustic environment as perceived by participants. Furthermore, Schafer describes a soundscape as composed of different types of sounds. Some reside in the background as 'keynote' sounds while others perform a 'signal' function and capture the attention of listeners. In much later research, Bull similarly described that sound does not possess the same quality as visual objects that can be attended to separate from each other [2]. As such, listeners can attend to particular sounds consciously, but their experience of individual sounds is shaped by all present sounds. Listening to music can add specific meaning to a situation [6], and this has fostered a development of tools to curate listening experiences. Previous work within HCI has investigated social practices emerging around digital music in homes [10]. Findings include a preference for digital music rather than listening from CDs or records. This enabled new ways of listening to music such as curating shared playlists and discovering new music on web-based platforms.

In a previous study on the relation between soundscape and situations, participants listened to outdoor recordings and were asked to rate the appropriateness of four predefined activities in relation to the sound [13]. Results showed that participants associated particular soundscapes with particular activities. For example, listening to sounds of single vehicles, participants rated bicycling as an inappropriate activity. The authors conclude that a soundscape can afford a certain set of actions. They also found that the activity with which the listener is engaged affects which sounds in the soundscape are paid attention to. Another study, based on questionnaire surveys in urban squares, similarly showed that preferences for particular sounds were dependent on respondents' use of the physical space [17]. At the same time, the soundscape of a physical space influenced how the space was used. Findings further included a tendency that preference for or annoyance with a particular sound depended on the situation in which the sound emerged. An outdoor concert might be perceived positively and attract people whereas the same music played from a store would elicit annoyance. Another aspect of soundscape evaluation is participants' expectations of how a place sounds. Previous research uses Truax's concept 'soundscape competence' to detail how prior experience affects behaviour as a result of characteristics of the soundscape [5]. With soundscape competence, the authors refer to a relation between a sound and the meaning the listener attaches to it. When in a familiar place, persons expect certain sound sources, a certain level of control, particular behaviour from nearby persons, etc.

With these studies in mind, activity and situation are central elements to evaluating technology which modifies users' perceived soundscape. The situations defined for a study of personal sound technologies necessarily affect participants' perception of the appropriateness of specific sounds. In other words, even though the study presented here is focused on experience of soundscapes, we infer from previous work that participants will weigh characteristics of the technologies delivering parts of the soundscape according to the situation they engage with.

3   Mapping Personal Sound Technologies

Personal sound technology is a term which spans across multiple speaker and headphone types. Common for all of them is the fact that they allow for a user to listen to something individually. This distinguishes personal sound technology from personalized sound. Where personalized sound connotes that a sound itself can be customized to each user, personal sound connotes a user controlling one or more sounds.

There are differences, though, in how technologies provide personal sound as detailed in Sect. 2. Some are worn on the user's body while some are wall-hanging speaker systems. While headphones generally provide users with options for cancelling or opening up to sounds from the physical environment, this might also soon be possible with speaker systems. Therefore, in order to investigate the experience of listening using personal sound technology in different situations, we first present a mapping of how these types of technologies relate to each other. This provides a systematic overview that we will later use as part of framing the experience of sound zone technology.

Figure 1 shows an illustration of how different types of personal sound technology relates to the user's peripheral acoustic environment. For each technology, the user receives a mix between reproduced sound and environment sounds. The left emphasizes the personal sound. The middle equally emphasizes personal sound and peripheral environment, but under the conditions of reproduction of the environment. Finally, the right also emphasises personal sound and peripheral environment, but with nothing covering the user's ears. For each type, we provide an example of a type of headphone or speaker that accomplishes the particular mix between reproduced sound and environment sound.

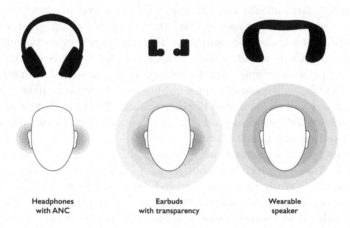

Headphones with ANC   **Earbuds with transparency**   **Wearable speaker**

Fig. 1. Each type of technology relates the user to the peripheral acoustic environment differently. Active noise cancellation headphones: only personal sound. Earbuds: personal sound and environment sounds through microphone. Body-worn speaker: personal sound and environment sounds at equal level.

With sound zone technology, the aim is to allow users to modify their soundscape to include or exclude particular sounds as well as limiting the area within which the included sounds can be heard. Different personal sound technologies share functionalities such as creating an individual listening experience, but as we illustrate in Fig. 1, they also result in different relations between the user and their environment. Sound zone technology could be constructed with similar different functionalities, motivated through different use situations [11]. Therefore, characterizing the resulting experience of using different personal technologies is useful as a reference for eventually characterizing the resulting experience(s) of sound zone technology.

3.1   Active Noise Cancellation

On-ear headphones or in-ear earbuds with Active Noise Cancellation (ANC) enable users to only listen to the sound played through the speakers. When the noise cancellation is activated, all sounds from the environment will, to some extent, be cancelled. Loud, high frequency sounds can still be heard in some cases. In relation to sound zones and personal listening, ANC headphones allow users to both isolate themselves from sounds played by other users and restrict their own chosen sound to be played within a private hearing range.

3.2   Transparency

Open earbuds allow users to listen to sound privately while still being able to hear sounds from the peripheral environment. In these cases, users are provided with a 'transparency' or 'hear through' mode which, instead of cancelling sounds, reproduces sounds from the environment. A microphone attached to the headphones records environmental sounds which are then played back to the user in real time. In relation to Fig. 1, they reproduce all sounds from the environment but, from the users' perspective, might also reproduce environmental sound recorded and composed prior to listening.

3.3   Wearable Speakers

Wearable speakers are an alternative to headphones and earbuds that allow for personal sound to be reproduced in a larger area than the users' ears. Users wear the speaker on their shoulders, and two speakers embedded on either side play sounds in an upwards direction. A waveguide is implemented between the speakers to enhance the sound through air pressure. These neck-worn speakers offer users a semi-private listening experience as other people in the same environment may be able to hear the sound from the speakers as well.

4   Method

Our research question to address in this study was: How are personal sound technologies experienced in various social situations with mixed personal and shared soundscapes? To investigate this, we had two particular aims: (1) gain insights into the use and experience of various personal sound technologies according to different situation types, and (2) find out how those technologies affect potential users' experience of quality and what quality encompasses. This entailed considerations into how we could enable participants to talk about the experience. Answering the research question, we conducted a qualitative study with emphasis on participants' experience of their soundscape in relation to different situations. In the study, we equipped participants with headphones or speakers to mimic the three relationships between user and environment described in Fig. 1. We also defined three situations in which participants increasingly need to engage with each other to explore the experience with different demands to their attention. In the following section, we provide details about participants, chosen headphones and speakers, and procedure of the study.

4.1 Participants

As we are concerned with social aspects of personal listening experiences, we conducted the study with two participants at a time to also allow for a discussion on how those technologies affect the social interaction that could occur in users' daily lives. We recruited 12 participants in pairs who knew each other prior to the study. We did so to limit the amount of time necessary for participants to feel comfortable talking to each other. Table 1 presents an overview of participants' age, identified gender, and relationship with each other. We sought differences in age and types of relationships in order to be inclusive to potential differences as relationship type potentially affects the experience of a situation and how participants choose to interact with each other. Only one pair had a particular interest in sound technology (Pair 1). Both expressed interest in buying headphones and speakers of a high quality. For Pairs 3 and 4, all four participants were regular users of one of our chosen technologies. None of the participants were familiar with sound zone technology.

Table 1. Study participants.

Pair #	Participants	Relation
1	Male (28) and female (26)	Romantic partners (7 years)
2	Male (38) and male (54)	Romantic partners (6 years)
3	Female (30) and female (28)	Coworkers (2 years)
4	Male (31) and male (31)	Coworkers (3 years)
5	Female (26) and male (26)	Friends (2 years)
6	Male (29) and male (32)	Coworkers (2 years)

4.2 Technology

We chose three technologies that each unfold an instance visualized in Fig. 1 corresponding to sound zone characteristics. These have assumed differences on three parameters: Participants' ability to (1) interact with each other, (2) hear the other participants' sound, and (3) hear sounds from the environment. We also chose technologies with good reproduced sound quality based on high and consistent frequency and dynamic range. This resulted in using the Bose QuietComfort 35, Beoplay E8 2.0, and Bose SoundWear Companion Speaker.

4.3 Procedure

We conducted the study in a room with a reverberation time matching the average domestic living-room [7]. We did so to match the physical setting with the situations presented to participants. The study was carried out in three parts. Each part investigated a particular type of technology in relation to three situations. For each part, the two participants wore the same set of headphones, earbuds, or wearable speakers. We counterbalanced the order of situations and technologies between each pair of participants. We defined the situations from two dimensions. First, they should have varying levels of necessary interaction between participants. Second, they should require varying levels of attention from participants. With this in mind, the situations were defined as follows: (a) Draw from a picture (2 min), (b) Play a specified card game (3 min), and (c) Plan a trip to a specified location (3 min).

Participants participated in the first situation individually. We asked them to redraw an image in front of them, thereby lessening the required attention compared to a situation where they were asked to draw from imagination. For the second situation, we asked them to play a card game they were already familiar with. This allowed us to investigate a situation where participants would interact with each other but they were not required to talk. For the third situation, we asked participants to plan a trip to a location they knew. This required them to both think about the elements of planning a trip as well as talk to each other. The inclusion of intense, social situations for all technologies was made to enable participants to discuss the different experiences between situations. The physical setup for each situation can be seen in Fig. 2.

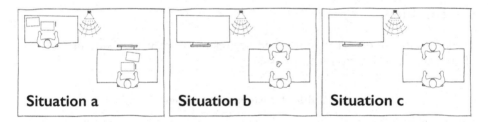

Fig. 2. The physical setup for each situation. Situation A was individual, and situations B and C were social. A speaker provided environment sound.

When participants had engaged with the specified situation, a follow-up, semi-structured interview was conducted. In this interview, we focused on clarifying different elements of the experience, specifically regarding (1) Sound quality, (2) Interacting with each other, (3) Attention to background sound, and (4) Disturbances, but with potential additional comments. We asked participants to reflect upon and describe their experience of each of these topics. The interviews took shape from participants' immediate responses to the initial topics.

Composition of Study Soundscape. Present in the study was each participant's personal sound, a kitchen environment sound played from a speaker on a wall of the room, participants' voices, and sounds from when participants or the facilitator moved. Together, this made up a complex soundscape, experienced by participants as a whole [2], which we then sought to dissect in the interviews. While participants wore the same type of technology in each part, they listened to different types of sound. One participant listened to a podcast featuring only speech by a male and a female voice, continued throughout the study. The other participant could choose a music playlist of three songs from a list of ten genres.

An issue with assessing the quality of an experience of a soundscape is that the assessment itself makes participants draw attention to sounds they would not necessarily have noticed consciously otherwise [4]. For that reason, we did not reveal the presence of sounds such as the background sound by asking about them directly. We counterbalanced the order of the technologies.

Data Analysis. The interviews were transcribed and analysed thematically [3]. Based on the mapping in Sect. 3, we expected findings concerning themes of 'personal sound', 'social interaction', 'awareness', and 'sound quality'. In the first iteration, we coded the data according to these themes as well as emerging themes. This resulted in 43 unique codes that were hierarchically organised into 8 themes. Following a second iteration, we consolidated two themes, 'awareness' and 'intrusiveness', which contained similar analytical points. Two themes, 'error' and 'setup', had very few occurrences and did not offer insights into the research question of this paper and were therefore disregarded.

5 Findings

Table 2 shows an overview of our findings related to characteristics of each type of speaker emerging from the analysis.

Table 2. Overview of findings.

Characteristic	ANC headphones	Open earbuds	Wearable speaker
Personal sound	+ Enabling immersion	− Volume	+ Drowning out environment − Focus on personal sound
Social interaction	+ Hand gestures − Dialogue	+ Dialogue − Sound over participant	+ Dialogue with volume control
Sound quality	+ Reproduction	− Reproduction	− Disturbing sound types
Awareness	+ Personal sound − Environment	+ Environment	+ Other participant
Preference	+ Individual activities − Social activities	+ Limited social interaction	+ Awareness − Comfort

5.1 Personal Sound

Participants modified their personal sound for two purposes: (1) Drowning out environment sounds and (2) achieving higher immersion. We found that they adapted the use particularly of the ANC headphones and the wearable speakers. For the earbuds, participants in five of the pairs expressed that they played the music or podcast at an undesirably low volume, but the technology did not allow them to increase it to a satisfactory level.

Modifying personal sound mainly had to do with participants' engagement with the individual situation (A). This occurred in instances where participants increased the volume of their personal sound for situation A, the individual drawing situation, but with the purpose of either supporting immersion or of drowning out other sounds. For the ANC headphones, a participant stated that he could increase the volume seeing as social interaction was not necessary. Another instance occurred for the wearable where the participant stated: *"When you [the other participant] moved over and started drawing, I turned up mine to the point where I could no longer hear yours."* (M2, Pair 4).

The personal sound sometimes affected participants' engagement with a situation by supporting it. One participant described the ANC headphones as built for shutting out the world. He elaborates: *"I really think these allow you to immerse yourself in stuff, because anything else is completely shut out."* (M1, Pair 6). In this case, the composition of the soundscape is described as very simple and that enables the participant to focus on what they are doing.

These findings regarding personal sound show that the personal sound or use of the technology gets modified according to what participants wish to attend to during a situation; that is, each within their own soundscape.

5.2 Social Interaction

Generally, participants sought to complete the descriptions of the situations, but they did so using different strategies and with different levels of communication according to both situation type and technology type. These findings concern (1) the ways participants chose to interact with each other given the individual soundscapes and the situations of the study, and (2) how use of the speaker technology was modified to ease this interaction.

For the earbuds, most participants described that they were able to speak to each other when engaged with situation C in which dialogue was necessary. However, some sought to use other strategies for communicating with each other for situation B where they interacted with each other, but dialogue was not required. One participant described her use of eye contact with the other participant as a way to negotiate the rules of the card game.

Similarly, for the ANC headphones, a participant stated for situation B that: *"You could just talk with your hands."*. He continues to say for situation A: *"You couldn't do that for the first situation."*. Not only did the participant choose to discontinue speaking with the other participant, he also chose to turn up the volume of his personal sound when situation B did not require any dialogue between participants.

As expected, the noise cancelling function of these headphones made dialogue difficult for participants. Elaborating on her experience, one participant described that, to her, this type of headphone would mainly be useful when alone. Furthermore, several participants either lowered the volume of their sound or raised their voice to be able to speak to each other. In these instances, participants prioritised being able to have a dialogue with each other over listening to their personal sound.

Participants in three pairs described speaking to each other as easy with the wearable speakers. They utilized the possibility to do so for both situation B and C which stands in contrast to the earbuds where participants could speak to each other but primarily only did so when necessary in situation C. Deciding to speak meant that participants typically chose to focus on the social interaction with the other participant as opposed to listening to their own sound even when the situation did not require them to do so. One participant said the following in relation to the card game (situation B) and the wearable speaker: *"It became an entirely different kind of game, because we were actually able to discuss whether or not this and that was right... I actually experienced looking at you [other participant] more instead being completely closed off."* (F2, Pair 3).

For easing social interaction, we found three instances where a participant turned off their sound or removed the ANC headphones when engaged with situation C in which participants jointly planned an imaginary trip. One participant in Pair 2 elaborated on this, saying that he did not see any benefit of listening to music while talking to the other participant. In other words, participants adapted their use of the technology to fit the social context of situation C when they could. In contrast, when they were wearing the earbuds and could not turn up the volume, they expressed a desire for higher volume of the personal sound, thereby placing lower priority on the social interaction.

In summary of our findings related to social interaction, participants would mainly choose to speak when possible; thereby prioritizing the other participant over sound. In some instances, participants developed other non-verbal strategies to successfully communicate with each other and prioritised the sound over the other participant.

5.3   Sound Quality

Sound quality was described by participants in terms of (1) sound reproduction and (2) type of sound. Only participants with a high interest in HiFi and speaker technology were affected in the way that the sound quality impacted their ability to focus on the sound. When listening to the podcast, one participant in Pair 1 said that the high sound quality of the ANC headphones helped him better focus on simultaneous activities in the situation; i.e. listening to the contents of the podcast and having a conversation with the other participant.

The way participants referred to their personal sound changed. Regarding the earbuds, one participant initially described her sound as a news podcast, stating that she was able to speak with the other participant. However, a few minutes later in the interview, the participant said: *"There shouldn't be any noise when you have to talk to each other"* (F2, Pair 3). Another participant provided the following comment about environment sounds while wearing the earbuds: *"There was a lot of background noise with an almost metallic timbre. I mean, you can hear a sort of input when people are talking. But with a metallic timbre, and I almost think, for example for the sound of putting the pen on the table, that it became louder and more distorted in a way. And that really disturbed the music."* (F1, Pair 1).

Our findings show that participants do not only refer to sound quality in terms of personal sound reproduction. They also relate quality to sound type. Determining the quality of what they listen to is dependent on these two factors.

5.4 Awareness

Our findings show that awareness of sounds was described by participants in (1) positive, indifferent, and negative ways based on how the personal sound and environmental sounds affected them, and (2) how it related to the situations with which they were engaged. The descriptions referred to awareness of both personal sound and background sounds, and how it was dependent on the particular combination of sounds. Different examples of how one type of sound demanded more attention than the other were given. This happened whether the demanding sound was their own or the other participant's.

Participants experienced that their level of tolerance changed according to type of situation. During situation A, they were aware of but not disturbed by the other participant's sound, but it became demanding during social situations for the wearable speaker. Described by one participant: *"For this [individual situation], you are only using visuals and your motor functions, but you don't have to hear anything, whereas if we are having a conversation about [trip destination] or [card game], our auditory sensory system is already divided."* (M1, Pair 6).

In some instances, participants intentionally ignored sounds. One participant described a situation where she felt in control of her attention in relation to her own personal sound; in this case a podcast: *"...if it had been someone yelling, or if it had been a voice I recognised, then I would have been disturbed. Then I would have directed my attention... Because I could hear it. But actually it wasn't interesting enough, so I just let it slide to the background."* (F2, Pair 3). In this instance, the participant is aware of an unwanted sound, but it is not intrusive to the experience. One participant commented about the podcast: *"It was easy to follow what they were saying. Even without focusing on it while simultaneously doing activities that demanded attention."* (M1, Pair 1). This instance also describes the personal sound as unintrusive, but not without the participant attending to it.

As expected, no participants noted any environment sounds for the ANC headphones. This was, unexpectedly, also the case for the wearable speakers. For the earbuds, some participants described the sounds from the peripheral environment as intrusive to their ability to listen to the personal sound. One participant explained: *"I didn't really focus on the quality of the music, but rather on anything else going on in the room, because I actually think that was louder. And also the sound of my own breathing. Suddenly, I sounded like Darth Vader while wearing them."* (F1, Pair 1). The other participant in Pair 1 continued: *"All the input that you're making gets transferred back to you through the headset which then plays it even louder."* (M1, Pair 1). Only one participant noticed the background sound that was added to the environment through a speaker. The participant mentioned this in the interview of the third part of the study but added that as soon as she noticed the sound consciously, she was also able to remember the sound being played previously.

These examples show that personal sound and environment sounds can both demand attention or be ignored. In some instances, such as the one described by M1 in Pair 1, the personal sound can be perceived as an activity in parallel to situations A, B, and C, whereas in other instances the personal sound resides on the same level as environment sounds.

5.5   Preference

Preference for particular speaker technologies depended more on the situation than technical characteristics. We found that preference was either expressed in relation to (1) situations, (2) the type of personal sound participants listened to, or (3) the comfort of the technology. One participant prioritised his preference the following way: *"I would say the [brand] over-ears for drawing. That way you could concentrate on that. And for talking, that neck thing."* (M1, Pair 5). This statement confirmed the expectations of how the technologies would perform in relation to individual versus social situations. Some participants even preferred noise cancellation over being able to talk to the other participant. In one instance, a participant experienced that she could achieve a satisfactory level of communication with the other participant using hand gestures, making her prioritise the comfortable wear of the ANC headphones over interaction with dialogue. Some also preferred the ANC headphones due to comfort, practicality of wear, and sound quality. Other participants' preferences differed from that.

One participant described his least favourite technology in relation to the type of sound he was listening to (a podcast): *"It wasn't that I felt distracted by sounds in the room, but because someone was talking, you could doubt whether it was someone from the outside or if it was something I heard in my ear. For that kind [podcast], I don't think those [earbuds] are good."* (M2, Pair 2). For other participants, the fact that the earbuds reproduced environmental sounds made them prefer these above other speaker technologies. One participant had experienced that, for the individual situation, the earbuds had enclosed her ears but for the social situations, she was able to focus on talking to the other participant.

The wearable speakers were preferred by some participants as a speaker. A number of participants described that they would use those as a regular speaker and not for personal sound. One participant, however, preferred the wearable speakers for the way they allow listeners to be open to the peripheral environment: *"I actually think I liked the neck thing best for most things. I think it was nice, because I also felt that those [ANC headphones] are really closed off. That makes the neck thing nice; the fact that it's more open."* (F1, Pair 5).

Our findings reveal that participants' preference is mainly determined by the situation they were engaged with. For personal sound technologies, the social aspect of the situation is especially essential.

6   Discussion

The aim of this study has been to investigate the experience of personal sound technologies in various situations with mixed personal and shared soundscapes. The findings show that the three technologies provide users with very different experiences. These findings are summarised in Table 2. The juxtaposition in the table allows us to compare and contrast characteristics between technologies.

Some of the differences between technologies that participants experienced confirmed expectations from previous research. Our findings show a trade-off in the awareness of environmental sound and the quality of the personal sound. When users cannot remove environmental sound, they are subjected to different types sound that can be perceived as disturbing. When isolated from the environment to a larger extent, the load on their awareness is minimised, but they also lack the ability to speak and carry out social activities in a situation. This confirms the mapping in Fig. 1.

6.1   Studying the Experience of Personal Sound

Our findings create a frame of reference for future work on personal sound technology. Achieving a personal listening experience can be done using a number of different technologies where sound zone technology is one potential option in the future. While these technologies are different, the experience can be studied from the same characteristics.

The vision of sound zone technology is to provide an experience of personal sound in which a user can choose which sounds should be present in their soundscape. Based on previous work describing what sound zone systems aim to offer users, cf. Sect. 2, and our findings, we can define five general characteristics of personal sound technology which are achieved in different ways by current products. First, sound zones offer users personal sound; i.e., a private listening experience [1,8]. Second, sound zones allow social interaction [11]. Third, the quality of the reproduced sound should be comparable to that which is reproduced through headphones [16]. Fourth, they allow users to be aware of their peripheral environment since they do not require headphones [11]. And finally, preference for these characteristics could be dependent on the context of use [4].

Using the technologies in our study as a proxy for sound zones, we illustrate the potential relations between user, environment, and other people as a continuum in Fig. 3. On the continuum, three instances are marked. In simple terms, these represent the extent to which the user can hear the peripheral environment. In more complex terms, they can be described by unfolding general characteristics of personal sound technology. One aim of the study presented here was to make such a characterisation. Rather than asking how much of the sound from the outside environment to let in to a user's personal listening experience, we expand the discussion on which sounds to include or exclude, as well as when. This is achieved through the themes of our findings.

A question following the representation in Fig. 3 is: In which ways are the chosen technologies representative of sound zone technology? Participants in the

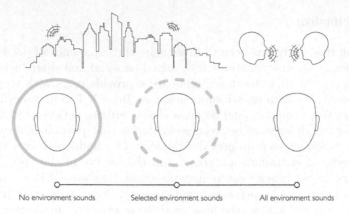

Fig. 3. The relation between user and environment, illustrated as a cityscape and dialogue, on a continuum from closed to open. Three instances are marked, representing no environment sounds, selected environment sounds, and all environment sounds.

study had to wear all three types of technologies which would not be the case for sound zone technology. However, each technology represents a different way sound zones could be envisioned and understood in terms of how closed off from the environment users would be. As such, our findings have provided a richer picture of how sound zones can be used in setups for personal listening.

The earbuds represent a place on the sound zone continuum where some sounds from the environment are selected, and some are not. In our study, the earbuds reproduced all environment sounds which could have had an effect since participants did not experience a choice between wanted and unwanted sounds from the environment. Being presented with that choice can lead users to become aware of sounds they would not otherwise have noticed as previously described in [16], cf. Sect. 2. Adding to that, our findings showed that except for one, participants were not aware of the background sound being played even though they were physically able to hear it. For future research, it would be interesting to provide users with a selection of background sounds to further study how their own choices on composing the resulting soundscape affects their awareness. Furthermore, valuable insights into how the background sound is delivered can be gained. For example, background sound played through headphones or earbuds might demand a different level of awareness compared to background sound played from a speaker located in a different position than the user.

6.2   Composing for Shared and Individual Soundscapes

Headphones modify users' perceived soundscape by introducing additional sound or removing sound from the environment. The three speaker types in our study enabled participants to modify the soundscape in different ways by either removing, reproducing, or allowing environment sounds. We observed how participants behaved during situations and discussed with them how the speakers had affected their behaviour. Our findings show that participants' ability to modify their soundscape affected what they wanted to achieve in certain situations. This adds to previous research describing the relation between soundscape and sound zone technology as an intervention [12].

Haas et al. found and described that users sometimes want to modify their soundscape by removing intrusive sounds when engaged in a situation [9], cf. Sect. 2. In their study, users described noise cancelling headphones as feeling unnatural and that, in many cases, they did not want complete silence. Therefore, they often filled the silence by playing music or other sounds that would be non-intrusive. The participants in our study were listening to sound but had the ability to turn it off. As such, silence was not the point of departure for the participants, and they had to make a conscious decision to turn off the sound or lowering the volume. Some participants chose to do that, and with our findings we add to the study by Haas et al. by showing that personal sound has different purposes such as enabling immersion in a specific activity and drowning out sounds from the peripheral environment.

In our findings, some participants were able to consciously filter out unwanted sounds, and they explained that the situation and surroundings are factors when they determine what is intrusive and what is not. This confirms previous research on urban soundscapes that showed a relationship between prior experience and expectations for which sounds should be present in a specific place [4,15]. Our findings add to this by demonstrating that, for personal sound technology, participants' filtering abilities are determined by the situations they are actively engaged in and are not limited to the physical space. This was also true for the cases where participants could not filter out unwanted sounds. The same sound could be referred to as music and noise. The situation affected participants' ability to filter out sound; in some cases, this was supported and in others, it was not. Participants might have had expectations to which sounds would be present in the room, resulting in a certain perception of the soundscape.

Our study included both individual and social elements to mimic a situation in which the level of social interaction changes. Compared to the study by Haas et al. [9], we show how these types of technologies fit into a social situation where usage is not only based on activities in which the user is alone or surrounded by strangers with whom they would not usually interact. In a domestic context, users can be surrounded by other people and, for that reason, do not necessarily want to be closed off completely to the peripheral environment. Haas et al. found that headphones signified to other people that the user does not want to be approached. Our findings showed this was different for wearable speaker technology. For example, one participant looked at the other participant more when the technology allowed her to hear the participant and the environment more. While some participants lowered their volume to better focus on speaking to the other participant, no one intended for their own sound to be intrusive to the other participant. As expected, for the individual situation, participants opted to turn up the volume of their own sound or tune out the sound.

Furthermore, the tolerance participants have for certain sounds changes according to situations. Participants defined some situations to be common experiences meant to be shared, and this resulted in a lower tolerance of sounds that make it difficult to interact verbally with each other, such as dialogue. The level of tolerance was also described in relation to how the sounds fit together. With this insight, we suggest that how closed a personal sound technology is to the environment should be determined by the type of sound listened to by individual users. This adds to previous research on appropriateness of activities [13] with the element of personal sound and importance of whether or not the situation was social. Our findings suggest that activity appropriateness is not only determined by the soundscape but also by engagement with other people.

The setup did not always represent a real situation. This was an expected comment due to the characteristics of the technologies which make it more or less inviting to speak to other people. While this conflict enabled participants to talk about what a real situation might look like, a direction for future work is to conduct similar studies in environments with which participants are familiar, such as their own homes or work places. This will allow for other situations that relate to a specific context for using the technology. It will also provide insights into the effect of expected and unexpected sounds on the experience of using personal sound technology.

7   Conclusion

In this paper, we have presented a qualitative study investigating experiences of personal sound technologies to make a frame of reference for future studies. We chose three technologies that relate the user to the environment and other people differently by either being closed or open. The result is a thematic characterisation of these speaker technologies based on users' experience of personal sound, social interaction, sound quality, awareness of peripheral environment, and preference determined from situation type.

As more variations of headphones and speakers for personal sound are developed, research on the effect on social interaction and how that can be supported by these technologies becomes increasingly important. The findings presented here suggest further work in this area. First, the study can be elaborated by using different types of sounds. Participants in our study described differences in how the sound affected their attention and ability to tune out the sound. Second, further research could limit the number of variables to assert causality. Third, the situation that participants engage in can be more closely related to real life with a setup that takes place in their own homes and during their daily routines. Fourth, different technologies that relate users differently to their environment can be investigated in order to describe other instances on the continuum. Finally, the characteristics emerging from this study can be quantified in more controlled lab settings.

References

1. Betlehem, T., Zhang, W., Poletti, M.A., Abhayapala, T.D.: Personal sound zones: delivering interface-free audio to multiple listeners. IEEE Sig. Process. Mag. **32**(2), 81–91 (2015)
2. Bull, M.: Sounding Out the City: Personal Stereos and the Management of Everyday Life. Berg, Oxford (2000)
3. Clarke, V., Braun, V.: Thematic analysis. In: Teo, T. (ed.) Encyclopedia of Critical Psychology, pp. 1947–1952 Springer, New York (2014). https://doi.org/10.1007/978-1-4614-5583-7
4. Brown, A.L., Kang, J., Gjestland, T.: Towards standardization in soundscape preference assessment. Appl. Acoust. **72**(6), 387–392 (2011)
5. Bruce, N.S., Davies, W.J.: The effects of expectation on the perception of soundscapes. Appl. Acoust. **85**, 1–11 (2014)
6. DeNora, T.: Music in Everyday Life. Cambridge University Press, Cambridge (2000)
7. Díaz, C., Pedrero, A.: The reverberation time of furnished rooms in dwellings. Appl. Acoust. **66**(8), 945–956 (2005)
8. Druyvesteyn, W.F., Garas, J.: Personal sound. J. Audio Eng. Soc. **45**(9), 685–701 (1997)
9. Haas, G., Stemasov, E., Rukzio, E.: Can't you hear me? Investigating personal soundscape curation. In: MUM 2018, pp. 59–69. ACM Press, New York (2018). https://doi.org/10.1145/3282894.3282897
10. Leong, T.W., Wright, P.: Revisiting social practices surrounding music. In: CHI 2013, pp. 951–960. ACM Press, New York (2013). https://doi.org/10.1145/2470654.2466122
11. Lundgaard, S.S., Nielsen, P.A.: Personalised soundscapes in homes. In: DIS 2019, pp. 813–822. ACM Press, New York(2019). https://doi.org/10.1145/3322276.3322364
12. Lundgaard, S.S., Nielsen, P.A., Kjeldskov, J.: Designing for domestic sound zone interaction. Pers. Ubiquit. Comput. 1–12 (2020). https://doi.org/10.1007/s00779-020-01387-2
13. Nielbo, F.L., Steele, D., Guastavino, C.: Investigating soundscape affordances through activity appropriateness. In: Proceedings of Meetings on Acoustics ICA 2013, vol. 19, no. 1, 8 p (2013). https://doi.org/10.1121/1.4800502
14. Nielsen, J.K., Lee, T., Jensen, J.R., Christensen, M.G.: Sound zones as optimal filtering problem. In: 2018 52nd Asilomar Conference on Signals, Systems, and Computers, pp. 1075–1079. IEEE, New York (2018)
15. Pompei, J.F.: The use of airborne ultrasonics for generating audible sound beams. Audio Eng. Soc. Conv. **47**(9), 726–731 (1998)
16. Schafer, R.M.: The Soundscape: Our Sonic Environment and the Tuning of the World. Alfred A. Knopf, New York (1994)
17. Yang, W., Kang, J.: Soundscape and sound preferences in urban squares: a case study in Sheffield. J. Urban Des. **10**(1), 61–80 (2016)
18. Yoon, S., Lim, Y., Lim, H., Kim, H.: Architecture of automatic warning system on urgent traffic situation for headphone users. Int. J. Multimed. Ubiquit. Eng. **7**(2), 421–426 (2012)

How Much is the Noise Level be Reduced? – Speech Recognition Threshold in Noise Environments Using a Parametric Speaker –

Noko Kuratomo[1,2]($\boxtimes$) ⓘ, Tadashi Ebihara[3] ⓘ, Naoto Wakatsuki[3],
Koichi Mizutani[3] ⓘ, and Keiichi Zempo[3] ⓘ

[1] Graduate School of Science and Technology, University of Tsukuba,
Tsukuba, Japan
[2] Research Fellow of Japan Society for the Promotion of Science, Tokyo, Japan
so.noko.sj@alumni.tsukuba.ac.jp
[3] Faculty of Engineering, Information and Systems, University of Tsukuba,
Tsukuba, Japan
zempo@iit.tsukuba.ac.jp

Abstract. As a technology that allows sound to be heard only in specific areas in public spaces, the directional sound of parametric speakers has been attracting attention. The parametric speaker is also expected to have a wide range of uses, in settings ranging from shopping malls to museums for presenting information sound. The purpose of this study is to measure evaluate the Speech Recognition Threshold (SRT) of parametric speakers and compare with that of loudspeakers at various noise levels through experiments. It can also reveal how much the parametric speaker can reduce the noise heard by non-target users, which is unavoidable with loudspeakers.

Through experiments, the volume required to transmit an informative sound to a particular listener is about 12.61 dBA less than the level necessary for the loudspeaker. Moreover, the SRT of the surrounding people is about 2.48 dBA higher than that for the loudspeaker. Based on the results, the volume received by people in the surrounding area, including environmental noise, was calculated, and the effect of noise reduction is discussed. This study provides important insights for the flexibility in the design of the sound space.

Keywords: Soundscape · Speech recognition · Parametric speaker

1 Introduction

The primary objective of soundscape design for public places is to create a comfortable space. Sound is an essential factor in the spatial comfort [7,17,19],which can thus be increased by reducing noise levels. One of the methods often used is

ⓒ IFIP International Federation for Information Processing 2021
Published by Springer Nature Switzerland AG 2021
C. Ardito et al. (Eds.): INTERACT 2021, LNCS 12933, pp. 542–550, 2021.
https://doi.org/10.1007/978-3-030-85616-8_31

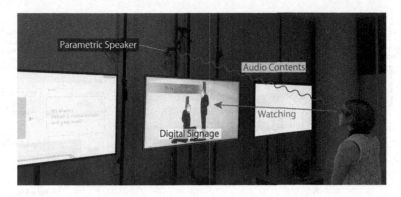

Fig. 1. One of the applications of the parametric speaker [9] : A system in which only the person viewing the advertisement can hear the sound by using parametric speakers improves the effectiveness of advertisements and spatial comfort.

masking noise with comforting sounds. For example, there are studies have examined the effects of playing sounds of streams and birds in traffic noise [6,15], and masking noise with the sound of fountains [14,18]. Since outdoor noise is uncontrollable, masking it increases the comfort level. In contrast, sounds with controllable volume, such as announcements of exhibits in a museum or advertisements on digital signage, are noisy to people who are not interested in them. In other words, unlike traffic noise, controllable sound is perceived by both people who need to hear it and those who do not, and both types of listeners are in the same space. When sound is emitted by a loudspeaker, it is perceived as noise by those who do not need it, and their comfort level is decreased. If the sound is masked with a comforting sound as a countermeasure, the people who need to hear it will be unable to do so.

Therefore, the directional sound of parametric speakers has been attracting attention as a technology that allows sound to be heard only in specific areas in public spaces. A parametric speaker is a device that arrays ultrasonic waves while transmitting a signal that demodulates them into audible sound by using the nonlinearity of their propagation through the air, resulting in audible sound with a narrow directionality [4,20]. Whereas conventional loudspeakers diffuse sound, parametric speakers emit sound in a straight line, which has the advantage of limiting the target area and causing less noise. Another feature of this system is that it is easier to localize than loudspeaker stereophonic sound due to reduced crosstalk [5].

One of the applications of the parametric speaker is the delivery of sounds that accompany advertisements on digital signage [9]. This study proposes a system in which only the person viewing the advertisement can hear the sound by using parametric speakers, as shown in Fig. 1. This system has been reported to improve the effectiveness of advertisements compared with those without sound while reducing noise and improving spatial comfort relative to the use of loudspeaker. However, the disadvantage is that it tends to be noisier than silence, and the advertising is registered by fewer people in the surroundings compared

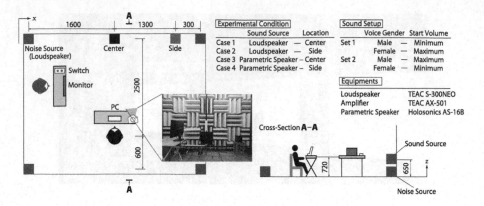

Fig. 2. The experimental environment and conditions.

with a loudspeaker. That is, there is a trade-off between usage effectiveness and spatial comfort when using parametric speakers.

Sound often contains linguistic information that the listener needs to understand, especially in situations using parametric speakers. The parametric speaker is also expected to have a wide range of uses, in settings ranging from shopping malls to museums. Therefore, it is important for the future sound design of public spaces to clarify how loud the emitted sound must be so that it can be understood in various noisy environments and what the noise level is at that time.

The purpose of this study was to quantitatively evaluate the degree of noise abatement. The Speech Recognition Threshold (SRT) of parametric speakers was measured and compared with that of loudspeakers at various noise levels through experiments. The threshold of understanding was calculated not only for the person receiving the spoken information but also for the people around them who were not meant to receive it. This information can be used to quantitate how much louder a parametric speaker must be compared with a loudspeaker when it is actually used in a public place. It can also reveal how much the parametric speaker can reduce the noise heard by non-target users, which is unavoidable with loudspeakers. This enables soundscape designers to evaluate the degree of contribution to spatial comfort. By examining environments ranging from quiet to noisy, such as museums and shopping malls, a variety of different conditions can be covered.

2   Experimental Environment

The experiment was conducted in an anechoic chamber to measure the SRTs of people who need information and those who do not. The experimental environment is described in Fig. 2. In the experiment, the sound was emitted by a parametric speaker and loudspeaker at various noise levels. For background noise, loudspeakers were placed in the four corners of the chamber to produce sound. The participants sat in chairs and judged whether they could hear the

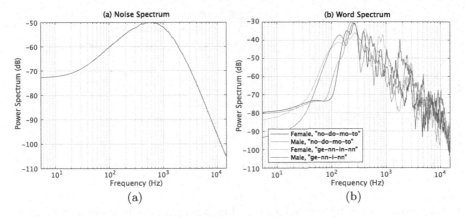

Fig. 3. Spectra – (a) Background noise, (b) Examples of the spoken word

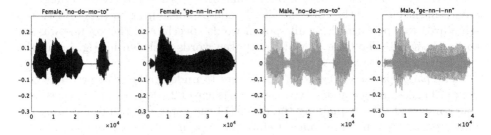

Fig. 4. Examples of the time plot of the spoken words : "nodomoto" means throat, and "genninn" means reason.

target sound. The loudspeaker and parametric speaker that emitted the target sound were to be installed in the center or at the sides. The speakers was placed in front of the participants for the center placement and out of their line of sight for the side condition, as shown in Fig. 2. A list of the equipment used is given in the table at the top right of Fig. 2.

The background noise was white noise with an FIR digital filter (according to ITU-T Rec. G.227). The spectrum of this noise is shown in Fig. 3(a). The noise volume was set at 20–80 dBA, and was changed by increments of 10 dBA. The volume is defined as the average volume measured by a sound level meter set up where the participants were sitting. For volume calibration, a 1 kHz sine wave was used. The sound was calibrated to a sound pressure equivalent to that of the background noise or the target sound.

SRT measurement experiments need to use native languages with uniform syllable and parenthetical densities. If the target sound is not in the native language [11–13], or if the number of syllables or the degree of familiarity varies [1, 2], the recognition threshold will decrease and accurate data will not be obtained. Since this experiment was conducted entirely with Japanese participants, the FW07 dataset [10] in Japanese was used for the transmitted sound. This dataset

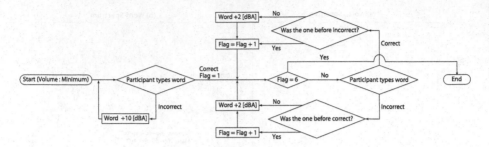

Fig. 5. Experiment procedure of the test started at the minimum volume.

contains words with four syllables and has been previously used in SRT experiments by Japanese researchers [8,16]. Since familiarity density [3] can also be selected, this experiment used a high familiarity word set to create a language environment close to that of daily life. Loudness normalization (ITU BS.1770-3 standard) was performed for all spoken words speech, and the volume was set to be the same. The time plot of the spoken words is shown in Fig. 4, and the spectrum is shown in Fig. 3.

The participants of this experiment were 14 undergraduate or graduate students (9 males and 5 females) with an average age of 22.64 years. The experiment was conducted after explaining the details of the experiment and obtaining the participants' consent in advance. Before the experiment, we conducted a sound field threshold measurement to confirm that the participants had normal hearing.

This experiment was reviewed and approved by the ethics committee of the University of Tsukuba (Faculty of Engineering, Information and Systems, Permission number: 2020R434).

3   Procedure

In the experiment, the words were played in an environment where background noise was always present. Participants typed the words that they heard on a PC. The researcher watched the input text by mirroring it to determine if it matched the actual words played and then used a switch to increase or decrease the volume. If the test started at the minimum volume, the sound was increased by 10 dBA every time a wrong answer was given. After that, the volume was decreased by 2 dBA when a correct answer was given and increased by 2 dBA after another wrong answer. Repeat these steps, and end the audio presentation if it turns into a wrong answer for the third time. These steps were repeated, and the audio presentation ended after a third wrong answer. This procedure was repeated but starting with the maximum volume, and the sound presentation was ended after the third correct answer. The volume at which the percentage of correct answers was 50% was set as the SRT, which was taken from the midpoint of the volume when the answer reversed from incorrect to correct or vice versa. The above experimental procedure is shown in Fig. 5.

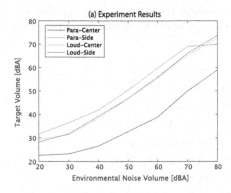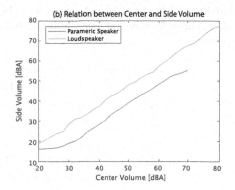

Fig. 6. (a) The SRT results for each speaker and location. High SRT is better for the Side because it is harder to hear; low SRT is better for the Center because it requires less volume. (b)The volume flowing to the side when the center receives the sound. The smaller the Side is than the Center, the less sound will flow into the Side.

There were four experimental conditions: a loudspeaker or parametric speaker was used; the speaker was placed in a central or lateral location; the test started at the minimum or maximum volume; and the words were read out loud in a male or female voice. The experimental conditions and sound settings are shown in the right corner of Figure 2. The volume of the target sound is defined as the average volume measured by a sound level meter placed where the participants were sitting with the speaker placed in the center of the room. For example, a target volume of 40 dBA means that this is the volume that the participant heard when the speaker was in the center, and the speaker output the same volume when it was at the side. The volume range was 20–80 dBA for the loudspeaker and 20–70 dBA for the parametric speaker on the basis of equipment and ear protection.

4   Results and Discussion

The SRT results for each speaker and location are shown in the Fig. 6(a). For the loudspeaker, the SRTs are almost the same between the center and side placements at all background volumes. The SNRs, which is the difference between the background noise volume and the SRT, and their average were calculated. The calculated results are about –1.44 dBA for the Center and –1.21 dBA for the Side. In other words, this implies that when the listener can understand the sound, the people around them can also hear the same content. This feature is appropriate for wide announcement applications. However, it is not suitable if sound is intended for only a specific individual or when the surrounding environment needs to remain quiet.

With the parametric speaker, the SRT is different between the center and side placements. The average SNR of the SRT is about –13.88 dBA for the Center and 1.27 dBA for the Side. The volume required to transmit an informative sound to

Table 1. The calculated volume received by people in the center and surrounding area, including environmental noise, and the differences between loudspeaker and parametric speaker.

Background	Loudspeaker			Parametric Speaker			Diff
	SRT	Side	Total	SRT	Side	Total	
20	29.27	27.27	28.02	22.59	14.10	20.99	7.02
30	31.41	29.38	32.71	23.21	14.65	30.12	2.59
40	38.34	36.23	41.52	26.59	17.66	40.03	1.50
50	46.80	44.58	51.10	32.68	23.09	50.01	1.09
60	56.16	53.83	60.94	38.84	28.59	60.00	0.94
70	65.20	62.75	70.75	49.98	38.52	70.00	0.75
80	72.71	70.17	80.43	58.98	46.54	80.00	0.43
unit:[dBA]							

a particular listener is about 12.61 dBA less than the level necessary for the loudspeaker. The results also show that people around the particular listener cannot hear much of the information in the sound. The phenomenon described as "whispering in the ear" by the participants of the experiment is thought to be due to the self-demodulating nature of parametric speakers as well as the fact that the SRT is quite small. Moreover, the SRT of the surrounding people is about 2.48 dBA higher than that for the loudspeaker. Furthermore, the volume flowing to the side when the center receives the sound is shown in Fig. 6(b). The average volume heard by a person at the side is −2.26 dBA lower than that heard by the person at the center for the loudspeaker and −10.92 dBA lower for the parametric speaker. There is a difference of about 8.66 dBA between the speakers.

Based on the above data, the volume received by people in the surrounding area, including environmental noise, was calculated. For example, in a 50 dBA environment, the SRT of the target person is 46.80 dBA for the loudspeaker. Based on a linear approximation of the volume relationship shown in Fig. 6(b), the volume received by the people around the target was calculated to be 44.58 dBA. This means that the people around the target listener are exposed to a combined noise level of 50 dBA + 44.58 dBA = 51.10 dBA. In contrast, the volume level at which the advertisement sound can be heard in a 50 dBA environment with the parametric speaker is 32.68 dBA. In this case, the surrounding people will receive 23.09 dBA, as indicated in Fig. 6(b). The overall noise level is 50 dBA + 23.09 dBA = 50.01 dBA. In other words, when changing from a loudspeaker to a parametric speaker, the people around the target listener hear about 1.09 dBA less sound. The same calculation reveals the differences in noise levels, as shown in Table 1. The smaller the background sound level, the larger the difference in the overall noise level. It can also be shown quantitatively that there is a difference at all background sound levels, as shown in Fig. 7. Compared with the loudspeaker, the parametric speaker is expected to improve the spatial

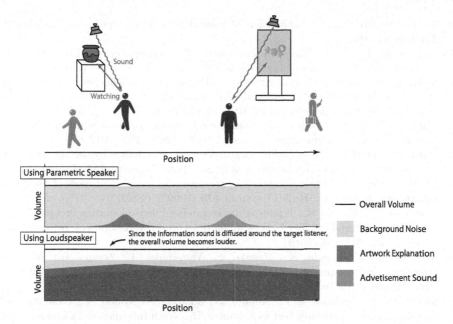

Fig. 7. Compared with the loudspeaker, the parametric speaker is expected to improve the spatial comfort level of non-target individuals, as they receive almost no unnecessary information. The overall volume is also reduced, which allows for more flexibility in the design of the sound space, such as adding other announcements or environmental sounds.

comfort level of non-target individuals, as they receive almost no unnecessary information. The overall volume is also reduced, which allows for more flexibility in the design of the sound space, such as adding other announcements or environmental sounds. In particular, it is quantitatively confirmed that it is possible to create a space design in a quiet environment such as a museum that allows people to listen to explanations without interfering with other viewers.

As a limitation, the background noise in the experiment was filtered white noise for generalization. This is a noise with small amplitude variation, whereas in real life, the amplitude can vary greatly (e.g., road traffic noise and speech announcements). It is necessary to investigate how the SRT changes in that case, especially when the words are delivered by parametric speakers. In addition, the anechoic room is a free sound field with no reverberation. In real life, reverberation is also a factor, so its influence needs to be studied in the future.

References

1. Amano, S.: Effects of lexicon and coarticulation on phoneme perception. J. Acoust. Soc. Jpn. (E) **14**(2), 91–97 (1993)

2. Amano, S., Kondo, T.: Estimation of mental lexicon size with word familiarity database (1998)
3. Amano, S., Kondo, T., Kato, K.: Familiarity effect on spoken word recognition in japanese. In: Proceedings of the 14th ICPhS. vol. 2, pp. 873–876 (1999)
4. Aoki, K., Kamakura, T., Kumamoto, Y.: Parametric loudspeaker–characteristics of acoustic field and suitable modulation of carrier ultrasound. Electr. Commun. Jpn (Part III: Fund. Electr. Sci.) **74**(9), 76–82 (1991)
5. Aoki, S., Toba, M., Tsujita, N.: Sound localization of stereo reproduction with parametric loudspeakers. Appl. Acoust. **73**(12), 1289–1295 (2012)
6. Hong, J.Y., et al..: Effects of adding natural sounds to urban noises on the perceived loudness of noise and soundscape quality. Sci. Total Environ. **711**, 134571 (2020)
7. Jo, H.I., Jeon, J.Y.: Effect of the appropriateness of sound environment on urban soundscape assessment. Build. Environ. **179**, 106975 (2020)
8. Kobayashi, Y., Kondo, K.: Japanese speech intelligibility estimation and prediction using objective intelligibility indices under noisy and reverberant conditions. Appl. Acoust. **156**, 327–335 (2019)
9. Kuratomo, N., Yamada, K., Masuko, S., Yamanaka, T., Zempo, K.: Effect of attention adaptive personal audio deliverable system on digital signage. In: SIG-GRAPHAsia 2019 Technical Briefs, pp. 118–121(2019)
10. Sakamoto, S., Yoshikawa, T., Amano, S., Suzuki, Y., Kondo, T.: New 20-word lists for word intelligibility test in Japanese. In: Ninth International Conference on Spoken Language Processing (2006)
11. Scharenborg, O., Coumans, J.M., van Hout, R.: The effect of background noise on the word activation process in nonnative spoken-word recognition. J. Exp. Psychol. Learn. Mem. Cogn. **44**(2), 233 (2018)
12. Scharenborg, O., van Os, M.: Why listening in background noise is harder in a non-native language than in a native language: a review. Speech Commun. **108**, 53–64 (2019)
13. Shimizu, T., Makishima, K., Yoshida, M., Yamagishi, H.: Effect of background noise on perception of English speech for Japanese listeners. Auris Nasus Larynx **29**(2), 121–125 (2002)
14. Skoda, S., Steffens, J., Becker-Schweitzer, J.: Road traffic noise annoyance in domestic environments can be reduced by water sounds. In: Forum Acusticum (2014)
15. Van Renterghem, et al..: Interactive soundscape augmentation by natural sounds in a noise polluted urban park. Landsc. Urban Plan. **194**, 103705 (2020)
16. Yamamoto, K., Irino, T., Araki, S., Kinoshita, K., Nakatani, T.: Gedi: Gammachirp envelope distortion index for predicting intelligibility of enhanced speech. Speech Commun. **123**, 43–58 (2020)
17. Yang, W., Kang, J.: Soundscape and sound preferences in urban squares: a case study in Sheffield. J. Urban Des. **10**(1), 61–80 (2005)
18. Yang, W., Moon, H.J.: Effects of indoor water sounds on intrusive noise perception and speech recognition in rooms. Build. Serv. Eng. Res. Technol. **39**(6), 637–651 (2018)
19. Yang, W., Moon, H.J.: Combined effects of acoustic, thermal, and illumination conditions on the comfort of discrete senses and overall indoor environment. Build. Environ. **148**, 623–633 (2019)
20. Yoneyama, M., Fujimoto, J.i., Kawamo, Y., Sasabe, S.: The audio spotlight: An application of nonlinear interaction of sound waves to a new type of loudspeaker design. J. Acoust. Soc. Am. **73**(5), 1532–1536 (1983)

Stress Out: Translating Real-World Stressors into Audio-Visual Stress Cues in VR for Police Training

Quynh Nguyen[1,2(✉)] ⓘ, Emma Jaspaert[3] ⓘ, Markus Murtinger[1,4],
Helmut Schrom-Feiertag[1] ⓘ, Sebastian Egger-Lampl[1] ⓘ, and Manfred Tscheligi[1,2] ⓘ

[1] AIT Austrian Institute of Technology, 1210 Vienna, Austria
{quynh-huong.nguyen,helmut.schrom-feiertag,
sebastian.egger-lampl}@ait.ac.at
[2] University of Salzburg, 5020 Salzburg, Austria
manfred.tscheligi@sbg.ac.at
[3] KU Leuven, 3000 Leuven, Belgium
emma.jaspaert@kuleuven.be
[4] USECON GmbH, 1010 Vienna, Austria
murtinger@usecon.com

Abstract. Virtual Reality (VR) training has become increasingly important for police first responders in recent years. Improving the training experience in such complex contexts requires ecological validity of virtual training. To achieve this, VR systems need to be capable of simulating the complex experiences of police officers 'in the field.' One way to do this is to add stressors into training simulations to induce stress similar to the stress experienced in real-life situations, particularly in situations where this is difficult (e.g., dangerous or resource-intensive) to achieve with traditional training. To include stressors in VR, this paper thus presents the concept of so-called 'stress cues' for operationalizing stressors to augment training in VR simulations for the context of police work. Considering the level of complexity of police work and training, a co-creation process that allows for creative collaboration and mitigation of power imbalances was chosen to access the police officers' knowledge and experience. We assert that stress cues can improve the training experience from the trainer's perspective as they provide novel interaction design possibilities for trainers to control the training experience. E.g., by actively intervening in training and dynamically changing the interaction space for trainees which also improves the trainee's experience. Stress cues can also improve the trainee's experience by enabling personalizable and customizable training based on real-time stress measurements and supplementing information for improved training feedback.

Keywords: Virtual reality · Contextual experience · Training experience · Police training · High stress · Stress cues · Stress cue interaction · Co-creation

C. Ardito et al. (Eds.): INTERACT 2021, LNCS 12933, pp. 551–561, 2021.
https://doi.org/10.1007/978-3-030-85616-8_32

1 Introduction

Virtual Reality (VR) provides a valuable platform for immersive training experiences, especially for high-stress professions like first responders where mistakes can cost lives [6]. The training of police first responders specifically has been the subject of continuous research (see e.g., [7]). Individual, contextual, societal, and organizational factors influence decision-making and acting in the field, making training conceptualizations a highly sophisticated endeavor. This makes it a particularly interesting interaction context for human-computer interaction (HCI) research.

The benefits of VR training include lower costs and higher safety compared to real-life training (see e.g., [10]). It also enables interactions in simulated contexts with high immersion and a sense of presence [11]. Unlike in real-life simulation training, VR also allows for the inclusion of vulnerable groups (e.g., children, elderly people) or dangerous equipment (e.g., explosive materials) [14].

However, to produce an ecologically valid VR training experience for police officers who have to regularly perform under stress, stress needs to be inducible. This can be achieved by augmenting the VR training scenario with stressors that add complexity to the scenario [12]. This allows for personalized training based on the trainee's learning goals, pace, needs, and time constraints. Stressors have been used in VR training, e.g., for stress inoculation training [24]. However, to the best of our knowledge, there is little to no research investigating how to operationalize stressors, i.e., how to transform 'descriptive' stressors into concrete, measurable, observable, and implementable elements in VR. Furthermore, there is little research on designing interaction concepts for trainers to easily affect the stress levels of trainees in VR training by using stressors.

Thus, our main goal is to investigate how the training experience of both trainer and trainee can be enhanced through the implementation of stressors in the complex context of police VR training. For this, we will address two research questions: (1) How can known real-world stressors be translated into audio-visual stress cues in VR training environments? (2) How can the overall concept for trainers interacting with the implementation of stressors in VR look like?

We followed a co-creation approach that iteratively involved stakeholders in the research and development process as experts of their professions and experiences [23]. This was done to gain insights into the complex world of police work and training and to facilitate a collaborative environment that can alleviate potential power imbalances (see e.g. [5]) that can exist in hierarchical and highly specialized structures like police organizations [19]. As its main contribution, the paper presents the concept of 'stress cues' as the operationalization of descriptive stressors into concrete, observable and implementable elements in VR to improve the training experience for both trainers and trainees. We also provide first ideas for how trainers could interact with stress cues during VR training with the help of a research prototype.

2 Related Work

2.1 Stressors in Virtual Reality Training of Police First Responders

First responder personnel is regularly put under significant stress due to threats to their psychological and physical wellbeing [13]. Stress can be defined as "any physical, cognitive or emotional reaction that causes physiological or mental tension and that may result in physical or emotional impairment" [2, p. 55] while stressors can be considered "internal or external demands imposed on or inherent" [16, p. 80] to the police officer or trainee. One way to support first responders is to provide operational training under stress to prepare for stressful situations and increase resilience. To do so, stressors for first responders need to be a) identified and b) operationalized for VR.

So far, police research has focused on identifying stressors that contribute to overall work stress in first responders (e.g., [1, 18]) rather than on acute situational stressors in the specific context of interventions in the field. Additionally, stressors that occur in the field are often formulated broadly, e.g., by the type of intervention (e.g., armed robbery) or refer to more general events or 'critical incidents' (e.g., officer-involved shooting). These indicate which types of interventions lead to general work stress, but do not indicate which stressors lead to acute stress during specific police interventions.

In virtual training under stress, stressors are used to achieve higher ecological validity. However, the concept remains underspecified for stressors in VR as well. In one review in the context of military stress training, stressors can take physical (e.g., lack of sleep, dehydration) and psychological forms (e.g., information overload) [17]. Another study on the selection of stressors in VR to train stress management skills, describes stressors only as generally 'stressful situations' [3]. Overall, there is little to no research on the transformation of stressors into concrete, observable and implementable elements for VR training. Particularly, there are no concepts on how to best design interactions for trainers for them to easily and quickly adjust stress levels in VR training with stressors to achieve a better training experience for trainees.

2.2 Interaction Design for Virtual Training Experiences

In VR training, trainees must physically and mentally engage with the training simulation. Especially in police training, trainees must demonstrate their ability to act quickly, decisively, and professionally in various high-risk scenarios. To increase the ecological validity of the training experience, real equipment like pepper spray, tasers, and firearms are virtualized as tangible, functional objects which the trainee can handle just as in real training [22]. While the trainees are immersed in the training scenarios, the trainers supervise the training from outside the VR. This context requires a simple interaction and interface design that makes it possible to observe the training and the trainees' response and to adapt the scenario quickly and with little mental effort.

Monitoring and supervisory intervention can be compared with contexts from flight monitoring, control centers, and decision support systems. But especially the training context provides a special challenge for HCI research because the digitalization and use of software represent a new application domain for trainers. While there is, to the best of our knowledge, no research yet on interaction design specifically for trainers, first approaches can be found for general training experience (e.g., [8, 25]).

2.3 Co-creation

For the development of new technologies, researchers in human-centered design argue that it can be highly beneficial to include the knowledge and opinions of people as experts of their professions, experiences, and lives [21]. As co-creation uses tools and techniques that engender people's creativity [20], it can aid in obtaining people's tacit knowledge which cannot be accessed easily through other means. This might be especially valuable in special contexts like law enforcement where successful work relies heavily on procedural and tacit knowledge. Furthermore, co-creative methods might be able to engender an equitable, collaborative environment that could equalize potential power imbalances that exist in police organizations [5] where hierarchical and highly specialized structures exist [19].

3 The Problem Context: The SHOTPROS Project

SHOTPROS investigates the influence of human factors (HFs) on decision-making and acting (DMA) of police officers under high-stress and in high-risk operational situations. The aim is to develop a training framework and a corresponding VR system concerned with improving the performance of DMA in high-stress and high-risk situations.

3.1 Used Methods for Developing the Stress Cue Concept

We organized six co-creation workshops at six law enforcement agencies (LEAs) across Europe. 60 police officers and trainers participated in the 1.5-day workshops. Several co-creation tools (e.g. brainstorming and co-designing with LEGO™-like building blocks) were used to facilitate active and creative participation. As suggested by previous research (see [5]), this helps to create a collaborative atmosphere, mitigate power-related biases in the structure of hierarchical, highly bureaucratized police organizations [19], and to yield participants' tacit knowledge. The participants generated possible HFs influencing stress of police first responders and developed VR scenarios for training DMA in stressful, high-risk situations. Based on the findings from the workshops and an additional co-creation session with representatives of all partner LEAs in SHOTPROS, a list of 40 stressors was created. The list items were ranked according to priority by one LEA trainer expert from each organization through an online survey. The ranked items were then used to iteratively develop the stress cues.

Further, trainers from all LEAs participated in its development by providing their needs and expertise for the training experience through online co-creation and feedback rounds. These interaction design ideas were then included in the VR prototype.

3.2 The Stress Cue Concept

As described earlier, a research gap currently exists on how to operationalize contextual factors that induce stress ('stressors') for training in VR and how to design interaction concepts describing how trainers can use these elements. So far, descriptions of stressors remain general which makes it difficult to implement them in interaction concepts. To close this gap, we introduce the concept of stress cues which operationalize descriptive stressors into concrete, observable and implementable elements in VR to improve the training experience for trainers and trainees. The concept also entails the following components: (a) A stress cue repository, (b) the interaction design for controlling and injecting the selected stress cues in the VE via a live editor, (c) a real-time stress measurement dashboard to evaluate and visualize stress cue effects on the trainee and (d) an after-action review (AAR) dashboard. In the following, each of the four components of the concept of stress cues will be explained.

Creation of Stress Cues in a Stress Cue Repository. Table 1 shows the ten collected stressors rated most relevant for inducing stress. A selection of these stress cues was implemented as audio-visual stimuli, i.e., as animated 3D objects with sound, into the VR prototype to visualize the interactive stress cue concept (see Fig. 1). The prototype will be used to collect feedback from end users, evaluate the concept of stress cues, and provide a baseline for co-creation with the end users on future design instantiations.

Table 1. Top 10 stressors elaborated and voted by the LEA partners.

Stressor	Description
Weapon (knife/gun)	The trainee looks into a room/vehicle and sees a knife/gun and a hand holding it
Crowd (approx. 30 people)	The trainee stands in front of a crowd of people (multiple crowd behaviors possible)
Unexpected weapons	An unknown person stands in the room and uses an ashtray or vase as a weapon
Aggressive dog	A dog barks and runs at the trainee
Blood	There are traces of blood in a room
Darkness	A closed room (or street) with no or very little light
Injured people	Showing people seriously injured
Loud unexplained noise	A door is banged shut after trainee walked inside the room./ In a closed room, the TV is running and producing loud sudden sounds
Scream	Screams are audible while the trainee is inside a closed room/or outside (e.g., on the street)
Unknown origin of smoke	Closed room gets filled with smoke

Interaction Design for the Stress Cues: The Stress Cue Live Editor. Following the implementation of stressors as stress cues into VR, one of the most important aspects to improve the training experience is to consider how the trainer could interact with and use the stress cues during training. Here, we propose a live editor where stress cues can be selected to influence the scenario in real-time with three interaction possibilities: (1) single selection to add a stress cue to the VR training scenario, (2) selection of multiple stress cues in parallel, and (3) generation of a stress cue sequence. For each stress cue, the characteristics and intensity can be defined (e.g., adjusting music volume or the level of aggressiveness of the dog). After selecting the manifestations of the stress cues, they are directly applied to the actual VR scenario.

Real-time Stress Measurement Dashboard and After-Action Review Dashboard. In the prototype, the stress level is determined through the trainee's heart rate variability (HRV), a recognized indicator of stress [9], with a Zephyr™ bio-harness which provides reliable and valid measurements of heart rate [15]. The stress level is displayed in the Stress Cue Live Editor, allowing trainers to get immediate feedback on the effect of the selected stress cues on the trainee's state. Through the integrated real-time stress measurement, the effect of single stress cues and cascading effects of stress cues combinations can be evaluated. This can help trainers in choosing augmentations for the scenario, improving training effectiveness. The after-action review (AAR) dashboard displays visualizations of the physiological stress level and behavioral trainee data through which the trainee's performance can be replayed and analyzed after training.

3.3   The Stress Cue Prototype

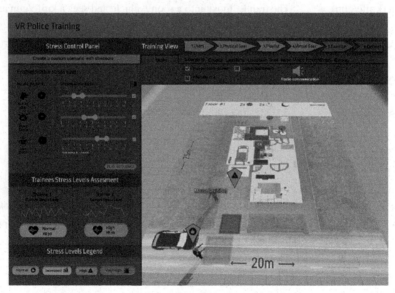

Fig. 1. Stress cue live editor showing stress levels of trainees and selected stress cues and control panel to add (1) single stress cues, (2) stress cues in parallel, or (3) in a sequence. Screens based on existing software by the VR partner RE-liON in SHOTPROS.

The question of how the training experience can be improved in the complex context of police work with stress cues guided the development of the prototype. Based on design ideas and feedback in the co-creation process, we prototypically integrated ideas for trainer interactions with the stress cues into the VR training system developed in SHOTPROS (see Fig. 1). The end user requirements revealed that an efficient, effective interaction and easy-to-use user interface design is needed. It allows for observations of the training and trainees' behavior and adaptations to the scenario by (de)activating stress cues rapidly with little mental effort.

At the top of the stress cue live editor (Fig. 1), the scenario execution control is shown at the 'exercise execution' stage. The main area is the 3D representation of two trainees in the VE, marked with symbols indicating position and stress level. Obstacles like walls are disabled for a better view of the trainees. On the left, the list of selected stress cues, the panel for stress cue control, color-coded stress levels of the trainees, and a legend depicts for the stress levels are depicted. The design meets the consulted trainers' requirements to keep the scenario display central and only use a border area for the live editor. Stress cues can be activated to induce immediate stress in trainees at any time individually by single play buttons for instant playback or in a sequence through 'play sequence' with an additional selection of the start and end on the timeline via sliders. Simultaneous playback of all stress cues is possible by pressing all play buttons in quick succession or by defining and playing a parallel sequence.

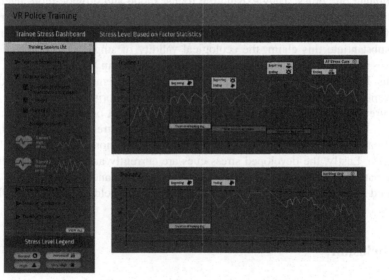

Fig. 2. After-action review dashboard for analyzing stress responses during the appearance of stress cues for trainees exposed to stress cues.

In the AAR dashboard (Fig. 2), the trainees' data is displayed. The response to the stress cues can be analyzed via a time diagram where stress cues and their active period are shown to align stress cues to stress responses. All (see Fig. 2, trainee 1) or selected stress cues (see Fig. 2, trainee 2, barking dog only) can be displayed. The level of stress can be viewed on the y-axis and is color-coded: green for normal, yellow for increased, orange for high, and red for very high stress.

4   Discussion and Future Work

This paper has described how a proposed operationalization of stress cues will enhance the training experience in the context of police work where contextual, individual, societal, and organizational factors interact with and influence decision-making and acting in the field, making training highly important but difficult to conceptualize. The co-creation process was described through which the stress cue concept was developed (research question 1). It showed how stressors in operative police work were translated into audio-visual stimuli and implemented in a VR prototype based on several iterations of co-creation and interaction design development. We suggest that the effective implementation of stressors not only includes audio-visual stimuli (i.e., the stress cues themselves) but also a VR interaction concept for the trainer, real-time stress measurements, and an AAR dashboard to fully operationalize stressors by making them objectively measurable (research question 2). To validate the proposed implementation empirically, we will evaluate the VR prototype in upcoming studies.

Ecologically valid stress cues can be of high added value to the training experience of any first responder (e.g. fire rescue, medical emergency services) in VR by giving trainers the possibility to manipulate the VE to achieve a stress level that is effective to the training outcomes. They expand the trainer mode and provide more interaction possibilities to actively intervene in the training and dynamically change the interaction space of the trainee, thus improving the training experience of trainee and trainer.

To substantiate this claim, the ecological validity of single and combinations of stress cues must be tested, as well as the effect of stress cues in VR compared to real-life situations. In addition to HRV, we plan to integrate measurements such as breath rate, eye movement, and pupillometry data (see e.g., [4]). An algorithm will use these inputs to measure and visualize experienced stress and the impact of stress cues in trainees. Moreover, future research could move towards automated stress cue additions through artificial intelligence algorithms based on the trainee's behavior and physiological stress response(s). Lastly, the developed stress cues are currently audio-visual stimuli only. Beyond that, additional stress inducement through olfactory and haptic feedback will be considered in future work, e.g. through vibrations of hand-held controllers or full-body VR suits.

5   Conclusion

This paper investigated how the training experience of LEA first responders can be improved to be more ecologically valid. Our research has shown that this can be achieved through the integration of stress cues in VR training. Therefore, we propose the translation of real-world stressors in the context of existing LEA first responder training into the concept of 'stress cues' in VEs. The use of stress cues could be especially beneficial in VR training because it provides various interaction possibilities for trainers. Stress cues are easily adaptable, manipulable, and controllable and thus allow for a personalization of training based on an individual trainee's training goals, capabilities, and needs. Training enhanced through ecologically valid stress cues will allow trainees to learn and train how to mitigate the effects of stress responses repeatedly with interchangeable, customizable stress cues. We see this approach as part of a future interaction design approach, as it aims to combine human experiences, interactions, and behavior with several human senses such as sight, hearing, but also smell, and touch.

Acknowledgments. This work is supported by the European Commission's Horizon 2020 Research and Innovation Programme (Grant number: 833572).

References

1. Abdollahi, M.K.: Understanding police stress research. J. Forensic Psychol. Pract. **2**(2), 1–24 (2002). https://doi.org/10.1300/J158v02n02_01
2. Alkus, S., Padesky, C.: Special problems of police officers: stress-related issues and interventions. Couns. Psychol. **11**(2), 55–64 (1983)
3. Bouchard, S., Baus, O., Bernier, F., McCreary, D.R.: Selection of key stressors to develop virtual environments for practicing stress management skills with military personnel prior to deployment. Cyberpsychol. Behav. Soc. Netw. **13**(1), 83–94 (2010). https://doi.org/10.1089/cyber.2009.0336
4. Brammer, J.C., et al.: Breathing biofeedback for police officers in a stressful virtual environment: challenges and opportunities. Front. Psychol. **12**(586553), 401 (2021). https://doi.org/10.3389/fpsyg.2021.586553
5. Cantoni, L., Marchiori, E., Faré, M., Botturi, L., Bolchini, D.: A systematic methodology to use lego bricks in web communication design. In: Proceedings of the 27th ACM International Conference on Design of Communication, pp. 187–192. Association for Computing Machinery, New York (2009). https://doi.org/10.1145/1621995.1622032
6. Fowlkes, J., Schatz, S., Stagl, K.C: Instructional strategies for scenario-based training: insights from applied research. In: SpringSim 2010: Proceedings of the 2010 Spring Simulation Multiconference, San Diego, vol. 32, pp. 1–5 (2010). https://doi.org/10.1145/1878537.1878571
7. Jaspaert, E., Vervaeke, G.: Het gebruik van virtual reality in de criminologie [The use of Virtual Reality in criminology]. In: Hardyns, W., Snaphaan, T. (eds.), Big data en nieuwe innovatieve methoden binnen de criminologisch onderzoek [Big data and new innovations in criminological research] (2020)
8. Kim, A.S.: Behind the starbucks counter: design solutions for utilizing virtual reality for collaborative training. In: Proceedings of the 37th ACM International Conference on the Design of Communication (SIGDOC 2019), pp. 1–5. Association for Computing Machinery, New York (2019). Article 29. https://doi.org/10.1145/3328020.3353938
9. Kim, H.G., Cheon, E.J., Bai, D.S., Lee, Y.H., Koo, B.H.: Stress and heart rate variability: a meta-analysis and review of the literature. Psychiatry Invest. **15**(3), 235–245 (2018). https://doi.org/10.30773/pi.2017.08.17
10. Merchant, Z., Goetz, E.T., Cifuentes, L., Keeney-Kennicutt, W., Davis, T.J.: Effectiveness of virtual reality-based instruction on students' learning outcomes in K-12 and higher education: a meta-analysis. Comput. Educ. **70**, 29–40 (2014). https://doi.org/10.1016/j.compedu.2013.07.033
11. Martín-Gutiérrez, J., Mora, C.E., Añorbe-Díaz, B., González-Marrero, A.: Virtual technologies trends in education. EURASIA J. Math. Sci. Technol. Educ. **13**(2), 469–486 (2017). https://doi.org/10.12973/eurasia.2017.00626a

12. Martin, G.A.: Automatic Scenario Generation Using Procedural Modeling Techniques. University of Central Florida (2012). https://stars.library.ucf.edu/cgi/viewcontent.cgi?article= 3151&context=etd
13. Mitchell, J.T.: Critical incident stress management: a comprehensive, intergrative, systematic, and multi-component program for supporting first responder psychological health. In: Bowers, C.A., Beidel, D.C., Marks, M.R. (eds.) Mental Health Intervention and Treatment of First Responders and Emergency Workers, pp. 103–128. IGI Global (2020). https://doi.org/10. 4018/978-1-5225-9803-9.ch007
14. Murtinger, M., Jaspaert, E., Schrom-Feiertag, H., Egger-Lampl, S.: CBRNe training in virtual environments: SWOT analysis & practical guidelines. Manuscript submitted for publication (2020)
15. Nazari, G., Bobos, P., MacDermid, J.C., Sinden, K.E., Richardson, J., Tang, A.: Psychometric properties of the Zephyr bioharness device: a systematic review. BMC Sports Sci. Med. Rehabil. 10(6), 1–8 (2018). https://doi.org/10.1186/s13102-018-0094-4
16. Ontrup, G., Vogel, M., Wolf, O.T., Zahn, P.K., Kluge, A., Hagemann, V.: Does simulation-based training in medical education need additional stressors? An experimental study. Ergonomics 63(1), 80–90 (2020). https://doi.org/10.1080/00140139.2019.1677948
17. Pallavicini, F., Argenton, L., Toniazzi, N., Aceti, L., Mantovani, F.: Virtual reality applications for stress management training in the military. Aerosp. Med. Hum. Perform. 87(12), 1021–1030 (2016). https://doi.org/10.3357/AMHP.4596.2016
18. Slate, R.N., Johnson, W.W., Colbert, S.S.: Police stress: a structural model. J. Police Crim. Psychol. 22, 102–112 (2007). https://doi.org/10.1007/s11896-007-9012-5
19. Sollund, R.: Obstacles and possibilities in police research. Outlines Crit. Pract. Stud. 7(2), 43–64 (2005). https://tidsskrift.dk/outlines/article/view/2103
20. Steen, M.: Tensions in human-centred design. CoDesign 7(1), 45–60 (2011)
21. Steen, M., Kuijt-Evers, L., Klok, J.: Early user involvement in research and design projects–A review of methods and practices. In: 23rd EGOS colloquium, pp. 1–21 (2007)
22. van den Hoven, E., Frens, J., Aliakseyeu, D., Martens, J.-B., Overbeeke, K., Peters, P.: Design research & tangible interaction. In: Proceedings of the 1st International Conference on Tangible and Embedded Interaction, TEI 2007, pp. 109–115. Association for Computing Machinery, New York (2007). https://doi.org/10.1145/1226969.1226993
23. Visser, F.S., Stappers, P.J., Van der Lugt, R., Sanders, E.B.: Contextmapping: experiences from practice. CoDesign 1(2), 119–149 (2005). https://doi.org/10.1080/15710880500135987
24. Wiederhold, B.K., Wiederhold, M.D.: Virtual reality for posttraumatic stress disorder and stress inoculation training. J. Cyberther. Rehabil. 1(1), 23–35 (2008)
25. Yigitbas, E., Heindörfer, J., Engels, G.: A context-aware virtual reality first aid training application. In: Proceedings of Mensch und Computer 2019 (MuC 2019), pp. 885–888. Association for Computing Machinery, New York (2019). https://doi.org/10.1145/3340764.3349525

What Is Fair? Exploring the Artists' Perspective on the Fairness of Music Streaming Platforms

Andres Ferraro[1] , Xavier Serra[1] , and Christine Bauer[2]([⊠])

[1] Universitat Pompeu Fabra, Barcelona, Spain
andres.ferraro@upf.edu
[2] Utrecht University, Utrecht, The Netherlands
c.bauer@uu.nl

Abstract. Music streaming platforms are currently among the main sources of music consumption, and the embedded recommender systems significantly influence what the users consume. There is an increasing interest to ensure that those platforms and systems are fair. Yet, we first need to understand what fairness means in such a context. Although artists are the main content providers for music platforms, there is a research gap concerning the artists' perspective. To fill this gap, we conducted interviews with music artists to understand how they are affected by current platforms and what improvements they deem necessary. Using a Qualitative Content Analysis, we identify the aspects that the artists consider relevant for fair platforms. In this paper, we discuss the following aspects derived from the interviews: fragmented presentation, reaching an audience, transparency, influencing users' listening behavior, popularity bias, artists' repertoire size, quotas for local music, gender balance, and new music. For some topics, our findings do not indicate a clear direction about the best way how music platforms should act and function; for other topics, though, there is a clear consensus among our interviewees: for these, the artists have a clear idea of the actions that should be taken so that music platforms will be fair also for the artists.

Keywords: Music artists · Fairness · Music streaming platform · Transparency · Quotas · Lack of control · Gender balance · Music context · Influencing taste

1 Introduction

Music streaming platforms are currently among the main sources of music consumption. What the users consume is strongly influenced by what is offered on the music platforms, and what is promoted through the algorithmic recommendations in particular. What the users consume, in turn, shapes the music streaming ecosystem at large. There is an increasing research interest in making the platforms and their recommendations fairer.

© IFIP International Federation for Information Processing 2021
Published by Springer Nature Switzerland AG 2021
C. Ardito et al. (Eds.): INTERACT 2021, LNCS 12933, pp. 562–584, 2021.
https://doi.org/10.1007/978-3-030-85616-8_33

Generally, the topic of fairness received particular attention in machine learning and artificial intelligence [35], focusing on the quantification of fairness and the algorithmic perspective. Research in the field of human-computer interaction (HCI), in contrast, studied the perception of fairness by taking the end consumers' perspective (e.g., [30,31,54]). In general, a large part of HCI research addresses the user who directly interacts with a (computational) system. Yet, also other humans are impacted by system design and HCI practices. Hence, it is crucial to consider also these groups' demands in design considerations.

Recommender systems connect and affect several stakeholders including consumers, the platform provider, item providers, and society [36]. While several potential sources of bias have been identified that may lead to unfairness (e.g., [22,40,57]), the focus of attention lies on algorithmic and data bias [8]. A recent review [43] highlights that existing literature tends to consider the implications for the receivers of the recommendations (i.e., end consumers) only. Thus, the research gap lies in considering the provider's interests (and the interests of the society at large) when assessing the ethical impact of recommender systems.

Addressing this research gap, this work focuses on the item provider's perspective on online platforms, which are an underrepresented group of humans in HCI research. This also holds for the music domain. Recommender systems play a prominent role in connecting users with content (and the artists behind this content) on such music platforms. While various studies (e.g., [12,37]) have investigated and shown that current music recommender systems (MRS) do not serve different user segments equally well, there is a research gap concerning the artists' perspective [9,10]. Besides being a so-far underrepresented group of humans in HCI research, music artists have limited opportunities for direct interaction with a music platform (in their role as an item provider)[1]; and yet, they are strongly affected by the design of such systems. While our long-term goal is to have music platforms that are perceived 'fair' from the various stakeholders' perspectives, this work zooms in music artists as the main item providers for music platforms. The concrete goal of this work at hand is to *understand the different dimensions of music platforms (and their recommender systems) that define fairness from the artists' perspective.*

To this end, we conducted semi-structured interviews with music artists from different countries and with varying popularity. Using a Qualitative Content Analysis as proposed by [41], we have (i) identified various aspects that show how the artists feel affected by the current music platforms and their integrated information retrieval and recommender systems components, and (ii) how such music platforms and systems could be improved concerning fairness. Only such understanding can ultimately lead to fairer music platforms that are not only optimized for the interests of the platform providers or the consumers. We deem our work a fundamental contribution to (i) understanding the impact that such music platforms have on artists from their perspective and (ii) understanding what the artists consider fair for them.

---

[1] Interaction is limited to providing recordings and some meta-data (e.g., title, tags).

The remainder of this work is structured as follows: First, we present the conceptual basis and discuss related work (Sect. 2). In Sect. 3, we detail the methods. Section 4 represents the major part of this paper, where we outline and discuss the issues and aspects that we derived from the interviews. As we illustrate the artists' concerns and ideas, we embody a completely novel contribution to the field. In Sect. 5, we discuss how the findings reflect the existing understanding of fairness and derive implications for the operationalization of recommender systems and interaction functionalities on music platforms. In Sect. 6, we summarize our work and point to future research directions.

2   Conceptual Basis and Related Work

A purely technical approach is not sufficient for defining and operationalizing fairness in practice, as seen in previous attempts in several fields [18,19,33,39]. Taking an information systems perspective, [27] emphasize that fair systems need to embrace people, technology, and organizations, and that unsolved challenges exist on all three dimensions. In other words, fairness cannot be operationalized with a lack of a definition or understanding of what fairness connotes in a certain context. The notion of fairness has evolved over time [35]; and particularly recent literature (e.g., [33,48]) emphasizes that for developing a good understanding of fairness in a given context, it is crucial to take a multidisciplinary point of view and listen to the opinions of the various stakeholders involved and affected.

2.1   Defining Algorithmic Fairness

There is a multitude of definitions of (algorithmic) fairness [35]. Two common definitions are 'group' and 'individual' fairness. Individual fairness reflects that similar individuals should be treated similarly. Group fairness ensures that people of a protected group should be treated in the same way as the rest of the population. While [21] clearly distinguishes those two concepts, other works (e.g., [15]) suggest that individual and group fairness are not contradictory and may be achieved simultaneously. In information retrieval, fairness is frequently defined in terms of *exposure* [14,47] or *attention* [49]. Thereby, [14] focus on individual fairness, whereas other works typically consider group fairness [47,49]. The idea of exposure of the artists could also be adopted for the music domain. Yet, it is not answered how a *fair exposure* should be operationalized or—on an even deeper level—what fairness actually means in the context of music platforms. To understand what fairness is from the artists' perspective, we need to involve artists. To the best of our knowledge, there is no public work that reaches out to artists to identify how they feel affected by current music platforms and how they believe the embedded recommenders systems could be improved to be fair for them.

2.2   Perception of Fairness in Algorithms

Besides defining algorithmic fairness, there is a wealth of studies investigating how people perceive and reason about the fairness of algorithms. When it comes to definition, people seem to prefer simple compared to complex ones [51].

In a survey investigating the general perception of fairness of automated decision-making systems, [31] found that people consider that systems make more objective decisions than humans and may also process larger amounts of information which would allow them to make fairer decisions. Yet, the respondents also noted that systems are limited concerning generalizability and modeling reality. Another survey [30] studied how people perceive the fairness of realistically-imperfect systems. As the respondents had contradictory opinions on systems, the authors conclude that is impossible to achieve a broad acceptance in society regarding the "right" fairness definition. The study also highlights that there is a general preference towards human judges compared to a system, even if the participants consider the systems fair or unbiased.

In an online experiment [54], participants rated algorithms according to their perception of fairness. The study found that participants rate systems as more fair if they are favored by it, even in cases where the algorithms were explicitly described to the participants as being very biased to a particular demographic group. This effect was present across various participant groups, in different levels depending on education level, gender, and other aspects of the participants.

In group discussions and interviews with traditionally marginalized groups in the US, [56] sought to understand these groups' perceptions of fairness in algorithms. This work highlights that the opinions regarding the fairness of algorithms vary depending on individual factors, context, different stakeholders' perspectives, and different framing of fairness. This can help to explain inconsistencies in some findings across studies on fairness perception. Further, this shows that the contextual factors should be taken into account when studying algorithmic fairness, supporting the idea of considering the interests of the different groups of stakeholders of the systems.

2.3 Bias and Fairness in Music Recommendation

Besides the general issues and considerations concerning fairness, the music platforms and their recommenders face specific challenges. Among others, the inherent popularity bias is widely discussed. In this section, we discuss related works that study how music recommender can affect artists.

The music market is a typical example of the long-tail economy [6,7] with a highly uneven distribution of demand for the most popular and the least popular items. Since Anderson [6,7] popularized the concept, there is an ongoing debate about whether online platforms indeed facilitate users to consume items in the long tail or, on the contrary, accentuate the 'superstar phenomenon' [46] where the popularity curve gets more skewed in the long-term [11,17,24]. Celma [16] was among the first to study how different recommenders may or may not promote the less popular items in the music domain. Also for other domains, [28] found that users tend to consume a reduced number of items when recommender systems are at play. While these works focused on the consumers' behavior, the findings clearly indicate that recommenders have an impact on item providers.

A study in the Spotify context [5] found that users who follow algorithmically-generated recommendations have reduced diversity in the content they consume.

In contrast, users who consume increasingly more diverse content, are those who reduce the algorithmic consumption and increase their organic consumption. As reducing the diversity in recommendations means that fewer artists get exposure and that it is more difficult for them to reach an audience, we believe that is important to also study the effect that algorithmically-generated recommendations can have on artists (e.g., [23,25]).

Based on the idea that many local artists tend to be obscure long-tail artists, there are research endeavors (e.g., [3,52]) to "localify" recommendations to promote local artists. Although technical approaches to localize music recommendations are proposed, the artists' perspective on such a goal or approach is not discussed. Another work by Spotify [55] studies music consumption on a country level. The latter study investigates how users from a country consume content from another country, and how this consumption pattern evolves and changes over time. The authors identify that language and geographical proximity potentially impact the consumption between countries. Yet, a more fine-grained investigation is needed where also the popularity of the artist is taken into account. Such an endeavor may allow drawing conclusions about the chances given to local artists for gaining a larger audience using these platforms.

Mehrotra et al. [42] acknowledge that fair music recommenders need to consider multiple stakeholders. They define the recommendation problem as a marketplace and consider the perspectives of the music consumers and the artists. Intending to achieve algorithmic fairness, they define a fairness metric for artists that they base on the popularity distribution in the recommendations. While that work points out that there are different ways of defining fairness, a rationale for their choice and definition are missing.

However, previous work rarely reaches out to artists and, to date, no work involves music artists for understanding how music platforms can be fair for them. Baym [13] builds on interviews with artists to investigate how digital technologies changed their interaction with the audience. Andersen and Knees [4] interview artists for investigating their assessment of algorithms and artificial intelligence in the music creation process; our work, in contrast, refers to recommenders for music consumers. Aguiar and colleagues [1,2] analyze how strategic decisions and recommenders embedded in music platforms affect music consumption behavior and the success of songs. Ferraro and colleagues [23,25] take an algorithmic approach to analyze the impact of MRS on users' behavior and how this affects different groups of artists. Holzapfel et al. [34] raise ethical implications in music information retrieval and conceptually illustrate how music platforms may negatively impact certain groups of artists.

3   Methods

To understand the artists' perspective on the current music platforms and their embedded MRS, we conducted semi-structured interviews with music artists. The interviews took place from December 2019 through March 2020. The interviews are part of our ongoing research to explore viable solutions for fairer music platforms and MRS, this work at hand focuses on understanding the artists' perspective on what represents a fair music platform.

We carried out 9 semi-structured interviews with music artists. According to research practice [20,44], the sample size is adequate and, more importantly, we reached a high level of thematic saturation [29] with the same topics being repeatedly mentioned across the interviews. The interviews were designed to last one hour in total for each interview including a brief and general introduction to MRS and music platforms. We used open questions with the aspiration that the artists would bring up their own ideas that might not be considered in the field before. In addition, we proposed specific alternatives to gather the artists' opinions on those alternatives.

In the following, we detail the interview process. The materials used for the interviews (i.e., invitation letter, consent form, first version of questions, final version of questions) can be found on Zenodo[2].

3.1 Interviews

Before the interviews, we informed that the data and results of the interviews will be kept anonymous at all times, which was important so the artists could feel free to share concerns regarding the music platforms or issues related to the music industry. In addition to the consent form, we asked the participants to fill out a short form with optional information about themselves that would be used to refer to their answers (i.e., age, gender, country, genre, popularity level, number of records/singles, years active in the music industry, contracts with labels). The first 10 min of the interview were used to explain the project's purpose and to give a general introduction to MRS and how these are integrated into current music platforms.

For the interview part, we defined a protocol to be used during the interviews which included a set of guiding questions and tentative question to encourage the interviewees to elaborate further. The protocol was developed so that each guiding question addressed and explored various topics and issues of how the music platforms might affect artists. As the first step in elaborating this guide, we started with collecting information and ideas about the general aspects of current music platforms that could affect artists. In a second step, we formulated questions to address the identified issues. Since the rich collection of potentially interesting issues had to be reduced to fit the time scope of an interview and to have (a narrower) focus, in the third step, each team member gave a score between 1 and 3 to each of the original 36 questions according to priority, with 1 being the highest priority. Afterward, the team discussed the 14 questions with differing scores until consensus was reached. Based on the agreement between the scores we defined a definitive list of guiding 21 questions (whereof we use 11 as main questions and 10 as sub-questions) to be used in the interview protocol (Table 1). Note, all interviews were held in Spanish and the materials provided to participants were all in Spanish.

---

[2] https://doi.org/10.5281/zenodo.4793395.

Table 1. Guiding questions in the interview protocol.

No.	Topic	Guiding question
1	Convey interest, gain trust	Do you use any platform to listen to music? What's your experience with it?
2	Reflecting	Do you think your career would be much different without these systems?
3	Lack of control	Which of your music tracks should be recommended more and which less?
4	Bias to more popular	There are groups of artists that are not recommended by the system because of different reasons. Do you see any alternatives for this?
5	Diversity	Music considered "niche music" is not recommended to many users, should the system nurture diversity (e.g., in terms of genres, styles, artists from all over the world, popular and not-yet-popular) or focus more on recommending what the user is familiar with?
6	Size of repertoire	If artist X has more music than the artists Y, do you think the system should recommend more music by artist X—or should the recommendation be independent of an artist's repertoire?
7	New artists	For a given user out of 100 recommendations, how many do you think should be new artists?
8	New music	Should your older songs be promoted more than your newer songs?
9	Country quotas	In a music platform that has more users from country X but more artists from country Y, the artists from X could be recommended more than artists from Y. What is the behavior that you expect from the system in that case?
10	Influencing the users	Currently, K-pop is the 7th most listened genre, over R& B and classical music. Such a popularity distribution could also refer to gender, country, or other aspects of the music. Do you think the systems should try to reproduce this behavior, or should try to provoke a change on it?
11	Income distribution	Do you think the current model based on number of streams is good or there could be a better model?

We note limitations of our interview design. First, while we cater for diversity, our sample is not representative of the population of music artists. The findings we report should, thus, be viewed as a deep exploration of our sample's beliefs and attitudes, but not as generalizing to the artist population as a whole. Yet, the findings indicate that we reached a high level of saturation with the same topics being repeatedly mentioned across the interviews. Second, while we assure anonymity in the presentation of the results, the interviewer naturally knows the participants' identity, which may have influenced participants such that some issues may not have been voiced. As some of the participants sometimes used strong language and addressed delicate issues, we believe that we were able to maintain a comfortable atmosphere with a high level of trust.

3.2   Participants

We recruited 9 music artists that we consider diverse—in the kind of music they perform, their popularity, location, age, and gender. Four of the participants are between 26–35 years old, four are between 36–45, and one is within the range 46–55. Seven are male and two are female. Most of these artists have many projects in parallel (one is a solo artist, the others work with many bands). The artists were born in four different countries (i.e., Australia, Spain, Russia, Uruguay) and started their careers in three different countries (i.e., Spain, Uruguay, Cuba).

The genres that the artists consider their music sum up to a total of 24. Examples are folk, pop, ska, punk-rock, dubstep, D&B, and world music. The number of years in the industry is between 4 and 25. The number of albums released ranges between one and ten. Five participants consider themselves 'independent artist', three have a contract with one of the three major labels (i.e., Sony, Universal, Warner), two have a contract with an independent label. Five artists consider themselves internationally known, four are known within their country. The specific information of each participant is given in Table 2, including the identifier that we use to refer to participants for quotes.

3.3   Processing and Analysis

Following the methodology of Qualitative Content Analysis [41], the interviews were recorded and transcribed, followed by developing an annotation scheme (i.e., coding) inductively from the transcriptions of the interviews, which we used to annotate the transcriptions accordingly.

The total duration of the recordings is 420 min, which transcribed correspond to 33,669 words. The annotation scheme was developed inductively from the transcriptions, where statements were used as the level annotations. Often, statements were on sentence level; yet, many sentences include two or more statements. Note that the annotation scheme was developed in English while the transcriptions were kept in their original language (i.e., Spanish). The development of the annotation scheme and the annotation of statements itself was an iterative process where we assigned a topic to a specific sentence and if it did not fit to any of the previous topics then a new one was defined. We iterate a total of 4 times and the final annotations were reviewed by a different person than the annotator to increase intercoder reliability.

The final annotation scheme includes a total of 15 overall topics that were obtained from 752 annotated text sections. In Table 3, we describe the topics with

Table 2. Information about the participants.

ID	Country	Age	Music styles	Audience	Gender	Contract
P1	Uruguay	46–55	Rock, Folk, Hip-Hop, Electronic	International	Male	Major label
P2	Uruguay	26–35	Rock, Hip-Hop, Reggae, Dub	Local	Male	Major label
P3	Uruguay	36–45	Ska, Punk/Rock, Dub, Dubstep, D&B	International	Male	Major label
P4	Spain	26–35	Indie, Rock	Local	Male	Independent
PF1	Cuba	36–45	World, Jazz, Cuban Music, Electronic	International	Female	Independent
PF2	Spain	26–35	Indie Pop, Singer-songwriter	Local	Female	Indie label
PN1	Uruguay	26–35	Alternative Rock/Indie, Progressive Rock	Local	Male	Independent
PJ1	Spain	36–45	Jazz, Free Improvisation	International	Male	Independent
PR1	Spain	36–45	Hip-Hop, Reggae, Blues, Salsa, Flamenco	International	Male	Indie label

Table 3. Details on the annotation scheme.

Topic	Description	Example of annotation
User view	Participant comments on using a music platform in the role of a music consumer	*PN1: "I usually read the artist's biography and the influences of an artist."*
Artist view	Participant expresses opinion from the point of view of their artist role.	*P2: "[...] it wouldn't hurt if the systems were More random, not that obvious—if you like 'Beatles,' I recommend 'Rolling Stones.'"*
Lack of control	Reference to giving more control either to the artists over the music presented, or to users over what they get recommended	*P2: "As an artist, I would love to have more freedom of action over my music on the platform."*
Diversity	Related to any aspect of diversity in the recommendation	*P3: "I would expect that the music platforms promote more diverse content"*
Context of music	Aspects related to information and presentation apart from the music; the context that it is embedded in	*P1: "There are songs that have history, [you cannot ignore that]."*
New music	Participant refers to artists new on a music platform or new music of existing artists.	*P2: " [...] it makes sense if half of the recommendations [made by the music platform are songs of] new artists."*
Popularity bias	Participant refers to aspects related to popularity bias of recommender systems or the music business	*P4: "The problem is [that] the recommender system systematically ignores all those potential artists because it is easier to recommend [what is more popular]."*
Influencing behavior/taste	Participant expresses opinion concerning music platforms' opportunity to influence users' listening behavior or music taste	*PF1: "In my opinion, you can't impose some [specific] Music to the users."*
Transparency	Refers to the need for information about how a music platform works and how its recommender system makes decisions	*PN1: "If a human makes that decision if he says 'I have a small store, I am going to put it this way,' I will understand it better than if an algorithm does it."*
Labels'/ platforms' interests	Participant refers to the interests of stakeholders such as the music platform providers or record companies	*P2: "[A platform] needs to take responsibility for its recommender system [...] Obviously, they are commercially not capable or not interested."*
Size of artists' repertoire	Participant distinguishes between artists with more or fewer songs or albums	*PR1: "If you have more songs, you have more chances to satisfy different audiences."*
Quotas for local music	Participant mentions regulations for local music such as Quotas for local artists on music platforms	*PR1: "Otherwise, you won't know what there is in your country."*
Gender balance	Participant talks about gender bias in the music industry or on music platforms, or how recommendations might be fair(er) from a gender perspective	*PN1: "[...] the population of the world is 50% women. So it would be ridiculous if the system wouldn't recommend it."*
Regulation of recommendations	Participant refers to regulations or policies for music platforms or their recommender systems	*P3: "[...] the question is if it should be imposed by the state [to promote local music]."*
Royalties distribution	Participant refers to royalties generated on music platforms or their distribution Among artists	*PF1: "It is absurd what [the platform] pays to the artists."*

an example annotation for each topic. Note, quotes are given as translations to English, whereas the interviews were held in Spanish. Table 4 presents the number of annotations per participant per topic.

Table 4. Statistics about annotations.

Topic	P4	PF1	P3	P2	P1	PN1	PJ1	PR1	PF2	Total
User view	8	1	5	8	6	5	4	2	7	46
Artist view	15	12	25	22	14	17	4	9	13	131
Lack of control	15	4	8	14	6	5	0	2	8	62
Diversity	5	2	8	6	4	2	1	3	8	39
Context of music	7	6	8	2	17	1	0	5	0	46
New music	12	6	7	8	6	14	6	10	13	82
Popularity bias	6	0	8	5	1	4	2	5	1	32
Influencing user behavior/taste	7	2	17	7	16	3	1	7	7	67
Transparency	7	0	11	13	2	6	0	2	2	43
Labels'/platforms' interests	8	4	14	17	13	5	5	11	5	82
Size of artists' repertoire	2	1	2	2	2	4	1	2	1	17
Quotas for local music	3	3	8	3	5	5	2	2	3	34
Gender balance	5	3	5	4	0	2	1	1	2	23
Regulations of recommendations	3	0	3	0	4	0	0	0	0	10
Artists' income distribution	3	1	4	9	4	4	3	7	3	38
Total	106	45	133	120	100	77	30	68	73	752

4 Results

In the first part of this section (Sects. 4.1 to 4.3), we present how the artists feel affected by current music platforms. Subsequently (Sects. 4.4 to 4.8), we discuss those topics that give direction on what the artists consider fair music platforms; in the paper at hand, we report those topics that were addressed by *all* participants. Table 5 provides an overview of these topics and summarizes what the participating artists deem necessary for future fair MRS.

4.1 Fragmented Presentation

The participants report that they do not find adequate the way they are presented on the music platforms.

Two artists (P2 and P3) mention that their artist profiles on the music platforms show old tracks at the top because those are the most-listened items over the years. *P3: "But it is something that I have done 10 years ago. [The platform] puts the most listened tracks. [...] and you have to scroll down to reach the latest album."*

Also, the context in which artists and their music are presented may affect their public image; e.g., the artist P3 refers to a feature that serves users with an automatically generated playlist (called "radio"). The "radio" of an artist is an infinite playlist that includes tracks of this artist and also music by other artists. P3 reports that the "radio" based on his band includes music that he does not like and features artists that he distances himself from ideologically. *P3: "I see things that I do not like and that I reject ideologically. Why appears [Band X]?"*

P3 explains that the band works hard on creating a certain public image—with the lyrics, the music, the art. The music platform then mixes it with something different. *P3: "I don't think the same people listen to it. That bothers me as an artist."*

P1 states that the current music platforms disconnect the music from its context. He points out that a song is inseparable from its social context. *P1: "Music—art—is a representation of people's sensitivity, it's a diary of people telling what happens." P1: "Listening to hip-hop from the '90s [is tied to] the slums of Los Angeles, of New York, and [to] what was happening at that time. That music comes from a place. It doesn't come out of nowhere."* P1 thinks that current music platforms do not provide much context of the music and emphasizes that including such information would enhance the experience. *P1: "[...] there are songs that have their history, their function. So the more information there is—who are the people who made that song, with whom, how, where, why they sing it—, I know it would be much richer."* Yet, P1 adds that some music may not convey any deeper message but exists for business reasons only. *P1: "[They are] made to sell more records."* He puts the example of the genre Reggaeton, for which he thinks that frequently the explicit video is the selling argument and not the music. In such a case, adding information about the context would not add much to the user experience.

4.2   Reaching an Audience

Another frequently mentioned issue is the difficulty to reach a larger audience, either because the artists are newcomers or when established artists enter a new music platform. This issue is usually known in recommenders systems as the item cold-start problem. While it has become easier than ever before to access an enormous amount of music, the artists (P2, PN1, PF1, PF2, PR1) state that it is not easy to discover less popular artists with current music platforms; it requires the user actively looking for those artists when encountering them via other sources such as magazines or interviews. PF1 feels that it is very difficult to reach a larger audience. *PF1: "If [a track] hasn't been listened to a number of times, it does not show up, and that means that it is not being recommended." PF2: "[...] if [the music platform] does not recommend things that [...] have rarely been listened to, then it enters a circle that never ends... it always goes... you will never be listened to more. Then you're stuck there until someone pays for you to have the promotion."* P2 also participates in a less-popular band project. He affirms that music platforms make it difficult for the users to reach the band. *P2: "[...] it would not hurt if the systems were more random, not that obvious—if you like 'Beatles,' I recommend 'Rolling Stones.'"*

PN1 underlines that the emergence of large music platforms changed the entire music industry, making it even more difficult for new artists to reach a larger audience. *PN1: "Before you could go [to a label,] with something super weird but super interesting that could catch their attention and take you on a tour [...]. [But now] it's not the music that sells. [If] you don't have followers, you don't have content, you have nothing, you're nobody, and that's why you* won't appear [in the recommendations]. You have to grow in a different way, through Instagram for example, which doesn't have anything to do [with music], and the value of music gets lost."

Also, PR1 points out the difficulty of getting visibility on the music platforms if the artist is not popular. Similar to PN1, PR1 argues that it was also hard for an artist to reach visibility before the emergence of music platforms. *PR1:* *"[...] in this business, there have always been many traps. The musician wants to make music, but it's a business. At first, you don't want to see it because you want to make music and you are happy. So for example, the old record companies used to have a monopoly before the [social] networks. You were only played on the radio if they paid for it. They said, '[This artist] has sold twenty thousand copies' but it was the record company itself that bought twenty thousand copies. [...] then everyone wanted to hear that [artist]." PR1: "On YouTube, there were companies that made it to reach the million [...] And I think that [happens] today too. You can buy visits [...]."* P3 adds that artists being excluded, making it hard to reach an audience, has happened ever since, and he provides an anecdote of Bob Marley going to a radio station to force them to play his songs. *P3: "They had Bob Marley and they didn't play it!"* P3 argues that artists who really want to reach an audience will find a way to do it. Yet, probably not through a music platform but using other digital mediums.

In conclusion, there is no clear consensus about the actions that music platforms should take to be fair in this context. Among the mentioned alternatives, we see that some artists (e.g., P1, P2, P4, PN1) suggest that the music platforms should have a minimum quota of starting artists that are recommended to all the users alike. Others suggest that new artists should use alternative ways to reach an audience.

4.3   Transparency

Several artists (P3, PN1, P1, P2, PR1, PF2) mention that the music platforms should be more transparent. P3 states that he does not understand how exactly the music platform promotes some artists more than others; e.g., in the automatic playlists or the curated playlists. *P3: "It would be nice if the platform was equitable, or fair, for everyone in that sense, because if I'm one of the largest bands in Uruguay, why I'm not in many of the playlists there? Is it the platform that doesn't want me there? Is it me doing something wrong? [...] Maybe the platform does not benefit much with what we do, so they discard us."* PF2 thinks that the music platforms should be more transparent towards the artists about how their recommendation system works and what the artists have to do for being recommended more often. PF2 thinks that this is particularly important for independent artists. *PF2: "[...] you are a bit naked there. You put your music on Spotify and mention in the concerts that they can listen [to your music], but you don't see any change. For example, no one explains to you that it is important that other people add your songs to their playlists so that the algorithm will recommend you."*

PJ1 feels that music platforms are profitable only for some of the stakeholders. The artist wonders what the goals of the music platforms are. *PJ1: "Is the goal for people to listen to music or is the goal to make money from it?" PJ1: "The people who invest in these things at the [...] powerful industry level, these people do make money from this. The others do not. [...] there is no middle class. There is an upper class and a lower class."*

Regarding transparency in algorithmic decisions, the artist PN1 mentions that although both humans and algorithms may be biased, a non-ideal decision made by a human may be easier to accept than one taken by an algorithm. *PN1: "[...] if a human makes that decision if he says 'I have a small store, I am going to put it this way,' I will understand it much more than if an algorithm does it."*

4.4   Influencing Users' Listening Behavior

One of our interests was to learn what the artists think about the music platforms' opportunities and power to influence the users' listening behavior. For example, by tailoring the music recommendations, a music platform could balance genres or consider a gender balance among the recommended artists. In an open question, which did not mention gender, all artists came up with the issue that content by female artists is not well represented. We found that all artists agreed that the music platforms should promote content by female artists to reach a gender balance in what users consume.

While there was clear consensus to influence users' listening behavior with respect to the artists' gender—to reach a balance—, there was also a clear agreement *not* to do so concerning the music style. For the latter, they think it is better not to influence the users. P2 suggests a gender balance in the recommendations. *P2: "[Platforms have] a huge responsibility in making recommendations. "* Regarding gender balance, PN1 states, *PN1: "[...] the population of the world is 50% women. So it would be ridiculous if the system wouldn't recommend them."* PN1 suggests a progressive change, which he thinks will prevent users to perceive it as something negative and leave the music platform. PF1 states that the system could enforce a 50% balance of male and female artists because many other factors different from gender, e.g., the music style, define whether someone will like what is recommended. Finally, PF2 considers that using quotas alone would not be enough, as there is a need for a change in education to have a bigger impact. However, she agrees that artists could be better off with quotas. *PF2: "As a female artist I would like the system to recommend my music to someone that only listens to the music of male artists."*

4.5   Popularity Bias

Researchers have put a lot of effort into reducing the popularity bias and improving the recommendations for items in the long-tail of the popularity distribution (e.g., [53]). Reaching out to the artists, we wanted to explore their perspective on that issue; whether or not they feel that current systems allow the users to access items of less popular artists; and how this could be improved in the future.

P4 states that it may be easier for the music platforms to recommend what is popular because it can satisfy the majority of the users. Yet, P4 points out, *P4: "The problem is [that] the recommender system systematically ignores all those potential artists [...]"*. P4 thinks that some users may be happy with the recommendation of the generally popular items, whereas others may not and probably leave the music platform. The users who are more passionate about music will not see any advantage in using such recommendations. *P4: "[...] it's wrong that you don't have the option to explore that long-tail. [You can't] take advantage of a recommender system if you want to [explore the long-tail]."* PR1 considers that the music platforms may generate higher revenues if they recommend popular artists, and may therefore not be interested in promoting less popular content.

Although strongly advocating the promotion of diverse content, PF2 speculates that this may again lead to having users listen to widely popular music. Therefore, she claims that the music platforms should prevent it, *PF2: "[...] otherwise, you will always end up listening to American music."*

All interviewees agree that it is crucial that the music platforms also recommend less popular music. They believe that the music platforms will harm the music culture if recommendations are limited to the most popular artists.

4.6 Artists' Repertoire Size

While popularity bias is a widely researched topic in the recommender systems community, and for MRS in particular, little attention is paid towards how the size of an artist's repertoire affects the probability of their songs being recommended to users. The artists' opinions arc divided concerning how a music platform should reflect the differences in the repertoire sizes. While three artists think that artists with larger repertoires should be more represented in recommendations (P1, PF1, PR1), four artists do not support that idea (P2, P4, P3, PF2), and two artists were indecisive (PN1, PJ1).

P1 argues that the higher number of records leading to an increased likelihood for an artist's items being recommended reflects what happens outside the music platforms. *P1: "[...] that's fine, the same thing happens in real life if someone makes 25 records, you will surely come across it at some point."* PJ1, P2, and P4, in contrast, argue that having more records should not be a reason for being recommended more often. *P2: "[...] I know so many amazing bands with only one album, it has 10 songs. And you will never get to those [being recommended]."* *PJ1: "This is delicate because there are big artists that have one album, or the opposite."* *P4: "Intuitively, I think it is unfair that an artist with more music is recommended more. [...] if an artist has 30 albums but they are all completely different from the previous ones, then it makes sense. But if there is an artist whose albums are all the same ...[it does not]."*

PR1 points out that artists with more songs are probably more diverse in their repertoire. So, it is more about the diversity than the size of the repertoire. *PR1: "If you have more songs you have more chances to satisfy different audiences."*

P3 states that an artist profile with more songs may leave the impression that the artist is in the music business for a long time, which may be a reason to recommend the artist more. But he adds that repertoire size should not be given such importance. PF2 adds that sometimes not all tracks of an artist are available on a particular music platform, so the repertoire size on the music platform would not reflect reality.

PN1 raises the issue that it may depend on the users' goals whether the artists' repertoire size matters. If a user wants to explore a new artist, then it is not useful to recommend to this user an artist with only a few songs. For users exploring on a track basis, the artists' repertoire size is irrelevant.

4.7   Quotas for Local Music

Today's most prominent music platforms operate in several countries, more or less globally. With the widely adopted collaborative filtering approaches for recommendations ("people who like that..., also like that..."), it may happen that the music preferences of users in countries with a large number of users may influence the algorithms' outputs globally. As a result, artists that are popular in countries with a smaller user number will have fewer chances to be recommended than artists that are popular in countries with a large number of users.

While there are studies investigating the existence of local trends on global music streaming (e.g., [55]) and recommendation approaches that account for country-specific music preferences (e.g., [12]), it is not clear whether and how current music platforms consider local repertoire. Similarly, outside the music platforms, some countries define quotas of local content for radio stations while other countries do not. Yet, such quotas for radio do not apply to online music platforms, specifically not for automatic recommendations.

We asked the artists about quotas, the desirability and applicability to have quotas on online music platforms, and for automatic recommendations in particular. We also asked for potential alternative solutions to deal with local content. Three artists mention that the recommenders should have quotas for local music. Other five artists were not sure whether quotas were the right solution but emphasized that it is important that the music platforms promote local content.

PR1 agrees with quotas and indicates that *PR1: "otherwise, you won't know what there is in your country."* PJ1 is ambivalent. On the one hand, he believes that it is not right to base such decisions on where a person is from, on the other hand, he sees the need to promote local artists because they are at a disadvantage from the start; and with quotas, they could make up for it over time.

P1 suggests abandoning the idea of defining locality in terms of countries because national borders are not necessarily cultural borders. He proposes to define locality within a radius of a user: Artists that are in a certain radius (e.g., within a radius of 5000 km) should be given a higher weight than artists outside that radius; and within the radius, different weights again, with higher weights for the closest artists. Yet, the same artist (P1) emphasizes that quotas are a necessary measure in some countries because, otherwise, local artists would not be able to make a living solely from music. Accordingly, he suggests that quotas should also apply to automatic recommendations and proposes to use a combination of country and radius. *P1: "[...] if you go to the border [between Uruguay and Brazil] [...], the Brazilian influence is greater than the Uruguayan one. So it seems to me that the radius is more representative for culture."*

PN1 considers it peculiar that there is a higher chance for the user to be presented with US artists compared to local ones, even if the latter are locally famous and popular. PN1 calls for more transparency and draws an analogy to the news sector. *PN1: "[...] it is like reading the news in the New York Times instead of the local newspaper. [...] you know that you're reading the New York Times or the local news. But you don't know whether it is an algorithm that makes the recommendation."*

PF2 and P4 argue against quotas because this could cause users to leave the music platform if they do not like local music. Yet, both emphasize giving importance to locality. P4 suggests giving individual users the chance to choose the degree of locality they want to have. PF2 suggests promoting local content by letting users indicate the countries they would like to receive recommendations from besides their own country. Artists could also be allowed to indicate in which countries they would like their music to be recommended. This would enable artists to reach other countries. *PF2: "As an artist, you could reach more countries if you are interested."*

P2 is unsure whether quotas are the ideal measure but emphasizes that the music platforms have responsibility for what their algorithms recommend. *P2: "[A platform provider] needs to take responsibility for its recommender system— [...] understand the situation. [...] Obviously, they are commercially not capable or not interested [...] but it would be great [...] if [they] find a way to link [...] a Yankee band with a Uruguayan band [...] make a connection that contributes. [...] [The platforms] have their share of responsibility for what they are showing or recommending. I don't know if there should be quotas [...] but [...] it would be great if there was something."*

P3 questions whether quotas should be enforced by law and suggests that music platforms take the responsibility for it. *P3: "The question is whether it should indeed be state-imposed. For things to be that way, do we have to impose it?" P3: "[the platform] should do what is ethically correct. [...] If I were Spotify [...] I would [promote local content] in every country."* While P3 voices concerns about whether the music platforms should be trusted in deciding what to promote more or what to promote less. Yet, for gender fairness and local content, P3 is confident that the music platforms could find the right balance.

Different from the common understanding of local quotas, PF1 suggests that it should be the opposite: Instead of having quotas for local music in smaller markets, there should be quotas in larger markets to include music from those smaller markets. In addition, PF1 points out that giving users the possibility to explore the country-specific music scene would be more beneficial for the artists. *PF1: "[...] provide the possibility to listen to what you have not listened to before. For example, 'what have I not listened to from Colombia?' 'What is underground in such a country?' If you give the local artists a voice and let them tell the story behind their music, that would be more interesting."*

4.8 New Music

New music may refer to (i) artists that are new to a user (thus, the discovery of artists) and also to (ii) a new track or album released by an artist that had already been part of the music platform.

Most of the interviewed artists agree that the artists should be in control of what tracks or albums get more recommended. In the case that they are not in control themselves, they strongly prefer a recommender system that puts more weight on their latest releases. PR1 states that every artist wants their new music to be promoted so that the world finds out they have a new release. *PR1: "[...] you do a promotion campaign to tell that you released more [content]. To tell the world, 'Hey! There is a new album!' [...] Like saying, 'Hello, I'm here.'"* Also, some artists feel more identified with what they are doing now compared to music they released many years ago, which is another reason for them to prefer the promotion of the latest release. *P3: "[...] it is something that I have done 10 years ago. [...] I don't know if I feel identified [with it]."*

For allowing users to discover artists that they are not yet familiar with, there is no clear consent either. While all agree—in varying degrees, though— that the music platforms should allow users to discover artists that they do not know, it remains unclear how the music platforms should do that. Most of the interviewed artists state that the user should be in control, having the opportunity to indicate that they want to discover new artists, and when they want to do so. *P2: "[...] being able to choose would be good. A button that says 'I'm open to new stuff' or 'Let me listen to what I want.' Because sometimes you want new stuff and sometimes you want something very specific."*

5 Discussion

Table 5 summarizes the concrete aspects in which the music platforms could be more beneficial for the artists. The results show that the artists' perspective on fairness relates closely to the end consumer's perspective on some aspects, whereas the interviews could also reveal that artists face problems that are not reflected in previous work on the consumer's perspective. The different roles (here, users vs item provider) may lead to varying perceptions of fairness (see [54]). For example, gender fairness is frequently also discussed from the consumer or societal perspective [50]. Our results make concrete that artists aim for *gender balance*. In contrast, the problems associated with the fragmented presentation (e.g., music presented detached from its context; artist profile may list tracks first that am artist does not identify with anymore), for example, accrue from the artist perspective. Furthermore, the results suggest that not all identified aspects that artists consider important for a fair music platform are directly linked to algorithmic fairness. For instance, the perceived lack of control and the demand that music is presented in a way so that its context is clear are not of algorithmic nature; rather, these are system design issues. Hence, the HCI community is called to address the needs of this so-far underrepresented group.

Table 5. Aspects to improve with most of the artists in agreement.

Topic	Description
Quotas for local music	Promoting local music
Gender balance	Expectation of gender balance in recommendations
Popularity bias	Recommending items in the long tail, Not only the most popular artists
Lack of control	Giving artists control concerning the tracks that are promoted; if not in control, preference for promotion of Latest releases
Transparency	Transparency about how the algorithms work; why is music Recommended or not
Influencing users' taste	The system should not influence the user's taste
Music in context	Music should be presented to users with information about its Context

For operationalization, we can build on the strong foundations of prior research. For instance, from the interviews, we understand that artists see the need to promote new and less popular artists. While collaborative filtering is commonly used in MRS, it is an approach that is prone to popularity bias. Content-based approaches based on the advancements in music information retrieval (see [45]) could be especially apt to promote new and less popular artists.

Furthermore, as different the topics of promoting local music and ensuring gender balance in recommendations seem the basis for their operationalization exhibit similarities. First, meta-data about both, the artists' regional or cultural affiliation as well as gender information, are available for popular artists (e.g., using sources such as Wikipedia or MusicBrainz), but scarce for new and less popular artists. Thus, while existing meta-data may be used, other approaches have to be leveraged to gather missing data; this may be challenging for new and less popular artists, in particular. Second, many works investigate the diversity or coverage of computed recommendations (see [38]), little is known about how to ensure an envisaged ratio of attributes (here: region, culture, gender). In [26], we proposed a re-ranking approach to gradually achieve gender balance. Similar approaches may be used for other attributes. Targeting ratios for multiple criteria is more complex.

In addition, the finding that artists perceive their profile presentation as being fragmented and that their music is presented detached from its context, are an inspiration and rationale to consolidate and structure information from dispersed sources, so that the music presentation can be enriched with this information and put into context. For new and less popular artists, but also for new music by established artists, it will be challenging to retrieve such information. Besides challenges concerning the operationalization for information retrieval and consolidation, it is subject to future research to investigate how such contextualized information should be presented so that it (i) puts the music into context as meant by the artist and (ii) is understandable and appealing to the user. This is a great opportunity to also address the artists' demand for more control and to add interaction functionality for this stakeholder. This functionality may be as simple as an interface to insert context information or correct information that was retrieved from other sources. Providing templates for visualizing context information may add control. Further, templates and functionalities to give the artist page a personal branding may be appreciated by artists because the visual representation has long been a strong component in the music field (e.g., album artwork, stage shows, the association of genres with colors, etc.).

6   Conclusions

We reached out to music artists and conducted semi-structured interviews to understand how they are affected by current music platforms and what improvements they deem necessary so that those music platforms are *fair* from the artists' perspective. Thereby, we paid particular attention to music recommender systems that are an integral part of today's music platforms. We conclude that the participating artists' perceptions and ideas are well aligned.

The interviewed artists agree on some aspects that are needed to make the music platforms fairer: 1) The artists call for better promotion of local music; 2) they agree that gender balance in the recommendations is indisputably expected; 3) the artists voice that music items in the long tail of the popularity distribution (not only the most popular artists) have to be included in the recommendations shown to users; 4) the participants advocate giving control to the artists over the tracks that are promoted or higher weighted in recommendations (if they are not directly in control, then they generally favor the promotion of their latest releases); 5) they request transparency about how the algorithms work, to understand why their music is recommended or not; 6) the artists consider a system that influences a user's taste (or attempts to do so) an undesired misuse; and 7) they would appreciate if the music platforms would be enriched with information that puts the music into context.

Besides the consensus on many topics, there is no clear direction for others: 1) There is no agreement concerning quotas for local content; 2) no clear majority whether the size of the artists' repertoire should be reflected in recommendations; 3) while the artists seem to agree that new artists should be given space on the music platforms, there is no agreement on how to operationalize this; and there is 4) no clear agreement whether a music platform should promote the discovery of artists previously unknown by a user. Overall, while there is a prevailing belief that music platforms would open up the long-tail to users and encourage them to consume more of those items, the interviews suggest that the long-tail items and artists remain obscure.

A limitation of our work relates to the chosen context. We deliberately drew the sample from a big and coherent music market (Spanish-speaking music market), which is geographically dispersed (Europe, North America, and South America), and where the artists are diverse in styles, career, and popularity.

While we could find shared ideas and opinions across the sample which is diverse in many aspects, the sample's perception could still be aligned from a cultural perspective (e.g., Uruguay and Spain are similar in most of Hofstede's cultural dimensions [32]). Yet, this defined setting (artists from Spanish-speaking countries) is a good opportunity for upcoming research to draw comparisons to other defined groups of artists. Future research may investigate the identified aspects in different contexts and more depth. Further, while we catered for some aspects of diversity in our sample of music artists, reaching out to a larger sample will allow for even more aspects of diversity (e.g., including artist of non-binary gender, considering solo artists, mixed-gender bands, mono-gender bands, various ethnic groups, artists dedicated to niche music). Although we reached thematic saturation, reaching out to a wider set of diverse artists may reveal additional topics or different viewpoints.

These caveats notwithstanding, our work gives direction towards relevant topics for fairness on music platforms and their integrated MRS. The findings indicate pathways towards fairer music platforms, whereas the concrete operationalization is subject to further research.

Naturally, the music domain has its specificities. Yet, our study results may inspire studies in other domains. First, our findings indicate that different roles may come with different fairness perceptions and requirements. Hence, we encourage studies in other domains where an item provider typically has several items and where a person is the face to the public for themselves, an organization, or a brand (e.g., sports, many technology companies). Second, our findings suggest that perceived unfairness also is tied to a lack of control. Likely, control may also be given with more opportunities for interaction.

Acknowledgments. This research was partially supported by Kakao Corp.

References

1. Aguiar, L.: Let the music play? Free streaming and its effects on digital music consumption. Inf. Econ. Policy **41**, 1–14 (2017). https://doi.org/10.1016/j.infoecopol.2017.06.002
2. Aguiar, L., Waldfogel, J.: Platforms, promotion, and product discovery: evidence from spotify playlists. Tech. rep, National Bureau of Economic Research (2018)
3. Akimchuk, D., Clerico, T., Turnbull, D.: Evaluating recommender system algorithms for generating local music playlists (2019). https://arxiv.org/abs/1907.08687
4. Andersen, K., Knees, P.: Conversations with expert users in music retrieval and research challenges for creative MIR. In: Proceedings of the 17th International Society for Music Information Retrieval Conference, ISMIR 2016, pp. 122–128 (2016)
5. Anderson, A., Maystre, L., Anderson, I., Mehrotra, R., Lalmas, M.: Algorithmic effects on the diversity of consumption on spotify. In: Proceedings of The Web Conference 2020, WWW 2020, pp. 2155–2165 (2020)
6. Anderson, C.: The long tail. Wired, January 2004. https://www.wired.com/2004/10/tail/

7. Anderson, C.: The Long Tail: Why the Future of Business is Selling Less of More. Hyperion, New York (2006)
8. Baeza-Yates, R.: Data and algorithmic bias in the web, New York, NY, USA (2016). https://doi.org/10.1145/2908131.2908135
9. Bauer, C.: Allowing for equal opportunities for artists in music recommendation: a position paper. In: Proceedings of the 1st Workshop on Designing Human-Centric Music Information Research Systems, wsHCMIR 2019, Delft, The Netherlands, pp. 16–18 (2019)
10. Bauer, C.: Report on the ISMIR 2020 special session: how do we help artists? ACM SIGIR Forum **54**(2), 1–7 (2020). http://sigir.org/wp-content/uploads/2020/12/p15.pdf
11. Bauer, C., Kholodylo, M., Strauss, C.: Music recommender systems challenges and opportunities for non-superstar artists. In: Proceedings of the 30th Bled eConference, Bled, Slovenia, pp. 21–32 (2017)
12. Bauer, C., Schedl, M.: Global and country-specific mainstreaminess measures: definitions, analysis, and usage for improving personalized music recommendation systems. PLOS ONE **14**(6), 1–36 (2019). https://doi.org/10.1371/journal.pone.0217389
13. Baym, N.K.: Playing to the Crowd: Musicians, Audiences, and the Intimate Work of Connection, vol. 14. NYU Press, New York (2018)
14. Biega, A.J., Gummadi, K.P., Weikum, G.: Equity of attention: amortizing individual fairness in rankings. In: The 41st International ACM Conference on Research & Development in Information Retrieval, SIGIR 2018, pp. 405–414 (2018)
15. Binns, R.: On the apparent conflict between individual and group fairness. In: Proceedings of the 2020 Conference on Fairness, Accountability, and Transparency, FAT* 2020, pp. 514–524 (2020). https://doi.org/10.1145/3351095.3372864
16. Celma, O.: Music recommendation and discovery: The Long Tail, Long Fail, and Long Play in the Digital Music Space. Springer, Heidelberg (2010). https://doi.org/10.1007/978-3-642-13287-2
17. Coelho, M.P., Mendes, J.Z.: Digital music and the "death of the long tail". J. Bus. Res. **101**, 454–460 (2019)
18. Cramer, H., Garcia-Gathright, J., Reddy, S., Springer, A., Takeo Bouyer, R.: Translation, tracks & data: an algorithmic bias effort in practice. In: Extended Abstracts of the 2019 Conference on Human Factors in Computing Systems, CHI EA 2019, pp. 1–8 (2019). https://doi.org/10.1145/3290607.3299057
19. Cramer, H., Garcia-Gathright, J., Springer, A., Reddy, S.: Assessing and addressing algorithmic bias in practice. Interactions **25**(6), 58–63 (2018)
20. Creswell, J.W., Poth, C.N.: Qualitative Inquiry and Research Design: Choosing Among Five Approaches. Sage Publications, Thousand Oaks (2016)
21. Dwork, C., Hardt, M., Pitassi, T., Reingold, O., Zemel, R.: Fairness through awareness. In: Proceedings of the 3rd Innovations in Theoretical Computer Science Conference, ITCS 2012, pp. 214–226 (2012). https://doi.org/10.1145/2090236.2090255
22. Farnadi, G., Kouki, P., Thompson, S.K., Srinivasan, S., Getoor, L.: A fairness-aware hybrid recommender system. arXiv preprint arXiv:1809.09030 (2018), https://arxiv.org/abs/1809.09030
23. Ferraro, A., Bogdanov, D., Serra, X., Yoon, J.: Artist and style exposure bias in collaborative filtering based music recommendations. In: Proceedings of the 1st Workshop on Designing Human-Centric Music Information Research Systems, wsHCMIR 2019, Delft, The Netherlands, pp. 8–10 (2019)
24. Ferraro, A., Jannach, D., Serra, X.: Exploring longitudinal effects of session-based recommendations. In: 14th ACM Conference on Recommender Systems, RecSys 2020, pp. 474–479 (2020). https://doi.org/10.1145/3383313.3412213

25. Ferraro, A., Jeon, J.H., Kim, B., Serra, X., Bogdanov, D.: Artist biases in collaborative filtering for music recommendation. In: Machine Learning for Media Discovery Workshop at International Conference on Machine Learning (ICML) (2020)
26. Ferraro, A., Serra, X., Bauer, C.: Break the loop: Gender imbalance in music recommenders. In: 6th ACM SIGIR Conference on Human Information Interaction and Retrieval, CHIIR 2021, New York, NY, USA, pp. 249–254. ACM (2021). https://doi.org/10.1145/3406522.3446033
27. Feuerriegel, S., Dolata, M., Schwabe, G.: Fair AI. Bus. Inf. Syst. Eng. **62**(4), 379–384 (2020). https://doi.org/10.1007/s12599-020-00650-3
28. Fleder, D., Hosanagar, K.: Blockbuster culture's next rise or fall: the impact of recommender systems on sales diversity. Manag. Sci. **55**(5), 697–712 (2009)
29. Guest, G., Bunce, A., Johnson, L.: How many interviews are enough?: an experiment with data saturation and variability. Field Methods **18**(1), 59–82 (2006). https://doi.org/10.1177/1525822X05279903
30. Harrison, G., Hanson, J., Jacinto, C., Ramirez, J., Ur, B.: An empirical study on the perceived fairness of realistic, imperfect machine learning models. In: Proceedings of the 2020 Conference on Fairness, Accountability, and Transparency, FAT* 2020, New York, NY, USA, pp. 392–402. ACM (2020). https://doi.org/10.1145/3351095.3372831
31. Helberger, N., Araujo, T., de Vreese, C.H.: Who is the fairest of them all? public attitudes and expectations regarding automated decision-making. Comput. Law Secur. Rev. **39**, 105456 (2020). https://doi.org/10.1016/j.clsr.2020.105456
32. Hofstede, G., Hofstede, G.J., Minkov, M.: Cultures and Organizations: Software of the Mind, vol, 3rd, revised. edn. McGraw-Hill, New York (2010)
33. Holstein, K., Wortman Vaughan, J., Daumé, H., Dudik, M., Wallach, H.: In: Improving fairness in machine learning systems: What do industry practitioners need? , New York, NY, USA (2019). https://doi.org/10.1145/3290605.3300830
34. Holzapfel, A., Sturm, B., Coeckelbergh, M.: Ethical dimensions of music information retrieval technology. Trans. Int. Soc. Music Inf. Retr. **1**(1), 44–55 (2018)
35. Hutchinson, B., Mitchell, M.: 50 years of test (un)fairness: lessons for machine learning. In: Proceedings of the Conference on Fairness, Accountability, and Transparency, FAT* 2019, pp. 49–58 (2019). https://doi.org/10.1145/3287560.3287600
36. Jannach, D., Bauer, C.: Escaping the McNamara fallacy: toward more impactful recommender systems research. AI Mag. **41**(4), 79–95 (2020). https://doi.org/10.1609/aimag.v41i4.5312
37. Kowald, D., Müllner, P., Zangerle, E., Bauer, C., Schedl, M., Lex, E.: Support the underground: characteristics of beyond-mainstream music listeners. EPJ Data. Science **10**(1) (2021). https://doi.org/10.1140/epjds/s13688-021-00268-9
38. Kunaver, M., Požrl, T.: Diversity in recommender systems - a survey. Knowl. Based Syst. **123**, 154–162 (2017). https://doi.org/10.1016/j.knosys.2017.02.009
39. Madaio, M.A., Stark, L., Wortman Vaughan, J., Wallach, H.: In: Co-designing checklists to understand organizational challenges and opportunities around fairness in AI. New York, NY, USA (2020). https://doi.org/10.1145/3313831.3376445
40. Marlin, B., Zemel, R.S., Roweis, S., Slaney, M.: Collaborative filtering and the missing at random assumption. arXiv preprint arXiv:1206.5267 (2012), https://arxiv.org/abs/1206.5267
41. Mayring, P.: Qualitative Content Analysis. In: A Companion to Qualitative Research, chap. 5.12, pp. 159–176. SAGE, London (2004)
42. Mehrotra, R., McInerney, J., Bouchard, H., Lalmas, M., Diaz, F.: Towards a fair marketplace: counterfactual evaluation of the trade-off between relevance, fairness & satisfaction in recommendation systems. In: Proceedings of the 27th ACM International Conference on Information and Knowledge Management, CIKM 2018, pp. 2243–2251 (2018). https://doi.org/10.1145/3269206.3272027

43. Milano, S., Taddeo, M., Floridi, L.: Recommender systems and their ethical challenges. AI Soc. (2020). https://doi.org/10.1007/s00146-020-00950-y
44. Morse, J.M.: Designing funded qualitative research. In: Handbook of Qualitative Research, pp. 220–235. Sage Publications, Thousand Oaks (1994)
45. Murthy, Y.V.S., Koolagudi, S.G.: Content-based music information retrieval (cb-mir) and its applications toward the music industry: A review. ACM Computing Survey **51**(3) (2018). https://doi.org/10.1145/3177849
46. Rosen, S.: The economics of superstars. Am. Econ. Rev. **71**(5), 845–858 (1981). http://www.jstor.org/stable/1803469
47. Sapiezynski, P., Zeng, W., E Robertson, R., Mislove, A., Wilson, C.: Quantifying the impact of user attention on fair group representation in ranked lists. In: Proceedings of The 2019 World Wide Web Conference, WWW 2019, pp. 553–562 (2019). https://doi.org/10.1145/3308560.3317595
48. Selbst, A.D., Boyd, D., Friedler, S.A., Venkatasubramanian, S., Vertesi, J.: Fairness and abstraction in sociotechnical systems. In: Proc. of the Conference on Fairness, Accountability, and Transparency, FAT* 2019, pp. 59–68 (2019). https://doi.org/10.1145/3287560.3287598
49. Singh, A., Joachims, T.: Fairness of exposure in rankings. In: Proceedings of the 24th ACM SIGKDD International Conference on Knowledge Discovery & Data Mining, SIGKDD 2018, pp. 2219–2228 (2018). https://doi.org/10.1145/3219819.3220088
50. Sonboli, N., Smith, J.J., Berenfus, F.C., Burke, R., Fiesler, C.: Fairness and transparency in recommendation: the users' perspective. arXiv preprint arXiv:2103.08786 (2021). https://arxiv.org/abs/2103.08786
51. Srivastava, M., Heidari, H., Krause, A.: Mathematical notions vs. human perception of fairness: a descriptive approach to fairness for machine learning, KDD 2019, New York, NY, USA, pp. 2459–2468. ACM (2019). https://doi.org/10.1145/3292500.3330664
52. Turnbull, D., Waldner, L.: Local music event recommendation with long tail artists (2018). https://arxiv.org/abs/1809.02277
53. Vall, A., Quadrana, M., Schedl, M., Widmer, G.: Order, context and popularity bias in next-song recommendations. Int. J. Multimed. Inf. Retr. **8**(2), 101–113 (2019). https://doi.org/10.1007/s13735-019-00169-8
54. Wang, R., Harper, F.M., Zhu, H.: Factors influencing perceived fairness in algorithmic decision-making: Algorithm outcomes, development procedures, and individual differences. In: Proceedings of the 2020 CHI Conference on Human Factors in Computing Systems, CHI 2020, New York, NY, USA, pp. 1–14. ACM (2020). https://doi.org/10.1145/3313831.3376813
55. Way, S.F., Garcia-Gathright, J., Cramer, H.: Local trends in global music streaming. In: Proceedings of the International AAAI Conference on Web and Social Media, vol. 14, pp. 705–714 (2020)
56. Woodruff, A., Fox, S.E., Rousso-Schindler, S., Warshaw, J.: A qualitative exploration of perceptions of algorithmic fairness. In: Proceedings of the 2018 CHI Conference on Human Factors in Computing Systems, CHI 2018, New York, NY, USA, pp. 1–14. ACM (2018). https://doi.org/10.1145/3173574.3174230
57. Yao, S., Huang, B.: Beyond parity: Fairness objectives for collaborative filtering. In: Proceedings of the 31st International Conference on Neural Information Processing Systems, NIPS 2017, pp. 2925–2934 (2017). https://doi.org/10.5555/3294996.3295052

You Sound Relaxed Now – Measuring Restorative Effects from Speech Signals

Yong Ma$^{(\boxtimes)}$ (iD), Jingyi Li (iD), Heiko Drewes (iD), and Andreas Butz (iD)

LMU Munich, Munich, Germany
{yong.ma,jingyi.li,heiko.drewes,andreas.butz}@ifi.lmu.de
http://www.medien.ifi.lmu.de

Abstract. The recently proposed *restorative environments* have the potential to restore attention and help against fatigue, but how can these effects be verified? We present a novel measurement method which can analyze participants' speech signals in a study before and after a relaxing experience. Compared to other measurements such as attention scales or response tests, speech signal analysis is both less obtrusive and more accessible. In our study, we found that certain time- and frequency-domain speech features such as short-time energy and Mel Frequency Cepstral Coefficients (MFCC) are correlated with the attentional capacity measured by traditional ratings. We thus argue that speech signal analysis can provide a valid measure for attention and its restoration. We describe a practically feasible method for such a speech signal analysis along with some preliminary results.

Keywords: Speech feature analysis · Attention measurement · Restoration

1 Why Measure Attention Restoration from Speech?

The increasing stress for humans in modern urban environments makes physical and mental recovery a vital research topic in human-centered computing. Studies indicate that the exposure to (virtual) natural environments can effectively restore attention [20] and mitigate the feeling of fatigue. Such a *restorative environment* could, for example, be used in automated driving and offer travellers a way of reconnecting with nature and mentally recharging during travel. To measure the effects of attention restoration, existing research mostly uses self-report questionnaires or response tests. However, these traditional approaches interrupt the flow of the experiment and influence the attention being measured. Other proposed attention detection methods use physiological sensors. For instance, eye movement can be used to gauge attention [7] and analyze its recovery. Signals from EEG [2,19] and ECG [4] can also effectively detect attention restoration, but are currently still much less convenient to measure. Analyzing the human speech signal may present a very unobtrusive and effective alternative.

© IFIP International Federation for Information Processing 2021
Published by Springer Nature Switzerland AG 2021
C. Ardito et al. (Eds.): INTERACT 2021, LNCS 12933, pp. 585–594, 2021.
https://doi.org/10.1007/978-3-030-85616-8_34

The idea of using speech signal processing (SSP) in the analysis of drowsiness or fatigue detection was introduced by Dhupati et al. [6]. SSP allows the automated detection and evaluation of certain mental states. More specifically, speech signals have been used for emotion detection and can also support the automatic assessment of mental recovery. Moreover, unlike physiological sensors that record data under constrained conditions, speech data can be recorded in completely natural and unpredictable situations [8]. This motivated us to combine speech feature analysis with an efficient speech segmentation algorithm [26] to detect and evaluate the attention restoration effect of restorative environments. More concretely, we investigated whether a user's speech signals, recorded in a traditional response test before and after a restorative experience, could provide an additional objective measure of the restorative effects and would align with the results of the response test and attention scale. Using traditional machine learning methods, we were also able to classify and predict different restoration levels based on speech features.

2   Background and Related Work

Our initial use case was measuring the restorative effect of an in-car restorative environment developed in another project [14]. In brief, our work there built on the paradigm of attention restoration [20], the effects of which are mainly measured by attention scales and response tests. The technical basis of our work is speech signal analysis and automatic speech segmentation. We will therefore briefly introduce related work from these two areas below.

2.1   Measuring Attention

Virtual Restorative Environments (VREs) aim to reduce stress and restore attentional capacities [25] by recreating scenes of natural beauty and peacefulness in VR. The timeline of a typical trial in attention restoration research consists of a stress-induction phase followed by a restoration phase [24]. Experimenters usually collect attention data at the beginning or between two phases as the baseline for comparison with the post-restoration data. Previous work tried to measure attention by established methods such as self-reporting scales and response tests [20]. However, these conventional measurements are inconvenient because they inevitably interrupt the flow of the experiment and also suffer from subjective factors. Furthermore, physiological signals such as heart rate [13] or other signals from mobile sensors [27] can also be used to measure attention recovery effects. As a less obtrusive measuring method, we propose to use speech signal analysis to detect and quantify attention restoration.

2.2   Speech Feature Extraction and Speaker Segmentation

Speech signal analysis means the analysis and processing of phonetic characteristics, generally including features in both the time- and frequency-domain [23].

Such audio features have also helped to analyze human social behavior and assess the state of humans' mental health [8], or enable automatic mood detection [16]. When looking for suitable signal features for measuring attention, we found that the time-domain features *speech entropy, short-time energy* and *speech intensity* can identify stress or fatigue [17]. The frequency-domain features *Mel Frequency Cepstral Coefficients (MFCC)* can indicate happiness or stress [15]. Thus, it seemed plausible that these speech features could also be used to measure other mental properties, such as attentional capacity.

A robust and reliable speaker segmentation will substantially improve the accuracy of the extracted features. Existing segmentation methods can be split into supervised and unsupervised algorithms. Supervised segmentation algorithms, such as the GMM method [18] and artificial neural networks [32], recognize the speaker's voice after being trained on it beforehand. Unsupervised segmentation algorithms detect the speaker's voice without prior training, for example, from time-domain [12] and frequency-domain [11] features. Other traditional voice segmentation methods are based on energy estimation [22] and hidden Markov models (HMM) [26]. Since we wanted to use recordings from previously unknown study participants, any supervised method that requires prior training on a specific voice was out of question. Based on the existing literature on fully automatic segmentation, we thus decided for an unsupervised speech segmentation.

3   Establishing Speech Signal Analysis as a Measure

Our original study used a within-subject design in which each participant experienced an in-car VRE. We collected subjective and objective attention measures both before and after the restorative experience and the control condition. As a side effect, we recorded speech signals during these measures. For the purpose of this paper, we then analyzed the correlation between these other measures of attention and the features of the recorded speech signal. We hypothesized that certain speech features would be correlated with the attention measures.

3.1   Apparatus, Participants and Experimental Procedure

The VRE was implemented in Unity 3D and installed on a standard PC connected to an Oculus Rift HMD. We used a separate noise cancelling headphone for audio output. A digital audio recorder was used to record speech signals at 48 kHz and 16 bit resolution. Speaker distance to the microphone was about 15 cm. Matlab 2017a and MIRtoolbox 1.7.1 were used for speech signal analysis. Our study procedure was approved by the local ethics review board(ID: EK-MIS-2020-011). We invited 21 participants (5 male) aged between 19 and 33 years (M = 26.7, SD = 4.0) to our lab. More than half of them had experience in driving and VR.

The study consisted of 7 steps as shown in Fig. 1. After a demographic questionnaire, we asked participants to fill the 13-item Attentional Function Index (AFI) questionnaire [5] as a subjective measurement of attention. As an objective measurement, participants were then asked to complete the Digit Span Backward test

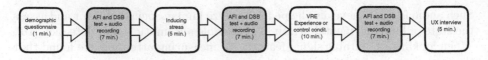

Fig. 1. Timeline of the study procedure.

(DSB) [30] on a computer and we simultaneously recorded their voice. The study was conducted in the quietest room of our lab to reduce background noise. In the third step, participants were shown a video clip of a traffic jam[1] to induce a context-specific type of stress [3] before the restorative experience. The purpose of this step was to ensure that participants were in a state of lowered attentional capacity. We then took the same measurements and recorded audio data again. In the fifth step, participants experienced the in-car restorative environment or (as a control condition) closed their eyes in VR for around 10 min [14]. After this intervention, participants were asked to complete the same tests, again recording their voice. To end the study, the experimenter conducted an interview asking participants to talk about their feelings during the restorative experience.

3.2   Methods Used for Speech Signal Analysis

We used the recorded speech data to explore the relationship between speech features and attention restoration. From the voice recordings of the DSB test, we selected the speech parts and extracted time- and frequency-domain speech features including short-time energy, zero-crossing rate, formant and MFCC. The processing pipeline is shown in Fig. 2 and explained below.

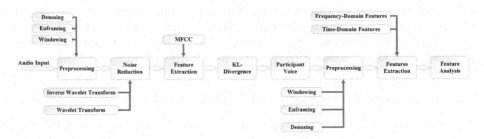

Fig. 2. Our signal analysis pipeline tightly integrates speech feature extraction and speaker segmentation.

In a preprocessing step, we denoised and enframed the audio data and defined a time window. For the frame size, we used 25 ms and a frame step of 10 ms. We included a 4-Daubechies wavelet transform [21,28] and its inverse transform for noise reduction and speech enhancement, and then extracted the MFCC feature. Then, we also computed the Kullback-Leibler Divergence (KL-Divergence) [31]

---

[1] https://www.youtube.com/watch?v=GlCazmVBUMg.

and used it, together with the extracted features, to reliably segment the data into speech and non-speech segments. Features for attention detection were only extracted from speech segments and forwarded to further processing. In speech features analysis, we mainly explore the relationship between the speech features and attention restoration effects, which includes Pearson correlation coefficient [1], significance test, visual comparison and attention restoration level classification.

4   Comparison to Traditional Measures

To verify our method, we compared it to the traditional, objective and subjective tests of attention. We used the Pearson correlation coefficient to determine whether there was a strong correlation between these attention measures and our method before and after the restorative experience. We also compared them using traditional machine learning to verify whether speech signal analysis can actually predict the effect of attention restoration. A strong correlation effect is reported for $r \geq 0.5$ and the accuracy in our machine learning method is above 0.85 in two-class and 0.7 in three-class classifications.

4.1   Results of the Traditional Measures

For the original study, the attention score as provided by the AFI reflects the participants' subjective evaluation of their attentional state at the moment. We observed a stronger average increase in the VRE condition compared to the control condition. In the VRE, participants on average gained 2.9 (SD = 7.6) points, compared to an increase of 1.4 (SD = 8.4) points in the control condition. In the VRE, also the absolute AFI score was slightly higher after the restorative experience (Mdn = 61) than before (Mdn = 59). Across conditions, we observed a slightly stronger improvement in the DSB test in the VRE condition than in the control condition: Participants improved their short-term memory by 0.16 (SD = 0.7) digits in the VRE, but only by 0.11 (SD = 0.5) digits in the control condition. Moreover, in the test after the VRE, participants achieved their best working memory span (M = 5.11, SD = 1.0) compared to all other DSB tests.

4.2   Results Based on Speech Signal Analysis

Comparison Using Pearson Correlation. As shown in Table 1, the time domain features short-time energy, zero-crossing rate, max peak in autocorrelation and 3 formants show a strong positive correlation with the AFI score. For the formants, we chose the first three frequency peaks in the spectrum which have a high degree of energy. These six speech features thus can be effectively used to analyze and assess the attention restoration in our experiment. In addition, the short-time energy and zero-crossing rate before the VRE experience were lower than after it. In other words, these two features seem to increase when participants go from a state of fatigue to a state of relaxation.

Table 1. Pearson Correlation Coefficients between various signal features and attention restoration as measured by the AFI score

Short-Time Energy	0.8994
Zero-crossing Rate	0.9192
Max peak in autocorrelation	0.9209
Formant 1	0.9209
Formant 2	0.5798
Formant 3	0.7515

Comparison Using Significance Tests. As shown in Fig. 3, the short time energy and zero-crossing rate before the VRE experience are slightly lower than after. We used a Wilcoxon Signed Rank Test [29] and found the difference to be significant between these two states in short time energy (p = 0.0453) and zero-crossing rate (p = 0.0475). This is consistent with the results of the conventional tests and means that these features can detect attention restoration effects. For all other extracted speech features, differences were not significant.

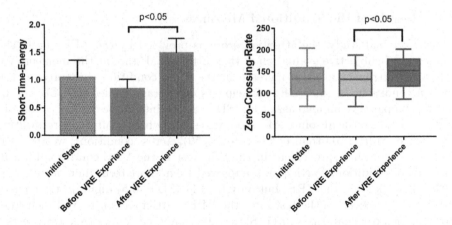

Fig. 3. Comparison of the features short-term-energy (left) and zero crossing rate (right) using a Wilcoxon Signed Rank test

Visual Comparison Using Spectrograms. From our data, we also computed spectrograms using a 128 channel Mel filter bank spanning 0 to 8 kHz (see Fig. 4). The left image shows data before the VRE and the right one after. The right spectrogram is visibly brighter than the left one, which suggests that this speech feature also is (positively) correlated to the attention restoration level and that such features can help to detect those levels.

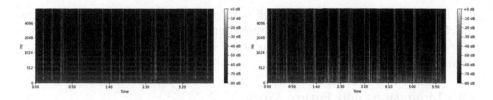

Fig. 4. Spectrograms of the MFCC feature before (left) and after (right) the VRE

Attention Restoration Level Classification. Using seven effective speech features which seemed to be correlated to attention restoration levels, we tested two traditional machine learning methods. Low attention levels represent the state before the VRE experience or control condition and high levels are the state after. The resulting accuracies for 2-class classifications were 0.92 and 0.88 respectively using the Support Vector Machines (SVM) [9] and the k-Nearest-Neighbours (KNN) [10] algorithms. Even if we define three different levels (after control condition, after VRE experience, and before), the accuracy of the SVM and KNN methods were 0.72 and 0.61, which still means that they can be used to recognize these three different states rather reliably.

5 Discussion, Limitations and Outlook

In the context of our research on attention restoration through VREs, we have found that speech signal analysis can potentially be used as an indirect measure for the effectiveness of restorative experiences. However, we are aware of certain limitations and found indications for necessary future work.

5.1 Discussion

In our original study, we had designed an evaluation procedure for the restorative effects of an in-car VRE. Through traditional attention measurements, we found that the studied VRE achieved low to moderate restorative effects in terms of improved attentional capacity and working memory. In addition to these established measures, we now also tested a novel evaluation method based on speech signal analysis: After extracting short-time energy and zero-crossing rate [12] in the time domain and MFCC [15] in the frequency domain with a preceding speaker segmentation, we conducted a correlation analysis and found these acoustic characteristics to be strongly correlated with the aforementioned traditional attention measures. This result was also confirmed by using significance tests on the change in these features and by visual comparison.

Furthermore, we found that traditional machine learning algorithms, such as KNN and SVM, can reliably detect and predict the measured attention restoration states from the recorded speech data. We therefore argue that speech signal analysis can be utilised to detect and evaluate the restorative effect in the same way as traditional measurements, such as attention scales or response tests.

The long term vision of this approach is to establish a fully automatic processing chain for measuring attention restoration levels based on audio data from interviews, which are conducted in a study anyway, or even using audio from voice interactions.

5.2   Limitations and Future Work

The relatively small number of participants in our study and the early stage of our speech signal analysis call for future studies confirming the precise relationship between an even more comprehensive set of speech features and attentional capacity or other mental properties. With regard to the voice recordings in the Digit Span Backward test, a chat-bot based on speech signal analysis could further improve the evaluation process by eliminating the human experimenter and eliciting better audio from participants who feel under less surveillance.

For now, all our analyses were done manually and after the study. In the future, we intend to iterate on our signal processing chain and eventually provide a fully automatic assessment system based on acoustic characteristics, which can, for example, effectively assess the restorative effects of VREs in real automated driving, but also provide attention measurements in other study setups. We expect that such a system will be generally applicable in a wide variety of contexts when measuring attention restoration levels.

6   Summary

While there is a growing emphasis on human wellbeing in designing interactive technologies, the corresponding evaluation methods have been less explored so far. In this paper, we explored an evaluation method for the attention restoration effects of an in-car VRE based on speech signal analysis. We compared this novel method to conventional measures in the form of subjective ratings of attentional capacity and objective performance in response tests. We developed and presented an initial version of a complete processing chain, including feature extraction and unsupervised speech segmentation. The results show that speech signal analysis can measure the restorative effects on attention and provide results that are consistent with the traditional measurements. We thus advocate the use of speech signal analysis as a novel HCI evaluation method, especially in measuring attention, but potentially for a wider range of mental parameters.

Acknowledgements. We thank all study participants for their time and effort, as well as our anonymous reviewers for their valuable feedback. Y.M.'s contributions were funded by the China Scholarship Council (CSC), grant number 201706070119.

References

1. Benesty, J., Chen, J., Huang, Y., Cohen, I.: Pearson correlation coefficient. In: Noise Reduction in Speech Processing, pp. 1–4. Springer, Vienna (2009). https://doi.org/10.1007/978-3-211-89836-9_1025

2. Biesmans, W., Das, N., Francart, T., Bertrand, A.: Auditory-inspired speech envelope extraction methods for improved EEG-based auditory attention detection in a cocktail party scenario. IEEE Trans. Neural Syst. Rehabil. Eng. **25**(5), 402–412 (2016)

3. Braun, M., Weiser, S., Pfleging, B., Alt, F.: A comparison of emotion elicitation methods for affective driving studies. Presented at the (2018)

4. Carreiras, C., Lourenço, A., Aidos, H., da Silva, H.P., Fred, A.L.N.: Unsupervised analysis of morphological ECG features for attention detection. In: Madani, K., Dourado, A., Rosa, A., Filipe, J., Kacprzyk, J. (eds.) Computational Intelligence. SCI, vol. 613, pp. 437–453. Springer, Cham (2016). https://doi.org/10.1007/978-3-319-23392-5_24

5. Cimprich, B., Visovatti, M., Ronis, D.L.: The attentional function index-a self-report cognitive measure. Psychooncology **20**(2), 194–202 (2011)

6. Dhupati, L.S., Kar, S., Rajaguru, A., Routray, A.: A novel drowsiness detection scheme based on speech analysis with validation using simultaneous EEG recordings, pp. 917–921. IEEE (2010)

7. Franěk, M., Šefara, D., Petružálek, J., Cabal, J., Myška, K.: Differences in eye movements while viewing images with various levels of restorativeness. J. Environ. Psychol. **57**, 10–16 (2018)

8. Gao, B., Woo, W.L.: Wearable audio monitoring: content-based processing methodology and implementation. IEEE Trans. Hum. Mach. Syst. **44**(2), 222–233 (2014)

9. Gunn, S.R., et al.: Support vector machines for classification and regression. ISIS Technical Report **14**(1), 5–16 (1998)

10. Guo, G., Wang, H., Bell, D., Bi, Y., Greer, K.: KNN model-based approach in classification. In: Meersman, R., Tari, Z., Schmidt, D.C. (eds.) OTM 2003. LNCS, vol. 2888, pp. 986–996. Springer, Heidelberg (2003). https://doi.org/10.1007/978-3-540-39964-3_62

11. Hogg, A.O., Evers, C., Naylor, P.A.: Speaker change detection using fundamental frequency with application to multi-talker segmentation, pp. 5826–5830. IEEE (2019)

12. Jalil, M., Butt, F.A., Malik, A.: Short-time energy, magnitude, zero crossing rate and autocorrelation measurement for discriminating voiced and unvoiced segments of speech signals, pp. 208–212. IEEE (2013)

13. Jiang, D., Hu, B., Chen, Y., Xue, Y., Li, W., Liang, Z.: Recognizing the human attention state using cardiac pulse from the noncontact and automatic-based measurements. Soft. Comput. **22**(12), 3937–3949 (2018)

14. Jingyi, L., Yong, M., Puzhen, L., Andreas, B.: A journey through nature: exploring virtual restorative environments as a means to relax in confined spaces. Association for Computing Machinery, New York, NY, USA (2021)

15. Joshi, D.D., Zalte, M.: Speech emotion recognition: a review. IOSR J. Electron. Commun. Eng. (IOSR-JECE) **4**(4) (2013)

16. Lam, K.Y., et al.: Smartmood: toward pervasive mood tracking and analysis for manic episode detection. IEEE Trans. Hum. Mach. Syst. **45**(1), 126–131 (2014)

17. Li, X., Tan, N., Wang, T., Su, S.: Detecting driver fatigue based on nonlinear speech processing and fuzzy SVM, pp. 510–515. IEEE (2014)

18. Maurya, A., Kumar, D., Agarwal, R.: Speaker recognition for Hindi speech signal using MFCC-GMM approach. Procedia Comput. Sci. **125**, 880–887 (2018)

19. Narayanan, A.M., Bertrand, A.: Analysis of miniaturization effects and channel selection strategies for EEG sensor networks with application to auditory attention detection. IEEE Trans. Biomed. Eng. **67**(1), 234–244 (2019)

20. Ohly, H., et al.: Attention restoration theory: a systematic review of the attention restoration potential of exposure to natural environments. J. Toxicol. Environ. Health, Part B **19**(7), 305–343 (2016)

21. Popov, D., Gapochkin, A., Nekrasov, A.: An algorithm of Daubechies wavelet transform in the final field when processing speech signals. Electronics **7**(7), 120 (2018)

22. Rocha, R.B., Freire, V.V., Alencar, M.S.: Voice segmentation system based on energy estimation, pp. 860–864. IEEE (2014)

23. Schuller, B.W.: Intelligent Audio Analysis. Signals and Communication Technology, Springer, Heidelberg (2013). https://doi.org/10.1007/978-3-642-36806-6

24. Stevenson, M.P., Schilhab, T., Bentsen, P.: Attention restoration theory ii: a systematic review to clarify attention processes affected by exposure to natural environments. J. Toxicol. Environ. Health Part B **21**(4), 227–268 (2018)

25. Stone, R., Small, C., Knight, J., Qian, C., Shingari, V.: Virtual natural environments for restoration and rehabilitation in healthcare. Virtual Augment. Real. Ser. Games Healthc. **1**, 497–521 (2014)

26. Sun, Y.X., Ma, Y., Shi, K.B., Hu, J.P., Zhao, Y.Y., Zhang, Y.P.: Unsupervised speaker segmentation framework based on sparse correlation feature, pp. 3058–3063. IEEE (2017)

27. Visuri, A., van Berkel, N.: Attention computing: overview of mobile sensing applied to measuring attention. Presented at the (2019)

28. Wieland, B., Urban, K., Funken, S.: Speech signal noise reduction with wavelets. Verlag nicht ermittelbar, Ph.D. thesis (2009)

29. Wilcoxon, F.: Individual comparisons by ranking methods. In: Kotz, S., Johnson, N.L. (eds.) Breakthroughs in Statistics, pp. 196–202. Springer, New York (1992). https://doi.org/10.1007/978-1-4612-4380-9_16

30. Woods, D.L., et al.: Improving digit span assessment of short-term verbal memory. J. Clin. Exp. Neuropsychol. **33**(1), 101–111 (2011)

31. Yang, Y., et al.: Kullback-Leibler divergence frequency warping scale for acoustic scene classification using convolutional neural network, pp. 840–844. IEEE (2019)

32. Yella, S.H., Stolcke, A., Slaney, M.: Artificial neural network features for speaker diarization, pp. 402–406. IEEE (2014)

Explainable AI

Effects of Interactivity and Presentation on Review-Based Explanations for Recommendations

Diana C. Hernandez-Bocanegra$^{(\boxtimes)}$ ⓘ and Jürgen Ziegler ⓘ

University of Duisburg-Essen, 47057 Duisburg, Germany
{diana.hernandez-bocanegra,juergen.ziegler}@uni-due.de

Abstract. User reviews have become an important source for recommending and explaining products or services. Particularly, providing explanations based on user reviews may improve users' perception of a recommender system (RS). However, little is known about how review-based explanations can be effectively and efficiently presented to users of RS. We investigate the potential of interactive explanations in review-based RS in the domain of hotels, and propose an explanation scheme inspired by dialogue models and formal argument structures. Additionally, we also address the combined effect of interactivity and different presentation styles (i.e. using only text, a bar chart or a table), as well as the influence that different user characteristics might have on users' perception of the system and its explanations. To such effect, we implemented a review-based RS using a matrix factorization explanatory method, and conducted a user study. Our results show that providing more interactive explanations in review-based RS has a significant positive influence on the perception of explanation quality, effectiveness and trust in the system by users, and that user characteristics such as rational decision-making style and social awareness also have a significant influence on this perception.

Keywords: Recommender systems · Explanations · Interactivity · User study · User characteristics

1 Introduction

Explaining the recommendations generated algorithmically by a recommender system (RS) has been shown to offer significant benefits for users with respect to factors such as transparency, decision support, or trust in the system [55,56]. Many approaches to explaining the products or services suggested by an RS have been based on ratings provided by other users or properties of the recommended items, approaches related to collaborative and content-based filtering methods [25,58]. More recently, fueled by the advances in natural language processing, user-written reviews have received considerable attention as rich sources of information about an item's benefits and disadvantages, which can be utilized for explanatory purposes. Reviews are, however, subjective, and may be inconsistent with the overall rating given by the user. Even when overcoming the

© IFIP International Federation for Information Processing 2021
Published by Springer Nature Switzerland AG 2021
C. Ardito et al. (Eds.): INTERACT 2021, LNCS 12933, pp. 597–618, 2021.
https://doi.org/10.1007/978-3-030-85616-8_35

challenge of processing noisy review texts, the question of which review-based information to show and how to present it is still largely open, partly due to the lack of empirical findings on how to best present review-based explanations, just as there is a general lack of user-centric evaluations of explanatory RS [44].

While as yet no overall theoretical model of explainable recommendations has been established, we propose to analyze explanations through the lens of argumentation theory which has produced a wide range of models of argumentation [5]. One class of these models defines logical structures with elements such as claims, or evidence to support or refute claims. A second class of models [63] have abandoned the idea of static argumentation models and propose a dialectical approach, focusing on the exchange of arguments within a dialogue between two parties. This approach led to the formulation of dialogue models of explanation [27,38,62], taking into account the social aspect of the explanatory process (an explainer transfers knowledge to an explainee [40]), which could facilitate the interactive provision of explanatory information in the form of a question-and-answer exchange. However, the practical application of dialogue models in explainable RS and their actual benefit from the users' perspective is yet to be determined.

Thus, grounding on argumentation theory and dialogue models of explanation, we formulated and tested an interactive approach to explanations based on reviews, that facilitates the exploration of arguments that support claims made by the system (i.e. an item is worth purchasing), while providing answers to some of their potential questions at different levels of detail (e.g. what was reported on [feature]?). To this end, we adopted the definition of interactivity by Steuer [54]: "extent to which users can participate in modifying the form and content of mediated environment in real time", and characterized the degree of interactivity of explanations through the Liu and Shrum dimensions of interactivity [35]: *active control* and *two-way communication*. The first is characterized by voluntary actions that can influence the user experience, reflected in our proposal by the possibility to use hyperlinks and buttons, that allow users to navigate explanatory information at will. The second refers to the ability of two parties to communicate to one another, reflected in our proposal by the ability to indicate the system which are their most relevant features, so the answers are adjusted accordingly.

While interactive explanations have been already addressed in the field of explainable artificial intelligence (XAI), their impact in explainable RS remains largely unexplored, as well as the empirical validation of their effects on users. Hence, we aimed to provide empirical evidence of the effect that an implementation of this approach may have on users' perception. More specifically, we evaluated users' perception in terms of the quality of explanations, and of the explanatory objectives: transparency, effectiveness and trust, as defined by [55], and aim to answer: **RQ1**: How do users perceive review-based explanations with different degrees of *interactivity*, in terms of explanation quality, and of the transparency, efficiency and trust in the system? We also aimed to test the combined effect of explanation interactivity and different presentation styles, particularly:

using only text, using a bar chart or using a table, to show, among others, the distribution of positive and negative comments on the quality of an item. Here, we were interested to inquire, for example, whether users who find a presentation style less satisfactory might benefit from interactive options that allow them to clarify their doubts. Thus: **RQ2**: How do different *presentation styles* influence users' perception of review-based explanations with different degrees of interactivity?

Furthermore, we addressed the influence that different user characteristics might have on the perception of the proposed approach. Regardless of its type, an explanation may not satisfy all possible explainees [52]. Moreover, individual user characteristics can lead to different perceptions of a RS [30,67], for which we assumed that this would also be the case for explanations, as discussed by [6,26,31]. Since a main objective of providing explanations is to support users in their decision-making, investigating the effect of different personal styles to perform such a process is of particular interest to us. Particularly, we focus on the moderating effect of the *rational* and *intuitive* decision making styles [24], the former characterized as a propensity to search for information and evaluate alternatives exhaustively, and the latter by a quick processing based mostly on hunches and feelings. Furthermore, since review-based explanations rely on the expressed opinions of other users, we investigated the effects of the extent to which users are inclined to adopt the perspective of others when making decisions, a trait defined as *social awareness* by [10]. We also considered *visualization familiarity*, i.e. the extent to which a user is familiar with graphical or tabular representations of information. Consequently, **RQ3**: How do individual differences in decision-making styles, social awareness or visualization familiarity moderate the perception of review-based explanations with different degrees of interactivity and presentation styles?

To address our research questions, we conducted a user study taking as example the hotels domain, since it represents an interesting mix between search goods (with attributes on which complete information can be found before purchase [42]) and experience goods (which cannot be fully known until purchase [42]). Such a product evaluation could benefit from third-party opinions [29,42], potentially rich in argumentative information that can be used for explanatory purposes.

Finally, the contributions of this paper can be summarized as follows:

- We formulate a scheme for explanations as interactive argumentation in review-based RS, inspired by dialogue models and argument structures.
- To test our research questions, we implemented an interface based on the proposed scheme, and a RS based on a matrix factorization model (i.e. EFM, [70]), and sentiment-based aspect detection, using the state of art natural language processing model BERT ([15]).
- We provide empirical evidence of the effect of review-based interactive explanations on users' perception, as well as the influence of user characteristics on such perception.

2   Related Work

Next, we will review work related to review-based explanations, interactive explanations in both explainable artificial intelligence (XAI) and RS, the use of dialogue models in contrast to static models of explanations, and the moderating effect of user characteristics on the perception of explainable RS.

Review-Based Explanations. Review-based explanatory methods leverage user generated content, rich in detailed evaluations on item features, which cannot be deduced from the general ratings, thus enabling the generation of more detailed explanations, compared to collaborative filtering (e.g. "Your neighbors' ratings for this movie" [25]) and content-based approaches (e.g. [58]). Review-based methods allow to provide: **1)** verbal summaries of reviews, using abstractive summarization from natural language generation (NLG) techniques [8,14], **2)** a selection of helpful reviews (or excerpts) that might be relevant to the user, detected using deep learning techniques and attention mechanisms [11,17], **3)** a statistical view of the pros and cons of item features, usually using topic modelling or aspect-based sentiment analysis [16,66,70], information that is integrated to RS algorithms like matrix or tensor factorization [4,64,70]) to generate both recommendations and aspect-based explanations.

Our evaluation is based on the third approach, and is particularly related to the model proposed by [70], since it facilitates getting statistical information on users' opinions, which has been proven to be useful for users [26,41], and can be provided in explanations with different presentation styles (strictly verbal or visual). Yet, the optimal way of presenting explanatory information, either in a textual (short summaries) or a graphical form (e.g. bar charts) remains unclear.

Interactive Explanations. In addition to display factors, a second factor could also influence users' perception of the explanations: the possibility of interacting with the system, to better understand the rationale for its predictions. Interactive explanations have been already addressed in the field of explainable artificial intelligence (XAI) (although to a much lesser extent compared to static explanations [1]). Here, the dominant trend has been to provide mechanisms to check the influence that specific features, points or data segments may have on final predictions of machine learning (ML) algorithms, as in [13,32,51]. However, the impact of such interactive approaches in explainable RS remains largely unexplored. More specifically, the dominant ML interactive approach differs from ours in at least two ways: 1) we use non-discrete and non-categorical sources of information, subjective in nature and unstructured, which, however, can be used to generate both textual and visual structured arguments 2) such approach is designed to meet the needs of domain experts, i.e. users with prior knowledge of artificial intelligence, while we aim to target the general public.

Effects of interactivity have been studied widely in fields like online shopping and advertising [35,53], and more specifically in the evaluation of critique-based RS, where users are able to specify preferences for the system to recalculate recommendations, which has been found to be beneficial for users [12,36,37]. Despite the intuitive advantages that interactivity can bring, interactivity does not always translate into a more positive attitude towards the system, since it also depends on the context and the task performed [35]. Nevertheless, it has also been shown that higher active control is beneficial in environments involving information needs, and a clear goal in mind [35], which is actually our case (i.e. deciding which hotel to book).

Dialogue Models of Explanation. To formulate and test our proposal, we set our focus on argumentative models that may enable the two-way communication desideratum. In contrast to static approaches to explanation, dialogue models have been formulated conceptually [2,38,47,60], allowing arguments over initial claims in explanations, within the scope of an interactive exchange of statements. Despite the potential benefit of using these models to increase users' understanding of intelligent systems [40,65], their practical implementation in RS (and in XAI in general) still lacks sufficient empirical validation [38,40,52]. This dialogical approach contrasts with other argumentative - though static - explanation approaches [3,9,26,33,69] based on static schemes of argumentation (e.g. [23,57]), where little can be done to indicate to the system that the explanation has not been fully understood or accepted, and that additional information is still required.

User Characteristics. We hypothesized (in line with [35]) that a number of user characteristics may moderate the effect of interactive functionalities, on the perception of explanations. Particularly, we aimed to test the moderating effect of decision-making styles and social awareness. In regard to the former, research has shown that it is determined significantly by preferences and abilities to process available information [19]. Particularly, we believe that users with a predominant rational decision making style would better perceive explanations with a higher degree of interactivity, than explanations with less possibility of interaction, given their tendency to thoroughly explore information when making decisions [24]. On the other hand, more intuitive users may not find the interactive explanations very satisfactory, given their tendency to make decisions through a quicker process [24], so that a first explanatory view would be sufficient, and it would not be necessary to navigate in depth the arguments that the system can offer. Here, [26] noted that rationality and intuition might not be diametrically opposed constructs. In their study, although most participants reported that they thoroughly evaluate the available information when making decisions, many of them also reported a tendency to use their intuition.

As for social awareness, and in line with results reported by [26], we hypothesize that users with a higher social awareness may perceive explanations with higher interactivity more positively, given their tendency to take into account the opinions of others, and to adjust their own using those of others, while choosing between various alternatives [50], which has been proved to be beneficial during decision making [68], and is facilitated by our approach.

Finally, in regard to presentation styles, visual arguments (a combination of visual and verbal information) may have a greater "rhetorical power potential" than verbal arguments, due (among others) to their greater immediacy (possibility of quick processing) [7]. This could especially benefit users with a predominantly intuitive decision-making style, due to their usually quick manner of making decisions, based mostly on first impressions [24]. However, users with lower visual abilities might benefit less from a presentation based on images or graphics [28,49]. Consequently, we believe that when exposed to graphic-based explanation formats, higher interactive explanations may be beneficial to users with lower visual familiarity, as they could access additional information to better understand the explanations provided.

3   Scheme for Explanations as Interactive Argumentation in Review-Based RS

To evaluate our research questions, we designed an interaction scheme for the exploration of explanatory arguments in review-based RS. A recommendation issued by a RS can be considered a specific form of a claim, namely that the user will find the recommended item useful or pleasing [18]. The role of an explanation is thus to provide supportive evidence (or rebuttals) for this claim. Claims are, however, also present in the individual user's rating and opinions, which may require explaining their grounds as well, thus creating a complex multi-level argumentative structure in an explainable RS, a concern also raised in [22]. To formulate an explanation scheme able to support this type of structure, we considered dialog-based explanation models [38,61,62], in which instead of a single issue of explanatory utterances, an explanation process is regarded as an interaction, where a user could indicate when additional arguments are required, to increase their understanding of system claims.

In this context, Walton [61,62] modeled explanation requests (user questions) and explanation attempts (a set of assertions as system response). On the other hand, Madumal et al. [38] noted that argumentation may occur within explanation, and modeled the shift between explanatory and argumentative dialog, as well as the explanatory loops that can be triggered, when follow-up questions arise. While this type of models may help to define the moves allowed within an explanatory interaction, they offer little indication of how the arguments within the interaction moves should be structured, to increase their acceptance by users. To this end, we rely on the scheme by Habernal et al. [23], an adaptation of the Toulmin model of argumentation [57], formulated to better represent the kind of arguments usually found in user-generated content. This scheme involves: claim (conclusion of the argument), premise (a general reason to accept a claim), backing (specific information or additional evidence to support the claim), rebuttal (statement that attacks the claim) and refutation (statement that attacks the rebuttal).

Our proposed scheme is shown in Fig. 1. Unlike Walton, who modeled explanatory movements as explanation requests and attempts, we considered an explanation process as a sequence of *argumentation attempts* (the system intends to provide arguments to explain something) followed by *argument requests* (the user ask the system to provide - follow-up - arguments that support the claim that user will find the recommended item useful). A missing element of Walton's model in our scheme is a feedback mechanism so that users can indicate whether

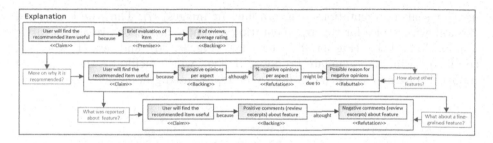

Fig. 1. Scheme for explanations as interactive argumentation in review-based RS. Blue boxes: argumentation attempts by the system, green boxes: argument requests by users. (Color figure online)

full understanding has been achieved, which is left for future work. The realization of our scheme as an user interface is depicted in Fig. 2. Here, design features like links and buttons enable argument requests by users, e.g.: the link "what was reported?" (Fig. 2b) fosters the interactive features *active control* (control on what aspects the system should focus on in its argumentation) and *two-way communication* (user communicates to the system that further argument backing is needed), which triggers a system argumentation attempt.

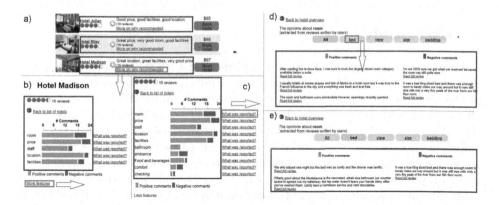

Fig. 2. Screenshots of system used in user study. Enclosed in blue: argumentation attempts; in green: argument requests. Orange arrows: sequence of allowed moves, pointing to the next interface. a) List of recommended items; clicking on "More on why recommended" displays: b–c) aggregation of comments by aspect; clicking on "What was reported?" displays: d) comments on chosen aspect; clicking a fine-grained feature button, displays: e) comments on chosen feature. c, d, e enabled only in study condition interactivity "high". (Color figure online)

An explanatory dialogue can take place both through verbal interactions and through a visual interface (non-verbal communication, or a combination of verbal and visual elements) [38,40]. As for presentation, while arguments are usually associated with oral or written speech, arguments can also be communicated using visual representations (e.g. graphics or images) [7]. Thus, we considered the following styles for the argumentation attempt "% of positive and negative opinions": 1) Table (Fig. 3a, 3b), bar chart (Fig. 3c, 3d), and text (Fig. 3e, 3f), the latter using the template proposed by [26], which facilitates the display of rebuttal statements, which can hardly be represented graphically.

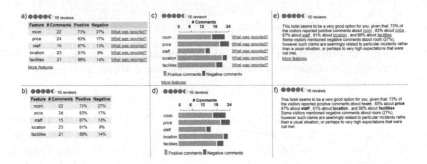

Fig. 3. Manipulation of *presentation* style in combination with *interactivity*, in user study. Left: *table*, middle *bar chart*, right *text*. Top: interactivity *high*, bottom: interactivity *low*.

4   User Study

To answer our research questions, we implemented a RS that reflects the scheme described in Sect. 3, and conducted a user study to compare users' perception of the overall system (in terms of the dependent variables (DVs): transparency, effectiveness and trust), and of the specific aspects of explanations (in terms of the DVs: explanation confidence, transparency, persuasiveness, satisfaction and sufficiency). As independent variables (IVs) we considered the factors *interactivity* and *presentation*. Possible values of IV interactivity are: "high" (users could make all possible argument requests, Fig. 1 and 2), and "low" (users could only make the initial argument request "more on why recommended?"). Possible values of IV presentation are: *table* (Fig. 3 a, b), *bar chart* (Fig. 3 c,d) and *text* (Fig. 3 e,f). The study follows a 3 × 2 between-subjects design, and each participant was assigned randomly to one of six conditions (combination of *interactivity* and *presentation* style). As covariates, we considered the user characteristics: rational and intuitive decision-making style, social awareness and visualization familiarity. We hypothesized:

H1: Users' perception of the system and its explanations is more positive when they are given explanations with higher interactivity.

H2: Users with a predominantly rational decision style perceive explanations with higher interactivity more positively than less rational decision makers.

H3: Less intuitive users perceive explanations with higher interactivity more positively, compared to more intuitive users.

H4: Users with greater social awareness perceive higher interactive explanations more positively than users with less social awareness.

H5a: Users with a predominantly intuitive decision-making style or **H5b** a greater visualization familiarity will prefer bar chart explanations over text explanations, regardless of interactivity.

H6: Users who are less familiar with data visualization will perceive explanations with higher interactivity more positively, particularly in the case of more challenging visualizations such as bar charts.

4.1 Questionnaires

Evaluation: We utilized items from [46] to evaluate the perception of system transparency (construct *transparency*, user understands why items were recommended), of system effectiveness [30] (internal reliability Cronbach's $\alpha = 0.85$, construct *perceived system effectiveness*, system is useful and helps the user to make better choices), and of trust in the system [39] ($\alpha = 0.90$, constructs *trusting beliefs*, user considers the system to be honest and trusts its recommendations; and *trusting intentions*, user willing to share information). We used the user experience items (UXP) of [31] to address explanations reception, which we will refer to as *explanation quality* ($\alpha = 0.82$), comprising: explanation confidence (user is confident that she/he would like the recommended item), explanation transparency (explanation makes the recommendation process clear), explanation satisfaction (user would enjoy a system if recommendations are presented this way), and explanation persuasiveness (explanations are convincing). We added an item adapted from [17] (explanations provided are sufficient to make a decision) to evaluate explanation sufficiency. All items were measured with a 1–5 Likert-scale (1: Strongly disagree, 5: Strongly agree).

User Characteristics: We used all the items of the Rational and Intuitive Decision Styles Scale [24] (internal reliability Cronbach's $\alpha = 0.84$ and $\alpha = 0.92$, respectively), the scale of the social awareness competency proposed by [10] ($\alpha = 0.70$), and the visualization familiarity items proposed by [31] ($\alpha = 0.86$). All items were measured with a 1–5 Likert-scale (1: Strongly disagree, 5: Strongly agree).

4.2 Participants

We recruited 170 participants (66 female, mean age 37.61 and range between 18 and 72) through Amazon Mechanical Turk. We restricted the execution of the task to workers located in the U.S, with a HIT (Human Intelligence Task) approval rate greater than 98%, and a number of HITs approved greater than 500. We applied a quality check to select participants with quality survey responses (we asked validation questions to check attentiveness within questionnaires, and questions related to the content of the system, e.g. "recommendations were based on: Opinions of celebrities, True/False", "The purpose of this question is to check attentiveness, please mark Disagree"). We discard participants with less than 10 (out of 12) correct answers, or no effective interaction with the system (checked in logs). The responses of 27 of the 197 initial participants were then discarded for a final sample of 170 subjects, statistical power of 90%, α =0.05, power value above conventional for adequacy of .80 are considered acceptable [45]; An 'a priori' type of analysis was performed in G*power software [21]. Participants were rewarded with $1.4 plus a bonus up to $0.40, depending on the length and number of arguments provided in their response to the question "Why did you choose this hotel?", and the extent to which those arguments referred to explanations and information provided by the system. Time devoted to the task by participants (in minutes): M = 10.88, SD = 1.62.

4.3 Procedure

Instructions indicated that a list of hotels reflecting the results of a hypothetical hotels' search and within the same price range would be presented (i.e. no filters to search hotels were offered to participants), and that they could click on the name of a desired hotel to see general information about it. However, we asked, as we were more interested in their views on the explanations given for each recommendation, to click on the "More on why recommended" links of hotels they might be interested in, and to explore the information provided. No further instructions were given regarding how to interact with the different interaction options, since we were interested to address to what extent the users used them or not. Users were instructed to indicate which hotel they would finally choose, and to write a few sentences reporting their reasons for it, for which a bonus up to $0.4 would be paid, depending on the quality of this response, with the aim of achieving a more motivated choice by the participants, as well as to encourage a more effective interaction with the system. We then presented a cover story, which sought to establish a common starting point in terms of travel motivation (a holiday trip). Next, we presented to the participants the system showing a list of 30 recommended hotels (sorted by predicted rating), and their corresponding personalized explanations (system implementation details in Sect. 4.4). Finally, evaluation and validation questions were presented, plus an open-ended one, asking for general opinions and suggestions about the explanations.

4.4 Dataset and Implemented System

Dataset and Aspect Annotation: ArguAna [59], includes hotel reviews and ratings from TripAdvisor; sentiment and explicit features are annotated sentence wise. We categorized the explicit features in 10 general features (room, price, staff, location, facilities, bathroom, ambience, food and beverages, comfort and checking), with the help of 2 annotators (Krippendorff's alpha of 0.72), aiming to train a classifier to detect the main aspect addressed in a sentence (e.g. "I loved the bedding" would be classified as *room*).

Aspect-Based Sentiment Detection: We trained a BERT classifier [15] to detect the general feature addressed within a sentence: we used a 12-layer model (*BertForSequenceClassification*), 6274 training sentences, 1569 test sentences,

F-score 0.84 (macro avg.). We also trained a BERT classifier to detect the sentiment polarity, using a 12-layer model (*BertForSequenceClassification*), 22674 training sentences, 5632 test sentences, F-score 0.94 (macro avg.). Classifier was used to **1)** consolidate the quality of hotels and relevance of aspects to users (see Figs. 2b, 2d), and **2)** to present participants with negative and positive excerpts from reviews regarding a chosen feature (Fig. 2d, 2e).

Explainable RS Method: We implemented the Explicit Factor Model (EFM) [70], a review-based matrix factorization (MF) method to generate both recommendations and explanations. The rating matrix (ratings granted by users to items) consisted of 1284 items and 884 users extracted from the ArguAna dataset (only users with at least 5 written reviews were included), for a total of 5210 ratings. Item quality and user preferences matrices were consolidated using the sentiment detection described previously. Each element of the former matrix measures the quality of the item for each aspect, while the elements of the latter measure the extent to which the user cares about an aspect. The number of explicit features was set to 10. Model-specific hyperparameters were selected via grid-search-like optimization. After 100 iterations, we reached an RMSE of 1.27, a metric used to measure the differences between dataset values and the values predicted by the RS model. Values of predicted rating matrix were used to sort recommendations, and shown within explanations (average hotel rating with 1–5 green circles). Values of quality matrix were used to calculate the percentages of positive and negative comments on aspects (Fig. 3).

Personalization Mechanism: To reduce implications of the *cold start* problem [48] (system does not have enough information about the user to generate an adequate profile and thus, personalized recommendations), participants were asked for the five hotel features that mattered most to them, in order of importance. The system calculated a similarity measure, to detect users within the EFM preference matrix with a similar order of preferences. Then the most similar user was used as a proxy to generate recommendations, i.e. we selected the predicted ratings of this proxy user, and used them to sort recommendations and features within explanations.

4.5 Data Analysis

We evaluated the effect that IVs (interactivity and presentation style) may have on 2 different levels: **1)** *overall system* perception (DVs explanation quality, and system transparency, effectiveness and trust), and **2)** perception of specific aspects of *explanations* (DVs explanation confidence, transparency, satisfaction, persuasiveness and sufficiency), and to what extent the covariates (user characteristics: rational and the intuitive decision making styles, social awareness and visualization familiarity) could influence such perception.

Evaluation scores (DVs' scores) for each individual were calculated as the average of the reported values for the scale items, in case of multi-item scales. Scores on "explanation quality" were calculated for each individual as the average of scores on specific aspects of explanations, and the covariates scores as the average of the reported values for items of every scale. Internal consistency

(Cronbach's alpha) was checked for system evaluation and user characteristics constructs (reported in Sect. 4.1).

Overall System Perception: Given that DVs are continuous and correlated (see Table 1), a MANCOVA analysis was performed. Subsequent ANCOVA were performed to test main effects of IVs and covariates, as well as the effect of interactions between them. Q-Q plots of residuals were checked to validate the adequacy of the analysis.

Perception of Explanations: DVs are ordinal (scores are the reported answers to single questionnaire items), thus we performed ordinal logistic regressions to test influence on DVs by predictor variables (IVs and covariates), no multi-collinearity was tested, as well as Q-Q plots of residuals. DVs are also correlated (see Table 2), so significant tests were conducted using Bonferroni adjusted alpha levels of .01 (.05/5).

Use of Interactive Options: Calculated based on system activity logs. A Mann-Whitney U test was used to compare distributions of users characteristics who used or not use such options.

5   Results

5.1   Evaluation and User Characteristics Scores

The average evaluation scores by presentation style and interactivity are shown in Tables 1 and 2. Distributions of the scores of rational ($M = 4.35$, $SD = 0.50$) and intuitive ($M = 2.59$, $SD = 0.98$) decision making styles, social awareness ($M = 4.04$, $SD = 0.53$) and visualization familiarity ($M = 3.23$, $SD = 0.95$) are depicted in Fig. 4a.

Table 1. Mean values and standard deviations of perception on the overall system, per *presentation* style and *interactivity* (n = 170), p < 0.05*, p < 0.01**; values reported with a 5-Likert scale; higher mean values correspond to a positive perception of the overall RS. Pearson correlation matrix, p < 0.001 for all coefficients.

Variable	Presentation						Interactivity				Correlation			
	Text		Table		Bar chart		Low		High		Variable			
	M	SD	M	SD	M	SD	M	SD	M	SD	1	2	3	4
1. Expl. Quality	3.98	0.52	4.10	0.56	4.07	0.70	3.92	0.61	4.17**	0.55				
2. Transparency	4.14	0.52	4.11	0.86	3.91	0.99	4.02	0.78	4.08	0.86	0.51	—		
3. Effectiveness	3.95	0.69	4.05	0.73	4.04	0.78	3.91	0.79	4.11*	0.67	0.67	0.75	0.56	—
4. Trust	3.91	0.60	3.99	0.58	3.97	0.72	3.86	0.67	4.05*	0.57	0.57	0.74	0.55	0.79	—

5.2   Overall System Perception

Interactivity: We found a significant multivariate effect of interactivity on overall system perception $F(4,157) = 2.68$, $p = .034$. Univariate tests revealed that

Table 2. Mean values and standard deviations of perception on explanation specific aspects, per *presentation* style and *interactivity* (n = 170), p < 0.05*, p < 0.01**; values reported with a 5-Likert scale; higher mean values correspond to a positive perception on the explanations. Pearson correlation matrix, p < 0.001 for all coefficients.

Variable	Presentation						Interactivity				Correlation				
	Text		Table		Bar chart		Low		High		Variable				
	M	SD	M	SD	M	SD	M	SD	M	SD	1	2	3	4	5
1. Expl. confidence	4.09	0.55	4.11	0.65	4.05	0.85	3.95	0.74	4.21*	0.62					
2. Expl. transparency	4.16	0.73	4.19	0.83	4.16	0.86	4.05	0.84	4.29*	0.77	0.60	—			
3. Expl. satisfaction	3.84	0.85	4.09	0.79	4.11	0.80	3.88	0.84	4.14*	0.77	0.40	0.53	—		
4. Expl. persuasiveness	3.84	0.71	3.96	0.71	3.93	0.82	3.82	0.71	4.00	0.77	0.64	0.47	0.45	—	
5. Expl. sufficiency	3.96	0.79	4.14	0.81	4.09	0.83	3.89	0.87	4.23**	0.71	0.40	0.44	0.50	0.45	—

interactivity significantly influences the perception of explanation quality $F(1,168) = 9.76$, $p = .002$, effectiveness $F(1,168) = 4.02$, $p = .047$, and trust $F(1,168) = 4.63$, $p = 0.033$. In all these cases, the average of every variable was higher for the *high* condition than for *low* condition (see Table 1).

Presentation Style: We found no significant main effect of *presentation* style.

Rational Decision-Making Style: We found a significant multivariate effect of rational style, $F(4,157) = 7.55$, $p < .001$. Univariate tests revealed a main effect of rational decision-making style on explanation quality, $F(1,168) = 20.27$, $p < .001$, system transparency $F(1,168) = 8.25$, $p = .005$, effectiveness, $F(1,168) = 26.76$, $p < .001$ and trust, $F(1,168) = 24.94$, $p < .001$. In all these cases, a positive trend was observed between these variables and the rational decision-making style, i.e. the higher the rational decision-making score, the higher the perceived explanation quality, the transparency, the effectiveness and the trust, independent of style or interactivity (Fig. 4b).

Social Awareness: We found a significant multivariate effect of social awareness, $F(4,157) = 6.41$, $p < .001$. Univariate tests revealed a main effect of social awareness on explanation quality $F(1,168) = 17.25$, $p < .001$, system transparency $F(1,168) = 12.57$, $p < .001$, effectiveness $F(1,168) = 22.85$, $p < .001$ and trust $F(1,168) = 18.02$, $p < .001$. In all these cases, a positive trend was observed between these variables and social awareness, i.e. the higher the social awareness score, the higher the perceived explanation quality, the transparency, the effectiveness and the trust, independent of style or interactivity (Fig. 4c).

5.3   Perception of Explanations

Interactivity: We found a main significant effect of interactivity; here, the odds of participants reporting higher values of explanation sufficiency when interactivity *high* was 2.30 (95% CI, 1.26 to 4.29) times that of interactivity *low*, a statistically significant effect, Wald $\chi2(1) = 7.32$, $p = .007$. We observed a similar pattern in relation to explanation confidence ($p = .017$), explanation transparency ($p = .043$) and explanation satisfaction ($p = .041$). However, this association (despite $p < .05$) is non-significant after Bonferroni correction (corrected $p < 0.01$).

Fig. 4. a) Kernel density estimate of user characteristics scores: rational and intuitive decision making styles, social awareness and visualization familiarity. b) Effect of rational decision-making style on the perception of the overall system (fitted means of individual scores). c) Effect of social awareness on the perception of the overall system (fitted means of individual scores).

Presentation Style: We found no significant main effect of *presentation* style.

Additionally, we observed a possible interaction ($p <= 0.05$, although non-significant after Bonferroni correction, corrected $p < 0.01$) between:

Rational Decision-Making Style and Interactivity: An increase in rational decision-making score was associated with an increase in the odds of participants under interactive *high* condition reporting higher values of explanation sufficiency, with an odds ratio of 3.20 (95% CI, 0.99 to 10.65), Wald $\chi2(1) = 3.81$, $p = .051$ (Fig. 5a).

Intuitive Decision-Making Style and Presentation Style: An increase in intuitive decision-making score was associated with an increase in the odds of participants under *bar chart* condition reporting higher values of explanation satisfaction, with an odds ratio of 2.40 (95% CI, 1.14 to 5.18), Wald $\chi2(2) = 5.67$, $p = .023$, compared to participants under *text* condition (see Fig. 5b).

Social Awareness and Interactivity: An increase in social awareness score was associated with an increase in the odds of participants under interactive *high* condition reporting higher values of explanation persuasiveness, with an odds ratio of 3.83 (95% CI, 1.20 to 12.34), Wald $\chi2(1) = 5.17$, $p = .023$ (Fig. 5c).

Visualization Familiarity and Interactivity: An increase in visualization familiarity score was associated with an increase in the odds of participants under interactive *high* condition reporting higher values of explanation satisfaction, odds ratio of 1.91 (95% CI, 1.03 to 3.58), Wald $\chi2(1) = 4.24$, $p = .039$ (Fig. 5d).

5.4   Use of Interaction Options

48% of the users assigned to the interactivity *high* conditions used at least one of the interaction options provided. 48.15% of participants used the 'more features' option when explanations were displayed using table, 26.92% using bar chart and 33.3% using text. 55.56% of participants used the 'what was reported' option when explanations were displayed as table, 50% as bar chart and 3.7% as text. And 22.22% of participants used the 'comments on specific features' option when

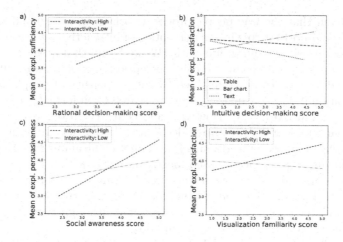

Fig. 5. Interaction plots (fitted means of individual scores) for perception of explanation: a) sufficiency, interaction between interactivity and rational decision-making style. b) satisfaction, interaction between presentation and intuitive decision-making. c) persuasiveness, interaction between interactivity and social awareness. d) satisfaction, interaction between interactivity and visualization familiarity.

explanations were displayed as table, 19.23% as bar chart and 3.7% as text. Additionally, a Mann-Whitney U test revealed that the average of visualization familiarity scores of users who used the interaction options ($M = 2.98$, $SD = 1.05$) is significantly lower than the score of those that did not use them ($M = 3.41$, $SD = 0.85$), $U(\mathrm{N}_{used} = 41, \mathrm{N}_{notused} = 44) = 678.50$, $p = .024$).

6   Discussion

In regard to our **RQ1**, our results show that greater interactivity has a significantly positive effect on users' perception, in terms of system effectiveness and trust, as well as of explanation quality, compared to explanations with lower interactivity, thus confirming our **H1**. We believe that the interactivity aspects addressed in our proposal could play a determining role in the observed effect, namely: active control and two-way communication, fostered in turn by design features such as links and buttons representing argument requests. Active control by enabling users to be in control of which argumentative content to display; two-way communication by enabling them to indicate the system which argumentative statements require further elaboration, and which features are of real relevance at the time of making the decision, an approach that might contribute to a better acceptance and understanding of explanations, as predicted by dialogue models of explanation [27,62].

However, the benefit and actual use of interactive options in review-based explanations might be influenced by individual differences, as discussed by [35] for the scope of online advertising and shopping. In particular, and regarding our

RQ3, we found that the way people process information when making decisions would play an important role in the perception of interactive review-based explanations. More precisely, and in line with **H2**, we found that greater interactivity might have a more positive effect on the perception of explanation sufficiency by more rational users, which is explained by the propensity of people with a predominant rational decision-making style, to search for information and evaluate alternatives exhaustively [24]. However, and contrary to our expectations, we observed that the degree of intuitive decision style did not moderate the effect of interactivity on users' perception, so we cannot confirm our **H3**. Here, despite the predominant quick process based mostly on hunches that characterize more intuitive decision-makers [24], we believe that looking at verbatim excerpts from other users' reviews may also be of benefit to them, to corroborate whether their hunches are aligned with the system's assertions, although they may not do so as extensively as less intuitive users would do.

Additionally, in line with our **H4** and results reported by [26], we observed that social awareness might moderate the effect of interactivity on explanation persuasiveness. Here, results suggest that participants with a higher disposition to listen and take into account others' opinions, tend to perceive higher interactive explanations as more persuasive, which seems a consequence of the possibility to read reports of personal experiences by customers, who have already made use of the recommended items. This represents a potential advantage in the evaluation of experience goods like hotels, which is characterized by a greater reliance on word-of-mouth [29, 42].

In regard to our **RQ2** and **RQ3**, and in line with **H5a**, our observations suggest that intuitive decision style might mediate the effect of presentation on explanation satisfaction, independent of interactivity. Particularly, explanatory arguments presented as a bar chart seemed to be perceived as more satisfactory to more intuitive users, than the presentation using a table or only text, presumably due to their greater immediacy [7], thus facilitating the rapid decision-making process that characterizes more intuitive users. However, and contrary to our expectations, we cannot conclude that users with more visualization familiarity will perceive the bar chart explanations better than the text-based ones (**H5b**). One possible reason could be that a text-based format makes it easier to visualize argumentative components as rebuttal and refutation, which could lead to a higher acceptance of an argument, as advocated by argumentation theory ([23]), but could hardly be expressed through graph-based formats.

Additionally, although users with lower visualization familiarity tended to use the interaction options more, we cannot confirm our hypothesis that those users would perceive graphic-based explanations (i.e. bar chart) better when more interactive options are offered, (**H6**). Actually, we found that users with more experience with data visualization reported a more positive perception for explanations with higher interactivity, independent of presentation style. We believe this is not due to difficulties understanding the explanations (as we thought would be the case for users with less visualization familiarity), but because higher interactivity facilitated a structured navigation and more appealing display of the data, which would not be as easy to process or useful if presented on a single static explanation.

Overall, we observed a main effect of rational decision-making style and social awareness in the perception of the system and all the proposed explanations. This suggests that review-based explanations seem to benefit more the users who tend to evaluate information thoroughly and take into account the opinions of others when making decisions, compared to users who use a more shallow information-seeking process.

Interactivity and Transparency Perception. Despite the main effect of interactivity on the overall perception of the system and its explanations, the mean perception of system transparency (user understands why items were recommended) is only slightly higher for the interactivity *high* condition than for the *low* condition. We believe that the reason might be two-fold: 1) Walton's [62] suggests to include an explicit mechanism to confirm effective understanding by the user, so that if this has not yet been achieved, the iterative cycle of user questions and system responses may continue. In consequence, we believe that a more flexible approach in which the user could, for example, write their own questions, rather than the bounded link-based options, might contribute in this regard. And 2) users may be also interested in understanding the reasons why the hotel x is better than hotel y. This would not only be in line with the view of authors who claim that the *why-questions* ask for a contrastive explanation ("why P rather than Q?") [27,34,40], but also concurs with some participants' suggestions, that options for comparison would be very useful.

Use of Interaction Options. We observed that almost half of participants under the condition interactivity "high" actually used the interaction options, although participants were not explicitly instructed to use them, so it can reasonably be inferred that their use was mainly voluntary. It is critical, however, that these options are named appropriately, indicating clearly their destinations (as stated by [20] guidelines), to increase the probability of their use, as evidenced by the lack of use of the option to read reviews excerpts in the *text* condition (Fig. 3e).

Additionally, some of the users assigned to the *low* interactivity condition pointed to 1) the lack of access to additional information in connection to the explanations (particularly customer reviews) as a disadvantage, with about a quarter of those participants writing suggestions on the subject, e.g. "I would prefer to read the actual reviews and understand why ratings were what they were", or 2) insufficiency of aggregated percentages of positive and negative opinions to adequately explain recommendations, e.g. "I feel they maybe could have a lot more information more on SPECIFICALLY what they say about the room instead of just an overall aggregation". In this regard, it is important to note though, that participants of all conditions had access to the full hotel reviews (they were included in the general view of each hotel).

Practical Implications. Our approach was specifically tested in hotels domain, however, since it allows users to navigate from aggregated accounts of other users' opinions to detailed extracts of individual reviews, we believe it might generalize adequately to domains that involve the evaluation of experience goods [43], and where the search for information is characterized by a greater reliance on word-of-mouth [29,42] for example restaurants, movies or books. Additionally, our findings lead to the following practical implications:

- Providing interactive explanations resembling an argumentative communication between system and user could contribute to a better perception of the system, which could be done using web navigation options, e.g. links or buttons, indicating a *why* or *what* questions to be answered by the system.
- Presenting both aggregated opinion statistics and excerpts of comments filtered by feature, as part of an interactive explanation, is a beneficial way to provide explanations sufficient in content, while avoiding overwhelming users with irrelevant data in a single step or screen.
- Given the practical difficulty of detecting user characteristics (e.g., decision-making style or visualization familiarity) by the system, we suggest interactive options to be considered, not only to provide in-depth arguments or to detect the relevance of features to the user, but also to modify the presentation style of argument components.

7   Conclusions and Future Work

In this paper, we have presented a scheme for explanations as interactive argumentation in review-based RS, inspired by dialogue explanation models and formal argument schemes, that allows users to navigate from aggregated accounts of other users' opinions to detailed extracts of individual reviews, in order to facilitate a better understanding of the claims made by the RS. We tested an implementation of the proposed scheme in the hotels domain, and found that more interactive explanations contributed to a more positive perception of effectiveness and trust in the system. We also found that individual differences in terms of user characteristics (e.g. decision-making style, social awareness and visualization familiarity) may lead to differences in the perception of the proposed implementation.

While our proposal suggests a first step towards an effective implementation of interactive explanations for review-based RS, we acknowledge that a major limitation of our approach is that the questions that users can ask are limited to a given set of pre-defined statements. To mitigate such a limitation, we will extend, in future work, our proposed scheme to support a wider range of questions, which can be asked by the user even in their own words. To this end, we plan to leverage advances of conversational agents (i.e. chatbots), natural language processing and natural language generation techniques, such as question answering and automatic summarization, to enhance the implementation proposed in this paper.

Likewise, we plan in the future to investigate the effect of contrastive dialog-based explanations of the type "Why P rather than not-P?". This type of explanation can be leveraged to enable users to influence the recommendation process itself, e.g. requesting for a more refined set of recommendations that better suit their preferences, based on an explanatory contrast between options. This might result in greater satisfaction with the overall system, as has been proven with interactive RS in the past, but this time from the explanations as such.

Acknowledgements. This work was funded by the German Research Foundation (DFG) under grant No. GRK 2167, Research Training Group "User-Centred Social Media".

References

1. Abdul, A., Vermeulen, J., Wang, D., Lim, B.Y., Kankanhalli, M.: Trends and trajectories for explainable, accountable and intelligible systems: an HCI research agenda. In: Proceedings of the 2018 CHI Conference on Human Factors in Computing Systems - CHI 2018, p. 1–18 (2018)
2. Arioua, A., Croitoru, M.: Formalizing explanatory dialogues. In: Beierle, C., Dekhtyar, A. (eds.) SUM 2015. LNCS (LNAI), vol. 9310, pp. 282–297. Springer, Cham (2015). https://doi.org/10.1007/978-3-319-23540-0_19
3. Bader, R., Woerndl, W., Karitnig, A., Leitner, G.: Designing an explanation interface for proactive recommendations in automotive scenarios. In: Ardissono, L., Kuflik, T. (eds.) UMAP 2011. LNCS, vol. 7138, pp. 92–104. Springer, Heidelberg (2012). https://doi.org/10.1007/978-3-642-28509-7_10
4. Bauman, K., Liu, B., Tuzhilin, A.: Aspect based recommendations: recommending items with the most valuable aspects based on user reviews. In: Proceedings of the 23rd ACM SIGKDD International Conference on Knowledge Discovery and Data Mining, pp. 717–725 (2017)
5. Bentahar, J., Moulin, B., Belanger, M.: A taxonomy of argumentation models used for knowledge representation. Artif. Intell. Rev. **33**(3), 211–259 (2010)
6. Berkovsky, S., Taib, R., Conway, D.: How to recommend?: user trust factors in movie recommender systems. In: Proceedings of the 22nd International Conference on Intelligent User Interfaces, pp. 287–300 (2017)
7. Blair, J.A.: The possibility and actuality of visual arguments. In: Tindale, C. (eds.) Groundwork in the Theory of Argumentation, vol. 21, pp. 205–223 (2012)
8. Carenini, G., Cheung, J.C.K., Pauls, A.: Multi document summarization of evaluative text. Comput. Intell. **29**, 545–574 (2013)
9. Carenini, G., Moore, J.D.: Generating and evaluating evaluative arguments. Artif. Intell. **170**, 925–952 (2006)
10. Casel: 2013 casel guide: Effective social and emotional learning programs - preschool and elementary school edition, collaborative for academic social and emotional learning (2013)
11. Chen, C., Zhang, M., Liu, Y., Ma., S.: Neural attentional rating regression with review-level explanations. In: Proceedings of the 2018 World Wide Web Conference on World Wide Web, pp. 1583–1592. International World Wide Web Conferences Steering Committee (2018)
12. Chen, L., Pu, P.: Critiquing-based recommenders: survey and emerging trends **22**(1–2), 3085–3094 (2014)
13. Cheng, H.F., et al.: Explaining decision-making algorithms through UI: strategies to help non-expert stakeholders. In: Proceedings of the 2019 CHI Conference on Human Factors in Computing Systems, pp. 1–12 (2019)

14. Costa, F., Ouyang, S., Dolog, P., Lawlor, A.: Automatic generation of natural language explanations. In: Proceedings of the 23rd International Conference on Intelligent User Interfaces Companion, pp. 57:1–57:2 (2018)
15. Devlin, J., Chang, M.W., Lee, K., Toutanova, K.: BERT: pre-training of deep bidirectional transformers for language understanding. arXiv preprint arXiv:1810.04805 (2019)
16. Dong, R., O'Mahony, M.P., Smyth, B.: Further experiments in opinionated product recommendation. In: Lamontagne, L., Plaza, E. (eds.) ICCBR 2014. LNCS (LNAI), vol. 8765, pp. 110–124. Springer, Cham (2014). https://doi.org/10.1007/978-3-319-11209-1_9
17. Donkers, T., Kleemann, T., Ziegler, J.: Explaining recommendations by means of aspect-based transparent memories. In: Proceedings of the 25th International Conference on Intelligent User Interfaces, pp. 166–176 (2020)
18. Donkers, T., Ziegler, J.: Leveraging arguments in user reviews for generating and explaining recommendations. Datenbank-Spektrum **20**(2), 181–187 (2020)
19. Driver, M.J., Brousseau, K.E., Hunsaker, P.L.: The dynamic decision maker (1990)
20. Farkas, D.K., Farkas, J.B.: Guidelines for designing web navigation. Tech. Commun. **47**(3), 341–358 (2000)
21. Faul, F., Erdfelder, E., Lang, A.G., Buchner, A.: G*power 3: a flexible statistical power analysis for the social, behavioral, and biomedical sciences. Behav. Res. Methods **39**, 175–191 (2007)
22. Friedrich, G., Zanker, M.: A taxonomy for generating explanations in recommender systems. AI Mag. **32**(3), 90–98 (2011)
23. Habernal, I., Gurevych, I.: Argumentation mining in user-generated web discourse. Comput. Linguist. **43**(1), 125–179 (2017)
24. Hamilton, K., Shih, S.I., Mohammed, S.: The development and validation of the rational and intuitive decision styles scale. J. Pers. Assess. **98**(5), 523–535 (2016)
25. Herlocker, J.L., Konstan, J.A., Riedl, J.: Explaining collaborative filtering recommendations. In: Proceedings of the 2000 ACM Conference on Computer Supported Cooperative Work, pp. 241–250. ACM (2000)
26. Hernandez-Bocanegra, D.C., Donkers, T., Ziegler, J.: Effects of argumentative explanation types on the perception of review-based recommendations. In: Adaptation and Personalization (UMAP 2020 Adjunct) (2020)
27. Hilton, D.J.: Conversational processes and causal explanation. Physcol. Bull. **107**(1), 65–81 (1990)
28. Kirby, J.R., Moore, P.J., Schofield, N.J.: Verbal and visual learning styles. Contemp. Educ. Psychol. **12**(2), 169–184 (1988)
29. Klein, L.: Evaluating the potential of interactive media through a new lens: search versus experience goods. J. Bus. Res. **41**, 195–203 (1998)
30. Knijnenburg, B.P., Willemsen, M.C., Gantner, Z., Soncu, H., Newell, C.: Explaining the user experience of recommender systems. In: User Modeling and User-Adapted Interaction, pp. 441–504 (2012)
31. Kouki, P., Schaffer, J., Pujara, J., O'Donovan, J., Getoor, L.: Personalized explanations for hybrid recommender systems. In: Proceedings of 24th International Conference on Intelligent User Interfaces (IUI 19), pp. 379–390. ACM (2019)
32. Krause, J., Perer, A., Ng, K.: Interacting with predictions: visual inspection of black-box machine learning models. In: Proceedings of the 2016 CHI Conference on Human Factors in Computing Systems, pp. 5686–5697 (2016)
33. Lamche, B., Adigüzel, U., Wörndl, W.: Interactive explanations in mobile shopping recommender systems. In: Proceedings of the 4th International Workshop on

Personalization Approaches in Learning Environments (PALE 2014), held in conjunction with the 22nd International Conference on User Modeling, Adaptation, and Personalization (UMAP 2014), pp. 92–104 (2012)

34. Lipton, P.: Contrastive explanation. Royal Inst. Philos. Suppl. **27**, 247–266 (1990)
35. Liu, Y., Shrum, L.J.: What is interactivity and is it always such a good thing? implications of definition, person, and situation for the influence of interactivity on advertising effectiveness. J. Advert. **31**(4), 53–64 (2002)
36. Loepp, B., Herrmanny, K., Ziegler, J.: Blended recommending: integrating interactive information filtering and algorithmic recommender techniques. In: Proceedings of the 33rd Annual ACM Conference on Human Factors in Computing Systems - CHI 2015, pp. 975–984 (2015)
37. Loepp, B., Hussein, T., Ziegler, J.: Choice-based preference elicitation for collaborative filtering recommender systems. In: Proceedings of the 32nd Annual ACM Conference on Human Factors in Computing Systems - CHI 2014, pp. 3085–3094 (2014)
38. Madumal, P., Miller, T., Sonenberg, L., Vetere, F.: A grounded interaction protocol for explainable artificial intelligence. In: Proceedings of the 18th International Conference on Autonomous Agents and Multiagent Systems, AAMAS 2019, pp. 1–9 (2019)
39. McKnight, D.H., Choudhury, V., Kacmar, C.: Developing and validating trust measures for e-commerce: an integrative typology. Inf. Syst. Res. **13**, 334–359 (2002)
40. Miller, T.: Explanation in artificial intelligence: insights from the social sciences. Artif. Intell. **267**, 1–38 (2018)
41. Muhammad, K.I., Lawlor, A., Smyth, B.: A live-user study of opinionated explanations for recommender systems. In: Intelligent User Interfaces (IUI 2016), vol. 2, pp. 256–260 (2016)
42. Nelson, P.J.: Consumer Information and Advertising. In: Galatin, M., Leiter, R.D. (eds.) Economics of Information. Social Dimensions of Economics, vol. 3. Springer, Dordrecht (1981). https://doi.org/10.1007/978-94-009-8168-3_5
43. Nelson, P.: Information and consumer behavior. J. Polit. Econ. **78**(2), 311–329 (1970)
44. Nunes, I., Jannach, D.: A systematic review and taxonomy of explanations in decision support and recommender systems. User Model User Adap. **27**, 393–444 (2017)
45. Perugini, M., Gallucci, M., Costantini, G.: A practical primer to power analysis for simple experimental designs. Int. Rev. Soc. Psychol. **31**(1)(20), 1–23 (2018). https://doi.org/10.5334/irsp.181
46. Pu, P., Chen, L., Hu, R.: A user-centric evaluation framework for recommender systems. In: Proceedings of the Fifth ACM Conference on Recommender Systems - RecSys 2011, pp. 157–164 (2011)
47. Rago, A., Cocarascu, O., Bechlivanidis, C., Toni, F.: Argumentation as a framework for interactive explanations for recommendations. In: Proceedings of the Seventeenth International Conference on Principles of Knowledge Representation and Reasoning, pp. 805–815 (2020)
48. Schein, A.I., Popescul, A., Ungar, L.H., Pennock, D.M.: Methods and metrics for cold-start recommendations. In: Proceedings of SIGIR 2002, pp. 253–260 (2002)
49. Schnotz, W.: Integrated model of text and picture comprehension. In: The Cambridge Handbook of Multimedia Learning, 2nd ed., pp. 72–103 (2014)
50. Sniezek, J.A., Buckley, T.: Cueing and cognitive conflict in judge advisor decision making. Organ. Behav. Hum. Decis. Process. **62**(2), 159–174 (1995)

51. Sokol, K., Flach, P.: LIMEtree: interactively customisable explanations based on local surrogate multi-output regression trees. arXiv preprint arXiv:2005.01427 (2020)

52. Sokol, K., Flach, P.: One explanation does not fit all: the promise of interactive explanations for machine learning transparency **34**(2), 235–250 (2020)

53. Song, J.H., Zinkhan, G.M.: Determinants of perceived web site interactivity. J. Mark. **72**(2), 99–113 (2008)

54. Steuer, J.: Defining virtual reality: dimensions determining telepresence. J. Commun. **42**(4), 73–93 (1992)

55. Tintarev, N.: Explanations of recommendations. In: Proceedings of the 2007 ACM Conference on Recommender Systems, RecSys 2007, pp. 203–206 (2007)

56. Tintarev, N., Masthoff, J.: Evaluating the effectiveness of explanations for recommender systems. User Model. User Adapt. Interact. **22**, 399–439 (2012)

57. Toulmin, S.E.: The uses of argument (1958)

58. Vig, J., Sen, S., Riedl, J.: Tagsplanations: explaining recommendations using tags. In: Proceedings of the 14th International Conference on Intelligent User Interfaces, pp. 47–56. ACM (2009)

59. Wachsmuth, H., Trenkmann, M., Stein, B., Engels, G., Palakarska, T.: A review corpus for argumentation analysis. In: 15th International Conference on Intelligent Text Processing and Computational Linguistics, pp. 115–127 (2014)

60. Walton, D.: The place of dialogue theory in logic. Comput. Sci. Commun. Stud. **123**, 327–346 (2000)

61. Walton, D.: A new dialectical theory of explanation. Philos. Explor. **7**(1), 71–89 (2004)

62. Walton, D.: A dialogue system specification for explanation. Synthese **182**(3), 349–374 (2011)

63. Walton, D., Krabbe, E.C.W.: Commitment in Dialogue: Basic Concepts of Interpersonal Reasoning. State University of New York Press, New York (1995)

64. Wang, N., Wang, H., Jia, Y., Yin, Y.: Explainable recommendation via multi-task learning in opinionated text data. In: Proceedings of the 41st International ACM SIGIR Conference on Research and Development in Information Retrieval, SIGIR 2018, pp. 165–174 (2018)

65. Weld, D.S., Bansal, G.: The challenge of crafting intelligible intelligence. Commun. ACM **62**(6), 70–79 (2019)

66. Wu, Y., Ester, M.: Flame: a probabilistic model combining aspect based opinion mining and collaborative filtering. In: Eighth ACM International Conference on Web Search and Data Mining, pp. 153–162. ACM (2015)

67. Xiao, B., Benbasat, I.: Ecommerce product recommendation agents: use, characteristics, and impact. MIS Q. **31**(1), 137–209 (2007)

68. Yaniv, I., Milyavsky, M.: Using advice from multiple sources to revise and improve judgments. Organ. Behav. Hum. Decis. Process. **103**, 104–120 (2007)

69. Zanker, M., Schoberegger, M.: An empirical study on the persuasiveness of fact-based explanations for recommender systems. In: Joint Workshop on Interfaces and Human Decision Making in Recommender Systems, pp. 33–36 (2014)

70. Zhang, Y., Lai, G., Zhang, M., Zhang, Y., Liu, Y., Ma., S.: Explicit factor models for explainable recommendation based on phrase-level sentiment analysis. In: Proceedings of the 37th International ACM SIGIR Conference on Research and Development in Information Retrieval, pp. 83–92 (2014)

Human-XAI Interaction: A Review and Design Principles for Explanation User Interfaces

Michael Chromik$^{(\boxtimes)}$ and Andreas Butz

LMU Munich, Munich, Germany
{michael.chromik,butz}@ifi.lmu.de

Abstract. The interdisciplinary field of explainable artificial intelligence (XAI) aims to foster human understanding of black-box machine learning models through explanation-generating methods. Although the social sciences suggest that explanation is a social and iterative process between an explainer and an explainee, explanation user interfaces and their user interactions have not been systematically explored in XAI research yet. Therefore, we review prior XAI research containing explanation user interfaces for ML-based intelligent systems and describe different concepts of interaction. Further, we present observed design principles for interactive explanation user interfaces. With our work, we inform designers of XAI systems about human-centric ways to tailor their explanation user interfaces to different target audiences and use cases.

Keywords: Explainable AI · Explanation user interfaces · Interaction design · Literature review

1 Introduction

Intelligent systems based on machine learning (ML) are widespread in many contexts of our lives. Often, their accurate predictions come at the expense of interpretability due to their black-box nature. As consequential predictions of these systems may raise questions by those who are affected or held accountable, there is a call for *"explanations that enable people to understand the decisions"* [85]. Hence, much research is conducted within the emerging domain of explainable artificial intelligence (XAI) and interpretable machine learning (IML) on developing methods and interfaces that human users can interpret – often through some sort of explanation. Often there is not a single explanation to be conveyed [1]. Therefore, the DARPA XAI program describes the XAI process as a two-staged approach. It distinguishes between the explainable model and the explanation user interface [37] and, thus, disentangles analyzing the ML model behavior from communicating it to the user. We define an *explanation user interface (XUI)* as the sum of outputs of an XAI system that the user can directly interact with. An XUI may tap into the ML model or may

© IFIP International Federation for Information Processing 2021
Published by Springer Nature Switzerland AG 2021
C. Ardito et al. (Eds.): INTERACT 2021, LNCS 12933, pp. 619–640, 2021.
https://doi.org/10.1007/978-3-030-85616-8_36

use one or more explanation generating algorithms to provide relevant insights for a particular audience. The design of interfaces that *"allow users to better understand underlying computational processes"* is considered a grand challenge of HCI research [86]. Shneiderman considers XUIs as a building block towards *human-centered AI* which aims *"to amplify, augment and enhance human performance"* instead of automating it [85].

However, most XAI research focuses on computational aspects of generating explanations while limited research is reported concerning the human-centered design of the XUI [85,89,102]. Similarly, resources targeting practitioners, such as UK's Information Commissioner's Office[1], who aim to provide practitioners with *"guidance [that] is practically applicable in the real world"*, do not touch on explanation user interfaces nor how to present them to users and instead propose *"...to draw on the expertise of user experience and user interface designers"*. A notable exception is Google's *People+AI Guidebook*[2] which presents case studies of explanations integrated into mobile apps. As the human use of computing is the subject of inquiry in HCI [73], our discipline *"should take a leading role by providing explainable and comprehensible AI, and useful and usable AI"* [105]. In particular, our community is well suited to *"provide effective design for explanation UIs"* [105].

To follow this call and to understand the current practices in the field, we took an HCI perspective and conducted a systematic literature review. The overarching research question (ORQ) of our work is to **survey how researchers designed XUIs in prior XAI work.** From there, we analyze the user interactions offered by the XAI systems and describe observed design patterns. Our work is guided by the following more specific research questions:

- RQ1: How can the different concepts of interaction in XAI be characterized?
- RQ2: What design principles for interactive XUIs can be observed?

The increasing demand for interpretable systems also raises the question how to present this interpretability to users. The contribution of this paper is two-fold: First, we provide a structured literature overview of how user interaction has been designed in XAI. Second, we outline design principles for human interaction with XUIs. Our work guides researchers and practitioners through the interdisciplinary design space of XAI from an HCI perspective.

2   Background and Related Work

2.1   Interaction in Surveys of Explainable AI

XAI is an umbrella term for algorithms and methods that extend the output of ML-based systems with some sort of explanation. The goal is *"to explain or to present [the ML-based system] in understandable terms to a human"* [27].

---

[1] ico.org.uk/about-the-ico/ico-and-stakeholder-consultations/ico-and-the-turing-consultation-on-explaining-ai-decisions-guidance/.

[2] pair.withgoogle.com/chapter/explainability-trust/.

Multiple reviews of the growing field of XAI exist. They formalize and ground the concept of XAI [1,3], relate it to adjacent concepts and disciplines [1,62], categorize methods [36,57], analyze the user perspective [33], review evaluation practices [65], or outline future research directions [1,3]. Most of these reviews acknowledge the importance of interaction for XAI only as a side note. For instance, Mueller et al. [65] consider an effective explanation to be *"an interaction"* and *"not a property of statements"*. Adadi et al. [3] state that *"explainability can only happen through interaction between human and machine"*. Abdul et al. [1] present research on interactive explanation interfaces as an important trajectory to advance the XAI research field. However, none of these reviews elaborates how this interaction could be described nor designed to inform researchers and practitioners. To our knowledge, none of the review look at XAI from an interaction design perspective.

On a broader level, there is a line of research on how to design the overall human interaction with AI-infused systems. For instance, Amershi et al. present guidelines for AI-infused systems [5]. While not explicitly addressing interpretability nor explanations, they point out the importance of making clear why the system did what it did in case of errors. However, their guidelines do not outline what this interaction could look like.

2.2 The XAI Pipeline and Explanation User Interfaces

The XAI process can be broken down into different steps. Murdoch et al. distinguish between the predictive accuracy, the descriptive accuracy, and the relevancy of an XAI system. *Predictive accuracy* is the degree to which the learned ML model correctly extracts the underlying data relationships. *Descriptive accuracy* (also referred to as fidelity) is the degree to which an explanation generation method accurately describes the behavior of the learned ML model. Both accuracies can be objectively measured. In contrast, the subjective *relevancy* describes if the outputs are communicated in a way that they provide insights for a particular audience into a chosen domain problem [67].

The DARPA XAI program illustrates the XAI process as a two-staged approach. It distinguishes between the explainable model and the explanation user interface [37]. The former addresses the predictive and descriptive accuracies, while the latter aims for relevancy. Such a two-staged approach disentangles the XAI process into analyzing the ML model behavior and communicating it to the user. Similarly, Danilevsky et al. [21] differentiate between explainability techniques and explainability visualizations. The former generates *"raw explanations"* typically proposed by AI researchers while the latter is concerned with the presentation of these *"raw explanations"* to users typically guided by HCI researchers. Most open-source methods for XAI provide a single explanation generation method. However, there is a growing number of explanation generation toolkits (e.g., AIX 360[3], Alibi[4], DALEX[5]) that combine multiple state-of-the-art methods in a uniform programming interface and thus enable rapid prototyping of XUI.

---

[3] https://aix360.mybluemix.net/.

[4] https://docs.seldon.io/projects/alibi/en/latest/.

[5] https://uc-r.github.io/dalex.

**In this work, we define an explanation user interface (XUI) as the
sum of outputs of an XAI process that the user can directly interact
with.** Shneiderman [85] outlines two modes of XUI. *Explanatory* XUIs aim to
convey a single explanation (e.g., a visualization or a text explanation). In contrast, *exploratory* XUIs let users freely explore the ML model behavior. They
are most effective when users have the power to change or influence the inputs.
Arya et al. [7] distinguish between static and interactive explanations. A static
explanation *"does not change in response to feedback from the consumer"*. In
contrast, interactive explanations allow *"to drill down or ask for different types
of explanations [...] until [...] satisfied"*.

3   Methodology

In line with our ORQ, our method for characterizing interaction in XAI was
to collect a corpus of publications using the structured search approaches by
Kitchenham and Charters [47]. We then analyzed the corpus regarding the interaction concepts followed by the authors as well as the design and interaction
functionalities offered to users.

To collect a corpus of candidate publications, we conducted a systematic
search in the *ACM Digital Library*. We limited our search to work that has
been published at venues relevant to HCI (*Sponsor SIGCHI*). Through initial
exploratory search, we obtained an initial understanding of relevant keywords,
synonyms, and related concepts that helped us to construct the search query.
Different terms are used to describe the field of XAI and XUI [1]. We focused on
publications that include user-centered artefacts with explicit forms of explanation for the underlying intelligent behavior. Our primary focus was on research
that builds on the potentials of current algorithmic explanation-generating XAI
methods and thus often self-identifies as *"XAI"* or *"explainable AI"*. To account
for the historic perspectives, we included *"explanation interface"* and *"explanation facility"*. These terms emerged in the 2000s from the recommender systems
community and have often been used as a umbrella term for user interfaces covering different explanatory goals [92]. Further, we were interested in research that
has a user focus and mentions some form of *"user interaction"*, *"user interface"*,
or aspects of *"usability"* or *"interactive"*. We prepended the terms interaction
and interface with *"user"* to distinguish them from feature interactions and system interfaces. While not covering the entire dynamic of this interdisciplinary
field, this scoping resulted in a diverse set of works from multiple decades that
put a focus on the user interface artefact. This resulted in the following search
query:

> [[All: "xai"] OR [All: "explainable ai"] OR [All: "explanation facility"]
> OR [All: "explanation interface"]] AND [[All: "user interaction"] OR [All:
> "user interface"] OR [All: usability] OR [All: interactive]]

We conducted the search procedure in December 2020, which returned a total of 146 results. We then analyzed the full-text of all results. We excluded 13 results without a contribution (i.e., proceedings, keynotes, workshop summaries). Publications included in our analysis had to present results from *constructive* [73] research that involved an XUI artefact (n = 57) or *conceptual* [73] research that addresses interaction in XAI (n = 34). Consequently, we excluded 28 results that were not related to XAI and 14 results that were related to XAI but did not present an XUI nor describe interaction. The review was conducted by the first author. The second author was consulted for feedback. Our final set for analysis consisted of 91 publications. We analyzed the selected publications and coded information about the reported XUI and user interactions in a database.

4   Concepts of Interaction in XAI

Following Hornbæk and Oulasvirta [42], *interaction* describes the interplay between two or more constructs. They analyzed the interplay between the constructs human and computer that were discussed in HCI research. From this, they derived seven concepts of interaction: interaction as information transmission, as dialogue, as control, as experience, as optimal behavior, as tool use, and interaction as embodied action. More narrowly, Miller frames XAI as one kind of a human-agent interaction problem where an *"explanatory agent [is] revealing underlying causes to its or another agent's decision making"* [62]. As such, it is about the interplay between a human user and an AI agent that is mediated through an XUI. Tintarev and Masthoff [92] distinguish seven explanatory goals: transparency (answer how the system works), scrutability (allow to question and correct the system), trustworthiness (increase user confidence), persuasiveness (convince user), effectiveness (help user making good decisions), efficiency (help user making decisions faster), and satisfaction (increase usability). As these may be conflicting with one another, designers of XUI *"need to make trade-offs while choosing or designing the form of interface"* [93].

We build on the interaction concepts of Dubin and Hornbaek [42] and apply them to human-XAI interaction. To answer RQ1 (How can the different concepts of interaction in XAI be characterized?), we analyzed the primary interaction concept that authors (implicitly) applied as part of their work. In particular, we focus on the interplay between a user and an AI system that is facilitated through a UI that leverages some kind of explanation to reach an explanatory goal. We abstracted from the purpose that the researchers used the XUI for and instead looked at how a user could interact with it. As such, we approached the concepts of interaction with an *artefactist approach* [90]. Below, we introduce each concept and relate them to surveyed publications. Table 1 summarizes our analysis.

4.1   Interaction as (Information) Transmission

This concept centers around maximizing the throughput of information via a noisy channel. The interaction is about selecting the best message for transmission from a set of possible messages [42]. It follows the *Shannon-Weaver* [84] model of communication according to which the sender transmits information to the receiver but in between noise is added to the original message (Fig. 1).

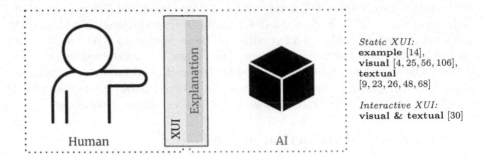

Fig. 1. XAI-interaction as (information) transmission is about presenting an accurate and complete explanation about the AI behavior.

Transfer to XAI: The goal of this interaction centers around presenting users with one complete explanation. Surveyed publications following this concept are mostly driven by the explanatory goal of transparency and acknowledge that *"algorithms should not be studied in isolation, but rather in conjunction with interfaces, since both play a significant role in the perception of explainability"* [25]. They emphasize either (i) the descriptive accuracy of an explanation to describe the underlying AI behavior [26,30,48,56,68] or (ii) the capacity of a single explanation style [4] or differences between explanation styles [9,14,23,25,83,106] to convey information about the behavior to the human. The message is noisy because it may be difficult or even impossible to fully describe the complexity of the AI in a human understandable way, such as with deep neural networks. Unlike interaction as a dialogue, this interaction is mainly about unidirectional communication by presenting a single and static explanation. The XUI is mainly used as a medium for transmitting this explanation.

Examples: Ehsan et al. [30] present real-time explanations about the actions taken by an autonomous gaming agent in the form of natural language rationales. Alqaraawi et al. [4] study whether saliency maps convey enough information to enable users to anticipate the behavior of an image classifier. Cai et al. [14] compared how well two example-based explanation styles could promote user understanding of a sketch recognition AI. Dodge et al. [23] and Binns et al. [9] study how much different textual explanation styles convey about underlying fairness issues of an ML system. Yang et al. [106] study the differences in spatial layout and visual representation of example-based explanations.

4.2 Interaction as Dialogue

This concept describes a cycle of communication of inputs/outputs by the computer and perception/action by a human. The interaction happens in stages or turns [42]. It tries to ensure a correct mapping between UI functions and the user's intentions and feedback by the UI to bridge the *gulf of execution* [69] (Fig. 2).

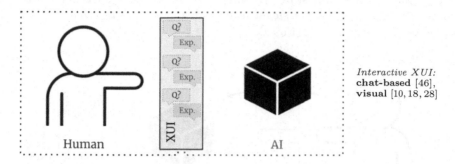

Fig. 2. XAI-interaction as dialogue is about facilitating an iterative communication cycle about the AI behavior.

Transfer to XAI: This concept acknowledges that a single explanation rarely results in a desired level of understanding [1]. Instead, it emphasizes the naturalness and accessibility of (often implicit or simplified) explanations. In contrast to interaction as embodied action, this concept is driven by the user, with the AI responding. Unlike interaction as control, this concept does not change the AI behavior. The goal of the interaction is to provide users with functionalities to gradually build a mental model of the AI behavior. We distinguish between inspection dialogues [10,18,28] and natural dialogues [46].

Inspection Examples: Exploratory dialogues allow the user to explore how (possibly hypothetical) changes in inputs lead to changes in the AI prediction or let the user inspect internals of the AI. The XUI is mostly about offering functionalities to iteratively request explanations of the same kind. Explanations have a high fidelity but are implicit. For instance, Cheng et al. [18] present an XUI that allows users to observe how the predictions of a university admission classifier change by freely adjusting the values of input features of applicants. Their exploratory approach was shown to improve users' comprehension although it required more of their time. Bock and Schreiber [10] present an XUI to inspect layers and parameters of deep neural networks in virtual reality. Similarly, Douglas et al. [28] visualize an AI agent's behavior in form of interactive saliency maps in virtual reality.

Natural Examples: Natural dialogues aim to *"lower the threshold of ability required to analyze data"* and thus make XUIs more accessible to end users of XAI. The XUI is about presenting functionalities to request different natural language explanations. The interaction is mostly driven by the human through questions. Explanations are explicit but simplified in the form of textual answers. Kim et al. [46] present an XUI that enables users to ask factoid questions about charts in natural language (e.g., *"What age had the lowest population of males?"*). The XUI provides the answer and an explanation how it was derived from the chart (e.g., *"I looked up 'age' of the shortest blue bar"*).

4.3   Interaction as Control

This concept supports a rapid and stable convergence of the human-computer system towards a target state. Building on *control theory*, the interaction is aiming *"to change a control signal to a desired level and updating its behavior according to feedback"* [42] (Fig. 3).

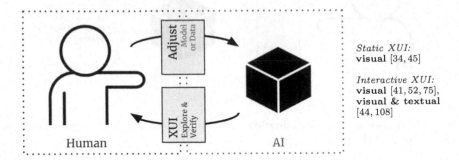

Static XUI:
visual [34, 45]

Interactive XUI:
visual [41, 52, 75],
visual & textual
[44, 108]

Fig. 3. XAI-interaction as control is about supporting a rapid convergence towards the desired AI behavior.

Transfer to XAI: This concept aligns with the ideas of interactive ML [29] and ML model tweaking. The XUI feeds control signals from the ML model to the human controller (feedback). These inform the controller how to change parameters of the ML model or its data so that the model adjusts its behavior (feedforward). The goal of the interaction is to reach the AI behavior desired by the controller. We found two streams of research that follow this paradigm. They can be distinguished by their targeted users: *AI experts* [41, 45, 52, 75, 78] or *AI novices* [34, 44, 108].

AI Expert Examples: Explanations are provided mainly on an abstract level as numbers and visualizations. The cycle of exploration and verification drives the process of understanding. The XUI is a standalone application facilitating this interaction while the actual model adjustments are performed in a separate UI (e.g., the development environment). For instance, [78] present an early XUI to debug rule-based expert systems by explaining why a rule was fired. Krause et al. [52] present the interactive visual analytics systems *Prospector*, that supports data scientists in understanding local predictions and deriving actionable insights on how to improve the ML model. They can (i) explore local predictions and simulate counterfactual changes by different ML models to support the formulation of tweaking hypotheses or (ii) verify how their implemented tweaking hypotheses change the prediction behaviour of the ML model. Hohman et al. [41] present *Gamut*, an XUI were *"interactivity was the primary mechanism for exploring, comparing, and explaining"*. User can link local and global explanations, ask counterfactual and compute similar instances. In contrast, Kaur et al. [45] show that the non-interactive XUIs of widely used explainability tools, such as InterpretML or SHAP, hinder experts to effectively control ML models.

AI Novice Examples: These XUI strive *"to effectively communicate relevant technical features of the [ML] model to a non-technical audience"* [108]. These XUIs provide explicit explanations to support the exploration. They also integrate controls for adjusting underlying the ML models without the need of a separate UI. Yu et al. [108] present an XUI for ML classification in the sensitive context of criminal justice. Their XUI enables designers and end-users to explore and understand algorithmic trade-offs based on an interactive confusion matrix and textual explanations. Further, it allows them to adjust model thresholds in a way that reflects their fairness beliefs (feedforward). Ishibashi et al. [44] present an XUI that synergetically combines low-level spectrograms with semantic thumbnails to interactively train a sound recognition AI. Fulton et al. [34] showcase how an XUI can be integrated into games for AI novices to generate usable data for AI experts.

4.4 Interaction as Experience

This concept considers human expectations towards a computer. It is closely related to *user experience* (UX) encompassing a person's emotions, feelings, and thoughts that may be formed before, during, or after interaction [53] (Fig. 4).

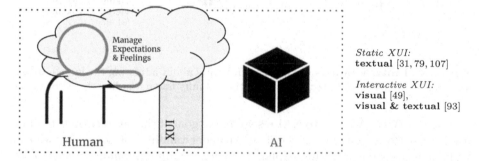

Fig. 4. XAI-interaction as experience is about managing expectations about the AI behavior.

Transfer to XAI: Applied to XAI, this interaction concept emphasizes managing the expectations and preferences of users about the AI. It centers around the explanatory goals of trust [49,77,79,107], satisfaction [93], and persuasiveness [31].

Examples: Knijnenburg et al. show that letting users inspect a recommendation process through an interactive XUI increased their perceived understanding and satisfaction. Tsai et al. [93] investigate the relation of user preferences about explanation styles and user performance. Their results suggest that XUIs preferred by users *"may not guarantee the same level of performance"*. Yin et al. [107] show that a user's trust is impacted by upfront information on the AI's predictive accuracy even after repeated interactions. Pushing this interaction concept, Eiband et al. [31] show with their XUI that even empty (so-called placebic) explanations can result in a soothing perceived understanding of users. As an intervention, Pilling et al. [77] outline a design fiction of an AI certification body that provides users with standardized AI quality marks (e.g., *"level 4: product is able to explain itself to users on request."*).

4.5   Interaction as Optimal Behavior

This concept centers around adapting the user behavior to better support their tasks and goals. It acknowledges that the interaction with the system is often constrained, and thus suboptimal. Users are trading off rewards and costs of an interaction. It builds around the idea of *bounded rationality* [87] according to which humans act as "satisficers" who strive for satisfying and sufficient solutions (instead of optimal ones) due to cognitive limitations (Fig. 5).

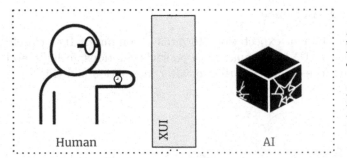

Fig. 5. XAI-interaction as optimal behavior is about adjusting the human behavior despite the cognitive or technical limitations of fully understanding the AI behavior.

Transfer to XAI: Applied to XAI research, the goal of the interaction is to guide users to reach a "satisficing" level of AI understanding for some downstream task. It focuses on providing explanations for *"training humans to have better interactions with AI"*, for example, when they face erroneous AI systems [99] or exhibit misconceptions caused by cognitive biases [97]. We distinguish between research that (i) examines limitations that occur during the interaction with an XAI [12,13,24,60,61,70,97] and (ii) designs interactions to better moderate these limitations [2,16,19,59,81,98,99].

Examples that Examine Limitations: Millecamp et al. [61] studied the impact of personal characteristics on the interaction and perception of XAI in a music recommender setting. They show that the perception and interaction with XUIs is influenced by a user's need for cognition (NFC) (i.e., their tendency to engage in and enjoy effortful cognitive activities). Nourani et al. [70] show that a user's first impression of an AI system influences their overall perception of the system. While a positive first impression may lead to automation bias, a negative first impression may result in a less accurate mental model. They call for XUIs that control a user's first impression and *"continually direct user attention to system strengths and weaknesses throughout user-system interactions"*. Similarly,

Bucinca et al. [12] highlight that the effectiveness of XAI is impacted by the design of the interaction itself. Thus, it is important to take *"into account the cognitive effort and cognitive processes that are employed [by the user]"* during their interpretation of explanations.

Examples that Moderate Limitations: Several of the works designed interactions that *"optimize the performance of the sociotechnical (human+AI) system as a whole"* [12]. For example, Wang et al. [98] provide confidence explanations to help users to gauge when or when not to trust an AI. Similarly, Schaekermann et al. [81] show that highlighting and textually explaining ambiguous predictions helps physicians to *"allocate cognitive resources and reassess their level of trust appropriately for each specific case"*. Abdul et al. [2] propose a visual explanation style that balances cognitive load and descriptive accuracy by limiting the visual chunks to be processed by the user. Further, they present a method to estimate users' cognitive load of explanations. Weisz et al. [99] teach users strategies to effectively interact with a limited capability chatbot in a banking and shopping context. Their interaction aims to explain to users why a chatbot may be unable to provide meaningful responses. For instance, explaining that the chatbot mapped the user's utterance to multiple low confidence intents because the utterance was poorly worded or ambiguous. Mai et al. [59] guide users through a military-inspired structured reflection process, called *after-action review* to understand the behavior of an AI agent. Accompanied by a visual explanation of AI decisions, the reflection process helped users to organize their cognitive process of understanding and kept them engaged.

4.6 Interaction as Tool Use

This concept centers around using computers to augment the user's capabilities beyond the tool itself. Following *activity theory*, the system influences the *"mental functioning of individuals"*. As such, AI can also be used as a tool for learning. For example, the social sciences use word embeddings as a diagnostic tool to quantify changes in society [35] (Fig. 6).

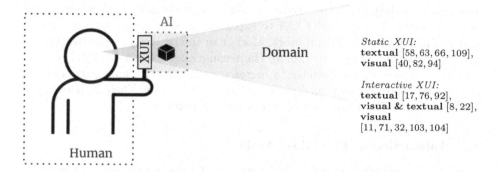

Fig. 6. XAI-interaction as tool use is about facilitating learning from the AI behavior about a given domain.

Transfer to XAI: Applied to XAI, this interaction concept helps humans to find hidden patterns and insights in domain-specific data. To facilitate this learning, some form of explanation is required. The XUI serves as a lens on a domain (beyond the AI behavior) that would otherwise be difficult to understand. In this way, the interaction contributes to augment human thinking.

Examples: Xie et al. [104] assist physicians analyzing chest x-rays of patients through an interactive mixed-modality XUI. Paudyal et al. [76] presents an interactive XUI for a computer-vision based sign language AI. The textual explanations provide learners with feedback on the location, shapes, and movements of their hands. Similarly, Schneeberger et al. [82] use an XUI to let users practice emotionally difficult social situations with a social AI agent. Das et al. [22] present an XUI which provides feedback on a chess player's intended moves. Their visual highlighting and textual explanations significantly improved the performance of chess players in a multi-day user study. They point out the importance of accompanying textual explanations for the AI reasoning. Only showing the visual explanation did not improve performance. Similarly, Feng et al. [32] support players by visually explaining evidences for each uncovered word of a quiz question. Xie et al. [103] use an interactive XUI with visual explanations to give game designers live-feedback on how challenging their created level designs are. Misztal-Radecka and Indurkhya [63] generate textual user stories for personas from large datasets to inform interaction designers about potentially relevant user groups.

Explainable Recommender Systems: In addition, most works on explainable recommender systems follow this interaction concept as their recommendations aim to give users insights about the recommender domain [40]. Some XUIs allow personalization by steering the recommendation behavior and thus, include aspects of the *interaction as control* concept. These user-initiated manipulations dynamically influence the recommendations and serve as a feedforward mechanism. However, users' focus is not about reaching an envisioned end state of AI behavior, but generating useful insights about the domain (or themselves). For example, O'Donovan et al. [71] present *PeerChooser*, an interactive movie recommender that enables users to provide "hints" about their current mood and needs by dragging movie genres closer or further away from their avatar. Bostandjiev et al. [11] use the XUI to explain a music recommendation process and to elicit preferences from users. Users can interactively adjust weights on the input and model level to explore the recommender. Chen et al. [17] present a preference-based recommender to increase users' product knowledge of high-investment products, such as digital cameras and laptops. Their XUI textually explains trade-offs within a set of recommended items.

4.7   Interaction as Embodied Action

This concept centers around collaboration and joint action with a computer. In 1960, Licklider formulated the vision of *man-computer symbiosis* in which *"men and computers [are] to cooperate in making decisions and controlling complex situations"* [55]. Humans may be amplified through collaboration with AI. However, effective collaboration goes beyond interaction. In this way, this concept builds on theories from the computer-supported cooperative work (CSCW) community, such as mutual goal understanding, preemptive task co-management and shared progress tracking [96] (Fig. 7).

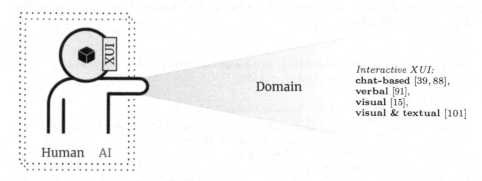

Fig. 7. XAI-interaction as embodied action is about establishing a joint understanding with the AI for an effective collaboration in a given domain.

Transfer to XAI: Applied to XAI, explanations are a crucial component for effective cooperation. A lack of explanatory communication resulted in dissatisfaction [38,72]. In this way, XUIs contribute to the augmentation of human actions. A symbiotic relationship for which this is especially important involves *autonomous systems*. Autonomous systems in high-risk scenarios have a high degree of autonomy and thus *"need to explain what they are doing and why"* [39]. In such a setting, it is crucial for humans and agents alike to communicate each other's capabilities and intended next steps with respect to a common goal, often in real-time. We identified XUIs which are not only about understanding AI agents (*interaction as transmission*), but which enabled them to also influence the agents' actions – and vice versa [15,39,80]. Unlike *interaction as control* the interaction is not only driven by the human controller, but by both parties [6,91,101].

Examples: Tabrez et al. [91] present an AI agent that analyzes the game decisions of a human collaborator in a collaborative game setting and verbally interrupts the human in case the common goal becomes unattainable because of a wrong move. The AI agent dynamically constructs a *theory of mind* of the human collaborator and provides tailored explanations that aim to correct their understanding of the game situation. Chakraborti et al. [15] present an XUI that coordinates mission plans between a semi-autonomous search and rescue robot and a human commander who has an incomplete and possibly outdated map of the robot's environment. Visual explanations are embedded as changes in the commander map. The commander can either request (i) an optimal plan by the robot and explanations for this plan, or (ii) a potentially suboptimal plan that is aligned with the commander's expectations. As such, the XUI reconciles potential mismatches about the plans between robot and commander. Hastie et al. [39] and Robb et al. [80] present an XUI that provides operators of autonomous underwater vehicles with why and why not explanations in realtime via a chat interface. Further, users can influence actions of the autonomous system through the XUI (e.g. setting reminders). Their XUI was reported to increase the situation awareness of operators and adjusted their mental model of system capabilities.

Table 1. Surveyed XAI publications categorized according to the different concepts of interaction by Hornbæk and Oulasvirta [42].

Interaction concept	Interaction Goal *applied to XAI*	References
Transmission	Present users with accurate or complete explanation about AI behavior. *Explanatory goal: transparency*	[4, 9, 14, 23, 25, 26, 30, 48, 56, 68, 106]
Dialogue	Facilitate natural and iterative conversation about AI behavior. *Explanatory goals: transparency, scrutability*	[10, 18, 28, 46]
Control	Support rapid convergence towards desired AI behavior. *Explanatory goal: effectiveness*	[34, 41, 44, 45, 51, 52, 75, 78, 108]
Experience	Manage expectations about AI behavior. *Explanatory goals: satisfaction, trust, persuasiveness*	[31, 49, 77, 79, 93, 107]
Optimal behavior	Adjust human behavior despite limitations of fully understanding the AI behavior. *Explanatory goal: efficiency*	[2, 12, 13, 16, 19, 24, 50, 59–61, 70, 81, 97–99]
Tool use	Facilitate learning from AI behavior about a given domain. *Explanatory goals: effectiveness*	[8, 11, 17, 22, 32, 40, 58, 63, 66, 71, 76, 82, 92, 94, 103, 104, 109]
Embodied action	Establish a joint understanding with the AI for an effective collaboration in a given domain. *Explanatory goal: effectiveness*	[15, 39, 80, 88, 91, 101]

5   Design Principles for Interactive XUI

In the last section, we described the general interplay between the XAI system and the user. Below, we will focus on the interactive qualities of the XUI itself. Vilone et al. define interactivity as *"the capacity of an explanation system to reason about previous utterances both to interpret and answer users' follow-up questions"* [95]. We expand this definition by building on the concept of *explanation facilities* that dates to the era of rule-based expert systems. Moore and Paris [64] proposed that a good explanation facility should, among others, fulfill the requirements of *naturalness* (explanations in natural language following a dialogue), *responsiveness* (allow follow-up questions), *flexibility* (make use of multiple explanation methods), and *sensitivity* (provided explanations should be informed by the user's knowledge, goal, context, and previous interaction). We analyzed our sample of XAI publications through the lens of these requirements to answer RQ2 (What design principles for interactive XUIs can be observed?). We found common interaction strategies and design recommendations [17,45,80,104] that address aspects of these requirements. We unify and present them as *design principles*. In interaction design, design principles are *"guidelines for design of useful and desirable products"* [20].

5.1   Complementary Naturalness

Consider complementing implicit explanations with rationales in natural language.

Why: Implicit visual explanations can accurately depict the inner workings of an AI but are often inaccessible to non-experts. In contrast, rationales in natural language are post-hoc explanations *"that are meant to sound like what a human [explainer] would say in the same situation"* [30]. Relaying facts through text may *"reassure users when system status might be uncertain or [...] obscure"* [80]. Combining visual cues with textual rationales can facilitate understanding and communicative effectiveness [30].

How: Kim et al. [46] outline a method that automatically generates explanations from visualizations through a template-based approach. Robb et al. [80] elaborate design recommendations on how to incorporate chat-based XUI for autonomous vehicle operators. For example, Yu et al. [108] provide users with a switch to change a visual explanation into verbose explicit sentences. Schaekermann et al. [81] complement quantitative low-confidence predictions with arguments in natural language to attract the attention of physicians. Sklar et al. [88] explain the reasoning behind an AI agent's actions through a chat-interface.

5.2   Responsiveness Through Progressive Disclosure

Consider offering hierarchical or iterative functionalities that allow follow-ups on initial explanations.

Why: Prior research indicated that there is a fine line between no explanation and too much explanation [61]. A user's individual need for cognition influences this threshold. Providing overly detailed explanations overwhelms users who may operate on a simpler mental model of the underlying AI.

How: Springer and Whittaker [89] recommend applying the interaction design pattern of *progressive disclosure*. It is about providing users only with high-level information and offering follow-up operations in case they are interested in further details[6] It resembles the *"progressive-step-by-step process"* demanded by [85]. As such, an XUI should (i) provide information on demand, (ii) hierarchically organize explanatory information, and (iii) keep track of the interaction with a user. For example, Millecamp et al. [61] provide a *Why?* button next to a recommendation. Clicking it provides a one-dimensional visual explanation in the form of a bar chart. If users are interested in additional details, they can click another button to receive a multi-dimensional visual explanation that compares multiple attributes of multiple recommendations in the form of a scatter plot. Krause et al. [52] use tooltips to summarize the most influential features and their sensitivity. If interested, users can drill down and freely explore these with partial dependence plots. Bock et al. [10] visualize a convolutional neural network in virtual reality. Progressive disclosure is realized through spatial distance. As the user approaches the network, more layers with finer granularity become visible. This design principle can also be implicitly implemented by enabling users to repeatedly adjust controls of the ML model [11,108] or input parameters [18,76] to progressively disclose local insights step-by-step.

5.3   Flexibility Through Multiple Ways to Explain

Consider offering multiple explanation methods and modalities to enable explainees to triangulate insights.

Why: Humans gain understanding in many ways. Paez [74] outlines them along a spectrum between understanding why (gained through observations and exemplifications) and objectual understanding (gained through idealizations and simplified models). In practice, there is often no best way to explain. For instance, a physician's *"differential diagnosis seldom relies on a single type of data"* [103]. In this way, explanation methods and modalities can complement each other.

How: This principle builds around the interaction design pattern of *multiple ways*[7], which is about *"providing an opportunity to navigate [...] in more than one manner"*. Multiple publications recommend addressing local and global explanation paradigms within one XUI [24,41,104]. This enables users to get an overview of the overall AI behavior and scrutiny of individual cases at the same time. To facilitate this navigation, Liao et al. [54] present a catalog of natural language questions that can technically be answered by current XAI methods.

---

[6] nngroup.com/articles/progressive-disclosure/.

[7] w3.org/tr/understanding-wcag20/navigation-mechanisms-mult-loc.html.

Covering multiple of them under a *"holistic approach"* [54] allows users to triangulate insights. For example, Xie et al. [103] present a three-stage explanation workflow that supports physicians in top-down or bottom-up reasoning. Their XUI can *"connects the dots"* and highlight how explanations at each stage relate to one another. Wang et al. [97] present a XUI that provides feature attributions and counterfactual rules in parallel to support multiple ways of reasoning. Hohman et al. [41] provide highly interconnected visual model-level and instance-level explanations side by side to *"flexibly support people's differing processes"*. Chen et al. [17] provide different explanatory views that allow users to examine recommended products from different angles.

5.4 Sensitivity to the Mind and Context

Consider offering functionalities to adjust explanations to explainees' mental models and contexts.

Why: Explanation needs of user evolve *"as one builds understanding and trust during the interaction process"* [54]. Further, prior beliefs and biases of users influence how they respond to different styles of explanations. This calls for *"a personalized approach to explaining ML systems"* [23].

How: This principle builds around the concept of *mixed-initiative interaction* [43], which emphasizes an interaction in which the human and the computer work towards the shared goal – fostering human understanding in the case of XAI. The timing of actions along the stages of grounding, listening, and interrupting is important for a successful interaction. To adapt its operations, an XUI needs to construct a computer model (or theory of mind [91]) of the user's mental model [65]. Despite its complexity, we found first examples. Tabrez et al. [91] estimate a human collaborator's beliefs in a collaborative game to identify explanation points. Other works [15,17,19], elicit preferences or beliefs to estimate a user's expected AI predictions (so called foils), e.g., so that counterfactual explanations can argument only regarding these. Wenskovitch et al. [100] present a method to infer user intent from interactions with visual explanations. Xie et al. [104] implement an *"urgent"* mode that can be toggled by physicians in a hurry to only see high confidence explanations with little system complexity.

6 Limitations and Outlook

Our review excluded publications outside the *ACM Digital Library* and the *SIGCHI* community. We are confident that our review covers many publications that emphasize the interaction design perspective of XAI. However, we probably have missed relevant applied research from adjacent XAI communities inside (e.g., FAccT) and outside (e.g., AIS) of *ACM*. Future work could extend our work with their learnings. Another promising direction for future research is constructive research that encompasses all presented design principles. None of the survey publications considered all design principles in one XUI. This makes sense as researchers try to limit and control variables for a rigorous evaluation of their research questions. However, with the emergence of open-source explanation-generating toolkits it would be a logical next step to explore reusable and customizable XUI frameworks. These could integrate multiple explanation methods under a human-centric interaction concept.

7 Summary

Interaction design has been discussed as an important aspect for effective explainability in XAI. Yet, so far, it has not been systematically analyzed. Starting from a systematically obtained set of XAI publications that mention user interfaces or user interaction, we derived seven concepts of human-XAI interaction. Further, we analyzed the presented XUI and consolidated proposed recommendations as design principles encompassing four recurring themes: naturalness, responsiveness, flexibility, and sensitivity. We contribute a categorization to describe XAI work not only by the intended target audience or domain of application, but also through the pursued interaction concept. Our survey provides a starting point for researchers and practitioners planning and designing human-centric XAI systems.

References

1. Abdul, A., Vermeulen, J., Wang, D., Lim, B.Y., Kankanhalli, M.: Trends and trajectories for explainable, accountable and intelligible systems. In: CHI 2018 (2018)
2. Abdul, A., von der Weth, C., Kankanhalli, M., Lim, B.Y.: COGAM: measuring and moderating cognitive load in ML model explanations. In: CHI 2020 (2020)
3. Adadi, A., Berrada, M.: Peeking inside the black-box: a survey on explainable artificial intelligence (XAI). IEEE Access **6**, 52138–52160(2018)
4. Alqaraawi, A., Schuessler, M., Weiss, P., Costanza, E., Berthouze, N.: Evaluating saliency map explanations for convolutional neural networks. In: IUI 2020 (2020)
5. Amershi, S., et al.: Guidelines for human-AI interaction. In: CHI 2019 (2019)
6. Andres, J., et al.: Introducing peripheral awareness as a neurological state for human-computer integration. In: CHI 2020 (2020)
7. Arya, V., et al.: One explanation does not fit all: a toolkit and taxonomy of AI explainability techniques. arXiv (2019)
8. Barria-Pineda, J., Brusilovsky, P.: Explaining educational recommendations through a concept-level knowledge visualization. In: IUI 2019 (2019)
9. Binns, R., Van Kleek, M., Veale, M., Lyngs, U., Zhao, J., Shadbolt, N.: It's reducing a human being to a percentage. In: CHI 2018 (2018)
10. Bock, M., Schreiber, A.: Visualization of neural networks in virtual reality using unreal engine. In: VRST 2018 (2018)
11. Bostandjiev, S., O'Donovan, J., Höllerer, T.: TasteWeights: a visual interactive hybrid recommender system. In: RecSys 2012 (2012)
12. Buçinca, Z., Lin, P., Gajos, K.Z., Glassman, E.L.: Proxy tasks and subjective measures can be misleading in evaluating XAI systems. In: IUI 2020 (2020)

13. Bunt, A., Lount, M., Lauzon, C.: Are explanations always important? A study of deployed, low-cost intelligent interactive systems. In: IUI 2012 (2012)
14. Cai, C.J., Jongejan, J., Holbrook, J.: The effects of example-based explanations in a machine learning interface. In: IUI 2019 (2019)
15. Chakraborti, T., Sreedharan, S., Grover, S., Kambhampati, S.: Plan explanations as model reconciliation: an empirical study. In: HRI 2019 (2019)
16. Chen, L.: Adaptive tradeoff explanations in conversational recommenders. In: RecSys 2009 (2009)
17. Chen, L., Wang, F.: Explaining recommendations based on feature sentiments in product reviews. In: IUI 2017 (2017)
18. Cheng, H.F., et al.: Explaining decision-making algorithms through UI. In: CHI 2019 (2019)
19. Chromik, M., Fincke, F., Butz, A.: Mind the (persuasion) gap: contrasting predictions of intelligent DSS with user beliefs. In: EICS 2020 Companion (2020)
20. Cooper, A., Reimann, R., Cronin, D.: About Face 3: The Essentials of Interaction Design. Wiley, Hoboken (2007)
21. Danilevsky, M., Qian, K., Aharonov, R., Katsis, Y., Kawas, B., Sen, P.: A survey of the state of explainable AI for natural language processing. arXiv (2020)
22. Das, D., Chernova, S.: Leveraging rationales to improve human task performance. In: IUI 2020 (2020)
23. Dodge, J., Liao, Q.V., Zhang, Y., Bellamy, R.K.E., Dugan, C.: Explaining models: an empirical study of how explanations impact fairness judgment. In: IUI 2019 (2019)
24. Dodge, J., Penney, S., Hilderbrand, C., Anderson, A., Burnett, M.: How the experts do it: assessing and explaining agent behaviors in real-time strategy games. In: CHI 2018 (2018)
25. Dominguez, V., Messina, P., Donoso-Guzmán, I., Parra, D.: The effect of explanations and algorithmic accuracy on visual recommender systems of artistic images. In: IUI 2019 (2019)
26. Donkers, T., Kleemann, T., Ziegler, J.: Explaining recommendations by means of aspect-based transparent memories. In: IUI 2020 (2020)
27. Doshi-Velez, F., Kim, B.: Towards a rigorous science of interpretable machine learning. arXiv (2017)
28. Douglas, N., Yim, D., Kartal, B., Hernandez-Leal, P., Maurer, F., Taylor, M.E.: Towers of saliency: a reinforcement learning visualization using immersive environments. In: ISS 2019 (2019)
29. Dudley, J.J., Kristensson, P.O.: A review of user interface design for interactive machine learning. ACM Trans. Interact. Intell, Syst (2018)
30. Ehsan, U., Tambwekar, P., Chan, L., Harrison, B., Riedl, M.O.: Automated rationale generation: a technique for explainable AI and its effects on human perceptions. In: IUI 2019 (2019)
31. Eiband, M., Buschek, D., Kremer, A., Hussmann, H.: the impact of placebic explanations on trust in intelligent systems. In: CHI EA 2019 (2019)
32. Feng, S., Boyd-Graber, J.: What can AI do for me? Evaluating machine learning interpretations in cooperative play. In: IUI 2019 (2019)
33. Ferreira, J.J., Monteiro, M.S.: What are people doing about XAI user experience? A survey on AI explainability research and practice. In: Marcus, A., Rosenzweig, E. (eds.) HCII 2020. LNCS, vol. 12201, pp. 56–73. Springer, Cham (2020). https://doi.org/10.1007/978-3-030-49760-6_4
34. Fulton, L.B., Lee, J.Y., Wang, Q., Yuan, Z., Hammer, J., Perer, A.: Getting playful with explainable AI. In: CHI EA 2020 (2020)

35. Garg, N., Schiebinger, L., Jurafsky, D., Zou, J.: Word embeddings quantify 100 years of gender and ethnic stereotypes. Proc. Natl Acad. Sci. **115**(16), E3635–E3644 (2018)
36. Guidotti, R., Monreale, A., Ruggieri, S., Turini, F., Giannotti, F., Pedreschi, D.: A survey of methods for explaining black box models. ACM Surv. **51**, 1–42 (2018)
37. Gunning, D.: DARPA's XAI program. In: IUI 2019 (2019)
38. Guzdial, M., et al.: Friend, collaborator, student, manager: how design of an AI-driven game level editor affects creators. In: CHI 2019 (2019)
39. Hastie, H., Chiyah Garcia, F.J., Robb, D.A., Laskov, A., Patron, P.: MIRIAM: a multimodal interface for explaining the reasoning behind actions of remote autonomous systems. In: ICMI 2018 (2018)
40. Herlocker, J.L., Konstan, J.A., Riedl, J.: Explaining collaborative filtering recommendations. In: CSCW 2000 (2000)
41. Hohman, F., Head, A., Caruana, R., DeLine, R., Drucker, S.M.: Gamut: a design probe to understand how data scientists understand machine learning models. In: CHI 2019 (2019)
42. Hornbaek, K., Oulasvirta, A.: What is interaction? In: CHI 2017 (2017)
43. Horvitz, E.: Principles of mixed-initiative user interfaces. In: CHI 1999 (1999)
44. Ishibashi, T., Nakao, Y., Sugano, Y.: Investigating audio data visualization for interactive sound recognition. In: IUI 2020 (2020)
45. Kaur, H., et al.: Interpreting interpretability. In: CHI 2020 (2020)
46. Kim, D.H., Hoque, E., Agrawala, M.: Answering questions about charts and generating visual explanations. In: CHI 2020 (2020)
47. Kitchenham, B., Charters, S.: Guidelines for performing systematic literature reviews in software engineering (2007)
48. Kleinerman, A., Rosenfeld, A., Kraus, S.: Providing explanations for recommendations in reciprocal environments. In: RecSys 2018 (2018)
49. Knijnenburg, B.P., Bostandjiev, S., O'Donovan, J., Kobsa, A.: Inspectability and control in social recommenders. In: RecSys 2012 (2012)
50. Kocaballi, A.B., Coiera, E., Berkovsky, S.: Revisiting habitability in conversational systems. In: CHI EA 2020 (2020)
51. Koch, J., Lucero, A., Hegemann, L., Oulasvirta, A.: May AI? Design ideation with cooperative contextual bandits. In: CHI 2019 (2019)
52. Krause, J., Perer, A., Ng, K.: Interacting with predictions: visual inspection of black-box machine learning models. In: CHI 2016 (2016)
53. Law, E.L.C., Roto, V., Hassenzahl, M., Vermeeren, A.P.O.S., Kort, J.: Understanding, scoping and defining user experience. In: CHI 2009 (2009)
54. Liao, Q.V., Gruen, D., Miller, S.: Questioning the AI: informing design practices for explainable AI user experiences. In: CHI 2020 (2020)
55. Licklider, J.: Man-computer symbiosis. IRE Trans. Hum. Factors Electron. **1**, 4–11 (1960)
56. Lim, B.Y., Dey, A.K.: Weights of evidence for intelligible smart environments. In: UbiComp 2012 (2012)
57. Linardatos, P., Papastefanopoulos, V., Kotsiantis, S.: Explainable AI: a review of machine learning interpretability methods (2020)
58. Ludwig, J., Geiselman, E.: Intelligent pairing assistant for air operation centers. In: IUI 2012 (2012)
59. Mai, T., et al.: Keeping it "Organized and Logical". In: IUI 2020 (2020)
60. Mikhail, M., Roegiest, A., Anello, K., Wei, W.: Dancing with the AI devil: investigating the partnership between lawyers and AI. In: CHIIR 2020 (2020)

61. Millecamp, M., Htun, N.N., Conati, C., Verbert, K.: To Explain or not to explain: the effects of personal characteristics when explaining music recommendations. In: IUI 2019 (2019)
62. Miller, T.: Explanation in artificial intelligence: insights from the social sciences. Artif. Intell. **267** 1–38 (2019)
63. Misztal-Radecka, J., Indurkhya, B.: Persona prototypes for improving the qualitative evaluation of recommendation systems. In: UMAP 2020 Adjunct (2020)
64. Moore, J.D., Paris, C.: Requirements for an expert system explanation facility. Comput. Intell. **7**, 367–370 (1991)
65. Mueller, S.T., Hoffman, R.R., Clancey, W., Emrey, A., Klein Macrocognition, G.: Explanation in human-AI systems. arXiv (2019)
66. Muhammad, K.I., Lawlor, A., Smyth, B.: A live-user study of opinionated explanations for recommender systems. In: IUI 2016 (2016)
67. Murdoch, W.J., Singh, C., Kumbier, K., Abbasi-Asl, R., Yu, B.: Definitions, methods, and applications in interpretable machine learning. Proc. Natl Acad. Sci. **116**, 22071–22080 (2019)
68. Musto, C., Lops, P., de Gemmis, M., Semeraro, G.: Justifying recommendations through aspect-based sentiment analysis of users reviews. In: UMAP 2019 (2019)
69. Norman, D., Draper, S.: User Centered System Design. New Perspectives on Human-Computer Interaction (1986)
70. Nourani, M., et al.: Investigating the importance of first impressions and explainable AI with interactive video analysis. In: CHI EA 2020 (2020)
71. O'Donovan, J., Smyth, B., Gretarsson, B., Bostandjiev, S., Höllerer, T.: PeerChooser: visual interactive recommendation. In: CHI 2008 (2008)
72. Oh, C., et al.: Understanding how people reason about aesthetic evaluations of AI. In: DIS 2020 (2020)
73. Oulasvirta, A., Hornbaek, K.: HCI research as problem-solving. In: CHI 2016 (2016)
74. Páez, A.: The pragmatic turn in explainable artificial intelligence (XAI). Minds Mach. **29**, 441–459 (2019)
75. Patel, K., Bancroft, N., Drucker, S.M., Fogarty, J., Ko, A.J., Landay, J.: Gestalt: integrated support for implementation and analysis in ML. In: UIST 2010 (2010)
76. Paudyal, P., Banerjee, A., Gupta, S.: On evaluating the effects of feedback for sign language learning using explainable AI. In: IUI 2020 (2020)
77. Pilling, F., Akmal, H., Coulton, P., Lindley, J.: The process of gaining an AI legibility mark. In: CHI EA 2020 (2020)
78. Poltrock, S.E., Steiner, D.D., Tarlton, P.N.: Graphic interfaces for knowledge-based system development (1986)
79. Pu, P., Chen, L.: Trust building with explanation interfaces. In: IUI 2006 (2006)
80. Robb, D.A., et al.: Exploring interaction with remote autonomous systems using conversational agents. In: DIS 2019 (2019)
81. Schaekermann, M., Beaton, G., Sanoubari, E., Lim, A., Larson, K., Law, E.: Ambiguity-aware AI assistants for medical data analysis. In: CHI 2020 (2020)
82. Schneeberger, T., Gebhard, P., Baur, T., André, E.: PARLEY: a transparent virtual social agent training interface. In: IUI, 2019 (2019)
83. Schuessler, M., Weiß, P.: Minimalistic explanations: capturing the essence of decisions. In: CHI EA 2019 (2019)
84. Shannon, C.E.: A mathematical theory of communication. Bell Syst. Tech. J. **5**, 3–55 (1948)
85. Shneiderman, B.: Bridging the gap between ethics and practice. ACM Trans. Interact. Intell. Syst. **10**, 1–31 (2020)

86. Shneiderman, B., Plaisant, C., Cohen, M., Jacobs, S., Elmqvist, N., Diakopoulos, N.: Confessions: grand challenges for HCI researchers. Interactions (2016)

87. Simon, H.A.: Models of Bounded Rationality: Empirically Grounded Economic Reason, vol. 3. MIT Press, Cambridge (1997)

88. Sklar, E.I., Azhar, M.Q.: Explanation through Argumentation. In: HAI 2018 (2018)

89. Springer, A., Whittaker, S.: Progressive disclosure. ACM Trans. Interact. Intell. Syst. (2020)

90. Stolterman, E., Wiltse, H., Chen, S., Lewandowski, V., Pak, L.: Analyzing artifact interaction complexity (2012)

91. Tabrez, A., Agrawal, S., Hayes, B.: Explanation-based reward coaching to improve human performance via reinforcement learning. In: HRI 2019 (2019)

92. Tintarev, N.: Explanations of recommendations. In: RecSys 2007 (2007)

93. Tsai, C.H., Brusilovsky, P.: Evaluating visual explanations for similarity-based recommendations: user perception and performance. In: UMAP 2019 (2019)

94. Vig, J., Sen, S., Riedl, J.: Tagsplanations: explaining recommendations using tags. In: IUI 2009 (2009)

95. Vilone, G., Longo, L.: Explainable artificial intelligence: a systematic review. arXiv (2020)

96. Wang, D., et al.: From human-human collaboration to human-AI collaboration. In: CHI EA 2020 (2020)

97. Wang, D., Yang, Q., Abdul, A., Lim, B.Y.: Designing theory-driven user-centric explainable AI. In: CHI 2019 (2019)

98. Wang, N., Pynadath, D.V., Hill, S.G.: Trust calibration within a human-robot team: comparing automatically generated explanations. In: HRI 2016 (2016)

99. Weisz, J.D., Jain, M., Joshi, N.N., Johnson, J., Lange, I.: BigBlueBot: teaching strategies for successful human-agent interactions. In: IUI 2019 (2019)

100. Wenskovitch, J., Dowling, M., North, C.: With respect to What? Simultaneous interaction with dimension reduction and clustering projections. In: IUI 2020 (2020)

101. Wiegand, G., Schmidmaier, M., Weber, T., Liu, Y., Hussmann, H.: I drive - you trust: explaining driving behavior of autonomous cars. In: CHI EA 2019 (2019)

102. Wolf, C.T.: Explainability scenarios: towards scenario-based XAI design. In: IUI 2019 (2019)

103. Xie, J., Myers, C.M., Zhu, J.: Interactive visualizer to facilitate game designers in understanding machine learning. In: CHI EA 2019 (2019)

104. Xie, Y., Chen, M., Kao, D., Gao, G., Chen, X.A.: CheXplain: enabling physicians to explore and understand data-driven medical imaging analysis. In: CHI 2020 (2020)

105. Xu, W.: Toward human-centered AI: a perspective from human-computer interaction. Interactions (2019)

106. Yang, F., Huang, Z., Scholtz, J., Arendt, D.L.: How do visual explanations foster end users' appropriate trust in machine learning? In: IUI 2020 (2020)

107. Yin, M., Wortman Vaughan, J., Wallach, H.: Understanding the effect of accuracy on trust in machine learning models. In: CHI 2019 (2019)

108. Yu, B., Yuan, Y., Terveen, L., Wu, Z.S., Forlizzi, J., Zhu, H.: Keeping designers in the loop: communicating inherent algorithmic trade-offs across multiple objectives. In: DIS 2020 (2020)

109. Zanker, M.: The Influence of knowledgeable explanations on users' perception of a recommender system. In: RecSys 2012 (2012)

Making SHAP Rap: Bridging Local and Global Insights Through Interaction and Narratives

Michael Chromik[✉]

LMU Munich, Munich, Germany
michael.chromik@ifi.lmu.de

Abstract. The interdisciplinary field of explainable artificial intelligence (XAI) aims to foster human understanding of black-box machine learning models through explanation-generating methods. In practice, Shapley explanations are widely used. However, they are often presented as visualizations and thus leave their interpretation to the user. As such, even ML experts have difficulties interpreting them appropriately. On the other hand, combining visual cues with textual rationales has been shown to facilitate understanding and communicative effectiveness. Further, the social sciences suggest that explanations are a social and iterative process between the explainer and the explainee. Thus, interactivity should be a guiding principle in the design of explanation facilities. Therefore, we (i) briefly review prior research on interactivity and naturalness in XAI, (ii) designed and implemented the interactive explanation interface *SHAPRap* that provides local and global Shapley explanations in an accessible format, and (iii) evaluated our prototype in a formative user study with 16 participants in a loan application scenario. We believe that interactive explanation facilities that provide multiple levels of explanations offer a promising approach for empowering humans to better understand a model's behavior and its limitations on a local as well as global level. With our work, we inform designers of XAI systems about human-centric ways to tailor explanation interfaces to end users.

Keywords: Explainable AI · Explanation interface · Interactivity

1 Introduction

Many decisions in our lives are influenced or taken by intelligent systems that leverage machine learning (ML). Whenever their predictions may have undesired or consequential impacts, providing only the output of the black box may not be satisfying to their users. Even if the prediction is accurate in regard to the underlying training data, users may distrust the system, have different beliefs regarding the prediction, or want to learn from individual predictions about a given problem domain. Thus, a need for understanding the ML model behavior arises [2]. The field of *explainable artificial intelligence (XAI)* develops novel

© IFIP International Federation for Information Processing 2021
Published by Springer Nature Switzerland AG 2021
C. Ardito et al. (Eds.): INTERACT 2021, LNCS 12933, pp. 641–651, 2021.
https://doi.org/10.1007/978-3-030-85616-8_37

methods and techniques to make black-box ML models more interpretable. Current XAI research mostly focuses on the *cognitive* process of explanation, i.e., identifying likely root causes of a particular event [21]. As a result, some notion of explanation is generated that approximates the model's underlying prediction process. Explanations may be textual, visual, example-based, or obtained by simplifying the underlying prediction model [3]. An approach widely used in practice is *explanation by feature attribution* [3]. Especially local explanations based on *Shapley values* [27] are widespread [4]. Feature attribution frameworks, such as SHAP[1], merely provide visual explanations and leave their interpretation entirely to the user. As such, they are targeting mostly ML experts, such as developers and data scientists. However, Kaur et al. [17] observed in their studies that even experts have an inaccurate understanding of how to interpret the visualizations provided by SHAP. Even if they are correctly interpreted by ML experts, they may still remain opaque to end users of XAI due to their technical illiteracy [6]. This applies especially to end users and subject-matter experts, who often have little technical expertise in ML. Thus, their interpretability needs require even more guidance and attention.

The main idea of this paper is to explore how to improve the accessibility of Shapley explanations to foster a pragmatic understanding [11,23] for end users in XAI. We believe that an important aspect required to address the call for *"usable, practical and effective transparency that works for and benefits people"* [1] is currently not sufficiently studied: providing end users of XAI with means of interaction that go beyond a single static explanation and that are complemented by explicit interpretations in natural language. As the human use of computing is the subject of inquiry in HCI [22], our discipline *"should take a leading role by providing explainable and comprehensible AI, and useful and usable AI"* [34]. In particular, our community is well suited to *"provide effective design for explanation UIs"* [34]. Our work contributes to the HCI community in two ways: First, we present and describe the interactive explanation interface artifact *SHAPRap* that targets non-technical users of XAI. Second, we report promising results from a formative evaluation that indicates that our approach can foster understanding. With this work, we put our design rationales up for discussion with our fellow researchers.

2   Related Work

We base our work in the interdisciplinary research field of XAI. It aims to make black-box ML models interpretable by generating some notion of explanation that can be used by humans to interpret the behavior of an ML model [31]. An ML model is considered a black-box if humans can observe the inputs and outputs of the model but have difficulties understanding the mapping between them. However, most works focus on computational aspects of generating explanations while limited research is reported concerning the human-centered design of the explanation interface. The social sciences suggest that the explanation

---

[1] github.com/slundberg/shap.

process should resemble a social process between the explaining XAI system (sender of an explanation) and the human explainee (receiver of an explanation) forming a multi-step interaction between both parties, ideally leveraging natural language [21]. Especially, in situations where people may be held accountable for a prediction-informed decision, they may have multiple follow-up questions before feeling comfortable to trust a system prediction. Abdul et al. emphasize that interactivity and learnability are crucial for the effective design of explanations and their visualization [1]. Widely used explainability frameworks, such as SHAP, present their explanations in the form of information-dense visualizations, however, they do not provide any interactivity nor guidance to support users in their interpretation process. As a consequence, even experienced ML engineers struggle to correctly interpret their output and often take them at face value [17]. Humans mostly explain their decisions with words [19]. Thus, it is intuitive to provide end users of XAI with explanations in natural language. We found first work that takes a human-centric perspective on XAI and encompasses interactivity and naturalness. Weld and Bansal [32] propose seven different follow-up and drill-down operations to guide the interaction. Liao et al. [18] compile a catalog of natural language questions that can technically be answered by current XAI methods. Covering multiple of them under a *"holistic approach"* allows users to triangulate insights. Reiter [24] discusses the challenges of natural language generation for XAI. Further, users have been shown to understand technical explanations better if they are complemented by narratives in natural language [9,10,13]. For instance, Gkatzia et al. improved users' decision-making by 44% by combining visualizations with statements in natural language [13]. Sokol and Flach [29] present *Glass-Box* an interactive XAI system that provides personalized explanations in natural language. Similarly, Werner [33] presents *ERIC* an interactive system that gives explanations in a conversational manner through a chat-bot like interface. Forrest et al. [12] generate textual explanations from feature contributions based on LIME [25].

3   SHAPRap

3.1   Scenario, ML Model, and XAI Method

Scenario. Our XAI system is centered in a decision-support situation in which the human decision-maker is accompanied by an intelligent and interpretable system. We put our study participants in the shoes of a private lender on a fictional crowd lending platform. We centered our study in a crowd lending domain because we assumed that the participants can relate to decisions about lending or investing personal money. Participants can see demographic information, loan details, and credit history of individuals that request a loan on the platform. Each request is accompanied by an "AI-based intelligent prediction" of the *default risk*, i.e., the probability that the borrower fails to service a loan installment some time during the loan period. The prediction is introduced as an "AI-based" feature that is based on machine learning from historic cases. We build on a tabular data set as many ML models deployed in practice build on this type of data [4,20]. We used the *Loan Prediction*[2] data set which consists of 614 loan requests with 13 columns. We relabeled two columns of the data set to be consistent with our scenario[3].

ML Model. We calculated the default risk prediction using a *XGBoost classifier*. Tree-based ensembles, such as XGBoost, are widely used in many real-world contexts because of their practicability [20]. However, they are considered black-box ML models. To limit the cognitive load for participants we chose to train our model on a subset of columns. We used only the seven categorical columns (5 binary, 1 ternary, and 1 with four possible values). We trained a binary XGB classifier with 100 decision trees and class probabilities as outputs. Other than that, we used the default hyperparameters of the *xgboost* package. The accuracy of the predicted default risk on our stratified validation set was 0.83.

XAI Method. In this work, we use the *SHAP (SHapley Additive exPlanations)* [20] framework to compute the model's feature contributions on a local and global level. SHAP belongs to the class of *additive feature attribution methods* where the explanation is represented as a linear function of feature contributions towards an ML prediction. The contributions are approximated by slightly changing the inputs and testing the impact on the model outputs. The framework unifies the ideas of other feature attribution methods (such as LIME [25]) with *Shapley values*, which originate from game theory [27]. Shapley explanations quantify the contribution of individual features values towards a prediction. For a single observation, they uniquely distribute the difference between the average prediction and the actual prediction between its features [20]. For example, if the average prediction over all instances in a dataset is 50% and the actual prediction for a single instance is 75%, SHAP uniquely distributes the difference of 25% points across the features that contributed to the instance's prediction. Despite their vulnerability to adversarial attacks [28] and potential inaccuracies [14], we consider Shapley explanations as relevant to end users for two reasons: (i) they can yield local and global insights because Shapley values are the atomic units of each explanation. As these units are additive, they may be aggregated over multiple predictions or features to learn about the model's global behavior, and (ii) the consistent and model-agnostic nature of Shapley values allows XAI designers to offer a uniform explanation interface to users even if the underlying data or ML model changes (Fig. 1).

3.2 Explanation Interface

Local Explanation View. The local explanation view resembles a spreadsheet-like user interface that is overlaid with a heat map of Shapley values for each feature

---

[2] datahack.analyticsvidhya.com/contest/practice-problem-loan-prediction-iii/.

[3] We re-framed the *Loan_Status* column to represent the default risk and the *Credit_History* column to represent a negative item on a credit report.

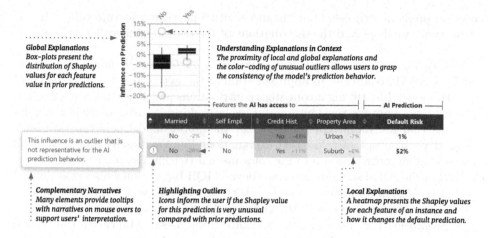

Fig. 1. The components of the *SHAPRap* explanation interface

of an instance. We support users' rapid visual estimation of feature contributions through preattentive processing based on a cell's hue [15]. Each cell is shaded depending on their direction and magnitude of contribution towards the prediction (red increases the loan request's risk of defaulting, while green decreases it). The local explanation view is *contrastive* [21] as it allows comparing variances *between* feature contributions for individual instances (*horizontal axis*). Further, as we show multiple local explanations next to each other, users can compare variances or regularities *within* feature values across multiple instances (*vertical axis*). To support this, users can sort each column by value to contrast instances with identical feature values.

Global Explanations View. Local explanations yield how an ML model derives its prediction for a single data instance. In contrast, global explanations help users to get an intuition how a model derives its predictions over multiple instances or an entire dataset (*global sample*). For each feature value, we provide a box-plot of how it contributed to the prediction for all instances in the global sample. A narrow box-plot indicates a more consistent prediction behavior, while a wider box-plot indicates that the contributions vary for the same feature value. These variances result from interactions with other features and may require additional judgment (see next paragraph). The distribution of Shapley values in the global view depends on the chosen global sample. If the sample is representative for the population that the ML model will be confronted with in a particular domain, the global view helps users understanding when its predictions are consistent and therefore predictable and when they are not. In practice, the global sample may be the entirety of predictions of an ML model after its deployment across all users, or (if data sparsity requirements apply) a sample of predictions that an individual user has previously been exposed to. Further, it would be possible to let users customize the global sample (e.g., only instances above a certain prediction threshold or instances with a particular feature value). In our prototype, we displayed the distributions of the training and validation sets.

Highlighting Outliers. A post-hoc *explanation by feature attribution* approach, such as SHAP, is always an approximation of the actual prediction behavior of an ML model. Identifying inconsistent contributions and communicating them to the user can improve their interpretation by making it easier to identify explanations that are more representative for the global model behavior. We built around the concept of role-based explanations [5]. We classify each instance's feature value contribution into the roles *normal* (within the *inter quartile range (IQR)* of the global sample), *unusual* (beyond IQR but within whiskers as defined by $\pm 1.5 \times IQR$), and *very unusual* (outliers beyond the whiskers). We highlight *very unusual* contributions in the global and local views as orange warning circles prompting the users to not generalize from these instances to the typical prediction behavior of the model. Further, these outliers may serve as starting points for analyzing feature value interactions. When hovering over an outlier, we highlight features of this instance that are *unusual* and thus provide hints which feature values may be interacting with each other.

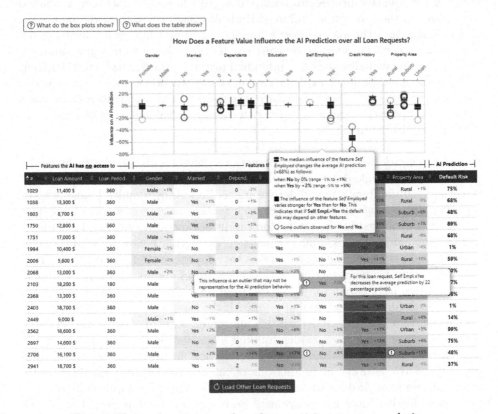

Fig. 2. The explanation interface that participants were exploring.

Complementing Narratives: It is not easy to understand the concepts of additive Shapley explanations just by looking at plots [17]. It might take some time to interpret a plot, and the user is likely to be overwhelmed at first. Thus, we automatically created textual explanations from Shapley values using a template-based approach and to support their interpretation of the local and global views. We provide users with on-demand textual explanations in form of tooltips on mouseovers for each feature box-plot, instance cell, outlier highlight, and column header. Further, we provided background information about the local and global views during onboarding and accessible through help buttons during interaction. This way, information redundancy can be avoided following the *progressive disclosure* paradigm [30].

4   Formative Evaluation

Method. We conducted a formative evaluation with 16 participants recruited through the online platform *Prolific*. We recruited participants with at least a graduate degree, English fluency, and an approval rate of 100%. 8 participants self-identified as female, 8 as male and were in the age groups 18–24 (3), 24–35 (9), and 35–54 (4). 11 participants agreed to use spreadsheets at least weekly, 6 knew how to read box-plots, and 4 had practical experience with ML. After introducing their role in the crowd lending scenario and the explanation views, users were asked to freely explore *SHAPRap* for 10 to 15 min (Fig. 2). Then, they rated their level of understanding on a 7-point scale[4] [8]. Afterwards, they completed a *forward prediction* quiz [7]. Participants had to simulate the AI prediction for 6 pre-selected loan requests with the help of the global explanation view. We randomly chose 6 instances with unique feature value combinations and at most two *unusual* contributions to assess participants' understanding of the typical prediction behavior. In the end, they rated the *explanation satisfaction scale* [16] and answered three open questions. On average, participants took 28.1 min (SD = 10.4 min) to complete the study and were compensated £5 per completion (=£10.67/h).

Results. Overall, our results indicate mixed reactions but show effective gains of pragmatic understanding for some participants. The explanation facility felt overwhelming at first, but the complementary elements of global, local, and textual explanations were considered as somewhat useful and sufficiently detailed to get a general idea about the typical prediction behavior. After exploring *SHAPRap*, participants on average rated their understanding as *"I understand which features are more important than others for the AI prediction"* (mean = 4.07, SD = 1.67). However, applying this understanding in the quiz turn out to be challenging for 6 participants as they scored worse than random guess (expected

---

[4] Level 1: *I understand which features the AI has access to and what the AI predicts as an output.*, Level 4: *I understand which features are more important than others for the AI prediction.*, Level 7: *I understand how much individual feature values influence the AI prediction and which feature values depend on others.*

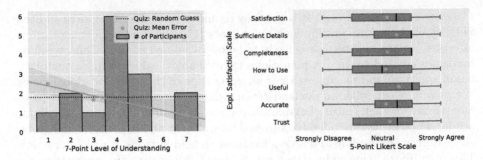

Fig. 3. *(left)* 11 participants perceived they understood at least which features were important for the prediction. 6 of them objectively proved their understanding via a lower than random mean error in a forward prediction quiz. *(right)* Results from the *explanation satisfaction scale.* The orange dots indicate the respective mean. (Color figure online)

error for a random guess was 1.8). For example, P5 *"understood what the box representations meant but found it hard to actually apply this data to the applicants. It might just require practice."* On a positive end, 6 participants rated their gained understanding as at least level 4 and proved this with low mean errors in the quiz (cf. Fig. 3). Participant P6 (no ML experience, mean error of 0.8) *"found the explanations quite complicated to follow but after studying the table and explanations it became clearer as to which factors were being used to measure the likelihood of defaulting on the loan."* P3 (extensive ML experience, mean error of 0.33) found *"the explanations were detailed, and it was interesting to see that credit history was the leading variable for default risk."* Multiple participants appreciated the complementary nature of the natural language explanations. Without them *"the graph was quite difficult to understand on its own"* (P6). P13 liked *"that the [textual] explanations are written simply, everyone would understand it"* and P9 appreciated that the *"language was simple"*. However, it seemed that narratives on a more aggregated or abstract level were missing to understand the bigger picture. P4 found *"this kind of explanations useful just to people who already have studied this but for people with different educational background this kind of explanations are not enough."* P5 suggested adding an executive summary for each loan request and the overall global view. Further, some participants were overwhelmed by the non-linear behavior and interactions of the ML model and seemed to expect to figure them out. P5 found *"the green and red increase/decrease for risk seemed simple and helpful at first, but there seemed to be very random correlations between different aspects."* Similarly, P10 stated: *"I am guessing there are so many intersecting correlations it's hard to read for a non-numbers person."*. This resonates with Rudin [26] that the term *explanation* is misleading as it suggests a full understanding can be reached even if we merely provide pragmatic approximations.

5   Summary

This paper presents the explanation interface *SHAPRap*, which supports end users in interpreting local Shapley explanations in the global context of *normal* and *unusual* model behavior. Further, it provides narratives using a template-based approach. With our work, we contribute to the development of accessible XAI interfaces that enable non-expert users to get an intuition about the probabilistic decision behavior of black-box ML models.

References

1. Abdul, A., Vermeulen, J., Wang, D., Lim, B.Y., Kankanhalli, M.: Trends and trajectories for explainable, accountable and intelligible systems: an HCI research agenda. In: CHI 2018 (2018). https://doi.org/10.1145/3173574.3174156
2. Adadi, A., Berrada, M.: Peeking inside the black-box: a survey on explainable artificial intelligence (XAI). IEEE Access (2018). https://doi.org/10.1109/ACCESS.2018.2870052
3. Barredo Arrieta, A., et al.: Explainable artificial intelligence (XAI): concepts, taxonomies, opportunities and challenges toward responsible AI. Inf. Fus. (2020). https://doi.org/10.1016/j.inffus.2019.12.012
4. Bhatt, U., et al.: Explainable machine learning in deployment. In: Proceedings of the 2020 Conference on Fairness, Accountability, and Transparency (2020). https://doi.org/10.1145/3351095.3375624
5. Biran, O., McKeown, K.: Human-centric justification of machine learning predictions. In: IJCAI 2017 (2017). https://doi.org/10.24963/ijcai.2017/202
6. Burrell, J.: How the machine 'thinks': understanding opacity in machine learning algorithms. Big Data Soc. (2016). https://doi.org/10.1177/2053951715622512
7. Cheng, H.F., et al.: Explaining decision-making algorithms through UI: strategies to help non-expert stakeholders. In: CHI 2019 (2019). https://doi.org/10.1145/3290605.3300789
8. Chromik, M., Eiband, M., Buchner, F., Krüger, A., Butz, A.: I think i get your point, AI! the illusion of explanatory depth in explainable AI. In: IUI 2021 (2021). https://doi.org/10.1145/3397481.3450644
9. Das, D., Chernova, S.: Leveraging rationales to improve human task performance. In: IUI 2020 (2020). https://doi.org/10.1145/3290605.3300789
10. Ehsan, U., Tambwekar, P., Chan, L., Harrison, B., Riedl, M.O.: Automated rationale generation: a technique for explainable AI and its effects on human perceptions. In: IUI 2019 (2019). https://doi.org/10.1145/3301275.3302316
11. Eiband, M., Schneider, H., Buschek, D.: Normative vs. pragmatic: two perspectives on the design of explanations in intelligent systems. In: IUI Workshops (2018)
12. Forrest, J., Sripada, S., Pang, W., Coghill, G.: Towards making NLG a voice for interpretable machine learning. In: INLG (2018). https://doi.org/10.18653/v1/W18-6522
13. Gkatzia, D., Lemon, O., Rieser, V.: Natural language generation enhances human decision-making with uncertain information. Presented at the (2016)
14. Gosiewska, A., Biecek, P.: Do not trust additive explanations. ArXiv (2020). https://arxiv.org/abs/1903.11420

15. Healey, C.G., Booth, K.S., Enns, J.T.: High-speed visual estimation using pre attentive processing. ACM Trans. Comput. Hum. Interact. (1996). https://doi.org/10.1145/230562.230563
16. Hoffman, R.R., Mueller, S.T., Klein, G., Litman, J.: Metrics for explainable AI: challenges and prospects. CoRR (2018). https://arxiv.org/abs/1812.04608
17. Kaur, H., Nori, H., Jenkins, S., Caruana, R., Wallach, H., Wortman Vaughan, J.: Interpreting interpretability: understanding data scientists' use of interpretability tools for machine learning. In: CHI 2020 (2020). https://doi.org/10.1145/3313831.3376219
18. Liao, Q.V., Gruen, D., Miller, S.: Questioning the AI: informing design practices for explainable AI user experiences. In: CHI 2020 (2020). https://doi.org/10.1145/3313831.3376590
19. Lipton, Z.C.: The mythos of model interpretability. ACM Queue (2016). https://doi.org/10.1145/3236386.3241340
20. Lundberg, S.M., et al.: From local explanations to global understanding with explainable AI for trees. Nat. Mach. Intell. (2020). https://doi.org/10.1038/s42256-019-0138-9
21. Miller, T.: Explanation in artificial intelligence: insights from the social sciences. Artif. Intell. (2019). https://doi.org/10.1016/j.artint.2018.07.007
22. Oulasvirta, A., Hornbaek, K.: HCI research as problem-solving. In: CHI 2016 (2016). https://doi.org/10.1145/2858036.2858283
23. Páez, A.: The pragmatic turn in explainable artificial intelligence (XAI). Mind. Mach. (2019). https://doi.org/10.1007/s11023-019-09502-w
24. Reiter, E.: Natural language generation challenges for explainable AI. In: Proceedings of the 1st Workshop on Interactive Natural Language Technology for Explainable Artificial Intelligence (NL4XAI 2019) (2019). https://doi.org/10.18653/v1/W19-8402
25. Ribeiro, M.T., Singh, S., Guestrin, C.: "Why should i trust you?": explaining the predictions of any classifier. Proceedings of the 22nd ACM SIGKDD International Conference on Knowledge Discovery and Data Mining (2016). https://doi.org/10.1145/2939672.2939778
26. Rudin, C.: Stop explaining black box machine learning models for high stakes decisions and use interpretable models instead. Nat. Mach. Intell. (2019). https://doi.org/10.1038/S42256-019-0048-X
27. Shapley, L.S.: A value for n-person games. Contributions to the Theory of Games (1953)
28. Slack, D., Hilgard, S., Jia, E., Singh, S., Lakkaraju, H.: Fooling lime and shap: adversarial attacks on post hoc explanation methods. Proceedings of the AAAI/ACM Conference on AI, Ethics, and Society (2020). https://doi.org/10.1145/3375627.3375830
29. Sokol, K., Flach, P.A.: One explanation does not fit all. KI - Künstliche Intelligenz (2020). https://doi.org/10.1007/s13218-020-00637-y
30. Springer, A., Whittaker, S.: Progressive disclosure. ACM Trans. Interact. Intell. Syst. (2020). https://doi.org/10.1145/3374218
31. Wang, D., Yang, Q., Abdul, A., Lim, B.Y.: Designing theory-driven user-centric explainable AI. In: CHI 2019 (2019). https://doi.org/10.1145/3290605.3300831
32. Weld, D.S., Bansal, G.: The challenge of crafting intelligible intelligence. Commun. ACM (2019). https://doi.org/10.1145/3282486

33. Werner, C.: Explainable ai through rule-based interactive conversation. In: EDBT/ICDT Workshops (2020). http://ceur-ws.org/Vol-2578/ETMLP3.pdf
34. Xu, W.: Toward human-centered AI: a perspective from human-computer interaction. Interactions (2019). https://doi.org/10.1145/3328485

Quantifying the Demand
for Explainability

Thomas Weber(✉) ⓘ, Heinrich Hußmann ⓘ, and Malin Eiband

LMU Munich, Frauenlobstr. 7a, 80337 Munich, Germany
{thomas.weber,heinrich.hussmann,malin.eiband}@ifi.lmu.de
http://www.medien.ifi.lmu.de

Abstract. Software that uses Artificial Intelligence technology like Machine Learning is becoming ubiquitous with even more applications ahead. Yet, the very nature of these systems has made it very hard to understand how they operate, creating a demand for explanations. While many approaches have been and are being developed, it remains unclear how strong this demand is for different domains, application types, and user groups. To assess this, we introduce a novel survey scale to quantify the demand for explainability. We also apply this scale to an exemplary set of applications, novel and traditional, in surveys with 212 participants, showing that interest in explainability is high in general for intelligent systems but also traditional software. While this validates the heightened interest in explainability, it also reveals further questions, e.g. where we can find synergies or how intelligent systems require different explanations compare to traditional but equally complex software.

Keywords: Explainable AI · XAI · Survey · Target group · Use case

1 Introduction

Data-driven applications have become one of the driving factors of our modern society. They use technology like Machine Learning to process large amounts of data, enabling functionality that was previously very hard to achieve. Many of these allow us to let computers take over tasks that would otherwise take human intelligence and much time. They are often, therefore, also referred to as "intelligent systems" [28]. Their – seemingly non-intelligent – counterpart is software that does not use, e.g., Machine Learning but relies on a clear set of instructions and algorithms for its defined execution.

While traditional software had been the only type for many years, recent improvements, particularly in processing power and storage, have allowed intelligent systems to become ubiquitous also. Their "decisions" influence how we find and consume information, what we buy, how we communicate, etc. Their success is unlikely to stop, too, with up-and-coming applications like autonomous driving and personalized diagnostics heavily relying on their capabilities.

ⓒ IFIP International Federation for Information Processing 2021
Published by Springer Nature Switzerland AG 2021
C. Ardito et al. (Eds.): INTERACT 2021, LNCS 12933, pp. 652–661, 2021.
https://doi.org/10.1007/978-3-030-85616-8_38

Naturally, intelligent systems thus can have a wide-ranging impact on our life. Understanding their effect on us and society, the ethical implications their use has, etc., is, therefore, an essential ability for us all. The sheer complexity of these systems still impedes this, though.

Making these complex systems more accessible is one of the goals of explainable AI (XAI) [14,15]. By providing explanations in various forms, this research branch hopes to allow people to understand how intelligent systems process data, make their decisions, and operate in general. While explanations of Machine Learning models often start from the technology, the human perspective is becoming more and more important [4,16,18,25]. This includes methods for designing and building explainability for all sorts of target groups [16,19,25,29].

One of the early questions in user-centred XAI must always be whether people do require and demand explanations of the systems they use. While often this demand appears logical, it is usually justified very qualitatively with the potential benefits of explanations. This, unfortunately, makes it very hard to quantify and compare this demand across different applications, groups, etc.

This paper contributes by introducing a survey scale in Sect. 3 for quantifying this *demand for explainability*. Not only does this allow for better justification of future explainability, but it also allows interesting comparisons. As an example and first application for this scale, we performed a high-level investigation into the difference between intelligent and traditional, non-intelligent systems.

The motivation for this comparison is that people have managed to use complex software systems for many years, often without explicit explanations. This begs the question of whether intelligent systems are, in this regard, fundamentally different to demand special attention. Depending on the differences and commonalities, it would also allow us to better find synergies between the specialized, emerging field of XAI and general, well-researched human-computer-interaction. We present the results of this first survey with 212 participants in Sect. 4 and subsequently discuss the implications.

2   Related Work

By design, AI or data-driven systems process volumes of data that are beyond human capabilities. While the concept of the learning process is fairly straightforward, understanding what an individual model has learned and how it comes to "decisions" is becoming more and more complex with the growing volume of input data. Explainable AI (XAI) is, therefore, a branch of research that aims to make these systems more explainable, interpretable, and understandable [15]. Over the years, people have developed many mechanisms, visualizations, and tools to provide explanations in some form on another [1,3,7,14,18–20,22,27].

However, many of the above methods to increase explainability can be very technology-focused making them not ideal for inexperienced end-users. As Miller et al. [23] highlight, this is exasperated by the fact that technology experts and the developers of these systems are often in charge of making them more understandable, which can lead to situations in which the end-users' demands are neglected.

There certainly are approaches to make AI more accessible [2,30] and how their effect from a user-centred perspective [25]. Unfortunately, though, a study by Hase et al. [17] found that the effect which current explanations have is not as much as one would hope to begin with. Furthermore, inadequate explainability can also have an adverse effect where the users believe they understand the system even though they do not [13,26]. Ehrlich et al. [9] also highlight the fact that with the uncertainty of data-driven systems, explanations may not always be beneficial, particularly in real-world scenarios when there may not be a correct choice, and situational judgement is required. A series of studies by Bunt et al. [5] furthermore indicates that explanations, while good, are not always considered worthwhile from the users' perspective. In fact, they found that their participants only desired explanations in about 7% of instances. At the same time, as Eiband et al. [10] explore, even placebo explanations can help.

All this suggests that explainability is not as simple as providing a nice explanation and all is well, but instead, some prior evaluation will be necessary to appropriately gauge when, how much, and what type of explanation is adequate.

3 Survey

The following section describes the survey and the scale to assess the demand for explainability as well as the aspects we took into account when designing it.

3.1 Demand for Explainability Scale

Since a survey of the literature yielded no readily available scale to measure the demand for explainability, we constructed our own.

To this end, we brainstormed an initial set of 30 questions related to explainability of software systems, which we narrowed down to 15 core questions based on the feedback of two experts for XAI and intelligent systems (see Table 1). All questions use five-point Likert scales.

After a pilot survey to eradicate comprehension issues, we used a first sample of 50 questionnaire answers for a factor analysis of those questions using R's *psych* package[1]. The factor analysis as a statistical method allowed us to determine which of our initial questions actually contribute to the intended topic and which are tangential [21].

The factor analysis revealed four factors (cf. Fig. 1) in our data with the loadings, as shown in Table 1. These values indicate how strongly the individual questions contribute to a common underlying topic. Visual analysis via a scree plot also supports the assumption that there are four factors. We concluded that the first group of questions actually pertains to the demand for explainability. The second may be considered to be about the system performance, the third appears to be about prior experience, and the last group covers the participants' perceived own expertise.

---

[1] https://www.rdocumentation.org/packages/psych/.

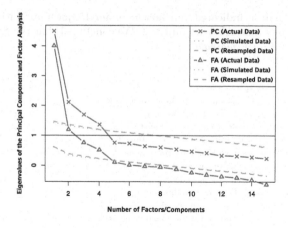

Fig. 1. The Scree plot, a method for visually identifying the number of factors during factor analysis, suggests four underlying factors.

We, therefore, considered only the first seven questions in the table as our scale throughout the remainder of this work. To see the scale work in practice, we then used it to gauge the demand for explainability for a number of software systems (as described below). We kept all 15 questions in, though, to re-run the factor analysis with a large data set, which yielded the same factors. This and a Cronbach's α of 0.88 for our scale indicate to us that the scale consistently measures what it is meant to.

3.2 Explainability of Different Types of Applications

To apply the scale in practice, we selected a number of software systems commonly found in the literature [6,11,12,14,19,24,29] for two comparisons.

First, we compared intelligent systems that people already use in their daily life to some that either still under research or used only in niche, experimental circumstances. With the explanations we provided for each of these systems, the participants could build an understanding of what an intelligent system is and thus had a point of reference and see intelligent systems, not as a vague concept but an everyday occurrence. For the systems not yet available, one would assume that the demand for explainability would be higher, already due to their unfamiliar nature, so it provided a good point of reference for comparison.

For the reasons mentioned at the beginning of this paper, we also chose to run a second comparison against more traditional software systems. The applications we used as examples in our surveys are, therefore, as listed in Table 2.

For each application, we asked how frequently people use it and only applied the scale to those applications which the participant would use only at least infrequently. So, the number of applications for which each participant provided feedback did vary slightly. To ensure a shared understanding of these applications, each was preceded by an example and a description which of its

Table 1. Factor analysis indicated four factors in our 15 questions with the loadings as shown. Values of less than ±0.3 are omitted. We concluded that the first six questions refer to the *demand for explainability*.

Question	Loadings
The systems needs to be explained more	0.833
I would benefit from an explanation of how the system works	0.785
The system should justify its decisions and its output	0.734
It is important that people understand how this system works	0.719
The system would be improved if it offered explanations for its behaviour	0.712
Understanding how the system works is important to me	0.658
I am interested in understanding the detailed internal workings of the system	0.608
I am willing to trust the output of the system	0.636
I would describe the system's behaviour as intelligent	0.485
In my experience, the system works as intended	−0.546
If the system did not work as intended, I would suffer negative consequences	−0.553
I have been in a situation where the system behaved contrary to my expectations	0.690
I frequently experience situations in which I do not understand why the System behaves the way it does	0.686
I have an idea of what factors might influence the behaviour of the system	0.729
I believe I am capable of understanding how this system works	0.689

features are relevant for the survey and may warrant an explanation. We also used these descriptions to explicitly differentiate between intelligent and non-intelligent applications, particularly for those applications where the line starts to blur.

Besides this the survey also included a section for demographic and background information and the technology affinity scale by Edison and Geissler [8]. For each application, we also had open, free-text questions ask whether participants saw specific issues that require explanations in order to have additional qualitative feedback to the quantitative measure of the scale.

We disseminated each survey, comparison to future and traditional applications, online over a two-week period each to a diverse group of students, employees, and alumni of our institution.

Table 2. The applications we used as examples for the different groups in our survey.

Current intelligent systems	Future intelligent systems	Traditional software
Online search engine	Autonomous driving	Operating systems
Social media platforms	Predictive policing	Web browser
Multimedia platforms	robotics	Email software
Online shops	Personalized medicine	Office applications
Navigation		Image manipulation software

4   Results

In total, 96 people completed the first survey comparing current and future intelligent systems, and another 116 contributed to the comparison to traditional software. In the following, we will explore these results of our survey scale.

Based on the demographic data, our survey participants provide us a sample of 94 males, 112 females, and six participants that chose not to disclose their gender. They tend to be on the younger side (mean: 24.8, sd: 5.7), which also shows in the education, where half had at most a high school education and a quarter had received a Bachelors degree, and in their professional experience, where a third indicated that they had less than a year of work experience (mean: 3.1, sd: 4.7). The technology affinity of our participants, measured on a range from 1 to 5, was decent, with an average score of 3.5 (sd: 0.9).

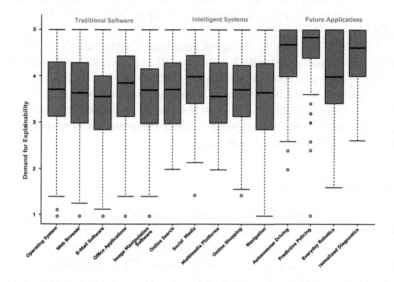

Fig. 2. The demand for explainability across the different applications.

Figure 2 now shows the demand for explainability across our selected applications. Overall the demand is medium to high and very consistent within each application group. Between those groups, we can clearly see a difference as the demand for explainability is at a consistently medium level (mean: 3.6, sd: 0.7) for applications that the participants already use, while for the applications that are not yet widely available, on the other hand, the demand is overall much higher (mean: 4.3, sd: 0.5). So we performed a hypothesis test to compare whether this difference between current and future applications is significant. With a Shapiro-Wilk-Test indicating a normal distribution of the data, the results of a subsequent ANOVA show a highly significant difference ($p < 0.001$) between these application types. Between traditional applications and available intelligent systems, we could not determine a significant difference ($p > 0.168$).

The quantification also allows us to better compare the demand for explainability between different participant groups. However, we could not determine any effect of age (corr. coeff: 0.055) or gender (t-test: $p > 0.62$) on the demand for explainability. Effects of education or professional experience also are negligible. The participants' technology affinity was ever so slightly correlated to the demand for explainability (correlation coefficient: 0.217) in general, although this results mostly from the traditional applications (correlation coefficient: 0.295) and not from the future applications (corr. coeff.: 0.091).

While the quantification alone is a good way for comparing two groups, it alone does not yet tell much about specific problems or solutions. This was very apparent in the qualitative list of issues that demand explainability which resulted from inductive coding of the qualitative answers. Concerns about data protection and privacy were raised 42 times for intelligent systems and only 5 times for traditional applications. Other issues were bias due to skewed data (29 intelligent/0 traditional systems), security risks (9/6) or the effect of undetected failures (23/20).

Based on their feedback in the open questions, participants also disagreed on what format explanations should have across all applications, with some requesting detailed technical explanations while others explicitly stated that this type of explanation would not help them. The presentation of explanations, however, was not a separate question and thus only some participants divulged their preference. Consequently, we cannot make reliable estimates of how prevalent these opinions are for different applications.

5   Discussion

Based on the data outlined in the previous section, we will briefly discuss the meaning and implications of these results.

As a high-level summary, it can be said that the demand for explainability appears to be consistently high across the board. This high interest in explainability certainly validates the increased interest in XAI and human-centered methods in general. On the other hand, the fact that for existing intelligent applications the demand is not significantly higher, suggests that with all the interest in new technology, existing software is still not sufficiently explained. A possible explanation for this may be that even software systems that do not use Machine Learning or similar technology have become so complex that from the perspective of the average user they do not differ to much from data-driven applications. So, maybe research on explainability should focus more on inherent complexity than on underlying technology. A future comparison to simpler systems may corroborate this.

One important factor that does play a role, though, is whether people already use an application, which leads to a slightly lower demand for explainability. This should come as no surprise, since the less they know about applications, the more information they need to understand it. People have gotten used to the software they use every day and are familiar with its capabilities and limitations.

The interesting point here is that many of these systems only have limited explanatory capabilities. This suggests that people are, in fact, capable of generating their own explanations even without explicit support. Whether these explanations are correct and sufficient is another question. Actively supporting the user still seems to be a worthwhile endeavor.

Considering the wide array of issue that our participant listed as in need of explanations, we can assume that not everyone needs the same explanations to be satisfied, though. The spectrum of issues is wide within single applications also. Furthermore, different participants gave different requirements for their explanations, strongly indicating that we will probably need multiple different explanations per application, target group, and use case, further pointing towards more user-centered approaches.

Which situation requires what type and level of explanation will need to be explored on an individual basis as our high-level assessment can only act as an early indicator. Clearly, there are many factors that have not yet been explored, like the influence of experience or personality. We, therefore, encourage future researchers and engineers to start not with the technology when building explanations but rather assess the demand quantitatively and qualitatively first and only then attempt to meet it.

6 Conclusion

In this paper, we introduced a survey scale to assess the demand for explainability in various software systems, domains and use cases. A quantification with such a test instrument is helpful for comparing systems, situations or user groups.

We tested this scale with an online survey where we recorded the general demand for explainability for various software systems, some of which use Machine Learning, some of which do not. This high-level evaluation validates the interest in XAI but it also points out the fact that intelligent systems are by no means the only software systems in need of better or more explanations.

Additional qualitative feedback from the survey also shows that there are some similarities in terms of what aspects need to be explained, but also some application-specific issues. Rather than building explanation form the technology side, this should encourage a user-centred perspective for explainability since there is no single solution that fits all situations or user groups. It also indicates that there might be strong synergies between more traditional Human-Computer-Interaction and XAI.

References

1. Adadi, A., Berrada, M.: Peeking inside the black-box: a survey on explainable artificial intelligence (XAI). IEEE Access **6**, 52138–52160 (2018)
2. Amershi, S., et al.: Guidelines for human-AI interaction. In: Brewster, S.A., Fitzpatrick, G., Cox, A.L., Kostakos, V. (eds.) Proceedings of the 2019 CHI Conference on Human Factors in Computing Systems, CHI 2019, Glasgow, Scotland, UK, 04–09 May 2019, p. 3. ACM (2019)

3. Barbalau, A., Cosma, A., Ionescu, R.T., Popescu, M.: A generic and model-agnostic exemplar synthetization framework for explainable AI (2020)
4. Bohlender, D., Köhl, M.A.: Towards a characterization of explainable systems. CoRR (abs/1902.03096) (2019)
5. Bunt, A., Lount, M., Lauzon, C.: Are explanations always important?: a study of deployed, low-cost intelligent interactive systems. In: Duarte, C., Carriço, L., Jorge, J.A., Oviatt, S.L., Gonçalves, D. (eds.) 17th International Conference on Intelligent User Interfaces, IUI 2012, Lisbon, Portugal, 14–17 February 2012, pp. 169–178. ACM (2012)
6. Cohen, I.G., Graver, H.: A doctor's touch: What big data in health care can teach us about predictive policing. SSRN Electron. J. (2019)
7. Du, M., Liu, N., Hu, X.: Techniques for interpretable machine learning. Commun. ACM 63(1), 68–77 (2019)
8. Edison, S.W., Geissler, G.L.: Measuring attitudes towards general technology: antecedents, hypotheses and scale development. J. Target. Meas. Anal. Mark. 12(2), 137–156 (2003)
9. Ehrlich, K., Kirk, S.E., Patterson, J.F., Rasmussen, J.C., Ross, S.I., Gruen, D.M.: Taking advice from intelligent systems: the double-edged sword of explanations. In: Pu, P., Pazzani, M.J., André, E., Riecken, D. (eds.) Proceedings of the 16th International Conference on Intelligent User Interfaces, IUI 2011, Palo Alto, CA, USA, 13–16 February, 2011, pp. 125–134. ACM (2011)
10. Eiband, M., Buschek, D., Kremer, A., Hussmann, H.: The impact of placebic explanations on trust in intelligent systems. In: Extended Abstracts of the 2019 CHI Conference on Human Factors in Computing Systems. CHI EA 2019, New York, NY, USA, pp. 1–6 Association for Computing Machinery (2019)
11. Eiband, M., Völkel, S.T., Buschek, D., Cook, S., Hussmann, H.: When people and algorithms meet: user-reported problems in intelligent everyday applications. In: Fu, W., Pan, S., Brdiczka, O., Chau, P., Calvary, G. (eds.) Proceedings of the 24th International Conference on Intelligent User Interfaces, IUI 2019, Marina del Ray, CA, USA, 17–20 March 2019, pp. 96–106. ACM (2019)
12. Gade, K., Geyik, S.C., Kenthapadi, K., Mithal, V., Taly, A.: Explainable AI in industry. In: Proceedings of the 25th ACM SIGKDD International Conference on Knowledge Discovery & Data Mining. KDD 2019, New York NY, USA, pp. 3203–3204. Association for Computing Machinery (2019)
13. Gaviria, C., Corredor, J.A., Zuluaga-Rendón, Z.: "if it matters, I can explain it": social desirability of knowledge increases the illusion of explanatory depth. In: Gunzelmann, G., Howes, A., Tenbrink, T., Davelaar, E.J. (eds.) Proceedings of the 39th Annual Meeting of the Cognitive Science Society, CogSci 2017, London, UK, 16–29 July 2017 (2017). cognitivesciencesociety.org
14. Goebel, R., et al.: Explainable AI: the new 42? In: Holzinger, A., Kieseberg, P., Tjoa, A.M., Weippl, E. (eds.) Machine Learning and Knowledge Extraction, pp. 295–303. Springer, Cham (2018)
15. Gunning, D., Stefik, M., Choi, J., Miller, T., Stumpf, S., Yang, G.: XAI - explainable artificial intelligence. Sci. Robotics 4(37) (2019)
16. Hall, M., Harborne, D., Tomsett, R., Galetic, V., Quintana-Amate, S.: A systematic method to understand requirements for explainable AI (xai) systems (2019)
17. Hase, P., Bansal, M.: Evaluating explainable AI: which algorithmic explanations help users predict model behavior? (2020)
18. Hoffman, R.R., Mueller, S.T., Klein, G., Litman, J.: Metrics for explainable AI: challenges and prospects. CoRR (abs/1812.04608) (2018)

19. Holzinger, A., Biemann, C., Pattichis, C.S., Kell, D.B.: What do we need to build explainable AI systems for the medical domain? CoRR (abs/1712.09923) (2017)
20. Lundberg, S.M., et al.: Explainable AI for trees: From local explanations to global understanding. CoRR (abs/1905.04610) (2019)
21. Mair, Patrick: Factor Analysis. In: Modern Psychometrics with R. UR, pp. 17–61. Springer, Cham (2018). https://doi.org/10.1007/978-3-319-93177-7_2
22. Melis, M., Demontis, A., Pintor, M., Sotgiu, A., Biggio, B.: SECML: a python library for secure and explainable machine learning (2019)
23. Miller, T., Howe, P., Sonenberg, L.: Explainable AI: beware of inmates running the asylum or: How I learnt to stop worrying and love the social and behavioural sciences. CoRR (abs/1712.00547) (2017)
24. Mittelstadt, B.D., Floridi, L.: Transparent, explainable, and accountable AI for robotics. Sci. Robotics **2**(6) (2017)
25. Ribera, M., Lapedriza, À.: Can we do better explanations? A proposal of user-centered explainable AI. In: Trattner, C., Parra, D., Riche, N. (eds.) Joint Proceedings of the ACM IUI 2019 Workshops co-located with the 24th ACM Conference on Intelligent User Interfaces (ACM IUI 2019), Los Angeles, USA, March 20, 2019. CEUR Workshop Proceedings, vol. 2327. CEUR-WS.org (2019)
26. Rozenblit, L., Keil, F.C.: The misunderstood limits of folk science: an illusion of explanatory depth. Cogn. Sci. **26**(5), 521–562 (2002)
27. Tjoa, E., Guan, C.: A survey on explainable artificial intelligence (xai): toward medical xai. Presented at the (2020)
28. Völkel, S.T., Schneegass, C., Eiband, M., Buschek, D.: What is "intelligent" in intelligent user interfaces?: a meta-analysis of 25 years of IUI. In: Paternò, F., Oliver, N., Conati, C., Spano, L.D., Tintarev, N. (eds.) IUI 2020: 25th International Conference on Intelligent User Interfaces, Cagliari, Italy, 17–20 March 2020, pp. 477–487. ACM (2020)
29. Wang, D., Yang, Q., Abdul, A.M., Lim, B.Y.: Designing theory-driven user-centric explainable AI. In: Brewster, S.A., Fitzpatrick, G., Cox, A.L., Kostakos, V. (eds.) Proceedings of the 2019 CHI Conference on Human Factors in Computing Systems, CHI 2019, Glasgow, Scotland, UK, 04–09 May 2019, p. 601. ACM (2019)
30. Wickramasinghe, C.S., Marino, D.L., Grandio, J., Manic, M.: Trustworthy AI development guidelines for human system interaction. In: 13th International Conference on Human System Interaction, HSI 2020, Tokyo, Japan, 6–8 June 2020, pp. 130–136. IEEE (2020)

Trust Indicators and Explainable AI: A Study on User Perceptions

Delphine Ribes[1]([✉]), Nicolas Henchoz[1], Hélène Portier[1], Lara Defayes[1],
Thanh-Trung Phan[4,5], Daniel Gatica-Perez[4,5], and Andreas Sonderegger[2,3]

[1] EPFL+ECAL Lab, Ecole Polytechnique fédérale de Lausanne, Lausanne, Switzerland
delphine.ribes@epfl.ch
[2] Bern University of Applied Sciences, Bern, Switzerland
[3] Université de Fribourg, Fribourg, Switzerland
[4] Idiap Research Institute, Martigny, Switzerland
[5] LIDIAP-STI, Ecole Polytechnique fédérale de Lausanne, Lausanne, Switzerland

Abstract. Nowadays, search engines, social media or news aggregators are the preferred services for news access. Aggregation is mostly based on artificial intelligence technologies raising a new challenge: Trust has been ranked as the most important factor for media business. This paper reports findings of a study evaluating the influence of manipulations of interface design and information provided in the context of eXplainable Artificial Intelligence (XAI) on user perception and in the context of news content aggregators. In an experimental online study, various layouts and scenarios have been developed, implemented and tested with 266 participants. Measures of trust, understanding and preference were recorded. Results showed no influence of the factors on trust. However, data indicates that the influence of the layout, for example implicit integration of media source through layout structuration has a significant effect on perceived importance to cite the source of a media. Moreover, the amount of information presented to explain the AI showed a negative influence on user understanding. This highlights the importance and difficulty of making XAI understandable for its users.

Keywords: Trust indicators · Fake news · Transparency · Design · Explainable AI · XAI · Understandable AI

1 Introduction

News aggregators are considered as one of the most phenomenal changes in the media industry over the last decade [1], leading to disruption of the content supply chain and therefore of the business models in the media industry. They can be considered as a curation of news from various media organisations [2]. This curation can be performed by machine based algorithms, human judgement or a mix of both. However, due to the volume of content processed, automation has gained in importance in recent years. In 2009, for instance, Google was already curating over 25000 media sources around the world without human assistance. The phenomenon continues to increase: according to the 2019

© IFIP International Federation for Information Processing 2021
Published by Springer Nature Switzerland AG 2021
C. Ardito et al. (Eds.): INTERACT 2021, LNCS 12933, pp. 662–671, 2021.
https://doi.org/10.1007/978-3-030-85616-8_39

Reuters report [3], across all countries, search engines, social media or news aggregators are the preferred services for news access. However, previous research [4, 5] has indicated the importance of trust for the acceptance and perceived usefulness of such tools. But the rise of automated aggregation generates new trust issues. First, the multiplication of sources and the ease of creating and sharing content has spawned the massive distribution of fake news [6]. Additionally, users may get confused by the variety of news sources [7]. Finally, coming along with the increasing complexity and opacity of aggregating algorithms, users may not understand how algorithms make decisions, resulting in a loss of confidence in the aggregation [8]. In this regard, the question arises as how trust and confidence can be influenced when designing interfaces.

The work presented in this paper aims at evaluating the influence of design measures in the particular context of news content aggregators and specifically the effect of layout design and algorithm transparency on user trust.

2 Background and Related Work

2.1 Trust Indicators

To address trust issues, various projects have been initiated. For example, following the US 2016 election, "The Trust Project" [9] was launched, putting forward a set of eight trust indicators with the objective to provide information on the news article (*e.g.* the source, the publication date, the funding). Similarly, other sets of indicators have been proposed [10]. Such indicators are used, for example, for the "Facebook context button". From the proposed list of indicators, the source appears to be essential to assess the reliability of the content [11–14] and evidence from literature [15] suggests that source visibility should be designed to favor visibility. In a more intrusive way, some social networks have launched warning labels such as the "Facebook disrupted label" or "warnings on misleading Tweets label". Their purpose is to inform readers about the veracity or the trustworthiness of the information. Whether produced manually by external and independent fact checking organisations or in a more automatic way based on mathematical models [16], they may be harmful if misused or used inadequately [17, 18].

2.2 Aggregation Algorithm Transparency

Transparent AI or eXplainable Artificial intelligence (XAI) systems provide understandable justifications for algorithm outputs [19]. XAI is considered critical for building trust with AI [20]. To successfully implement a XAI system, it is important to determine the XAI system goals, the information to be explained and the way it is explained [21]. In the particular context of news content aggregators, the goal for the XAI system is to make the user understand why a content has been aggregated and how well the content matches the user search criteria. In this regard it has been suggested that information should be explained and represented in a simplified way in case that users are AI-novices [22]. In addition, it should be designed in an engaging way [23] and encourage users to interact with and further inspect the result [24]. In addition, previous research on automation has shown that the accuracy of the automated system (also referred to as automation reliability) considerably influences trust and usage behaviour [25]. Furthermore, research on technology acceptance has shown the important role of system usefulness and ease of use [26].

2.3 The Present Study

In order to address the above-mentioned research question, different versions of an AI-based news content aggregator prototype for an important national event (i.e. winegrowers' festival) were developed. The versions differed with regard to detail of explanation of the AI (level of XAI) and the visual representation of the results (design manipulation). With regard to the design manipulation, it was expected that the visual organisation of the content based on its source (i.e. curated heritage archives, news media archives, or social media) would lead to an increase in trust in the result of the content aggregator compared to an unstructured presentation. In a similar vein it was hypothesized that increasing detail of explanation of the AI would lead to a better understanding and hence to higher trust ratings.

3   Method

3.1   Participants

A total number of 226 participants (mean age of 32.38, SD = 13.74, ranging from 18 to 80 yrs., 128 women, 94 men and 4 identifying themselves differently) were recruited for this study. About half of participants (N = 108) were students while the other half consisted of employees working in various domains.

3.2   Experimental Design

We conducted an online experiment following a 2×3 between-subjects design, with the factors 'XAI' (detailed explanation vs. short explanation vs. no explanation) and design (source order vs. rank order). Figure 1 shows the different experimental manipulations. In a second stage of the study, one variable (*Perceived relevance of the interface design*) was recorded and analysed as repeated measures variable.

For the manipulation of the level of XAI in the *short explanation* condition, a color-coded matching rate number (CCMRN) in percentage was presented for each search result, together with the relevant keywords next to the aggregated content. This information helps understanding the prioritisation of the content and the accuracy with which the content matches the user search. In the *detailed explanation* condition, the same information as in the short explanation condition was presented. Furthermore, users could obtain additional information on content features, keywords extracted from indexation as well as success rate in percentage regarding the AI indexation by clicking on a button labeled "+ display more details". In the *no explanation condition*, no information regarding matching rate and search performance was presented.

In the *source order* condition of the design manipulation, search results were organized with regard to the source they were extracted from. The different sources of content were: "heritage" for content originating from curated cultural heritage archives such as museums, "news media" for content being produced by national and regional news and television companies, and "social network" for content being generated by users on platforms such as Instagram and Facebook. This version of the news aggregator interface was designed to clearly indicate the source of the presented content. Therefore, results were sorted into labeled and color-coded columns, each column representing a media type. The search results within each column were organized with regard to their matching rate with the search keywords, with high-matching content being placed on top of the column. Each column could be scrolled individually while the title always stayed visible. In the *rank order* condition, search results were ordered with regard to matching with the search keywords, without being organized by source. However, the source of the content was indicated by a color code in the description.

Fig. 1. Representation of the different interfaces as a function of XAI (detailed explanation vs. short explanation (without the purple) vs. no explanation (without the purple and salmon - top image) and design (source order vs. rank order - bottom image). (Color figure online)

3.3 Measures

Trust in the search results was assessed with the items 'Do you trust the results obtained by this search engine?', 'Did you find the results obtained by this search engine relevant?',

'Did you find that the images that came up in the search matched the keywords?' with a scale ranging from 1 'not at all' to 7 'absolutely'.

Perceived adequacy of the sorting order was assessed with the item 'Would you have liked to change the order in which the images appeared?' using a Likert scale ranging from 1 'not at all' to 7 'absolutely'.

Perceived usefulness of citing the source was assessed with the item 'Do you find it useful to have the source of the content cited?' on a scale ranging from 1 'not at all' to 7 'absolutely'.

Subjective understanding of the CCMRN was assessed with the item 'Did you understand what the matching rate number represents?' on a scale ranging from 1 'not at all' to 7 'absolutely'. Two screenshots displaying two different CCMRN (one with a low value and one with a high value) with their associated content were shown above the item.

Objective understanding of the CCMRN was assessed with the item 'Try to explain, as simply as possible, how this matching rate number is calculated'. Participants' answers were coded into three categories, 1: not understood, 2: moderately understood, 3: understood.

Perceived usefulness, trustworthiness and interest in the CCMRN was assessed with the items 'Do you find the matching rate number to be a useful indicator?', 'Do you trust this indicator?' and 'Would you like to have an indicator like this when doing online search?' on a scale ranging from 1 'not at all' to 7 'absolutely'.

Perceived accuracy of the CCMRN was assessed with the item 'Do you find that the percentages shown match the similarity between the search keywords and the found content?' on a scale ranging from 1 'not at all' to 7 'absolutely'.

Perceived usefulness, trustworthiness and interest in the detailed explanation available was assessed with the items 'Does this information help you to understand how the matching rate number is calculated?', 'Would you like to have access to this kind of information the next time you do an online search?', 'Do you trust this information' on a scale ranging from 1 'not at all' to 7 'absolutely'. A screenshot displaying the content together with its associated CCMRN and its associated details was displayed above the item.

As a repeated measures variable, *Perceived relevance of the interface design* was assessed by asking the participants 'Do you find it relevant to sort the results according to the interface below? on a scale ranging from 1 'not at all' to 7 'absolutely'. The question was asked twice. First, a screenshot of the source order interface was displayed and then, a screenshot of the rank order interface was displayed.

Additional variables such as perceived usefulness, relevance and accuracy of human indexation versus AI indexation were recorded but are not explicitly reported in this publication and will be part of a future publication.

3.4 Procedure

Participants recruited via institutional mailing lists and social media were equally distributed over the six experimental conditions. They answered an online questionnaire before and after seeing one of the online versions of the interface. They were asked to use a desktop computer or a laptop to complete this online-study. The search query feature was removed in order to control for results quality (i.e. all participants obtain the same search result interface for a maximal experimental control). Before launching the user interface, a text was displayed explaining the context of the search and indicating the keywords used in the search, which were 'parade', 'smile', and 'child'). The time to complete the survey was about 30 min.

3.5 Statistical Analysis

Data was analysed with two-factorial ANOVAs with post-hoc analyses using Sidak corrections. Data regarding the *perceived relevance of the interface design* was analysed with a three-factorial mixed ANOVA with the two questions regarding the relevance of the design versions (source order vs. rank order) as repeated measures variables. The link between two measures was calculated using the Pearson correlation.

4   Results

Trust in the Search Results. Participants in the source order condition tended to trust the results more ($M = 4.91$, $SE = 0.12$) than participants in rank order condition ($M = 4.69$, $SE = 0.12$) but the difference is not significant, $F(1, 220) = 1.70$, $p = .19$, $\eta^2 = .01$. Interestingly, no significant differences regarding participants' trust in search results were found for the XAI manipulation ($F < 1$), and also the interaction of the two factors did not reach significance level ($F < 1$). Since no interaction effect reached significance level for all the dependent variables, they are not reported for the following dependent variables.

Perceived Adequacy. Participants in the source order condition were significantly less inclined to change the order in which the search results were presented ($M = 3.59$, $SE = .18$) than those in the rank order condition ($M = 4.20$, $SE = .18$), $F(1, 220) = 5.53$, $p = .02$, $\eta^2 = .03$. No significant difference was found for the XAI manipulation $F(2, 220) = 1.45$, $p = .23$, $\eta^2 < .01$.

Perceived Relevance of the Interface Design. The repeated measures comparison of the two design versions (source order vs. rank order) indicated significantly higher ratings for the source order ($M = 5.28$, $SE = .10$) compared to the rank order ($M = 3.74$, $SE = .12$), $F(1, 220) = 113.41$, $p < .001$, $\eta^2 = .34$. Both between-factors did not influence this measure, $F_{design} < 1$; $F_{XAI}(2, 220) = 1.52$, $p = .22$, $\eta^2 = .014$.

Perceived Usefulness of Citing the Source. Participants in source order condition (S-) found it significantly more useful ($M = 6.58$, $SE = .10$) to have the source cited than participants in the rank order condition ($M = .30$, $SE = .10$), $F(1, 220) = 3.94$, $p = .048$, $\eta^2 = .02$). No significant differences were found for the XAI manipulations ($F < 1$).

Subjective Understanding of the CCMRN. Participants in the source order condition rate their understanding significantly higher ($M = 5.63$, $SE = .15$) than participants in the rank order condition ($M = 5.18$, $SE = .15$), $F(1, 220) = 4.45$, $p = .036$, $\eta^2 = .02$. No significant difference was found for the XAI manipulation ($F < 1$).

Objective Understanding of the CCMRN. No significant differences were found for the design manipulation ($F < 1$), while the effect of XAI reached significance level $F(1, 220) = 3.16, p = .044, \eta^2 = .03$. Sidak-corrected post-hoc comparisons indicated that participants in the detailed condition explained significantly less well how the *CCMRN* is calculated ($M = 2.38, SE = .08$) compared to participants in the short explanation ($M = 2.66, SE = .08; p = .04$), while the comparisons with no explanation condition ($M = 2.58, SE = .08$) did not reach significance level. There is a positive relationship between subjective and objective understanding of the *CCMRN*, $r = .27, p < .001$ indicating that participants who subjectively think they understood the *CCMRN* were better able to explain it.

Usefulness, Trustworthiness and Interest in the CCMRN. No significant differences were found for the design manipulations $F(1, 220) = 1.2, p = .26, \eta^2 = .006$ nor for the XAI manipulations $F(2, 220) = 2.2, p = .11, \eta^2 = .02$.

Perceived Accuracy of the CCMRN. No significant differences were found for the design manipulations ($F < 1$) nor for the XAI manipulations ($F < 1$).

Perceived Helpfulness, Trustworthiness and Interest in the Detailed Explanation. No significant differences were found for the design manipulations $F(1, 220) = 1.2, p = .26, \eta^2 = .006$ nor for the XAI manipulations $F(2, 220) = 2.2, p = .11, \eta^2 = .02$.

5   Discussion and Conclusion

This study addressed the effect of design manipulations and XAI on user trust and understanding. Surprisingly, results indicate that user trust is not influenced by the proposed design manipulations. We believe there are several reasons for this. The first one may be the content used. The winegrowers' festival is a popular event whose media content may not be prone to fake news, whatever the source. Therefore, the implemented design manipulations might have shown little influence on trust. To pursue efforts in understanding the influence of interface design on user trust, it might be important to conduct additional research with the suggested design manipulations on different content more connotated to include fake news (e.g. political, ecological or economical information). The second explanation for the unexpected outcomes may be due, as discussed in [15], to the similitude in the presentation of the content for both design conditions, resulting in a comparable effect on trustworthiness of the design manipulations. We manipulated the design of results sorting, either by source or by ranking order but the presentation format of the content remained identical for both conditions (*i.e.* position of the image or video within the content, size of the content, size of the elements surrounding the content), leading to a similar effect on user trust. Finally, the lack of effect on user trust might be due to the visibility of the sources in both conditions. Since the source appears to be essential to assess the reliability of the content [11–14], the effect on trust remains the same as long as the source is clearly highlighted.

While the proposed manipulations of XAI and design did not influence trust ratings, they did show an effect on subjective and objective understanding of the CCMRN. For participants in the detailed explanation condition, a discrepancy was observed between their subjective and objective understanding of the CCMRN: in the detailed explanation condition, participants performed worse in explaining the CCMRN. Nevertheless, they rated their subjective understanding similarly when compared to the other two XAI conditions. This indicates that providing an additional amount of information does not automatically lead to a better understanding of the AI system. Similar findings were presented in previous research where it was shown that XAI systems must be designed in a tailored way as otherwise this too much information can erode trust [25]. We observed however that the understanding of the CCMRN is not converted at this point into an effect on trust. This could be due to the fact that participants found it difficult to imagine the meaning of a percentage score. It would therefore be interesting to test the effect using only the red-orange-green colour code, the highlighted keywords, or a sentence as proposed in [25, 27, 28]. We believe that the effect on comprehension would be comparable, but users would be more inclined to use it. Surprisingly, we found that participants in the *source order* condition rated their subjective understanding of the CCMRN higher compared to participants in the *rank order* condition, but their objective understanding was similar. In the *source order* condition, results are sorted into categories and displayed as columns which can be scrolled individually. On the contrary, in the *rank order* condition, results are scrolled all together. The clear organisation in three separate columns might facilitate the reading and comprehension of the relevant information, which helped participants to focus on the meaning of the presented information.

Interestingly, the design manipulations showed effects on specific user perceptions. Participants in the *source order* condition found it more important to present information about the source in addition to the content compared to participants in the *rank order* condition. This corroborates results found in previous research [15] indicating the importance of clearly indicating the source of aggregated content in order to favor its visibility. However, as the results of this study indicate, the way the source is highlighted is also an important factor to influence people's perception of its importance. Moreover, results indicated that participants in this study preferred the *source order* layout. As for the subjective and objective understanding of the CCMRN, the proposed source order layout made the content easier to read, which might have influenced their preference ratings.

Limitations of this study are that results are based on data of a popular event dataset in Switzerland and hence need to be interpreted within this cultural context. Moreover, results are based on self-report data, which must be taken into account when interpreting the results [29].

To conclude, the presented study established a connection between layout design and user understanding. More specifically, we related the sorting of news into column categories to the importance of citing the source. This knowledge is useful in the fight against misinformation when designing news content aggregators. The results of this study also demonstrated a link between the amount of information provided to explain AI and the understanding of the AI, indicating that more information does not forcefully lead to a better understanding. In this regard, the real challenge for the future development of XAI environments might not be to make the system explainable but to make it understandable for the person that is supposed to use and trust it.

This project has received funding from the Initiative for Media Innovation based at Media Center, EPFL, Lausanne, Switzerland.

References

1. Lee, A.M., Chyi, H.I.: The rise of online news aggregators: consumption and competition. Int. J. Media Manage. **17**(1), 3–24 (2015). https://doi.org/10.1080/14241277.2014.997383
2. Isbell, K.: The rise of the news aggregator: legal implications and best practices. SSRN Electron. J. (2012). https://doi.org/10.2139/ssrn.1670339
3. Newman, N.: Reuters Institute Digital News Report 2019, p. 156 (2019)
4. Oechslein, O., Haim, M., Graefe, A., Hess, T., Brosius, H.-B., Koslow, A.: The digitization of news aggregation: experimental evidence on intention to use and willingness to pay for personalized news aggregators. In: 2015 48th Hawaii International Conference on System Sciences, HI, pp. 4181–4190, January 2015. https://doi.org/10.1109/HICSS.2015.501
5. Innovation in News Media World Report 2018. WAN-IFRA. https://wan-ifra.org/insight/inn ovation-in-news-media-world-report-2018/. Accessed 16 Apr 2021
6. Rubin, V.L., Chen, Y., Conroy, N.K.: Deception detection for news: three types of fakes. Proc. Assoc. Inf. Sci. Technol. **52**(1), 1–4 (2015). https://doi.org/10.1002/pra2.2015.145052 010083
7. Reuters Institute Digital News Report 2017, p. 136 (2017)
8. European Commission: Final report of the high level expert group on fake news and online disinformation. Shaping Europe's digital future - European Commission, 12 March 2018. https://ec.europa.eu/digital-single-market/en/news/final-report-high-level-exp ert-group-fake-news-and-online-disinformation. Accessed 14 Dec 2020
9. The Trust Project Homepage. https://thetrustproject.org/
10. Zhang, A.X., et al.: A structured response to misinformation: defining and annotating credibility indicators in news articles, p. 10 (2019). https://doi.org/10.1145/3184558.3188731.
11. Kiousis, S.: Public trust or mistrust? Perceptions of media credibility in the information age. Mass Commun. Soc. **4**(4), 381–403 (2001). https://doi.org/10.1207/S15327825MCS0404_4
12. Hovland, C.I., Weiss, W.: The influence of source credibility on communication effectiveness. Public Opin. Q. **15**(4), 635–650 (1951). https://doi.org/10.1086/266350
13. ACUNA, T.: The digital transformation of news media and the rise of disinformation and fake news. EU Science Hub - European Commission, 25 April 2018. https://ec.europa.eu/jrc/ en/publication/eur-scientific-and-technical-research-reports/digital-transformation-news-media-and-rise-disinformation-and-fake-news. Accessed 14 Dec 2020
14. Pornpitakpan, C.: The persuasiveness of source credibility: a critical review of five decades' evidence. J. Appl. Soc. Psychol. **34**(2), 243–281 (2004). https://doi.org/10.1111/j.1559-1816. 2004.tb02547.x
15. Kim, A., Dennis, A.R.: Says who?: how news presentation format influences perceived believability and the engagement level of social media users. In: 51st, Hawaii, vol. 43, Issue 3, pp. 1025–1039 (2018)
16. Zhou, X., Zafarani, R.: Fake news: a survey of research, detection methods, and opportunities, 1 (2018). http://www.journalism.org/2017/09/07/news-use-across-social-media-platfo rms-2017/
17. Pennycook, G., Rand, D.G.: The implied truth effect: attaching warnings to a subset of fake news stories increases perceived accuracy of stories without warnings. SSRN (2017). https:// doi.org/10.2139/ssrn.3035384
18. Clayton, K., et al.: Real solutions for fake news? measuring the effectiveness of general warnings and fact-check tags in reducing belief in false stories on social media. Polit. Behav. **42**(4), 1073–1095 (2019). https://doi.org/10.1007/s11109-019-09533-0

19. Gunning, D.: Explainable artificial intelligence (XAI). Mach. Learn. 18
20. Shin, D.: The effects of explainability and causability on perception, trust, and acceptance: implications for explainable AI. Int. J. Hum. Comput. Stud. **146**, 102551 (2021). https://doi.org/10.1016/j.ijhcs.2020.102551
21. Mohseni, S., Zarei, N., Ragan, E.D.: A multidisciplinary survey and framework for design and evaluation of explainable AI systems, arXiv181111839 Cs, August 2020. http://arxiv.org/abs/1811.11839. Accessed 08 Apr 2021
22. Lage, I., et al.: Human evaluation of models built for interpretability. In: Proceedings AAAI Conference Human Computation Crowdsourcing, vol. 7, no. 1, October 2019. Art. no. 1
23. Muir, B.M.: Trust between humans and machines, and the design of decision aids. Int. J. Man Mach. Stud. **27**(5), 527–539 (1987). https://doi.org/10.1016/S0020-7373(87)80013-5
24. Kulesza, T., et al.: Explanatory debugging: supporting end-user debugging of machine-learned programs. In: 2010 IEEE Symposium on Visual Languages and Human-Centric Computing, pp. 41–48, September 2010. https://doi.org/10.1109/VLHCC.2010.15.
25. Kizilcec, R.F.: How much information? Effects of transparency on trust in an algorithmic interface. In: Conference Human Factors Computing Systems, pp. 2390–2395 (2016). https://doi.org/10.1145/2858036.2858402
26. Venkatesh, V., Bala, H.: Technology acceptance model 3 and a research agenda on interventions. Decis. Sci. **39**(2), 273–315 (2008). https://doi.org/10.1111/j.1540-5915.2008.00192.x
27. Eslami, M., et al.: I always assumed that I wasn't really that close to [her]: reasoning about Invisible Algorithms in News Feeds. In: Proceedings of the 33rd Annual ACM Conference on Human Factors in Computing Systems, New York, pp. 153–162, April 2015. https://doi.org/10.1145/2702123.2702556.
28. Wang, W., Benbasat, I.: Recommendation agents for electronic commerce: effects of explanation facilities on trusting beliefs. J. Manage. Inf. Syst. **23**(4), 217–246 (2007). https://doi.org/10.2753/MIS0742-1222230410
29. Podsakoff, P.M., MacKenzie, S.B., Lee, J.-Y., Podsakoff, N.P.: Common method biases in behavioral research: a critical review of the literature and recommended remedies. J. Appl. Psychol. **88**(5), 879–903 (2003). https://doi.org/10.1037/0021-9010.88.5.879

Author Index

Printed in the United States
by Baker & Taylor Publisher Services